Faith-Based Violence and Deobandi Militancy in Pakistan

.

Jawad Syed • Edwina Pio • Tahir Kamran • Abbas Zaidi
Editors

Faith-Based Violence and Deobandi Militancy in Pakistan

palgrave
macmillan

Editors
Jawad Syed
University of Huddersfield
Huddersfield
United Kingdom

Tahir Kamran
Government College University
Lahore, Pakistan

Edwina Pio
Auckland University of Technology
Auckland, New Zealand

Abbas Zaidi
School of the Arts & Media
University of New South Wales
Australia

ISBN 978-1-349-94965-6   ISBN 978-1-349-94966-3   (eBook)
DOI 10.1057/978-1-349-94966-3

Library of Congress Control Number: 2016951736

Cover illustration: © Godong / Alamy Stock Photo

Printed on acid-free paper

This Palgrave imprint is published by Springer Nature
The registered company is Macmillan Publishers Ltd. London

ENDORSEMENTS

"This is a most timely volume which provides historical depth and nuance to the understanding of Islamic militancy and violence in Pakistan. Such an awareness is often lacking in contemporary analyses. The empirical data provided in a series of incisive and insightful chapters enables an informed account to emerge of the causes and consequences of the growing influence of Deobandi Islam within the country and its transnational linkages. The volume enables the reader to grasp the complex factors which reduce the space for pluralism, despite inherited traditions of tolerance. The book is a must read for everyone seeking to understand contemporary Pakistan and to assess its future trajectory."
Professor Ian Talbot, University of Southampton, UK

"This book is a landmark in scholarship on Islam, Pakistan and militancy. It will provide necessary insights into the genesis of violence in the name of religion and sect which scholars, ordinary readers and decision-makers can use to understand why Pakistan's name is often in the headlines for the wrong reasons."
Professor Tariq Rahman, HEC Distinguished National Professor, Dean, School of Liberal Arts and Social Sciences, Beaconhouse National University, Lahore, Pakistan

ACKNOWLEDGEMENTS

The editors thank the University of Huddersfield and the Interfaith Unity for Tolerance for their generous support of this project. The editors also thank the anonymous reviewers for providing critical and constructive comments on various chapters. Special thanks are due to a worthy reviewer whose contribution is no less than an editor but who chooses to remain anonymous for personal reasons. The editors also wish to thank Palgrave Macmillan, the commissioning editor and her team for their support at various stages of this book—right from its conception to the end product in your hands.

CONTENTS

EDITORS' AND CONTRIBUTORS' BIOGRAPHIES

EDITORS' BIOGRAPHIES

Tahir Kamran is Professor and Head of the Department of History at Government College University Lahore, Pakistan. During 2013–2015 he was the Iqbal Fellow at the University of Cambridge, UK, as a professor in the Centre of South Asian Studies. He has authored four books and has written several articles specifically on the history of the Punjab, sectarianism, democracy and governance.

Edwina Pio is New Zealand's first Professor of Diversity and a Fulbright alumnus. She works at the Faculty of Business and Law of Auckland University of Technology, New Zealand, and is Visiting Professor at Boston College, Massachusetts, USA. She is a co-director of the Global Centre for Equality and Human rights (GCEHR). She seeks to change the parameters of diversity initiatives, specifically with respect to ethnicity, gender and religion. She has numerous publications in journals and books, including *Sari: Indian Women at Work in New Zealand* (inaugurated by John Key, Prime Minister of New Zealand) and *Work & Worship.*

Jawad Syed is Professor of Organisational Behaviour and Diversity Management at the University of Huddersfield, UK. His main academic interests are gender, race and diversity in organizations, international human resource management, business ethics and organizational knowledge. He is the founder and co-director of the Global Centre for Equality and Human Rights (GCEHR). He is also a programme chair of the Gender, Race and Diversity in Organisations strategic interest group of the European Academy of Management. He has co-edited the following books: *Managing Cultural Diversity in Asia: A Research Companion* (2010), *Managing Gender Diversity in Asia: A Research Companion* (2010), *Human Resource Management in a Global Context: A Critical Approach* (Palgrave Macmillan, 2012) and *Managing Diversity and Inclusion: An International Perspective* (2015).

Abbas Zaidi has worked as a journalist and teacher in Pakistan, Brunei Darussalam and Australia. He is based in Sydney, where he tutors in media studies and academic writing at various universities. He is the author of *Two and a Half Words and other Stories* (Savvy Press, 2012) and *Language Shift: Sociolinguistic Lives of Two Punjabi Generations in Brunei Darussalam* (Classic Books, 2013).

CONTRIBUTORS' BIOGRAPHIES

Naeem Ahmed is an associate professor in the Department of International Relations, University of Karachi, Pakistan. He was a recipient of a Fulbright predoctoral scholarship at the University of Cincinnati, Ohio, USA, in 2003. He was also the recipient of a Fernand Braudel IFER postdoctoral fellowships in Paris, France, in 2013. He is widely published in national and international research journals. His field of research is religious extremism and terrorism, with particular reference to Pakistan.

Faiza Ali is a senior lecturer at Liverpool Business School. She has more than ten years of experience in teaching and research. Her areas of research include diversity management, gender equality, work–life balance, sexual harassment and intersectionality in the workplace. In particular, she is interested in exploring issues and challenges faced by women in Muslim-majority countries such as Pakistan, Turkey and Bangladesh.

Thomas K. Gugler has been a research fellow at the Zentrum Moderner Orient in Berlin, Germany, and in the Department for Near Eastern Studies at the University of Vienna, Austria. He is currently working on a project entitled "Culture and Plurality in Contemporary South Asia" at the Cluster of Excellence "Religion & Politics", University of Muenster, Germany. His academic publications include *Mission Medina* (2011) and *Ozeanisches Gefühl der Unsterblichkeit* (2009).

Arshi Saleem Hashmi is an associate professor at the National Defence Universitys, Islamabad, Pakistan. She has been a Yale World Fellow and Rotary International Peace Fellow. She has studied at the American University, USA, the Johns Hopkins University, USA, Quaid-e-Azam University Islamabad and Kennedy School of Government's Executive Education programme at Harvard University, USA. She has also worked with the United States Institute of Peace, Pew Forum on Religion and Public Life, the Institute of Regional Studies and the University of Karachi, Pakistan.

Pervez Amirali Hoodbhoy is a nuclear physicist, essayist and national security analyst. He taught at Quaid-e-Azam University's physics department for 40 years before becoming Professor of Physics and Mathematics at Forman Christian College University, Lahore, Pakistan, where he teaches.

Humayun Kabir is an assistant professor in the Department of Political Science and Sociology at North South University, Dhaka, Bangladesh. Prior to this he taught at Hiroshima Jogakuin University. He also served as a postdoctoral research fellow for three years at the Graduate School for International Development and Cooperation, Hiroshima University. His research interests revolve around Islam, religious clergy, madrassas and the Muslim minority community in South Asia. Publications include book chapters in several edited volumes, including *Religion and Representation: Islam and Democracy* (2015) and *The Moral Economy of Madrasas: Islam and Education Today* (2011). His research findings on madrassas, ulema (Islamic clerics), Islamism, identity politics and conflict in modern South Asia have been published in various international journals, including *Contemporary South Asia* and *South Asia*.

Raza Mir is Professor of Management at William Paterson University, USA. His research mainly concerns multinational corporations, and issues relating to power and resistance in organizations. He also studies organizational philosophy and has co-edited *The Routledge Companion to Philosophy in Organization Studies*. He recently served as Chair of the Critical Management Studies Division of the Academy of Management.

Mohammad Ali Naquvi is a community activist and social justice advocate based in central New Jersey, USA. Over the past 15 years he has worked to build intra-faith coalitions in the American Muslim community and joint initiatives with communities of colour. As Advocacy Director for Husayn Center for Social Justice, he attempts to empower the urban community in the capital city of Trenton, New Jersey, to bring about transformative social change.

Fatima Z. Rahman is an assistant professor in the Department of Politics and Chair of Islamic World Studies at Lake Forest College, USA. She has published articles in *Australian Journal of Political Science, Polity* and *Interdisciplinary Journal of Research on Religion*. Her research interests include Islam and politics, Islam and minorities, and Middle East politics.

Zulqarnain Sewag is an Urdu poet and a researcher of public policy and contemporary affairs. He regularly contributes to Pakistani and international English daily newspapers and magazines on diverse contemporary issues. His research paper "Sectarian Rise in Pakistan: Role of Saudi Arabia and Iran" was published in 2015. His Urdu poetry book *Sehra mein chagal* is forthcoming.

Liyakat Takim is a professor and the Sharjah Chair in Global Islam at McMaster University in Hamilton, Canada. A native of Zanzibar, Tanzania, he has spoken at more than 80 academic conferences and authored 100 scholarly works on diverse topics such as reformation in the Islamic world, the treatment of women in Islamic law, Islam in the USA, the indigenization of the Muslim community in the USA, dialogue in post-9/11 America, war and peace in the Islamic tradition, Islamic law, Islamic biographical literature, the charisma of the holy man and shrine culture, and Islamic mystical traditions. He teaches a range of courses on Islam and offers a course on comparative religions. His first book is *The Heirs of the Prophet Charisma and Religious Authority in Shi'ite Islam* (SUNY, 2006), his second is *Shi'ism in America* (New York University Press, 2009) and he is currently working on his third, *Ijtihad and Reformation in Islam*. He has taught at several US and Canadian universities and is actively engaged in dialogue with different faith communities.

Sam Westrop is the Research Director for Americans for Peace and Tolerance, a senior fellow of the Gatestone Institute, and a regular commentator featuring on British and US television and radio on the topics of extremism and terrorism. He runs the organization Stand for Peace, which monitors political and religious extremist networks in the UK.

List of Figures

LIST OF TABLES

CHAPTER 1

Introduction: An Alternative Discourse on Religious Militancy

Jawad Syed

*What droppeth at dawn is not the dew. It's the tears that the night
sheddeth for the aggrieved.*

*(Shah Abdul Latif Bhittai 1689–1752.
Translated by Jawad Syed)* *.

Increasingly, policy-makers, leaders and research scholars around the globe
are recognizing the need to attend to the potential threat that faith-based
radicalization and extremism pose to individuals, communities and societies, even if in some instances the threat is not clearly identifiable. Pakistan,
the world's sixth most populous country with more than 192 million
inhabitants (Government of Pakistan 2015), has a diverse population in
terms of faith, sect, ethnicity and other forms of identity (Syed 2008).
In recent years, systematic faith-based violence there has reached unprecedented levels in terms of death and destruction for Sunni Barelvis, Sufis,
Shias, Ahmadis, Christians, Hindus and other communities. Addressing
this issue is of global importance.

---

* (Bhittai, S.A. 2006. *Spiritualism in the Poetry of Shah Abdul Latif Bhittai*.
Compiled and Translated by Munawar Arbab (Halo). Edited by Fahmida
Hussain. Karachi: University of Karachi)

J. Syed (✉)
University of Huddersfield, Huddersfield, UK

© The Editor(s) (if applicable) and The Author(s) 2016
J. Syed et al. (eds.), *Faith-Based Violence and Deobandi
Militancy in Pakistan*, DOI 10.1057/978-1-349-94966-3_1

In almost all incidents of faith-based violence and suicide bombings, militant groups such as the Pakistani Taliban (known as Tehrik-i-Taliban Pakistan [TTP]), Lashkar-e-Jhangvi (LeJ, Army of Jhangvi), Sipah-e-Sahaba Pakistan (SSP, also operating as Ahle Sunnat Wal Jamaat or ASWJ) and affiliated militant outfits, with overlapping, shared memberships and blurred boundaries, are involved. Almost without exception, these militants belong to the Deobandi subsect of Sunni Islam and are involved in attacks on fellow Sunni Muslims, in addition to attacks on non-Sunni and non-Muslim communities (Fair 2015a, b). There is also evidence of attacks on relatively moderate Deobandi scholars and other incidents of intra-Deobandi violence (*The News* 2014). On a global level there is some evidence of Deobandi militancy in other regions, including in the West and the Middle East in support of Al-Qaeda, and the so-called Islamic State in Iraq and Syria (ISIS, also known as ISIL [Islamic State of Iraq and the Levant] or Daesh).

Some analysts have pointed out that Deobandi militant outfits are not isolated offshoots but also enjoy the support of a wider network of Deobandi religiopolitical parties, clerics, *madrassas* (religious schools or seminaries), and at least some sections of the populace and security establishment. According to Siddiqa (cited in Zia 2013), the LeJ is part of the larger Deobandi network that is connected with other groups, such as the SSP, Jaish-e-Muhammad (JeM), Harkat-ul-Mujahideen (HuM) and Harkat-ul-Jihad al-Islami (HUJI). Also, it has the Tableeghi Jamaat and Jamiat Ulema-e-Islam–Fazl (JUI-F) network to depend on. Over the years it has become stronger and it is now in the process of establishing itself politically. However, its violent contingent will continue to exist and expand. In fact, it will be able to justify itself and camouflage better due to this mainstreaming.

Siddiqa notes that

> LeJ and the Deobandi network has expanded quite well in parts of North Punjab and most of South Punjab. They are now getting into Sindh as well. They are focused on their ideology, which means the strengthening of a Sunni state that sees the minorities in a certain role. Minorities will always be considered as half citizens.

Reporting her personal observation of the growing influence of radical Deobandism, Siddiqa states, "I have been to villages that follow the JeM and the LeJ in South Punjab, for instance, where they express displeasure of the Shias and Barelvis. The Shias are considered a greater enemy than the Barelvis who are only treated as yet as fools who ought to be corrected" (Ayesha Siddiqa, interviewed by Zia 2013, paras 15–18).

Given the Pakistani state's emphasis on assimilative national identity, incidents of sectarian attacks are either ignored or under-reported, with little mention of the common denominational identity of the perpetrators. In view of the historical support given to Deobandi and Salafi jihadist groups by the Pakistani security establishment, there is also some evidence of a lack of will on the state's part to bring the perpetrators to justice. Similar neglect is also evident in the Pakistani media. Zaidi (2014) laments the way in which the mainstream media neglects Deobandi militancy and the suffering of victim communities. He urges the victim communities to unite and to take a principled and sustained stand to defeat *takfiri* (apostatizing) violence.

It may be noted that Deobandis, despite their allegiance to the Hanafi school of jurisprudence, are heavily influenced by the ultraorthodox Takfiri (a fanatic Muslim who considers other Muslim sects or groups infidels due to religious or political differences and justifies violence against them) and jihadist ideologies of Ibn Taymiyyah (1263–1328) and Muhammad ibn Abd al-Wahhab (1703–1792). Such influences pre-date the origins of the Darul Uloom Deoband in 1867. Therefore, Deobandis are closer to Salafis or Wahhabis in their inclination to takfiri, sectarian and jihadist militancy.

Owing to the Deobandis' better organization and resources (in contrast to those of Sunni Sufis and Barelvis), their ideology remains influential in Pakistan, with little room or tolerance for other sects and faiths. Kamran (2014) notes that Pakistan's national narrative is predicated on a specific religious identity, thereby excluding those adhering to other identities. "Sometimes one laments the attempts to include minorities in the national narrative as a futile exercise. In fact, their exclusion has taken on a horrific form and they are being exterminated." Kamran suggests that marginalization is not only limited to non-Muslims but also stretches to "othering" within Islam. He argues that "once non-Muslims were driven to the margins in the country, the wedge of differentiation was turned to other sects". He refers to the dominant Deobandi direction of the national narrative in Pakistan. Furthermore, he notes that the mention of Ahmad Sirhindi (alias Mujaddid Alf Sani) (1564–1624), Shah Waliullah (1703–1762) and Shabbir Ahmed Usmani (1887–1949) as the architects of the ideology that underpins state nationalism testifies to the overwhelming sway of Deobandi ideas in Pakistan. As a way forward, Kamran recommends a new national narrative, particularly with regard to the discourse on religion, and he highlights the need for an alternative discourse with an all-inclusive humane character.

In April 2016, BBC Radio 4 broadcast two extensive episodes titled The Deobandis highlighting the armed sectarian and jihadist groups of Deobandis which are not only active in South Asia but also in the UK and elsewhere. The program shows that Deobandi Islam is intentionally isolationist and that its strict beliefs put it at odds with modern mainstream societies and beliefs. It also points towards the Deobandis role in intra-Muslim sectarianism and show how some senior Deobandi leaders in the West have links to the proscribed militant organisations (BBC, 2016).

This volume documents and highlights the Deobandi dimension of extremism and its implications for faith-based violence and terrorism. This dimension of radical Islam remains largely ignored or misunderstood in mainstream media and academic scholarship. The book addresses this gap. It also covers the Deobandi diaspora in the West and other countries, and the role of its radical elements in transnational incidents of violence and terrorism. It is interdisciplinary in nature and cuts across the fields of politics, religion, history, media studies, anthropology and governance.

In the context of violence and terrorism in South Asia, Fair (2015a) points towards generic and vague discourses that are often used in mainstream media and analyses. She argues that

> While most commentators on Pakistan's dire internal security situation tend to use the anodyne descriptors of "Islamist", "terrorist", or even "sectarian militants" to describe these groups, these expressions suffer from considerable under-specification. In fact, the groups that are primarily engaged in this kind of Islamist domestic violence against Pakistanis in and out of government are almost exclusively Deobandi, one of the five major interpretive traditions of Islam in Pakistan.[1]

The problem with generic or vague terms such as "Islamist", "terrorist" and "Sunni" is that they (1) deflect attention from the specific Deobandi (South Asian) and Salafi/Wahhabi (transnational) identity of the vast majority of militants; and (2) provide legitimacy to the Deobandi/Salafi militancy. Deobandi and Salafi subsects combined represent a tiny minority within the global Sunni population.[2] Within the Salafi and Deobandi population, the takfiri jihadist militants represent a fraction of these subsects although many of their top clerics and ideologues hold and spread takfiri and jihadist ideologies.

A recent report by the European Parliament (EP) reveals how Salafi/ Wahhabi groups based in the Middle East are involved in the support of, and supply of arms to, militant groups around the world. The work, commissioned by the EP's Directorate-General for External Policies, warns about these organizations and claims that "no country in the Muslim world is safe from their operations ... as they always aim to terrorise their opponents and arouse the admiration of their supporters" (EP 2013). Similar discoveries were made in a leaked cable from the US Consulate in Lahore that stated that "financial support estimated at nearly 100 million USD annually was making its way to Deobandi and Ahl-e-Hadith [Salafi] clerics in the region from 'missionary' and 'Islamic charitable' organisations in Saudi Arabia and the United Arab Emirates ostensibly with the direct support of those governments" (Dawn 2011). In light of these developments, parliamentarians in the USA and the UK, such as Congressman Ed Royce and Lord Eric Avebury, have demanded close monitoring of Deobandi madrassas and a strict ban on the madrassas and outfits involved in militancy (Avebury 2013; PTI 2015).

The specific identification of the radical Deobandi and Salafi militants is useful to isolate them from the majority of peaceful Sunni and Shia Muslims. This provides direction to governmental resources so that they can focus on those outfits, mosques, madrassas, charities, media and social media channels that are associated with these ideologies.

In spite of extensive scholarship and developments in the field of religion and terrorism over the last few decades, not much attention has been paid to the significant role played by Deobandi ideology and organizations in incidents of violence in Pakistan and other countries. While some notice has been taken of Salafi or Wahhabi militancy and its ideological, political and financial roots in Saudi Arabia and other Arab countries, there is no such focus Deobandism. This is despite the fact that Deobandi outfits are reported to be responsible for up to 90 percent of violence and terrorism in Pakistan (Hussain 2010) and are known to be active in other countries, such as the UK, the USA, Iraq, Syria and Afghanistan.

Indeed, as Metcalf (2011) notes, many of Pakistan's Deobandi clerics are supportive of the Taliban, which shares their sectarian orientation. Metcalf argues that the emergence of the Pakistani Taliban suggests a commonality of goals with the Afghan Taliban, and that Pakistani militant organizations have demonstrably been linked to actions beyond Pakistan, Afghanistan and Kashmir. She acknowledges that, in recent decades, militancy and terrorism in Pakistan, including militancy on the part of Deobandis, has escalated, and also that the Taliban identify as part of the Deobandi school of thought (Metcalf 2002). Many of the Taliban studied in Deobandi schools (madrassas), but one senior spokesman for the Taliban in his conversation with Metcalf went so far as to declare, "Every Afghan is a Deobandi."

However, instead of taking a clear stance against Deobandi militant outfits, such as the Taliban, SSP/ASWJ and JeM, senior Deobandi clerics in Pakistan and India have resorted to a discourse that shifts the blame of Deobandi militancy towards "Zionists and Western crusaders" (Sikand 2008). For example, in the much publicized anti-terrorism convention held at Deoband in 2008, the conference's organizer and rector of the Darul Uloom Deoband, Maulana Marghubur Rahman, castigated "Zionist forces" for spreading terrorism throughout the world to promote Western and Israeli imperialism, and suggested that Jews and Christians might be behind many terrorist attacks, including in India. He insisted that no Muslim would engage in terrorist activities because this would hurt Muslims more than others, hence "it is unrealistic and even impossible for them to be terrorists". Several other speakers at the convention repeated similar arguments in their approach to terrorism (Sikand 2008).

In his critical evaluation of the Darul Uloom's stance towards terrorism, Yusuf Ansari writes in the Urdu daily *Hindustan Express* that none of the clerics who condemned terrorism in general at the convention "named a single terrorist organization and condemned it". He sees it as unfortunate that Deobandi clerics fail to explicitly mention, leave alone condemn, Al-Qaeda, the Taliban and similar groups. Ansari says,

> The question arises as to why those ulema [clerics] who condemn terrorism as anti-Islamic did not say a thing about these groups. Is it that in their eyes these groups' actions do not constitute terrorism? While the speakers at the convention explicitly condemned America for its terrorism, why did they not themselves also introspect and look within?

In conclusion, Ansari argues that it is not enough to denounce terrorism as anti-Islamic, and that terrorist organizations must be specifically named and sternly condemned (cited in Sikand 2008).

This denialist and conspiracy theory attitude is also a characteristic of Pakistani Deobandi clerics who vaguely condemn terrorism but continue to ally themselves with leaders of banned terrorist outfits, such as the SSP/ASWJ, and continue to support the Taliban. For example, in recent years, three Deobandi-dominated outfits—namely, Mutahida Deeni Mahaz,

Difa-i-Pakistan Council and the Wafaq-ul-Madaris Al Arabiya—included the ASWJ/SSP and its leadership within their fold. Similarly, in December 2009, Mufti Rafi Usmani, the Grand Mufti of Pakistani Deobandis, held the US security company Blackwater responsible for the attack on the Ashura procession in Karachi in which more than 45 Shia and Sunni Muslims were killed (*Geo TV* 2009). This was in spite of the fact that the police investigation revealed that the attack was in fact the work of Jundallah, a Deobandi terror group (Tanoli 2015), one of several aliases of the SSP/ASW/LeJ network.

Indeed, Deobandis are quite pragmatic in being aligned to centres of power and resources in the relevant country—for example, their alignment with secularism and the Indian National Congress in 1947 in India. Similarly in Pakistan, Deobandi clerics aligned themselves with the ruling establishment when they started the process of Islamizing the country through the Objectives Resolution (1949) and Islamization (late 1970s and beyond). The Deobandis aligned themselves with the Pakistan Army during and after the Afghan Jihad (1980s), with the Bharatiya Janata Party (Hindu nationalist party ([BJP]) more recently (Fareed 2014) and with Saudi Arabia since the very rise of the Wahhabi establishment. As Metcalf (2002) describes, most striking about Deoband-type movements is the extent to which politics is an "empty box", which is filled expediently and pragmatically depending on what seems to work best in any given situation. In a Muslim–majority context—that is, Pakistan, with unprecedented access to power and resources, Deobandi clerics and organizations in Pakistan have demonstrated a disturbing behaviour in their ambiguous and obtuse approach to religious violence and intolerance.

Kamran (2014) describes the phenomenon as "political Islam" and argues that its full articulation in the subcontinent happened in 1831 when Syed Ahmed and Shah Ismael waged *jihad* (holy war) against Sikh rulers of the Punjab and North West Frontier Province (NWFP, currently Khyber Pakhtunkhwa [KPK] and Federally Administered Tribal Areas [FATAs]). Notably their jihad was not only against Sikh rulers but also against "impure" Sufi practices within the local Muslim population in Pashtun areas and elsewhere. Kamran argues that though their movement failed to achieve its goal of establishing a caliphate, the ideology sustained itself. The gradual displacement of Sufi-ideology Islam was a conspicuous outcome. With the advent of the Deobandi denomination in 1867, political Islam institutionalized itself as a movement. This institutionalization and its effects are visible today in the shape of an enormous network of Deobandi madrassas, a very organized proselytizing group (Tablighi Jamaat), political parties, pressure groups (e.g., Jamiat Ulema-e-Hind [JUH, Organization of Indian Islamic Scholars] and JUI) and militant outfits (e.g., Taliban, TTP and ASWJ/LeJ). Kamran argues that literal Islam with takfir (excommunication) and exclusion were the abiding features of the Deobandi movement. By forging pan-Islamic links, this form of Islam went from strength to strength. For example, through the establishment of the and its active role in the Khilafat Movement (1919–1926), the upholders of political Islam carved out a permanent niche for themselves. Through the Khilafat Movement, Deobandi political Islam acquired maturity that was subsequently articulated through the Islamist politics of agitation. Alavi (2002) argues that "the Khilafat Movement implanted the religious idiom in the modern Indian Muslim politics for the first time". He refers to the adverse implications of the movement for the South Asian Muslim community and the key role played by the Deobandi clerics in using religion for political purposes. Kamran (2014) notes that as the core principal of their politics, the agitation tended to give way to communal violence, which was relatively contained within India. Given a Muslim-majority context in Pakistan with access to corridors of power and a significant demographic presence, violence came to be the centrepiece of their strategy. Enabled by a large network of Deobandi madrassas, Tablighi Jamaat and religiopolitical groups, in addition to Saudi funding and the Pakistani establishment's support, Deobandi clerics took off their secular cloak and worked for the Islamization and "purification" of Pakistan. This was also witnessed in the anti-Ahmadi movement in the 1950s (Kamran 2014), and during the onslaught against Sunni Sufis, Barelvis, Shias and other communities in the post-Afghan Jihad years.

In light of recent high-profile incidents, such as the Peshawar Army Public School (APS) massacre (2014), the Lahore church massacre (2015), the Shia Hazara massacres in Quetta (2010–2014), the Sunni Sufi shrine massacres in Lahore, Karachi and Dera Ghazi Khan (2010–2011), the Ahmadi mosque massacre in Lahore (2010) and the Zikri shrine massacre in Avaran (2015), there is a need to more deeply examine the historical, ideological and political roots of Deobandi militancy and the role of Deobandi madrassas and outfits in such incidents of violence. There is also a need to examine how Pakistan and other countries could develop a comprehensive response to such radicalization and violence in order to create an inclusive and pluralistic society. In any society, people of diverse faiths and cultures should peacefully co-exist, feeling equally valued and protected.

Despite the fact that Pakistan was created as an independent homeland for Muslims, its founders were quite pluralistic in their approach to nation-building. Founded by a Shia Muslim, Quaid-i-Azam Muhammad Ali Jinnah (1876–1948), the country had a Sunni leader, Prime Minister Liaquat Ali Khan (1895–1951). Moreover, its first law minister, Jogendra Nath Mandal (1904–1968), was a Hindu, and its foreign minister, Sir Muhammad Zafarullah Khan (1893–1985), was an Ahmadi. The country's founder and first governor-general, Jinnah, thus expressed his commitment to the equal rights of all people, notwithstanding their religion, caste or creed, in his first presidential address to the Constituent Assembly of Pakistan in 1947:

> You are free; you are free to go to your temples, you are free to go to your mosques or to any other place or worship in this State of Pakistan. You may belong to any religion or caste or creed—that has nothing to do with the business of the State ... In course of time Hindus would cease to be Hindus, and Muslims would cease to be Muslims, not in the religious sense, because that is the personal faith of each individual, but in the political sense as citizens of the State.[3]

However, in the subsequent decades, the country could not uphold these pluralistic and egalitarian values. The recurring martial laws and the suppression of political parties, the gradual ascendancy of Islamist ideologies, the anti-Ahmadiyya movement of the 1950s, the anti-Shia violence since the 1980s, the forced takeover of Sunni Sufi/Barelvi mosques since the 1980s (ICG 2007), and the state patronage of the Deobandi and Salafi ideologies during and after the Afghan Jihad paved way for the persecution of and violence against not only non-Muslims but also Sunni Sufi, Barelvi, Shia and other denominations of Islam.

What started out as faith-based militancy by radical Deobandi groups against the Shias, Sunni Sufis, Barelvis and other religious groups has now metastasized into violence against the entire state. The cancer of takfirism seems to devour everything within its wake, including even the host—that is, the state. That is precisely what has happened in Pakistan. From the Moon Market blasts in Lahore in 2009, to the suicide attack on a volleyball match in Lakki Marwat in 2010 and the schoolchildren massacre in Peshawar in 2014—all these heinous crimes were committed by the Taliban and their various Deobandi affiliates and avatars. Even the Sri Lankan cricket team were not spared by the SSP/LeJ in 2009. These are just a few examples of the various indiscriminate attacks targeting innocent Pakistani civilians and foreigners regardless of which faith background or ethnicity they belonged to. Similarly, the army and police have been targeted by the same nexus of interconnected militant groups on countless occasions. The fatal assaults against high-ranking police officers, such as Ashraf Marth in Gujranwala (1997), Sifwat Ghayur in Peshawar (2010) and Chaudhry Aslam in Karachi (2014), were proudly claimed by these groups, as were the attacks on various military establishments, such as the General Headquarters (GHQ) in Rawalpindi (2009), Naval Station Mehran in Karachi (2011) and the air force base in Kamra (2012). These militants have also killed progressive political leaders and icons, such as Mohsin Naqvi (1996), Benazir Bhutto (2007), Shahbaz Bhatti (2011), Bashir Bilour (2012) and Shuja Khanzada (2015).

According to a report issued by Minority Rights Group International (MRGI 2015), religious minorities in Pakistan face systematic violence and persecution at the hands of militant groups, as well as high levels of social marginalization. The report clearly mentions Deobandi militant groups such as the SSP, the LeJ, the TTP, Lashkar-i-Islam and others, which attack, threaten and abduct minorities.[4]

Pakistan's Hindu community has experienced a shrinking population since Partition (in 1947) (HAF 2005). Hindus are estimated to constitute about 1.6 percent of Pakistan's population. Spread all over the country, most of them are in Sindh province with a major presence in Tharparkar, Mirpur Khas, Sanghar and Umerkot districts (Babar 2006; HAF 2005). For centuries, Hindus have been an integral part of the indigenous population of Pakistan and, in many instances, they participate actively and alongside the Muslim traditions of Sufism and Muharram (Raza 2015). Yet in recent times they have faced increasing marginalization and persecution. In 2013 the grave of a Hindu man was dug up and desecrated by a mob incited and led by the proscribed radical Deobandi group the ASWJ in the Pangrio area of Sindh (Reuters 2013).

There is some concern that the traditionally pluralistic social fabric of Sindh is under threat from the recent proliferation of Deobandi and Ahle-Hadith/Salafi madrassas (Siddiqa 2015). Coinciding with the mushrooming of these madrassas are the increasing reports of abduction and forced conversions of Hindu girls to Islam (*India Today* 2014). Siddiqa (2015) argues that the concentration of Deobandi and Salafi madrassas in areas with a Hindu population, opened with funding from the Gulf, have contributed to the process of social conversion. Not surprisingly, tension vis-à-vis religious minorities and instances of Eid Milad-un Nabi (a Sunni Sufi festival) being forcibly stopped have increased.

Mariana Babar (2006) highlights the issue of kidnapping and the forced conversions of Hindu girls. In one such example, in 2005, a Hindu couple in Karachi received a letter from their three missing daughters informing them that they had converted to Islam and were required as per Islamic *sharia* law not to live with infidels, including their Hindu parents. The letter bore the address of a Deobandi madrassa, Taleem ul Islam, based in Karachi. The Hindu community feels that it is the Islamists' agenda to drive out non-Muslims from Pakistan. A Hindu member of Pakistan's Parliament said on the floor of the House that "Several religious parties are reportedly behind the move to convince the people that it is their responsibility to get rid of infidels from Pakistan" (Babar 2006).

The plight of the Hindu community has only deteriorated in recent years. Minority Rights Group International (MRGI) (2015) reports that in 2014 the community experienced an alarming increase in attacks on places of worship. While a total of nine Hindu temples were attacked during 2013, five were targeted in March 2014 alone.

Similarly, Pakistan's indigenous Sikh community has also faced attacks at the hands of the Taliban and allied militant groups. According to a US State Department report on religious freedom, there are some 20,000 Sikhs residing across Pakistan (USDOS 2008).

On 6 September 2014, Harjeet Singh, the owner of a herbal medicine store in the Peshawar, was target killed. On 4 September 2014, another Sikh, Amarjeet Singh, was stabbed to death in Mardan. In August 2014, militants fired on members of the Sikh community in Peshawar, killing one and injuring two others. Sikhs are also exposed to kidnapping threats from militant groups. The kidnappers demand unaffordable sums and then kill the victim if they aren't paid. In February 2014, two Sikh businessmen were kidnapped in Dera Ismail Khan. They were released after allegedly paying a hefty ransom (Ahmad 2014). In January 2013, a 40-year-old Sikh was kidnapped by the militant group Lashkar-e-Islam in Khyber Agency (FATA). He was later beheaded, and his mutilated body was dumped in a sack with a note accusing him of spying for a rival group (*Times of India* 2013). In 2010, two Sikh men were beheaded by the Taliban in FATA. The choices given to them were stark: pay the hefty ransom or convert to Deobandi Islam (UPI 2010).

In addition to the routine attacks and target killings, the Sikh community in Peshawar and FATA report that they are often required to pay the Islamic *jizya* tax (poll tax on non-Muslim subjects) to militant groups (*The Express Tribune* 2014). It seems that the shadows that were first cast by Syed Ahmad's jihadist militancy against the Sikhs in the Khyber Pakhtunkhwa (KP)P/FATA region in the nineteenth century have re-emerged in the twenty-first century.

There is also some evidence of Deobandi support of ISIS, Al-Qaeda and other transnational terrorist movements. One recent example is the San Bernardino attack (Syed 2015). On 2 December 2015, 14 people were killed and 22 injured in a terrorist attack in San Bernardino, California. Syed Rizwan Farook and his wife, Tashfeen Malik, targeted a Department of Public Health event of about 80 employees. Farook was a US citizen of Pakistani descent who was a health department employee. Tashfeen Malik was a Pakistani-born resident of the USA. Farook used to frequent a Deobandi mosque while his wife was radicalized via the same route as scores of Pakistanis—that is, the harsh, stark and literalist Saudi-funded school of Wahhabism, and its South Asian variant, Deobandism. Tashfeen Malik and her family are said to have links to Lal Masjid (a radical Deobandi mosque in Islamabad), the SSP (DW 2015) and Dr Farhat Hashmi's Al-Huda Institute, known for spreading extremist Wahhabi/Deobandi ideology among South Asian Muslim women.

Declan Walsh (2015) reports in *The New York Times*:

> Relatives and neighbours said that, after some years in Saudi Arabia, Ms. [Tashfeen] Malik's father, Gulzar, rejected the Barelvi school of Sunni Islam that his family had traditionally practiced, and turned to the stricter Deobandi school. He stopped returning home for weddings, and his children, including Ms. Malik, did not meet their Pakistani relatives.

This is a major challenge currently facing Pakistan and other Muslim-majority nations. Historically peaceful and tolerant, Sunni Muslims (Sufis, Hanafis, etc.) are gradually being exposed to and radicalized by ultraorthodox Salafi and Deobandi ideologies, embracing the twisted notions of takfir and jihad.

A similar discovery was made by a former Department of Homeland Security employee, Phil Haney, who tracked members of the Deobandi movement with which Farook and Tashfeen Malik were affiliated. Haney worked for the department in Atlanta and at the US Customs and Border Protection's National Targeting Centre, where he researched people and groups that might be linked to terrorism. He identified members of the Deobandi movement and its various subgroups, such as Tablighi Jamaat and al-Huda, as they travelled into and out of the USA. It should be noted that Dar Al Uloom Al-Islamiyah of America mosque, frequented by Syed Farook, belongs to the Deobandi sect. Tashfeen Malik studied with Al-Huda in Pakistan. Hanley said that after more than six months of tracking the Deobandi movement, Homeland Security halted the investigation at the urging of the State Department's Office of Civil Rights. In a televised interview with Megyn Kelly of Fox News, Haney said that if he had been allowed to continue his investigation, Tashfeen Malik's visa application could have been flagged for greater scrutiny (*The Federalist* 2015).

Boone (2015) notes that Al-Huda specializes in attracting middle-class, educated women to discussions about a puritanical form of Islam that critics say is akin to the Deobandism of the Taliban or the Wahhabism of Saudi Arabia. Boone reveals that Tashfeen Malik's family had abandoned their traditional Sufi-based Barelvi Islam that is credited with being relatively tolerant.[5] He (2015) suggests that the family were radicalized towards the hardline Deobandi/Wahhabi ideology due to their residence in Saudi Arabia. Tashfeen Malik's father, Gulzar Ahmad Malik, moved his family to Saudi Arabia when his daughter was just a young girl.

As a matter of fact, the Deobandi connections to ISIS were evident long before the San Bernardino massacre. In November 2014, a public video was released by female students of Jamia Hafsa, a Deobandi madrassa in Islamabad, paying allegiance to Abu Bakr al-Baghdadi, the so called caliph of ISIS. In that video the girls invited ISIS to lead their takfiri jihadist movement in Pakistan. The video clip was owned and endorsed by Abdul Aziz, a senior Deobandi cleric of Islamabad's Lal Masjid. Aziz said that he respected Daesh and identified with its mission. Aziz admitted that the female students had prepared the video with his consent. The principal of the madrassa, Umme Hassan, reportedly endorsed the statement, saying that the girls were justified in declaring support for ISIS (Khan 2014).

Back in 2007, Aziz had made the headlines when he led violent demonstrations in favour of sharia law in Pakistan and in support of the Taliban. The standoff resulted in a military operation against Lal Masjid, in which scores of Deobandi militants and security personnel lost their lives.

There is also some evidence of the presence of Deobandi militants in Syria and Iraq. Security analysts contend that LeJ, Pakistan's most powerful Deobandi militant group, is fighting for ISIS in Iraq (Kugelman 2015). According to an estimate, as many as 500 Pakistani militants are currently in Iraq and Syria in support of ISIS and other militant groups (Neuman 2015). The Australian police are currently investigating the case of Omarjan Azari, the man arrested in Sydney who pleaded guilty to sending funds to ISIS. Azari revealed that he had sent more than $15,000 to help get people from Pakistan into Syria as fighters (Safi 2015).

The ISIS–Deobandi connection was also evident in the aftermath of the brutal execution of American journalist James Foley in August 2014. ISIS demanded the release of Aafia Siddiqui in its proposed prisoner exchange. Siddiqui, a Pakistani woman imprisoned in Texas on terrorism charges, is eulogized by Deobandi militants, but outside Pakistan, relatively few people say much about her. This suggests the presence and/or influence of Pakistanis within ISIS's ranks.

Mangla (2014) reports, "Before ISIS militants executed journalist James Foley in a grisly video posted online this week, they made several demands of the United States in exchange for his freedom. One was the release of Aafia Siddiqui, a Pakistani scientist who is currently in prison in Texas for 86 years."

James Foley's execution and the demand by his killers to release Aafia Siddiqui confirmed the links between Pakistan's Deobandi terrorists groups and ISIS. According to *The Nelson* (2014), "A call for her release would indicate Isil has a contingent of Taliban veterans from Afghanistan and Pakistan."

Robert Fisk (2014), in analysing the British Muslim identity of James Foley's killer, writes about this connection: "But the political origin of Indian Muslims—and here I'll use the frontiers of the old British India— surely provide a clue to the origins of the "Islamic State" which … Abu Bakr al-Baghdadi, has created. I suspect these roots lie in the Deobandis."

It is noteworthy that the Darul Uloom Deoband madrassa was founded in 1867 in the aftermath of two failed jihadist movements—that is, Shamli jihad led by Qasim Nanotvi; and other Deobandi pioneers who, instead of supporting and swearing allegiance to Mughal Emperor Bahadur Shah Zafar (whom they considered a lesser Muslim due to his Sufi beliefs) waged their independent jihad and for a short while established an "Islamic state" in the Shamli and Thana Bhawan region. Before the Shamli jihad, Deobandi icons Syed Ahmed (1786–1831) and Shah Ismail (1779–1831) had led a jihadist militancy, with the full knowledge and permission of the British colonial rulers, against the indigenous Sikh kingdom of the Punjab and Khyber Pakhtunkhwa (then the North West Frontier Province. They were fiercely resisted by indigenous Pashtun Muslims and finally crushed by the Sikh army in 1831 (Moj 2015). These two jihadist misadventures and, a few decades later, the Khilafat Movement (1919–1926) confirmed the Islamist political ambitions of the Deobandi movement and its leaders. It was only towards the end of the twentieth century that the Deobandis were able to establish their long-ambitioned sharia state in the shape of the Islamic Emirate of Afghanistan (1996–2001), commonly known as the Taliban.

Post-Partition, Fisk (2014) notes, the Deobandis became far more important and powerful in the Muslim-majority land of Pakistan. Indeed, their power gained impetus during the Afghan Jihad and reached its climax in the shape of the Taliban emirate in Afghanistan. Fisk notes that while the Deobandis restricted women, opposed Muslim hierarchies, and rejected the Shia and other communities, the Taliban "were to take these beliefs to an extreme which the original Deobandis would never have recognised". In Afghanistan, the Taliban were behaving as puritanical fascists, considering debate as little more than heresy. By 1998, Taliban groups along the Afghan–Pakistan border were punishing sinners with stoning and amputation, killing Shia Muslims and forcing women to adopt Islamist dress. Fisk remarks that the ideology and tactics of the Taliban are comparable to those of ISIS.

The links between ISIS and the Deobandis have also been witnessed in Kashmir where ISIS flags have been seen in Islamist rallies. According to a media report (Chastain 2014), a local leader said,

We are unable to control the youth who are drifting towards the Deobandi school of thought, which is more or less aligned to Wahabi (Wahhabi) sect … This is a disturbing trend in the Kashmir Valley, which is predominately of Barelvi thought. The trend in the coming future may disturb the social fabric and trigger sectarian clashes.

In Pakistan, ASWJ affiliates have already declared their affiliation with ISIS. According to a recent report (Rafiq 2014),

In recent years, anti-Shia militants have already done this in Quetta and Karachi, with bomb attacks on Shia residential communities. Already, social media accounts associated with the anti-Shia SSP (now known as Ahle Sunnat Wal Jamaat Pakistan) avidly promote the Islamic State's activities inside Iraq and Syria. And small groups of Pakistani jihadists have posted videos of themselves swearing allegiance to Abu Bakr al-Baghdad.

ISIS is found to be involved in terrorism within Pakistan. The Safoora Goth massacre in Karachi (13 May 2015), in which 46 Ismaili Shias were killed in cold blood, is believed to have been carried out by local Deobandi operatives of ISIS. According to *Aaj News* (10 July 2015), the attack was made on the direct orders of Abdullah bin Yousuf, who heads the Punjab and Karachi chapter of ISIS. The confession came from Tahir Minhaj (alias Sain), one of the main accused in the attack. Minhaj further revealed that ISIS wall-chalking in the city was done under Saad Aziz's supervision. Saad Aziz is a co-accused of the Safoora massacre and was also involved in the murder of Sabeen Mahmud, a civil society activist in Karachi. Saad Aziz said that Sabeen Mahmud was killed because of her statement against Moulana Abdul Aziz of Lal Masjid (*Indus News* 2015). Saad Aziz is revealed to be a follower of Deobandi hate cleric Haq Nawaz Jhangvi (founder of SSP), and he translated and published his takfiri/sectarian speech in an online magazine, *Al-Rashideen* (*The Express Tribune* 2015).

In June 2014, the Pakistan military started Operation Zarb-e-Azb, a joint military offensive being conducted by the Pakistan Armed Forces against various militant groups, including the TTP, LeJ, Al-Qaeda, Jundallah and allied organizations. In 2015, government statistics showed that major terrorist attacks had declined by 70 percent, and Pakistanis were flocking back to shopping malls and restaurants (Craig 2015). However, there is still a long way to go in order to enforce the ban on ASWJ, and to arrest and bring to justice all major TTP/ASWJ leaders. The attacks on persecuted communities have declined marginally but are still almost routine. For example, on 13 December 2015, a bomb blast killed 23 people in Parachinar, most of them Shia Muslims (Hussain 2015). Prior to that, in October 2015, at least 22 Shia and Sunni Muslims and a Hindu were killed in an attack on a Muharram procession in Jacobabad (*BBC News* 2015).

In recent years the plight of persecuted and target-killed faith groups has been noted by human rights organizations, which are beginning to document cases of Deobandi militancy in Pakistan. Perhaps the most detailed account is presented in the 2014 Human Rights Watch (HRW) report entitled *We are the Walking Dead* (HRW 2014). Besides presenting a moving account of what may be described as a pregenocide of Shia Muslims, the report highlights the Deobandi nexus of militant groups that engage in violence against the Shias. Amnesty International too has highlighted the target killing of Shias in a 2013 report (Amnesty International 2013). This identifies the Deobandi militant group, the LeJ, as the main perpetrator in these attacks. The assaults on Sunni Sufis, Shias and other communities have also been noted by other international organizations and leaders. For example, United Nations (UN) Secretary General Ban

Ki Moon highlighted and condemned the massacres of Shia Muslims in Pakistan in his statement issued on 23 October 2015 (UN 2015). Similarly, in his 2012 address to the UN, US President Barack Obama condemned the incitement against "Sufi Muslims and Shiite pilgrims" (The White House 2012). However, despite these high-level statements, there has been a dearth of exhaustive studies to document the scale and extent of violence facing these groups, except for a few voluntary efforts by the persecuted communities.

Notwithstanding the lack of consolidated research on this topic, at least some attention has been paid to Deobandi militancy in recent years. For example, in a public lecture at the World Affairs Council, C. Christine Fair (2015b) highlighted the Deobandi dimension of violence and terrorism:

> In Islam, just like there are in Christianity and Judaism, there are many interpretive traditions. Most of the militants that we are talking about come from one [tradition] and that is called Deobandism, and it is important to know this because all of the groups of Deobandis have a common ideological infrastructure, e.g., mosques, madrassas and religious scholars who issue *fatwas* [religious decrees] to justify what they do and these also become really important recruiting networks, and they also have ties to Deobandi political parties.

Fair (2015b) further notes that the vast majority of groups operating against Western interests in Pakistan and Afghanistan are Deobandis. She reports that in 2001, when the USA forced the Pakistanis to support its war on the Taliban, many of the Taliban's Deobandi allies turned against the Pakistani state even though the state had originally been its patron. As an example of Pakistan's Deobandi militants' alliance with the Afghan Taliban, Fair refers to the US cruise missile attack on an Al-Qaeda camp in Khost in 1988 that killed some members of Pakistani militant organizations. Fair further states:

> So they [the Pakistani Deobandi militants] felt that the Taliban had finally achieved a *sharia* under their ideological umbrella and the [Pakistani] state was being forced by Americans to undermine this amazing accomplishment. So these Deobandi organizations, some of them stayed loyal to the Inter-Services Intelligence [ISI, Pakistan's intelligence agency], many of them did not. And those groups began targeting the Pakistani state and began doing this actually at the end of 2001 and early 2002. And with this begins the emergence of what started to operate in 2007 under the banner of Pakistani Taliban [TTP]. Now Pakistani Taliban, think about them as this is as a kaleidoscope, you look at it, flick it, you look at it again, you see some thing else. When Pakistanis talks

about their own Taliban, they will often simply call them Taliban to deliberately confuse you. So you need to understand these are different organizations, they have overlapping membership, they have overlapping [Deobandi] ideology, but they are in many ways distinct in terms of what their goals are and what their areas of operation are. (Fair 2015b, video transcript)

The Deobandi–Al-Qaeda connection resurfaced in December 2015, when Indian security agencies arrested the head of Al-Qaeda in the Indian Subcontinent (AQIS), Sanaul Haq, alias Maulana Asim Umar, one of the most wanted terrorists in India. Educated at the Dar-ul-Uloom Deoband madrassa, from where he graduated in 1991, Haq fled to Pakistan, where he studied at the Jamia Uloom-e-Islamia, a Deobandi madrassa in Banuri Town, Karachi, that has produced several takfiri jihadists, including Masood Azhar (Jaish-e-Muhammad), Azam Tariq (SSP/ASWJ), Qari Saifullah Akhtar (Harkat-ul-Jihad al-Islami) and Fazl-ur-Rehman Khalil (Harkat-ul-Mujahideen). Haq was identified on the basis of the interrogation of an arrested Deobandi cleric, Abdul Rehman, who had been tasked to sett up "AQIS recruitment networks" in India. Abdul Rehman holds two PhDs in Arabic and Islamic studies from Deoband, and he runs a madrassa in the Tangi area of Cuttack district (Jha 2015; Swami 2015).

This book highlights the common ideology and overlapping membership of Deobandi militant outfits with a specific focus on faith-based violence in Pakistan. It develops and synthesizes academic research on this topic and highlights its relevance to issues of human rights and equality. It illuminates the multilevel challenges facing persecuted communities along societal, political and individual dimensions.

It also takes into account the intersectionality of religion with other dimensions of identity. In some instances, religion is intertwined with ethnicity, thus adding another layer to faith-based discrimination and persecution. This phenomenon occurs in the case of radicalized Deobandi Pashtuns and Balochs in Pakistan, some of whom may be intolerant of Shia Hazaras due to differences in both faith and ethnicity. In this specific instance, the Hazara ethnicity (Changezi 2015) provides an identification marker, which enables the persecuted community to be both ghettoized and targeted. According to Hussain (2010), an ethnic breakdown reveals that 35 percent of arrested terrorists are Pashtuns, who comprise about 15 percent of Pakistan's population. There is also an issue of how religion intersects with gender and/or class, adding to the complex and multilayered nature of discrimination and intolerance. An intersectional approach allows for the investigation of individual experiences at the nexus of religion and other social identities. It recognizes the problematic nature of the matrix of domination for minoritized or persecuted individuals (Cho et al. 2013; Collins 2004).

This volume is envisaged to be an essential guide and reference text on faith-based militancy and terrorism in Pakistan and across the globe. It is expected that governmental and international organizations—for example, the UN, the European Union (EU), human rights groups and the media—will refer to it to develop an informed and nuanced understanding of the subject.

It is also expected to be of widespread interest and value to those concerned with Pakistan, South Asia and faith, interfaith or political violence. It will serve to inform those countries (particularly the UK, the USA and South Africa) where Deobandi influence has taken hold and is growing. Any state concerned about militant organizations shaped or influenced by Deobandi ideas and organizations will find this a useful guide to analyse these concerns under an academic light.

The volume offers a combination of theoretical and empirical chapters, comprising critical literature reviews, conceptual analyses and empirical insights that interrogate and explore the issue of Deobandi militancy and faith-based violence. It uses a variety of research designs and interdisciplinary approaches to present a holistic perspective on the topic.

KEY QUESTIONS

While the above issues are discussed the following are some of the key questions addressed in the book:

1. To what extent is Deobandi ideology responsible for faith-based hatred and violence in Pakistani society?
2. What is the historical approach of Deobandism to heterogeneity, pluralism and tolerance within and outside Islam? To what extent does Deobandism expect or enforce uniformity or assimilation over other faiths and sects?
3. To what extent are the elements of takfir (excommunication) and jihad an integral part of Deobandi ideology?
4. To what extent is Deobandi ideology influenced by Salafi/Wahhabi ideology? In the context of the history of militancy in Islam, are there any similarities between takfiri Deobandis and the Khawarij?
5. To what extent is the governmental, institutional or informal support from Pakistan, Saudi Arabia, the USA and other countries, during and after the Afghan Jihad era, responsible for the rise of Deobandi militancy?

6. What is the role of Deobandi seminaries (madrassas), mosques and religiopolitical groups in the rise of Deobandi militancy?
7. What is the extent of the influence and power of Deobandi madrassas, religiopolitical parties, militant outfits, pressure groups and lobbies in Pakistan and other countries?
8. To what extent does the mainstream media maintain silence or dilute Deobandi militancy against Sunni Sufis, Barelvis, Shias, Christians, Ahmadis and other communities? To what extent are certain religious identities tabooed or silenced in the Pakistani media and society?
9. To what extent are the usual Sunni–Shia, Saudi–Iran, Islam–West and Muslim–Christian binaries appropriate to examine Deobandi militancy in Pakistan and elsewhere? Is there a sectarian violence equally evident between Deobandis and Barelvis/Shias/Christians/Ahmadis?
10. To what extent are the issues of blasphemy and takfir (apostatizing) intertwined with faith-based violence and persecution?
11. What are the implications of intersectionality of faith with other forms of identity such as gender, ethnicity and social class? In particular, how do women of persecuted communities suffer as a result of militancy and terrorism?
12. What is the role of the Deobandi diaspora in the West in the radicalization of ordinary Sunni Muslims and in subsequent acts of violence?
13. What can be done to reform Deobandi ideology, madrassas and other institutions to make them productive and harmonious elements of Pakistani and other societies?

While many, if not all, of the above issues are discussed to varying extents and detail in this book, it is acknowledged that some of them deserve further in-depth scholarship and merit a dedicated research volume in their own right. It is our hope that this volume will encourage and enable future researchers to extend scholarship in this field.

ORGANIZATION AND OVERVIEW OF CHAPTERS

Comprising 18 chapters, the book has been organized in a logical and easy-to-follow manner, beginning with the South Asian context and then expanding to the evolution of an international Deobandi movement. The volume highlights how such a development has implications for faith-based militancy within both a Pakistani and an international context. It also deals with the representation of Deobandism in the media, its links to the Salafi/ Wahhabi school of Saudi Arabia, its implications for women, and the current debates regarding countermeasures both within and outside Pakistan.

In "Could Pakistan Have Remained Pluralistic?" (Chapter 2), Pervez Hoodbhoy speculates whether Pakistan could have been different from how it is today, or whether an extraordinarily violent birth in 1947, inspired by religious nationalism, made the present inevitable. In this context, he examines three important questions. First, although Pakistan was formed on the basis of Muslim identity, might it have still remained an imperfect but de facto secular and pluralist state—perhaps like India or Bangladesh—where religious minorities may feel discriminated against but are relatively secure? Second, what historical events were principally responsible for the slide into the present epoch of radicalism and intolerance? And third, can Pakistan become an Islamic state in the not too distant future and what would that mean for its people? Hoodbhoy argues that if the caliphate ever comes to be, the axe would fall not only on non-Muslim minorities but also on several communities that are currently considered Muslim would see themselves characterized as non-Muslim.

In "The Genesis, Evolution and Impact of 'Deobandi' Islam on the Punjab: An Overview" (Chapter 3), Tahir Kamran delineates the process that culminated in the proliferation of the Deobandi version of Islam in Punjab that eventually led to the formation of terrorist organizations in the closing years of the twentieth century. He argues that the gradual spread of Deobandi influence was not in consonance with the composite cultural ethos that was intrinsic to Punjab. Kamran notes that the Deobandis are still in a minority but that the aggressive articulation of their religious beliefs has given them such leeway that it is possible to think that the creation of Pakistan was in fact to their advantage.

In "Covering Faith-Based Violence: Structure and Semantics of News Reporting in Pakistan" (Chapter 4), Abbas Zaidi argues that although hard news reporting is considered to be the most objective of all journalistic genres, it may often be biased. Using the appraisal model within the systemic-functional linguistics paradigm, Zaidi shows that the reporting in Pakistan can be as biased as any other journalistic genre. His chapter focuses on a case study where the Shias of Pakistan were victims of a Deobandi terror campaign. However, through its reporting, the media portrayed the Shias as the aggressors and the Deobandis as the victims.

In "Historical Roots of the Deobandi Version of Jihadism and Its Implications for Violence in Today's Pakistan" (Chapter 5), Arshi Saleem

Hashmi argues that the Deobandi movement seems to have multiple objectives. The Deobandi *ulema* (clerics) moved closer to politics and created the JUH in 1919. However, even before that, in 1914, Maulana Mahmudul Hassan, chancellor at Darul Uloom Deoband, conceived a movement for the liberation of India by which armed units would be deputed to organize the Pakhtuns of the tribal areas and rally support in Afghanistan to provide a convenient point for the Turkish army to open up a new front against the British. The movement was rooted in the politics of pan-Islamism, but its founders highlighted the differences in their militaristic outlook and criticized the politics of the non-violent movement, which dominated the nationalist Indian arena at that time. Hashmi notes that one of the important and dominant pillars of the Deobandi school of thought is a sacred right and obligation to go to any lengths to wage jihad so as to protect Muslims anywhere in the world. She argues that after the creation of Pakistan, religiously motivated violent Deobandi groups openly declared and claimed militancy, and they established a reign of terror in the country against various sects within Islam and people of other faiths.

In "Experiences of Female Victims of Faith-Based Violence in Pakistan" (Chapter 6), Faiza Ali uses an intersectional lens to document and highlight the Sunni Sufi, Shia and Ahmadi women's experiences of faith-based violence in Pakistan. She takes into account the intersectionality of faith with gender and ethnicity, particularly in the context of the Hazara Shia community of Quetta and the target killings of the Sunni Sufi, Shia and Ahmadi communities in other parts of Pakistan. Drawing on in-depth interviews with affected women, Ali considers the sociological and psychological aspects of faith-based violence and its intersectional implications.

In "Marked by the Cross: The Persecution of Christians in Pakistan" (Chapter 7), Edwina Pio and Jawad Syed argue that Christians in Pakistan are trapped between their religious faith and Islamic extremism, and are the victims of persecution. Christians have deep roots in Pakistan dating from the nineteenth century, and most of them are in the grip of economic and political poverty. They also bear the brunt of anti-Western sentiment in the world of Islam. In current-day Pakistan, mob violence resulting in injury and death, burning and killing of individuals, shooting during church services, rape, sexual abuse, kidnapping and forced conversion are some of the atrocities experienced by adherents to the Christian faith. Discrimination takes place against a background of religious extremism, the violation of minority rights, and often state-sanctioned jihadist discourse, with powerful figures remaining silent on issues of religious persecution and violence. Pio and Syed argue that while Christians in Pakistan do not have to pay the jizya and in theory are allowed to practice their religion, Islamic sharia law, including but not limited to the blasphemy law, facilitates their discrimination and constant persecution in their homes and places of worship.

In "Pakistan: A Conducive Setting for Islamist Violence against Ahmadis" (Chapter 8), Fatima Z. Rahman argues that Ahmadis continue to face persecution and violence, which dates back to Pakistan's independence. She argues that Islamist groups inspired by Deobandi theology, who are against other religious minorities, are largely responsible for perpetrating the violence against Ahmadis. Rahman argues that Ahmadis are particularly easy and vulnerable targets of Islamist terrorism because of enabling conditions created by the state's sanctioning of persecution as well as public opinion strongly prejudiced against Ahmadis.

In "Barelvi Militancy in Pakistan and Salmaan Taseer's Murder" (Chapter 9), Jawad Syed focuses on Barelvi-related violence and Salmaan Taseer's murder. He argues that the tragic murder of Punjab Governor Taseer in 2011 raises questions about the extent of Sunni Sufi or Barelvi extremism and the resultant militancy. In view of the significant support for Taseer's murderer by a section of Barelvis, there is a need to probe Barelvi militancy in terms of its current capability and future potential. Syed offers such probing, as well as an account of violence facing Sunni Sufis and Barelvis at the hands of Deobandi militants.

In "The Shias of Pakistan: Mapping an Altruistic Genocide" (Chapter 10), Abbas Zaidi critically examines the Shia genocide taking place in Pakistan. Claiming that the existing definitions of genocide are monolithic grand narratives, he refines the definition by contextualizing it with reference to the Shia genocide. One of the salient features of his proposal is that it explores genocide as being altruistic. Zaidi also investigates how power alignments play their part in defining genocide.

In "The Intra-Sunni Conflicts in Pakistan" (Chapter 11), Zulqarnain Sewag notes that people from different religious, sectarian and cultural backgrounds have peacefully co-existed in the area called Pakistan today. Sufis were the forerunners of peace. However, as they weakened, their place was filled by religious extremists. Sewag notes that in the historical course of Islam, there have been two major divisions: the Sunnis and the Shias. However, with the emergence of Darul Uloom Deoband in 1867 and the Barelvi movement in 1904, the mild intra-Sunni differences escalated into intra-Sunni conflicts, especially after

the Afghan Jihad of the 1980s, the 9/11 attacks, and incessant expor-
tation of Wahhabi ideology and funding from the Middle East to the
Deobandi and Ahl-e-Hadith (Salafi) groups. As a result, the Sunnis are
at daggers drawn with each other, with the traditional Sufis or Barelvis
usually on the receiving end. Sewag argues that if the intra-Sunni
differences are not addressed, they might irreparably damage the pluralistic nature of Pakistani society.

In "Genealogical Sociology of Sectarianism: A Case Study of Sipah-e-
Sahaba Pakistan" (Chapter 12), Tahir Kamran discusses the example of
SSP to argue that the causes other than ideological divide are important in
tracing the genealogical sociology of the militant organization. Different
groups and stakeholders involved in the conflict deploy multiple strategies
to further their interests. SSP represented more than just a violent struggle
against the Shia sect. Historically it was also a legacy of Ahrar; socially
it was a confrontation of urban nouveau riche in collaboration with the
migrant community, who were politically dispossessed by the Shia landlords; and, in a much wider context, it served as a means to counter the
Iranianization of Pakistan—the agenda set forth by General Zia ul Haq
and the military establishment with the aid of Saudi Arabia. Hence at various levels the same organization acted with multiple guises, purposes and
functionalities by serving the interests of various groups and states.

In "Islamization and Barelvis in Pakistan" (Chapter 13), Thomas
K. Gugler notes that the citizens of Pakistan are facing a massive terrorist
threat, in particular by both ISIS and the Taliban. He addresses the theological differences between Barelvis and Deobandis that in parts already
hint at the reasons why modern jihadism is somehow characteristic of
Deobandis, but not in an equal manner for Barelvis. Gugler argues that
forces other than just theology are the Wahhabi factor and its means of
realpolitik in funding conservative madrassas as well as the state policy of
supporting jihadist militancy for foreign policy projects and objectives.
The Peshawar APS massacre in 2014 was a clear statement of the fact that
the state has to act more efficiently to confront terrorist activities and to
find a solution for these seemingly religiously motivated attacks against
state and society. Gugler argues that the National Action Plan alone does
not yet seem to offer sufficient meaningful reasons for optimism. He suggests that one apparent strategy to fight Islamist extremism is the revival
of Pakistan's pluralist traditions of Islamic piety.

In "Fighting the Takfiris: Building an Inclusive American Muslim
Community by Countering Anti-Shia Rhetoric in the USA" (Chapter 14),

Raza Mir and Mohammad Ali Naquvi argue that the dominant problem concerning Muslims in the USA continues to be emerging Islamophobia, a racist tendency that denies any intra-Islamic heterogeneity in its construction of Muslims. However, recent events have brought a lot of sectarian tensions within Muslims to the fore, particularly in the shape of rising Salafi/Wahhabi and Deobandi puritanism, which manifests itself as an intolerance both of intra-Islamic heterogeneity and of non-Muslim faiths. Mir and Naquvi map the arc of this growing anti-Shia rhetoric in the USA, which can trace horizontal transnational connections to similar, well-developed movements in South Asia and the Middle East. They also provide counterexamples of pan-Islamic harmony in the US sphere. Finally, they offer suggestions regarding how Muslim groups that are opposed to extremist ideologies can assist in developing intrafaith initiatives to combat extremist outfits, whose anti-Shia rhetoric is the tip of a very dangerous iceberg in the USA.

In "The 'Othering' of the Ahmadiyya Community in Bangladesh" (Chapter 15), Humayun Kabir notes that the Ahmadiyya community has been historically subject to "othering" by the mainstream Muslims who are strongly antithetical to the Ahmadi belief in the prophethood of Mirza Ghulam Ahmad (1835–1908). Distinctive in the process of "othering", as delineated in this chapter, is that earlier the nature of resistance against the Ahmadiyya community was limited to theological debates, reform and preaching activities, but now it is becoming increasingly intolerant, hostile and violent. Kabir captures the shift from the Bengali Deobandis' preaching (tablighi) and reformist activities that began to construct the Ahmadiyya community as religiously "other" in Brahmanbaria, which is where the country's first Ahmadiyya Jamaat was established in 1912, to the rise of more politically charged violent persecution of the Ahmadiyya community in the 1980s, the beginning of the desecularization of the Bangladeshi state. He argues that the hate campaign against and persecution of the Ahmadiyya community tends to undermine the inclusive and syncretized religious traditions in Bangladesh, and that this is the result of the rise of political Islamic forces and their gradual strength in popularizing the demands for the sanctity of Sunni Islam—that is, the Deobandi/ Wahhabi variant of it. Kabir claims that the increased persecution of the Ahmadiyya community is bound to happen if the state fails to demarcate the boundary between religion and politics, and if the liberal-democratic forces continue to maintain an alliance with the Islamists and bow to their popular Islamist demands.

In "Hidden in Plain Sight: Deobandis, Islamism and British Multiculturalism Policy" (Chapter 16), Sam Westrop argues that the tendency of government, the media and academia to treat British Islam as one homogenous bloc has led to extremist strains of Sunni Islam, particularly the Deobandis, exerting increasing influence over British Muslims, to little protest from a naïve political elite. While some Deobandi groups maintain isolation from mainstream society, others—borrowing the tactics employed by Islamist groups—have attempted to exploit state multiculturalism policy, to work within public bodies and to learn to practise, in front of the media, a more tolerant rhetoric. Westrop argues that despite these differences in tactics, the hardline rhetoric taught by almost all Deobandi seminaries and clerics in the UK, some backed by Salafist monies, has served to fuel extremist ideas and has seemingly contributed towards the radicalization of Muslim youth.

In "Violence and the Deobandi Movement" (Chapter 17), Liyakat Takim examines the genesis and development of the movement, the key figures who shaped its ideology, and its religious basis and affiliation. He then discusses Deobandi militancy and violence in a transnational context, and documents and highlights the role of Deobandi ideology in the global spread of intolerance and extremism as an affiliate of or ally to the Salafi-Wahhabi ideology. Takim also explains why certain ideological differences exist and the role of the Deobandis in promoting violence and extremism. He also presents some examples of Deobandi violence, such as the group's participation in the 7/7 bombings in London and similar incidents of terror in the West, its contribution to Al-Qaeda terrorism and, more recently, its role as transnational warriors of ISIS in Iraq and Syria. The chapter also discusses the Deobandi movement's collusion with the SSP (the army of the companions of the Prophet) in its sectarian warfare against the Shi'is in Pakistan.

In "Pakistan's Counterterrorism Strategy: A Critical Overview" (Chapter 18), Naeem Ahmed critically evaluates the counterterrorism strategy of Pakistan, which it adopted after the 9/11 attacks in order to combat terrorism, unleashed by Al-Qaeda and the homegrown terrorist network of militant jihadi and sectarian groups, following the Deobandi takfiri ideology. He argues that despite the security operations in the tribal areas, the ability of Pakistan-based terrorist groups to plan and execute terror attacks has not been significantly damaged. The terror network, its strength and its structure have so far remained intact. Moreover, security operations have not reduced the bigger threat, which is now emanating from the urban-based militant sectarian groups, comprising well-educated and ideologically motivated hardcore terrorists. The chapter suggests that the success of Pakistan's counterterrorism strategy largely depends on implementing strong measures to neutralize violent extremist ideology. These measures include reforming madrasas that have become the nurseries of extremism and terrorism; establishing a punitive regime by improving the criminal justice system and further strengthening the anti-terrorism regime; launching counter-radicalization programmes to prevent the production of terrorists; introducing reforms in the public education sector to curb religious hatred and the enemy image of neighbouring countries; and redefining Pakistan's India-centric national security paradigm, which seeks support from militant jihadist groups.

Unique Features

Notwithstanding certain limitations (e.g., the need for further in-depth scholarship on some of the themes touched upon in this volume), this book has a number of unique features. First and foremost, it offers a departure from an Anglo-American view of sweeping generalizations (e.g., Islamist, terrorist or Sunni) or false mainstream binaries (e.g., Islam–West, Sunni–Shia, Saudi–Iran, Salafi–Sufi) to a more contextual, nuanced and informed understanding of terrorism and violence in Pakistan and on a global scale. The fact that most of the contributors are of Pakistani/South Asian heritage or have a contextual and critical understanding of the situation on the ground further adds to the credibility of the contributions, thus filling a niche in this domain. An international audience is likely to benefit from a deeper understanding of the issues presented herein.

The innovative aspect of this book is its focus on the Deobandi element of religious violence in Pakistan and elsewhere, a crucial aspect which some other works broach but only superficially as part of a larger project. This volume not only engages with recent scholarship but also includes works of an array of established and emerging scholars. The methodology of choosing a fresh approach is to collectively develop research and evolve the existing narrative in this domain.

In addition to theoretical and ideological analyses, the book offers valuable statistical data, empirical examples and critical case studies to illustrate the nature and extent of Deobandi militancy. It also evaluates the role of the state, the media and religious institutions in the spread of faith-based intolerance. Another unique feature is the book's consideration of the intersectionality of faith/sect with gender, social class and ethnicity, and its adverse implications for certain communities. Finally, it not only emphasizes the Deobandi dimension of terror but also offers recommendations for anti-terrorism, resolutions and, ultimately, peace.

This volume comes at a time when there is a dire need for new and effective discourses on terrorism. The specific identification of Deobandi militancy (in South Asia) and Salafi/Wahhabi militancy (internationally) instead of the perpetuation of generic, vague and lumping descriptors such as "Islamists", "terrorists" and "Sunni" is crucial when public voices are calling for "something to be done" about religious violence. A first step in that process is to understand the Deobandi phenomenon, including the role of Saudi Arabia and the USA in supporting such jihadi militants during the War in Afghanistan. This support was in collusion with the General Zia regime in Pakistan, a point which many in the West and mainstream media tend to forget.

AUDIENCE OF THE BOOK

The book is intended for an understanding and open audience including, but not limited to, government policy-makers, non-governmental organization (NGO) workers, terrorism analysts and consultants, peace and conflict studies scholars, and human rights activists. It will be of equal interest to academics and students in the fields of religious and ethnic studies, international relations, geopolitics, anthropology, sociology, political science, governance, diaspora studies, community studies, Islam, South Asia, media studies, peace and conflict studies, and diversity management. In other words, it has an interdisciplinary content and audience.

NOTES

1. Here, Fair is referring to the Sunni Sufi/Barelvi, Shia, Deobandi, Salafi/Ahl-e-Hadith and Ahamdiyya communities.
2. Deobandis do not exist outside South Asia except as diaspora in a few countries. Salafis are largely concentrated in Saudi Arabia and Qatar, and in small numbers in other countries. In Pakistan, Sunni Sufis and Barelvis represent around 60 percent of the Muslim population, 20 percent are Shias, 15 percent are Deobandis and 4 percent are Ahl-e-Hadith or Salafi (Bedi 2006). In Egypt, Salafis are no more than 6–7 percent of the population (*The Week* 2015). Even in Saudi Arabia, the hub of Wahhabi power, the Salafis/Wahhabis are estimated to be between 22 percent and 40 percent of the population (Izadi 2013; Schwartz n.d.).

The most prevalent Sunni subsects are Hanafi (dominant in South and Central Asia, Turkey and Egypt), Maliki (North, West and East Africa) and Shafii (South East Asia, East Asia). However, the Hanbali Salafis are concentrated only in Saudi Arabia and a few tiny sheikhdoms of the Persian Gulf (UNC 2009). Notwithstanding their numerical minority, Salafis are indoctrinating an increasing number of Sunni Muslims of Hanafi, Maliki and Shafii backgrounds owing to generous Saudi and Qatari funding (Blair 2014).

3. Muhammad Ali Jinnah's first presidential address to the Constituent Assembly of Pakistan on 11 August 1947. See Allana, G. (1969). *Pakistan Movement Historical Documents*. Karachi: Department of International Relations, University of Karachi, pp. 407–411.

4. Singh (2015) notes that the LeJ is aligned with groups such as the TTP, Jaish-e-Mohammad and Al-Qaeda, and that it advocates the destruction of the Shia sect, Christianity, Hinduism and Judaism.

5. Deobandis and Salafis allege that the Barelvi traditions of visiting shrines, honouring deceased saints and listening to Sufi devotional music that has characterized Islam in South Asia for centuries is blasphemous (Boone 2015).

References

Aaj News. (2015). ISIS involved in Safoora bus attack, July 10. http://aaj.tv/2015/07/isis-involved-in-safoora-bus-attack/

Ahmad, A. (2014, September 30). The killing of the Sikhs. *The Diplomat*. Available at: http://thediplomat.com/2014/09/the-killing-of-the-sikhs/

Alavi, H. (2002, November 2–9). Misreading partition road signs. *Economic and Political Weekly*. Available at: http://www.sacw.net/partition/alaviNov2002.html

Amnesty International. (2013, February 18). Pakistan: Authorities must do more to protect Hazara community from deadly attacks. *Amnesty International*. Available at: http://www.amnestyusa.org/news/news-item/pakistan-authorities-must-do-more-to-protect-hazara-community-from-deadly-attacks

Avebury, L. (2013, February 25). Hazara massacres. *The Huffington post*. Available at: http://www.huffingtonpost.co.uk/lord-avebury/hazara-massacres_b_2757747.html

Babar, M. (2006, January 23). Sindh's stolen brides. *Outlook India*. Available at: http://www.outlookindia.com/article/sindhs-stolen-brides/229886

BBC (2016). The Deobandis. By Owen Bennet Jones. BBC Radio 4, April 5-12. Available at: http://www.bbc.co.uk/programmes/b07766zw.

BBC News. (2015, October 23). Pakistan unrest: Suicide bomber kills Shia marchers in Jacobabad. *BBC News.* Available at: http://www.bbc.co.uk/news/world-asia-34622989

Bedi, R. (2006). *Have Pakistanis forgotten their Sufi traditions?* Singapore: International Centre for Political Violence and Terrorism Research, IDSS.

Blair, D. (2014, October 4). Qatar and Saudi Arabia 'have ignited time bomb by funding global spread of radical Islam'. *The Telegraph.* Available at: http://www.telegraph.co.uk/news/worldnews/middleeast/iraq/11140860/Qatar-and-Saudi-Arabia-have-ignited-time-bomb-by-funding-global-spread-of-radical-Islam.html

Boone, J. (2015, December 7). San Bernardino shooter's 'hardline' Islam not an outlier in native Pakistan. *The Guardian.* http://www.theguardian.com/us-news/2015/dec/07/tashfeen-malik-pakistan-conservative-islam-isis-san-bernardino-shooting

Changezi, S. H. (2015, November 15). Zabul opportunists. *Dawn.* Available at: http://www.dawn.com/news/1219735/zabul-opportunists

Chastain, M. (2014, August 1). Islamic State flag confuses government and separatists in India. *Breitbart.* Available at: http://www.breitbart.com/Big-Peace/2014/08/01/Islamic-State-Flag-Confuses-Government-and-Separatists-in-India

Cho, S., Crenshaw, K. W., & McCall, L. (2013). Toward a field of intersectionality studies: Theory, applications, and praxis. *Signs, 38,* 785–810.

Collins, P. H. (2004). Learning from the outsider-within: The sociological significance of black feminist thought. In S. Harding (Ed.), *The feminist standpoint theory reader: Intellectual and political controversies.* New York: Routledge.

Craig, T. (2015, September 8). In Pakistan, a prime minister and a country rebound—at least for now. *The Washington Post.* Available at: https://www.washingtonpost.com/world/asia_pacific/in-pakistan-a-prime-minister-and-a-country-rebound--at-least-for-now/2015/09/07/4661049e-5173-11e5-8c19-0b6825aa4a3a_story.html

Dawn. (2011, May 21). 2008: Extremist recruitment on the rise in south Punjab madrassahs. *Dawn.* Available at: http://www.dawn.com/news/630656/2008-extremist-recruitment-on-the-rise-in-south-punjab-madrassahs

DW. (2015, December 5). The deadly link between San Bernardino and Pakistan. *DW.* Available at: http://www.dw.com/en/the-deadly-link-between-san-bernardino-and-pakistan/a-18897198

EP (European Parliament). (2013). *The involvement of Salafism/Wahhabism in the support and supply of arms to rebel groups around the world.* Brussels: Directorate-General for External Policies of the Union.

Fair, C. C. (2015a, July 20). *Does Pakistan have a Madrasah problem? Insights from new data.* Available at SSRN: http://ssrn.com/abstract=2468620

Fair, C. C. (2015b, March 4). Pakistan, the Taliban and Regional Security. Public Lecture. *World Affairs Council.* Available at: http://www.worldaffairs.org/media-library/event/1422

Fareed, M. F. (2014, February 28). Deoband cleric declares support for Narendra Modi. *The Indian Express*. Available at: http://indianexpress.com/article/cities/lucknow/deoband-cleric-declares-support-for-modi/

Fisk, R. (2014, August 24). Isis's skill in exploiting social media is no reason for US leaders to start talking about the apocalypse. *The Independent*. Available at: http://www.independent.co.uk/voices/comment/isiss-undoubted-skill-in-exploiting-social-media-is-no-reason-for-us-leaders-to-start-talking-about-9688438.html

Geo TV. (2009, December 30). Blackwater involved in Karachi catastrophe, says Mufti Usmani. *Geo TV.* Available at: http://www.geo.tv/12-30-2009/55868.htm

Government of Pakistan. (2015). Population, labour force and employment. *Government of Pakistan.* Available at: http://www.finance.gov.pk/survey/chapters_15/12_Population.pdf

HAF (Hindu American Foundation). (2005). *Hindus in South Asia and the diaspora: A survey of human rights.* Available at: http://www.hafsite.org/pdf/hhr_2005_html/pakistan.htm

HRW (Human Rights Watch). (2014, June 29). "We are the Walking Dead": Killings of Shia Hazara in Balochistan, Pakistan. *Human Rights Watch.*

Hussain, S. E. (2010). *Terrorism in Pakistan: Incident patterns, terrorists' characteristics, and the impact of terrorist arrests on terrorism* (PhD Thesis, Penn Dissertations Paper 136). http://repository.upenn.edu/edissertations/136

Hussain, M. (2015, December 13). At least 23 killed, 30 injured in Parachinar blast. *The Express Tribune.*

ICG (International Crisis Group). (2007, March 29). *Pakistan: Karachi's Madrasas and Violent Extremism.* International Crisis Group.

India Today. (2014, 18 April). *1,000 Christian, Hindu girls forced to convert to Islam every year in Pakistan: report.* http://indiatoday.intoday.in/story/1000-christian-hindu-girls-forced-to-convert-to-islam-every-year-in-pakistan-report/1/353608.html

Indus News. (2015, July 12). Safoora tragedy accused reveals association with ISIS: JIT report. *Online Indus.* Available at: http://www.onlineindus.com/safoora-tragedy-accused-reveals-association-with-isis-jit-report/

Izady, M. (2013). *Demography of religion in the Gulf.* Gulf 2000 project, Columbia University. Available at: http://gulf2000.columbia.edu/

Jha, R. (2015, December 9). Al-Qaida's India chief comes from freedom fighters' family. *The Times of India.* Available at: http://timesofindia.indiatimes.com/india/Al-Qaidas-India-chief-comes-from-freedom-fighters-family/articleshow/50239495.cms

Kamran, T. (2014, November 30). Is apolitical Islam possible? *The News.* Available at: http://tns.thenews.com.pk/is-apolitical-islam-possible

Khan, A. (2014, December 15). No regret over supporting IS, says Lal Masjid cleric. *The Express Tribune.* Available at: http://tribune.com.pk/story/806711/no-regret-over-supporting-is-says-lal-masjid-cleric/

Kugelman, M. (2015, February 25). How serious is the ISIS threat to South Asia? *The Express Tribune*. Available at: http://blogs.tribune.com.pk/story/26350/how-isis-could-become-a-potent-force-in-south-asia-how-serious-is-isiss-threat-to-south-asia/

Mangla, I. S. (2014, August 22). Who is Aafia Siddiqui, The woman ISIS wanted in exchange for journalist James Foley? *International Business Times*. Available at:http://www.ibtimes.com/who-aafia-siddiqui-woman-isis-wanted-exchange-journalist-james-foley-1666822

Metcalf, B. D. (2002). 'Traditionalist' Islamic activism: Deoband, Tablighis, and *Talibs*. SSRC essay. Available at: http://essays.ssrc.org/10yearsafter911/traditionalist-islamic-activism-deoband-tablighis-and-talibs/

Metcalf, B. D. (2011). *"Traditionalist" Islamic activism: Deoband and Deobandis, ten years later*. SSRC paper, Available at: http://essays.ssrc.org/10yearsafter9 11/%E2%80%9Ctraditionalist%E2%80%9D-islamic-activism-deoband-and-deobandis-ten-years-later/

Moj, M. (2015). *The Deoband madrassah movement: Countercultural trends and tendencies*. London: Anthem Press.

MRGI (Minority Rights Group International). (2015, July 2). State of the World's minorities and indigenous peoples 2015—Pakistan. *Minority Rights Group International*. Available at: http://www.refworld.org/publisher,MRGI,ANN UALREPORT,PAK,55a4fa494,0.html

Neuman, P. R. (2015, January 26). Foreign fighter total in Syria/Iraq now exceeds 20,000; surpasses Afghanistan conflict in the 1980s. *ICSR*. http://icsr.info/2015/01/foreign-fighter-total-syriairaq-now-exceeds-20000-surpasses-afghanistan-conflict-1980s/

PTI. (2015, December 17). US lawmaker seeks shutting down of Deobandi madrasas in Pakistan. *The Economic Times*. Available at: http://economictimes.indiatimes.com/news/international/world-news/us-lawmaker-seeks-shutting-down-of-deobandi-madrasas-in-pakistan/articleshow/50216173.cms

Rafiq, A. (2014, July 28). Will the Islamic state spread its tentacles to Pakistan? *The Diplomat*.Availableat:http://thediplomat.com/2014/07/will-the-islamic-state-spread-its-tentacles-to-pakistan/

Raza, H. (2015, March 5). Mithi: Where a Hindu fasts and a Muslim does not slaughter cows. *Dawn*. Available at: http://www.dawn.com/news/1167315

Reuters. (2013, October 8). *Religious tension in Pakistan as Muslims dig up Hindu grave*. http://www.reuters.com/article/us-pakistan-hindus-grave-idUSBRE9970EF20131008

Safi, M. (2015, December 16). Man arrested in Sydney raids pleads guilty to sending funds to Isis. *The Guardian*. Available at: http://www.theguardian.com/australia-news/2015/dec/16/funds-meant-for-isis-was-to-help-fighters-get-from-pakistan-to-syria-sydney-court-hears

Schwartz, S. (n.d). *Stephen Schwartz discusses Wahhabism*. http://www.sullivan-county.com/immigration/schwartz.htm

Siddiqa, A. (2015, March 3). The madressa mix: Genesis and growth. *Dawn*. Available at: http://www.dawn.com/news/1166039

Sikand, Y. (2008). Reflections on Deoband's anti-terrorism convention. *Economic and Political Weekly, 43*, 13–15.

Singh, S. (2015, July 30). A terrorist's killing in Pakistan—The background. *The Indian Express*. http://indianexpress.com/article/explained/a-terrorists-killing-in-pakistan-the-background/

Swami, P. (2015, December 17). Head of al-Qaeda in Indian Subcontinent is from Uttar Pradesh. *The Indian Express*. Available at: http://indianexpress.com/article/india/india-news-india/head-of-al-qaeda-in-indian-subcontinent-is-from-up/

Syed, J. (2008). The representation of cultural diversity in Urdu-language newspapers in Pakistan: A study of Jang and Nawaiwaqt. *South Asia: Journal of South Asian Studies, 31*(2), 317–347.

Syed, J. (2015, December 8). From Karachi to San Bernadino: In quest of an alternative discourse on terrorism. *The Huffington Post*. Available at: http://www.huffingtonpost.co.uk/jawad-syed/san-bernadino-karachi-terrorism_b_8740002.html

Tanoli, I. (2015, October 24). Five years on, Ashura bombing suspects still at large. *Dawn*. Available at: http://www.dawn.com/news/1215128

The Express Tribune. (2014, January 26). The shoes I walk in: Minorities blame growing discrimination for the loss of a feeling of fellowship. *The Express Tribune*. Available at: http://tribune.com.pk/story/663510/the-shoes-i-walk-in-minorities-blame-growing-discrimination-for-the-loss-of-a-feeling-of-fellowship/

The Express Tribune. (2015, May 22). Saad Aziz confesses to Sabeen's murder for holding Valentine's Day rally. *The Express Tribune*. Available at: http://tribune.com.pk/story/890555/saad-aziz-confesses-to-sabeens-murder-for-holding-valentines-day-rally/

The Federalist. (2015, December 10). *Blockbuster allegation: DHS, State halted investigation into Islamist group linked to San Bernardino terrorists*. http://thefederalist.com/2015/12/10/dhs-state-halted-investigation-into-islamist-group-linked-to-san-bernardino-terrorists/

The News. (2014, February 13). Armed struggle against Pakistan is un-Islamic: Fazl. *The News*.

The Week. (2015, January 19). What is Salafism and should we be worried by it? *The Week*. Available at: http://www.theweek.co.uk/world-news/6073/what-is-salafism-and-should-we-be-worried-by-it

The White House. (2012, September 25). *Remarks by the President to the UN General Assembly*. Available at: https://www.whitehouse.gov/the-press-office/2012/09/25/remarks-president-un-general-assembly

Times of India. (2013, January 9). Kidnapped Sikh man beheaded in Pakistan's tribal belt. *Times of India*. Available at: http://timesofindia.indiatimes.com/

world/pakistan/Kidnapped-Sikh-man-beheaded-in-Pakistans-tribal-belt/articleshow/17951666.cms

UN (United Nations). (2015, October 23). Ban condemns terrorist attacks in Pakistan on religious holiday. *Un News Centre*. http://www.un.org/apps/news/story.asp?NewsID=52365#.VnXAg5OLTBI

UNC (University of North Carolina). (2009). *Jurisprudence and law—Islam reorienting the veil*. University of North Carolina. Available at: http://veil.unc.edu/religions/islam/law/

UPI. (2010, February 22). *Report: Two Sikhs beheaded in Pakistan*. Available at: . http://www.upi.com/Top_News/International/2010/02/22/Report-Two-Sikhs-beheaded-in-Pakistan/UPI-87261266842522/

USDOS (US Department of State). (2008). *International religious freedom report 2007*. Available at: http://www.state.gov/j/drl/rls/irf/2007/90233.htm

Walsh, D. (2015, December 6). Tashfeen Malik was a 'Saudi girl' who stood out at a Pakistani university. *The New York Times*.

Zaidi, A. (2014, December). Lessons of the Rawalpindi Ashura tragedy. *Viewpoint Online*. Available at: http://www.viewpointonline.net/site/component/content/article/37-columnnews/3510-lessons-of-the-rawalpindi-tragedy-.html

Zia, F. (2013, February 24). "LeJ's ideology is to strengthen a Sunni state": Interview with defense and security analyst Dr Ayesha Siddiqa. *The News*. Available at: http://jang.com.pk/thenews/Feb2013-weekly/nos-24-02-2013/spr.htm#1

CHAPTER 2

Could Pakistan Have Remained Pluralistic?

Pervez Hoodbhoy

In this chapter I shall speculate whether Pakistan could possibly have been different from what it is today, or whether an extraordinarily violent birth in 1947, inspired by religious nationalism, made the present inevitable. In this context, three important questions suggest themselves:

1. Although Pakistan was formed on the basis of Muslim identity, might it have still remained an imperfect but de facto secular and pluralist state—perhaps like India or Bangladesh—where religious minorities may feel discriminated against but are relatively secure?
2. What historical events were principally responsible for the slide into today's radicalism and intolerance?
3. Can Pakistan become an Islamic state in the not too distant future? What would that mean for its people?

Pakistan's early years were tolerably good for those non-Muslims who still remained within the borders of the newly emergent Muslim state. A massive transfer of population across borders had dislocated tens of millions, but the English-speaking native elite from the days of the Raj were still firmly in command in both India and Pakistan. Religious right-wing

P. Hoodbhoy (✉)
Forman Christian College, Lahore, Pakistan

© The Editor(s) (if applicable) and The Author(s) 2016
J. Syed et al. (eds.), *Faith-Based Violence and Deobandi
Militancy in Pakistan*, DOI 10.1057/978-1-349-94966-3_2

parties in Pakistan that opposed equal citizenship rights, in particular Jamaat-e-Islami and Deobandi forces, did not yet have enough members with sufficient education or skills to be significant players in governing the new country.

Consequently, many non-Muslims continued with their positions in the civil service, armed forces, and various high civilian posts. In his celebrated August 11, 1947 speech, the founder of Pakistan, Mohammed Ali Jinnah, assured them that they "may belong to any religion or caste or creed; that has nothing to do with the business of the State". This received reinforcement with his appointment of Jogendra Nath Mandal, a Hindu, as Pakistan's first law minister. While a few of Jinnah's close associates vehemently disagreed in private, Ahmadis were legally Muslims and well placed in official positions. Jinnah's choice of Chaudhry Zafarullah Khan, an Ahmadi, as the first foreign minister of Pakistan, carried a strong message of reassurance for Ahmadis.

However, the initial religious unity did have its limits. The Shia–Sunni divide became apparent when the prayers at Jinnah's state funeral were led not by a Shia aalim, as is the custom among Shias, but instead by a Sunni Deobandi aalim, Shabbir Ahmed Usmani. Nevertheless, the centuries-old Sunni–Shia dispute was then mostly in cold storage. That Shias were deviants from the Islamic faith was certainly whispered, but it was rarely broadcast from the minarets.[1]

That gentle past is well behind us. Less than two years after the country's birth, the Objectives Resolution required citizens to be identified on the basis of their religion. In 1953, Lahore was engulfed in anti-Ahmadi riots, leaving hundreds dead. Then, in 1956, Pakistan underwent a name change and became the Islamic Republic of Pakistan. Nevertheless, its constitution still subscribed to a diluted form of pluralism. Karachi, Lahore, and Quetta were culturally diverse metropolises. Several non-Muslims, such as Flight Commander Cecil Chaudury and Wing Commander Mervyn Leslie Middlecoat, were prominent in the list of heroes of the Indo-Pakistani War of 1965.

It was sometime in the 1970s that the relative open-mindedness of early Pakistan began to fade. From a softer, syncretic, and accommodative form of South Asian Islam, Pakistan's trajectory shifted towards a harder, literal, and exclusionary form of Arabized Islam, largely of Deobandi persuasion. As Kamran describes it, the "Deobandi denomination epitomised the scriptural interpretation of Islam. Ulema like Imdadullah Muhajir Makki, Rahmatullah Kairanwi and later on Anwar Shah Kashmiri played a role in bringing local version(s) of Islam in line with the way it was practised and professed in Hijaz and Egypt. In the 20th century, the war of Tripoli [the Tripolitan War (1801–1805)] and, later, the First World War (1914–1918) helped crystalise the pan-Islamic episteme."[2] According to a PhD thesis on terrorism in Pakistan, around 90 percent of religious terrorists are Deobandi by faith and many of them are Pashtun by ethnicity.[3]

However, one must be careful not to ascribe the shift entirely to the Deobandi version of the faith. One notes that Barelvis are today the strongest champions of the blasphemy law, a weapon that non-Muslims have come to fear like nothing else. The centrality that religion has acquired today in matters of eating, drinking, apparel, and culture cannot be attributed to the efforts of any one Muslim sect.

Now, with hundreds of attacks having occurred on their places of worship and a feeling that society at large discriminates against them, large sections of Pakistan's Christian, Hindu, Ahmadi, and Parsi communities have chosen to emigrate rather than live their lives on the margins. Many Christians and Hindus have changed their names to Muslim ones in the hope of concealing their identity. Ironically, Ahmadis were among the strongest proponents of the division of India, but today they are undoubtedly the most scared, and the most strongly discriminated against. Those who remain are fearful, conscious that any dispute with "real" Muslims could instantly result in their being falsely accused of blasphemy.

Liberal Pakistanis are often quick to attribute the country's changed texture to 11 years of General Zia-ul-Haq's rule (1977–1988). They blame him for overturning Jinnah's alleged vision of a modern, secular state and inserting instead an atavistic, radicalized version. But this accusation hangs too great a weight on too slender a thread. No individual can change a country's direction unless it was already prepared. Zia received support from not just the army and clergy but also from wide swathes of the population. His death in an air crash did not lead to a discontinuity of policy. All subsequent democratic and military governments maintained mind-twisting education as part of their education policies and failed to reduce the role of religion in matters of the state. Today, secularism in Pakistan still seems remote and unattractive to most Pakistanis, although proponents try in vain to prove that it actually means having a plurality of religions rather than no religion.

Pakistan's situation is mirrored across the Muslim world. Today's Syria, Iraq, and Libya are hell holes for minorities, while in Egypt the Coptic minority remains endangered. Surely those situations would have still come to be, even if Zia-ul-Haq had never existed. It surely makes little sense to try to link the Iranian Revolution of 1979 or the rise of Da'ish in 2014 with events in South Asia 70 years earlier. Clearly, considering matters related to the Islamic faith is absolutely essential.

To be sure, pluralism and secularism are under attack in many countries, including non-Muslim ones. In Israel the early Zionists had claimed commitment to universalistic ideals, but aggressive Jewish exclusivism now dominates. In India the secularism of Jawaharlal Nehru has waned with the rise of Hindutva forces, and Christians and Muslims are constantly reminded of their minority status by the government of Narendra Modi. In Myanmar, the tiny community of Rohingya Muslims lives in constant fear. And in China, the Uighur Muslims have been slapped with outright denials of religious freedom.

This return to primal behavior is interesting from a sociological perspective and is a challenge to understand. In evolutionary terms, cooperation between humans, rather than conflict between them, has been responsible for all progress. But now, reversion to ethnic, racial, national and religious characteristics is increasingly dominant in most parts of the Islamic world. This may have an explanation in terms of fiercer competition for resources, excessively rapid urbanization, the psychological insecurity induced by the explosive speed of technological and scientific progress, or the enhanced ability of religious and ethnic zealots to spread hate messages through the internet and mass media. However here we shall not explore these deeper matters any further.

Instead a more direct, case-specific approach will be taken here. Understanding Pakistan's present condition calls for a framework that is cognizant of the history of pluralism in Islam, together with the limits on equal citizenship placed by Islamic doctrines and injunctions. We shall then deal with the specific circumstances surrounding the carving of a Muslim majority state out of united India; the political trajectory followed by Pakistan until 1979 (the year of the Soviet invasion of Afghanistan); and the zigzag path that it has followed. Towards the end we shall speculate on where Pakistan might be headed.

PLURALISM IN ISLAMIC HISTORY

Religious pluralism in its broadest sense refers to the belief that a diversity of beliefs and practices should be accommodated within a society with equal citizenship rights. It must be distinguished from toleration, which allows only for co-existence with those with whom one has a fundamental disagreement. On the other hand, pluralism corresponds to a worldview wherein one's religion is not the sole source of truth, and where at least some truths and true values exist in other religions. One may further disaggregate pluralism into inter-religious pluralism and intrareligious pluralism. The latter relates to other religions, and the former to sects within the same religion.

Islamic history contains significant episodes where toleration, but sometimes also pluralism, was considered normal. Moorish Spain is the prime example.[4] Between 711 and 1492, a melding of Christian, Jewish and Muslim traditions created a unique culture. Each group contributed its best, thrived and prospered, while maintaining its separate religious tradition. Churches, synagogues, and mosques were open to worshippers; those who were atheists co-existed with believers. Moorish Spain was different from other Muslim civilizations in Arab or Persian lands because of the co-existence of different faiths, so it is considered to be the epitome of a state based on universal principles, capable of accommodating and accepting citizens irrespective of their faith.

Another example is that of the great Moghul emperor Akbar-i-Azam.[5] Born in 1542, Akbar was a Sunni Hanafi Muslim who has come to symbolize religious syncretism and adaptation. From the fifteenth century, a number of rulers in various parts of India had adopted policies of religious tolerance to lessen communal disharmony between Muslims and Hindus. These sentiments were further encouraged by the teachings of popular saints, such as Guru Nanak, Kabir, and Chaitanya. Persian poets such as Rumi, Hafiz, and Sadi advocated human sympathy and a liberal outlook. One of Akbar's first actions after gaining control of the administration was the abolition of jizya. Akbar met Portuguese Jesuit priests and sent an ambassador to Goa, requesting them to send two missionaries to his court so that he could understand Christian doctrines better.

South Asia's Muslim societies have a long tradition of charismatic Sufi masters, such as Mansur al-Hallaj and Jalaludin Rumi, who invested in the concept of subjugating the self (jihad bi nafsihi) to the service of the Creator and His creation. Allah, they argued, must be worshiped not out of duty or fear but because he loved his creation and was loveable. Many dedicated their lives to the service of the weak and needy. In searching for that divine love, Sufi Muslims pray at shrines, venerate local saints, sing, and dance themselves into ecstatic oblivion. In India, some Sufi saints continue to be revered by Muslims and Hindus alike.

CAN ISLAMIC DOCTRINE ACCOMMODATE PLURALISM?

Abundant historical precedents, some of which are mentioned above, demonstrate that Muslim societies have been tolerant and pluralistic. But is pluralism actually sanctioned by Islamic teachings or even consistent with them? There is considerable scope for opinion here. Owing to a lack of an unchallengeable religious authority, grand questions such as "Does Islam permit a pluralistic state?" are fundamentally unanswerable in Sunni Islam. Unlike in Catholicism, where the Pope provides absolute authority, Islam lacks a central figure who is acceptable to all sects. Only a living caliph can formally adjudicate, but, in spite of Abu Bakr Al-Baghdadi being a claimant, no such individual is accepted by any significantly large fraction of Muslims today.

One must therefore revert to the sole point of agreement between all Sunni Muslims and all Shia Muslims—the Qur'an. Accepted by all Muslims as the unaltered word of God, it is the final authority in matters of adjudication. On the other hand, the life of the Prophet, as recorded in the Hadith, is considered important by most Muslims. But since there are errors of transmission, it is not considered to be authoritative at the same level. No arguments from outside Islam have validity because, as a faith, Islam is a set of immutable principles that does not need compatibility with anything other than itself.

When argued in the light of the Qur'an, intrareligious pluralism is certainly permissible. No Muslim sects are defined in the Qur'an because, as is well known, the division into Sunni and Shia sects came about roughly 25 years after the death of the Holy Prophet and arose because of the dispute about succession. Muslims can therefore legitimately argue that there is no room for sectarian conflict in pristine Islam.

Inter-religious pluralism is more complicated. On the one hand, the injunctions *la ikraha fi-din* (there is no compulsion in religion) and *lakum dinukum, wa liya din* (to each his own faith) are often cited as proof that Islam supports individual choice. In fact, modernist Muslims frequently quote this to prove that Islam can co-exist within a secular sphere and that it is a belief system that can combine with any political order of your choice. However, the matter cannot be considered resolved because if Islam does permit religious freedom then an individual who is born a Muslim, or has converted to Islam, should be allowed to leave the religion. But a dominant interpretation is that this amounts to *irtidad* (apostasy), for which most Islamic scholars agree the penalty is death.

Three important elements of the Islamic faith need clarification by consensus. Without their explicit rejection, pluralism is impossible to achieve within a state that purports to be run by Qur'anic principles. They are the concepts of jizya (penalty), *zimmi* (non-Muslims), and *but-shikinee* (destruction of idols).

Jizya is a protection tax levied on zimmis living under Islamic regimes, affirming that their legal status is not that of a full citizen. Maulana Abul Ala Mawdoodi, a subcontinental religious aa'lim of Indian origin, whose influence extends deep into the Middle East, states that "acceptance of the Jizya establishes the sanctity of their lives and property, and thereafter neither the Islamic state, nor the Muslim public have any right to violate their property, honor or liberty".[6] He draws inspiration from Qur'anic verses such as:

> Qur'an 9.05: When the sacred months are past [in which a truce had been in force between the Muslims and their enemies], kill the idolaters wherever you find them, and seize them, besiege them and lie in wait for them in every place of ambush; but if they repent, pray regularly and give the alms tax, then let them go their way, for God is forgiving, merciful.

> Qur'an 9.29: Fight those who do not believe in God or the Last Day, and who do not forbid what has been forbidden by God and His Messenger [Muhammad], and those among the People of the Book who do not acknowledge the religion of truth until they pay tribute [jizya], after they have been brought low.

As Mawdoodi emphasizes, jizya is a symbol of humiliation and submission because zimmis should not be regarded as full-fledged citizens of the Islamic state even if they are natives to the country. Zimmis are not allowed to build new churches, temples, or synagogues. They are allowed to renovate old churches or houses of worship provided that they do not add any new construction. "Old churches" are those which existed prior to Islamic conquests and are included in a peace accord by Muslims. Construction of any church, temple, or synagogue in the Arab Peninsula (Saudi Arabia) is prohibited. It is the land of the Prophet and only Islam should prevail there. Yet Muslims, if they wish, are permitted to demolish all non-Muslim houses of worship in any land they conquer.

As a monotheistic religion, Islam does not tolerate idol worship. The destruction of idols (but-shikinee), considered mandatory for Muslims, puts literalist Islam at odds with religions such as Hinduism and Buddhism.

Idols deserving to be destroyed include statues (the Golden Calf in particular), persons (including Jesus), gods other than Allah, as well as Jinns and Satan. The Qur'an states: "Make war on them until idolatry shall cease and God's religion shall reign supreme" (Surah 8:36).

Mawdoodi, who is a Hanifite, expresses an opinion towards Christians different from those of Wahhabi school. He says:

> In their own towns and cities zimmis are allowed to do so [practice their religion] with the fullest freedom. In purely Muslim areas, however, an Islamic government has full discretion to put such restrictions on their practices as it deems necessary.[7]

Not surprisingly, the destruction in 1024 of idols in the Somnath Temple in Gujrat made Mahmud Ghazni a hero for many Muslims on the Indian subcontinent. His achievement is powerfully eulogized by popular twentieth-century Muslim writers, such as Nasim Hijazi. But Hindus bitterly resent the damage to their temples by the many Muslim raiders from Arabia. The Somnath episode was used by Hindu fundamentalists as their justification for destroying the Babri mosque in 1992. Thousands of Muslims were killed in the subsequent riots. Idol destruction continues in modern times: Afghanistan's Taliban regime destroyed the 2000-year-old Buddhas of Bamyan. Condemnation from the Muslim world was sparse.

Defying the literalists, and accepting the risk of being labeled as apologists, some important Muslim scholars have argued that inter-religious pluralism is indeed consistent with Islam.

MODERNIST INTERPRETATIONS

There are many passages in the Qur'an that are harsh with regard to Jews and idolatry. Reading them, it appears that the caliphate is committed to perpetual war against Judaism, Hinduism, and Buddhism. At the risk of being dismissed as apologists, some important modern Muslim scholars have sought to understand Islam in a way that allows an escape from this stark conclusion.

The modernist logic is exemplified by the Islamic scholar Fazal-ur-Rahman.[8] He insists that the *asbab al-nuzul* (the historical circumstances surrounding a specific revelation) should be used to examine any particular Qur'anic verse. Thus "historical Islam and normative Islam" are to be separated. He states that the multitude of Qur'anic revelations took place "in, although not merely for, a given historical context". Muslims must recognize the essential feature in the revelation which is not only meant for the specific context in which it was revealed but is also intended by the Creator to "outflow through and beyond that given context of history". He says that the Qur'an must be resurrected from the accumulated debris of tradition, precedents, and culture of the past millennium.

Rahman summarizes his methodology as follows:

> In building any genuine and viable Islamic set of laws and institutions, there has to be a two-fold movement: First one must move from the concrete case treatments of the Quran—taking the necessary and relevant social conditions of that time into account—to the general principles upon which the entire teaching converges. Second, from this general level there must be a movement back to specific legislation, taking into account the necessary and relevant conditions now, obtaining.[9]

From Rahman's point of view, slavery, polygamy, jizya, zimmi, and but-shikinee are all anachronisms that made sense only around the time of the Prophet. A few scholars, such as Javed Ghamidi, use similar arguments for softening the Islamic Penal Code, such as the death penalty for apostasy, and stoning to death for adultery.

Rahman's views are similar to those of other liberal Muslim thinkers of a decade ago, such as Syed Ameer Ali, Abul Kalam Azad, Asaf Ali Fyzee, and Taha Hussain. But do they constitute the "correct" Islam or, instead, mere apologia? It is impossible to say. What can be said accurately is that the earlier trend towards increasing acceptance of modernity has effectively been reversed since the 1970s. Now literalists and anti-pluralists, such as Mawdoodi, Qutb, Hassan Al-Banna, and Ayatollah Khomeini, are those who are largely seen speaking for Islam.

Muslims have responded to widely differing environments and rapidly shifting historical circumstances, proving themselves to be highly compatible with all the major types of polities, and varied forms of social and economic organization. Islam as a world-historical religion has unquestionably succeeded in implanting itself in a variety of societies and cultures, from the tribal-nomadic to the centralized bureaucratic to the feudal-agrarian to the mercantile-financial and to the capitalist-industrial.

However, textually and formally, literalist Islam does not appear to permit any real degree of integration of non-Muslims into a Muslim society. That Muslims have frequently lived together peacefully with other religious communities should not be confused with this fact. A clear dichotomy exists between faith and practice, with practice being more accommodative of pluralism than the faith.

ISLAMIC STATE: AN IMAGINED COMPULSION

Many Islamically motivated movements across the world today seek the creation of an Islamic state out of the conviction that they can truly practice their faith only in such a state. Among them are Da'ish, Taliban, Boko Haram, Al-Shabab, and the Muslim Brotherhood. The leader of Kashmiri separatists and a member of the Jamaat-e-Islami, Syed Ali Shah Geelani put it succinctly: "It's as difficult for a Muslim to live in a non-Muslim society as it is for a fish to live out of the water."

However, what an Islamic state actually is and how it would be governed remains unclear. Its proponents have yet to convince the majority of Muslims that their vision is the correct one. Nowhere is this more apparent than in the Islamic Republic of Pakistan. Though formally an Islamic state, it is engaged in a bitter war against those who accuse it of being Islamic only in name.

Throughout history, the nature of the Islamic state has been sharply disputed. The Holy Qur'an, the source of all authority for Muslims, does not speak of an Islamic state. Lacking specific guidance from the Holy Book, Islamic scholars have created their own understandings of what an Islamic state should be. Abul Hasan al-Mawardi (974–1058), a scholar in service of the Abbasid rulers and one of Islam's first political theorists, justifies the need for a religious state and writes of "A leader through whom he [Allah] provided for the deputyship of the Prophet", meaning a caliph who would be God's vice-regent on earth. But this connection between state and religion is refuted by other scholars, such as the greatest Muslim historian and social anthropologist of all times, Ibn Khaldun:

> Some wrongly assume the imamate to be the pillars of the state. It is one of the general public interests. The people are delegated to take care of it. If it were one of the pillars of faith, it would be something like prayer, and Muhammad would have appointed a representative, exactly as he appointed Abu Bakr to represent him in prayer.[10]

Agreeing on al-Mawardi's need to unite state and religion, the ideological founder of the Jamaat-i-Islami, Maulana Abul Ala Mawdoodi, conceptualized yet another vision of an Islamic state nearly 900 years later.

The head of such a state, he said, should be a pious Muslim male who would Islamize the nation and make better Muslims of his subjects. Sovereignty would lie with Allah, not the people. And, said Mawdoodi, the newly discovered ideology of secularism was the enemy of the Islamic state, as were people such as Jinnah and others whom he regarded as creatures of Western culture. The Jamaat-e-Islami, founded by Mawdoodi, has wings in Pakistan and Bangladesh. It inspires millinerian movements across the Muslim world.

The advocates for establishing an Islamic utopia are passionate but their different schools of thought disagree vehemently—even violently—about its nature. Had the Qur'an defined even the broad outlines of statehood, such controversies would have been stilled. But the Holy Book is totally silent on matters of state and politics. In fact, there is no word for "state" in the Arabic language. That which comes closest is *dawlah*, but this acquired its specific meaning based on the European concept of a geographically defined nation-state, with origins that can be traced back to the 1648 Treaty of Westphalia.

Nevertheless, some say that an Islamic system of governance is a fact of history, conceived and brought into existence by the Prophet Muhammad, who, after his migration to Medina, negotiated an accord with various Jewish and pagan tribes called Misaq-e-Medina. But the Misaq was a document, brilliantly conceived as it was, that had served only imminent needs. Through a process of consultations, the Prophet had apportioned various rights and responsibilities upon Muslims, Jews, Christians, and pagans. As a salutary consequence it brought to an end the bitter intertribal fighting between Aws and Khazraj of Medina.

Though crafted by Islam's founder, it was far removed from the kind of blueprint needed for the running of a modern economy and an apparatus for governance. Nevertheless, extravagant claims have persisted throughout history. Most recently, Tahir-ul-Qadri, a Canadian-Pakistani cleric and politician who has persistently agitated to overthrow the elected Government of Pakistan, has written a PhD dissertation on the Misaq. He claims that its 63 items make it the first written constitution of human history.[11] Others refer to the Misaq as a charter.

Whatever the correct description, at best, Medina was a protostate and the Misaq covered only matters that were immediately important to establishing the Holy Prophet's rule. While the original document has long been lost, bits and pieces of it can be found in the works of early scholars, such as Ibn Ishaq's *Sirat-al-Rasool-Allah*. Inspecting the 63 listed clauses in Qadri's thesis, the Misaq does not at all read like a constitution. Instead it deals with the following sets of issues: settling various blood feuds between tribes; payment of ransoms; restrictions on killing of believers at the instigation of non-believers; guaranteeing life protection for Muslims and Jews; rules for sanctioning revenge killings; rules for apportioning war expenses between Muslims and Jews; declarations of equality between different Jewish tribes; prohibition of treachery; and denial of shelter for women (unless agreed to by their families).

Misaq-e-Medina did not attempt to anticipate what the future might bring. In fact, it dealt strictly with those issues which were important for a small group of tribes. The estimated population of Mecca and Medina combined was, at the time of the Prophet, smaller than that of a typical neighborhood of Cairo or Karachi. The Misaq contains no hint of a taxation system, police or army, nor does it mention administrative units or jails. It does not offer any concept of territorial governance or defense. Each tribe was expected to follow its customs and traditions. In those days it was assumed that intertribal wars would continue forever, and all adult tribal men would take part in defending their tribal interests. The only law prevalent was that of *qisas* (retaliation).

Crucially, this "first constitution" is silent on how the state's ruler is to be chosen and what might be legitimate cause for his removal. Nor does it specify the limits of his power or that of the *shura* (consultative body). Did the shura have the necessary power to choose a caliph? Would there be an executive, a judiciary, or government ministries, and what would their functions be? It is therefore hard to accept that the Misaq is a document relevant to the running of a state, particularly in modern times.

The absence of guidelines meant that death of the Holy Prophet—who did not specify either his successor or even a procedure for determining one—created an enduring schism regarding the question of who would be the next leader of the faithful. The first three caliphs were companions of the Prophet: Abu Bakr (632–634), Omar (634–656), Osman (644–656), and, lastly, Hazrat Ali (599–661), the holy prophet's cousin and son-in-law and the fourth Caliph. The selection of the second and third caliphs was done largely by their dying predecessors according to tribal law. Only one—Abu Bakr—died a natural death. Three of the four rightly guided caliphs were assassinated, including one (Osman) who was brutally lynched by a mob while he was reading the Qu'ran. This suggests the lack of internal consensus even among those who had been close to the Holy Prophet, and an unstable political order.

The procedural vacuum led to a bitter power struggle within—the political establishment of the time had come apart. The tragedy of Karbala, which followed the succession by Yazid, created the enduring division between

Sunni and Shia Islam, which is responsible for much of the blood that flows in wars today. Yazid was elected by a tribal dynastic tradition rather than consensus. For Sunnis, Yazid was just another caliph, but for the Shia, he is the devil.

These historical conflicts suggest that any attempt in present times to create an Islamic state—which must necessarily be a caliphate—will involve conflict on an immense scale. Regardless of who would be the caliph, there is the question of what kind of rules would prevail. How would they impact upon states with populations of a hundred million Muslims or more, each with diverse Muslim sects? The caliphate would require non-Muslim minorities to be marginalized, silenced, forced to emigrate, or physically eliminated. This amounts to a flight of human capital. A diverse population contributes greatly in economic terms, but religious pluralism is impossible in the Islamic state of Mawdoodi and Qutb—even theoretically.

The legal system in an Islamic state, if derived from the principle of sharia, would be very different from laws that are prevalent in a modern society. For example, blood money would be a way for the rich to avoid punishment, even for capital crimes. Retaliation qisas and blood money *diyat* are means by which the rich can buy away their crimes. Examples in modern times show that this would violate the principles of natural justice.

- For example, Raymond Davis, a temperamentally violent Central Intelligence Agency (CIA) operative stationed in Pakistan, went on a killing spree in Lahore, shooting one of his victims in the back.[12] However, thanks to the intervention of the US Embassy, which paid the blood money to the victims' relatives, he was able to escape scot-free.
- Similarly, serial murderers and sex fiends have been arrested by the Pakistani police and convicted in court, but then set free because of forced out-of-court settlements and qisas.[13] In one case, a man killed his wife but arranged for their children to pay the blood money and was set free.

Prescribed blood money rates vary from country to country. The current rates in Saudi Arabia are listed below:[14]

- 300,000 riyals if the victim is a Muslim man
- 150,000 riyals if a Muslim woman
- 50,000 riyals if a Christian or Jewish man
- 25,000 riyals if a Christian or Jewish woman
- 6,666 riyals if a man of any other religion
- 3,333 riyals if a woman of any other religion

PAKISTAN: EARLY BEGINNINGS

Given the divergence that exists between different interpretations of Qur'anic verses, it is fair to ask what the founder of Pakistan, Mohammed Ali Jinnah, actually had in mind when he was mobilizing the Muslim masses to create a state only for Muslims. Lacking a clear understanding of either history or theology, Jinnah interchangeably called for an Islamic state and a Muslim state. This has left a legacy of confusion. Just as confusing is the fact that almost all religious parties in undivided India, including the Jamaat-e-Islami, had vociferously opposed the creation of a new state out of India. Some scholars, such as Maulana Abul Kalam Azad, argued that Muslims could and should live together with others, while others feared losing their local constituencies if India was divided. Yet others were bitterly critical of the Muslim League's (ML's) leadership, and Jinnah in particular.

Paradoxically, Jinnah was the most Westernized political leader in Indian Muslim history.[15] He was culturally and socially far more at ease with the high society of cosmopolitan Bombay and metropolitan London than with those he led and represented. His Urdu (the "Muslim" language of India) was barely understandable. A connoisseur of fine wines and hams, his living style was the very opposite of those whom he sought to inspire. Therefore he had to be recast in a different image, so Pakistan Television, under Zia's instructions, filled screens across the country with a steady stream of profound pieties emanating from a stern, sherwani-clad man. Jinnah had miraculously morphed into a deep-thinking Islamic scholar. Gone were his elegant suits from Savile Row, as was any reference to his marriage to a Zorastrian woman who refused to convert to Islam.

Two of Jinnah's oft-quoted speeches suggesting a secular outlook, delivered around the time of Partition, were slyly concealed from the public media during the Zia years:

> You are free; you are free to go to your temples, you are free to go to your mosques or to any other place of worship in this State of Pakistan. You may belong to any religion or caste or creed—that has nothing to do with the business of the State ... You will find that in course of time Hindus would cease to be Hindus and Muslims would cease to be Muslims, not in the religious sense, because that is the personal faith of each individual, but in the political sense as citizens of the State.[16]

Similarly, Jinnah came out forcefully against theocracy:

> Pakistan is not going to be a theocratic state to be ruled by priests with a divine mission. We have many non-Muslims-Hindus, Christians and Parsis—but they are all Pakistanis. They will enjoy the same rights and privileges as any other citizens and will play their rightful part in the affairs of Pakistan.[17]

The above-quoted speeches unequivocally demonstrate Jinnah's preference for secularism over theocracy in one important sense of the word: a secular state is necessarily neutral in matters of religion, and it neither supports nor opposes any particular set of religious beliefs or practices. The speeches led many Pakistani liberals to argue that Jinnah had envisioned Pakistan as a secular Muslim-majority country.

But secularism is just as much about the nature of law as it is about the state treating all religions equally. As a philosophy, secularism is fundamentally a post-Enlightenment belief that laws governing human activities and decisions should be based on the concept of reasonableness, not on the orders of some alleged divine authority. Secular laws are devised by humans according to their perception of society's needs. Because needs change according to times and circumstances, the laws in a secular society must necessarily change from time to time rather than being decreed once and for all.

Jinnah never called for Pakistan to be a secular state—not publicly, at least. However, there is evidence that he privately pledged (to an American diplomat) that Pakistan would be a "secular state", using these words. His statements from the 1930s onwards do not show any occurrence of the word "secular". Even when confronted by journalists, he would avoid a straight answer.

Why did Jinnah fight shy of expressing his beliefs openly and forthrightly? The answer lies in political realities. Had he campaigned for a liberal, secular Pakistan—and that too in competition with the secular Indian National Congress under the leadership of Jawaharlal Nehru—he would have certainly lost the leadership of the Pakistan Movement, which was based on communalism. So Jinnah opted for ambiguity, hoping that people in his ML would not notice his lifestyle too much. But, even if they did, he thought that the contribution that he was making to the welfare of Muslims—by helping to level the playing field—would dominate everything else. Behind everything else was an unstated hope that a liberal, secular Pakistan would one day follow once the messy business of Partition was over with. And so it was unnecessary to raise the issue of secularism now.

While liberal, modernist Muslims seek to downplay his words, the fact is that Jinnah alluded many times to an Islamic state. For example, in a broadcast address to the people of the USA in February 1948, he described Pakistan as "the premier Islamic state". Given who he was, what could he have really meant?

Jinnah was a lawyer par excellence and an adept leader of men, but he was no scholar of Islam. In fact, he knew no Arabic or Persian. He wrote no book or treatise, and his speeches do not suggest any real familiarity with Islamic history or jurisprudence. When he spoke on matters of the Islamic state, he often used the terms "Muslim state", "Islamic state", and sometimes simply "state". He made no specific reference to the Hadith, or to the works of classical Muslim scholars. Instead he made generalized normative statements about such a state being just, caring, and consistent with cultural practices. Maybe this was just as well for given the difficult subject matter.

Although Jinnah's choice of words was often loose and imprecise, he certainly had an eye on the audience that he was addressing. For instance, in a press statement on July 31, 1947, addressed to the FATAs, he said:

> The Government of Pakistan has no desire whatsoever to interfere in any way with the traditional independence of the Tribal Areas. On the contrary, we feel as a Muslim State, we can always rely on [the] active support and sympathy of the tribes.

At the conclusion of this statement, Jinnah chose to use the term "Islamic state":

> In the end, I would appeal to all the different elements in the NWFP and in the Tribal Areas to forget past disputes and differences and join hands with the Government of Pakistan in setting up a truly democratic Islamic State.

The real problem, however, goes beyond Jinnah's lack of scholarship in Islam. There has never been a consensus on what an Islamic state is, and it is unlikely that there ever will be.

PAKISTAN AFTER ZIA

Shortly after the coup, in 1978 the law minister of Zia-ul-Haq's military regime and the inventor of "doctrine of necessity", A.K. Brohi, fired a full broadside at politicians belonging to the political parties of Pakistani's nationalities. Supporting Zia's claim that nationalist identities are alien to Islam, and that Pakistan was created on the basis of religion alone, he wrote:

> Pakistan is a successor state to British India, which had a unitary, rather than a federal form of Government. First there was a Centre, which extended to peripheral parts (now forming Pakistan) and it was this Centre, which delegated powers to the provinces for the sake of administrative convenience. Thus, when Pakistan was founded, it retained its unitary character. Subsequent federalization was merely a result of Center's progressive decentralization rather than a product of voluntary surrendering of partial sovereignty by the constituent parts of Pakistan. Furthermore, Pakistan was founded on the basis of religion and religion alone. It can be kept together only by the cementing force of Ikhwan. There are no nationalities in Pakistan or, for that matter, anywhere else; and the idea of nationalities is subversive.[18]

In Pakistan's early years, Hindus, Christians, and Parsis were formally the religious minorities. The Ahmadis were added in 1974. Voices to expel from Islam smaller Muslim communities, such as the Ismailis and Zikris, became louder with time. This was expanded further to Shias, and later to the Sunni Barelvis. The use of religion in matters of the state was now beginning to have serious consequences.

Zia's Islamization plans had generated many enthusiastic guardians, including self-appointed ones. Hence, upon assuming power, every subsequent national leader—Benazir Bhutto, Nawaz Sharif, Pervez Musharraf, and Asif Ali Zardari—was wary of touching, much less undoing, Zia's steps. Even if their personal inclination and sense of justice caused them occasional discomfort, they calculated that the cost of tampering with any law that appealed to Islam would be too great. Nawaz Sharif, at least in his earlier tenure, had a strong religious streak and played around with the idea of having sharia law in Pakistan.

The deference of Pakistani leaders to *mullah* (religious cleric) power was not new. The instinctive response of leaders under stress is to seek appeasement. A whisky-drinking, mercurial Zulfikar Ali Bhutto had suddenly become Islamic in his final days as he made a desperate, but ultimately unsuccessful, attempt to save his government and life. A fearful Benazir Bhutto did not challenge the anti-woman Hudood and blasphemy laws during her two premierships. Her Western education and personal lifestyle notwithstanding, she made no attempt to undo laws that affected Pakistani women that were incompatible with modern ideas of justice.

General Pervez Musharraf was the only one bold enough in the post-Zia era to publicly espouse a more "modern" and "moderate" Islam. The relief was felt by many. Heads of government organizations were no longer required to lead noon prayers, as in the 1980s; female announcers with undraped heads freely appeared on Pakistan Television; thickly bearded stewards were replaced by female flight attendants on Pakistan International Airlines (PIA) flights; the first women fighter pilots were inducted into the Pakistan Air Force; and hundreds of women prisoners arrested on charges of fornication under the Hudood Ordinances were released. Many had spent years awaiting trial.

Although Musharraf played to the US gallery, his personal instincts were undeniably liberal. Well before September 11, 2001—on April 21, 2000 to be specific—he had announced a new administrative procedure for registration of cases under the Blasphemy Law 295-C. This law, under which the minimum penalty is death, had frequently been used to harass religious minorities as well as personal opponents. To reduce such occurrences, his modified procedure would have required authorization from the local district magistrate for registration of a blasphemy case. A modest improvement at best, it could have ameliorated some of the worst excesses.

But this commitment was less than firm. Some 25 days later, under the watchful glare of the mullahs, Musharraf hastily climbed down, saying, "As it was the unanimous demand of the ulema, mashaikh and the people, therefore, I have decided to do away with the procedural change in the registration of FIR [First Information Report] under the Blasphemy Law".[19]

This was the beginning of his other retreats. In October 2004, as a new system for issuing machine-readable passports was being installed, the government declared that henceforth it would not be necessary for passport holders to specify their religion. The Islamic parties swiftly reacted, denouncing it as a grand conspiracy aimed at secularizing Pakistan and destroying its Islamic character. But even before the mullahs took to the streets, the government lost nerve and the volte-face was announced. On March 24, 2005, the minister of information, Sheikh

Rashid (later associated with Imran Khan's Pakistan Tehreek-e-Insaf [PTI, Movement for Justice] in 2015), said that the decision to revive the religion column was a good one, otherwise "Qadianis and other apostates would be able to pose as Muslims and perform pilgrimage in Saudi Arabia".

In early July 2006, Musharraf directed the Council of Islamic Ideology to draft an amendment to the controversial Hudood Ordinances, put in place by General Zia-ul-Haq in 1980. This was not repealed by any of the civilian governments that ruled from 1988 to 1999. Under the Hudood Ordinances, Pakistani law prescribes death by stoning for married Muslims who are found guilty of extramarital sex (for unmarried couples or non-Muslims, the penalty is 100 lashes). The law is exact in stating how the death penalty is to be administered:[20]

> Such of the witnesses who deposed against the convict as may be available shall start stoning him and, while stoning is being carried on, he may be shot dead, whereupon stoning and shooting shall be stopped.

Musharraf proposed amending the Hudood Ordinances and opened them up for parliamentary discussion in early September 2006. Some suspected that part of the gain would be political: he might be seeking to split the parliamentary opposition to government policies in Balochistan, where the insurgency had pitted that province against the Punjab. On the other hand, he expected outrage from some of his allies, fundamentalists of the Muttahida Majlis–e–Amal (MMA, United Council of Action), the main Islamic parliamentary group that commanded majorities in the provincial assemblies of the NWFP and Baluchistan. Indeed, their reaction to the initiative was precisely as anticipated. MMA members tore up copies of the proposed amendments on the floor of the National Assembly and threatened to resign en masse. However, long before any threats by the Islamic opposition were carried out, Musharraf's government scuttled its own initiative. This retreat doomed the bill to obscurity.

Other Pakistani leaders in the Musharraf government were anxious to establish their religious credentials. Shaukat Aziz, a former Citibanker who was chosen to be prime minister, made a call for nationwide prayers for rain in a year of drought. At an education conference in Islamabad, he rejected the suggestion of a moderate Islamic scholar, Javed Ghamdi, that only schoolchildren in their fifth year and above should be given formal Islamic education. Instead, Aziz proposed that Islamic religious education should start as soon as children enter school. The government's education policy now requires Islamic studies to begin in the third year of school, a year earlier than in the previous policy.

Other ministers competed with the president and prime minister to show their Islamic zeal. The federal minister for religious affairs, Ijaz ul Haq (Zia-ul-Haq's son), speaking at the launch of a book authored by a leading Islamic extremist leader entitled *Christian Terrorism and the Muslim World*, argued that anyone who did not believe in jihad could be neither a Muslim nor a Pakistani. He then declared that given the situation facing Muslims today, he was prepared to be a suicide bomber.

Musharraf's other ministers felt even less need to show a liberal face. The health minister, Mohammad Nasir Khan, assured the Upper House of Parliament that the government could consider banning female nurses looking after male patients in hospitals. This move arose from a motion moved by female parliamentary members of the MMA. Maulana Gul Naseeb Khan, provincial secretary of the MMA, was among those holy men to whom women's bodies are of particular concern. He said, "We think that men could derive sexual pleasure from women's bodies while conducting an electrocardiogram or ultrasound." In his opinion, women would be able to lure men under the pretext of these medical procedures. Therefore, he said, "to save the supreme values of Islam and the message of the Holy Prophet (PBUH [peace be upon him]), the MMA has decided to impose the ban". Destroyed or damaged billboards with women's faces could be seen in several cities of the North West Frontier Province (now the KPK) province because the MMA deemed the exhibition of unveiled women as unIslamic.

Musharraf's "enlightened moderation" turned out to be largely cosmetic. Many felt that his decisions were more for US consumption than out of real worry for the growing forces of religious extremism. A standing ovation from the Council for Foreign Relations must surely have boosted his ego.

More generally, duplicity became the military's de facto foreign policy: even as it formally withdrew its support for the Taliban, it continued to actively support and train anti-India extremist groups on Pakistani soil. The membership of these jihadist groups largely subscribed to the Deobandi/Salafi/Wahhabi schools. Most were bitterly anti-Shia, while some considered worship at shrines, practiced by Barelvi Muslims and others, as heretical. Shrines became their targets, preferred because of their proximity compared with distant and dangerous India.

The challenge from the mosque, however, was becoming unbearable. In 2007, Islamabad's Red Mosque launched a full-scale insurrection against the Pakistani state. This had to be quelled with the loss of well over 200 lives, including more than a dozen elite Special Service Commandos. The madrassa associated with the Red Mosque had terrorized the capital city, kidnapping alleged prostitutes and trying them in an Islamic court. In 2015, Islamabad was fearful of the dozens of madrassas spread across the city. There were an estimated 30,000 in Pakistan.

Musharraf's government was followed by that of the ostensibly liberal Pakistan Peoples Party (PPP), led by Asif Ali Zardari. It took no initiative to curb the enormous power of the religious establishment and the madrassas. In fact, following the Red Mosque episode, every government has been shy about addressing this sensitive subject. The message from the mosque is strident: the reader is invited to sample typical *khutbas* (sermons) recently recorded in villages and towns across Punjab.[21] A little before Friday prayers is when the mullah makes his call to arms—sometimes literally. Islam, he says, has to be everywhere and not confined to the mosque. Even if the ulema frequently and ferociously differ among themselves, they are unified in demanding that the Qur'an and the Hadith must determine economics, politics, and family laws as well as govern lifestyle issues, such as dress, food, personal hygiene, marriage, family relations, and even daily routine. They warn that Islam—whose expression is the sharia—is a complete code of life and not just another theology like Christianity, Judaism, or Hinduism. The faithful must die and, if necessary, kill to establish this truth.

In 2015, the nervousness of the government of Nawaz Sharif was not without reason, as the following episode demonstrates. When the minister of information, Parvaiz Rasheed, spoke at the Karachi Arts Council that May, he stated the self-evident. Without explicitly naming madrassas, he said that large numbers of factories mass-produce ignorance in Pakistan through propagating *murda fikr* (dead knowledge). They use loudspeakers as tools, leaving well over 2 million young minds ignorant and confused. The early tradition of Muslim scholars and scientists was very vibrant and different, he said, but now blind rote learning and the use of books such as *maut ka manzar—marnay kay baad kya hoga?* (specter of death—what happens after you die?) is common.

The speech was extempore and the minister rambled, yet he set off a firestorm. He was accused of making fun of Islamic books and Islamic teachings, and clerics across Pakistan competed to denounce him. Made by an extremist sectarian outfit, the ASWJ, banners on Islamabad's roads appeared. They demanded that Rasheed be publically hanged. Taken down by the police, the banners reappeared elsewhere. The police accosted those putting them up, but withdrew after being confronted by youthful stick-bearing students from an illegally constructed madrassa in Islamabad's posh F-6/4 area—one of scores of other such madrassas in the city. The police chief expressed his views frankly: he was not equipped to take on religious extremists and suicide bombers.

The pressure on Rasheed was unbearable. Many, including the minister of defense, rushed to offer explanations and excuses for his May 3 speech. Privately they agreed with him but taking a public position was another matter. Rasheed retreated and apologized, claiming that he had been misunderstood. He was later seen at a *dastarbandi* (graduation) ceremony at the Al-Khalil Qur'an Complex in Rawalpindi, where he distributed prizes to madrassa students who had memorized the Qur'an. By doing so, he showed his lack of keenness to follow Governor Salman Taseer into martyrdom.

The Parvaiz Rasheed episode starkly illustrates the present condition of state, society, and politics in Pakistan today. One can take from it some important conclusions.

First, the urban-based clerical establishment grows bolder by the day, believing that it can take on even sitting ministers or, if need be, generals. It has many tanks and nuclear weapons, but didn't Islamabad's Lal Masjid (Red Mosque)—now grandly reconstructed—finally triumph over Pakistan's army? Even though the clerics lost 150 students and other fighters, the then army chief sits in the dock, accused of quelling an armed insurrection against Pakistan and killing one of its ring leaders. Chastened by this episode and others, the establishment now seeks to appease the mullah. Not a single voice in government defended the information minister.

Second, by refusing to own the remarks of its own information minister, the government has signaled its retreat on a critical front—madrassa reform. This part of the National Action Plan to counter terrorism involves financial audits of madrassas, revealing funding sources, curriculum expansion and revision, and monitoring activities. Some apparent urgency was injected following an off-the-cuff remark earlier this year by the interior minister, Chaudhry Nisar, that about 10 percent of madrassas were extremist. Even if only 3 percent are extremist, this suggests that there are many hundreds of such seminaries. Plans for dealing with them have apparently been shelved once again.

Third, one sees that open television access was given to clerics and other hardliners who claimed that Rasheed had forfeited his right to be called a Muslim. This is clear incitement to murder since a good fraction of society believes that apostates need to be eliminated. Such ideological extremism on television is far too common these days to deserve much comment. Still, it is remarkable that a serving minister—and, in particular, the minister of information and communications—was allowed to be targeted.

PAKISTAN EMBRACES PETRODOLLAR ISLAM

The oil embargo of 1973 resulted in massive wealth pouring into the coffers of Saudi Arabia and the Gulf states. In spite of spending sprees, such as buying jet airliners with gold-plated commodes for sheikhs and princes, there was plenty left over to propagate the ideology of the Kingdom of Saudi Arabia—Wahhabism. Saudi Arabia provided an estimated "90% of the expenses of the entire faith".[22] Pakistan has been a key recipient of Saudi largesse.

Wahhabism, the hardline literalist Islam of Saudi Arabia in the eighteenth century, started as a reaction to Shia'ism and Sufism. Wahhabis, who are indistinguishable from Salafis, see their version of Islam as normative and other forms of Islam as deviant. In its early years, they succeeded in destroying all shrines, together with historical monuments and relics left over from the early days of Islam.

Inspired by Imam ibn Hanbal, Ibn Taimiyya, Shah Waliullah, Maulana Mawdoodi, Syed Qutb, and many others, Wahhabis see Islam principally through the Penal Code. Religious pluralism is unacceptable. This must be contrasted with the more accommodative Islam of Sufis and poets such as Shah Abdul Latif, Sachal Sarmast, Baba Farid, Hafiz Shirazi, Maulana Rumi, and Shams-i-Tabrizi, who are widely revered as saints of peace and toleration. Historically, Sufis were responsible for much of Islam's rapid spread after its initial military conquests in the seventh and eighth centuries. The Kurds of Iraq, Iran, and Turkey were also converted in this way and still maintain their brand of folk Islam. Wahhabism fiercely attacked the syncretism of popular Islam, claiming that it arises from an ignorance of the Qura'nic teachings. On the Indian subcontinent the only strain of Islam that comes close to Wahhabism is Ahl-e-Hadith. It shares the Wahhabist hatred of shrine worshippers, whom it equate with idolaters. This back-to-the-Qur'an line has gained ground because today more individuals can read the abundant religious literature and be influenced by it.

The purpose of Saudi Arabia's massive global network of charities, preachers, and teachers is to create alliances and legitimize its claim to being the leader of Islam, both at home and abroad. As the keepers of the Holy Places, they have made inroads by offering funds to local communal Islamic organizations that influence public life, education, knowledge, and rituals. Islamic communities made vulnerable by distress—Palestine, Kashmir, Bosnia, Chechnya, Central Asia, and Egypt—are particularly targeted.

The export of Wahhabism as a religious duty has been blessed by many prominent Saudi religious scholars, such as the Saudi Grand Mufti, Sheikh Abd Al Aziz Bin Baz, who died in 1999. His teachings and Islamic jurisprudence are to be found in many Islamic centers and mosques around the world. They are posted on hundreds of radical Islamic websites of terror organizations. His teaching and books are available and have been part of the radical Islamic indoctrination curriculum in jihadi training camps. Baz demonized other Muslims and demanded their expulsion. He called for a global *da'awah* (invitation to Islam), insisted on a wealth tax to support the Afghan jihad, and claimed that the sun circled the earth rather than the other way round.

Sheikh Baz was just one of the many Saudi ulema who have called for Saudi financing of radical Islamic institutions across the world. This funding has impacted the content of their literature, skewing it in favor of Salafist-Wahhabist thinking. Local ulema are invited to perform Hajj and Umra pilgrimages on Saudi expenses. When they return to their institutions, they are facilitated in producing low-priced books, audiotapes, videocassettes, and compact discs. Many Islamic charities and other organizations operate their own websites. A key purpose of this outreach is to attack the West and rival Muslim groups, including Sunni organizations. Local beliefs and practices are sternly condemned as "aberrant" on account of differences in their methods of performing rituals and various rules governing a range of issues related to normative personal and collective behavior.

Though indifferent to the suffering of fellow Muslims in their neighborhood, Saudi Arabia has put its financial resources behind the export of its religious ideology overseas. Oil is cheap and the Saudi economy was hurting in 2015, but with almost unlimited dollar reserves stashed all over the world, the famed profligacy of Saudi and Gulf sheikhs remained undiminished. Even as desperate refugees fled Syria and Iraq for European countries, and impoverished Yemenis were blown up in Saudi-led airstrikes, their spending binges continued to make waves. A beach in the French Riviera was closed to accommodate a 1,000-person party during the vacation of the 79-year-old Saudi monarch, King Salman bin Abdulaziz. Then, during his visit to Washington DC, the entire Four Seasons Hotel was occupied. All this came at a time when the world was reeling with shock over the photograph of a drowned Syrian toddler lying facedown on a beach. Although Saudi Arabia has closed its doors to Syrian refugees, it has offered to build 200 mosques for them in Germany.

The mechanisms used to spread Salafi-Wahhabi Islam are varied.[23] Some funding comes directly from the state coffers, but wealthy princes, businesses, and ulema channel money to shadowy groups across the world. This pays for satellite channels, scholarships for students in universities and madrassas, and to bring over large numbers of influential political leaders and ulema to Saudi Arabia for short periods.

In Indonesia, Saudi Arabia has established institutions such as the LIPIA College in Jakarta. These are fountainheads of Salafism and Wahhabism, located in an environment that was hitherto accustomed to a syncretic form of Islam.

In Bangladesh the fundamentalist Jamaat-e-Islami, an offshoot of its Pakistani wing, has relentlessly sought to subvert the country's secular character. Following the murder of its founder, Sheikjh Mujibur Rahman, it has received Arab assistance in many invisible ways through Saudi-assisted NGOs. A strong Saudi presence is evident in financial institutions. The Islamic Bank of Bangladesh Limited (IBBL) was founded in 1975 at the initiative of Fuad Abdullah Al Khatib, the Saudi ambassador to Bangladesh.[24] One of its directors, Mir Quasem Ali, was awarded the death sentence in 2014 for war crimes committed in 1971, including murder and torture. He was Saudi Arabia's "money man" in Bangladesh, and a director of both the IBBL and the NGO Rabita al-Alam al-Islami. The Jamaat also controls 14 other banks, of which the IBBL is the largest, and one of the three largest banks in South Asia. About 60 percent of the IBBL's shares are held by Saudi individuals and institutions. The Jamaat has recently moved into the insurance sector as well, entering into a collaboration agreement with the Far Eastern Islamic Insurance Corporation.

In Pakistan, Saudi influence is ubiquitous. Former Saudi intelligence chief Prince Turki bin Sultan was on the mark when, speaking about Pakistan and Saudi Arabia, he said, "It's probably one of the closest relationships in the world between any two countries." Both countries are

Sunni and conservative, and both have ruling oligarchies (though one is dynastic and the other military). They were the first to recognize and support the Taliban regime in Afghanistan. Their relationship with the USA has a strong similarity: their populations strongly resent what they see as a master–client relationship. The International Islamic University (IIU) in Islamabad is a bastion of Wahhabism, with a president who is Saudi national, appointed by Saudi Arabian authorities, and who speaks no English or Urdu. He was appointed after Saudi Arabia's government demanded the removal of his predecessor, a demand that President Zardari was forced to implement.[25] Several notorious terrorists are known to have a close association with the IIU.

Although the Saudi government denies directly funding jihadist groups in Kashmir, but there is scarcely any doubt that such denial is to blur the direct aid to jihad 940 groups such as Jamaat-ud-Dawah (also known as Lashkar-e-Tayyaba). From time to time there are reports in the inter-Arab and the international press that indicate that the Saudi-based charities transfer funds for jihad causes in Kashmir and invite the leaders of the jihad groups to Saudi Arabia.

Petrodollar funding for madrassas and mosques has steadily worked in favor of the hardliners, enabling a rapid spread of Deobandi Islam. The supposedly apolitical Tablighi Jamaat (TJ) religious movement, headquartered in Raiwind near Lahore, has annual congregations that rank in size as second only to those of the Hajj pilgrimage. With an estimated following of 70–80 million people of Deobandi persuasion, this brand of Islam has spread across Southwest Asia, Southeast Asia, Africa, Europe, and North America. In France it has about a 100,000 followers, and by 2007, Tabligh members were attending 600 of Britain's 1,350 mosques. Tablighis despise mystical Islam, which they equate with idolatry and ancestor worship.

The TJ represents only the tip of the religious iceberg. Attendance at mosques has skyrocketed, as has adherence to prayers, fasting, and other rituals. In Pakistan, an observer who grew up in a military family notes that "until the late seventies, the mosques located at the armed forces bases were 90 percent Ahle Sunnat Wal Jama't [Sufi], 8 percent Deobandi, and 0 percent Salafi. Currently 85 percent of the mosques are Deobandi or Salafi, and less than 10 percent are Ahle Sunnat Wal Jama't."[26] Steadily the culture of the mosque is defeating the culture of the shrine.

CONCLUSION AND PROGNOSIS

Imagine that on the eve of the 1979 Soviet invasion of Afghanistan there had been a socialist government in Pakistan that was sympathetic rather than hostile to the Soviets. Suppose that it had spurned US inducements to start a religious war against the "infidel" invaders, refused to team up with Saudi Arabia to create the *mujahideen* (those engaged in jihad) in newly made madrassas, and instead allied itself with the communist government in Kabul. How different would history have been? How would this have impacted pluralism—or the lack of it—in Pakistan?

It is, of course, impossible to say with certainty, but here's my guess. Minus Zia-ul-Haq, Pakistan would likely have continued as an imperfect pluralistic state, but only for so long. Pakistani workers returning from Saudi Arabia and the Gulf states were already bringing back with them not just new wealth but also new religious ideas and attitudes that were inimical to pluralism. The failure of the Pakistani state to provide education would have encouraged the growth of Wahhabi-Salafi-Deobandi madrassas even without the need for mujahideen fighters. The strength of religious forces was already apparent when Bhutto was obliged to retreat in 1974. Moreover, the country's powerful military has always needed India as its adversary in order to keep itself as the dominant force in Pakistan. It is therefore likely that, as in 1965, the army would have used religiously inspired fighters to bleed India after Delhi ham-handedly manipulated the 1987 elections in Indian-held Kashmir. One surmises that Zia was part of a broader stream of history; the transition to the radicalized present would have come anyway.

And what of the caliphate? Nostalgia for the days of Muslim grandeur—enormously attractive to young Muslims—was abundant then as it is now. Movements such as the Hizb-ut-Tahrir, which agitate for a global caliphate, draw strength from the fact that most Muslims across the world think of themselves as Muslims first, and then as citizens of their respective countries. In Pakistan this may be especially true.[27] Drawing conclusions from a British Council survey conducted in 2009, *The Telegraph* says:

The report found that three-quarters of respondents identified themselves foremost as Muslims, with just 14 per cent describing themselves primarily as a citizen of Pakistan. Only 10 per cent have a great deal of confidence in national or local government, the courts or the police and just one third advocate democracy for the country.[28]

Corroborating the above survey, another, this time conducted by *Express Tribune*, found that a majority of Pakistan's internet users say that they consider themselves "Muslim first" (49 percent) and "Pakistani" second (28 percent), while the rest (23 percent) voted "Other".[29] A Pew Global Attitudes Survey found that 43 percent of Turks consider themselves Muslim first and only 29 percent as Turks first. A majority of Muslims in six countries want Islam to be part of political life.[30]

Yet, in spite of such public enthusiasm, it is unlikely that Pakistan will move too far from its steady trajectory and become an Islamic sharia state headed by a caliph. Even if some charismatic person were somehow to seize power and declare himself caliph, there would be the eternal question of which rules should prevail. For Pakistan's Sunni majority, the choice would be between any one of the four brands of sharia—Hanafi, Sha'fi, Maliki, and Hanbali. If one Sunni faction succeeded in imposing one form of sharia, competing factions could accuse it of heresy or apostasy. Assassinations in Pakistan of Deobandis by Barelvis, and Barelvis by Deobandis, suggest that this is not mere hypothesis. The Shiites, of course, do not recognize any kind of sharia and would be outcasts in any such dispensation.

For women, the situation would be even more unbearable. Pakistan's Council of Islamic Ideology (CII) has made clear what women should expect under the sharia dispensation.[31] This has included the abolition of the age limit for a girl's marriageability, thus making child marriages permissible. A man would not need his wife's permission for another marriage, whether that be the second, third, or fourth. The CII declared that Islam had given the woman the right to separate from her husband, but another marriage could not be a valid reason for doing so. It also ruled that DNA is insufficient evidence for rape.

If the caliphate ever comes to be, the axe would first fall on non-Muslim minorities. They would be marginalized, silenced, forced to emigrate, or physically eliminated. And, without doubt, several communities that are currently considered Muslim would see themselves characterized as non-Muslim. The destruction of precious human capital would take many decades to recover from. At best the caliphate would be a brief, bloody moment in Pakistan's history before some cataclysmic implosion.

NOTES

1. The anti-Shia content of current sermons can be gauged from the approximately 200 Friday sermons delivered recently in Punjabi villages and towns that have been recorded, translated, and categorized at www.mashalbooks.org.

2. *Pan-Islamism and the nation-state,* Tahir Kamran, The News, September 27, 2015.

3. *Terrorism in Pakistan: Incident Patterns, Terrorists Characteristics, and the impact of terrorist arrests on terrorism,* Syed Ejaz Hussain, Penn Dissertations, (2010).

4. *The Ornament of the World: How Muslims, Christians, and Jews Created a Culture of Tolerance in Medieval Spain,* Maria Rosa Menocal, Back Bay Books, 2003.

5. *The Mughals of India,* Harbans Mukhia, John-Wiley & Sons, 2004.

6. *The Rights of Non-Muslims in Islamic State,* Syed Abul Ala Mawdoodi, Islamic Publications, LTD. Lahore, Pakistan, 1982.

7. Mawdoodi, ibid.

8. *Islam and Modernity–Transformation of an Intellectual Tradition,* Fazlur Rahman, University of Chicago Press, 1982.

9. Fazlur Rahman, ibid.

10. *The Muqaddimah,* Ibn Khaldun, translated by Franz Rosenthal, Princeton University Press, 1969, p 169.

11. *Constitutional Analysis of the Constitution of Medina,* Dr. Muhammad Tahir-ul-Qadri, Islamic Library.

12. *Raymond Davis was acting head of CIA in Pakistan,* The Telegraph, February 22, 2011.

13. *Forced out-of-court settlements, qisas, allow murderers and rapists to go free,* Dawn, December 6, 2014.

14. http://s1.zetaboards.com/anthroscape/topic/5675939/1/

15. Jinnah of Pakistan, Stanley Wolpert, Oxford University Press 1984.

16. Aug 11, 1947, Jinnah's address to the First Constituent Assembly http://www.pakistan.gov.pk/Quaid/speech03.htm

17. Jinnah's broadcast address to the people of the United States of America, Feb 1948, http://www.pakistan.gov.pk/Quaid/speech25.htm

18. A.K. Brohi, Dawn, October 1978.

19. General Pervez Musharraf, Dawn, May 17, 2000.
20. The Offence of Zina (Enforcement of Hudood) Ordinance, 1979. Ordinance No. VII of 1979, February 9, 1979.
21. *Message from the mosque,* www.mashalbooks.org
22. *What Is Saudi Arabia Going to Do?* Dawood al-Shirian, 2003Al-Hayat, May 19, 2003.
23. *How Saudi Petrodollars Fuel the Rise of Salafism,* France 24, September 29, 2012.
24. *The Economics of Islamic Fundamentalism in Bangladesh,* May 28, 2015, Amitava Mukherjee.
25. 'Saudi pressure' forced Zardari to sack IIUI rector, The Tribune, November 16, 2016.
26. *Wahabization- Salafization of Pakistan and Muslim Ummah: Fighting the Terrorists But Supporting Their Ideology,* Abul Hassaan, October 23, 2009, http://www.islamicsupremecouncil.com/bothways.htm
27. *Muslim-Western tensions persist,* Pew Global Attitudes Survey, 21 July 2011.
28. British Council: Pakistan facing 'frightening' demographic disaster, The Telegraph, 20 Nov 2009.
29. Tribune survey: Online Pakistanis 'Muslims first', 'Pakistani second', Express Tribune, 16 February, 2012.
30. *Most Muslims want democracy, personal freedoms, and Islam in political life,* Pew Research Global Attitudes Project, 10 July 2012.
31. *Muslim women cannot object to husbands' marriages,* Dawn, 22 Oct 2014.

CHAPTER 3

The Genesis, Evolution and Impact of "Deobandi" Islam on the Punjab: An Overview

Tahir Kamran

Introduction

Deobandis are a very powerful group because they have weapons and financial support from the Middle East, and logistical support from the state of Pakistan. This has resulted in a proliferation of their *madaris* (seminaries), which has made them more powerful. According to Deeni Madaris Report (1988), produced by the Ministry of Education, "out of a total 2,891, 717 belonged to Barelvis, 47 to Shias, and the salafi Ahle Hadith had 161, Jamat-i-Islami and independent madrasas accounted for 97. The rest were Deobandi madrasas." In addition, Deobandis "are the most militant in their demands for the Pakistani state to become truly Islamic—as they would define it" (International Crisis Group 2002, p. 29; Cohen 2003, p. 10). They were in the vanguard of the movement against the Ahmadiyya community that was eventually declared non-Muslim in 1974 and also orchestrated anti-Shia sectarian violence in the 1980s and 1990s.

T. Kamran (✉)
Department of History, Government College University, Lahore, Pakistan

© The Editor(s) (if applicable) and The Author(s) 2016
J. Syed et al. (eds.), *Faith-Based Violence and Deobandi Militancy in Pakistan*, DOI 10.1057/978-1-349-94966-3_3

It is important to briefly explain here the spatial context of the Deobandi creed so that the politics of exclusion as professed by Deobandis can be understood. As Juan R.I. Cole (1988), in the eighteenth and nineteenth centuries, Shia'ism (Usuli denomination) had prospered in Awadh and its surrounding areas. It was largely at the behest of Nawab(s) of Awadh that the Shia denomination came to have an overwhelming impression on Lucknow and beyond (Cole 1988, pp. 152–157). The emergence of the Deobandi version of Islam and particularly the exclusionist/sectarian trend which subsequently became quite discernible appeared to be a reaction to Shia dissemination in Awadh in particular and the United Provinces in general. That was the context in which Shah Abdul Aziz wrote *Taufa ithna-i-Ashari*, (Gift to the twelvers), which was a refutation of the Shia sect (Rizvi 1986, p. 72). That fact provides us with some perspective on the sectarian streak of the Deobandi condemnation of Shia'ism.

Reverting to the parties and factions representing militancy in the Deobandi creed, the JUI is the largest Deobandi political party, and such terrorist organizations as Harkat-ul-Mujahideen (HM), Jaish-i-Muhammad (JM), the SSP and the LeJ have umbilical links with it. Not only have these organizations been active in Kashmir and other parts of India but more importantly, since 2007, they have persistently mounted a challenge to the writ of the Pakistani state (Devji 2008). In July 2007, Deobandi clerics' formidable armed resistance to state agencies from Lal Masjid, located in the very heart of Islamabad, demonstrated their potential to throw down the gauntlet to the state's authority. With the emergence of the TTP and its allied groups as a result of the operation silence that was carried out on Lal Masjid, the very existence of the Pakistani state came under existential threat. Curiously enough, most of the abovementioned organizations are thoroughly entrenched in Punjab. To make sense of the phenomenon of the Deobandi creed, the emphasis of this study is on the important Deobandi ulema from the Punjab, the *madaris* and particularly the religious exclusionism that Deobandis orchestrated generally.

The protagonists of Deobandi thought owe a good deal to the Majlis-i-Ahrar-i-Islam (established in 1929), which acted as an instrument of political articulation for them in Punjab. Ulema such as Ahmed Ali Lahori, Qazi Ehsan Ahmed Shujabadi and Ataullah Shah Bokhari unleashed their anti-British political activism through Majlis-i-Ahrar from its inception. Therefore Ahrar also finds a place in this chapter to provide a better understanding of the evolution of the Deobandi influence on the province's politics. The Deobandi political influence grew in the wake of Partition of India, as is evident from the study of the Deobandi literature. The impact it had on the political and social formation of the province will also be a focus of this study.

Thus far the Deobandi influence on Punjab has been studied only tangentially by historians such as David Gilmartin (1988) and Ian Talbot (1988, 2005). Similarly, Tariq Rahman (2004), Ali Riaz and Mumtaz Ahmed have carried out studies of considerable worth but their focus is limited to the evolution and functioning of madaris; they have not exclusively scrutinized Deobandis and their looming influence in Punjab. Hence in the contemporary era when religious extremism is attracting considerable scholarly attention, the Deobandi movement merits a thorough inquiry. This chapter is divided into four sections. The first deals with the historical background, explaining the displacement of the *pir–murid* (master–disciple) relationship and the emergence of the Darul Ulum Deoband. The second section, on Deobandi incarnations, discusses the political activism of Deobandi ulema. The third, investigating Deobandis in Punjab, mentions the proliferation of Deobandi madaris in the province and important leaders who preached the Deobandi version of Islam. The last section is about the Deobandi militant organizations and violence.

HISTORICAL BACKGROUND

The most outstanding feature of "popular Islam" (Eaton 1978, p. 74) in Punjab and Sind has been all the permeating influence of Sufis and shrines over the centuries. The pir–murid relationship acquires particular salience in the sociopolitical rural setting. Although mosques and *maulvis* (prayer-leaders) abound in the villages, they could hardly have substituted for "a pervasive ideal of religious authority" that a pir embodies and the shrines as "sites of special access to religious power" or *barakat* (blessings) (Eaton 1978, p. 76). According to popular belief, barakat (spiritual charisma) is transmitted from one generation of the pir's living descendants to another. Barakat is "perhaps best understood as an almost blood-like substance that flows through the veins of a pir and endows him with what Max Weber called 'charismatic authority' " (Ibid.). The pir's shrine also epitomizes sanctity that it derives by virtue of the *baraka* it inherits from the pir itself. The pir, "the spiritually saturated holy man", creates a bond with the murid through *bait*, a pact of spiritual allegiance. Thus the former formalizes his role vis-à-vis the latter. The pir performs a dual function: he not only fulfils the "mundane desires" of the murid but also acts as a mediator between him and Allah.

Apart from exercising spiritual influence, the pirs in Punjab and Sind possessed large landholdings which "ideally placed (them) to play a leading role in rural politics" (Talbot 1988, p. 21). Over time, many shrines in Multan, Lahore, Pak Pattan, Dera Ghazi Khan and other parts of Punjab acquired enormous property through *inam/muaafi* land grants given to shrine by the state and considerable *waqf* (endowments) donated by devotees. From the eleventh century onwards, most of the rulers granted various shrines large swathes of land as a matter of policy called *madad-i-muash*, meant to secure the *sajjada nishin's* (hereditary administrator's) loyalty. Large landholdings became instruments not only of economic affluence but also political authority for the many who collaborated with the British. The British colonial government from the second half of the nineteenth century abandoned the official patronage previously extended to the mosques, temples and shrines through Act XX of 1863. However, to establish a link with the "rural hierarchies of mediation", a structure was created by the government whereby the local authorities and cultures could be incorporated into the empire. Therefore the imperial ideology from 1857 onwards warranted an alliance with many of the rural shrines despite the official policy stating otherwise.

Throughout the Muslim rule in North India, "ulema, as teachers, interpreters of religious law, and theologians, were closely linked to political power" (Jones 1989, p. 57). Their economic and political fortunes "waxed and waned with the rise and fall of Islamic (Muslim) Empires" (Gardezi 2004, p. 76). The Mughal decline and the onset of British rule threatened their status as state functionaries. The reaction of the ulema to the Mughal downfall and the advent of British rule was markedly different from that of the sajjada nishins of Punjab. In this era of sociopolitical transition, the influence of many sajjada nishins remained intact in their respective localities but for the ulema it was catastrophic. For them "it signaled the disappearance of the cultural axis around which the entire Indian Islamic system was developed" (Gilmartin 1988, p. 53). With the crumbling of Muslim authority, "the ulema thus faced a new dilemma in defining the practical meaning of Islamic community in India" (Smith 1963, pp 42–43). Not only did the meanings of the Islamic system undergo a tectonic shift, as Smith argues, but the responsibility for the system's maintenance was assumed solely by the ulema class. Hence "a serious reorientation among many of the Delhi's leading ulema" (Gilmartin 1988, p. 53) ensued, beginning with Shah Waliullah (1704–1762) in the eighteenth century. During the second half of the nineteenth century, the movements of Islamic revivalism led to the realignment of "ulema class interests with the fortunes of [the] Islamic community rather than the state" (Jones 1989, p. 57).

It was in this context that Hafiz Syed Abid Hussain established Darul Ulum in 1867 at Deoband in the United Provinces. In 1915, a British official, Meston, described Darul Ulum as "a most impressive place, very like what one imagines some of the great universities of the middle ages to have been" (Robinson 1994, p. 266). Set up in an old mosque, the Chatta Masjid, under a shadowy pomegranate tree, it was strikingly distinct from earlier madaris. "Much of the organizational form was adopted from British institutions and then modified to fit the needs of Deoband" (Jones 1989, p. 58). The fact that the people were independent of kin ties and that they received donations from the general public were the two primary traits that meant that the institution had modernist bearings, which set it apart from other religious seminaries of the subcontinent. Darul Ulum had an independent infrastructure of its own. It was run by professional staff, and its students were admitted to study a defined curriculum and were supposed to take an examination for which they were awarded a degree at the convocation every year. It had its classrooms and a central library. Over time, it had many affiliated colleges, overseen by Darul Ulum's own graduates. The examining body too comprised Deobandi ulama.

The staff at Darul Ulum had specific roles as teachers, administrators and councillors. Erudition in Arabic was a fundamental criterion in the selection of the teachers. However, Persian teachers too were recruited but the faculty of Arabic held precedence over them "in pay and prestige" (Metcalf 1982, p. 95; Jullundri n.d., pp. 141–184). Initially the number of teaching staff did not exceed 12. The institution's administration consisted of a *sarparast* (rector) who acted as a patron, the *muhtamim* (chancellor) in charge of the day-to-day administration and a *sadr mudarris* (principal), responsible for overseeing the system of instruction. Qasim Nanutwi (1833–1877) and Rashid Ahmed Gangohi (1829–1905) were its early patrons. In 1892 the position of *mufti* an Islamic scholar who is authorized to issue fatwa (religious edicts) was added. He was "to supervise the dispensation of judicial opinions on behalf of the school" (Metcalf 1982, p. 95). Darul Ulum had a consultative council that included the administrators and seven additional members. Gradually the council became more influential than the staff and administration. By 1887 the consultative council was vested with all of the decision-making power.

The Darul Ulum curriculum was quite similar to what was being taught at other madaris in South Asia, known as Dars-i-Nizami. That curriculum was first introduced by Mullah Nizamuddin Sihalvi (d. 1747), who was a scholar of some repute in Islamic jurisprudence and philosophy in Lucknow (Ahmad n.d., p. 107). All madaris adhering to Sunni *fiqh* (Islamic jurisprudence) followed Dars-i-Nizami, which

> [consisted] of about twenty subjects broadly divided into two categories: *al ulum an-naqliya* (the transmitted sciences), and *al-ulum al-aqliya* (the rational sciences). The subject areas include grammar, rhetoric, prosody, logic, philosophy, Arabic literature, dialectical theology, life of the Prophet, medicine, mathematics, polemics, Islamic law, Jurisprudence, *ahadith*, and tafsir (exegesis of the Qur'an). (Ahmad n.d., p. 103)

Interestingly, only 8 out of 20 subjects of the curriculum can be regarded as purely religious. The rest were meant (1) to prepare students for civil service jobs and (2) to help them to have a better understanding of the religious scriptures. Darul Ulum attracted mostly poor students, unlike the *ashraf* (elites), who preferred the Muhammadan Anglo Oriental College in Aligarh.

Darul Ulum was financed by the Muslim princes of Hyderabad, Bhopal and Rampur, to mention a few who patronized learning and "extend[ed] their bounty across the border to their fellows in British India" (Metcalf 1982, p. 96). Similarly, big landlords from the United Provinces dispensed some of their wealth for altruistic causes by lending monitory support to Darul Ulum Deoband. However, these grants had no element of certainty. Ulema were not willing "to accept British grant-in-aid, for such help was precarious and carried the taint of its non-Muslim source" (Ibid., p. 97). Therefore, with extreme care, a network of donors was created "who formed a base not only for financial support but for dissemination of their teachings" (Ibid.). Many supporters pledged annually the contributions which formed the major part of Darul Ulum's income. The amount of the contribution was not fixed, nor was the specificity of the donor's religious and sectarian persuasion considered important (Rizvi 2005, p. 152).

DEOBANDI INCARNATIONS

In Sind, as Sarah Ansari (1992, pp. 78–79) argues, due to the pan-Islamism and particularly "the involvement" of Sindhi pirs in the Khilafat Movement (1919–1924), the system of colonial control was considerably shaken. From the late nineteenth century, Sindh had become "more integrated into all-Indian systems of communications, of trade and ideas". In the changed situation, several Sindhi pirs forged close links with pan-Islamic leaders in various parts of the subcontinent. Most important of these connections was the involvement of a certain group of pirs with Deobandi ulema. By the turn of the twentieth century, networks of religious seminaries stretching from Bhachundi on the Sind–Punjab border, via Haleji and Amrot near Sukkur, to Goth Pir Jhando, north of Hyderabad, had emerged as outposts of Deobandi influence in Sindh. In the case of the areas constituting North India, the traditional religious forms with sajjada nishins and shrines having mediatory agency was disapproved of by Deobandi ulema. Here my focus will be on the political activism of the Deobandi movement.

Ubaidullah Sindhi (1872–1944) is deemed to be the harbinger of Deobandi activism in Punjab and Sind (Azad 2002, pp. 19–87). Born to Sikh parents from Sialkot, Sindhi embraced Islam at the tender age of 15 in Muzaffargarh on August 29, 1887. Immediately afterwards he travelled to Sindh and took the oath of allegiance with Pir Hafiz Muhammad Sadiq at Bharchundi, thus his spiritual training began. From Bharchundi, Sindhi proceeded to Deoband in September 1888. There he came under the tutelage of Mehmud ul Hassan (1851–1922), who was instrumental in stirring the Deobandi movement to political activism. Sindhi proved himself worthy of Mehmud ul Hassan's attention when he successfully formed Jamiat ul Ansar, a student body at Deoband in 1909. The group was meant to organize Deobandi scholars both in the country and elsewhere. Besides setting up madrassas—Dar ul Irshad (established in 1901) in Goth Pir Jhanda, Nawab Shah District in Sind and Nazarath ul Maarif (established in 1912) in Delhi—he also played a pivotal role in *Tehrik i Reshami Roomal,* a silk letter conspiracy in 1915. This movement merits a mention here for two reasons. First, the area of its operation was mostly Punjab, and, second, it provides us with the first testimony of Deobandi activism in the region. Through a collaborative effort with Amir Amanullah Khan, the ruler of Afghanistan, a plan was hatched to oust the British from India with the help of Turkey. Sindhi was overseeing the operational side of that movement. Unfortunately for the Deobandi activists, the whole plan was leaked and most of those involved were arrested. One may however assert that despite the failure of the Tehrik i Reshmi Rumal, Punjab had a taste of anticolonial misadventure which was a Deobandi undertaking (Qureshi 1988, pp. 839–840).

In 1919, the Deobandi ulema formed themselves into a political group immediately after the commencement of the Khilafat Movement (1919–1924), which aimed to prevent the British from abolishing the Khilafat Movement in Turkey after the First World War. Thus the JUH came into existence, with Mehmud ul Hassan and Abul Kalam Azad as its central figures. The Khilafat Movement in synchrony with the Non-Cooperation Movement reconfigured all India politics in two ways. First, they brought politics to the masses, and, second, they enabled ulema to secure significant positions in the public arena. The movement had an extraordinary resonance in North India and to a lesser extent influenced urban Punjab. Lahore, Sialkot and Gujranwala were tangibly stirred by the anti-British sentiments during the early 1920s on the issue of the Khilafat Movement. During the same period, Deobandi stalwarts in Punjab, such as Ubaidullah Sindhi, Ata Ullah Shah Bokhari, Habib ur Rehman Ludhianvi and Ahmed Ali Lahori, began their political careers. They assumed centrality by inculcating an exclusionary version of Islam in their politics. In particular, their major rallying cry was *Khatam-i-Nabuvat* (finality of prophethood), used extensively in the condemnation of Ahmedhis ab initio. The concept gained the greatest significance after the Ahmedya sect emerged in the late 1890s (Ali 1973). The Ahmadis allegedly refuted the very idea of the last prophethood, which was considered to be one of the fundamentals of Islam.

Comprising Punjabi dissidents of the Khilafat Committee Punjab, Majlis-i-Ahrar-i-Islam (Mirza 1975, pp. 81–4) followed the puritanical and agitation style of politics in the 1930s. Maulana Zafar Ali Khan, Maulana Daud Ghaznavi, Syed Ataullah Shah Bokhari, Chaudhri Afzal Haq, Maulana Mazhar Ali Azhar, Khawja Abdul Rehman Ghazi, Sheikh Hassam-ud-din and Maulana Habib-ur-Rehman Ludhianvi constituted the core leadership of the Ahrar. Most of them were orators of extraordinary calibre who could spellbind their audience for hours. Although it was a composite organization representing all Muslim segments, the core ideology and principal leaders, such as Ataullah Shah Bukhari and Habib-ur-Rehman Ludhianvi, adhered to Deobandi Islam. It had an entrenched following among the lower-middle-income echelon of urban Muslim populace and particularly among the artisans of the Lahore, Amritsar and Sialkot districts of Punjab.

The Ahrar's agitations for the rights of the Muslims of Kashmir, who were suffering under the oppressive rule of the maharajah, are not properly acknowledged in the contemporary Pakistani historiography. The 1931 activities raised the Ahrar party's popularity in urban Punjab to an unprecedented level (Ludhyanvi 1968). This was because of the presence of large

Kashmiri Muslim communities in such cities as Amritsar, Lahore and Sialkot, where Ahrar had a substantial following. It was followed by another movement for the rights of poor Muslims in Kapurthala State, which further raised its profile and popularity. It lasted until the Masjid Shahid Ganj issue (A contested site between Muslims and Sikhs that led to disputes between the two religious communities) in Lahore, which irreparably undermined Ahrar's political standing in the province. The post-Shahid Ganj era was quite chequered for Ahrar because its electoral strength plummeted, nevertheless, the impact that some of its leaders—particularly Bokhari—had, had a lasting resonance. In the United Provinces (UP), Tabarra agitation and the Madhe-Sahaba (in 1937–39) (The madh-i sahaba, a tradition wherein the Sunnis recited verses praising the four rightly-guided caliphs and other companions of the Prophet. The tabarra is a Shia tradition of criticizing or in some extreme cases cursing the first three caliphs who, according to the Shia, deceitfully deprived the Prophet's son-in-law and cousin, Ali, of his right to succession (Kamran, 2009, 62)). Movement drove a wedge of sectarian animosity quite deep between the Sunnis and the Shias. A large number of Ahraris from Punjab travelled to Awadh especially to court arrest. In the 1940s, sectarian animosity was papered over as the Pakistan Movement had gained momentum, thus mitigating the sectarian sentiments. Calm had also set in because the failed campaign of Hakumat-i-Illahiyah, vigrously orchestrated by Ahrar, had left it absolutely crestfallen.

The political scenario in the 1940s had an unsettling affect on the Deobandi movement. The ML's call for a separate Muslim state drove a wedge into Deobandis' top ranks. Hussain Ahmed Madni, Abul Kalam Azad and Habib ur Rehman Ludhianvi stuck to the nationalist position of the Indian National Congress and the JUH. However, a few ulema diverged from the avowed standpoint of the nationalists. To them, Muslim separatism was a preferred course to safeguard their interests. Consequently, a parting of the ways took effect in 1945 when Shabbir Ahmed Usmani, Ehtasham ul Hassan Thanvi, Zafar Ahmed Usmani and Mufti Muhammad Shafi conglomerated and founded the JUI, which espoused the cause of the ML.

In 1949 the Deobandi ulema activated the Ahrar, which staged a comeback as Majlis-i-Tehafuz-i-Khatam-i-Nubuwwat. Its sole aim was an anti-Ahmadi campaign, which eventually culminated in anti-Ahmadiyya riots in 1953. However, sectarian differences could not be ironed out permanently because they kept recurring, finally culminating in the establishment of the SSP on September 8, 1985. Sectarian militants such as Haq Nawaz Jhangvi (1952–1990), the founder-leader of the SSP, and many of his close companions, such as Zia-ur- Rehman Farouqi, have acknowledged the legacy of Attaullah Shah Bukhari and his colleagues in Majlis-e-Ahrar.

DEOBANDIS IN THE PUNJAB: ULEMA AND MADARIS

When Haji Muhammad Abid started the fundraising for Darul Ulum, 12 percent of the total funds were raised from Punjab during the first 20 years of its existence (Metcalf 1982, p. 236). According to Gilmartin, financial support came mostly from the urban centres where the influence of saint and shrine was somewhat marginal (Gilmartin 1988, p. 54). Similarly, Punjab is reported to have been quite significant in the recruitment of students for Darul Ulum in its early years. However, concrete information about the number of students from Punjab remains doubtful as even Barbara Metcalf (1982) has hardly anything worthwhile to impart in this regard. With the aid of a map, she refers to the spread of the madaris affiliated to Deoband across Punjab by 1890. Lahore, Gujranwala and Peshawar were the centres mentioned on the map where such madaris were set up (p. 134). No further detail is given regarding their founders, and the names of those institutions are not recorded. Saleem Mansur Khalid, however, reveals that Madrasa-i-Rashidia at Jullundur was founded in 1897, and another madrasa, Madrasa-i-Naumania, was established in 1907 (Khalid 2004, p. 101). With regard to the ulema, it appears that Hussain Ali of Wan Bhachran (1866–1943) in Mianwali District was the earliest recorded scholar going to Darul Ulum Deoband (Rahi 1998, p. 159). He was Maulana Rashid Ahmed Gangohi's student in 1895 and learnt the ahadith from him. He was also instructed in the exegesis of the Qur'an by Maulana Mazhar Nanutwi, and logic and philosophy by Maulana Ahmed Hassan Kanpuri. In 1915 he returned to his village, Wan Bhachran, and began professing the Deobandi brand of Islam (Rahi 1998). For the locals, he zealously emphasized unequivocal faith in *Tauhid* (monism) and the Qur'an as the fundamental source to ascertain the truth. As well as preaching he wrote extensively but, owing to his extremist views, his writings remain unnoticed or mentioned only briefly even in the narratives of Deobandi scholars. Ghulamullah Khan (1909–1980), a scholar of great erudition and the founder of Taleem ul Quran, a renowned madrasa in the northern Punjab, chose to be his disciple. Similarly, Maulana Abdul Haleem Qasimi (1920–1983) went to learn Qura'nic translation from Hussain Ali.

In the early twentieth century, Abdul Rahim Raipuri (1853–1919), a Naqshbandi pir, and Maulana Ashraf Thanvi wielded considerable influence in Punjab. Abdul Rahim Raipuri was born in Tigri, a town in Ambala District. He therefore may be considered to be the earliest Deobandi *alim* (Scholar) with a Punjabi background. However, he spent most of his life in Ganga-Yumna valley, teaching in various madaris, such as Mazahir ul Ulum Sahranpur and Delhi. Many of his successors, such as Shah Abdul Qadir Raipuri, Shah Abdul Aziz Raipuri and Saeed Ahmed Raipuri, set up madaris in Lahore and Sargodha by the name of Idara Rahimia Ulum-i-Qurania.[1] The network of Nizam ul Madaris ur Rahimia is very extensive: there are innumerable affiliated madaris throughout Pakistan (Azad 2006). Unlike other Deobandis, these madaris disapprove of violence and organize peaceful protest movements.

Ahmed Ali Lahori (1886–1962), one of the renowned Deobandi alim, rose to the revered status of Sheikh ul Tafsir because his exegesis of the Qur'an was regarded as the most authentic, lucid and comprehensive by the followers of the Deobandi segment.[2] Not only was he held in high esteem because of his contribution as the founder of such institutions as Anjuman-i-Khudam ud Din and Qasim ul Ulum, but his scholarly works, particularly in the realm of tafsir, had a significance of their own. Ahmed Ali was instructed by renowned scholars and Sufis such as Maulana Abdul Haque, Maulana Ubaidullah Sindhi and Maulana Ghulam Muhammad Deenpuri. He was initiated into the Qaderia order and came under the spiritual tutelage of Maulana Deenpuri through an oath of allegiance (bait) in 1895 (Rehman n.d., p. 23). However, Sindhi was his guardian and spiritual guide. Therefore he zestfully took part in the anti-colonial struggle and in the process went to Kabul in 1921, but it soon returned. He went to jail seven times for his denunciation of the British.

Ahmed Ali completed his education at Madrisa-i-Dar ul Irshad in Sind and started teaching there immediately afterwards. Later on he was summoned to Delhi by Maulana Sindhi, where he was made *naib nazim* (deputy administrator) of Madrisa-i-Nazarat ul Maarif, Delhi. In 1917 he moved to Lahore and started imparting Qur'anic lessons to the general public in a mosque opposite Sheranwala School. However, an important phase in his career as an *alim-i-din* (religious scholar) began when he founded Anjuman-i-Khudam ud Din. Promotion and dissemination of the Qur'an and *sunna* (the tradition of the Prophet) were enunciated as fundamental aims of the *anjuman* (assembly) (Bokhari 1999, p. 249). Hence the precedence of scriptural Islam was underscored, and the popular

Islam epitomized through the primacy of saint and shrine was termed as *bidat* in Ahmed Ali's teachings. Sticking to the fundamentals of Islam was exhorted among Muslims. Fazal-i-Haq, a student of Nazir Ahmed Dehlvi, and Abu Muhammad Ahmed, a student of Rashid Ahmed Gangohi, were made anjuman's members, and Ahmed Ali became its *amir* (head). Madrisa-i-Qasim ul Ulum was founded under the auspices of Anjuman-i-Khudam ud Din in 1924. Its grandiose building was constructed in Line Subhan Khan, Sheranwala Gate, Lahore, which was completed in 1934. A *madrassa* for girls was also built in 1945 at the same location (*Daily Ausaf*, April 2007). Madrisa Qasim ul Ulum, known for learning via *tafsir ul Qur'an* (the exegesis of the Qur'an), has instructed approximately 80,000 scholars of Islam.

Ahmed Ali remained politically active as he developed a close affinity with Ahrar when it launched the Kashmir movement in 1931. He ardently espoused agitation against the high handedness of the *maharaja* (king) against the Kashmiri Muslims. After Pakistan's creation, he was instrumental in collecting funds (to the tune of thousands of rupees) for jihad in Kashmir, and he went to Muzaffarabad to deliver the funds with his son Ubaidullah Anwar (1926–1985) (Arshad 2006, p. 673). Hence the Deobandi penchant for jihad in Kashmir has a historical context. Ali was also at the forefront of the agitation launched against the British principal of Maclagan Engineering College, Lahore, who desecrated the Prophet of Islam. Although he was arrested on charges of inciting unrest, the British government had to give in and all rusticated students were restored (Rehman n.d., p. 42). Ahmed Ali was elected amir of the JUI, West Pakistan, on October 8 and 9, 1956. In June 1957, *Tarjman ul Quran*, "the Jamiat's organ", was launched by Ahmed Ali in Lahore (Rehman n.d., pp. 41–42). Anjuman Khudam ud Din and Qasim ul Ulum continued their founder's legacy even after his death in 1962. Both of them sustained reputation as the prime institution for earning of Qur'an and its tafsir..His son Ubaidullah Anwar, an ingenuous exegete in his own right, stepped into the big boots of Maulana Ahmed Ali. Like his father, Ubaidullah Anwar was associated with the JUI all his life. At the time of his death, he was its *naib amir* (deputy head). Currently both institutions—Anjuman Khudam ud Din and Qasim ul Ulum—are "in the capable hands of Maulana Ajmal Qadri under whose vigilant oversight *Anjuman* and *Madrasa* are moving from strength to strength" (Mazhar Moin, personal communication, August 2007). The Qur'an and the tradition of the Prophet were the fundamental postulates that anjuman has always emphasized without meaning any insolence to Sufi tradition. Hence the practice of religious rituals was circumscribed strictly to the confines of the Islamic scriptures. Ultimately, not only religious instruction but also playing a proactive role in politics was the legacy of the JUH, which was kept alive by Ahmed Ali and his successors. Therefore Anjuman Khudam ud Din and Madrasa Qasim ul Ulum contributed significantly to advancing the cause of political (radical) Islam. Maulana Ahmed Ali and Ubaidullah Anwar's preoccupation with the JUI alludes to the implicit, if not explicit, support for jihad in Afghanistan and Kashmir.

Apart from Lahore, Ludhiana and Jullundur were the two districts where Deobandi Islam found a conducive environment. Ulema from Ludhiana, particularly Maulana Muhammad and Maulana Muhammad Abdullah, came under the spotlight when they took the lead in denouncing Mirza Ghulam Ahmed, the founder of the Qadiani sect, as a *kafir* (a non-Muslim, a disbeliever).[3] After graduating from Deoband, Maulana Muhammad Abdullah came to Ludhiana and started teaching at the famous Madrasa Azizia. Later on he moved to Madrasa Allah Walla along with his son Mufti Naeem Ludhianvi (1890–1970), and he remained engaged in teaching the ahadith. However, Abdullah's lasting contribution was the establishment of Madrasa Darul Ulum Naumania. Habib ur Rehman Ludhianvi was the most renowned of all Deobandi *ulema* from Ludhiana. He was a Deoband graduate and a favourite student of Habib ur Rehman Usmani and Anwar Shah Kashmiri. In 1919 he entered politics and began addressing public meetings along with Shabbir Ahmed Usmani (1885–1949) when the Khilafat Movement had just begun. He remained very active in the politics throughout his life. He also was one of the chief protagonists of Majlis-i-Ahrar. In the annals of the Ahrar movement he is remembered as *raiul ahrar* (leader of Ahrar). Astoundingly, Habib ur Rehman stayed in Ludhiana instead of migrating to Pakistan. His sons still live in East Punjab and are engaged in *tabligh* (preaching). Maulana Muhammad Abdullah (sajjada nishin, Khanqah Sirajia Kundian District Mianwali),[4] Maulana Muhammad Ibrahim (Mian Channu) and Master Taj ud Din Ansari were the prominent figures who migrated from Ludhiana (Hussaini 2004, p. 378). Maulana Rashid Ahmed Ludhianvi (b. 1922) rose to prominence as an alim and a jurist.

Maulana Faqirullah Raipuri Jullunduri (1878–1963) and Maulana Khair Muhammad Jullunduri (1891–1970) were both Deoband graduates and celebrated scholars. Both ulema also shared the kinship bond.

They belonged to the Arain *biradri* (clan). This signifies an important fact that initially the Deobandi brand of Islam attracted the lower and lower-middle echelon of the Muslim urban Punjabi populace. Faqirullah received his early education from Jamia Rashidia, Raipur, which was modelled on Darul Ulum Deoband and Mazahir ul Ulum Saharanpur, and was founded by Maulana Muhammad Saleh. Later on he went to Darul Ulum Naumania, Lahore, and then to Deoband for higher learning. In 1908 he returned to Jullundur and started teaching at his alma mater, Jamia Rashidia. There he was entrusted with the task of shaping the future of such youngsters who attained prominence in the days to come, such as Rashid Ahmed Salfi, Habib ur Rehman Ludhianvi, Muhammad Ali Jullunduri, Abdul Jabbar Hissarvi and Maulana Khair Muhammad Jullundri (Hussaini 2004, p. 207). At the time of Partition, Faqirullah migrated to Pakistan and settled in Sahiwal (Montgomery) District ,where he revived Jamia Rashidia, which, in a few years time, became one of the prime institutions of Deobandi learning. Besides Khair ul Madaris, it is the only prominent madrasa which was set up in Jullundur and revived in West Punjab after Partition. Faqirullah was succeeded by his sons, Abdullah, Qari Lutfullah and Fazal Habibullah. Abdullah shot to fame as a scholar in the ahadith, and, after his death, a dispute over the Jamia's succession led the authorities to close it down. Since 9/11 it has continuously been subjected to raids by law-enforcement agencies (Rana Iqtidar Abbas, personal communication, August 2007).

Khair Muhammad Jullundri was born in Nakodar Tehsil. He began his education at 7 and continued until he was 20,in 1911. During those years he travelled extensively in Punjab and North India. Eventually he settled down at Madrasa-i-Faiz Muhammadi, Jullundur. He came under the spiritual shadow of Ashraf Ali Thanwi through bait. Through the persuasion of his *murshid* (teacher), Maulana Khair Muhammad, he established Madrasa-i-Khair ul Madaris in Alamgiri Mosque, Attari Bazzar, Jullundur, which was inaugurated on March 9, 1931 (Khairul Madaris n.d.). Until his death in 1943, Khairul Madaris continued functioning under the patronage of Ashraf Ali Thanvi, who also suggested its name (Bokhari 1999, p. 230). After Partition, Maulana Khair Muhammad moved to Pakistan and settled in Multan. With the ardent support of his student and naib, Maulana Muhammad Ali Jullunduri, Khair ul Madaris was revived on October 18, 1947, in Multan. There, Maulana Shabbir Ahmed Usmani was its patron but only for a brief period because he died in 1949 (Ibid.). Khair ul Madaris flourished in leaps and bounds, and eventually it came to be known as "the national centre of Deobandi educational activity" (The State of Sectarianism in Pakistan, April 18, 2005, p. 15). Khair Muhammad was a keen theologian with a passion for Islamic learning and was he devoid of any political ambition. However, he was one of a few Deobandi ulema who espoused the Pakistan Movement. After the creation of Pakistan, when the JUI was reorganized with Shabbir Ahmed Usmani as its patron, Ahmed had been elected as its president. However, after a short while he resigned because he did not find politics to his taste. However, he participated in putting together 22 points at the meeting of ulema at Karachi, which were presumed to be the basis for the Islamic constitution. Moreover, he also took part in "*Tehrik-i- Khatum-Nabuwwat* and strived for the promulgation of Islamic system in the country" (Bokhari 1999, p. 231).

Khair ul Madaris was on a firm footing when Maulana Khair Muhammad died on October 22, 1970. Currently it is being managed by Khair Muhammad's grandson, Maulana Qari Hanif Jullunduri, who matches his predecessors neither in scholarship nor in spiritual excellence and charisma.[5] The gory incident of Lal Ubaidullah in July 2007 has substantially undermined his reputation and integrity among Deobandi people. Khairul Madaris is nevertheless regarded as a prototype for other seats of Islamic learning within the country to emulate. The role of Khairul Madaris in exacerbating the sectarian cleavage in Pakistan will be addressed later in this chapter.

Partition accrued some benefit to Deobandis because the JUI remained a political force to be reckoned with.[6] Since 1947, mushrooming of the madaris illustrated Deobandi ascendancy, which bolstered the political profile of the JUI. All of its leadership emerged from madaris, so they shared the commonality of class along with creed, particularly until the late 1970s. Similarly, the student body at the madaris belonged to the lower-middle and lower strata. Hence the madaris were no less than a lifeline for the JUI. From Partition onwards until 2003, 120 religious schools were emerging every year. In 1947, Pakistan had 245 religious schools, whereas in 2000 the number had reached 6,761, then increasing to 6,870 by September 11, 2001.[7] Vali Nasr contends that the proliferation of Deobandi, Brelwi and Ahl-i-Hadith madaris began in 1970s, and in Punjab the rise in the number of seminaries "has been most notable". They multiplied "three and a half times between 1975 and 1996, from over 700 to 2,463". Of these, 750 were "classed as aggressively sectarian" (Table 3.1).[8]

Table 3.1   Madaris of various sects (1988)

Province/Region	Deobandi	Beralvi	Ahl-e- Hadith	Shia	Others	Total
Punjab	590	548	118	21	43	1,320
NWFP	631	32	5	2	8	678
Sindh	208	61	6	10	6	291
Balochistan	278	34	3	1	31	347
Azad Kashmir	51	20	2	–	3	76
Islamabad	22	20	–	2	3	47
Northern areas	60	2	27	11	2	102
Total	1,840	717	161	47	96	2,861

Source: Ministry of Education, Islamabad, 1988. Quoted in Khalid (2004, p. 150)

There are three principal reasons for the phenomenal growth of (particularly Deobandi) madaris. First is the funneling of funds from Persian Gulf monarchies and particularly from Saudi Arabia. These regions viewed "the turn of Pakistan's politics towards the Left in the late 1960s and the early 1970s with alarm, and supported all kinds of Islamic activities with the aim of strengthening Islamic institutions and ideology as a bulwark against the Left" (Nasr 2000). The doubts of the rulers of Arab states were dispelled by taking concrete measures. Nevertheless, the support for "Islamic activism" continued. In due course "the linkages between Islamic organizations and groups in the Persian Gulf monarchies and those in Pakistan had become entrenched, and operated independently of government control" (Ibid., p. 144).The Pakistani ulema and madaris were the biggest beneficiaries from these "religious and intellectual bonds that became embedded in institutional contacts and networks of patronage" (Ibid.). Barbara Metcalf (2004) argues that the madaris "were not only a resource in domestic politics but at times found themselves engaged in a kind of surrogate competition between Saudis and Iranians as each patronized religious institutions likely to support their side" (p. 276). Second, the Afghan Jihad contributed very significantly to the mushroom growth of the madaris. The militarization of madaris in the 1980s at the behest of the USA and Saudi Arabia (Burki 1998, pp. 82–83) later proved to be a Frankenstein for the Pakistani state and the entire Western World. Third, Ziaul Haq (1922–1988), himself a Deobandi and a son of a cleric from Jullundur, quite zestfully pursued the policy of Islamization and in the process strengthened madrasa networks and the ulema by doling out huge funds to them. After 1980 the madaris also received *zakat* (a religious tax) (Malik 1996, pp. 85–119). In addition, madrasa graduates were accommodated within the public services

Table 3.2 Evolution of Madaris in Pakistan

Province/Region	1947	1960	1980	1988	2000
Punjab	121	195	1,012	1,320	3,153
NWFP	59	87	426	678	1,281
Sindh	21	87	380	291	905
Balochistan	28	70	135	347	692
Azad Kashmir	4	8	29	76	151
Islamabad	–	1	27	47	94
Northern areas	12	16	47	102	185
FATA	–	–	–	–	300
Total	245	464	2,056	2,861	6,761

Source: Ministry of Religious Affairs, Islamabad, 1988, 2000. Quoted in Khalid 2004, p. 145). (Figures of 1980 are based on reports of 1979)

because their degrees were accorded equivalent status to degrees from secular institutions. This resulted in a substantial increase in the number of madrasa students (Table 3.2).

However, before explicating further the rapid growth of madaris, it is appropriate to mention two important seminaries—Jamia Ashrafia and Jamia Madnia—both located in Lahore.

Jamia Ashrafia was set up by Maulana Mufti Muhammad Hassan who was a student (Khalifa-e-Arshad) of Maulana Ashraf Ali Thanwi, after whom the madrasa was named.[9] The school practised a non-jihadi and immaculately peaceful creed. "However, many teachers of the madrassas not only have connections with Jehadi organizations, they are actively involved in Jehadi activities" (Rana 2004, p. 522). This madrasa and the adjacent mosque exercise tremendous influence on the affluent urban class of Lahore, and its administration avoids getting embroiled in any political controversy.

On September 14, 1947, Jamia Ashrafia was founded in an old quadrangular three-storey building in Nila Gunbad Anarkali at the centre of a thickly populated area of Lahore. Scholars of immense repute—namely, Maulana Rasool Khan, Maulana Idrees Kandhalvi and Mufti Jamil Ahmed Thanvi taught there. In 1957 the staff and students were moved to a new campus on Ferozepur Road, Lahore. Today the main campus comprises a large mosque, a huge administrative and teaching block, two spacious boarding houses, a hospital and quite a number of residences for the employees. After the death of Mufti Muhammad Hassan in 1961, his son, Mufti Muhammad Obaidullah, a graduate of Darul Ulum Deoband, became *rai-sul jamia* (head of the educational institution). The madrassa is affiliated to with the Wafaq ul Madaris ul Arbia (aboard of Islamic education for more than 7,000 madaris). With branches and affiliated madaris spread all over Pakistan, Jamia Ashrafia has more than 1,500 male and 500 female scholars just at its Lahore branch (retrieved from http:ashrafia.org.pk/jamia.htm).

Jamia Madnia is another Deobandi madrasa in Lahore, founded by Maulana Syed Hamid Mian (1926–1988) in the 1950s. Syed Hamid Mian was the son of renowned Deobandi alim Maulana Syed Muhammad Mian, who hailed from Sahranpur (UP).[10] Five years after Partition he moved to Pakistan and started teaching at Jamia Ashrafia. However, he decided to establish his own madrasa, which he eventually did in the Bhatti Gate, Lahore. It gradually developed into an important institution of learning of the ahadith. Abbass Najmi, a keen student of Deobandis in Pakistan, ranks Jamia Madnia as more influential than any madrasa after Khairul Madaris, Multan, because it has churned out numerous scholars of the ahadith and fiqh.

Returning to the mushroom growth of madaris, interestingly they multiplied by 2,745 percent during 55 years of Pakistan's history up to 2003.[11] In 1988 the number of Deobandi madaris in Punjab reached 590 out of a total of 1,320, then rose to 972 with 80,120 students in 1996 (Khalid 2004, p. 150; *Herald*, October 1996, p. 56). Curiously enough, Deobandi madaris expanded by quite a large number towards south Punjab because, out of 972, 595 madaris were in three districts: Multan, Dera Ghazi Khan and Bahawalpur. Similarly, Wafaq ul Madaris ul Arabia (established in 1959), which is a regulatory body of Deobandi madaris, is also in Multan. This trend was quite discernible even before Partition, and was strengthened considerably with the establishment of Khairul Madaris. Some other important seminaries established in South Punjab were Jamia Abbasia, Bahawalpur, Qasimul Ulum, Multan, Darul Ulum, Kabirwala, Madrasa Qasimul Ulum, Faqirwali, Madrasa Ashraful Ulum, Rahimyar Khan, Makhzanul Ulum and Khanpur. The ubiquity of the saint and shrine culture, poverty, and very few institutions of secular education were arguably the main reasons for this proliferation in the region.

Deobandi Militant Organizations and Violence

The dialectics in which Deobandis were playing antithesis to the exponents of local Islam were articulated through saint and shrine symbolism. In this connection the website of Khairul Madaris makes interesting reading:

> Geographically, Multan is situated in the heart of Pakistan and possesses a great historical significance. But the people of not only Multan as a seat

of learning, but of the whole southern Punjab were in the past decades, a prey to general ignorance and innovatory rituals practiced in the name of Islam. Under these circumstances, the new Khair-ul-Madaris at Multan proved to be a light house in a stormy night whose light began to spread not only through Punjab but also to the recesses of the whole Islamic world (Retrieved from http://www.khairulmadaris.com.pk/e-branches. htm.).

It was quite obvious that not only Multan but most of south Punjab was awash with shrines as the sites of devotional practices, which Deobandi puritanism was quite determined to wipe out. This may be one of the important factors in the spread of Deobandi seminaries in overwhelming number towards the south. Seminaries in southern Punjab were instrumental in paving the way for Deobandi Islam to displace the syncretic ethos reflected in the local version of Islam. In addition, they played a vital role in turning the region into the biggest recruiting ground for the jihadi *lashkars* (militiamen) operating in Afghanistan and Kashmir. Ayesha Siddiqua Agha is spot on when she says, "Bahawalpur is one of the few districts which have contributed as much to Jihad as some districts in the frontier district" (Agha 2006). Similarly, while identifying the causes of the mushroom growth of the madaris in divisions such as Multan, Dera Ghazi Khan and Bahawalpur, Jamal Malik (1996) contends:

As their infrastructure is poor, there are few important industries and less urbanization; in short, they do not have a high level of development. They are however more integrated in their traditional systems of social order and social security and thus are possibly more cohesive than "modern areas". These divisions are marked by large landed properties and a high number of small farmers or landless peasants (p. 185).

With so little allocation of funds on human resource development, alongside overlooking the social and economic disparity in the southern areas, the ruling elite helped to create a conducive environment for madaris to proliferate. More alarming is the growing militancy among the madara graduates. The SSP, the LeJ and the HA have had operational bases in the south. Stalwarts such as Masud Azahar and Abdul Rashid Ghazi (*naib khateeb* (junior cleric) at Lal Masjid, who was killed in July 2007 by law-enforcement agencies) hailed from Bahawalpur and Rajanpur, respectively.

Although many scholars consider the Afghan Jihad as a catalyst in engendering militancy, along with the outbreak of the Islamic Revolution in Iran (1979), the historical context in which the phenomenon of militancy grew, and later on gathered momentum, has not been unravelled. While studying Deobandi militancy, reference should be made to couple of watershed points that galvanized Deobandi activism in Pakistan. First, the anti-Qadiani movement was launched in 1953, Ahrar in the garb of Majlis-i-Tahafuz-i-Khatm-i-Nubuwwat (established in 1949) being the vanguard of the whole episode that resulted in the imposition of martial law in Lahore. The protest movement—Rast Iqdam (direct action) was quelled through a military action under the command of General Azam Khan. Deobandi activism, however, was stemmed for two decades. The anti-Ahmadi impulse nevertheless remained alive and smouldering beneath the surface and ignited again in 1974 in the wake of the Rabwa incident (Kamran 2015). The Ahmadis were declared non-Muslims by Zulfiqar Ali Bhutto's regime through an amendment to the 1973 Constitution, which appeared to work as a shot in the arm for the Deobandi leadership. The successful finale of the anti-Ahmadi movement had a lasting impact on Deobandis, who found encouragement and held on to their extremist views and militant agenda. Later on the new Deobandi leadership (e.g. Haq Nawaz Jhangvi and Manzoor Ahmed Chinioti) founded organizations that were avowedly sectarian and militant in nature. The role of the Afghan Jihad in providing the necessary wherewithal and motivation to such organizations can also not be refuted (Ahmed 2004).

The first of these organizations was the SSP, which was dedicated exclusively to fighting shi'ism, which it considered to be non-Muslim because of members' irreverence towards the companions of the Prophet (Kamran 2009; Abbas 2002). The Iranian Revolution in 1979 and the mobilization of the Shia community in Pakistan provided the basic motive to Haq Nawaz Jhangvi and his associates to form the SSP. The Afghan Jihad in the 1980s provided a conducive environment for the organization's growth and it went from strength to strength. According to many sources, Saudi Arabia had been the main sponsor of the sectarian organization. The assassination of its founder, Haq Nawaz Jhangvi, in February 1990 led to a string of murders and random attacks against Shias, including many Iranian officials living in Pakistan.[12] Most of the SSP's top leadership were assassinated (i.e., Zia-ur-Rahman Farooqi, Isar-ul-Qasmi and Azam Tariq). The organization also sent armed volunteers to help the Taliban in Afghanistan from 1998 onwards.

The LeJ was a splinter group of the SSP comprising more radical Deobandis (Kamran 2009). The LeJ was founded in 1994 by Raiz Basra, a veteran of the War in Afghanistan and a close associate of Haq Nawaz Jhnagvi, Akram Lahori and Malik Ishaq. All three died an unnatural death. While alive they gave the law-enforcement agencies an extremely hard time. The LeJ targeted Shia leaders, intellectuals and professionals. Based in Kabul until the fall of the city in November 2001, it was accused by the Government of Pakistan of plotting an attack on the then prime minister, Nawaz Sharif, in 1999. It had been a nemesis for the Hazara community in Baluchistan simply because it adheres to Shia faith. Malik Ishaq masterminded the terrorist attack on the Sri Lankan cricket team in Lahore in 2009. In addition, he was responsible for scores of assassinations and targeted killings. On July 29, 2015, he was killed in Muzzaffargarh when he tried to escaped from police custody.

In 1991, Fazal ur Rahman Khalil (a Pushtun) and Masud Azher, a young Pakistani cleric from Bahawalpur, established Harkat-ul-Ansar (HA) by merging Harkat-ul-Mujahadeen and Harkat-ul-Jihad. The outfit was joined by many Pakistani volunteers (especially from Punjab) who went to Afghanistan to support the mujahideen. Later on its attention was switched to Kashmir. A former US intelligence officer, Julie Sirrs, carried out a survey in 2000 which revealed that the "foreigners captured by military commander Masud in north east Afghanistan shows that 39 percent of the 113 prisoners were affiliated with Harkat-ul-Ansar" (Sirrs 2001). In October 1997 the US State Department declared it a terrorist organization, so it changed its name to the HM.

The JM is another Deobandi militant organization which is a brainchild of Maulana Masud Azhar. In 1994, Masud Azhar was jailed for his militant activities in Indian-held Kashmir. On December 24, 1999, a plane from an Indian airline was hijacked and brought to Qandhar. The hijacker obtained the release of Masud Azhar. He remained under the protection of the Taliban for some time and then returned to Pakistan and founded the JM in Islamabad (Lal Masjid) in February 2000. Many members of the Harkat-ul-Mujahidin and of the SSP are presumed to have joined the JM for ethnic reasons. Punjabis sided with Masud Azhar while Pushtuns stayed with Fazal-ur-Rehman Khalil. Oliver Roy (n.d)attributes the pattern of suicide attacks to the JM. In December 2000 a young Muslim from Birmingham, Muhammad Bilal, launched a suicide attack on the Indian army in Srinager, the first incident of its kind (retrieved from Metcalf 2004, pp. 236–64).

Religious intolerance was markedly exacerbated with the introduction of the Blasphemy Law in 1982 by Zia ul Haq. Until then, Section 295 A provided protection for the religious feelings of all the communities irrespective of their religious affiliation, and the perpetrator was to be punished with ten years in prison or a fine. Zia enforced Ordinance XX and made 295 B part of the Pakistan Penal Code (PPC) in 1982. In 1986 he inserted 295 C in the PPC, which brought minorities to a position of unprecedented invulnerability, particularly the Ahmedhi community, which was particularly excluded from the social mainstream. However, along with the Ahmadis, Muslims and Christians also fell victim to the Blasphemy Law, which was used mostly with malicious/ulterior motives. Many of the allegations were brought either to favour a business transaction or to settle personal scores (Gabriel 2007). The law has been a social bane to Pakistan, which cannot repeal simply because of the enormous pressure exerted on the state by the religious right and Deobandis, which, as described above, are the most zealous supports of that law.

Conclusion

The linear trajectory of this narrative, while mapping the growth of the Deobandi sect in Punjab, must not obscure the primacy of pirs in the contemporary sociopolitical setting of the province. Undoubtedly, the maulvi and madrasa nexus has expanded exponentially over the years at the expense of both saint and shrine, and the spiritual excellence that they epitomized. Nevertheless, saint and shrine have sustained their supremacy at least in the rural areas of the Punjab. Historically, saints of Punjab fitted well into the client–patron network of the colonial rulers, a tradition that continued undeterred until now. Conversely, Deobandi maulvis and madaris have been clamouring for *sharia* to be promulgated from the very outset. The success of the anti-Qadiani movement in the 1970s, Zia's bid to legitimize his military rule, the Afghan Jihad and the Islamic Revolution in Iran (1979) contributed a great deal in the Deobandi upsurge. US and Saudi aid changed the class character of Deobandi exponents. It should be reiterated here that the Deobandi movement represented the lower-middle and lower classes particularly in Punjab. However, Deobandi groups became more militant and markedly sectarian, frequently challenging the writ of the state in the 1990s. Recently, the Lal Masjid and Jamia Hafza incident in Islamabad, and the way in which the Ghazi brothers exhorted the government to implement sharia, typify religious extremism.

Defiance towards the state, the spiralling of sectarian hatred and suicide bombing are tactics deployed by Deobandi militants that have substantially unhinged the state apparatus in Pakistan. One explanation for the proliferation of Deobandis in South Punjab is the region's feudal character. Having no alternative ideology such as Marxism or liberalism, or even the language symbols which may challenge the feudal stranglehold, Deobandi (or sectarian) militancy remains one of the few ways to counter it. Hence, Deobandi denomination was a roaring success in the districts, such as Bahawalpur and Rahim Yar Khan. The quantum of autonomy that the madaris have enjoyed for the last 25 years makes it increasingly difficult for the Pakistani state to establish its own writ. Even proposals for curriculum reforms and the registration of madaris are defied vigorously.

Notes

1. Raipur is a small town near Saharanpur (UP) where Shah Abdul Rahim Raipur established Khanqah-i-Aliya Rahimia Raipur, which later on became one of the leading centres of Deobandi learning. Shah Saeed Ahmed Raipuri, the fourth Sheikh after Abdul Rahim, replicated it in Lahore in 2001 under the name Idara Rahimia Ulum-i-Qurania (Azad 2006, p. 199).
2. Maulana Ahmed Ali Lahori (1886–1962) was born in the small town of Jalal in Gujranwala District. The town is situated to the east of Gaghaar Railway Station. His father, Sheikh Habib Ullah, converted to Islam from Sikhism and adhered to the Chishtia order. Ahmed Ali had three brothers: Hafiz Muhammad Ali, Maulvi Aziz Ahmed and Hakim Rashid Ahmed (Rehman n.d, pp. 19–27; Malik 2005).
3. Maulana Muhammad and Maulana Muhammad Abdullah were brothers from Ballia Walli, Ludhiana District. Abdullah earned considerable acclaim as a scholar. Sitting at the feet of Muhammad Hassan Amritsari, Mehmud ul Hassan and Anwar Shah Kashmiri were students of the ahadith (Rahi 1998, pp. 346–347). Mujahid Hussaini (2004) states that according to the Prophet, one of the traditions— "re-incarnation of Messih (Jesus Christ or Hazrat Issah) would come to pass at a place by the name of *Ludh*". Hence Ghulam Ahmed chose Ludhiana for the final announcement of his prophethood (p. 377).
4. Khanqah Sirajia is one of only two Deobandi *khanqahs* (hospices with Sufi as its central figure) in Punjab, with the other at Sargodha by the name of Khanqah-i-Aliya Raipur.

5. Maulana Muhammad Sharif Jullunduri (the second son of Khair Muhammad) took over as an administrator of Khair ul Ulum after the Maulana Khair Muhammad's death in 1970. He died in Mecca on September 7, 1981. It therefore fell on the young shoulders of Hanif Jullunduri to manage the affairs of the seminary (Bokhari 1999, p. 444).

6. Since independence, JUI has developed strong roots in Baluchistan and the Frontier. As a result it has performed more consistently in the polls than the other religious parties. It formed coalition governments with the National Awami Party (NAP) in both provinces, although these were dismissed by Zulfiqar Ali Bhutto. This experience led the JUI to take its place in the anti-PPP Pakistan National Alliance in 1977. However, the JUI, under Maulana Fazlur Rehman's leadership, distanced itself from the Zia regime and took its place in the 11-party Movement for the Restoration of Democracy (MRD), launched in February 1981. Five years later, Maulana Fazl ur Rehman was appointed its convener. Despite the collapse of the MRD before the 1988 elections, the JUI remained in opposition to the Islami Jamhoori Ittehad (IJI) and captured eight seats in the National Assembly. The JUI remains opposed to the Islamist approach of the IJI, but its greatest rivalry is with the Barelvi and Shia Islamic groupings (Talbot 2005, p. 451).

7. From 1988 to 2000 the number of religious schools increased by 236 percent. The majority of these schools belonged to the Sunni-Deobandi denomination (Rahman 2004, pp. 77–98).

8. The apprehensions of the Arab rulers were somewhat assuaged when Prime Minister Z.A. Bhutto (1926–1979) purged his party of the leftist elements (Nasr 2000, p. 142).

9. Maulana Mufti Muhammad Hassan was born in Malpur near Hassan Abdal. He received his early education in his native town and then proceeded to Dar ul Ulum Deoband and became a worthy disciple of Ashraf Ali Thanvi. He learnt the ahadith from Anwar Shah Kashmiri. Later he moved to Amritsari and took up a teaching assignment at a well-known seminary, Jamia Naumania. On Partition he migrated to Lahore and founded Jamia Ashrafia, which is a prime Deobandi seminary in Punjab (*The Daily Jang*, special ed., April 27, 2007).

10. Hamid Mian received religious instruction from scholars such as Abdus Sami Deobandi, Abdul Khaliq Madni, Mufti Muhammad Shafi and Hussain Ahmed Madni (Bokhari 1999, p. 457).

11. According to a report compiled by the Interior Ministry, the number of students in those seminaries was around 1.5 million by 2003.

12. Haq Nawaz belonged to Mauza Chela Thana Massan *tehsil* (sub-district) and Jhang District. He was born in 1952 and hailed from the Sipra clan with a very small land holding. His father, Wali Muhammad, was a known *khojji* (tracker / spotter) of the area. Haq Nawaz could not go beyond fourth grade in school. He was then sent to Hafiz Jan Muhammad to learn the Qur'an by heart, which he did in two years. Hafiz Jan Muhammad persuaded him to go to Masjid Shiekhan Wali in Abdul Hakim (currently in Khanewal District). There he learnt the art of recitation from Qari Taj Muhammad and also acquired a knowledge of grammar. Then he spent five years at Darul Ulum, Kabirwalla, and was greatly influenced by Maulana Manzur Ahmed, who was a famous Deobandi scholar of the area. Lastly, he went to Khair ul Madariss, Multan, to learn the ahadith. He remained there for seven years. Then he had a brief stint as *imam* (prayer leader in a mosque) at Toba Tek Singh. He came to Jhang in 1973 as a khateeb of Masid Mohalla Piplianwalla. Interview from Haq Nawaz' s elder brother, Mehr Sher Muhammad, and his cousin, Hafiz Muhammad Nawaz, Mauza Chela, Jhang (Kamran 2009).

REFERENCES

Abbas, A. (2002). *Sectarianism: The players and the game.* Lahore: South Asia Partnership-Pakistan.

Abbas, R. I. (2007, August 1). "Emergence of Deobandis" [Personal interview].

Agha, A. S. (2006, December 25). Bahawalpur's two ends. Retrieved August 17, 2007, from http://archives.dailytimes.com.pk/editorial/25-Dec-2006/view-bahawalpur-s-two-ends-dr-ayesha-siddiqa

Ahmed, K. (2004, August 13–19). Maulana Chinioti the great apostatiser (1931–2004). *Friday Times.*

Ahmad, M. (n.d.). Madrassa education in Pakistan and Bangladesh. Retrieved September 17, 2007, from http://www.apcss.org/Publications/EditedVolumes/ReligiousRadicalism/PagesfromReligious

Ali, M. (1973). *The Ahmadiyyah movement* (S. Tuffail, Trans. & Ed.). Lahore: Ahmadiyyah Anjuman Ishaat Islam.

Ansari, S. (1992). *Sufi saints and state power: The pirs of Sind, 1843–1947.* Cambridge: Cambridge University Press.

Arshad, A. (2006). *Bees barrey musalman.* Lahore: Maktaba-i-Rashidia.

Azad, M. (Ed.). (2002). *Khutbat wa maqalat.* Lahore: Dar ul Tehqiq wa Ishaat.

Azad, M. (2006). *Mashaikh-i-Raipur: Khanqah-i-Aliya Rahimia Raipur aur mashaikh Raipur ka taaruf.* Lahore: Dar ul Tehqiq wal Ishaat.

Bokhari, H. (1999). *Akabir-i-Ulema-i-Deoband.* Lahore: Idara-i-Islamiat.

Burki, S. (1998). *A revision history of Pakistan.* Lahore: Vanguard Books.

Cohen, S. (2003). The Jihadist threat to Pakistan. *The Washington Quarterly, 26,* 5–25. Delhi: Oxford University Press.

Cole, J. R. I. (1988). *Roots of North Indian Shi'ism in Iran and Iraq: Religion and State in Awadh: 1722–1859* (pp. 152–157). Berkeley: University of California Press.

Deeni Madaris Report (1988). Citation in ICG Asia Report No. 36. pp. 9. International Crisis Group (ICG), Pakistan: Madrasas, Extremism and the Military Asia, 2002, Islamabad.

Devji, F. (2008). Red Mosque. *Public Culture, 20*(1), 19–26.

Eaton, R. (1978). The profile of popular Islam in the Pakistani Punjab. *Journal of South Asian and Middle Eastern Studies, II*(I), 74–92.

Gabriel, T. (2007). *Christian citizens in an Islamic state: The Pakistan experience.* Aldershot: Ashgate.

Gardezi, H. (2004). Religion, ethnicity, and state power in Pakistan: The question of class. In D. Allen (Ed.), *Religion and political conflict in South Asia.* Westport: Greenwood Press.

Gilmartin, D. (1988). *Empire and Islam: Punjab and the making of Pakistan.* London: IB Tauris.

Herald. (1996). October issue.

Hussaini, M. (2004). *Ulma-i-Deoband: ahid saz sakhsiat.* Faisalabad: Seerat Markaz.

International Crisis Group. (2002). *Pakistan: Madrasas, extremism and the military.* Islamabad/Brussels: International Crisis Group Report.

International Crisis Group. (2005). *The state of sectarianism in Pakistan* (Asia report, No.95). Brussels: International Crisis Group.

Jones, K. (1989). *Socio-religious reform movements in British India* (Cambridge history of India). Cambridge: Cambridge University Press.

Jullundri, R. (n.d.). *Bartanvi hind mein muslamanon ka nizam-i-taleem.* Lahore: Idara-i-Saqafat-i-Islamia.

Kamran, T. (2009). Contextualizing sectarian militancy in Pakistan: A case study of Jhang. *Journal of Islamic Studies, 20,* 55–85.

Kamran, T. (2015). The prehistory of religious exclusionism in contemporary Pakistan: Khatam-i-Nubuwwat, 1889-1953. *Modern Asian Studies, 49*(6), 1840–1874. doi:10.1017/S0026749X14000043.

Khairul Madaris. (n.d.). Retrieved September 17, 2007, from http://www.khairulmadaris.com.pk/e-branches.htm.

Khalid, S. (2004). *Deeni madaris mein taaleem:kaifiat, masail, imkanat.* Islamabad: Institute of Policy Studies.

Ludhyanvi, T. (1968). *Ahrar Aur Tehrik-e-Kashmir 1932.* Lahore: Maktaba-i-Majlis-e-Ahrar Islam.

Malik, J. (1996). *Colonization of Islam: Dissolution of traditional institutions in Pakistan.* Lahore: Vanguard Books.

Malik, A. (2005). *Dastan-i-Khawada- i-Maulana Ahmed Ali Lahori.* Lahore: Urdu Bazaar.

Metcalf, B. (1982). *Islamic revival in British India: Deoband, 1860–1900.* Princeton: Princeton University Press.

Metcalf, B. (2004). *Islamic contestations: Essays on Muslims in India and Pakistan.* New Delhi: Oxford University Press.

Mirza, J. (1975). *Karwan-i-Ahrar* (Vol. i). Lahore: Maktaba-i-Tabsara.

Moin, M. (2007, August 1). "Emergence of Deobandis" [Personal interview].

Nasr, S. (2000). The rise of Sunni militancy in Pakistan: The changing role of Islamism and the ulama in society and politics. *Modern Asian Studies, 34,* 139–180.

Qureshi, I. (1988). *A short history of Pakistan.* Karachi: University of Karachi.

Rahi, A. (1998). *Tazkirah-i-ulema-i-Punjab* (Vol. ii). Lahore: Maktaba-i-Rehmania.

Rahman, T. (2004). *Denizens of alien world: A study of education, inequality and polarization in Pakistan.* Karachi: Oxford University Press.

Rana, M. (2004). *A to Z of Jehadi organizations in Pakistan* (S. Ansari, Trans.). Lahore: Mashal Books.

Rehman, H. (n.d.). *Sheikh ul Tafsir Hazrat Maulana Ahmed Ali Lahori aur un key khulfa.* Lahore: Pakistan Book Centre.

Rizvi, S. A. A. (1986). *A socio-intellectual history of the Isna-Ashari Shi'is in India.* New Delhi: Munshiram Manoharlal Publishers.

Rizvi, M. (2005). *Tarikh-i-Dar–u-Ulum Deoband: Bar- i- saghir key musalmanon ka sab sey bara karnama.* Lahore: Idara-i-Islamyat.

Robinson, F. (1994). *Separatism among Indian Muslims: The politics of the United Provinces' Muslims, 1860–1923.* Delhi: Oxford University Press.

Roy, O. (n.d.). Islamic radicalism in Afghanistan and Pakistan. Retrieved September 20, 2007, from H:sectarianismThe Islamic threat.htm.

Sirrs, J. (2001). *The Taliban foreign fighters: A report prepared for the committee for a free Afghanistan*. Washington: Committee for a Free Afghanistan.

Smith, W. (1963). The 'Ulama' in Indian politics. In C. Philips (Ed.), *Politics and society in India*. London: George Allen & Unwin.

Talbot, I. (1988). *Punjab and the Raj*. Delhi: Manohar.

Talbot, I. (2005). *Pakistan: A modern history*. London: Hurst & Company.

The Daily Ausaf. (2007, April). Almi anjuman-i-khudam ud din ka seh mahi ijtamah.

The Daily Jang. (2007, April 27). Special edition.

CHAPTER 4

Covering Faith-Based Violence: Structure and Semantics of News Reporting in Pakistan

Abbas Zaidi

INTRODUCTION

"Media" is a broad category comprising many genres that are distinctive in their functional distribution. All of them, however, give an account of, say, a happening to their readers. People in general understand, say, an incident in the light of how the media portrays or represents it (Carrabine 2008; Fourie 2008; Biagi 2014).[1] Genres such as leaders are considered persuasive because they often take a position for or against an incident or issue and, therefore, cannot be categorized as neutral. Thus an editorial is defined as "a considered opinion of a newspaper on an issue of public importance" (Breuer and Napthine 2008, p. 126). Hard news reporting, on the other hand, is characterized by stories that "aim to inform the community about events and happenings and to provide citizens with the information they require to be able to participate as fully informed citizens in the democratic process" (Bainbridge et al. 2011, p. 454). Thus hard

A. Zaidi (✉)
University of New South Wales, Kensington, NSW, Australia

© The Editor(s) (if applicable) and The Author(s) 2016
J. Syed et al. (eds.), *Faith-Based Violence and Deobandi Militancy in Pakistan*, DOI 10.1057/978-1-349-94966-3_4

news reporting is considered far more objective than other media genres (see Section 2.1 below).

This chapter explores Pakistani newspapers' hard news reporting of faith-based violence in the country. It endeavours to find out if the hard news reporting favours or disfavours a denominational community and, what strategies are opted to do so. The central thesis of the chapter is:

> *Hard news reporting of faith-based violence in Pakistan heavily favours the Deobandis and disfavours the Shias.*

As an aside, it may be noted that it is not just the Shias who are disfavoured by the media. All the denominational communities in Pakistan—for example, the Ahmadis, Christians, Hindus, and Barelvi Sunnis—are disfavoured when violence perpetrated on them by the Deobandis is reported. However, to make this study manageable and in-depth, the focus will be set on just one community: the Shias of Pakistan. The justification for choosing the Shia community is (1) despite the Shias being a persistent target of persecution in Pakistan (see, e.g., Butt 2010; Voth 2014; Rajan 2015), very little scholarly work on their condition as victims of faith-based violence exists; (2) the contributions of the Shias in the creation of Pakistan have been more than those of any other community: Pakistan's founder, Muhammad Ali Jinnah, was a Shia (see, e.g., Nasr 2006; Rieck 2015; Ruthven and Wilkinson 2015); and, (3) historically, the Shias have been a significant group and their contribution to the cultural-intellectual history of the Indian subcontinent have been enormous (see, e.g., Rizvi 1986; Hasnain and Husain 1988; Jones 2011). Thus a probe into a genocidal assault on such a community should be a matter of academic, intellectual, and public, interest.

In Pakistan, a good deal of work has been done on various aspects of the media (e.g., Akhtar 2001; Niazi 2010; Farwell 2011; Ali 2012; Shaikh 2013). However, very few Pakistani scholars have researched the media's role in reporting faith-based violence. The present study is the first attempt of its nature, and it is hoped that it will encourage native scholars to work on the media's coverage of violence to which communities other than the Shias are regularly subjected.

Below is the contextual elaboration of the thesis:

1. A University of Pennsylvania research study has concluded that, in Pakistan, 90 percent of terrorism is committed by Sunni Deobandi

militant groups (Hussain 2010). Almost all terrorist groups in Pakistan are Deobandi. Some representative examples are the SSP/ASWJ, Jandullah, the JM, the LeJ, and HM. It may be noted here that all these groups are officially banned.[2] Despite the overwhelming extent of Deobandi terrorism and despite Deobandi spokesmen taking responsibility for persistent terrorist attacks, the media almost always hides the Deobandi identity of the attackers.

2. According to Global Security, the sectarian break-up of the population of Pakistan is: Shias 18 percent, Ismailis 2 percent, Ahmediyas 2 percent, Barelvis 50 percent, Deobandis 20 percent, Ahle Hadith 4 percent, and other minorities 4 percent.[3] The Shias and the Ismailis constitute one sect. The Shias are also known as "Twelvers" and the Ismailis as "Seveners". Historically the Twelvers have been known as the Shias—a denominator retained in this chapter. The first seven spiritual-political imams, or leaders, of the Shias and the Ismailis are the same. The Shia line of imamhood extends to 12. Because of this divergence over the institution of the imams, these two Shia subsects have evolved separately from each other, but they share the same origin and ideology in the person of Ali bin Abu Talib, cousin and son-in-law of Prophet Muhammad (for details, see Momen 1987; Meherally 1991; Daftary 1998; Ladha 2008). Thus the total population of the Shias in Pakistan is 20 percent.

   The Barelvis and the Deobandis are Sunni but have deep theological rifts. The Deobandis are close to the Salafis/Wahhabis of Saudi Arabia in their literalist interpretation of the Qur'an. The Barelvis, in contrast, have a wider interpretation of Islam. They practice the subcontinental version of Sufism. They visit shrines of holy personalities and believe that these personalities can intercede with God on their behalf. To the Deobandis, just like the Salafis, visiting shrines is heresy. The Deobandi and the Barelvi sects apostatize each other (see, e.g., Sahni 2010; Malik 2011; Bokhari 2013). The Barelvis have also been subjected to Deobandi violence. Despite the intense Barelvi–Deobandi divide, the media characterizes Deobandi violence against the Shias as "Sunni" and thus creates a false Shia–Sunni binary (see the following sections for details).

3. The media seldom identifies the victims' sectarian identity if they are Shia.

4. If the victims of terrorism belong to the Deobandi sect, the media identifies them as Deobandis.

5. The media reports Shia killing in one of three ways: denial, obfuscation, and justification. By denial I mean that the media explicitly or implicitly claims that not Shias but "people", "men", "pilgrims", or ethnic "Hazaras" are being killed. This happens when the media either does not report Shia killing at all or deliberately hides Shia victims' sectarian identity. By obfuscation I mean that the media portrays Shia killing in terms of a Shia–Sunni binary in which both sects are shown to be equally involved in violence. By justification I mean that the media portrays the Shias as heretics, blasphemers, and agents provocateurs operating on behalf of foreign powers and thus deserving of violence being done to them.

6. Sectarian communities such as the Amhadis, Barelvi Sunnis, Christians, and Hindus have an 'advantage' that is denied the Shias. If Ahmadis, Christians, or Hindus are attacked, they are clearly identified with reference to their places of worship (a church or temple), or their neighbourhood (Youhanabad and Rabwa/Chenab Nagar, respectively, Christian and Ahmadi neighbourhoods and thus well known all over Pakistan).

The thesis and its elaboration above may be further clarified by considering a few examples that show how the media positions the reader vis-à-vis acts of terrorist violence. For instance, on 25 May 2014 an Ahmadi doctor visiting Rabwa/Chenab Nagar from the USA was killed. Pakistan's three top English-language newspapers' headlines read thus:

Daily Times: US doctor shot dead in Rabwa[4]
Dawn: US-based Ahmadi doctor shot dead in Punjab[5]
Express Tribune: Ahmadi doctor killed in Chenab Nagar[6]

Two out of the three headlines clearly identify the sectarian identity of the Ahmadi doctor. For a Pakistani reader, the first headline will be as identifying of the doctor's sect as the other two because Chenab Nagar is the world centre of the Ahmadis and is synonymous with the Ahmadi faith.

On 21 September 2013, the Taliban attacked a Christian church in Peshawar. The same newspapers' headlines reported the attack thus:

Daily Times: Peshawar Church attack: Protestors demand justice[7]
Dawn: Twin church blasts claim 80 lives in Peshawar[8]
Express Tribune: 78 killed, over 100 injured in Peshawar church attack[9]

Again, from the headlines, it is clear that the victims of the attack were Christians. On 15 February 2015, a leader of the banned Deobandi group the ASWJ was killed in Rawalpindi. The ASWJ has a one-point agenda—that is, to have the Shias of Pakistan declared apostates. Its leaders have persistently justified Shia killing. For instance, in an interview with the *Friday Times*, the President of the ASWJ, Ahmed Ludhianvi, declared:

> Sectarianism has nothing to do with Shia killing. It is not correct to regard Shia killing as sectarian killing. Shouting "Shias are Infidels!" is just a slogan like "Food, Clothing and Shelter."[10]

"Kafir" means "infidel" and. In the Pakistani context, a "Kafir" stands for blasphemy and a challenge to God, and must be eliminated. This is how the same newspapers reported the killing:

> *Daily Times*: Protests as ASWJ leader shot dead; another escapes attack[11]
> *Dawn*: ASWJ local leader killed in Rawalpindi, central leader attacked in Karachi[12]
> *Express Tribune*: ASWJ leader shot dead[13]

On 1 July 2012, suicide bombers struck the most revered Barelvi shrine of Data Darbar in Lahore. The headlines of the three newspapers clearly identified the shrine being attacked:

> *Daily Times:* Triple suicide attacks kill 40 at Data Darbar[14]
> *Dawn:* At least 40 die in attack on Data shrine in Lahore[15]
> *Express Tribune:* Thirty five killed at Data Darbar blast[16]

On 10 January 2013, in a bombing attack, the LeJ, the militant wing of the ASWJ, killed 93 Shias in Quetta. The three newspaper headlines reported it thus:

> *Daily Times*: Death rains on Pakistan[17]
> *Dawn*: At least 93 lives lost in Quetta explosions[18]
> *Express Tribune*: Black Thursday: Bloodbath in Quetta[19]

There is no reference to who died. The *Daily Times'* headline does not even say where death "rained". On 7 June 2015, five Shias were killed by the LeJ.[20] The same newspapers obfuscated their sectarian identity by foregrounding their ethnic identity. The headlines were the same, as if a ready-made headline had been reproduced:

Daily Times: Five Hazara men gunned down in Quetta[21]
Dawn: Five Hazara men gunned down in Quetta[22]
Express Tribune: Five Hazara men gunned down in Quetta[23]

METHODOLOGY

The analyses undertaken in this chapter are based on insights offered by the Appraisal framework, which is Martin and White's (2005) extension of Michael Halliday's Systemic-Functional Linguistics (Halliday 1977, 1994; Halliday and Mathiessen 2014). The foundational argument of Systemic-Functional Linguistics is that language is a "system for making meanings" (Halliday 1994, p. xvii). It is through using the resources provided by language that people construct social reality. Hasan clarifies the Systemic-Functional Linguistics approach to language by positing that language is not just the creation of meaning but its "validation". She explains the notion of validation by saying that language grows "inter-organically" and meaning is "validated through the practices of other members of community" (Hasan in Cloran et al. 1996, pp. 22–23).

Meaning is created when language functions on three levels simultaneously: experiential, interpersonal, and textual.[24] The experiential function is about how language references events, incidents, issues and so on. Interpersonal function is about how language is used to influence relationships between interlocutors. The textual function is about how a message is coded—that is, whether the message is written or spoken, and how thematic prominence is given to ideas, issues, and subjects.

The Appraisal framework derives from the interpersonal function of Systemic-Functional Linguistics. Halliday and Matthiessen (2014, p. 33) explain the interpersonal function thus: (1) the roles played by interactants in a communicative situation; and (2) the values that the interactants bring with them to the communicative situations. The interpersonal function includes institutional, status, and affective roles. "In the act of speaking," according to Halliday, "the speaker adopts for himself a particular speech role, and in doing so assigns to the listener a complimentary role which he wishes him to adopt in his turn" (Halliday 1994, p. 68).

Thus the interpersonal function of language is to influence people. According to Marin and White (2005, p. 1) appraisal is concerned with:

the interpersonal in language, with the subjective presence of writers/speakers in texts as they adopt stances towards both the material they present and those with whom they communicate. It is concerned with how writers/speakers approve and disapprove, enthuse and abhor, applaud and criticise, and with how they position their readers/listeners to do likewise. It is concerned with the construction by texts of communities of shared feelings and values, and with the linguistic mechanisms for the sharing of emotions, tastes and normative assessments. It is concerned with the construction by texts of communities of shared feelings and values, and with the linguistic mechanisms for the sharing of emotions, tastes and normative assessments. It is concerned with how writers/speakers construe for themselves particular authorial identities or personae, with how they align or disalign themselves with actual or potential respondents, and with how they construct for their texts an intended or ideal audience.

Appraisal deals with how evaluative language is used by people/texts to position their interlocutors to their points of view through the resources called Attitude, Engagement, and Graduation. Attitude employs the subresources of Affect, Judgement, and Appreciation to position the audience to take a particular view of "participants, actions, happenings and state-of-affairs therein depicted" (White 2006a, p. 37). Affect deals with how texts construe positive or negative emotions about persons, ideas, or objects. Judgement is about how texts create evaluative stances towards human behaviour. Appreciation is about how texts create evaluative posturing about various phenomena. Taken together, these three subresources position readers to view objects of a discourse negatively or positively. Affect, Judgement, and Appreciation can be explicit or implicit, or inscribed or invoked (for more details, see the following section).

Engagement is about how attitudes are sourced and the voices played around discourse. Through strategies such as modality, projection, polarity, and adverbial comments, writers advance axiological positions and try to influence their readers about those positions. Through specific use of Engagement, writers decide whether to expand (heteroglossia) a discussion or contract it (monoglossia). Heteroglossic stances admit of various, even contrary, points of view. Monoglossic stances do not entertain opposing points of view. Graduation "attends to grading phenomenon whereby feelings are amplified and categories blurred" (Martin and White 2005, p. 35). Graduation is about how an interpersonal message can be graded or intensified through the use of force (how high or low something is in terms of intensity), and focus (how sharp or soft a comment or opinion can be in terms of affective intentionality and prototypicality).

The analyses below are based on White's development of the Appraisal framework with reference to hard news reporting (White 1997, 1998, 2003, 2005, 2006a, b, 2009, 2011, 2012; White and Thomson 2008). The justification for using his work as the frame of reference is its explanatory reach to account for both the form and the content of hard news reporting (see the following section).

Hard News Reporting: Structure and Semantics

The nature of hard news reporting was briefly indicated at the beginning of this chapter. In this section, a few remarks will be made about structural and semantic features of hard news reporting.

Because of their currency, relevance, and impact on society, incidents related to violence are often given frontal prominence (see, e.g., Freedman 2002; Boyle 2005). In generic terms, such coverage is known as hard news reporting, or hard news reports. Hard news reports, according to Bell (1990, p. 14), are the "staple product" of journalism. In the words of Bednarek and Caple (2012, p. 96), hard news reports are "characteristically associate[d] with news discourse". Wheeler (2005, p. 84) says that hard news reporting is "the bread and butter of the paper and involves important stories that affect people's lives". Probably the most important reason for some scholars' according hard news reports such a central place is because they (1) deal with happenings; and (2) do not, unlike opinion pieces, set out with an explicit axiological stance or agenda. Thus they are far more objective than other media genres. In other words, hard news reports are:

> primarily grounded in a material event such as an accident, natural disaster, riot or terrorist attack, and those grounded in a communicative event such as a speech, interview, report or press release. (White 1997, p. 101)

Most media scholars have dismissed claims about the objectivity of hard news reports (e.g., Goatly 2000; Hammersley 2006; Campbell et al. 2012). Work done in the traditions of critical discourse analysis (e.g., van Dijk 1988a, b; Hodge and Kress 1993; Fairclough 1995a, b; Clark 2007; Richardson 2007; Trask 2007) and Systemic-Functional Linguistics (e.g., Trew 1979; Iedema et al. 1994; Martin and White 2005; Bednarek 2006a, b) adopts linguistic frameworks to unpack bias in news reports.

Despite the claims that hard news reports are not objective, they are considerably more balanced and nuanced than other journalistic genres such as editorials and opinions. In their work on objectivity and subjectivity in various media genres, Martin and White (2005) did not find any explicit attitudinal content in their hard news report data. In other genres, however, there were explicit attitudinal stances to various degrees. In the light of their findings, Martin and White formulated what they characterized as "Journalistic voices". These voices are divided into "Reporter voice," "Correspondent voice," and "Commentator voice" Martin and White (2005, p. 173). The explicit attitudinal content in the three voices are none, minimal, and maximum, respectively. Thus of all the journalistic genres, hard news reports are the least subjective.

Scholars have posited schematic structures of hard news reporting. For instance, Bednarek and Caple (2012, p. 96) state that the structure of a hard news report is:

Headline^ Intro/Lead^ Body/Lead Development[25]

"Lead Development" is a vague expression because "development" often implies linearity, which is often not the case with hard news reporting.

Bell (1991, p. 150) posits an elaborate structure of hard news reports:

Abstract^ Orientation^ Evaluation^ Complication^Resolution

As shown below, Bell's proposed structure is too deterministic: it does not work for short news reports at all.

This chapter draws on the schematic structure of hard news reports proposed by White (1997, p. 121), which comprises a Nucleus and its Satellites. He calls his proposed structure "orbital". He does not use the "^" symbol because the satellites do not occur linearly. The Nucleus comprises the headline and the lead, and the rest of the report comprises Satellites, which refer back to the Nucleus. The Satellites serve the following functions: Appraisal (evaluation), Cause and Effect (giving reasons and consequences of a happening etc.), Contextualization (the social context of a happening etc.), and Elaboration (details of a happening etc.). As the Satellites are not linear, they can come in any order depending on the intention of the reporter. They can be shown visually, thus (the double-headed arrows stand for the recursiveness of the Satellites) (Fig. 4.1).

White (1997, 2006a, 2012) discusses a number of semantic features of hard news reports based on Attitude, Engagement, and Graduation,

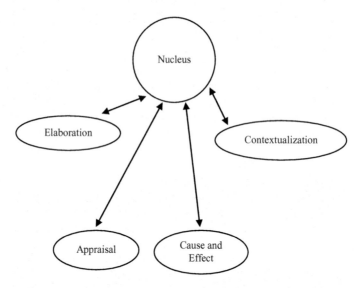

Fig. 4.1 Nucleus and its satellites

as discussed above. A few of those features relevant to this study will be referenced below. These are Attitudinal inscription and invocation, Agency and affectedness, Attribution, Authorial endorsement, Authorial distancing, and Evidential standing. A brief elaboration of these features is given here:

Attitudinal Inscription and Invocation Inscriptions are words and expressions which explicitly show a reporter's view of an event, issue, or person (e.g., corrupt, terrorist, brutal, and repressive). In contrast, invocations are evaluative without being so overtly. White (1997, 2006a) gives the following examples of invocation from his data:

(1) "George W. Bush delivered his inaugural speech as the United States President who collected 537,000 fewer votes than his opponent." There is nothing explicitly evaluative about the statement but it invokes a negative judgment of Bush, whose democratic legitimacy is subtly challenged on account of his getting over half a million fewer votes than his opponent.

(2) "Telstra has withdrawn sponsorship of a suicide prevention phone service—just days after announcing a $2.34 billion half-yearly profits." Again, there is nothing explicitly evaluative about the statement but

the factual expression "just days after" gives a negative evaluation of Telstra.

Agency and Affectedness This feature is about who initiates an action and who is affected by it. For instance, saying, "10 demonstrators killed" does not tell the reader who did the killing. Thus there is no agency in this statement. In contrast, saying, "Police killed 10 demonstrators" shows both agency (police) and the affected (demonstrators).

Attribution The way reporters attribute statements shows whether or not they are taking responsibility for a state of affairs. For instance, a reporter can use "says" or "states" with reference to a source in order to show their neutrality. They can use "claims" and "illustrate" to maintain dialogic expansion (a different view is possible) and dialogic contraction (a different view is not possible), respectively. Attribution serves many functions. Information is attributed to authorities when the purpose is to make it authentic. Information is attributed to respectable sources to give it moral standing. Attribution also helps to construe specific points of view. If the media sources a statement from an interested party, it means that it is siding with that party by giving prominence to its point of view.

Authorial Endorsement This is about a reporter's support of someone or something. For instance, in "The government has rightly passed the anti-terror legislation", the word "rightly" is indicative of the reporter's support of the legislation.

Authorial Distancing When a reporter is opposed to a state of affairs, certain lexical items may be used. In "The government has acted unlawfully", "unlawfully" shows the reporter's distance from the government action.

Evidential Standing Evidential standing is about how a reporter tries to position the reader favourably or unfavourably by referencing sources that may be credible or incredible. In "Nobel Laureates have supported the view that...", "Nobel Laureates" give a positive evaluation of the view because they enjoy great respect and authority.

Data and Data Analysis

The data for this chapter come from Pakistan's mainstream newspapers. These are national dailies which do not have any parochial readership targets. In other words, they are the national print media and address readership across the board. Since this study is about the hard news reporting of faith-based violence in Pakistan, very few examples from other genres will be used. When such examples are used, their status will be ancillary to the hard news reports. As will be made clear below, in hard news reporting it is features such as Agency and affectedness and Attribution that dominate. Given the limitations of space available, the focus of the analyses below will be these two features.

Every claim made in this chapter is backed by evidence from media reports. However, given the limitations of space, some of the reports will be paraphrased instead of quoted verbatim. For instance, in the very beginning of sections 3.2 and 3.3, the relevant reports have been paraphrased. The sources of the paraphrasing—that is, the media reports—have been identified in the footnotes.

Caveat

This study should also be noted for its limitations. My original intent was to carry out a multimodal analysis of hard news reporting in Pakistan. I had to drop the plan because despite my repeated efforts, none of the Pakistani newspapers or magazines responded to my requests for using the visuals published by them.[26] However, I have indicated where I have used and analysed a photograph.

Systemic-Functional Linguistics is a complex and technically sophisticated linguistic theory. Halliday himself has said that it is "an extravagant theory, not a parsimonious one" (Halliday 1994: xix). It has inspired thousands of articles, papers, books, seminars, conferences, dissertations, and theses. Given its scope and limitations, this chapter offers only a basic outline of the theory. Since this study is intended to be a work of scholarship, the analyses below will be rigorous but without technical jargon.

Appraising Faith-Based Violence Against The Shias

It was indicated above that the media reports violence against the Shias in terms of denial, obfuscation, and justification. One way to analyse the media coverage of such violence can be to look for relevant hard news reports to support the thesis of this chapter. This may provoke a pick-and-choose type of objection. In order to counter such an objection and with a view to illustrating the media's across-the-board anti-Shia and pro-Deobandi bias, this chapter will set its focus on one incident.

The Ashura Incident in Rawalpindi: A Summary

Called the Ashura, the 10th of Moharram in the Islamic calendar is the most significant and tragic day in Shia beliefs and practices. It was on this day that Hussain bin Ali, a grandson of the Prophet Muhammad, was martyred along with his sons, brothers, and companions by the ruler Yazid's army. Every year, Shias all over the world commemorate the Ashura by staging mourning processions.

On Friday 15 November 2013, the Shias of Rawalpindi held the yearly Ashura procession. When the mourners were near Taleem ur Koran, a Deobandi mosque-cum-seminary, its imam began the Friday sermon by denouncing Hussain bin Ali and praising Yazid. He also called the Shias "kafirs". It should be noted that on the 10th of Moharram, all mosques are legally bound not to use loudspeakers or make provocative speeches; only the regular daily call to prayer, the *azzan*, is allowed to be recited.

The Shia mourners began to shout slogans against Yazid. At this point, shots were fired from the mosque, resulting in the killing of eight Shias on the spot (see below for details). As a result, some of the Shia mourners set the mosque on fire. Since the fire was immediately extinguished, the front of the mosque was burnt but nothing was damaged inside. However, the media reported this incident from the Deobandi point of view. For instance, Fig. 4.2 shows a claim made on a Deobandi Facebook page.

Had the inside of the mosque been burnt down, the Deobandis would have shown some burnt copies of the Koran as evidence. They did not. The Deobandi leaders also claimed that the Shias had slit the throats of 12 seminary students. The media reported that the bodies of the slain seminary students had been taken to their home villages. Only the following day at a press conference did the chief of the Rawalpindi clarify that not a single seminary student had been killed (see below for details). However, the media continued to conceal facts.[27]

A photograph was published by *Newsline* showing Ahmed Ludhianvi, the head of the ASWJ, addressing the madrassa students and calling for the destruction of the Shias of Pakistan. It was taken two days after the 'burning' of the mosque-seminary. The photograph shows, contrary to Deobandi/media claims, that only the front of the mosque was damaged (for the photograph and the accompanying article, see Shehzad, 19 December 2013).

Fig. 4.2 The ASWJ factsheet about the 'destruction' caused by the Shias. (Translation: "The latest report of Shia barbarity: 190 people martyred; 12 slaughtered; 150 injured; 70 whereabouts unknown; 3500 copies of the Koran and 5000 copies of the Hadith martyred; 1 mosque and 1 seminary martyred [i.e., destroyed]; 150 shops burnt down; Wake up Sunnis! May Allah create more Riaz Basras [a Shia assassin and a founder of the Lashkar-e-Jhangvi; he was killed in a gunfight with the police in 2012]; Wake up Riaz Basra!")

Media Reports of the Incident [28]

An appraisal analysis of the headlines of various newspapers is given in Table 4.1.

As can be seen, the headlines make no reference to who the agent of the violence was and who the affected was. The media bias is clear in the reports. For instance, in its lead, *Daily Times*, a liberal English-language newspaper, portrayed the Shias as agents of violence and the Sunnis as affected. The agency has been highlighted and the affectedness underlined:

> Fighting erupted in the garrison city of Rawalpindi when a procession of **Shias marking the Ashura** coincided with a sermon at a nearby Sunni mosque. **Angry Shia protesters attacked** the <u>Sunni mosque and seminary,</u> [Shias] **torching** its building and an adjacent cloth market, where workers on Saturday were still battling to extinguish the fire completely.[29]

In that it does not admit a contrasting point of view, the lead is mono-glossic—that is, dialogically contracting. The Shias are portrayed as having acted violently and destroyed property. The authorial endorsement is invoked too. Many biased presuppositions and innuendos are packed into the lead:

Table 4.1 Newspaper headlines covering the Ashura tragedy

Newspaper	Headline	Appraisal	Comment
Daily Express	Two groups clash in Rawalpindi; curfew imposed	Negative judgment of both groups for doing violence	Obfuscation No distinction between aggressor and aggressed Both groups equally involved in violence
Daily Times	Curfew imposed in Rawalpindi after 10 killed in clashes; army called in Multan, Chishtian	Negative judgment of both groups for doing violence	Obfuscation No distinction between aggressor and aggressed Extreme violence: 10 killed Both groups equally involved in violence
Dawn	Rawalpindi violence kills nine; curfew back on after 4-hour-break	No agent or target of violence Affect of fear	Obfuscation No reference to human agency Anthropomorphic violence
Express Tribune	Rare curfew in Rawalpindi after deadly clashes	Focus: rare curfew Negative appreciation of incident (clashes)	Obfuscation No reference to human agency
Jang	Two groups clash near Foara Chowk in Rawalpindi, 7 die	Negative judgment of both groups for doing violence	Obfuscation No reference to aggressor or target Binary of violence
Nawa-e-Waqt	Rawalpindi: Two groups clash, 10 killed, 90 injured, curfew imposed	Negative judgment of both groups for doing violence	Obfuscation No reference to aggressor or target Binary of violence
The News	Rawalpindi: Curfew reimposed after brief respite; clashes toll up to 9	Negative judgment of both groups for doing violence	Obfuscation No reference to aggressor or target Binary of violence
The Nation	Army called in after deadly clashes	Fear and force (deadly)	Obfuscation No reference to aggressor or target

1. The fight was between the Shias and the Sunni, not between the Shias and the Deobandis.
2. The Shias were the culprits because they provoked the violence.
3. It was a procession on the street versus a sermon given in the mosque.
4. The Shias were "angry," but no such emotion is attributed to the Deobandis, which by implication means that they were solemn and busy praying.

5. The heretical status of the Shias is confirmed because they burnt down a mosque and a seminary.
6. The Shias are not only anti-Islam, they are anti-business too because they burnt down a cloth market.
7. As the workers were trying to extinguish the fire started by the Shias, the latter continued to set things on fire and thus endangered the lives of the workers.
8. The workers tried, probably unsuccessfully, to extinguish the fire started by the Shias.
   Conclusion: the Shias are the enemies not just of religion but of society too.

Dawn's report too supported the claim of 'unprovoked' Shia violence:

> Incidents of arson were also reported during the time of the clash in which shops in a cloth market in the city's Raja Bazaar and a seminary were set alight.[30]

The Daily Express reported that the participants of the Ashura procession—that is, the Shias—were the agents of violence. The Shia agency has been highlighted and the affectedness of the rest underlined:

> **The mourners [i.e., the Shias] snatched guns** from the policemen on duty and [**they**] **began firing** at the mosque. Later **they set** cloth and leather markets on fire. The fire was so intense that fire department failed to extinguish it. Soon everything was burnt down costing millions of rupees. **The violent mob** did not even spare the passers-by. **They even** attacked journalists and the police.[31]

The Shias were shown to be irrational and enraged mourners determined to destroy everything without provocation. In such a short paragraph, the number of the affected is unusually high: the mosque, the markets, the passers-by, the journalists, and the police. Thus in one go the Shias are portrayed as having subjected everything to intense violence.

All the newspapers stated that the deaths, between 7 and 10, were the result of the clash, but it was falsely claimed that the people killed were Sunnis. It was reported that the Shias had killed adults and little children who were students of the seminary housed in the Sunni mosque. The front-page coverage was given to an anti-Shia Deobandi cleric, Mufti Naeem, who, at a press conference, claimed that the Shias had killed scores of Sunni worshippers and students.[32] At the same press conference, Mufti Naeem denounced the formation of an inquiry commission to investigate the incident: "Everyone knows who the culprits are. The inquiry commission is part of an international conspiracy!" He concluded his press conference with the threat: "Either hang the culprits or we will decide on our own what to do!"[33]

Giving such prominence to an avowed Shia hater is symptomatic of the media bias. Subsequent to the mufti's claim about the dead bodies of the students killed by the Shias, the newspapers produced some "facts". It was reported that the victims of the violence were Sunnis. The Shia agency has been highlighted, and the false Shia–Sunni binary underlined below:

> **Shia mourners beat to death** three men from the seminary for insulting them. As a result, <u>clashes erupted between Shias and Sunnis</u>.[34]

Jang did not say who was involved in the violence. It reported that two groups fought near Raja Bazar, and it identified the "protesters" who went on a rampage, burning and destroying places.[35] In its report, *The Nation* claimed that the Shias had assaulted the Sunnis. It did not give the Shia point of view but gave ample space to the imam, who provoked the incident in the first place. In the report, all of the attributions are sourced from the Deobandi clerics; no Shia view is given a voice. The attributions have been highlighted below:

> **Seminary head Ashraf Ali**, at a press conference, claimed a total of 14 students were killed while 106 others injured in the attack. **He and other clerics** belonging to Jamiat Ahl-e-Sunnat sought action against the attackers. **JUI-F district Amir Abdul Ghafar Toheedi** told this scribe that attackers slaughtered three children of the seminary. Those killed in the seminary attack included Mehmood son of Atta Muhammad, Inayat Ullah son of Irfan, Awais son of Ziaul Hassan, Alam Zeb son of Baaz Ullah, Zaat and Muhammad Arif sons of Shah Muhammad, Fateh Zar Khan son of Zinda Khan, Saqib son of Wajid and Ilam Khan son of Aziz Khan. Names of five other deceased could not be ascertained.[36]

The Nation backed its Shia–Sunni obfuscatory report with an editorial. It referred to the Shias as "Crazed mobs" who "wander the streets seeking revenge". As a result of the Shia violence, "people are dead, security personnel are attacked, markets are set on fire".[37] It condemned "a regressive ideology" which "laments progress, modernity, education, basic human rights, and everything else that stands in its path to annihilation".

Only foreign news sources such as Reuters and *International Business Times* reported that the Ashura violence had cost Shia lives only.[38]

Reporting the Protests [39]

The media portrayed the Shias as the aggressors in the Rawalpindi 'attack'. The following day, it reported the protests against the 'attack'. These were Deobandi and Salafi protests led by the ASWJ. The Barelvi parties refused to participate, calling the protests a pure Deobandi issue, and not a Sunni or Islamic one. But the media continued to portray them as Sunni protests.

Table 4.2 gives an Appraisal summary of the headlines about the protests.

The claims made in the headlines about the peaceful protests conceal the fact that they were preceded by a campaign of arson and killing of Shia properties and lives (see below). From the lyrical "Groundswell"[40] to the pseudofactual "Lawyers strike,"[41] every headline tried to position the readers from the Deobandi point of view; no voice was afforded for the Shias.

An *Express Tribune* report sourced a speaker at the Deobandi protest rally against the "Shia violence" and its link outside Pakistan thus:

> "Hezbollah [of Lebanon] is active in the country," [the Deobandi] speaker said, "Their flags were seen at the procession when the tragedy occurred."[42]

The structural features of the report are highlighted below:

Religious Parties Announce 3-Day Mourning

ISLAMABAD—Following the Ashura Day clashes in Rawalpindi, the religious parties of the country have announced to observe November 22 (Friday) as a protest day and also three days mourning starting from today. [**contextualization**]

These factions in their separately held meetings also appealed Chief Justice of Pakistan [CJP] to take notice of these clashes and asked the government to confine all these religious meetings and "Ashura processions" to its worship places. [**elaboration**]

On the other hand, the government side, apart from holding meetings to review law and order situation in the country with special reference to Rawalpindi incident, also contacted religio-political parties to discuss the post-violence situation. [**elaboration**]

Table 4.2 Appraisal summary of the headlines about the protests

Newspaper	Headline	Appraisal	Comment
Daily Express	Lawyers strike, speakers demand arrest of culprits	Positive judgment for Deobandis Negative judgment for wrongdoing Shias (culprits)	Those who know law have sided with the people who are on the right side. This is why, the law should be made operative and culprits arrested No identity of the lawyer was given who were Deobandi and Salafi carrying posters of their sectarian parties
Daily Times	Day of protest	Affect: the entire nation is angry	The entire country protested
Dawn	Protests across Pakistan against Rawalpindi sectarian violence	Negative judgement against Shias Positive judgment for Deobandis	The entire country is aggrieved over Shias aggression
Dunya	Peaceful protests all over the country	Positive judgment for Deobandis	The protesters are restrained and mature as opposed to the violent Shias
Express Tribune	Groundswell of protests against Pindi unrest	Positive appreciation for the Deobandi protests	There is a lot of good will for the upsurge of feelings against the Shia violence
Jang	Those responsible for Rawalpindi tragedy must be hanged, say the protesters	Positive judgment of Deobandis Negative affect about those responsible for tragedy (Shias)	He protesters have respect for law and are demanding a legal action
Nawa-e-Waqt	Peaceful protests all over the country	Positive judgment of Deobandis	The entire country showed restraint
The News	Wafaqul Madaris [Deobandi organisation managing its seminaries] observing countrywide 'protest day' against Pindi carnage	Positive judgment for Deobandis Negative affect about the Shias (carnage)	Good/religious teachers and students are doing something solemn (observing) in connection with an ultimate cruel act (carnage)
The Nation	Rawalpindi Incident: Protest Demonstrations Countrywide	Positive appreciation of the protest	The entire country involved and unified in protest (mark the singular "protest" as opposed to "protests")

Minister for Interior Chaudhary Nisar Ali Khan made a telephonic contact with Jamiat Ulema-e-Islam (JUI-F) chief Maulana Fazlur Rahman and Maulana Samiul Haq to discuss the post-violence situation in the city. [elaboration]

Whereas the religious party Wafaq-ul-Madaris, after a day-long deliberation, reached consensus to observe the coming Friday as a protest day against the Rawalpindi clashes. [elaboration]

They termed imposition of curfew in the city an attempt to hide the facts from people of the country. Over 50 students of the religious seminary were still missing, they feared. [elaboration]

Expressing serious concern, they said that neither the central government nor the provincial government formally contacted them on this sad incident. [elaboration]

"Wafaq-ul-Madaris will announce next strategy after the funeral prayers of persons who died in this tragic incident," said a party member while talking to The Nation. [elaboration]

Condemning the government's mismanagement, they also said warned of consequences if proper justice was not provided to them. They also recalled that Wafaq-ul-Madaris had time and again had asked the government to restrict Ashura processions to some specific area. They also urged the government to take proper notice of the situation and nab the responsible involved in this incident as soon as possible.

Meanwhile, Ahle-e-Sunnat-Wal Jamat Pakistan in a different meeting appealed to the CJP to take notice of the Rawalpindi incident. [appraisal]

They also appealed to the government to confine religious meetings and Ashura processions should be confined to its worship places. [elaboration]

"We have time and again brought into the notice of the government that armed processions are dangerous for country," said the ASWJ chief. [appraisal]

Agencies add: Maulana Samiul Haq called for a DPC meeting on Monday to discuss Friday's violence in Rawalpindi. [elaboration]

Talking to journalists at Darul Uloom Haqqani in Akora Khattak on Saturday, Sami asked for a fair and impartial investigation into the "heinous violence" and appealed to the Chief Justice of Pakistan Iftikhar Muhammad Chaudhry to take suo motu notice. [appraisal]

He expressed disappointment over the silence of the Punjab government regarding the issue. [appraisal][43]

The report is a complete whitewash of the Shia view and identity. All of the generic resources—that is, the Satellites, Appraisal, Contextualize, and Elaboration—work in favour of the Deobandi militants. All of the parties and organizations mentioned are Shia-hating Deobandi. All of the leaders mentioned are Deobandi. The Chief Justice of Pakistan (CJP) at the time was also a Deobandi, who in the Shia perception had always acted against their interest and in the interest of the Deobandis.[44] The interior minister's ruling Pakistan Muslim League is a political ally of all the Deobandi parties, including the ASWJ. Maulana Samiul Haq, known as the Father of the Taliban, is the head of the seminary where the likes of Mullah Omar were educated and trained for the Afghan Jihad. Thus, according to the above report, it is the Deobandi parties that demand justice; it is the Deobandi leaders who hold meetings and reach "consensus" regarding the future line of action; it is the Deobandi leaders who appeal to the CJP for action; and it is their students who are "still" missing. There is no report about the Shia protesters. All this leads to one conclusion: the only voice of reason is the Deobandi voice. No reference is made to what the Shia leaders had to say about the incident. It is only to the anti-Shia leaders that the media affords an opportunity to condemn "heinous violence". The media portrayal of the Rawalpindi event is that it was an all-out Shia attack on Sunnis.

Table 4.3 summarizes how the mainstream newspapers of Pakistan reported the protests.

The Media's Verdict through Attribution

In this section, closer attention is paid to how the newspaper reports utilized attributions to position the readers against the Shias.

Few newspapers reported what the Shias had to say about the Rawalpindi incident. All of the statements were sourced from anti-Shia quarters. Below is a report from *The Nation*, with attributions/sourcing being highlighted:

Rawalpindi Incident: Protest Demonstrations Countrywide

Various religious parties hold rallies and protest demonstration against the Raja Bazaar, Rawalpindi, incident across Pakistan.

According to details, firing at a protest demonstration in provincial capital of KPK injured five people.

Table 4.3 Summary of newspaper reports on the protests

Newspaper	Appraiser	Appraised/Target	Summary of the report
The Nation[a]	Sunni	Shias	Peaceful protests by all religious parties. Traders went on strike to show their solidarity with the protesters
Express Tribune[b]	Sunni	Shias	The protests against the tragedy were legal and peaceful
Dawn[c]	Sunni	Shias	Protesting parties comprised ASWJ, Wafaqul Madaris, Pakistan Ulema Council, the Jamaatud Dawa, the Jamaat-i-Islami and other religious groups
The News[d]	Sunni	Shias	The protests against the Pindi carnage were peaceful
Daily Times[e]	Sunni	Shias	The protests caused no trouble or negative development
Jang[f]	Sunni	Shias	Protests staged all over the country. Protesters and relatives of those killed demanded justice and compensation for the lives and property destroyed
Dunya[g]	Sunni	Shias	The protests all over the country were peaceful
Nawa-e-Waqth	Sunni	Shias	Islamic parties staged peaceful protests. Resolutions were passed against terrorists. The masses participated in the protests
Daily Express[i]	Sunni	Shias	Every Islamic group protested. Lawyers observed strike in solidarity with the protesters

[a]"Rawalpindi Incident: Protest Demonstrations countrywide," *The Nation*, 22 November 2013: http://www.nation.com.pk/pakistan-news-newspaper-daily-english-online/islamabad/22-Nov-2013/rawalpindi-incident-protest-demonstrations-countrywide

[b]"Groundswell of protests against Pindi unrest," *Express Tribune*, 23 November 2013: http://tribune.com.pk/story/635856/groundswell-of-protests-against-pindi-unrest/

[c]"Protests across Pakistan against Rawalpindi sectarian violence," *Dawn*, 23 November 2013: http://www.dawn.com/news/1057851/protests-across-pakistan-against-rawalpindi-sectarian-violence

[d]"Wafaqul Madaris observing countrywide 'protest day' against Pindi carnage," *The News*, 21 November 2013:http://www.thenews.com.pk/article-127324-Wafaqul-Madaris-observing-countrywide-protest-day-against-Pindi-carnage

[e]"Day of protest," *Daily Times*, 23 November 2013: http://www.dailytimes.com.pk/default.asp?page=2013\11\23\story_23-11-2013_pg3_1

[f]"Rawalpindi tragedy: Various religious parties protest in Lahore," *Jang*, 22 November 2013: http://jang.com.pk/jang/nov2013-daily/22-11-2013/u16086.htm

[g]"Peaceful protests all over the country," *Dunya*, 22 November 2013: http://dunya.com.pk/index.php/dunya-headline/202017_1#.Uo9WqsRjUdo

[h]"Peaceful protests all over the country," *Nawa-e-Waqt*, 23 November 2013: http://www.nawaiwaqt.com.pk/national/23-Nov-2013/259725

[i]"Lawyers strike, speakers demand arrest of culprits," *Daily Express*, 23 November: http://www.express.com.pk/epaper/PoPupwindow.aspx?newsID=1102023292&Issue=NP_LHE&Date=20131123

Protest demonstrations and rallies were organized in Rawalpindi, Karachi, Peshawar, Lahore, Faisalabad, Multan and Gujranwala.

Addressing the participants of rally after offering Jummah prayers in Taleem-ul-Quran Seminary, leader of Ahle Sunnat Wal Jamaat (ASWJ) **Ahmed Ludhyanvi said** that the Raja Bazar tragedy took place due to the irresponsibility of administration.

He demanded of the Punjab government to immediately arrest culprits involved in Rawalpindi incident.

He further said that we own all the cities of Pakistan and we can't allow anybody to damage the properties.

Difae Pakistan Council and traders bodies also carried out a peaceful protest.[45]

There is not a single reference to what the Shias had to say about the Rawalpindi incident. All of the sources of information, responses, and statements came from anti-Shia Deobandis.

There were a few exceptions, however. Below is the *Express Tribune* report on the protests. The Deobandi sourcing has been highlighted and the Shia sourcing underlined:

Peaceful Protests: Protests against Rawalpindi Tragedy Remain Peaceful

LAHORE: The Ahle Sunnat Wal Jamaat (ASWJ) and the Majlis-i-Wahdat-al-Muslimeen (MWM) held rallies in front of the Press Club and Karbala Gamay Shah on Friday to protest the Rawalpindi tragedy. Heavy police contingents had been deployed at the venues as a precaution to avoid any untoward incident but the protests were relatively peaceful.

The ASWJ's rally was held in front of the Lahore Press Club and went on for four hours. Nearly 1,000 people joined the rally.

Security SP [superintendent of police] Ali Salman Khan told *Express Tribune* that the administration had approved the timing and venue of the protest. Operations DIG [deputy inspector general] Rana Abdul Jabbar said more than 700 policemen had been deployed at the Press Club.

The protest was called by ASJW Lahore ameer Maulana Hussain Ahmad, divisional president Maulana Muhammad Jameel Muawiya, provincial president Maulana Shamsur Rehman Muawiya, the International Khatam-i-Nabuwwat Movement, the Jamatud Dawa, the Muttahida Majlis-i-Ahle Sunnat Deoband and the Jamiat-i-Talaba-i-Arabia.

The demonstrators carried placards and banners condemning the Rawalpindi tragedy. **Speakers at the rally demanded** the government bring the perpetrators to justice. If the government does not restrict mourning to the imam bargahs, the ASWJ will do that, **speakers said.**

They criticized what they called the administration's failure to maintain law and order during Ashura.

They demanded an impartial inquiry of the incident. **They asked** the government to restrict mourning to imam bargahs.

The speakers said that if the government did not take immediate action against those responsible for the incident, ASWJ workers will take to the streets. **They demanded** compensation for the losses incurred in the incident.

The police officials on duty at the procession must be terminated, **the speakers said.**

"Hezbollah is active in the country," **a speaker said,** "Their flags were seen at the procession when the tragedy occurred."

The Majlis-i-Wahdat-al-Muslimeen (MWM) too held a sit-in in front of Karbala Gamay Shah. Over 2,000 people, including women and children, attended the protest.

MWM Punjab secretary general Allama Abdul Khaliq Asadi said the government was trying to incite sectarian violence. He asked the Supreme Court to take notice of the incident.

"Ashura mourners have never perpetrated terrorist acts," he said. "We are always the target."

He said those demanding that mourning be confined to imam bargahs "are delusional". Allama Raja Nasir Abbas Jafri said the government should deal with terrorist organizations and religious parties differently.

Allama Abuzar Mehdavi accused the law minister of hindering the investigation of the tragedy. He said terrorist organizations pretending to be religious parties were responsible for sectarian violence in the country.

As many as 600 policemen were deployed outside Karbala Gamay Shah. Operations DIG Rana Abdul Jabbar said that over 10,000 policemen had been deputed in the city. He said metal detectors and walk-through gates had been installed at entry points at senstive imam bargahs and mosques. The Lahore police also held a flag march on The Mall, starting from the Punjab Assembly to Secretariat Chowk.[46]

There are 10 attributions to the Deobandis as opposed to 7 to the Shias, which is not a significant difference. What is significant is that the

Shia cognitive stance is less sophisticated than the Deobandi one: the Shias say, ask, and accuse. In contrast, the Deobandis have a larger linguistic repertoire at their disposal: they say, ask, demand, condemn, and criticize. They also raise placards which refer to their civic sense of protesting. Also of significance is that the Shias complain of violence and terrorism, but the Deobandis raise wider issues which have a lot of intellectual content: (1) they are legal minded; (2) they want justice through an impartial inquiry; and (3) they are peaceful.

The report published in *Dunya* gives complete agency and attributive sourcing to the Deobandis:

Protest Processions All Over the Country End Peacefully

On the call of Ahle Sunnat Wal Jamat and Federal Arabic Seminary Alliance, protest processions were taken out all over the country. The processions ended peacefully and no untoward incident took place.

Activists [of Ahle Sunnat Wal Jamat and Federal Arabic Seminary Alliance] protested against the Rawalpindi slogans and shouted. Later, **they dispersed peacefully. The protesters offered** Friday prayers and then protested in the Guru Mandir area in Karachi. Processions of various sizes came together. **The activists were carrying** their party flags and protested. **They offered** *asr* prayer also. The **leaders of Ahle Sunnat Wal Jamat and World Congress for the Finality of Prophethodd addressed** the protesters. **They demanded** that the government get the warring parties to the negotiation table. In Lahore, **members of various parties protested and condemned** the Rawalpindi tragedy. Later, **they staged** a protest in front of the Lahore press Club and condemned the Rawalpindi tragedy. **They offered** the *asr* prayer on the road. **The participants sat** on the road for a long time and blocked traffic. **Their leaders addressed** them and **demanded** quick investigation into the incident. In Rawalpindi, **leaders of religious parties took out** a procession from the [the well-known Deobandi] Red Mosque. **They staged** a sit-in and **raised their voice against** the Rawalpindi incident. Later, **they dispersed** peacefully. In Quetta, the protesters were **led by [an Ahle Sunnat Wal Jamat leader] Ramzan Mengal. The protesters condemned** the Rawalpindi tragedy and dispersed after being addressed by their leaders. In Faisalabad, **the protesters took out** a rally where **speakers demanded** the arrest of those responsible for the Rawalpindi incident.[47]

Thus the only voices and points of view that the media emphasized and gave authenticity were those of the Deobandi sect whose leaders and followers were portrayed as good Muslims who did not forget to pray, even on the road, despite being extremely sad and angry.

The media further gave authenticity to these voices by backing them with the anti-Shia statement of the Punjab Law Minister, Rana Sanaulla, in the Punjab assembly. Sanaulla is known for his barely concealed links with the Deobandi terrorist organizations, such as the banned SSP and LeJ.[48] This is the statement which the media published prominently without questioning its veracity:

> He [Rana Sana] invited the opposition members to sit together if they wanted to know what preparations had been made. He told the House that the culprits who had invaded the mosque and set the markets ablaze had already been identified through CCTV [closed-circuit television] footages and that some of them had been taken in custody.[49]

However, Sanaulla and the government investigators never identified a single Shia who had "invaded" the mosque. The media, then or later, never questioned the authenticity of Sanaulla's claim.

From Friday to Friday: The Media Cover-Up

Between Friday 15 November 2013 and Friday 22 November 2013, violence took place all over Pakistan. The media portrayed it as a peaceful Sunni protest against Shia violence. Not a single newspaper reported how the violence had started or how it was organized.

One day before the Rawalpindi incident, the ASWJ called upon its activists to gather in the Taleem ur Koran mosque and stop the Shia protest. Figure 4.3 shows the related tweet, which the media never discussed.

At a press conference after the Rawalpindi event, the interior minister said that a day before the Ashura procession, the CCTV cameras around the mosque-cum-seminary had been disabled. Neither the minister nor the media tried to find out who was behind the act.[50]

Hours after the Rawalpindi incident, a number of Shia mosques were damaged or burnt down in different parts of Pakistan. The media only reported "some violence" in the cities of Multan and Chishtian and blacked out the complete burning down of three Shia mosques (and copies of the Koran there) in Rawalpindi alone. According to *Daily Times*

Shion k tabbaraa'e juloos ko Rokny K Liay
Kal Tmam Sathi Broz JUMA 10:00 AM Taleem ul Quraan Raja Bazaar phnchy
Zimdaron ki shrkat Lazmi hy

11/14/2013, 11:45 AM

Fig. 4.3 The ASWJ tweet calling upon its supporters to attack the Shia procession. (Translation: "To stop the blasphemous Shia procession, all friends are required to gather in Taleem ul Koran on Friday, 10 in the morning. The attendance of responsible people is mandatory.")[58]

Separately in Multan, at least 12 people were injured when Sunnis took to the streets to protest the Rawalpindi incident, leading to clashes with Shias who fired warning shots in the air, a senior police official told Agence France Presse (AFP).

The Multan administration later called in the army to control the situation. A person was killed and two others were injured in the clash in Multan's Nala Wali Muhammad area, according to Online news agency.

Following the clash, it added, angry mobs blocked city roads by setting fire to tyres. In neighbouring Chishtian, a Shia mosque was partially damaged and several shops were destroyed when Sunnis torched it in retaliation to the violence in Rawalpindi.

Several shops were also torched in Chishtian as tensions spread to Haroonabad and Bahawalnagar.[51]

Contrary to the fact that the Barelvis refused to take part in the protests, the media insisted on calling it a Sunni protest. Significantly, only the Sunnis, not the Deobandis, "took to the streets", but it was the

Shias who fired the warning shots. No identification is made of the person killed and the dozen or so injured. Apparently a Shia mosque was only "partially damaged", but no account was given of the several shops destroyed; they were all Shia shops. Again, the fact that several Shia shops were burnt down in Chishtian is concealed.[52] The attack on the Shias, their shops, and their mosque was justified because it was "retaliation" for the Rawalpindi tragedy.

It was only when the Deobandi Taliban came into action that the media began to report violence against the Shias, but, even then, the violence was reported according to the Shia–Sunni binary.

The Taliban began a campaign of violence against the Shias after the Rawalpindi incident, killing a number of Shias and burning down Shia mosques and businesses. They began by destroying a Shia mosque in Karachi, killing 9 Shia on the spot and injuring 50. Later, 7 more Shias died in hospital, which was not reported at all.[53]

Daily Times obfuscated the motives behind the bombing. Its reporter quoted a source thus: "it was difficult to say immediately whether Shias were the target because Sunnis also lived near the blast site".[54]

But it was the Taliban who took responsibility for the attack and said that they had killed the Shias of Karachi to avenge the Rawalpindi tragedy:

TTP Claims Responsibility for Twin Bomb Attacks in Karachi

KARACHI: The Tehrik-i-Taliban Pakistan (TTP) claimed responsibility Saturday for twin bomb attacks in Karachi overnight that killed at least seven people and wounded at least 28 others.

Shahidullah Shahid, a spokesman for umbrella group TTP, told AFP that the attacks in Karachi were carried out in revenge for violence in Rawalpindi on November 15.

He said the attacks were aimed at Shias in Karachi, and vowed further violence.

"It was to avenge the Rawalpindi incident, we will carry out more such attacks to avenge the killing of Sunnis," Shahid told AFP by telephone from an undisclosed location.

Fighting erupted in the garrison-city of Rawalpindi, which neighbours the capital Islamabad, earlier this month when a procession by Shia Muslims to mark the most important day of the mourning month of Muharram coincided with a sermon at a nearby Sunni mosque.

The groups clashed with each other, TV cameramen and security forces.

Officials said 11 people were killed and more than 60 injured while a Sunni mosque and seminary and an adjacent cloth market were burnt, with Sunni groups blaming Shia protesters.

Thousands of people in major cities across the country, including Karachi, protested amid high security on Friday after Sunni groups called for demonstrations against the Rawalpindi violence.

The explosions overnight in Karachi Friday took place within minutes of each other in the city's bustling, predominantly Shia neighbourhood of Ancholi.

Karachi, a city of 18 million people which contributes 42 per cent of Pakistan's GDP [gross domestic product], is rife with murder and kidnappings and has been plagued with sectarian, ethnic, and political violence for years.

The TTP has been behind hundreds of bomb and gun attacks that have fanned instability in Pakistan, killing more than 6,500 soldiers, police and civilians since 2007.[55]

Even when the Taliban (i.e., the Deobandis) made it clear that they were responsible for the Shia killing, *Dawn* continued to portray it as a Shia–Sunni binary in its report:

Thousands of people in major cities across the country, including Karachi, protested amid high security on Friday after Sunni groups called for demonstrations against the Rawalpindi violence.

Details of the Taliban campaign against the Shias were given only by some Shia websites.[56]

CONCLUSION

As pointed out at the beginning, this study is the first of its kind and, given the limitation of space, its focus is narrow. What is true of the media's role in the Shia genocide in Pakistan is equally true of its role in the persecution of other sectarian communities. The media does not exist in a vacuum. Various factors behind journalistic complicity in the Shia genocide, or for that matter the persecution of other communities in Pakistan, needs to be probed using scholarly paradigms as opposed to journalistic musings and commentaries. For instance, the role of how the likes of Saudi Arabia, Qatar, and the United Arab Emirates fund terrorism in Pakistan can rewardingly be investigated.[57] Work can also be done on the media's links to these and other terror-sponsoring sources.

This study has discussed both the English- and Urdu-language hard news reporting using White's framework. However, close structural-semantic attention was paid only to the English-language reports. The Urdu-language reports were explored in attitudinal terms only. A separate study is needed to find out if White's framework can account for Urdu-language reporting. *Prima facie*, with some additions, White's framework should account for Urdu hard news reporting both structurally and semantically. However, an Urdu-specific study needs to be done to verify this.

Another issue worth exploring is that of voice. Some of the hard news reports discussed here may not qualify for any of the three voices posited by Martin and White (2005). There may be a possibility of exploring a new voice. I would suggest a "transformative" voice for those reports (and other media genres) that deny the existence of issues, incidents, or facts. Or, it may be the case that the notion of the commentator voice can be extended to incorporate the transformative voice. A separate study is required to explore this issue too.

NOTES

1. "Media" is used as singular throughout this chapter because of its uniform coverage of faith-based violence in Pakistan.
2. See the report on these banned outfits: "212 organisations formally banned by Pakistan," *Express Tribune*, 28 June 2015: http://tribune.com.pk/story/911295/212-organisations-formally-banned-by-pakistan/
3. Global Security: http://www.globalsecurity.org/military/intro/islam-barelvi.htm. Also see, Ahmed 2011, 82.
4. "US doctor shot dead in Rabwa," *Daily Times*, 27 May 2014: http://www.dailytimes.com.pk/E-Paper/lahore/2014-05-27/page-1
5. "US-based Ahmadi doctor shot dead in Punjab," *Dawn*, 26 May 2014: http://www.dawn.com/news/1108691
6. "Ahmadi doctor killed in Chenab Nagar," *Express Tribune*, 26 May 2014:http://tribune.com.pk/story/713250/ahmadi-doctor-killed-in-chenab-nagar/
7. "Peshawar Church attack : Protestors demand justice," *Daily Times*, 23 September 2013: http://archives.dailytimes.com.pk/karachi/23-Sep-2013/peshawar-church-attack-protestors-demand-justice

8. "Twin church blasts claim 80 lives in Peshawar," *Dawn*, 22 September 2013: http://www.dawn.com/news/1044668
9. "78 killed, over 100 injured in Peshawar church attack," *Express Tribune*, 22 September 2013: http://tribune.com.pk/story/607734/ fifteen-dead-in-suicide-attack-outside-peshawar-church/
10. "Sectarianism has nothing to do with recent terrorism in Pakistan," *The Friday Times*, March 15-21 2013: http://www.thefridaytimes. com/beta3/tft/article.php?issue=20130315&page=5
11. "Protests as ASWJ leader shot dead; another escapes attack," *Daily Times*, 16 February 2015: http://www.dailytimes.com.pk/ national/16-Feb-2015/protests-as-aswj-leader-shot-dead-another-escapes-attack
12. "ASWJ local leader killed in Rawalpindi, central leader attacked in Karachi," *Dawn*, 15 February 2015: http://www.dawn.com/news/ 1163772
13. "ASWJ leader shot dead," *Express Tribune*, 16 February 2015: http://tribune.com.pk/story/839043/aswj-leader-shot-dead/
14. "Triple suicide attacks kill 40 at Data Darbar," *Daily Times*, 2 July 2010: http://archives.dailytimes.com.pk/main/02-Jul-2010/triple-suicide-attacks-kill-40-at-data-darbar
15. "At least 40 die in attack on Data shrine in Lahore," *Dawn*, 2 July 2010: http://www.dawn.com/wps/wcm/connect/dawn-content-library/dawn/the-newspaper/front-page/06-terrorists-tear-into-heart-of-lahore-40-die-in-attack-on-data-shrine-270-rs-01
16. "Thirty five killed at Data Darbar blast," *Express Triune*, 2 July 2010: http://tribune.com.pk/story/25061/three-blasts-at-data-darbar/
17. "Death rains on Pakistan," *Daily Times*, 11 January 2013: http:// www.dailytimes.com.pk/default.asp?page=2013%5C01%5C11%5Cst ory_11-1-2013_pg1_1
18. "At least 93 lives lost in Quetta explosions," *Dawn*, 11 January 2013: http://www.dawn.com/news/777830/at-least-93-lives-lost-in-quetta-explosions
19. "Black Thursday: Bloodbath in Quetta," *Express Tribune*, 11 January 2013: http://tribune.com.pk/story/492456/black-thursday-bloodbath-in-quetta/
20. It should be pointed out that the LeJ has always accepted killing the Shias, declaring that they will continue to kill them. See the following sections for more details.

21. "Five Hazara men gunned down in Quetta," *Daily Times*, 8 June 2015: http://www.dailytimes.com.pk/E-Paper/Lahore/2015-06-08/page-1/detail-1

22. "Five Hazara men gunned down in Quetta," *Dawn*, 8 June 2015 : http://www.dawn.com/news/1186849/five-hazara-men-gunned-down-in-quetta

23. "Five Hazara men gunned down in Quetta," *Express Tribune*, 8 June 2015: http://epaper.tribune.com.pk/DisplayDetails.aspx?ENI_ID=11201506080144&EN_ID=11201506080065&EMID=11201506080019

24. Technically, these functions are called metafunctions.

25. "^" means "followed by".

26. *Daily Times, Dawn, Express Tribune, Jang, Dunya, The Nation, Newsline,* and Yahoo!

27. Only the journalist Asma Shirazi tried to show what actually happened. The above details come from her report. Here is a link to her televions programme about what actually happened in Rawalpindi: http://www.youtube.com/watch?v=HS74NQlFIMQ. Here is another video which shows what actually happened in Rawalpindi on the Ashura day: http://lubpak.com/archives/296545

28. This section is based on the following news reports: "Curfew imposed in Rawalpindi after 10 killed in clashes; army called in Multan, Chishtian," *Daily Times*, 17 November 2013: http://www.dailytimes.com.pk/default.asp?page=2013\11\17\story_17-11-2013_pg1_1

    "Rawalpindi violence kills nine; curfew back on after 4-hour-break," *Dawn*, 17 November 2013: http://www.dawn.com/news/1056553/rawalpindi-violence-kills-nine-curfew-back-on-after-4-hour-break

    "Army called in to quell clashes in Multan, Chishtian," *Dawn*, 16 November 2013: http://www.dawn.com/news/1056574/army-called-in-to-quell-clashes-in-multan-chishtian

    "Rawalpindi: Curfew reimposed after brief respite; clashes toll up to 9," *The News*, 16 November 2013: http://www.thenews.com.pk/article-126657-Rawapindi:-Curfew-reimposed-after-brief-respite;-clashes-toll-up-to-9

    "Clashes at Moharram procession, police fails to control," *Daily Express*, 17 November 2013: http://www.express.com.pk/epaper/PoPupwindow.aspx?newsID=1102017355&Issue=NP_LHE&Date=20131117

"Two groups clash near Foara Chowk in Rawalpindi, 7 die," *Jang*, 16 November 2013: http://jang.com.pk/jang/nov2013-daily/16-11-2013/main.htm

"Two groups clash in Rawalpindi; curfew imposed," *Daily Express*, 17 November 2013: http://www.express.com.pk/epaper/PoPupwindow.aspx?newsID=1102017355&Issue=NP_LHE&Date=20131117

"Rawalpindi: Two groups clash, 10 killed, 90 injured, curfew imposed," *Nawa-e-Waqt*, 17 November 2013: http://www.nawaiwaqt.com.pk/E-Paper/Lahore/2013-11-17/page-1/detail-13

"Rare curfew in Rawalpindi after deadly clashes," *Express Tribune*, 17 November 2013: http://epaper.tribune.com.pk/DisplayDetails.aspx?ENI_ID=11201311170132&EN_ID=11201311170082&EMID=11201311170019

29. "Curfew imposed in Rawalpindi after 10 killed in clashes; army called in Multan, Chishtian," *Daily Times*, 17 November 2013: http://www.dailytimes.com.pk/default.asp?page=2013\11\17\story_17-11-2013_pg1_1

30. "Rawalpindi violence kills nine; curfew back on after 4-hour-break," *Dawn*, 17 November 2013: http://www.dawn.com/news/1056553/rawalpindi-violence-kills-nine-curfew-back-on-after-4-hour-break

31. "Clashes at Moharram procession, police fails to control," *Daily Express*, 17 November 2013: http://www.express.com.pk/epaper/PoPupwindow.aspx?newsID=1102017355&Issue=NP_LHE&Date=20131117

32. He is the head of Jamia Binoris which has produced some of the most notorious Taliban.

33. "The Administration is equally responsible; Wafaqul Madaris will deliberate line of action," *Dunya*, 17 November 2017: http://dunya.com.pk/index.php/city/karachi/2013-11-17/257268#.UogD7cRjUdo

34. "Curfew imposed in Rawalpindi after 10 killed in clashes; army called in Multan, Chishtian," *Daily Times*, 17 November 2013: http://www.dailytimes.com.pk/default.asp?page=2013\11\17\story_17-11-2013_pg1_1

35. "Two groups clash near Foara Chowk in Rawalpindi, 7 die," *Jang*, 16 November 2013: http://jang.com.pk/jang/nov2013-daily/16-11-2013/main.htm

36. "Army called in after deadly clashes," *The Nation*, 17 November 2013: http://www.nation.com.pk/E-Paper/Lahore/2013-11-17/page-1/detail-0

37. "Please, no more," *The Nation*, 17 November 2013: http://www.nation.com.pk/E-Paper/Lahore/2013-11-17/page-6/detail-0

38. Akinyemi, Aaron. (16 November 2013). Gunmen Kill Eight Shia Muslims in Pakistan. *International Business Daily*: http://www.ibtimes.co.uk/shia-muslim-pakistan-rawalpindi-targeted-killings-taliban-522705. Accessed on 10 November 2015; and Hassan, Syed Raza. (15 November 2013). Eight killed in Pakistan in attack on Shi'ite procession. Reuters: http://www.reuters.com/article/2013/11/15/us-pakistan-sectarian-violence-idUSBRE9AE12Q20 131115#XbCYIQU352lv1tVX.97. Accessed on 10 November 2015.

39. This section is based on the following news reports and opinion pieces:

    "Peaceful protests all over the country," *Dunya*, 22 November 2013:http://dunya.com.pk/index.php/dunya-headline/202017_1#.Uo9WqsRjUdo

    "Wafaqul Madaris observing countrywide 'protest day' against Pindi carnage," *The News*, 21 November 2013: http://www.the-news.com.pk/article-127324-Wafaqul-Madaris-observing-countrywide-protest-day-against-Pindi-carnage

    "Peaceful protests: Protests against Rawalpindi tragedy remain peaceful," *Express Tribune*, 23 November 2013: http://tribune.com.pk/story/635774/peaceful-protests-protests-against-rawalpindi-tragedy-remain-peaceful/

    "Day of protest," *Daily Times*, 23 November 2013: http://www.dailytimes.com.pk/default.asp?page=2013\11\23\story_23-11-2013_pg3_1

    "Protests across Pakistan against Rawalpindi sectarian violence," *Dawn*, 23 November 2013:http://www.dawn.com/news/1057851/protests-across-pakistan-against-rawalpindi-sectarian-violence

    "Lawyers strike, speakers demand arrest of culprits," *Daily Express*, 23 November: http://www.express.com.pk/epaper/PoPupwindow.aspx?newsID=1102023292&Issue=NP_LHE&Date=20131123

    "Groundswell of protests against Pindi unrest," *Express Tribune*, 23 November 2013: http://tribune.com.pk/story/635856/groundswell-of-protests-against-pindi-unrest/

    "Rawalpindi Incident: Protest Demonstrations countrywide," *The Nation*, 22 November 2013: http://www.nation.com.pk/pakistan-news-newspaper-daily-english-online/islamabad/22-Nov-2013/rawalpindi-incident-protest-demonstrations-countrywide

"Peaceful protests all over the country," *Nawa-e-Waqt*, 23 November 2013: http://www.nawaiwaqt.com.pk/national/23-Nov-2013/259725

"Those responsible for Rawalpindi tragedy must be hanged, say the protesters," *Jang*, 23 November 2013: http://jang.com.pk/jang/nov2013-daily/23-11-2013/main.htm

40. "Groundswell of protests against Pindi unrest," *Express Tribune*, 23 November2013:http://tribune.com.pk/story/635856/groundswell-of-protests-against-pindi-unrest/

41. "Lawyers strike, speakers demand arrest of culprits," *Daily Express*, 23 November: http://www.express.com.pk/epaper/PoPupwindow.aspx?newsID=1102023292&Issue=NP_LHE&Date=20131123

42. "Peaceful protests: Protests against Rawalpindi tragedy remain peaceful," *Express Tribune*, 23 November 2013: http://tribune.com.pk/story/635774/peaceful-protests-protests-against-rawalpindi-tragedy-remain-peaceful/

43. "Religious parties announce 3-day mourning," *The Nation*, 17 November 2013: http://www.nation.com.pk/E-Paper/Lahore/2013-11-17/page-3/detail-10

44. There is a considerable collection of media reports on the role of the anti-Shia role of the chief justice. Those interesting in reading the report are referred to the following section of the web site *Let Us Build Pakistan*: https://lubpak.com/?s=iftikhar+chaudhry.

45. "Rawalpindi Incident: Protest Demonstrations countrywide," *The Nation*, 22 November 2013: http://www.nation.com.pk/pakistan-news-newspaper-daily-english-online/islamabad/22-Nov-2013/rawalpindi-incident-protest-demonstrations-countrywide

46. "Peaceful protests: Protests against Rawalpindi tragedy remain peaceful," *Express Tribune*, 23 November 2013: http://tribune.com.pk/story/635774/peaceful-protests-protests-against-rawalpindi-tragedy-remain-peaceful/

47. "Peaceful protests all over the country," *Dunya*, 22 November 2013: http://dunya.com.pk/index.php/dunya-headline/202017_1#.Uo9WqsRjUdo

48. A collection of media reports on Rana Sanaulla's links to banned Deobandi outfits can be found here: https://lubpak.com/?s=Rana+sana

49. "Emotional scenes in PA as Op plea to debate Rawalpindi riots denied," *The Nation*, 30 November 2013: http://www.nation.com.pk/pakistan-news-newspaper-daily-english-online/editors-picks/30-Nov-2013/emotional-scenes-in-pa-as-op-plea-to-debate-rawalpindi-riots-denied

58. This tweet appeared on many Deobandi Twitter accounts. It was removed from some of those accounts but can still be viewed on at least two official accounts of the ASWJ: https://twitter.com/SKnewsPK/status/401167454660866048; and https://twitter.com/SKnewsPK/status/401167454660866048

50. See, for example, "Rawalpindi revelations: CCTV cameras were killed prior to mob violence," *Express Tribune*, 17 November 2013: http://tribune.com.pk/story/632855/Rawalpindi-revelations-cctv-camera-were-killed-prior-to-mob-violence/

51. "Curfew imposed in Rawalpindi after 10 killed in clashes; army called in Multan, Chishtian," *Daily Times*, 17 November 2013: http://www.dailytimes.com.pk/default.asp?page=2013\11\17\story_17-11-2013_pg1_1

52. This comes from a personal communication with Aamir Hussaini, a Multan-based journalist friend who witnessed these incidents in Multan and nearby Chishtian.

53. See the following reports as examples of obfuscation and denial: "Back to back bomb blasts in Karachi kill six, injure 28 people," *Express Tribune*, 22 November 2013: http://tribune.com.pk/story/635738/back-to-back-explosions-in-karachi-injure-15-people/; "Twin blasts leave nine dead in Karachi," *The News*, 23 November 2013: http://www.thenews.com.pk/article-127471-Twin-blasts-leave-nine-dead-in-Karachi

54. "Seven killed in twin bombings in Karachi," *Daily Times*, 23 November 2013: http://www.dailytimes.com.pk/default.asp?page=2013\11\23\story_23-11-2013_pg1_4

55. "TTP claims responsibility for twin bomb attacks in Karachi," *Dawn*, 23 November 2013: http://m.dawn.com/news/1058047/ttp-claims-responsibility-for-twin-bomb-attacks-in-karachi

56. See, for example, "Rawalpindi Ashura procession under attack, Shiites burnt alive, mosques, imambarhags and markets incinerated," *Shiite News*, 16 November 2013: http://www.shiitenews.org/index.php/pakistan/item/2614-rawalpindi-ashura-procession-under-attack-shiites-burnt-alive-mosques-imam-bargahs-and-market-incinerated

57. "US embassy cables: Hillary Clinton says Saudi Arabia 'a critical source of terrorist funding,'" *The Guardian*, 5 December 2010: http://www.theguardian.com/world/us-embassy-cables-documents/242073

"Hillary Clinton memo highlights Gulf states' failure to block funding for groups like al-Qaida, Taliban and Lashkar-e-Taiba," *The Guardian*, Monday 6 December 2010: http://www.theguardian.com/world/2010/dec/05/wikileaks-cables-saudi-terrorist-funding

Cartalucci, Tony, "Destroying a nation state: US-Saudi funded terrorists sowing chaos in Pakistan," *Global Research*, 24 December 2013: http://www.globalresearch.ca/destroying-a-nation-state-us-saudi-funded-terrorists-sowing-chaos-in-pakistan/5323295

"Recipient of foreign funds: Tough hunt for Punjab to identify madrassas," *Express Tribune*, 3 February 2015: http://tribune.com.pk/story/831973/recipient-of-foreign-funds-tough-hunt-for-punjab-to-identify-madrassas/

References

Ahmed, I. (2011). Religious nationalism and minorities in Pakistan: Constitutional and legal bases of discrimination. In I. Ahmed (Ed.), *The politics of religion in South and Southeast Asia* (pp. 81–101). London: Routledge.

Akhtar, R. S. (2001). *Media, religion, and politics in Pakistan*. Karachi: Oxford University Press.

Ali, Y. A. (2012). *A comparative analysis of media and media laws in Pakistan*. Lahore: Sang-e- Meel Publications.

Bainbridge, J., Goc, N., and Tynan, L. (2011). *Media and journalism: New approaches to theory and practice*. Melbourne: Oxford University Press.

Bednarek, M. (2006a). *Evaluation in media discourse: Analysis of a newspaper corpus*. London: Continuum.

Bednarek, M. (2006b). Epistemological positioning and evidentiality in English news discourse: A text-driven approach. *Text and Talk, 26*(6), 635–660.

Bednarek, M., & Caple, H. (2012). *News discourse*. London: Continuum.

Bell, A. (1990). Audience and reference design in New Zealand media language. In Allan Bell and Janet Holmes (Ed.), *New Zealand ways of speaking English*. (pp. 165–194). Wellington: Victoria University Press.

Bell, A. (1991). *The language of news media*. Oxford. Basil Blackwell.

Biagi, S. (2014). *Media/Impact: An introduction to mass media*. Melbourne: Cengage Learning.

Bokhari, K. (2013). Jamat-i-Islamic in Pakistan. In J. L. Esposito & E. E.-D. Shahin (Eds.), *The Oxford handbook of Islam and politics* (pp. 574–586). Oxford: Oxford University Press.

Boyle, K. (2005). *Media and violence: Gendering the debates*. London: Sage.

Breuer, I., & Napthine, M. (2008). *Persuasive language in media texts.* Elsternwick: Insight Publications.

Butt, U. (2010). Pakistan's salvation: Islam or Western inspired secular-liberal democracy? In U. Butt (Ed.), *Pakistan's quagmire: Security, strategy, and the future of the Islamic* (pp. 9–28). New York: Continuum.

Campbell, C. P., LeDuff, K. M., Jenkins, C. D., & Brown, R. A. (2012). *Race and news: Critical perspectives.* New York: Routledge.

Carrabine, E. (2008). *Crime, culture and the media.* Boston: Polity Press.

Clark, C. (2007). A war of words: A linguistic analysis of BBC embed reports during the Iraq conflict. In N. Fairclough, G. Cortese, & P. Ardizzone (Eds.), *Discourse and contemporary social change* (pp. 119–140). Bern: Peter Lang.

Cloran, C., Butt, D., & Williams, G. (1996). *Ways of saying, ways of meaning: Selected papers of Ruqaiya Hasan* (p. 22). London: Cassell.

Daftary, F. (1998). *A short history of the Ismailis: Traditions of a Muslim community.* Edinburgh: Edinburgh University Press.

Fairclough, N. (1995a). *Critical discourse analysis: The critical study of language.* London: Longman.

Fairclough, N. (1995b). *Media discourse.* London: Edward Arnold.

Farwell, J. P. (2011). *The Pakistan cauldron: Conspiracy, assassination & instability.* Washington, DC: Potomac Books.

Fourie, P. J. (2008). The effects of mass communication. In P. J. Fourie (Ed.), *Media studies: Media history, media and society* (pp. 228–268). Cape Town: Juta & Co.

Freedman, J. L. (2002). *Media violence and its effect on aggression: Assessing the scientific evidence.* Toronto: University of Toronto Press.

Goatly, P. A. (2000). *Critical reading and writing: An introductory coursebook.* New York: Routledge.

Halliday, M. A. K. (1977). Ideas about language. *Aims and perspectives in linguistics.* Applied Linguistics Association of Australia: Occasional papers Number 1, p. 37.

Halliday, M. A. K. (1994). *An introduction to functional grammar* (2nd ed.). London: Edward Arnold.

Halliday, M. A. K. & Mathiessen, C. M. I. M. (2014). *Halliday's introduction to functional grammar,* revised by Matthiessen, M. I. M. New York: Routledge.

Halliday, M. A. K and Mathhiessen, C. M. I. M. (2014). *Halliday's Introduction to Functional Grammar.* London: Routledge.

Hammersley, M. (2006). *Media bias in reporting social research?: The case of reviewing ethnic inequalities in education.* New York: Routledge.

Hasnain, N., & Husain, S. A. (1988). *Shias and Shia Islam in India: A study in society and culture.* New Delhi: Harnam Publications.

Hodge, R., & Kress, G. (1993). *Language as ideology* (2nd ed.). London: Routledge.

Hussain, S. E. (2010). *Terrorism in Pakistan: Incident patterns, terrorists' characteristics, and the impact of terrorist arrests on terrorism.* Unpublished PhD thesis. University of Pennsylvania. Available online: http://repository.upenn.edu/edissertations/136

Iedema, R., Feez, S., & White, P. R. R. (1994). *Media literacy*. Sydney: NSW Department of School Education.

Jones, J. (2011). *Shi'a Islam in colonial India: Religion, community and sectarianism*. Cambridge: Cambridge University Press.

Ladha, M. (2008). *A portrait in pluralism: The Aga Khan's Shia Ismaili Muslims*. Edmonton: Brush Education Inc.

Malik, A. (2011). *Political survival in Pakistan: Beyond ideology*. London: Routledge.

Martin, J. R., & White, P. R. R. (2005). *The language of evaluation: Appraisal in English*. Basingstoke: Palgrave/Macmillan.

Meherally, A. (1991). *A history of the Agakhani Ismailis*. Calgary: Detselig Enterprises.

Momen, M. (1987). *An introduction to Shi`i Islam: The history and doctrines of Twelver Shi`ism*, reprint edition. New Haven: Yale University Press.

Nasr, V. (2006). *The Shia revival: How conflicts within Islam will shape the future*. New York: W.W. Norton.

Niazi, Z. (2010). *The press in chains* (2nd ed.). Karachi: Oxford University Press.

Rajan, V. G. J. (2015). *Al Qaeda's global crisis: The Islamic state, takfir and the genocide of Muslims*. New York: Routledge.

Richardson, J. (2007). *Analysing newspaper: An approach from Critical Discourse Analysis*. New York: Palgrave Macmillan.

Rieck, A. T. (2015). *The Shias of Pakistan: An assertive and beleaguered minority*. London: C Hurst & Co Publishers.

Rizvi, S. A. A. (1986). *A socio-intellectual History of the Isnā'Asharī Shī'īs in India: 7th to 16th century A.D., with an analysis of early Shī'ism* (Vol. 2). New Delhi: Munshiram Manoharlal Publishers.

Ruthven, M., & Wilkinson, G. (2015). *The children of time: The Aga Khan and the Ismailis*. London: I.B. Taurus.

Sahni, A. (2010). Pakistan. In B. M. Rubin (Ed.), *Guide to Islamist movements* (Vol. 2, pp. 347–360). New York: E.M. Sharpe.

Shaikh, R. (2013). *Strangling liberty: Media in distress in Pakistan*. Kolkata: Frontpage Publications.

Shehzad, M. (2013, 19 December). The war within. *Newsline*.

Trask, R. L. (2007). *Language and linguistics: The key concepts*. New York: Routledge.

Trew, T. (1979). Theory and ideology at work. In R. Fowler, B. Hodge, G. Kress, & T. Trew (Eds.), *Language and control* (pp. 94–116). London: Routledge & Kegan Paul.

van Dijk, T. A. (1988a). *News as discourse*. Hillsdale: Erlbaum.

van Dijk, T. A. (1988b). *News analysis: Case studies of international and national news in the press*. Hillsdale: Erlbaum.

Voth, B. (2014). *The rhetoric of genocide: Death as a text*. Lanham: Lexington Book.

Wheeler, S. (2005). Beyond the inverted pyramid: Developing news-writing skills. In R. Keeble (Ed.), *Print journalism: A critical introduction* (pp. 83–94). New York: Routledge.

White, P. R. R. (1997). Death, disruption and the moral order: The narrative impulse in mass-media hard news reporting. In F. Christie & J. Martin (Eds.), *Genres and institutions: Social processes in the workplace and school* (pp. 101–133). London: Cassell.

White, P. R. R. (1998). *Telling media tales: The news story as rhetoric.* Unpublished Ph.D. University of Sydney, Sydney.

White, P. R. R. (2003). Beyond modality and hedging: A dialogic view of the language of intersubjective stance. *Text—Special Edition on Appraisal, 23*(3), 259–284.

White, P. R. R. (2005). Subjectivity, evaluation and point of view in media discourse. In C. Coffin & K. O'Halloran (Eds.), *Grammar, text and context: A reader* (pp. 229–257). Arnold: London.

White, P. R. R. (2006a). Evaluative semantics and ideological positioning in journalistic discourse. In I. Lassen (Ed.), *Image and ideology in the mass media* (pp. 45–73). Amsterdam/Philadelphia: John Benjamins.

White, P. R. R. (2006b). Evaluative semantics and ideological positioning in journalistic discourse—a new framework for analysis. In I. Lassen (Ed.), *Mediating ideology in text and image: Ten critical studies* (pp. 37–68). Amsterdam: John Benjamins.

White, P. R. R. (2009). Media power and the rhetorical potential of the 'hard news' report—Attitudinal mechanisms in journalistic discourse. In M. Enell-Nilsson & N. Nissila (Eds.), *Proceedings of the VAKKI symposium XXIV: Language and power* (pp. 30–49). Finland: University of Vaasa.

White, P. R. R. (2011). Appraisal. In J. Zienkowski, J.-O. Östman, & J. Verschueren (Eds.), *Discursive pragmatics* (pp. 14–36). Amsterdam/Philadelphia: John Benjamins.

White, P. R. R. (2012). Exploring the axiological workings of 'reporter voice' news stories—Attribution and attitudinal positioning. *Discourse, Context and Media, 1,* 57–67.

White, P. R. R., & Thomson, E. A. (2008). News journalism in a global society. In E. A. Thomson & P. R. R. White (Eds.), *Communicating conflict: Multilingual case studies of the news media* (pp. 1–14). London: Continuum.

CHAPTER 5

Historical Roots of the Deobandi Version of Jihadism and Its Implications for Violence in Today's Pakistan

Arshi Saleem Hashmi

To understand the peculiar nature of extremist religious violence witnessed in recent history in Pakistan, the influence of Deobandi interpretation and its role in the indoctrination of young minds cannot be put aside. One of the explanations is state patronage of the specific school of thought that helped to achieve the grand objective of defeating the Soviets, through mujahideens who were trained and educated in Deobandi madrassas and followers of this school of thought. The 1953 anti-Qadiani movement declaring Ahmadis non-Muslim placed the foundation for the political mobilization of religious intolerance in the country. Later, the Jamat-e-Islami-led Nizam-e-Mustafa movement in 1977 against Zulfikar Ali Bhutto's government also contributed to the aggressive nature of religious extremism. However, the grandiose empowered and violent politics of ultraorthodox Sunni Islam based on the Deoband school started emerging post-1991, when it was not the old traditional Deobandis demanding "Islamization " in the state but new, violent groups—believers in a very narrow interpretation of religious text—declaring their political

A.S. Hashmi (✉)
National Defence University, Islamabad, Pakistan

© The Editor(s) (if applicable) and The Author(s) 2016
J. Syed et al. (eds.), *Faith-Based Violence and Deobandi Militancy in Pakistan*, DOI 10.1057/978-1-349-94966-3_5

powers not in the parliament (because religious groups never received a significant number of votes in elections) but in society. This led to many unofficial alliances between local politicians (not really members of any religious party) and individuals from various militant organizations. Most of these empowered violent groups were Deobandis. Because of the alliance and political patronage, legislation for pluralism was rejected outright. It was only in 2007 that a major decision was taken to debate the Hudood Ordinances, and some of the laws regarding women were removed, including the right to be a full witness. Still the pressure was such that the legislators could not amend or discuss the blasphemy law, so it remains as it was when first inducted. It was only after 2008 that some major changes started taking place. However, a paradigm shift in terms of changing the national narrative towards religious extremism came only after the 2014 Peshawar APS massacre. The military action against the Pakistani Taliban as well as extremist religious groups affected the discourse about the role of religion in the country. However, the real change can only come when the state policy of not tolerating or accommodating a particular religious sect remains consistent, and, given the multisectarian religious dynamics, patronage of the Deobandi sect by successive regimes has been tantamount to creating cleavage in the religiously polarized society.

In recent history, particularly since the 1970s, countries with Muslim-majority populations have witnessed the rise of Islam as a political ideology, and militant groups using ultraorthodox Sunni ideology in different parts of the world, pressurizing the political forces in their domestic political showgrounds. The dominance of these religiopolitical forces has produced many questions, including about their relationships with conventional foundations. Over the years, societies with a Muslim majority have experienced infrequent religious revivalist movements that have placed emphasis on the need for the spiritual sanitization of the supporters, but militancy is definitely different from this renaissance and has extensive consequences. Violent Islamic extremism pursues "political objectives" and "provides [a] political response to today's societal challenges by imagining a future, the foundations for which rest on re-appropriated, reinvented concepts borrowed from the Islamic tradition".[1] Violent Islamic extremism is therefore essentially a political phenomenon and by no means simply an Islamic one. The proponents of extremist ultraorthodox Islamic groups highlight explicit courses of action to improve their political power, and implement various strategies to declare themselves on the social and political plane. In sharp contrast to the fundamentalists, who are concerned first with the erosion of religion and its proper role in society, Islamists focus on politicoeconomic interests.[2] For Islamists, "a true Islamic society—and flowing from this, a just, prosperous and strong one—is not simply comprised of pious Muslims; it requires an Islamic state or system".[3]

In the subcontinent, the notion of puritanical Islamic values and preserving the religion from influences in a multireligious society was taken up by the Deobandi movement. Deobandism is a nineteenth-century Indian school of Islam that rose to prominence during the time of British rule in India, and it was always more severe and strict than the milder South and South East Asian Islam.[4] Deobandis were very much politically dynamic; they did take part in mass movements, such as the Non-Cooperation Movement along with the Indian National Congress against the British Raj. In comparison with Barelvis, Deobandis were more active in the political domain. The three most important pillars of the Deobandi school of thought are based on the interpretation that a Muslim's first loyalty is to their religion and only then to the country of which they are a citizen or a resident; that a Muslim recognizes only the religious frontiers of their *ummah* (community of Muslims) and not the national frontiers; and that they have a sacred right and obligation to go to any country to wage jihad to protect the Muslims of that country. These three points pertinently define the ideological obligation that followers of the Deobandi sect carry with them. Because of their political activism, Deobandis on the platform of JUH actively worked for the Khilafat Movement following the idea of the great Muslim ummah. Gandhi's involvement added political importance but his endorsement was based on anti-British politics and not on a borderless religion-based nationalism. It is generally assumed that the politicization of religion and the role of the Deobandis started in the late 1970s with General Zia-ul-Haq's Islamization process, but the split within JUH presents a different picture. Jamal Malik states in *Colonization of Islam* that

> when *Jamiat e Ulema Hind* rejected the idea of Pakistan and other religious parties and scholars were also not in favor of a state for Muslims on western ideas, there was a group of Deobandi Ulema who supported the idea of Pakistan and they were present right from the beginning to support Islamization in Pakistan.[5]

So the Deobandis who supported the creation of a separate Muslim state already had an idea of a theocratic state which did not become a reality after independence and M.A. Jinnah came up with his idea of a Muslim state but not necessarily an Islamic one. It was only after Jinnah's death that the Deobandi members of the House managed to get the Objectives Resolution passed, and that paved the way for the Islamization process and a dominant role of Islam in Pakistan.

ARE DEOBANDIS INSPIRED BY WAHHABISM?

The term "Wahhabism" has connotations of an extreme or fundamentalist, pan-Islamic political agenda. It is commonly used by those who write about political Islamic movements as well as in the media around the world. Where a definition for Wahhabism can be found, it is usually a repetition of the same themes: "Saudi Arabia", "Bin Laden", "Ibn Abd al-Wahhab" and "purist Muslim".[6] Wahhabis believe in the Hanbali school of thought and Wahhabism is based on Muhammad bin Abd al-Wahab's teachings, which are followed by the House of Saud. These teaching are based on the Salafi school of thought, so all Wahhabis are Salafis but not all Salafis are Wahhabis. Salafism is widely practised in Saudi Arabia, and, because of its proselytization, followers of the Salafi school are found in many parts of the world with their intolerant, narrow interpretation of Islam. Salafism is an ultraconservative, orthodox movement based on the teachings of Imam Ahmed bin Hanbal and Ibn Taymiyyah. The Salafi school is often divided into three categories: the purists (or quietists), who avoid politics; the activists, who get involved in politics; and the jihadists, who believe in taking action. Modern-day proponents of jihad in the form of violent action believe in the Salafi movement. They also believe the eighteenth-century scholar Muhammad bin Abd al-Wahhab and many of his students to have been Salafis.

Although Saudi Arabia is commonly thought of as aggressively exporting Wahhabism, it is in fact Salafi teachings and indoctrination of different schools in the Sunni sect throughout the world but particularly in the Middle East, South Asia, South East Asia and Northern Africa. Saudi Arabia officially patronized many organizations and headquartered them its kingdom, but many of the guiding figures were foreign Salafis. The best known of these organizations was the Muslim World League, founded in Mecca in 1962, which distributed books and cassettes by al-Banna, Qutb and other foreign Salafi luminaries. Saudi Arabia successfully courted academics at al-Azhar University, and invited radical Salafis to teach at its own universities.[7]

King Faisal's embrace of Salafi pan-Islamism resulted in cross-pollination between Ibn Abd al-Wahhab's teachings on tauhid, *shirk* (idolatry) and bidat (and Salafi interpretations of ahadith (the sayings of Muhammad).

The juxtaposition of these two schools laid the foundation of contemporary political Islam in the Middle East as well as South Asia.[8] The ideology has extended to young and old, from children's madrassas to high-level scholarship through books, fellowships and mosques.

The Deobandi are a Muslim religious revivalist movement that emerged in India in reaction to the apparent threat to Islam from many influences that include both Western colonialism and Hinduism. Like the Wahhabis, the Deobandis believe that certain Sufi-related practices—such as seeking the mediation of saints and being innovative—as un-Islamic. Also, like the Wahhabis, they give superiority to the jurisprudence of former Islamic scholars rather than that of later ones. The concept of jihad is also more open to the Wahhabi understanding and thought than the Sufi's conception of jihad. In present-day Pakistan, followers of the Deobandi school of thought, which include the Taliban and the Lashkar-i-Tayeba (LT), are heavily influenced by Salafi teachings that began entering the country in the mid-1980s, along with money that helped to build madrassas all over Pakistan.[9] To say that Wahhabism and Deobandism are the same is factually incorrect but, in practice, violent political religious groups were found following the Wahhabi and Salafi school because both require Muslims to adhere to the original teachings with very narrow interpretations. Major violent Deobandi groups in Pakistan that have received funding from various Salafi groups include the LeJ, the SSP, Tehrik-e-Taliban Pakistan and Afghan Taliban in Pakistan.

Wahhabism, Ahl-e-Hadith and Ahle Sunnat

Within the Sunni doctrine, the Ahl-e-Hadith subsect established in the early twentieth century in India is the most conservative and strict. Enthused by an eighteenth-century scholar, Muhammad bin Wahhab of Saudi Arabia, Ahl-e-Hadith (commonly referred to as Wahhabis, or Salafis) came into existence as a response to the disparity between the Deobandis and the Barelvis. In 1906, Imam Ahmad Reza Khan of Bareilly advanced the teachings of the Barelvis, formally known as Ahl-e-Sunnat wa Jamaat.[10] This was a flexible alternative to the strict path followed by the Deobandis. In contrast, the Ahl-e-Hadith movement went for a more orthodox and conventional approach. After 1947, the supporters and followers of the Ahl-e-Hadith school of thought established three separate commissions to carry on their organizational work: one in India and two in the provinces of Pakistan.[11]

In 1948 the Pakistan Markazi Jami'at-e-Hadith was founded in Lahore. The Nikhil Banga O Assam Jami'at-e-Hadith (All Bengal and Assam Jami'at-e-Hadith) formed in Calcutta in 1946 shifted its headquarters to a northern city in what was then East Pakistan. The Anjuman-e-Ahl-e-Hadith was formed in West Bengal in 1951, with the result that, two years later, the Ahl-e-Hadith movement renamed itself East Pakistan Jami'at-i-Ahl-e-Hadith. In 1956 its headquarters were shifted to Dhaka. Followers of the Ahl-e-Hadith school preserved their presence and remained visible in what was then West Pakistan, but they were organizationally weak. Until his death, Abdullahil Kafi al-Quareshi led the East Pakistan committee. Dr Abdul Bari, a university lecturer, assumed the leadership in 1960. After the independence of Bangladesh, like many other religious organizations, Ahl-e-Hadith disappeared from the public scene.[12]

In post-1971 Pakistan, the Jamiat Ahl al-Hadith gained a great deal from Saudi support, and it represents one of the most radicalized elements within the Sunni fundamentalist sects in Pakistan. Inspired by Sayyed Ahmad, it wanted to bring Islam back to the purity of the original faith according to the Qur'an and the ahadith. The Ahl al-Hadith have formally claimed to be distinct from the Wahhabis, but their beliefs and practices have much in common with the dominant creed of Saudi Arabia, and in Pakistan they are often referred to as Wahhabis or Salafis. While the Ahl al-Hadith insists that they do not follow any one of the four schools of Islamic jurisprudence, they have moved progressively closer to the Hanbali interpretation, which is also the basis of Wahhabi practices. Their interpretation of Islam is puritanical and legalistic, and they reject all manner of perceived deviations and "idolatrous" practices that they claim have crept into the other major traditions. While their numbers are believed to be small—one tentative assessment by the International Crisis Group places them at 6 percent of the Muslim population of Pakistan—they have exercised disproportionate influence and demonstrated a great capacity for violence in recent years.[13]

SHAH WALIULLAH'S LEGACY

In principle, Shah Waliullah was little different from his contemporary, Islamic thinker Muhammad bin Abd-al-Wahab (1703–1787) of Saudi Arabia, who had also launched an Islamic revivalist movement. Wahab, who is regarded as one of the most radical Islamists, has a range of followers in India. He "regarded the classical Muslim law as sum and substance of the faith, and therefore, demanded its total implementation".[14] Waliullah also supported the rigidity of Wahab for strict compliance of Sharat (Islamic laws), and shariatization was his vision for Muslim India. He maintained that "in this area (India), not even the tiniest rule of that sharia should be neglected, this would automatically lead to happiness and prosperity for all". However, his theory of the rational evaluation of Islam was only a sugar-coated version of Islamic fundamentalism for tactical reasons. Glorifying the history of Muslim rule as a triumph of the faith, Waliullah attributed its downfall to the failure of the community to achieve literal adherence to Islamic scriptures. His movement for Islamic revivalism, backed by the ideology of pan-Islamism, was for the political unity of Indian Muslims. However, his religiopolitical ideology created a permanent crack in Hindu–Muslim relations in the subcontinent. Subsequently, non-Muslims of the region viewed his political concept of Islam as an attempt to undermine the self-pride and dignity of integrated Indian society.

The religiopolitical theory of Waliullah was quite inspiring for Indian Muslims, including members of Wahhabi movement. It drew popular support from the ulema, who were the immediate sufferers from the declining glory of Muslim rule in the subcontinent. The popular support for his ideology "has seldom been equaled by any Muslim religious movement in South Asian subcontinent".[15] He was of the view that the lost glory of the faith could be restored if Muslims adhered to the fundamentals of Islam literally.

The Sepoy Mutiny of 1857 was a turning point in the history of Islamic fundamentalism in India. With its failure, Indian Muslims lost all hope of restoring Muslim power in India. However, successive ulema in their attempt to keep the movement alive turned towards the institutionalized Islamic movement. Some prominent founders of the Darul Uloom Deoband, such as Muhammad Qasim Nanauti and Rashid Ahmad Gangohi, drew further inspiration from the religiopolitical concept of Shah Waliullah, as well as from Wahhabi ideology, and they set up an Islamic madrassa at Deoband in UP on 30 May 1866. It grew into a higher Islamic learning centre and in 1879 it assumed the present name of Dar-ul-Uloom (abode of Islamic learning). For the last 135 years, Dar-ul-Uloom, which was more of a movement than an institution, has been carrying the tradition of the Wahhabi movement of Saudi Arabia and of Waliullah of Delhi. Even Sir Sayid Ahmad drew inspiration from the tactical moderation of Islam from Walli Ullah in launching the Aligarh movement. The Muslim politics that we see today at Aligarh Muslim University are deeply influenced by the Islamic thought of Waliullah.

According to Dr Sayed Riaz Ahmad, a Muslim writer, the Muslim leaders, such as Maulana Abul Kalam Azad and Abul A'la Maududi, who participated in the freedom movement were followers of the Wahhabi school and carried the tradition of Waliullah with slight adjustments. Thus the nostalgic appeal to Muslim fundamentalism had a direct or indirect influence from Waliullah on the overall psyche of Indian Muslims. Unfortunately, the fundamentalist interpretation of Islam by Waliullah gradually widened the gap of mistrust between Hindus and Muslims of the subcontinent.

The combination of the Islamic extremism of Muhammad bin Abd al-Wahhab and the religiopolitical strategy of Waliullah has become the main source of inspiration for the Islamic terrorism that we see today. So long as Muslim leaders and intellectuals do not come forward and re-evaluate the eighteenth-century interpretation of faith, any remedy for the resolution of ongoing emotional disorder in society is only a remote possibility. It is the social obligation of intellectuals to awaken the moral and economic strength of the entire society without any religious prejudice.

Niblock determined that the more conservative circles of Saudi Wahhabism had for a long time perceived an affinity between Wahhabism and the Deobandi movement, from which the Taliban sprang. Some Wahhabis, indeed saw the Deobandis as their closest equivalent in South Asia. On this basis, Saudi private and charitable funding had flowed to the madrassa run by the Doebandi movement in Pakistan since the 1970s.[16] Wahhabism is deemed to have links with the Deobandi school of the Indian subcontinent and to have begun to infiltrate Western nations, including the UK. The purist Islamic perspective is seen to have influenced a large number of mosques within the UK, where hate speeches are allegedly delivered, in which curses are sought against the "enemies of Islam", including Christians and Jews.[17]

The Tablighi movement's rapid penetration into non-Muslim regions began in the 1970s and coincided with the establishment of a synergistic connection between Saudi Wahhabis and South Asian Deobandis. While Wahhabis are indifferent to other Islamic schools, they single out Tablighi Jamaat for praise, even if they disagree with some of its practices, such as a willingness to pray in mosques that house graves. The late Sheikh 'Abd al 'Aziz ibn Baz, perhaps the most influential Wahhabi cleric of the late twentieth century, recognized the Tablighis' good work and encouraged his Wahhabi brethren to go on missions with them so that they could direct and give advice to them.[18]

Charles Allen in his study gives a detailed account of the rise of Syed Ahmed and his followers, especially in the mountains of the Khyber Pass. He writes:

"The internal zeal and remarkable success that attended the preaching of Sayyid Ahmad indicates an unusual personality. Reform of Muslim practices is a serious matter; and as it then engaged the attention of some of the best minds of Muslim India, so it still forms a matter of earnest concern for those advanced leaders of Muslim thought who would like to see Islam purged of all the hurtful, degrading, and un-Islamic practices that keep it from being fashioned on more rational and progressive lines. Since these reforming doctrines went right to the heart of the everyday life of Muslims in the villages of India, the approach of a "Wahabi" preacher was as likely to create a storm as to produce a following".[19]

The Pushtun were already indoctrinated by the Wahhabi-influenced Deobandi school of thought. It was this group that was ready to take up the "holy war" against the infidel Soviets. Charles' account further proves this. He writes

The influence of the so-called Wahabi Movement still continues in two directions; one is in the organizations that it has left behind and the other in the effects on the development of the larger orthodox group. Traces of the original community left by Sayyid Ahmad are still to be found on the North –West Frontier, as are also similar traces of the schools of Shari'at Allah and Karamat Ali found in Bengal; but the most vigorous line of descent goes by the name of the Ahl-e-Hadith "People of Tradition."[20]He further states that "The leaders of the Ahl-i-Hadith sect declare that it is no way related to the founder of the Wahabi Movement of Arabia: but, however vigorously they may deny any connection, the spirit and the aims of this group appear to be identical with those of the Najdi reformer."[21]

VIOLENT OR NON-VIOLENT? EXAMINING THE NATURE OF DEOBANDI ISLAM

The Deobandi movement can hardly be seen as having a clearly defined goal. Rather, it seems to have multiple objectives. It was to a great extent a conservative movement. The Deobandi ulema moved closer to politics and created the JUH in 1919. This occurred amid competition with other organizations that were politically active for the independence of India.

The prominent leaders of the JUH included senior Deobandi clerics, such as Maulana Mahmudul Hassan (1851–1920) and Maulana Hussain Ahmed Madni (1879–1957), the latter being president until his death in 1957. The JUH's strategy was to adopt a non-violent approach against British rule in order to gain independence for India.[22]

In 1914, Maulana Mahmudul Hassan, chancellor at Darul Uloom Deoband, conceived a movement for the liberation of India by which armed units would be deputed to organize the Pakhtuns of the tribal areas, and rally support in Afghanistan in order to destabilize the British Indian government and provide a convenient point for the Turkish army to open a new front against the British. The movement was rooted in the politics of anti-colonialism and pan-Islamism galvanized by the start of the First World War, but the founders of the movement highlighted the differences in their militaristic outlook and the politics of non-violent non-cooperation which dominated the nationalist Indian arena at that time.[23]

The Deobandis formally subscribe to the Hanafi school of Islamic jurisprudence. They emphasize a puritanical interpretation of Islam that rejects the strong proclivities to syncretism that are characteristic of local, pre-Islamic and Sufi influences, which mark much of South Asian Islam. In 1919, Deobandi leaders created a political front, the JUH. The issue of the demand for the creation of Pakistan split the JUH, and so the JUI came into being under the leadership of Mawlana Shabbir Ahmed Usmani in 1945. The JUI united supporters of Partition, who lent their support to the dominant political group favouring the division of British India along religious lines: the ML. The JUI and a variety of Deobandi formations, including the Tablighi Jamaat, have been immensely influential both socially and politically in Pakistan, even as they have directly contributed to and shaped the course of sectarianism, extremism and militancy in, and exported from, the country.[24]

RADICALIZATION IN PAKISTAN: ZIA REGIME, MUSLIM LEAGUE AND DEOBANDI ALLIANCE

The radicalization of the Deoband movement in Pakistan can be traced back to the policy of conservative re-Islamization instituted by General Zia-Ul-Haq after his seizure of power in Pakistan in 1977. It was afterwards nurtured by the hardening stance of the Pakistani state and of the radical movements which shared the same enemies—namely, India, the communists and, to a lesser extent, the Shiites. However, the "militants" in due course turned to autonomous action and imposed their own strategy.[25]

After Pakistan was established as an independent Muslim state, it was further divided into many ethnic identities. The country was fragmented by the splits between the Sunni majority and the Shia minority. The Sunni doctrine was further divided into three main groups: Deobandi, Barelvi and Ahli Hadith. Each of these doctrines has its own schools and mosques, and has generated its own political parties. The parties have spawned radical spinoffs, many of which have been active in jihadist violence. Such violence has been most closely associated with the Deobandi and Ahli Hadith groups, both of which have seen their influence expand since the mid-1970s. The Deobandi has been favoured by the Government of Pakistan, and the Ahli Hadith by Saudi Arabia.[26]

Until 1979, the relation within Sunni doctrine (Deobandi, Barelvi and Ahl-e-Hadith) and between Shia and Sunni remained friendly and calm. The first case of sectarian violence emerged in 1953, when the Jaamat-i-Islami launched a violent campaign against the small Ahmadiyya community. The process of Islamization by Zia-ul Huq set free the forces of sectarianism and helped them to spread throughout the country. Following this, the civilian governments continued to exploit sectarian differences and used militant sectarian groups for their short-term benefit.[27]

Being a minority, the Shia population maintained a low profile on the political scene in the early days of the country but later extended implicit support to the secularist PPP, led by Zulfiqar Ali Bhutto. In addition, the two major Sunni groups—Deobandis and Barelvis—organized their political parties in the 1940s. The Deobandis, who were opposed to the establishment of Pakistan, formed the JUH in 1945, and broke away from their parent organization after 1947 to form the JUI, while the Barelvis formed the Jamaat-i-Ulema-i-Pakistan (JUP) in 1948. The political influence of these parties was far more limited than their sectarian following. The election results of 1970 bear testimony to this fact—each secured only seven seats. In fact, the results demonstrated that religious or sectarian identity had very little political appeal to the Pakistani population. For instance, the non-sectarian Islamist political party, the Jamaat-i-Islami (JI), did not do well either: it won only four seats.[28] The Islamization process, with the strict and authoritarian implementation of Sunni laws by Zia ul Haq, also raised sectarian differences.

The growing strength of the Shia population bothered the Sunni conservatives as well as two regional powers: Saudi Arabia and Iraq. Iraq was at that time engaged in a bloody war with Iran with the support of the West, especially the USA. For Saudis, the main challenge was to enclose the Iranian brand of Islamism within Iran by freezing the Sunni identity in countries around Iran and through building a "Sunni wall" around Iran.[29] Riaz Ali believes that "Saudis did this by providing funds to madrassas of the Ahl-e-Hadith in point of view of a counterbalance."[30]

Deobandis undertook immediate and aggressive action by founding the Sawad-e-Azam Ahl-e-Sunnat (Greater Unity of the Sunnis), and demanded that Pakistan be declared a Sunni state, and Shias as non-Muslim. In 1985, the Anjuman-e-Sipah-i-Sahaba (ASS, Society of the Army of the Prophet's Companions), later to become the SSP, was formed in Punjab to encourage violence against the Shias as its main objective.[31] The virulence of its expression and actions was unparalleled. The SSP, although apparently an independent organization, was strongly connected to the JUI until 1989. (The SSP entered into mainstream politics in 1990. The organization was renamed Millat-i-Islami after being banned in 2002.) Zia's regime extended support to the SSP to deal with growing Shia political influence, making it an integral part of its anti-Iran policy at home, and engaging it in raising fighters for the War in Afghanistan. The SSP gradually spread to the southern parts of the province from its base in the central region.[32]

The politicians associated with the Ahl-e-Hadith faction created a militant group in 1988, the LT (renamed Jamaat Dawa in 2002 after being banned by the government). The LT, which grew out of the Markaz Dawa-wal Irshad, comprised veterans of the War in Afghanistan and soon became engaged in violence both at home and in Kashmir. A spiral of violence was unleashed by the SSP and the LT. This resulted in a backlash from the Shia community: a militant group named the Sipah-i-Muhammed (SM, Army of Mohammed in Pakistan) was founded in 1991. As the SSP moved to the mainstream and was trying to tone down its violent rhetoric, a split occurred and some members formed a more aggressive organization, the LeJ, in 1994. The organization was named after Haq Nawaz Jhangvi, the founder of the SSP, to demonstrate that it is carrying on the work of Jhangvi, who was assassinated by his adversaries. By then the Barelvis had their own militant groups: Sunni Tehrik (ST) and the Anjuman Sipah-i-Mustafa (ASM). The Tehrik-i-Jafria Pakistan (TJP) was banned by the government in 2002 but then revived under the banner of Tehrik-i-Islam (TIP).[33]

RELIGIOPOLITICAL SCENARIO

The advent of 1970 brought great changes with it. The former East Pakistan voted in favour of the pro-autonomy Awami league supporting Mujeeb ur Rehman. In West Pakistan it was Zulfikar Ali Bhutto's party that won the elections. The political confrontation on the transfer of power led to civil disturbance and chaos. The civil war in East Pakistan brought India into the picture, and the political crisis turned into the Indo-Pakistan War and culminated in the creation of Bangladesh in 1971. Najum Mushtaq in his paper "Islam and Pakistan" writes:

> the idea of a nation based on religion, transcending ethnic diversity and bridging the geographic distance, fell apart. The leftover West Pakistan assumed the title of Pakistan. Refusing to learn the lessons of the post-independence 25 years, the framers of the new constitution led by Bhutto continued to play the religion card. The new constitution of Pakistan was full of Islamic content. General Zia ul-Haq, who toppled Bhutto in 1977, further strengthened these Islamic provisions. His 11-year rule coincided with the final decisive juncture in the Cold War: the Soviet invasion of Afghanistan and the U.S.-sponsored jihad led by Zia's Islamized Pakistan.[34]

Mushtaq adds:

> The Zia government introduced new laws based on ultra-orthodox Sunni interpretations of Islam and formulated Islamic rules and regulations for every institution. It thus subjected all sectors of society—from education to the media and from the cultural policies to official rules of business—to an Islamic code of conduct. Sectarianism flourished. This growing army of extremists in Pakistan fought the anti-Soviet Afghan jihad alongside the Arabs and Afghans and then served the cause of jihads from India to Bosnia to Chechnya. The next generation of the same mujahedeen groups is now the main protagonist in America's war on terrorism. The momentum of militancy created by Zia has continued after his demise in 1988. The semi-civilian rule of Nawaz Sharif and Benazir Bhutto could do little to stem the tide of Sunni militancy which has taken a two-track approach to advance its cause: at home against the Shias and other minorities and internationally against western targets. During the Musharraf period many of them have turned against the military itself.[35]

Murtaza Haider in his article published in *Dawn* explains

Whereas the population increased by 29 per cent during 1972 and 1981, the number of graduates from religious schools in Pakistan increased by 195 per cent during the same period. This resulted in an oversupply of graduates from religious schools who had limited employment prospects. The military and civil governments that followed the Zia regime also did little to address the dramatic increase in the number of *madrassas* and the students enrolled in such institutions. The number of *madrassas* jumped from 2,800 in 1988 to 9,900 in 2002. The Deobandi madrassas saw the largest increase during that period reaching a total of 7,000 institutions. In fact, the increase in the number of Deobandi madrassas was higher than the number of all other madrassas combined.[36]

JIHAD-E-AKBAR TO JIHAD-E-ASGHAR: POLITICIZATION OF THE NOTION OF JIHAD

There is enough empirical evidence to support the idea that the zealous Islamization during the 11-year rule of General Zia conferred a specific religious tone on various social and political phenomena in that era. In a purely religious context, Jihad-e-Akbar (the greater Jihad) is about controlling one's ego and fighting against one's vices. Jihad-e-Asghar (smaller Jihad) is basically the last option where armed struggle against the enemy is allowed in certain circumstance. Unfortunately the emphasis of the Zia regime was Jihad-e-Asghar, encouraging armed struggle against the infidels (Communist), i.e., Soviet forces in Afghanistan.

DEOBANDI–TALIBAN NEXUS

The traditionalist Deobandi networks appeared to be playing an important and recognizable role in Afghanistan. Indeed, as a rule, Taliban networks stem from old or newly created Deobandi networks.[37] The Taliban are Sunni Muslims, influenced by the Deobandi school of thought. After 1947, at the time of independence and Partition, when the Muslim areas of colonial India were established as the separate state of Pakistan, the centres of Deoband learning shifted to the Pakistani cities of Karachi, Lahore and Peshawar. Afghans were a part of steady stream of scholars travelling to Deoband and later to Pakistani madrassas to receive the teachings of the Deobandi school. The Taliban were the heirs to this tradition.[38]

Afghan students generally join Deobandi madrassas because of historical links between the Afghan ulema and the Dar Ul-Uloom Deoband madrassa in India. Even today the relationship between this madrassa and the Pakistani Deobandi movement is limited. Christophe Jaffrelot writes, "Under the generic term Deobandi one finds, in fact, different kinds of discourses and one cannot overestimate the education of their Ulema and the coherence of their ideology."[39]

Most of the Taliban ulema were educated in the NWFP (now KPK) during the war against the Soviets. In particular, the Darul Uloom Haqqaniyah in Akora Khattak, NWFP (KPK), has trained some of the most important cadres of the movement. There are strong links of solidarity between the ulema trained in this madrassa and its Taliban students. The ulema who are in control of the Taliban movement have a strong sense of group identity. Besides the presence of the Afghan Taliban, Pakistani madrassas are directly linked to the War in Afghanistan because participation in jihad is seen as a natural next step for its students. Most of the volunteers are Afghan but some Pakistani students also participate in jihad. The latter generally come from the NWFP and Baluchistan, and occasionally from Sindh or Punjab.[40]

The post-1979 wave of jihadism and violent intolerance among the Deobandi groups has much to do with Jamia Uloom-e-Islamia (situated in Binori Town, Karachi). The school continues the tradition of Darul Uloom Deoband. It has been often described as the "fountainhead of Deobandi militancy" in Pakistan because of its role in helping to establish and sustain a number of jihadi organizations, including the HuM, the JeM and the SSP.[41] A generation of former students has spread a web of similar jihadi madrassas across the country that pay allegiance to the Binori Town madrassa, and seek its guidance and support. The Jamia Uloom e-Islamia at Binori Town has worn the mantle of jihadi leadership since the days of the anti-Soviet jihad.[42] Abdul Rasheed, a Binori Town graduate and founder of the Al-Rasheed Trust, and Binori Town leaders Shamzai and Yusaf Ludhianvi, helped to establish the Jaish-e-Mohammed in 2000, which is headed by Masood Azhar, a former Binori Town student and teacher. The SSP, the Deobandi militant organization which pioneered organized sectarian militancy countrywide, was also backed by the Binori Town madrassa. Such support is particularly important because it translates into the support of the Deobandi sect countrywide.[43]

Jamiat-e-Ulema-e-Islam-S and Jamiat-e-Ulema-e-Islam-F

The JUH and JUI both look towards Darul Uloom Deoband for allegiance, though their political ideology differs from each other. As Barbara Metcalf explains

> In the final years of colonial rule, a minority group among the *Deobandi Ulama* dissented from support for the secular state and the privatization of religion espoused by the Indian nationalist movement. They organized, instead, as the *Jamiat Ulema-i-Islam* to support the Muslim League and the demand for a separate Muslim state. In independent Pakistan after 1947 they became a minor political party led by *Ulama* and a voice in the on-going debate over the nature of the Pakistani state. Should it be the secular state presumably intended by its founders, or a state meant to be shaped in accordance with Islam? The JUI has never had more than minute popular support, and the content of the party's programs over the years, it is probably fair to say, has been a fairly simplistic call for the dominance of Islam in public life.[44]

Like other Pakistani parties, the JUI has been subject to factional splits, joining together the personalities more than the issues, and there were perhaps half a dozen splits and reorganizations during its first half century.[45] Hence JUI was further divided into the Maulana Samiul Haq and Maulana Fazalur Rehman groups (JUI-S and JUI-F).

The increase in the number of madrassas in the 1980s corresponded with the arrival of almost 3 million Afghan refugees. The madrassas located along the frontier frequently provided the only education available to the immigrant boys. One school in particular, the Madrasa Haqqaniya in Akora Kathak near Peshawar, trained many of the top Taliban leaders. These sometime students (singular *talib*, plural *taliban*) were shaped by many of the core Deobandi reformist causes, all of which were further encouraged by Arab volunteers in Afghanistan. Ahmed Rashid, a longtime observer, says that the teaching was "An extreme form of Deobandism, which was being preached by Pakistani Islamic parties in Afghan refugee camps in Pakistan."[46]

SUNNI ORTHODOXY

The religious nexus that binds Deobandism and Wahhabism together had political aspirations during the Zia period:

> The Wahabi school of thought is predominant in Saudi Arabia. However, it should be emphasized that a vast majority of Muslims in Pakistan do not adhere to either Salafist or Wahabi traditions. The Deobandis opposed the

formation of Pakistan on the lines of a modern nation-state and regard themselves as the main voice of Sunni Islamic orthodoxy in Pakistan. In their beliefs, particularly their emphasis on Sharia, the Deobandis echo many of the puritanical Sunni Wahhabi traditions of Islam.[47]

The creation of the JUI in Pakistan made it socially relevant within the polity in the state:

> The Jamiat-e-Ulema-Islam (JUI) is the political organization of orthodox Sunni Muslim clerics and is led by Maulana Fazlur Rehman, who is the son of JUI's founder Maulana Mufti Mehmood. The Islamist JUI and Jamaat-i-Islami are also socially relevant—even if they are restricted to narrower ethnic and sectarian pockets—because their histories are linked to social and political developments in their areas of influence.[48]

"Jamiat Ulema-e-Islam, better known by its abbreviation, JUI is a hard-line Islamist party, widely considered a political front for numerous jihadi organizations ... pro-Taliban, anti-American and spiked with promises to implement Shariah, or Islamic law."[49]

The Deobandi school completely rejects Sufism (and its local Barelvi version) and the rituals held at shrines. This has been witnessed in a number of incidents: the attack on the Bari Imam Shrine in 2005[50]; the Sipah-e-Sahaba suicide attack on the shrine of Pir Rakhel Shah in the remote village of Fatehpur in Jhal Magsi District in Balochistan[51]; Haji Baba Turangzai's shrine in Safi tehsil in Mohmand Agency being taken over by 200 militants on 31 July 2007[52]; the Lal Masjid incident in July 2007; the killing of 40 people in suicide attacks on Data Darbar Lahore in July 2010[53]; the attack on Abdullah Shah Ghazi Shrine in Karachi in October 2010;[54] and many other examples of sectarian violence resulting from the intolerance and lack of acceptability of other schools by the Deobandis.

The Role of Deobandis in Pakistani Politics and Their Influence on Public Policy

The Deobandi parties played a major role in the legislative process of the period, augmenting an "Islamic" constitution of 1973 that had little to do with what Jinnah had imagined for Pakistan.Consequently, Zia introduced controversial Islamic legislation such as *Hudood* (Islamic codes), and other measures that included *zakat* (compulsory alms-giving), *ushr* (agricultural tax), Islamic banking, and blasphemy laws through a handpicked and non-party undemocratically "elected" *Majlis-e-Shura* (Parliament), which gave indemnity to his actions that were illegal according to the 1973 Constitution.[55]The 1973 Constitution was contradictory to what Jinnah was propagating before independence. Murphy and Rashid Malik in "Pakistan Jihad: The Making Of Religious Terrorism" write:

> In his efforts to promote an independent Muslim State, Jinnah was opposed by Muslim religious parties and groups namely *Deobandis* as well as the *Jamiat-i-Ulema-i-Islam*, *Jamaat-e-Islami* and other religious oriented groups. They were the supporters of Congress's notion of undivided and united India ... Jinnah's vision of Pakistan as a tolerant, modern, Islamic democratic State was later hijacked by religious elements who found in the new State an opportunity to advance their causes along conservative religious lines. From within and outside the State, religion was thus being used as a tool in advancing the political motives of religious parties and groups. The constitutional debate, the role of religious minorities, Islamisation, and *Sharia* were some of the examples that explained such trends and tendencies, which partly contributed toward the rise of religious extremism.[56]

In addition to the political activism of the Deobandis, the group played a major role in all spheres of political decision-making during the Zia era. Hussain Haqqani writes, "Islamists were appointed to important government positions in the judiciary, civil services, and educational institutions. Sharia courts were established to try cases under Islamic law, while Islamization was promoted through the government supported media."[57]

Zia raised a rhetoric of religion that plucked the masses' hearts and pleased the ulema, who in return would provide him with an ideological justification and mbrella to rule. Dr Hasan Askari writes that, in the 1978 cabinet formation,

> parties which accepted representation in the federal cabinet included Pakistan Muslim League (PML), *Jamiat-ul-Ulama-Islam* Pakistan (JUIP), Pakistan Democratic Party (PDP) and *Jamaat-i-Islami* ... However, this was the first time for the *Ulema* and other religious parties to be associated with power structure of the government. If one glances through the past record of the *Ulema* and religious parties, it appears that they had failed to win a substantial majority in any elections. Once in the government, they vehemently started advocating the establishment of a religious state bordering on theocracy rather than a modern democratic Islamic state. Such a point of view was helpful to the military government to sidetrack the demand of early Elections during 1979–85.[58]

State Patronage of Sunni Orthodoxy

The Zia regime patronized Islamic groups to further the concept of jihad. The USA helped General Zia to sustain his foreign policy and as a result ensure the continuity of his regime. Though one cannot say that US support was the only factor in consolidating the regime, it certainly contributed to endorsing his policies through financial and diplomatic support. Dietrich Reetz in his work "Migrants, Mujahedin, Madrassa Students" writes:

> It was particularly General Zia-ul-Haq who, with the express consent and encouragement of Western nations, and the U.S. in particular, politicized Islam to stabilize his own hold on power. During his reign several Islamic actors allowed themselves to be instrumentalized hoping to advance their own ideological objectives. This state intervention grossly "distorted" the Islamic field and created new players, institutions and concepts which later on acquired an identity and life of their own.[59]

After Zia's death and the resulting 1988 elections, Benazir Bhutto became Prime Minister of Pakistan. However, she was unable to alter the Islamic colour that her predecessor had given to the state, so she continued with most of his policies. "A major stumbling-block to the Bhutto government turned out to be the existence of the constitution as amended by General Zia-ul-Haq. An attempt by the PPP to have the constitutional changes of 1985 declared null and void by the Supreme Court, failed."[60] This resulted in a number of political crises, including a rift between the prime minister and President Ghulam Ishaq Khan: and central authority versus provincial autonomy.

Under Nawaz Sharif's government (1990–1993), the national conservative saw the continuation of the preceding Islamist policies. The period was marked by the Gulf crisis, with Iraq's invasion of Kuwait. The intial decision to send troops to Saudi Arabia was taken by the interim government of Ghulam Mustafa Jatoi. However, this decision was upheld by the incoming Nawaz Sharif government. The new government had found itself in a situation where the army chief had taken a position that was almost totally opposed to that of the government.[61]

SECTARIAN CONFLICT LEADING TO VIOLENCE

The real beginning of sectarian violence first ignited during the time of the Iranian Revolution and the Islamization process by Gen Zia in 1979. This was completely at odds with the ingredients of Zia's Islamization process because it was focused entirely on implementing Sunni laws and principles. Thus a rift took place between the two communities.[62] The crucial moment in the Shia–Sunni radicalization was basically the Iranian Revolution in 1979 and General Zia's dissemination of zakat and ushr ordinances under Sunni Islamic law in 1980. This Sunni law was in conflict with the Shia laws, leading to a protest campaign by the Shia community against the decision. In the 1980s, sectarian politics was growing and it drastically shifted towards Shia–Sunni violence. As a result of pressure on the Shias in Pakistan due to Deobandi social and political empowerment, Shia activism in the country took a new turn as a reaction to Deobandi activism, which was locked on to declare all Shia as non-Muslims. In the 1990s there were many sectarian battles, especially in the northern areas of Pakistan, including Parachinar and Hangu. Sometimes the situation even looked like a civil war. Many hundreds of people were killed in these clashes and sometimes army and paramilitary forces were called to restore peace.[63] General Zia's government turned a blind eye to the Sunni (mostly Deobandi and Salafi) Afghan mujahideen and their local Sunni cohorts to cut down the Turi Shias of upper Parachinar for obstructing the use of their territory as a launching pad against the Soviet-backed government in Kabul.[64] It is on the record that in most of the sectarian violence the militant organizations of the Deobandi school of thought were involved.

POLITICS OF FATWA AND HATE SPEECH FUELLING SECTARIAN VIOLENCE

The Deobandis are not the only ones who issue fatwas, but their role has been quite confusing. There is no doubt that the religious edicts for individuals and organizations seeking legal opinion or Islamic legitimacy for their actions also fuels sectarian tension, the reason being the nature of the fatwas. While some requests for opinions pertain to personal matters, such as marriage and inheritance issues, most relate to matters of sect and creed. With online and print availability, the reach of such fatwas—particularly those about sectarian differences—to people is unrestricted. Most of the fatwas reveal a mediaeval mindset. Since madrassas compete to win over members of rival sects, this intense intermadrassa competition fuels sociopolitical conflicts even within families and neighbourhoods in a city. According to International Crisis Group's research, the work of Yusuf Ludhianvi of the Binori Town madrasa is perhaps the most widely read among the Deobandi fraternity. His landmark work, *Ikhtilaf-e-Ummat aur Sirat-e-Mustaqeem* (Dissent in the Ummah and the Right Path), a critique of Barelvi, Shia, Ahle Hadith, Salafi and JI's Maulana Maududi's religious creed, is considered a masterpiece of Deobandi theology and is widely used. After examining Shia literature, Ludhianvi concluded that there was no doubt about the infidelity of Shias, and they were excluded from Islam: Shia'ism is a religion contrary to Islam. In fact, he propounded the same opinion about all Islamic sects other than the Deobandi. Similarly, the Deobandi extremists of the SSP and the LeJ revere Haq Nawaz Jhangvi, whose fiery speeches are an integral part of every activist's collection.[65]

JIHAD WITHIN JIHAD: *COLLAPSE OF THE SOVIET UNION AND SHIFT OF POLICY OF JIHAD*

With the Soviet invasion of Afghanistan, there was a change in the internal and external dynamics of the region. Pakistan politically pressurized Russia to withdraw, alongside covertly supporting the Afghan Mujahideen in Afghanistan—also funded by the USA, which at last forced the USSR to leave Afghanistan. After the Soviet withdrawal, Pakistan had to face a number of external and internal threats and challenges. In these complex and uncertain circumstances, Pakistan was left alone in the middle to deal with all the issues.[66] After the Soviet Union withdrew from Afghanistan, a power struggle began between the mujahideen and Najibullah's government. Pakistani intelligence supported the mujahideen in overthrowing the government[67] but it was not until 1992 that this was achieved. The Soviet Union continued its support of Najibullah's government while the USA withdrew its support for the mujahideen.[68]

FROM ANTI-SOVIET UNION TO ANTI-USA: THE AL-QAEDA–TALIBAN NEXUS

After 11 September 2001, Pakistan faced a difficult scenario. Owing to its continuous support of the Taliban, it was already facing condemnation from the international community. It had two options at that time: to side with the USA in the fight against Al-Qaeda, or to have pro-Taliban policies and face international isolation and denunciation. Pakistan kept the notion of national interest and turned around its Taliban and Afghan policies.

In its shift following 9/11, Pakistan began to support the US-led coalition forces in their military operations inside Afghanistan. Since the US invasion of Afghanistan, the Pakistan military has been actively involved in hunting down Al-Qaeda members in the tribal belts of the country.[69] As a result, the Taliban has gradually reduced its dependence on Pakistan and has started looking for support elsewhere, including strengthening its ties with Osama Bin Laden. During the 1990s, Bin Laden established a camp in Jalalabad. He supported the Taliban financially and also sent many Arab-Afghans to take part in the Taliban's military operations, which it had started in the North.

The relations between the Taliban and the USA became worse, especially after the former offered refuge to Bin Laden. The events of 9/11 shook the whole world and Al-Qaeda was held responsible for arranging the twin towers attacks in particular. Thus in October 2001 the USA launched a military operation to crack down on Al-Qaeda.[70]

The Tehrikeek-e-Taliban in Pakistan had sprung out of the residue of the mujahideen after the withdrawal of the Soviet Union from Afghanistan. These mujahideen formed a large number of groups in Pakistan, Afghanistan and Kashmir, and the TTP is also one of those factions.[71] There is a strong argument about categorizing the TTP as takfiris. E. Sivan analysed the situation of Talibanization, emphasizing that the TTP has adopted the takfiri doctrine of Taqi ad-Din Ahmad Ibn Taymiyyah, and revived by Sayyid Mawlana Abul Ala Mawdudi and Sayyid Qutb.[72] The Islamic scholars consider the takfiris as "heretics of Islam".

DEOBANDIS' VIOLENT STRUGGLE TO PRESERVE THE POLITICAL STATUS OF PAKISTAN

Preserving the religious influence within the governing system of Pakistan has been an key aim among religious factions. This has in turn helped such entities to redeem their social and political objectives in the fluctuating political realm of the country.

The Deobandis, with increasing mushroom growth of their institutions all across Pakistan, have been struggling to maintain the same political edge in the system as mentioned above. This struggle, starting in the mid-1970s, initially to counter the Soviet influence in the country, developed into an extreme form of struggle for Islamization and the eradication of other factions of non-Islamic religions. The Deobandis were heavily funded by national as well as international sources, and the general enmity between Shia and Sunni sects culminated in a disastrous and violent movement of power in the country.

Since the 1990s, with the advent of the War in Afghanistan and the intrusion of the Taliban in Pakistan, Deobandi groups have been known for their religious violent activities. Especially in areas such as KPK and Baluchistan, these groups gained power as well as a stronghold in the FATA. The TTP not only attacked the westerners but also the local people and the Shiite community. It was known to be largely supported by extremist religious groups established in Punjab, who were actively involved in Afghanistan and India as well. Groups such as the SSP and the LeJ have been the principal allies of Al-Quaida. They have provided weapons, recruits, finances and other resources to the Pakistani Taliban, and they were involved in violent attacks targeted at the militant FATA.[73] Another organization that has gained significant attention in religious politics is the JUI, which is further subdivided into different leaderships, most prominent of which are Mualana fazl-ur-Rehman and Maulana Sami-ul-haq's. The JUI has a strong hold on religious politics, especially in the regions of KPK and Baluchistan. It has had strong political support since the Zia regime and up until now has been capable of putting pressure on the establishment where needed.

In 1999 the JUI led a street protest against the Lahore peace process between Nawaz Sharif and the Indian Prime Minister, Vajpayee. The organization is rigorously devoted to imposing strict sharia law in the country and has condemned all efforts at secularization. Maulana Sami-ul-Haq (known as the Father of Talibans) has referred constantly to its agenda of a strict and binding Islamic sharia law.[74]

These organizations, in the surge of maintaining political status and resisting sectarian supremacy, have aggravated the situation to create a more violent environment. Incidents in Karachi marked with the political hold of the Muttahida Quami Movement (MQM) speak of the horrors of sectarian divide and political unrest. The assassination of the governor of Punjab, Salman Taseer, was a sorry tale of extremism etched in the roots of the society where he was assassinated by his own security guard, who was a staunch Sunni Muslim and declared that the governor made blasphemous comments against Islam and so was fit to be put to death.

The Lal Masjid incident (2007) was also an unfortunate event reflecting Islamic extremism and the extent of militancy in the country. A madrassa run by pro-Taliban leaders, Maulana Abdul Aziz and Maulana Abdul Rashid Ghazi, who sought to overthrow the establishment of General Pervaiz Musharraf quite rigorously, came under attack from the government in its efforts to eliminate pro-Taliban terrorist factions. The issue remains under discussion between different scholars regarding whether it was strategic planning or a reaction to Islamic extremism. Pervez Hoodboy writes:

> The *Lal Masjid* crisis is a direct consequence of the ambivalence of General Musharraf's regime towards Islamic militancy. In part it comes from fear and follows the tradition of appeasement. Another part comes from the confusion of whether to cultivate the Taliban—who can help keep Indian influence out of Afghanistan—or whether to fight them.[75]

This series of organizations and incidents defines the violent political struggle of religious groups to maintain their status of political power. However, within this power struggle, sectarian violence and terrorist activities continue to threaten the national security of the country. Owing to their immense historical importance, seminaries such as Darul Uloom could today act as a constructive platform on which to debate the political, religious, economic and social challenges confronting Muslims in Afghanistan, Pakistan and India, and simultaneously to engage in dialogue with non-Muslims. Likewise, in order to retain their past glory, Deobandi scholars will themselves have to take the initiative to evolve and reform the institutional structures of their seminaries so as to creatively and effectively respond to the contemporary challenges facing South Asia's Muslims.[76] However, the continuous patronage and growth of the Deobandi institutes may cause the ongoing sectarian violence to intensify. It is only reasonable to suggest that such organizations need to be checked and controlled thoroughly in time to limit their contributions towards the fragmentation of society.

The current "Islamic identity" appears to be narrow and self-destructive rather than an overarching concept of *amn* and *salamti* (peace and security); it is more of a myopic view of Islam versus the rest of the world. Unfortunately Pakistan became the victim of strict and inflexible policies. It is not race, geography or problems associated with those factors that have defined these policies, as is assumed by some in Pakistan, but the

deliberate construction of a geopolitical situation, the formation of enemies, the creation of alliances and confronting others that has resulted in
the problems that the country is now facing.

NOTES

1. Denoeux, Guilian. "The Forgotten Swamp." *Middle East Policy* 9, no. 2
   (June 2002), mepc.org/public_asp/journal_v019/0206_denoeux.asp.
2. Marty, Martin E., and R. Scott Appleby, eds. *Fundamentalisms
   Comprehended*. Chicago: University of Chicago Press, 1995.
3. Bubalo, Anthony, and Greg Fealy. *Between the Global and the Local:
   Islamism, the Middle East and Indonesia*. Washington, D.C.: Saban
   Center for Middle East Policy, Brookings Institution, 2005.
4. Marquand, Robert. "The Tenets of Terror." *Christian Science
   Monitor*, 18 October 2001.
5. Jamal Malik, Colonization of Islam. (Lahore, Vanguard Books-1996)
   p. 48.
6. Anis Ghani Kotia. 'Muhammad ibn Abd al-Wahhab and Sufism: A
   study into the reasons behind and a remedy for increased violent radicalization among British Muslims'. Masters Dissertation. Islamic
   College for Advanced Studies and Middlesex University. 2010. Pg:7.
7. Trevor Stanley, "Understanding the Origins of Wahhabism and
   Salafism", James Town Foundation publication: Terrorism Monitor
   Volume: 3 Issue: 14, July 15, 2005.
8. For more details about Wahhabi and Salafism, see Mark Durie, "Salafis
   and the Muslim Brotherhood: What is the difference?", June 6, 2013,
   published by Middle East Forum and Moussalli, Ahmad (January 30,
   2009). *Wahhabism, Salafism and Islamism: Who Is The Enemy?* A
   Conflicts Forum Monograph. p. 3.
9. Op cit, 165, pg - 173.
10. Not to be confused with the Deobandi militant outfit, the ASWJ,
    which is a reincarnation of the SSP.
11. Riaz Ali, *Faithful Education/Maddrasaaaha in South Asia*, Rutgers
    University Press, USA. 2008. p. 123.
12. p. 124.
13. Barry Rubin. *Guide to Islamist Movements*. M.E. Sharpe Inc. 2010.
    p. 349.
14. Qamar Hasan, " Muslims in India: Attitudes Adjustments and
    Reactions", Northern Book Centre, New Delhi 1987, p-3.

15. Mohammad Yusuf Abbasi, "The Genesis of Muslim Fundamentalism in British India, Indian Institute of Applied Political Research 1987, p-5.

16. Tim Niblock. *Saudi Arabia: Power, Legitimacy and Survival.* Routledge. 2006. Pg: 157.

17. Anis Ghani Kotia. 'Muhammad ibn Abd al-Wahhab and Sufism: A study into the reasons behind and a remedy for increased violent radicalization among British Muslims'. Masters Dissertation. Islamic College for Advanced Studies and Middlesex University. 2010. Pg:4.

18. "Fatwa of Shaykh 'Abdul-'Azeez ibn Baaz regarding the Jamaa'ah at-Tableegh," *fatwa-online.com*, 1993. Cited in Alex Alexiev. *Tablighi Jamaat: Jihad's Stealthy Legions.* Middle East Quarterly. 2005, pp. 3–11.

19. Murray T. Titus, Islam in India and Pakista: A Religious History of Islam in India and Pakistan, (New Delhi, Munshiram Manoharlal Publishers- 2005) p- 193.

20. Ibid.- pg 195.

21. Ibid.

22. Farhang Morady, Ismail Siriner (eds). Globalization, Religion & Development. IJOPEC (International School of Politics & Economics). 2011.

23. Sana Haroon. *Frontier of Faith: Islam in the Indo-Afghan Borderland.* Columbia University Press 2007. Pg:93.

24. Barry Rubin. *Guide to Islamist Movements.* M.E. Sharpe Inc. 2010. Pg: 348.

25. Mariam Abou Zahab, Olivier Roy. Islamist Networks: The Afghan-Pakistan Connection. Columbia University Press. 2002. Pg: 22.

26. Monte Palmer & Princess Palmer. *Islamic Extremism: Causes, Diversity, and Challenges.* Rowman & Littlefield Publishers. 2008. Pg 126.

27. Riaz Ali, *Faithful Education/Maddrasaaaha in South Asia*, Rutgers University Press, USA. 2008. Pg 108.

28. Ibid., pg 108.

29. Nasr, Seyyed Vali Reza. "Islam, the State, and the Rise of Sectarian Militancy in Pakistan." In *Pakistan: Nationalism without a Nation?* Edited by Christophe Jaffrelot, 85–114. New Delhi: Monohar, 2002.

30. Riaz ali, *Faithful Education/Maddrasaaaha In South Asia*, Rutgers University Press, USA. 2008. Pg 109.

31. Ibid.

32. Ibid., pg 110
33. Ibid., pg 110.
34. Najum Mushtaq, "Islam and Pakistan", in John Feffer (Editor), *Foreign Policy In Focus*. December 21, 2007 http://www.fpif.org/articles/islam_and_pakistan.
35. Ibid.
36. Murtaza Haider. How and Why Madrasa Graduates gravitate towards militancy and extremism. 2011. http://urdutahzeeb.net/articles/blog1.php?p=12809&more=1&c=1&tb=1&pb=1.
37. Antonio Giustozzi (ed) Decoding the new taliban: insights from the afghan field. Columbia University Press. 2009.
38. Roland Jacquard, In the name of Osama Bin Ladin: Global terrorism and the Bin Ladin brotherhood. Duke University Press. 2002. pg: 38.
39. Christophe Jaffrelot. Pakistan : Natioalism without a nation. Manohar publishers and distributors, New Delhi. 2002. Pg: 168.
40. Ibid.
41. Pakistan: Karachi's Madrasas and Violent Extremism-Asia Report N°130, March 29, 2007 published by the International Crisis Group.
42. Mumtaz Ahmad, "Continuity and Change in the Traditional System of Islamic Education: The Case of Pakistan" in Baxter and Kennedy (eds) "Pakistan 2000", Lexington Books.
43. Pakistan: Karachi's Madrasas and Violent Extremism-Asia Report N°130, March 29, 2007 published by the International Crisis Group.
44. Metcalf, Barbara. Traditionalist Islamic Activism: Deoband, Tabligh and Talib, ISIM papers, International Institute for the study of Islam in modern world, 2002.
45. Sayyid A.S. Pirazda, *The Politics of the Jamiat Ulema-i-Islam Pakistan 1971-77* (Karachi: Oxford University Press, 2000).
46. Ahmed Rashid, *Taliban: Militant Islam, Oil and Fundamentalism in Central Asia*. (New Haven: Yale University Press, 2000), p. 88.
47. Ibid.
48. Haris Gazdar. "Pakistan's Precious Parties." *Economic and Political Weekly*, 9 Feburary 2008: 8–9.
49. Nicholas Schmidle. "Next-Gen Taliban." *The New York Times*, 6 January 2008. http://www.nytimes.com/2008/01/06/magazine/06PAKISTAN-t.html?_r=1&pagewanted=all).
50. *Dawn*, 28 May 2005.
51. *Daily Times*, 20 March 2005.

52. Saba Imtiaz, Iftikhar Firdous. "Targeting symbols of spirituality." *The Express Tribune*, 25 September 2010 http://tribune.com.pk/story/54204/targeting-symbols-of-spirituality/).
53. *Express Tribune*, 2 July 2010.
54. Express Tribune, October 7, 2010.
55. Richard Kurin. "Islamisation in Pakistan: a view from the country-side." *Asian Survey 25, no.8*, August 1985: 852–62.
56. Dr Eamon Murphy & Dr Ahmad Rashid Malik. "Pakistan Jihad: The Making Of Religious Terrorism." *IPRI Journal IX, no.2*, Summer 2009: 17–31.
57. HusainHaqqani. *Pakisan: Between Mosque and Military.* Washington, D.C.: The Brookings Institute Press, 2005.
58. Hassan Askari Rizvi. *Military and Politics in Pakistan.* Progressive Publishers, 1974.
59. Dietrich Reetz. "Migrants, Mujahedin, Madrassa Students: The Diversity of Transnational Islam in Pakistan." *South Asia-Chronicle*, January 2011: 182.
60. Olivier Immig and Jan Van Heugten, "A Taste of Power: Uneasy Reign of Benazir Bhutto-1988-1990" *immigvanheugten*, 1994: 4.
61. Op cit, 261.
62. Nicholas Howenstein. The Jihadi Terrain in Pakistan: An Introduction to the Sunni Jihadi Groups in Pakistan and Kashmir. *Pakistan Security Research Unit (PSRU)*. Research report 1, 5th February 2008. http://spaces.brad.ac.uk:8080/download/attachments/748/resrep1.pdf.
63. Irfani, Suroosh. Pakistan's Sectarian Violence: Between the "Arabist Shift" and Indo-Persian Culture in *Religious Radicalism and Security in South Asia.* Edited By Satu P. Limaye Mohan Malik Robert G. Wirsing. Asia-Pacific Center for Security Studies Honolulu, Hawaii.
64. Khaled Ahmed, "When the State Kills," *Friday Times*, September 2001.
65. Pakistan: Karachi's Madrasas and Violent Extremism-Asia Report N°130, March 29, 2007 published by the International Crisis Group.
66. Babar Shah. *Afghanistan Policy: An Evaluation.* http://www.issi.org.pk/old-site/ss_Detail.php?dataId=56.
67. Ibid.
68. Stephen Tanner, *Afghanistan: A military History from Alexander the Great to the fall of the Taliban* (USA: Da Capo Press, 2002), 208.

69. Pakistan: Madrasas, Extremism and the Military, *ICG Asia report.* (Islamabad/Brussels, 2002).
70. Khawar Hussain,. *Pakistan's Afghanistan Policy.* Naval Postgraduate School Monterey, California. 2005, Master's Thesis.
71. H. Abbas, *Pakistan's Drift into Extremism, Allah, the Army and America's War on Terror.* (London: M. E. Sharpe, 2005).
72. E. Sivan, *Radical Islam: Medieval Theology and Modern Politics,* New Haven/London, Yale University Press, 1985, pp. 90f.
73. *Pakistan: Millitant Jihadi Challenge.* International Crisis Group, 2009.
74. "Islamic Parties in Pakistan." *Crisis Group.* December 12, 2011.http://www.crisisgroup.org/~/media/Files/asia/south-asia/pakistan/216%20Islamic%20Parties%20in%20Pakistan.pdf.
75. PervezHoodbhoy. *Three quarks daily.* July 12, 2009. http://3quarksdaily.blogs.com/3quarksdaily/2007/07/preventing-more.html.
76. Luv Puri. "Deoband's battle for survival and relevance." *Himal SouthAsian.* December 2009. http://www.himalmag.com/component/content/article/700-deobands-battle-for-survival-and-relevance.html.

CHAPTER 6

Experiences of Female Victims of Faith-Based Violence in Pakistan

Faiza Ali

Faith-based violence is on the rise in Pakistan. In particular, people of certain faiths, such as Shias, Sunni Barelvis or Sufis, Ahmadis and Christians are the main target of such violence. There is no doubt that the victims' families suffer an unbearable personal, emotional and economic loss. However, women affectees may have different and more profound experiences compared with male family members. Their experiences of faith-based violence may differ based on the intersection of their gender with the faith, sect, ethnicity or class that they belong to. Recent news reports have also highlighted the experience of female victims of ISIS in Iraq, such as the persecution and violence facing Yezidi, Kurd, Shia and Sunni women (e.g., Moaveni 2015). The aim of this chapter is to highlight and identify the experiences of female victims belonging to Sunni Sufi, Shia an Ahmadi communities who are affected by faith-based militancy in Pakistan. In recent decades, Deobandi militant groups—namely, the Taliban, the LeJ, the SSP and their affiliates—have attacked not only government institutions and security forces but also, and particularly, certain faith communities.

In their recent study of the depression levels of affectees of war and terrorism in Pakistan with respect to gender, Ahmad et al. (2014) found

F. Ali (✉)
Liverpool Business School, Liverpool John Moores University, Liverpool, UK

that the victims score high on the depression scale, and the prevalence of depression is particularly high among women in comparison with men. The study further revealed that men show a decrease in symptoms of depression faster than women after benefiting from psychological interventions (Ahmad et al. 2014). However, the study is based mainly on quantitative data and does not provide an in-depth picture of experiences of affectees, in particular women. This chapter seeks to address this gap.

The term "intersectionality" refers to the critical insight that gender, ethnicity, class and so on operate not as unitary, mutually exclusive entities but rather as reciprocally constructing phenomena (Collins 2015). Prins (2006) argues that a useful mechanism of multiple axes of intersectionality can only be explained through the narration of multilayered stories of intersection of gender with other forms of identity. All identities are performatively produced in and through narrative enactments that include the precarious achievement of belonging (Phoenix and Pattynama 2006). For Prins (2006), the constructionist approach treats identity as more a point of narration in which the subject is "both actor in and co-author of our own life story" (p. 281).

Within the constructionist approach, identity is perceived as a matter not of naming but of narration. Identity cannot be grasped by a list of characteristics that informs us about the "what" of a person. It is about "who" someone is, and that, as Hannah Arendt (1998) suggests, can only be shown through storytelling. On the one hand, our stories of ourselves and others are only partly of our own making: we enter a stage that is already set, and our lives for the most part follow the course of already available narrative scripts. On the other hand, our stories are multilayered and contradictory: the scripts of gender, faith, ethnicity and class play a constitutive role, but never in the same way, never as mere determining factors.

With regard to the situation of faith-based violence in Pakistan, the US Commission on International Religious Freedom (USCIRF 2015) recommends that Pakistan be designated a "country of particular concern" in view of systematic violence against Shias, Christians, Ahmadis and Hindus there. While Shia Muslims in all parts of Pakistan have experienced violence at the hands of Deobandi militants, the case of Hazara Shias of Quetta is particularly important given the scale of violence facing them, and also because of the intersection of faith (Shia) with ethnicity (Hazara), which makes them more vulnerable to violence from militants. Hazaras, predominantly Shia Muslims by faith, are ethnically Mongolian, with oriental features and light skin—different from much of Pakistan's population. The vast majority of Hazaras are Shia Muslim and are therefore declared "heretics" (i.e., kafir or *murtad* [apostate]) by the Darul Uloom Deoband in India and its militant followers in Pakistan, such as the LeJ and the SSP. Quetta's Hazara Shia community seems to be on the frontline of Pakistan's battle with violent extremism. The BBC (2013) reports the case of Ruqsana Bibi, a Hazara Shia woman of Quetta, who lost three of her four sons in a terrorist attacks. The walls of her modest home are filled with family pictures. She sits on the floor holding three frames, each containing a picture of one of the children that she has lost (*BBC News* 2013). For Ruqsana Bibi and many other female victims, the loss is not only emotional and personal but also economic and social in a society where men are the breadwinners.

Ordinary Sunni Muslims too have suffered at the hands of faith-based violence by Deobandi Islamist groups in Pakistan. Not unlike other communities, their stories are those of suffering, as well resilience and resistance. On 9 October 2013, a 15-year-old, Malala Yousafzai (a Sunni Muslim of Pashtun ethnicity, and a Nobel Prize laureate), was brutally attacked in the Swat region of Pakistan on her way home from school—shot in the head at point-blank range by the Taliban. Her only crime was the insistence on girls' right to education, and opposition to the Taliban's brutalities against women and other groups. Luckily, Malala survived the brutal attack. She continues to lead a worldwide movement to educate girls, and has become an international symbol of courage and hope. Before the Taliban attempted to kill her, Malala had been reaching out to people and spreading her message by using a pseudonym to write a blog, for *BBC Urdu*, about women's rights and life under the Taliban. Since surviving the deadly attack, she has doubled her efforts and raised awareness about education in countries where access to schools is denied (Bailey 2014).

Ahmadi women's stories and suffering are no different. An Ahmadi girl tearfully recalls the loss of her own father, who was slaughtered along with 87 Ahmadis in what remains the most gruesome attack on the group in Pakistan's entire history. The attack took place in Lahore on 29 May 2010. She was 16 when her father was killed, and, for her at least, the memories of his life are vivid and raw, and the wound from his departure still fresh (*Ahmad* 2015).

In May 2015, 47 Ismaili Shia Muslims, including 16 women, were shot dead during an attack on a bus in Karachi (*BBC News* 2015). The Ismaili Shias are considered to be a very peaceful community, and are also known for their charity projects in Pakistan and other countries. The ISIS-inspired Deobandi militants who massacred the Ismaili men didn't spare the 16 Ismaili women either. It's hard to imagine the suffering of those women's families, particularly those with young children.

In the following section I review the literature on the topic of intersectionality to understand the justification of using this lens. This is followed by the empirical section.

LITERATURE REVIEW

The concept of intersectionality is a study of overlapping or intersecting social identities and related systems of oppression, domination or discrimination (Crenshaw 1991). The theory takes into account different social and cultural categories, such as gender, race, class, religion, caste, age and other axes of identity that interact on multiple and often simultaneous levels. This framework can be used to understand how systemic injustice and social inequality occur on a multidimensional basis (Crenshaw 1989). Intersectionality holds that the classical conceptualizations of oppression within society, such as racism, sexism, classism and belief-based bigotry, do not act independently of one another. Instead, these forms of oppression are interrelated, creating a system of oppression that reflects the "intersection" of multiple forms of discrimination (Knudsen 2006).

According to Knudsen (2006), intersectionality is a theory

> to analyse how social and cultural categories intertwine. The relationships between gender, race ethnicity, class, nationality and so forth are examined on multiple levels to explicate various inequalities that exist in society. They are not independent of one another but instead are interrelated forms of oppression that are manifested in multiple forms of discrimination. (p. 61)

Rather than looking at the majority culture, the theory of intersection reflects the minority culture: "The concept can be a useful analytical tool in tracing how certain people seem to get positioned as not only different but also troublesome and, in some instances, marginalized" (Staunæs 2003a, p. 101).

Perspectives on multiple minority identities include additive, multiplicative and interactionist, as well as intersectionality (Parent et al. 2013). "[A]dditive perspectives reflect the notion that minority identity statuses (e.g., class, race and gender) act independently and combine additively to shape people's experiences", with researchers from this perspective using the term "double jeopardy" to explain the additive effect (Parent et al. 2013, p. 640). Like the additive perspectives, multiplicative or interactionalist perspectives assume that the various identities can be conceptualized and operationalized, in study terms, as separate dimensions that, in this case, function multiplicatively—for instance, with one minority identity exacerbating the effect of another (Parent et al. 2013). The additive and multiplicative perspectives tend to be pursued via quantitative research.

Brah and Phoenix (2013, p. 82) argue that intersectionality has encouraged new ways of thinking about multiplicity in power relations: recognition that "race", social class and sexuality differentiate women's experiences has disrupted notions of a homogeneous category "woman" with its attendant assumptions of universality that served to maintain the status quo in relation to "race", social class and sexuality while challenging gendered assumptions.

The concept of intersectionality in a "conflict zone" such as Pakistan, where there is less religious tolerance, may increase the complexity of issues and challenges faced by the people of that area. Any conflicts, whether natural or man-made, have multiple and differential impacts on men and women because their experience of conflict is mediated through their gender. In Pakistan, women are socially positioned as subordinate to men (Ferdoos 2005). They do not have equal access to opportunities, resources and power. Owing to their lower social and economic position, they are more vulnerable and have less capacity to cope with the impact of conflicts, and human and natural disasters (Bari 2010; Ali and Knox 2008). It is well documented that women's vulnerabilities are exacerbated in conflict situations, such as war and terrorism (Niarchos 1995). Women face much harsher conditions resulting from terrorism and other similar situations. Several research studies conducted in the areas of peace, conflict and wars across the world show that not only the impact but also the perceptions and perspectives of men and women of conflicts are clearly gendered (Bari 2010; Jawaid et al. 2014). In general, women are perceived as passive victims of wars/conflicts who do not play any active role in initiating or participating in these events (Liebling-Kalifani et al. 2007).

In Pakistan, women are the neglected category in the analysis of the War on Terror, and the growing religious extremism and militancy (Bari 2010). Men and women are both affected by growing Deobandi militancy in Pakistan. However, their experiences are distinctly different. Hardly any significant effort is being made to document the gender differentials of the impact of the War on Terror. Since the impact of religious militancy on men and women is different, it is likely that the understanding and prescriptions for counterterrorism are also different.

In recent years the Darul Uloom Deoband has delivered numerous fatwas which undermine women's freedom. Notably, women cannot preach or deliver sermons; working women cannot mix with male colleagues; women must wear a *burqa* (veil or cover for the whole body); triple *talaq* (divorce) uttered through a mobile phone is valid; women cannot serve as *qazis* (judges); talking to one's fiancé on the phone is *haram* (forbidden); adolescent girls over 13 years of age cannot ride bicycles; it is undesirable for women to drive a car; women shouldn't contest elections and must observe *purdah* (the veil); co-education is impermissible. Other fatwas stipulate that Muslims shouldn't work in banks; modelling and acting are offences; watching cartoons on television is unlawful for children; donating blood and organs is haram; photography is sinful; celebrating birthdays is not allowed; a person blaspheming against the Prophet Muhammad should be killed; a body scan is impermissible; and life insurance is illegal (*Indian Express* 2013). Such kinds of practice further restrain women's mobility in social and economic activities, especially after the death of their financial supporter.

In a study conducted with men and women who faced the Taliban's terrorism in Pakistan in the Swat region, it was revealed that all men, women and children suffered from the social, economic and political impact of religious militancy. However, women were disproportionately affected owing to their dependent socioeconomic position in local cultures. Women's experience of Deobandi militancy/Talibanization was fundamentally different from that of men. Men suffered from physical violence. Women, on the other hand, were not allowed to live as autonomous human beings. Their survival was made dependent on the presence and support of the men in their lives. They were not allowed to go out of their homes under any circumstances without being accompanied by a *mehram* (a man related by blood). Women not only lost their access to education, health and other social services but also their sternly restricted mobility made their physical existence precarious and completely dependent on men. Women from conflict areas experienced the worst form of patriarchy (Bari 2010). However, this study does not take into account the complex nature of different intersectional issues, such as ethnicity, class and faith.

In light of the above discussion, it can be argued that women face different issues and challenges based on their gender, class, faith and ethnicity. Their experiences when faced with extreme issues of terrorism need to be explored carefully to understand the complexity of their challenges, and also how they cope differently to overcome such barriers. In this context, this chapter aims to answer the following research questions:

- How has faith-based militancy affected Pakistani women from diverse faith backgrounds?
- How do these women cope with such issues and challenges?

METHODOLOGY

The present study is based on an analysis of primary and secondary sources of information. The nature of analysis is qualitative due to the use of the intersectionality lens. Qualitative studies tend to be central to the intersectionality perspective, which assumes that multiple identities are not divisible as separate dimensions so that interlocking identities, which are unique for each individual, construct novel and distinctive experiences (Parent et al. 2013; Collins 2015).

The primary sources included semistructured interviews with women based on their gender and faith. In total 10 interviews were conducted: 5 with Shia women, of whom 2 were Hazara Shias; 3 with Sunni Barelvi or Sufi women; and 2 with Ahmadi women. All of them had lost an immediate family member in a terrorist attack. Owing to the sensitive nature of the topic, it was not easy to collect information from women who were victims of terrorism in one way or another. Some refused to be involved for a number of reasons (e.g., fear of raising their voice, emotional trauma). However, participation was purely voluntary and the ethical aspects of anonymity, privacy and wellbeing were duly considered in the data-collection process.

Secondary sources were also used to retrieve relevant information. For this purpose, different sources were investigated—for example, credible news articles and international institutions' reports. For the Hazara Shia women, in addition to carrying out two interviews, I also analysed the latest report by HRW, which contains a number of interviews with the Hazara Shia women.

Participants for the primary data were recruited using my personal networks using snowball and criterion sampling methods. These methods were deemed appropriate because of the personal nature of the questions and also in view of access issues. A semistructured, in-depth, qualitative interview protocol (see Appendix) was used to investigate and explore the issues and challenges facing the participating women. The questions sought to encourage them to share their experiences of, perceptions about and reflections on their experiences. An open-ended format was used, allowing participants to control the depth and breadth of information shared. The semistructured format provided a deeper understanding of the key issues. This methodology also presented an opportunity to ask follow-up questions to clarify, and elicit additional, information.

FINDINGS

The findings of this study can be divided into three main themes: social impact, economic impact and coping strategies. Each describes different experiences of Hazara Shia, non-Hazara Shia, Sunni Barelvi and Ahmadi women who have been a victim of faith-based violence.

Social, Emotional and Psychological Impact

From the analysis of primary and secondary data it is evident that women face a huge emotional and social ordeal as a result of faith-based violence. However, it is also important to consider individual circumstances. In this section I shall discuss the emotional experiences of women of different sects and ethnicities.

Although all of the women had experienced emotional trauma, Hazara Shia women had faced the strongest impact of violence. That is because some families lost more than one family member. Here is an account of a Shia Hazara woman:

> what is the reality? How many of you can relate to 5 dead bodies being taken out of a house—father, brothers, sons. What do the women of that house go through? What is the future of these women? Of the Shia Hazara women?

The data suggest that the Hazara Shia women continue to face threats of violence from Deobandi militant outfits, such as the LeJ and the SSP, even after losing their family member/s to these terrorists. For example, one Hazara Shia widow explained to HRW how she continues to receive threats after her husband's murder:

> After his death, I used his cell for a while and I started getting calls. They were all taunting and sometimes even vulgar and obscene. The first one came the night that Abid died—the man asked "How do you feel now?" After a while I just shut the [phone card] off.

The kind of emotional experience that Hazara women go through might be very different for women of a different class or sect. The entire Hazara community is under attack, so they have similar experiences. For example, a woman who lost her brother in a suicide attacks said:

> Our entire neighbourhood is full of homes grieving the dead and tending to the maimed. There were bits of human flesh on our rooftops and our courtyards. It was horrific.

Similarly, another Hazara Shia Muslim woman who lost her brother said:

> He was the youngest child in the family. The most loved one. The most protected one. Ever since he has gone we are all paranoid. Scared for each other's security. It has made us *bitter and angrier* in general.

The emotional trauma faced by Hazara families is compounded by the fact that they already know that their life is in danger. So in addition to mourning their loved ones, they continue to live in fear of death all the time, unlike the case of women living in Lahore or Karachi, for example. A Shia Hazara woman said that her father's murder followed numerous threats from the militants:

> A few days before his death, my father warned my brothers and several of his friends and acquaintances about their safety; he asked everyone to take extra security precautions. This was because he had received threats from the Lashkar-e-Jhangvi.

Other Shia women (non-Hazara) who are victims of terrorism also go through a great deal of emotional trauma. For example, according to a woman who lost not just her husband (a Shia Muslim) but also her school-going child,

> They say time is a great healer. For a mother who has lost a child, I doubt if it is. I would know. I lost my eleven-year-old son, along with my husband to the bullets of terrorists almost two years ago. The pain has not diminished, if at all it has grown—and I know that this is a burden I will carry as long as I live. (Haider 2015)

Although some families get social support, it may not be enough given the intensity of the loss. Consistent and prolonged help is needed by such families. According to the same woman who lost her husband and child,

> There is so much they can do, but at that time, it is impossible for a grieving family to be able to articulate their needs. So they say thank you and after the traditional forty days of mourning, they are more or less left to cope on their own. The extended family members continue to lend support, but very soon they too become exhausted. They wish you to "get over it", "to get on with life", "to move on". But that is easier said than done. (Haider 2015)

It is important to note that in this particular case the family seems to be well off. However, this may not be the case with the majority of victims' families who may not be financially sound or may not have good communication skills. This is evident from the fact that there are very few examples where victim women wrote articles to convey their point of view or experience in the media, such as in newspaper articles. There are certain families who not only have lost their family member/s but also are taking care of injured individuals. The emotional and psychological circumstances of such families might be very different from those of the people mentioned above. For example, a Shia woman from Parachanar who lost her father and her sister became paralysed as a result of the injuries that she sustained in the attack. She said:

> It's not much difficult to deal with other things, yes my father left us very early. Somehow we have come out of trauma. We are moving forward in life. But the most difficult thing is (to) see the loss of my sister. It is really painful to see my sister aged 31 (at that time she was 28) in paralysis. She lost the quality of life. It is actually a great loss for her children when they see their mother dependent on others and she cannot look after them. At that time her children were aged 9, 7 and 5 (she is mother of three children, 2 daughters and a son).

Sunni Barelvi (Sufi) women who lost family members also have to deal with a great emotional loss. A mother who lost her 30-year-old son in a suicide bomb attack at a Barelvi mosque recalled:

> That was greater tragedy than our imagination which we faced and we have lost our bread winner not only but I lost my son, his bride lost his husband, his sister lost his loving and caring brother and his younger brother lost his father like brother. Impact of this loss was emotional, psychological and socially but also economical.

Ahmadi women face similar emotional and psychological trauma. One of the participants who lost her father-in-law (who was also her uncle) said that the family had to go through great emotional trauma. Further threats to her husband caused her to leave the county as an asylum seeker. According to her,

> My father-in-law (also uncle) was a great man. He went for Friday prayers when his mosque was attacked. We came to know through news. My husband (victim's son) kept looking for him in the hospitals. When he found his it looked like he was in stable condition but after few hours we came to know that he died of his injuries Life changed after that. He was the head of our joint family and used to do all important chores for us. After him, we did not know how to get along with our life.

From the interviews it was evident that the Ahmadi victims received considerable emotional, social and financial support from their community. However, other people, such as neighbours, did not provide support to Ahmadis because of their faith and sectarian biases:

> We along with other affected families got full support from our *Jamaat* (the Ahmadiyya community). However, we did not get much support from non-Ahmadi people such as our neighbours as they do not like mingling with us because of our faith. We do understand that and don't want to complain about it.

The above examples provide an overview of the social impact of terror attacks on women of different sects, ethnicity and class. In the following section, different experiences with respect to economic constraints are presented.

Economic Impact

Pakistan is a male-dominated society where women are considered to be no more than second-class citizens (Ferdoos 2005). It is evident that women spend most of their time in the house and, owing to purdah, do not have much exposure to male strangers. Confronting the "male world" is therefore a traumatic experience that they find difficult to face (Syed et al. 2005). Most women have never been alone to a bank, a government office, a bookshop or even a hospital (Ferdoos 2005). The inability to interact with male strangers is closely intertwined with the purdah system, which again is based on the absence of concepts for mixed social interaction, and the perception of relationships between *na-mehram* (non-blood related) men and women as predominantly sexual ones (Ali and Kramar 2015; Ferdoos 2005). Men are the considered to be the breadwinners (Ali 2013). Hence, women, who are lose their financial supporters such as husband, brother, and father or son face immense difficulty dealing with day-to-day financial issues.

In case of Hazara Shia women, the level of difficulty is severe. This is because Quetta is already an economically less privileged area and the Hazara Shia face a continuous threat to their lives from Deobandi militants, as a result of which they are confined to a specific area. According to one Hazara Shia,

> I can't even go to the market to buy vegetables or sugar without fearing for my life so I take what I get within a one block radius, however overpriced and whatever the quality. It's like living in jail. (Thacker 2014)

In this particular context, Hazara Shia women who are victims of terrorism face extreme economic consequences owing to the loss of their financial supporters. The surviving family members of LeJ killings are often impoverished by the death of the family breadwinner. Sughra, the widow of Mohammed Zaman, who was killed in the 6 November 2012 Spinney Road taxi attack, described the economic impact of her husband's murder:

> I don't know whom to turn to for help. I just have no source of income. My family and my mother in particular have been kind and have been supporting me thus far. But I know that they will not be able to continue for very long as they themselves are extremely poor. Soon, I shall have no money to send my children to school. My children and I, we may be here now but you should already consider us dead. If the LeJ does not kill us, poverty will. (HRW 2014)

Below are the painful words of a Hazara young woman (published on 31 December 2012 in the *International Herald Tribune*) who lives in Quetta:

> What is the future of these women? Of the Shia Hazara women? When they step outside the four walls of their homes once the men have been slaughtered, to earn a living because they have no other choice, vultures start circling. These are men who have been directly or indirectly responsible for lifting the roof off their heads. Responsible for killing the men in their lives. They offer help to these women in exchange for not cash but kind. I am one of those women. (Zahidi 2012)

Non-Hazara Shia women who are victim of terrorism also face financial difficulties. However, their economic situation may not be as severe as that of the Hazara Shia women. For example, the following account describes the circumstances of a widow of a Shia doctor in Punjab:

> A widow may suddenly find herself dealing with issues she was previously completely unfamiliar with, from household maintenance, budget management and generating income to creating new family dynamics and nurturing vulnerable relationships. A widower may find himself suddenly facing the prospect of raising young children on his own. In all cases, a whole new hierarchy and support system has to be developed. From dealing with hospital reports and banks, to something as simple as eating a meal, the family needs friends. (Haider 2015)

Further, financially privileged Shia women may not be in need of governmental financial compensation. One such woman who lost her brother said:

> Some people might need financial support and for them the government must compensate. But for us, I could never touch the money that was paid against my brother's blood. Perhaps economic independence gives you that privilege.

Sunni Barelvi women also face financial constraints. A Sunni Barelvi woman who lost her son in a suicide attack at a Barelvi seminary in Lahore described her financial difficulties:

> Due to death of our sole breadwinner my younger son quit his study and got a job after great effort and he thus managed to win bread for us. Government had announced to give [compensation] and we received a cheque worth Rs 500,000 which was cashed after 5 month.

She further expressed her feelings:

> That was greater tragedy than our imagination which we faced. We have lost our breadwinner not only, but I lost my son, his bride lost her husband, his sister lost her loving and caring brother and his younger brother lost his father like brother. The impact of this loss was huge not just emotionally, psychologically and socially but also economically.

However, in certain instances where there was more than one breadwinner in a family, the economic impact was not as profound or there was also an element of resilience. A Sunni Barelvi woman who lost her husband in a targeted attack said:

> My husband used to contribute to running our house but he was not the sole bread earner of our family. My son is an employee at the [company name], member of some provincial official religious bodies and he gets salaries. There are some properties on rent so we did not face much difficulty in running our house, and not much financial hardship we faced after the death of my husband.

In the case of Ahmadi women, the situation seems to be different from women of other sects when it comes to economic issues. The interviews suggested that Ahmadi victim families receive not just emotional but also financial support from their *jamaat* (registered community of Ahmadis). For example, an Ahmadi woman who lost her uncle/father-in-law in a mosque attack said:

> When my uncle got killed in an Ahmadi mosque attack in Lahore, we received continuous support from our *Jamaat*. Our local community leaders provided food for three months to all 85 families so that they don't have to be worried about guests etc. In addition to this women who were left without their husband or economic supporters were provided with the same amount of money which they used to receive from their husband/father/ brother before the incident. Their children went to the same schools without any worry of school fee. Our religious leader ordered to take care of all such vulnerable families. Further, he asked all affected families to refuse to receive any kind of government support.

The above results provide a general understanding of the economic situation of women of different sects.

Coping Strategies

This section focuses on the coping strategies of women affected by militancy: how they adapt, react and reflect on their experiences after losing their loved ones.

In the mainstream media, Hazara Shia women are a visible presence when it comes to protest against terrorism. In the past the Pakistani nation witnessed these Hazara women sitting next to the dead bodies of their loved ones and demanding justice. The women were shown on national and international media protesting with the full support from their family. One such young Shia Hazara woman bravely raised her voice in the following manner:

> I must share what it means to be a Shia Hazara. Today, I am going to share a bit of my story—the story of me and my people. When one of us comes in front of you, you mostly label us Chinese or Korean. Our complexions are not like yours, neither is our race or genetic composition. We are the "others". And our pain is that of the others. We are Pakistanis but not considered a part of you. Very few will raise their voice for us, even when 27 of us are taken off a bus and are shot and killed just because we are Shias. Just because we have Mongol-like features. Just because we migrated here from Afghanistan. But what is the reality? How many of you can relate to 5 dead bodies being taken out of a house—father, brothers, sons. What do the women of that house go through?

National and international media witnessed a strong representation of Shia Hazara women in the protest of February 2013, when 84 Shia Hazara lost their lives in a suicide attack.

Non-Hazara Shia women also use their agency to deal with such situations. One participant informed me that she used social media for activism, but that did not help for long:

> Sometimes I talk about him like he's still there. Sometimes, I open his facebook and cry. Sometimes I text him. I used to vent out my anger through social media activism. I have had so many bitter arguments with so many people over the course of these 5 years. But then I deactivated social media and distanced myself from people.

Another Shia woman, who lost her son and husband, started a group called Grief Directory to help other families and mothers of victims. In her words,

> I intend to start this Grief Directory as a small step in my own journey of survival. It may help ease my pain if I know I am helping others who are in a similar situation as me. We share a bond of pain and loss and it is important to know we are not alone. The Grief Directory is envisioned as a coordinating mechanism to provide voluntary service to aggrieved families. Once a family registers with the directory, a list of their needs will be formulated with the help of the family members depending on their unique circumstances. These needs will be matched with people volunteering their services or time. (Haider 2015)

A Shia woman helped her brother to deal with many issues after the death of their father:

> It was a great loss when my father departed suddenly but it did not cause any serious financial difficulty because we had other sources of income as well. But yes after that incident my family went through many problems. There were matters which needed much resolve and courage. It was difficult for my brother to look after everything. However I and my brother together handled the situation.

Another Shia girl, 12-year-old Mehzar Zehra, is an inspiration for Pakistani women. On 30 November 2012 her father, Syed Nazar Abbas, had just picked her up from school in Karachi when two takfiri Deobandi militants appeared on a motorbike and opened fire. Her father died on the spot while she was critically injured. The case was initially highlighted by the media, and Mehzar was likened to Malala Yousufzai because they were both young girls—the first going to school, the second returning—but then Mehzar's case gradually disappeared from the news (Tarar 2012).

When doctors first saw Mehzar, they patiently explained to her mother that her daughter would have to live on a ventilator—for life. Over the next 38 days she was rushed to the intensive care unit three times, switching on the ventilator and then switching it off, waiting for something to happen. Her condition was serious: a bullet had ruptured both of her lungs, another had damaged her spinal cord and yet another had skimmed past her wrist. She was still in shock.

Less than a year later, on 23 March 2013, Mehzar attended a martyrs conference in Karachi in a wheelchair. In her speech she addressed the takfiri Deobandi militants:

> You think you will stop us? No! My father was killed because he was a Shia Muslim but the ritual of mourning and chest beating [Muharram rituals] will never stop. We will never stop remembering Imam Hussain and his family. I am thankful to my nation for their prayers for my recovery and I demand from government to fulfil its promise and send me abroad for my further treatment so that I can walk again and serve my nation.

Because of her suffering, perseverance and stance on human rights, Mehzar is regarded as Pakistan's Anne Frank. Through her strong spirit she is an inspiration to many people.

Dozens of Sunni, Shia and others mothers of students who were killed in the Peshawar APS massacre by Deobandi militants on 16 December 2014 are struggling with such great loss. The majority of them, when shown in the media, demand justice from government. One mother complained:

> Why don't they hang the culprits in public so that the mothers of martyred children can see and feel relieved to some extent?

The incident shook the whole country. However, for the mothers of those children, the pain is neverending. One mother said:

> It's the pain which will only finish with my death

The parents formed a Shuhada (Martyrs) Foundation to support each other. They also demanded justice from the government and armed forces. Another parent of a slain student, Akhtar, formed an NGO in his name to help him feel better: "I started an NGO in his name in Swabi around February this year." Aiman Khan Shaheed APS Welfare Society will work on education, women's development, child labour, poverty, and sports welfare. My martyred son loved a sport, that's why I included sports in it." he explained. Akhtar says he wants Aiman's NGO to help vulnerable segments of society, spread knowledge and remove poverty (Qayyum 2015).

The interviews suggest that Ahmadi women face similar struggles when it comes to coping strategies. When a massacre of Ahmadis took place in Lahore in 2010, the Ahmadiyya community TV channel interviewed all 85 victim families. Some information was gathered from those interviews. Overall it seems that Ahmadi women, despite their grief, are resilient and express pride in their martyrs. A widow said:

> I feel proud of my husband as he is a martyr. I also feel very comfortable when I come to know that our *Hazoor* [Ahmadis' religious leader (*khalifa*)] is on our side and pray for us.

Another aged mother who lost her son said with tears in her eyes:

> Alhamdollillah [all praise to Allah], everyone knows how a mother feels on the death of her son but ... Alhamdollillah, Alhamdollillah.

DISCUSSION

This chapter examines the social and economic impact on the lives of women who are the victims of Deobandi militancy. It also discusses their coping strategies were also discussed. I used the intersectionality lens of gender and religious belief to provide a unique understanding of the issues faced by such women. For this purpose Shia Haraza, Shia (non-Hazara), Sunni Barelvi and Ahmadi women were interviewed. Also, secondary sources of data were used to retrieve relevant information. The chapter suggests that although all three faith groups (Shia, Sunni and Ahmadi) are a target for Deobandi militancy, their experiences differ based on their gender, faith and ethnicity.

The murder of a family member at the hands of terrorists is a painful experience for anyone. The data analysis reveals that Shia Hazara women face a great deal of psychological and social trauma compared with Sunni Barelvi and Ahmadi women. One reason for this is that the majority of those interviewed had lost more than one member of their families, and even then they are under constant threat from the Deobandi militants of LeJ. From Shia Hazara women's accounts, the feeling of helplessness is clear. The case of Shia (non-Hazara) women is similar but with less intensity. Their families are also under constant threat, which leads to psychological pressure. Ahmadi women are provided with not just social but financial support from their *Jamaat*. Non-Ahmadi communities, including neighbours (mainly Sunni Muslims), tend to discriminate against Ahmadis on the basis of their faith.

In terms of economic impact, Shia Hazara women are once again the most affected. Although losing a family's financial supporter could be difficult for any family, this is particularly hard for Shia Hazara women. One reason is that Hazaras are financially weak because they live in an economically deprived area (Quetta). Further, the male family members face continuous threats to their lives, so they are confined to a small area and unable to find appropriate means of employment. In fact, hundreds of male Shia Hazaras have been killed in recent years, thus complicating the social, emotional and economic suffering of the women. Increasingly, members of the Hazara community have been compelled to live a fearful existence of restricted movement that has created economic hardship and curtailed access to education. This oppressive situation has prompted large numbers of Hazara to flee Pakistan for refuge in other countries (HRW 2014). Women who lack a man in their family may find it further difficult to survive as a result of harsh economic conditions. Shia women also face financial issues and, because of the patriarchal society, find it difficult to do outside chores. An important point to consider is that regardless of their gender or faith, all affected women face similar economic issues. However in all three cases, social class and the number of surviving males with employment play an important role.

With the loss of a family member it is very difficult to carry on with day-to-day activities. However, life needs to go on for those who are left behind. The study's findings suggest that women affected by terrorism use different ways of resilience and agency as their coping strategies. Shia Hazara women are very visible when it comes to protest. Pakistan witnessed one of such protest by Shia Hazara women when they sat next to the dead bodies of their loved ones who had been killed in a suicide attack. Shia women also show their agency through different methods, such as social activism and writing articles for newspapers. Sunni Barelvi and Ahmadi women are not very vocal when it comes to protests, but there is some evidence of their involvement in NGOs, with the support of their male family members, especially among Sunni Barelvi women. Ahmadi women and men who are affected by terrorism follow the advice of their religious leader. The majority of women, especially mothers who have lost their sons, feel proud of being related to a martyr. This may reduce the pain of losing a loved one and help them to carry on with the life. Some Ahmadi women find peace from being affiliated spiritually to their religious leader, Mirza Masroor Ahmad. Shia women also use spirituality to cope with the painful situation that they face, remembering the great sacrifice of their third divine leader, Imam Hussain.

The interviews indicate that there is a lack of clarity about who is behind the attacks that have taken away women's loved ones. While most women referred to the Taliban, the LeJ and the SSP, the Sunni Barelvi women clearly referred to the Deobandi identity of militants. Interestingly, an Ahmadi woman said that she had heard the word "Deobandi" for the first time during the interviews. One reason for this lack of awareness is that Deobandi clerics and outfits generally present themselves as Sunni or Ahle Sunnat, which makes it hard for ordinary people to distinguish them from the majority of peaceful Sunni Barelvi and Sufi Muslims.

RECOMMENDATIONS AND CONCLUSION

The intersectionality lens is important when it comes to investigating the experiences of women affected by Deobandi militancy because their experiences differ based on their gender, ethnicity, class and faith. The stories and incidents presented here offer a brief account of the complex and challenging experiences and suffering of women of victim communities in Pakistan. Based on semistructured interviews, the chapter documents women's experiences as victims of violence and highlights their coping strategies. It maps out the social and economic impacts on, and the coping strategies of, women with multiple dimensions: gender, faith, ethnicity and social class. Policy-makers and institutions such as government, NGOs and the security forces need to have an understanding of the complexity of these issues based on intersectionality, especially in the case of woman-headed households.

Based on this study the following recommendations are offered. First, it is important that gender-, faith- and class-aware approaches are used in compensation policies and packages that are offered by the federal and provincial governments to those who are directly or indirectly affected by terrorism. As gender plays a determining role in people's ability to access education, employment, healthcare and other opportunities, gender-specific approaches are the only way to provide equal opportunities to reintegrate them into society.

Second, development policies and programmes ought to have a clear gender focus. It is important that special efforts are made to include women's voices and concerns in all national and community-level decision-making processes in the reconstruction of conflict areas. Women-focused programmes and projects should also be initiated. However, these should be transformative in nature and should be able to move beyond addressing women's immediate needs to bring a long-lasting structural change so as to transform gender relations.

Finally, since Deobandi militancy has resulted in a high mortality rate among men and left many women as widows, female-led households need special attention. Government should also consider providing suitable training and employment opportunities to these women to alleviate their economic hardship.

Appendix: Semistructured Interview Protocol

1. Demographic information: Faith, sect, age, gender, marital status, number of children and ages (if any), relationship with victim, qualification, employment status, social class (upper, upper-middle class, lower-middle class, poor), city of residence?

2. Explanation of personal loss: What was your relationship to the victim? How and when did you lose them? What happened?
3. Economic consequences: Did you lose a breadwinner from your house? How are you coping with the financial constraints?
4. Emotional consequences: How did this loss affect you emotionally?
5. Societal role in terms of support: Do you get financial and emotional support from other family members, friends and neighbours or community groups?
6. Government/NGOs' role in terms of support: Do you receive any financial support from government or NGOs?
7. Coping strategies: How are you dealing with this loss?
8. How do you see the future for you, your children and your family?
9. Were the perpetrators of the violence brought to justice?
10. To what extent are you satisfied with the government's efforts to apprehend and punish the perpetrators?
11. What can the government and security agencies do to stop militancy and terrorism?

REFERENCES

Ahmad, U. (2015). Remember the Ahmadis of Lahore, remember the forgotten. *Dawn News*.http://www.dawn.com/news/1184975/remember-the-ahmadis-of-lahore-remember-the-forgotten. Accessed on 30 May.

Ahmad, S., Hayat, M., Ahmed, S., & Sajid, I. M. (2014). Gender differences in depression among the affectees of war on terrorism and the role of psychological interventions in the rehabilitation. *Pakistan Journal of Criminology, 6*(2), 95–112.

Ali, F. (2013). A multi-level perspective on equal employment opportunity for women in Pakistan. *Equality Diversity and Inclusion, 32*(3), 289–309.

Ali, F., & Knox, A. (2008). Pakistan's commitment to equal employment opportunity for women: A toothless tiger? *International Journal of Employment Studies, 16*, 39–58.

Ali, F., & Kramar, R. (2015). An exploratory study of sexual harassment in Pakistani organisations. *Asia Pacific Journal of Management, 32*(1), 229–249.

Arendt, H. (1998). *The human condition*. Chicago: Chicago University Press (Orig. pub. 1958).

Bailey, G. (2014). The power of Malala. *International Social Work, 57*(1), 75.

Brah, A., & Phoenix, A. (2013). Ain't IA Woman? Revisiting Intersectionality. *Journal of International Women's Studies, 5*(3), 75–86.

Bari, F. (2010). *Gendered perceptions and impact of terrorism/talibanization in Pakistan.* Islamabad: Henrich Boll Stiftung.

BBC News. (2013). Hell on Earth: Inside Quetta's Hazara community by Muin Azhar. http://www.bbc.co.uk/news/world-asia-22248500. Accessed on 22 May 2015.

BBC News. (2015). Pakistan gunmen kill 45 on Karachi Ismaili Shia bus. http://www.bbc.co.uk/news/world-asia-32717321. Accessed on 15 May 2015.

Collins, P. H. (2015). Intersectionality's definitional Dilemmas. *Annual Review of Sociology.* doi:10.1146/annurev-soc-073014-112142.

Crenshaw, K. (1989). Demarginalizing the intersection of race and sex: A black feminist critique of antidiscrimination doctrine, feminist theory and antiracist politics. *The University of Chicago Legal Forum, 140,* 139–167.

Crenshaw, K. W. (1991). Mapping the margins: Intersectionality, identity politics, and violence against women of color. *Stanford Law Review, 43*(6), 1241–1299.

Ferdoos, A. (2005). *Social status of urban and non-urban working women in Pakistan: A comparative study.* Unpublished PhD thesis, University of Osnabrueck, Osnabrueck.

Haider, F.A. (2015). The grief directory, published in *The News.* Available at: http://www.thenews.com.pk/Todays-News-9-293745-The-grief-directory

HRW (Human Rights Watch) Report. (2014). We are the walking dead: Killings of Shia Hazara in Balochistan, Pakistan. Available at: https://www.hrw.org/sites/default/files/reports/pakistan0614_ForUplaod.pdf

Jawaid, I., Haneef, K., & Pooja, B. (2014). Women, the victim of modern forms of terrorism: An introspection. *International Journal of Interdisciplinary and Multidisciplinary Studies, 1*(5), 49–59.

Knudsen, S. (2006). Intersectionality: A theoretical inspiration in the analysis of minority cultures and identities in textbooks. In E. Bruillard, M. Horsley, B. Aamotsbakken (Eds.), *Caught in the web or lost in the textbook* (pp. 61–76), 8th IARTEM conference on learning and educational media, held in Caen in October 2005. Utrecht: IARTEM.

Liebling-Kalifani, H., Marshall, A., Ojiambo-Ochieng, R., & Kakembo, N. M. (2007). Experiences of women war-torture survivors in Uganda: Implications for health and human rights. *Journal of International Women's Studies, 8*(4), 1–17.

Moaveni, A. (2015, November 22). ISIS women and enforcers in Syria recount collaboration, anguish and escape. *The New York Times,* Available at: http://www.nytimes.com/2015/11/22/world/middleeast/isis-wives-and-enforcers-in-syria-recount-collaboration-anguish-and-escape.html

Niarchos, C. N. (1995). Women, war, and rape: Challenges facing the international tribunal for the former Yugoslavia. *Human Rights Quarterly, 17*(4), 649–690.

Parent, M. C., DeBlaere, C., & Moradi, B. (2013). Approaches to research on intersectionality: Perspectives on gender, LGBT, and racial/ethnic identities. *Sex Roles*, 68(11–12), 639–645.

Phoenix, A., & Pattynama, P. (2006). Intersectionality. *European Journal of Women's Studies, 13*(3), 187–192.

Prins, B. (2006). Narrative accounts of origins: A blind spot in the intersectional approach? *European Journal of Women's Studies, 13*(3), 277–290.

Qayyum, M. (2015). #Neverforget: The wedding bells that will never ring. *Express Tribune*. Available at: http://tribune.com.pk/story/880914/neverforget-the-wedding-bells-that-will-never-rin

Staunæs, D. (2003). Where have all the subjects gone? Bringing together the concepts of intersectionality and subjectification. *NORA: Nordic Journal of Women's Studies*, 11(2), 101–110.

Syed, J., Ali, F., & Winstanley, D. (2005). In pursuit of modesty: Contextual emotional labour and the dilemma for working women in Islamic societies. *International Journal of Work, Organisation and Emotion, 1*(2), 150–167.

Tarar, T. (2012). That little girl. *The Daily Times*. Available at: http://archives.dailytimes.com.pk/editorial/09-Dec-2012/view-that-little-girl-mehr-tarar

Thacker, P. (2014). Pakistan's Hazara: 'It's like living in jail'. *Aljazeera News*. Available at: http://www.aljazeera.com/humanrights/2014/12/pakistan-hazara-it-like-living-jail-2014123114655754509.html

USCIRF (US Commission on International Religious Freedom). (2015). Annual report, Washington, DC: USCIRF. Available at: http://www.uscirf.gov/sites/default/files/USCIRF%20Annual%20Report%202015%20%282%29.pdf

Zahidi, F. (2012). Hazara Shias lose all hope in Pakistan. *International Herald Tribune*. Available at: http://tribune.com.pk/story/486883/a-story-of-the-others-hazara-shias-lose-all-hope-in-pakistan/

CHAPTER 7

Marked by the Cross: The Persecution of Christians in Pakistan

Edwina Pio and Jawad Syed

INTRODUCTION

A focus on freedom of religion is evident in a speech by Pakistan's founder Muhammad Ali Jinnah in 1947. He said, "You are free; free to go to your temples, you are free to go to your mosques or to any other places of worship in this state of Pakistan. You may belong to any religion or caste or creed that has nothing to do with the business of state" (cited in Syed 2008a, p. 109). In an interview in 1948, Jinnah further clarified:

> Minorities to whichever community they may belong will be safeguarded. Their religion or faith or belief will be secure. There will be no interference of any kind with their freedom of worship. They will have their protection with regard to their religion, faith, their life, their culture. They will be, in all respects, the citizens of Pakistan without any distinction of caste or creed." (cited in Cowasjee 2000, para. 7)

However, over the last few decades, Pakistan has consistently been placed in the top ten countries for violating minority rights (Minority

E. Pio (✉)
Auckland University of Technology, Auckland, New Zealand

J. Syed
University of Huddersfield, Huddersfield, UK

© The Editor(s) (if applicable) and The Author(s) 2016
J. Syed et al. (eds.), *Faith-Based Violence and Deobandi Militancy in Pakistan*, DOI 10.1057/978-1-349-94966-3_7

Rights Group International 2010). Discrimination takes place against a background of religious extremism, often state-sanctioned Jihadist discourse, a legal code which has blasphemy laws and powerful figures remaining silent on issues of persecution and violence. Furthermore, there is active dissemination of negative stereotypes of minorities, and religious clerics tend to foment fundamentalist thinking and action, often resulting in mob violence against minorities (Dilawri et al. 2014; Syed 2008b). These acts of violence, hate speech and discrimination are indicators of issues in many layers of society, and they pertain to human rights and governance (Dilawri et al. 2014). Reports from various human rights organizations, such as United Nations Human Rights High Commissioner, HRW, Amnesty International, Freedom House, Asian Human Rights Commission, Minority Rights International and the US State Department, confirm that, particularly since the mid-1990s, minorities are being persecuted in Pakistan (Open Doors World Watch List 2015; Raina 2014). Minority communities in Pakistan, such as the Ahmadis, Christians and Hindus, are just 0.22, 1.59 and 1.60 percent of the total population, respectively (based on the 1998 census), yet the number of people being victimized is proportionately huge and suggests targeted, rather than random, events (Raina 2014). In theory, Christians are allowed to attend church services and to practice their religion, except for evangelization and proselytization pertaining to the conversion of Muslims (Gregory 2012), but the reality paints a different picture.

This chapter will focus on Christians in Pakistan, who are trapped between their religious faith and Islamic extremism, and are the victims of persecution. Mob violence resulting in injury and death, burning and killing of individuals, shooting during church services, rape, sexual abuse, kidnapping and forced conversion are some of the atrocities experienced by Christians in current-day Pakistan.

While census figures indicate approximately 2.8 million Christians in Pakistan, or 1.59 per cent of the total population of 174 million, these have been contested and various sources suggest that the number could be up to 6 million (Ballard 2012; BBC 2013; Gregory 2012; Home Office 2015; Malik 2002; Raina 2014; Sookhdeo 2002; World Bank 2014). The majority of Christians are in Punjab, though there are also large populations in Sindh, Islamabad and KPK. For example, there are 54 villages in Punjab and 4 in Sindh where the majority of the population consists of Christian communities. The cities of

Karachi, Lahore and Faisalabad are home to many Christians. There are an equal number of Catholics and Protestants among the Christians of Pakistan, and there are approximately 500 churches across the country. The Church of Pakistan is the largest Protestant community, uniting four churches: the Anglican, Methodist, Presbyterian and Lutheran churches. Other Protestant churches include the United Presbyterian Church and the Salvation Army. Moreover, evangelical churches, such as Baptists, Seventh-Day Adventists, Full Gospel Assemblies Church and the Pentecostal Church exist in Pakistan. There are also a number of smaller churches and offshoots. The Catholic Church has had a long local history, and its superior organization and outreach makes it a very influential Christian institution in Pakistan (Raina 2014). While the majority of Christians in Pakistan experience poverty as their daily fare, there are a few in Pakistan's politicomilitary elite and urban middle class for whom the experience of discrimination can be brushed off, in contrast with the Christian majority. In fact the Government of Pakistan, in its effort to show that it does not persecute Christians, has pointed out the Christian presence in the ruling elite and higher ranks of the armed forces (Gabriel 2008). Yet despite this effort, many Christians with professional qualifications are seeking to flee the country and live overseas (Ballard 2012) because the rhetoric many not match the reality.

However, it is important to acknowledge that Islamic teachings are not monolithic, so interpretations of Islam differ, ranging from mystical traditions, moderate views, peaceful views, and extremist views and actions (Malik 2008). Additionally, many of the poor in urban and rural areas in Pakistan tend to experience powerlessness, insecurity, bondage and intimidation, and many religious minorities, including Christians, fall into this category of the poor (Gregory 2012; Zaidi 1988). Therefore poverty and powerlessness are important considerations when exploring the persecution of Christians in Pakistan, as also is the fact that not all Christians in Pakistan fall into the lower socioeconomic strata. The Zardari–Gilani government (2008–2013) sought to revitalize the Ministry of Minorities, introducing a package of measures to promote minority welfare, and in 2009 it appointed Shahbaz Bhatti, a prominent Christian human rights activist, as Pakistan's federal minister for minority affairs and raised this post to cabinet level. However, Bhatti was assassinated as a result of his attempts to modify the blasphemy laws.

DEEP ROOTS

Christians have deep roots in Pakistan. For example, elite Christians from Goa have been in Karachi for more than a century. In this cosmopolitan city, symbols of Christianity are evident, such as St. Patrick's Cathedral, Holy Trinity Cathedral, St. Andrew's Church, St. Anthony's Church and the Seventh Day Adventist Hospital. A number of these magnificent buildings hark back to the British era when Pakistan was part of India (Dawn 2010a). Other indicators of Christianity include schools (e.g., Saint Joseph College), hospitals and health facilities (e.g., the Holy Family Hospital and the Mary Adelaide Leprosy Centre). One can also find smaller symbols of Christianity, such as a crucifix hanging from the rear-view mirror of a taxi or rickshaw, religious stickers plastered on the back of a school van, or a cross on small, ordinary buildings, which are churches in the poorer sections of Karachi in Esa Nagri in Gulshan-i-Iqbal and Pahar Ganj in North Nazimabad. Many of the Karachi's elite schools were established by Christian missionaries, and, over many decades, their students have reached top professional positions in Pakistan and so garner a great deal of respect among the general Pakistani populace (Gregory 2012; Hephaestus Books 2011). Karachi's Christian community consists of Goan Christians, many of whom reside in Saddar around St. Patrick's and are generally in the upper echelons of society, and Punjabi Christians, who are generally on the lower rungs of the socioeconomic scale. In other parts of Pakistan there exist educational institutions, such as Kinnaird College for women, and Forman Christian College, both in Lahore (Ballard 2012). Missionary-supported hospitals can still be found in many of Pakistan's major cities, where they provide excellent medical services, and the Christian schools are a passport for the children of the elite to gain admission to foreign universities, so these institutions are protected (Ballard 2012).

Before British rule in Punjab, the jurisdiction of the previous ruler, Maharaja Ranjit Singh, was plurireligious, with Muslims, Sikhs and Hindus living in harmony, though the maharaja himself was a Sikh (Ballard 2012). The western area of Punjab subsequently became Pakistan. However, harmony was undermined owing to various political factions which utilized religion as a platform, and some authors believe that the present-day situation in Pakistan regarding anti-Christian sentiment is more a matter of politics rather than a theological shift (O'Keefe 1998). With the arrival of the British in the late nineteenth century, many arid regions of Punjab were made arable via a canal network, and Capuchin friars established agricultural settlements for the newly converted Christians (Walbridge 2003). In this century, Christians continue to be concentrated around these so-called canal colonies in Lahore, Multan and Sargodha (Walbridge 2003). Thus Christians in Pakistan have come to live there as a result of various historical events (Neil 1970), and they may in fact have had a longer presence in the country than some of the Muslims who crossed over to during Partition (O'Brien 2006).

Portuguese and Armenian traders are recorded in Lahore from 1606, and they are the first recorded Christians in Punjab (Raina 2014). Goan Christians who were Catholics moved from the Portuguese Estado da India to Karachi during the time of the British, and they have Portuguese names, such as Cornelius, Misquita, Fonseca, Pereira and Mascarenhas. In 1862, St. Joseph's Convent school was built in Saddar; in 1878, St. Patrick's cathedral was built there too; and the Goa-Portuguese Association was established in 1886 and changed its name to the Karachi Goan Association in 1936. Many of the Goan Christians form the elite among the Christians and they are a prosperous minority (Khan 2012; Rodrigues 2013; Zaidi 1988, 2011). For example, Manuel Misquita was one of Karachi's first elected mayors after the formation of Pakistan; Frank D'souza set up Pakistan's railway system in 1947 upon Jinnah's request; Toilentine Fonseca is generally credited for the musical score of Pakistan's national anthem; Brigadier Mervyn Cardoza was decorated with the Tamgha-e-Khidmat, as also was Blasé Mascarenhas, who retired as Intelligence Bureau Deputy Director; Sydney Pereira was head of the Atomic Energy Commission; and Jack Britto and Rony Gardner were both Olympic hockey players. Pakistan's first non-Muslim, and certainly most respected, Chief Justice of the Supreme Court was Justice A.R. Cornelius. Julius Salik is a famous Pakistani Christian and activist for minority rights. In 1996 he founded the World Minorities Alliance to advocate for the social status of minorities. That same year he was nominated by Prime Minister Benazir Bhutto for the Nobel Peace Prize. Saleem Raza, S.B. John, A. Nayyer and Benjamin Sisters are all famous singers belonging to the Christian community.

The vast majority of Pakistani Christians are converts from the lowest castes within the Hindu caste system (Raina 2014). They work as cleaners, caretakers and sweepers. The Hindi-Urdu term *chuhra* in old Hindustani dictionaries refers to a scavenger, the lowest caste or a village servant, disposing of excrement and trash, and removing animal corpses left on the roadsides—jobs which would pollute the upper castes. During Partition, some of these low castes who had converted to Christianity took refuge in the Christian areas of cities such as Lahore to escape Hindu-dominated India (Ballard 2012; Pinault 2008; Walbridge 2003). They were employed as leather workers and sweepers, plus many worked as agricultural labourers, and were they were considered impure and regarded as untouchables. In 1873, American Presbyterians converted these lower castes—Chuhras—believing that they would be better off without the caste system. Other lower castes, such as the Chamars, Jhiwars and Malis, followed suit and converted to Christianity (Raina 2014). These historical antecedents have resulted in Christians in general being referred to by the insulting term *musalli*, which means immoral, low caste and polluted (Ballard 2012). Unfortunately, conversion did not change their social status and they continue to be vulnerable to exploitation, violence, eviction and forced conversion to Islam (Walbridge 2003).

Another point to consider in the position of Christians in Pakistan is the Islamic or Arabic notion of *dhimmi*. This refers to the unbeliever who pays the jizyah tax and accepts lower status in an Islamic society/state for the privilege of living in there and following their own religion. Their status is generally that of a second-class citizen, with restricted freedoms. These could include inequalities with regard to taxes and penal law, and refusal of their testimony by Muslim courts. Dhimmi also means that the individual accepts subjugation and that they are allowed to reside in a Muslim country, despite the fact that they are unbelievers.

The notion of dhimmi, coupled with the stigma of lower castes and the amendments to Sections 295 and 298 of the Pakistan Penal Code, has rendered Pakistan's religious minorities substantially more vulnerable to persecution and violence, along with the fact that those who perpetuate such violence are rarely brought to appropriate justice (Ballard 2012). In recent decades, while organized and systematic violence by radical Deobandi militant outfits has been witnessed against Sunni Barelvi and Sufi Muslims, as well as Shia Muslims, the situation of Pakistan's minority Christian community is no better. As constant victims of persecution, allegations of blasphemy, violence, forced conversions, insults and discrimination, Christians also face problems in getting decent employment and, as a result, they often end up getting a job which is lower than their education status, something that further impedes their progress in life. Stereotypically, working as a sweeper or janitor is considered to be a trademark profession for Pakistani Christians. With few opportunities in employment or for economic prosperity, and frequent attacks on their lives and property, their lives in general have not improved, which reduces their self-esteem and exacerbates their identity crisis. It is not uncommon to see ordinary Muslims expressing contempt for their Christian employees, colleagues or neighbours. Some Christians face blatant faith-based discrimination, such as being denied a home to rent just because of their faith.

ISLAMIC EXTREMISM AND CHRISTIANS

Despite the fact that Pakistan's 1973 national Constitution ensures full rights of all communities as equal citizens, there are certain blatantly faith-discriminatory provisions, such as the fact that the Constitution does not allow any non-Muslim to be president or prime minister of the country. Article 41 states, "A person shall not be qualified for election as President unless he is a Muslim of not less than 45 years of age and is qualified to be elected as member of the National Assembly." Article 91 stipulates a Muslim-faith requirement for the prime minister (NA 2012). Moreover, in many instances, members of parliament and other public bodies, including non-Muslims, are required to swear allegiance to Islamic ideology, the foundation stone of Pakistan, as a part of their oath. In addition, non-Muslims are barred from being judges in the Federal Shariat Court, which has the power to strike down any law that is deemed un-Islamic.

Curricula and textbooks in Pakistan tend to promote perspectives that reinforce negative stereotypes and thus encourage prejudice and discrimination, in particular towards religious minorities, as well as towards the West (Nayyar and Salim 2005). Christians are disadvantaged in university admissions because they do not know the Qur'an by heart (Ballard 2012). Religiously motivated violence is endemic and the perpetrators are rarely brought to justice. Fabricated charges, torture and beatings are common (Open Doors World Watch List 2015; USCIRF 2013).

Muhammad Ali Jinnah, the founder and first leader of independent Pakistan, had a vision of a mainly Muslim identity for Pakistan, but which also protected minorities through equal treatment (Ballard 2012). The first Constitution of Pakistan, adopted in March 1956 (almost a decade after the country's birth) designated the country as an Islamic republic. Pakistan has ratified international conventions linked to freedom of religion and belief, such as the elimination of all forms of racial discrimination in 1965; a convention against torture and other cruel, inhuman or degrading treatment or punishment in 1984; and a convention on the rights of the child in 1989. In his first speech to the new nation on the very day of independence, the country's new Governor General, Mohammed Ali Jinnah, nailed his colours very firmly to the mast of secularism when he argued that "You may belong to any religion or caste or creed ...". His presidential address outlined a vision of a state where "religion or caste or creed ... has nothing to do with the business of the State", where "no matter to what community he belongs, no matter what relations he had with you in the past, no matter what is his colour, caste or creed, he is first, second and last a citizen of this State with equal rights, privileges and obligation ...", and where "we are all citizens and equal citizens of one State" (Jinnah 1948). Yet conditional citizenship, not equality, was to be the fate of minority communities in Pakistan (Raina 2014).

In 1973 the democratic government of the PPP, under the leadership of Prime Minister Zulfikar Ali Bhutto, ceded extensive political territory to the Islamists, accommodating many of their demands, while crushing secular and nationalist parties. Bhutto banned alcohol, moved the weekly holiday from Sunday (associated with Christianity by the Islamists) to Friday and had the Constitution redrafted to reaffirm Pakistan's identity as an Islamic republic (Bari 2009).

After Bhutto, Pakistan's military dictator, General Muhammad Zia-ul-Haq's (in power 1977–1988) politics opened the doors of the state more widely to Islam and began the introduction of sharia elements in governance and the law (Gregory 2012). Zia's introduction of strict sharia punishments for blasphemy offences in Articles 295 and 298 of the Pakistan Penal Code is most often deemed to be responsible for the persecution of religious minorities (Raina 2014). Pakistan's blasphemy law includes Section 295-B (offence: defiling etc. of a copy of the Holy Qur'an; maximum punishment is a life term, and the accused can be arrested without a warrant); Section 295-C (offence: whoever defiles the sacred name of the Holy Prophet Muhammad shall be punished with death, or imprisonment for life, and shall also be liable to a fine; mandatory death penalty). Such laws help to foment religious intolerance and extreme violence in their invocation, and blasphemy accusations are frequently directed at religious minorities. They are also used to settle personal scores and land disputes. Simply debating the blasphemy laws is considered to be blasphemy.

The PPC has its origins in British colonial rule and was enshrined in Pakistan's three constitutions (1956, 1962 and 1973). The 1973 Constitution, widely considered to be the most liberal, contains certain provisions for religious minorities, a number of which clearly have as their intent the provision of safeguards them. Sharia benches were introduced into Pakistan's High Courts from 1979 to rule on whether any existing law or provision of the law was "repugnant to Islam", and to amend any laws found to be so. This became a powerful mechanism for amending the 1973 Constitution, and for eroding the checks and balances within the PPC. In 1979, General Zia introduced the Islamic Hudood Ordinances, which imposed penalties for offences against the "boundaries" set by God in the Qur'an, such as drinking alcohol, taking drugs, theft and sexual crimes (Ballard 2012; Gregory 2012; Khan 2012).

General Zia-ul-Haq's regime's amendments placed special emphasis on the promotion of a puritanical and intolerant form of Deobandi/Salafi Islam; called for harsher punishments for offences against Islam; and required trials under Section 295 to be presided over by a Muslim judge. Changes were made to the blasphemy laws in the PPC (Section 295), in 1982 adding Section 295–B, which provides for mandatory life imprisonment for desecrating the Qur'an; amending Section 295C (1986), imposing the death penalty, or a life sentence, on anyone who "by words, either spoken or written, or by visible representation, or by any imputation, innuendo, or insinuation, directly or indirectly, defiles the sacred name of the Prophet Muhammad. The blasphemy law is a handy instrument that is often abused to settle land disputes or to curtail the freedom of religion, thoughts and beliefs (Khan and Rafi 2014). Many Christians have found themselves accused of blasphemy or Hudood crimes on the basis of nothing more than the say-so of one or more Muslim accusers, and charges are often fabricated (Blood 2009). Allegations of blasphemy can be applied on the thinnest of grounds; even a rumour of blasphemy can lead to the complete destruction of a whole community (Walbridge 2003).

General Pervez Musharraf (in power 1999–2007) set out a political and social agenda which initially appeared to be moderate in its outlook and intentions for Pakistan. As part of this, he stated unequivocally that in Pakistan, "minorities enjoy full rights and protection as equal citizens in the letter and spirit of true Islam" . Musharraf tried to amend the way the blasphemy law was implemented, as well as to ensure that senior police officers were obliged to investigate allegations of blasphemy to see if they could be substantiated before the alleged blasphemer(s) were arrested and charged (Gregory 2012). However, he was unsuccessful because there was pressure from Islamic groups and religious lobbies, and the forces set in motion by the former dictator, General Zia-ul-Haq (Ballard 2012).

Promoting Hate

Christians in Pakistan are not required to pay the jizya, and in theory are allowed to practise their religion, yet they have attracted hate, as evidenced by various discriminatory practices, as well as killings and constant persecution in their homes and places of worship. The constitutional and legal position makes Christians de facto unequal under the law, an inequality which includes Christian testimony being entirely excluded from some courts at the discretion of the judges, their testimony being granted less weight than Muslim testimony and, in practice, penalties for convicted Christians being more severe than those for Muslims for an equivalent crime. Hate is also facilitated by the blasphemy laws, the Hudood Ordinances and the Qanoon-e-Shahadat (law of evidence). Instances of persecution may be based on hearsay, the word of one or more persons and the fact that there are personal grievances, including issues of land, women and labour. Furthermore, blasphemy accusations are not investigated in detail, the victims of persecution are often killed in jail, police intervention is often non-existent and the law is flouted (Ballard 2012).

Terrorist and militant groups, typically of Deobandi origins, are becoming increasingly violent, as shown by incidents such as the bombing of the Marriott Hotel in Islamabad in September 2008, the attacks on the Sri Lankan cricket team in Lahore in March 2009, the attack on the police headquarters in Lahore in May 2009, the assault on the Pakistan Army's General Headquarters in October 2009, and another on the Pakistan naval base at Mehran in Karachi in May 2011 (Gregory 2012). Deobandi and Salafi (or Ahle Hadith) madrassas churn out violence through their jihadist and intolerant teachings, and this is perpetrated not only in Pakistan but also across its borders (Gregory 2012). Neofundamentalist Deobandi militant groups, such as the SSP, the LeJ, the JeM and, more recently, the TTP, target local Christian communities (Gregory 2012)

The UN Commission for Human Rights and Amnesty International figures for 2000–2007 suggest that, for reasons of faith, between 30 and 50 Christians are subjected to violent death in Pakistan each year and two to three times that number suffer serious injury. Beyond that, many hundreds are falsely imprisoned, and many thousands are subjected to serious physical abuse, intimidation and threat at the hands both of some of the majority Muslim communities and of elements of the state and local authorities, indicating widespread violence against Christians across the length and breadth of Pakistan. Christians also bear the brunt of anti-Western sentiment in the world of Islam. They find that their churches are locked up and inaccessible, or have been burnt or demolished, and there are bureaucratic delays, corruption and opposition involved in the maintenance and construction of churches (Catholic News Agency 2012). In some instances, Christian families have to flee their homes due to threats from Islamic militants that they must convert to Islam or face dire consequences (Khan and Rafi 2014). Radical Sunni groups have also exploited the situation of the PPC and police inefficiencies, using trials for religious offences to rally their call for more members for their cause (Ballard 2012).

Specific examples of persecution over the years are detailed below

In 1993, Salamat Masih, 11, Manzoor Masih, 38, and Rehmat Masih, 44, were accused of writing blasphemous remarks on a wall belonging to a mosque. In 1994, Manzoor Masih was killed outside the District and Sessions Court after exiting a hearing. Salamat Masih and Rehmat Masih were injured but survived. In 1995, Salamat Masih, 14, and Rehmat Masih, 46, received the death penalty. However, at a higher judicial review, Lahore High Court acquitted them, given that the accused were not familiar with Arabic. The bench included Justice Arif Iqbal Hussain Bhatti and Justice Chaudhry Khurshid Ahmad. (Justice Arif Iqbal Hussain Bhatti was later assassinated in 1997 in his chambers at Lahore High Court.)

In 1997, widespread riots took place in Shantinagar, following accusations of blasphemy against a Christian, during which a Christian village and 14 churches were burnt down (Walbridge 2003).

In 1998, Ayub Masih was sentenced to death for allegedly making blasphemous remarks. He was accused by a neighbour of stating that he supported the controversial British writer Salman Rushdie, author of *The Satanic Verses*. However, the Lahore High Court suspended his sentencing. His lawyer was able to prove that the accuser had used the conviction to force Masih's family off their land and then acquire control of the property. The case received international attention after Bishop John Joseph committed suicide on 6 May in front of parishioners at the court house in protest of the death penalty handed to Ayub Masih.

In 2000, Younus Shaikh, a physician, was charged with blasphemy on account of remarks that students claimed that he made during a lecture. A judge ordered that Shaikh should pay a fine of Rs 100,000 and that he be hanged. Shaikh was later acquitted by the court and fled Pakistan for asylum in Europe.

In 2003, Samuel Masih, a Christian, was accused of defiling a mosque by spitting on its wall. While in prison, he contracted tuberculosis and was transported to hospital. While in police custody he was killed by a police officer, who claimed that it was his duty as a Muslim to kill Masih.

In 2005 a number of Christian churches and schools in the city of Faisalabad were destroyed when Muslim preachers urged the people to "take revenge" after a Christian allegedly burnt pages of the Qur'an. It was reported that hundreds of Christians were forced to flee the town as a crowd thousands strong, wielding axes and sticks, set fire to five churches, a dozen houses, three schools, a dispensary, a convent and two parsonages. The incident took place just as the English cricket team were touring Pakistan and preparing to play a test match in Faisalabad.

In 2006 a Pakistani Christian named Shahid Masih was arrested and jailed for allegedly committing blasphemy. In 2006, two Christian men were sentenced to 10 years in prison for allegedly burning pages from the Qur'an. The allegation apparently arose from a dispute over land. They were subsequently acquitted by the High Court.

In 2009, members of the SSP torched Christian homes and killed Christians in the Gojra and Korian areas of Punjab. The reason for the violence was that a Christian had allegedly defiled a copy of the Qur'an. In 2010 the Lahore High Court ordered the release of Zaibun Nisa, a woman who was jailed in 1996 on a charge of blasphemy (having allegedly defiled a copy of the Quran) because of the lack of evidence (*Dawn* 2010b).

In a high-profile case registered in 2009, Aasia Bibi, a Christian woman, was accused of blasphemy. She was sentenced to death in 2010 but her case is pending confirmation by the Supreme Court. She is the first Christian woman to be sentenced to death by hanging on a charge of blasphemy. The case has sparked international reactions (*Dawn* 2010b; Guerin 2010). It was taken up by Salmaan Taseer, then Punjab governor, and then Shahbaz Bhatti (a Christian), federal minister for minorities, both of whom were killed in 2011 in targeted attacks for supporting Asia and recommending amendments to the blasphemy law (Hashim 2014). In an article in *The Guardian* published in the aftermath of Shabaz Bhatti's assassination, Peter Preston wrote:

> Now here's one especially dismal thing among many others, because it tests principle as well as feeble political resolve. Shahbaz Bhatti, Islamabad's minister for minorities, is assassinated outside his home by four assailants who

leave Taliban tracts behind them. Bhatti was a Christian, speaking out for an increasingly oppressed minority and ceaselessly advocating the repeal of Pakistan's blasphemy laws. So the Christian peasant farm-worker and mother of four, Aasia Bibi, whose case crystallises the whole sorry debacle, remains in prison and in fear for her life (Preston 2011).

Walsh (2011) wrote in *The Guradian* about his visit to Rawalpindi, where he saw a giant poster over the windows of a house, depicting a heroic warrior on a gallant white steed. The warrior was Malik Mumtaz Hussain, alias Qadri, the police bodyguard who gunned down the Punjab governor Salmaan Taseer, and this was his house. Malik Mumtaz was an elite force commando and there was a note on his file that he should be removed from VIP security duty on the day when the killing occurred, but his commando colleagues of the Punjab police silently stood by as he pumped 26 bullets into his target (Ballard 2012). A few days before Taseer's murder, Ibad Dogar, a senior political leader of the ruling Pakistan Muslim League-Nawaz (PML-N) and an ex-leader of the banned Deobandi terror outfit, the SSP/ASWJ, had announced a Rs 20 million bounty to assassinate Taseer for siding with an alleged blasphemy-accused Christian woman, Aasia Bibi. Apparently all Islamic clerics refused to lead Taseer's funeral, apart from a Sunni Barelvi cleric, Maulana Afzal Chishti, who stepped up. Few government officials attended (Gregory 2012).

In ominous developments, Karachi Christian churches were sprayed with pro-Taliban graffiti, and through 2010 and 2011, Taliban militants thought to be from within Karachi's Pashtun community carried out violent attacks on Christian communities in the city, killing at least eight Christians and injuring many others (Gregory 2012).

In 2012, Rimsha Masih, a Christian girl, reportedly 11 or 14 years old, and an illiterate with mental disabilities (Downs syndrome), was accused of blasphemy for burning pages from a book containing Qur'anic verses. The allegation came from a Muslim cleric who has subsequently been accused by the police of framing the girl. The girl, and later the cleric, were both arrested and released on bail.

In 2013, in the Toba Tek Singh area of Punjab province, a Christian youth, Sajjad Masih, was sentenced to life imprisonment and fined Rs 2 million. According to the prosecution, he had sent mobile phone messages insulting Muslim religious personalities. This blasphemy case, involving phone messages, is the first of its kind in Pakistan (*ICN* 2013).

In 2013, Boota Masih was killed in Karachi on the charge of blasphemy (*PCP* 2013).

In November 2014, a Christian couple, Sajjad and his wife Shama Masih, were accused of desecrating the Qur'an. They were beaten and then burnt to death in Kot Radhakishan, a village near Lahore (Hashim 2014). The victims were poor brick-kiln workers who were burnt alive in the presence of hundreds of Muslim onlookers, including helpless policemen (Jillani 2015).

In addition to the abovementioned cases of alleged blasphemy, there is evidence of systematic violence against Pakistan's Christian minority.

On 28 October 2001, 18 Christains and a Muslim policeman were killed in St. Dominic's Roman Catholic Church in Bahawalpur by Deobandi militants suspected of being affiliated with JeM.

On 18 March 2002, 5 were killed and 41 injured in a church attack in Islamabad. The victims incuded a US diplomat's wife and daughter.

On 5 August 2002, LeJ militants attacked the Murre Christian School, killing six people.

On 9 August 2002, LeJ militants threw grenades into a chapel in the grounds of a Christian hospital in Taxila, killing 4, including 2 nurses and a paramedic, and wounding 25 men and women.

On 25 September 2002, gunmen shot dead six people at a Christian charity (Peace and Justice) in Karachi's central business district. They entered the third-floor offices of the Institute for Peace and Justice (IPJ) and shot their victims in the head. All of the victims were Pakistani Christians. Karachi police chief Tariq Jamil said that the victims had had their hands tied and their mouths covered with tape.

On 25 December 2002, two burqa-clad gunmen tossed a grenade into a Presbyterian church during a Christian sermon in Chianwala in East Pakistan, killing three girls.

In November 2005, 3,000 extremists attacked Christians in Sangla Hill in Pakistan and destroyed Roman Catholic, Salvation Army and United Presbyterian churches. The attack was sparked by allegations of the violation of blasphemy laws by a Pakistani Christian named Yousaf Masih.

In February 2006, churches and Christian schools were targeted in protests over the publication of the Jyllands-Posten cartoons in Denmark, leaving two elderly women injured and many homes and much property destroyed.

In August 2006, a church and Christian homes were attacked in a village outside Lahore in a land dispute. Three Christians were seriously injured and one was reported missing.

In July 2008 during a prayer service, a Muslim mob stormed a Protestant church on the outskirts of Karachi, denouncing the Christians as "infidels" and injuring several, including a pastor.

The 2009 Gojra riots were a series of violent pogroms against Christians by extremist Deobandi Muslims. On 31 July 2009, hundreds of fanatics belonging to the SSP attacked a Christian locality in Punjab's Gojra city and burnt alive eight members of a family, besides setting ablaze dozens of houses. Five of those killed were women and children, who could not run to save their lives when their house was attacked. The anti-Christian riots were triggered by reports of desecration of the Holy Qur'an by some Christians, which eventually proved false.

On 2 March 2011, Federal Minister for Minorities Affairs Shahbaz Bhatti, a Roman Catholic and an outspoken critic of the blasphemy law, was shot dead on a busy road in the federal capital, Islamabad. Responsibility for the assassination was placed with the Punjabi Taliban (LeJ). A pamphlet found where Batti was killed claimed that he had been assassinated because of his opposition to the blasphemy law. A few weeks earlier, Tahir Ashrafi, a controversial Deobandi cleric known for hateful remarks against Ahmadis and Shias, made a fiery public speech against him in which he threatened Bhatti with physical violence if he did not refrain from his opposition to the blasphemy law. Ashrafi also played a key role in the release of the LeJ terrorist Malik Ishaq from jail. A militant of LeJ, Abdullah Umar Abbasi, was later arrested by the police in connection with Bhatti's murder.

On 29 April 2011 at least 20 people, including police officials, were wounded as 500 Muslim demonstrators attacked the Christian community in Gujranwala city.

On 30 May 2011, Maulana Abdul Rauf Farooqi and other clerics of the JUI quoted "immoral Biblical stories" and demanded a governmental ban on the Bible. Maulana Farooqi said, "Our lawyers are preparing to ask the court to ban the book."

On 23 September 2012, a mob of protesters in Mardan, angry at the anti-Islamic film *Innocence of Muslims*, set on fire a church, St. Paul's high school, a library, a computer laboratory and the houses of four clergymen, including that of Bishop Peter Majeed.

On 12 October 2012, Ryan Stanton, a Christian boy of 16, went into hiding after being accused of blasphemy, and after his home in Karachi was ransacked by a crowd. Stanton stated that he had been framed because he had rebuffed pressures to convert to Islam.

On 3 December 2012, the Punjabi Taliban (an affiliate of the LeJ/SSP) killed Bargeeta Almby, a 72-year-old female Christian charity worker from Sweden, who was shot in the Model Town area of Lahore for allegedly backing two Christian priests who had been accused of committing blasphemy. Model Town is the same area from where Warren Weinstein, a 71-year-old Jewish American US Aid official, was abducted on 13 August 2011 by armed men, who later handed him over to the TTP (*The News* 2014).

On 9 March 2013, a violent mob forced 170 Christian families to flee the Joseph Colony Lahore, before setting ablaze dozens of houses over allegations that a Christian resident of the area had committed blasphemy.

On 22 September 2013, at least 80 Christians were killed and dozens injured in a suicide attack by the Taliban/LeJ at the historic All Saints Church in Peshawar.

On Sunday 15 March 2015, TTP/LeJ suicide bombers attacked two churches in Lahore. At least 16 Christians were killed and 75 people sustained severe injuries in twin blasts near Saint John Catholic Church and Christ Church in the Youhanabad area. Once again, a Deobandi militant outfit, an offshoot of the TTP, calling itself Jamatul Ahrar, admitted that it had carried out the attack.

FRAGMENTED FUTURES

While a country created in the name of Islam was bound to give preference to its Muslim citizens, the situation of Christians and other minority groups became particularly bad after the state patronage of the ultraorthodox Deobandi and Salafi Islam during the military rule of General Zia-ul-Haq (Syed 2008b). This, along with state's active deployment of jihadist groups and madrassas for strategic objectives in Afghanistan and Kashmir, has enabled faith-based intolerance and violence. Veteran Pakistani columnist Ayaz Amir (2014) notes that the Deobandi school of thought used to co-exist easily and without conflict with other denominations and sects of Islam in Pakistan. The occasional sectarian clash did occur, but it was rare. However, under the impact of the Afghan Jihad, in which Deobandi religious parties stood at the forefront, sectarianism and bigotry acquired harder edges, leading to the rise of faith-based violence. He asks: In this situation, what should the Christians of Pakistan do?. Given that the Pakistani state has shown its inability to protect them, should they as good Christians continue to turn the other cheek, as they have done since the country's birth, or should they resort to active resistance? Amir (2014) notes that the blasphemy law and its increasing misuse is no longer a question of the sanctity of religion or the honour of the Prophet. More than anything else it is a reflection of the growing weakness of the Pakistani state and its inability to fulfil its primary responsibility of protecting the life, honour and property of its citizens.

In the post-9/11 world, the threat of violence against Christian and other minorities as a result of blasphemy is real in Muslim-majority countries, particularly those states affected by the US-led War on Terror. The threat is often used as a justification for the law, especially in calls for certain groups to be prosecuted. Such a threat merely illustrates the destructive potential of the privileging of a certain point of view above others, and the dangers of imposing state sanctions against opinions (Ross 2012). Driven by religious and political motivations, as well as xenophobia, the "othering" and persecution of minorities is a sore issue in many societies. In multiethnic and multifaith societies, it is relevant to consider Kahn's (2005) problem with multiculturalism—that is, the fact that such societies are torn between two instincts: one is to protect basic human rights, which must be defined and may therefore reek of bias; and the other is to allow groups to say and do things which might be perceived as being fundamentally wrong.

There is also evidence of transnational "othering" and persecution of Christians in at least some Muslim majority countries in the aftermath of 9/11. In March 2015 it was reported that the Grand Mufti of Saudi Arabia was calling for the demolition of all churches in the Arabian Peninsula and other countries. The statement is particularly serious because of the influential status of the Grand Mufti over Sunni Muslims, particularly those of Salafi and Deobandi backgrounds. He is the chief religious authority of the Kingdom of Saudi Arabia, home to the two holiest mosques of Islam, appointed by the Saudi government. Thus his statement could be seen as a quasiformal policy of a government and its elites, who are known for funding the transnational jihadist networks, Deobandi and Salafi mosques and seminaries (Lucie-Smith 2015).

Peaceful protests, such as the human chain of both Christians and Muslims in Lahore around a church, two weeks after the massacre of the people in All Saints Church in September 2013, present a more harmonious picture of Pakistan (Shaukat 2013)—one that Christians and perhaps the majority of Pakistanis desire. In a similar gesture of interfaith harmony, Shia Muslims of Multan distributed Christmas gifts to more than 700 Christian families in December 2013 (Jafri 2013). The route to such harmony could be through engaging with civil society and security agencies, legal reform, defining what constitutes hate speech, addressing issues of forced conversion and marriages, ending bonded labour, facilitating interfaith dialogue, increasing awareness of minority issues with media representatives and law-enforcement agencies, and emphasis on the promotion of diversity and inclusion in schools and madrassas through curricula and textbooks.

In the context of greater protection of minorities, and since the focus of this chapter is on Christian minorities, it is pertinent to end with the story of Parvez Henry Gill, a Pakistani businessman in Karachi (Washington Post 2015). Gill says he was sleeping when God crashed into one of his dreams and gave him a job: find a way to protect Christians in Pakistan from violence and abuse. To actualize his dream he is building a 14-storey cross at the entrance to Karachi's largest Christian cemetery (Gora Qabristan Cemetery, which dates back to the British colonial era), towering over thousands of tombstones that are often vandalized. Gill says that he hopes it can convince the members of Pakistan's persecuted Christian minority that someday their lives will get better. The cross will be 42.67 metres tall and 12.8 metres wide. Gill says that it will be the largest in Asia.

Christians have been fleeing Pakistan in droves in recent years amid a wave of horrific attacks against them. Gill says that "every few weeks" he hears from Christians who plan to move out of Karachi because of threats. The signs of that abuse are obvious at the cemetery. Although thousands of headstones have been neatly aligned over the past 150 years, a settlement has encroached on the cemetery, covering dozens of graves. Its residents toss garbage into the graveyard, and crosses and statues are frequently desecrated. Gill hopes that the cross will encourage more Christians to remain in Pakistan, perhaps even achieving the same success that his family has found. Gill's 97-year-old father, Henry, owned wheat and cotton fields in Punjab. His family has a long history of generosity, including helping thousands of poor children pay for education and covering the costs of more than 100 eye operations for the blind.

The blasphemy law continues to haunt the lives of non-Muslim minorities, and particularly Christians, in Pakistan (Benjamin 2014). As el-Gaili (2004) notes, nations may not choose to protect their minorities, particularly if this means that their own powers are limited or regulated. Yet protection of the most vulnerable sections of a population should be what truly matters to society and to nations, and in the ultimate analysis to our fragile world.

REFERENCES

Amir, A. (2014, November 7). What should Pakistani Christians do? *The News.* Availableat:http://www.thenews.com.pk/Todays-News-9-282746-What-should-Pakistans-Christians-do

Ballard, R. (2012). *The Christians of Pakistan: A historical overview and an assessment of their current position.* Manchester: Centre for Applied South Asian Studies.

Bari, S. (2009, January 22). The state and status of women. *The News.*

BBC News. (2013, September 23). Who are Pakistan's Christians? *BBC News,* Available at: http://www.bbc.co.uk/news/world-asia-india-24201241

Benjamin, L. T. (2014). The life of a Christian in Pakistan. *GMA Blog.* Available at: http://gmablog.org/2014/10/12/the-life-of-a-christian-in-pakistan/

Blood, P. R. (2009). *Pakistan-U.S. relations* (Congressional Research Service). Washington, DC: Congressional Research Service.

Catholic News Agency. (2012, January 13). Bishop denounces government bulldozing of Pakistan church and school. *Catholic News Agency.*

Cowasjee, A. (2000, July 9). The sole statesman—4. *The Dawn.* Available at: http://www.dawn.com/news/1072307

Dawn. (2010a, December 26). The Christian contribution. *Dawn.* Availble at: http://www.dawn.com/news/593854/the-christian-contribution-2

Dawn. (2010b, December 8). High profile blasphemy cases in the last 63 years. *Dawn.*Availableat:http://www.dawn.com/news/589587/high-profile-blasphemy-cases-in-the-last-63-years

Dilawri, S., Salim, A., Saleem, M., & Ishfaw, H. (2014). *Searching for security: the rising marginalization of religious communities in Pakistan.* London: Minority Rights Group International.

el-Gaili, A. T. (2004). Federalism and the tyranny of religious majorities: Challenges to Islamic federalism in Sudan. *Harvard International Law Journal, 45*(2), 511–521.

Gabriel, T. (2008). *Christian citizens in an Islamic state: The Pakistan experience.* Aldershot, UK: Ashgate.

Gregory, S. (2012). Under the shadow of Islam: The plight of the Christian, minority in Pakistan. *Contemporary South Asia, 20*(2), 195–212.

Guerin, O. (2010). Pakistani Christian Asia Bibi 'has price on her head'. *BBC.* Available at: http://www.bbc.com/news/world-south-asia-11930849

Hashim, A. (2014, November 5). Pakistani Christian couple killed by mob. *Al Jazeera.* Available at: http://www.aljazeera.com/news/asia/2014/11/pakistani-christian-couple-killed-mob-2014115154959911691.html

Hephaestus Books. (2011). *Christian schools in Pakistan.* London: Hephaestus Books.

Home Office. (2015). *Country information and guidance—Pakistan: Christians and Christian converts.* London: Independent Advisory Group on Country Information (IAGCI).

ICN (Independent Catholic News). (2013, July 15). Pakistan: Christian sentenced to life imprisonment for 'blasphemous text'. *ICN*. Available at: http://www.indcatholicnews.com/news.php?viewStory=22951

Jafri, O. (2013, December 23). Is that Santa at the door? No, its the Shia community of Multan. *The Express Tribune*. Available at: http://tribune.com.pk/story/649581/is-that-santa-at-the-door-no-its-the-shia-community-of-multan/

Jillani, S. (2015, September 1). New cross symbolic for Pakistan's Christians. *BBC News*. Available at: http://www.bbc.co.uk/news/world-south-asia-33929859

Jinnah, M. A. (1948). *Quaid-i-Azam Mahomed Ali Jinnah: Speeches as Governor-general of Pakistan, 1947–48*. Karachi: Pakistan Publications.

Kahn, P. (2005). *Putting liberalism in its place*. Princeton: Princeton University Press.

Khan, S. (2012). The blasphemy laws: A Pakistani contradiction. Available at: http://www.wpsa.research.pdx.edu/meet/2012/khan.pdf

Khan, M. S., & Rafi, G. (2014). Religion, politics and the Christians of Pakistan: Is KPK a better option to live? *Middle-East Journal of Scientific Research, 21*(6), 975–983.

Lucie-Smith, A. (2015, March 19). Saudi Arabia's Grand Mufti wants churches destroyed – it's time for the West to rethink relations. *Catholic Herald*. Available at: http://www.catholicherald.co.uk/commentandblogs/2015/03/19/how-can-the-west-keep-up-good-relations-with-saudi-arabia-when-its-chief-religious-leader-wants-churches-destroyed/

Malik, I. H. (2002). *Religious minorities in Pakistan* (Vol. 6). London: Minority Rights Group International.

Malik, J. (2008). *Madrasas in South Asia. Teaching terror*. Oxon: Routledge.

Minority Rights Group International. (2010). *State of the world's minorities 2010*. London: Author. Available at: http://www.minorityrights.org/6138/state-of-the-worlds-minorities/stateof-the-worlds-minorities-2008.html

NA (National Assembly). (2012). The constitution of the Islamic Republic of Pakistan. Available at: http://www.na.gov.pk/uploads/documents/1333523681_951.pdf

Nayyar, A. H., & Salim, A. (2005). *The subtle subversion: The state of curricula and textbooks in Pakistan*. Islamabad: Sustainable Development Policy Institute.

Neil, S. (1970). *The story of the Christian church in India and Pakistan*. New York: Eerdman Press.

O'Brien, J. (2006). *The construction of Pakistani Christian identity*. Lahore: Research Society of Pakistan.

O'keefe, M. (1998, October 25). Violence, injustice keep Pakistan's Christians living in fear in Lawless society. Available at: www.rider.edu/files/CCM-Violence.pdf

Open Doors World Watch List. (2015). Christian persecution in Pakistan. Available at: http://www.opendoorsusa.org/christian-persecution/world-watch-list/pakistan

PCP (Pakistan Christian Post). (2013, September 17). A Christian killed by throat cutting in Pakistan on accusation of blasphemy. Available at: http://www.pakistanchristianpost.com/headlinenewsd.php?hnewsid=4482

Pinault, D. (2008). *Notes from the fortune-telling parrot: Islam and the struggle for religious pluralism in Pakistan*. London: Equinox.

Preston, P. (2011, March 2). Shahbaz Bhatti's assassination is a bleak counterpoint to Cairo. *The Guardian*.

Raina, A. K. (2014). Minorities and representation in a plural society: The case of the Christians of Pakistan, South Asia. *Journal of South Asian Studies, 37*(4), 684–699.

Rodrigues, M. (2013). Goans of Pakistan. http://www.goansofpakistan.org/milestone.htm

Ross, R. (2012). Blasphemy and the modern, "secular" state. *Appeal, 17*(3), 3–19.

Shaukat, A. (2013, October 6). Human chain formed to protect Christians during Lahore mass. *Express Tribune*. Available at: http://tribune.com.pk/story/614333/muslims-form-human-chain-to-protect-christians-during-lahore-mass

Sookhdeo, P. (2002). *A people betrayed: The impact of Islamization on the Christian community in Pakistan*. Fearn: Isaac Books.

Syed, J. (2008a). Pakistani model of diversity management: Rediscovering Jinnah's vision. *International Journal of Sociology and Social Policy, 28*(3/4), 100–113.

Syed, J. (2008b). The representation of cultural diversity in Urdu-language newspapers in Pakistan: A study of Jang and Nawaiwaqt. *South Asia: Journal of South Asian Studies, 31*(2), 317–347.

The News. (2014, November 8). Christians in Punjab keep on suffering heavily. *The News*. Available at: http://www.thenews.com.pk/Todays-News-2-282940-Christians-in-Punjab-keep-on-suffering-heavily

USCIRF (United States Commission on International Religious Freedom). (2013). Religious Freedom Report on Pakistan 2012–13. Full text of the report. Available at: http://www.uscirf.gov/sites/default/files/resources/2013%20USCIRF%20Annual%20Report%20(2).pdf

Walbridge, L. S. (2003). *The Christians of Pakistan: The Passion of Bishop John Joseph*. Oxon: Psychology Press.

Walsh, D. (2011, December 11). Pakistan: Bombs, spies and wild parties. *The Guardian*.

Washington Post. (2015, May 19). Pakistani business man Parvez Henry builds a hug bulletproof cross in Karachi. Available at: http://www.stuff.co.nz/world/middle-east/68658066/Pakistani-businessman-Parvez-Henry-Gill-builds-a-huge-bulletproof-cross-in-Karachi.

World Bank. (2014). Pakistan: Total population. *World Bank Country Data*. Available at: http://data.worldbank.org/country/pakistan

Zaidi, S. A. (1988). Religious minorities in Pakistan today. *Journal of Contemporary Asia, 18*(4), 444–457.

Zaidi, A. (2011). Christian sportsmen who represented Pakistan. *The News*. Available at: http://blogs.thenews.com.pk/blogs/2011/12/christian-sportsmen-who-represented-pakistan/

.

CHAPTER 8

Pakistan: A Conducive Setting for Islamist Violence Against Ahmadis

Fatima Z. Rahman

INTRODUCTION

Ahmadis, members belonging to the Islamic minority sect Ahmadiyya, continue to be subjected to ongoing persecution and violence in Pakistan. The campaign against Ahmadis led by Deobandi Islamist groups has a long history, dating back to Pakistan's independence. Violence against Ahmadis has been systematically occurring since the 1953 Lahore riots. At the time, the Deobandi Islamist group Majlis-i-Ahrar, along with the fundamentalist cleric Maududi and his Islamist party, the JI, instigated the torture and murder of thousands of Ahmadis, as well as the destruction of Ahmadi property in Punjab. Since then, Islamists have perpetrated acts of terrorism against the Ahmadi community, with one of the most recent massacres occurring in 2010 in Lahore.

Islamist groups inspired by Deobandi theology are largely responsible for perpetrating the violence against Ahmadis because they are against other religious minorities. However, the Deobandi Islamist groups are able to easily target the Ahmadis with exceptional force, compared with other minorities, because the state sanctions the persecution of Ahmadis, and the broader Pakistani public supports their oppression. The predominant attitude in

F.Z. Rahman (✉)
Department of Politics and Chair of Islamic World Studies,
Lake Forest College, Lake Forest, IL, USA

© The Editor(s) (if applicable) and The Author(s) 2016
J. Syed et al. (eds.), *Faith-Based Violence and Deobandi Militancy in Pakistan*, DOI 10.1057/978-1-349-94966-3_8

209

Pakistan towards Ahmadis is a strong intolerance because they are viewed as deviants who have apostatized from Islam. Unlike other religious minorities, Ahmadis are viewed as apostates, and apostasy according to most strands of Islam, including the Deobandi Muslim school of thought, is one of the gravest sins and crimes, punishable by death. In the case of Ahmadis, this apostate status is prescribed to them based largely on their reverence for the founder of the Ahmadiyya movement, Mirza Ghulam Ahmad. This reverence for Mirza Ghulam Ahmad is viewed by most Pakistanis as heretical. In this chapter I argue that Ahmadis are particularly easy and vulnerable targets of Islamist terrorism because of enabling conditions created by the state's sanctioning of persecution, as well as public opinion strongly prejudiced against Ahmadis.

I begin by discussing the theological beliefs of Ahmadis, which distinguish them from other Muslims. To understand the prevailing attitude in Pakistan towards Ahmadis, it is necessary to know the beliefs of the Ahmadi community because it is Pakistani society's intolerance of these beliefs that fuels its animosity towards them. Most Pakistanis view these beliefs as both heretical and blasphemous, creating a strong hostility towards the Ahmadi community. Next I look at the major Deobandi Islamist groups that are responsible for spreading anti-Ahmadi propaganda, inciting and committing systematic violence against the Ahmadi community. This section describes the Deobandi theology that the Islamist groups follow, which is an extremely austere and intolerant version of Sunni Islam. It also explains how the theology inspires Deobandi Islamist groups, as well as others influenced by it, to perpetrate violence against Ahmadis. In the next section I present one of the major enabling conditions for Islamist violence against Ahmadis: state-sponsored persecution. The laws in the Pakistani Constitution and the PPC are presented, as well as Pakistan's electoral policies that legalize the persecution of Ahmadis. The section that follows presents the second enabling condition: the public's prejudiced view of Ahmadis. I illustrate how the state panders to Pakistani society's intolerance of Ahmadis by creating laws and policies that discriminate against them. Then I discuss some of the worst acts of violence against Ahmadis, highlighting the primary role of Deobandi Islamists and the state's lack of political will to stop the terrorism. This is followed by a discussion of the media's role in perpetuating the violence. I conclude by arguing that the prospects for a reduction in violence against the Ahmadis are grim. Islamists will continue to terrorize Ahmadis in the future because the influential actors in the state and in society share the Islamists' intolerance of Ahmadis.

THE AHMADIYYA SECT: ESTABLISHMENT AND BELIEFS

The Ahmadis belong to the contemporary Islamic sect, the Ahmadiyya movement, which was founded in 1888 in the Indian subcontinent by Mirza Ghulam Ahmad. Ahmad established the movement in an effort to reform corrupted Islamic teachings by emphasizing the pluralistic, tolerant, and peaceful aspects of the Qur'an and Islam's founding (Ahmad 2007; Ali 1996; Faruqui 1983).

In addition to the recognition of Mirza Ghulam Ahmad, some of the theological beliefs of Ahmadis differ from those of other Muslims. In particular, Ahmadis interpret much of the Qur'an metaphorically: they reject all forms of violence in the name of religion, they reject deference to clerics, and they reject many of the laws of sharia that most Muslims view as sacrosanct (Rahman 2014, p. 409). It is the reverence given to Mirza Ghulam Ahmad as a prophet by the larger subcommunity of the Ahmadiyya sect, as well as theological differences, that cause most Muslims in Pakistan to view Ahmadis as deviant apostates and non-Muslim.

There are two subcommunities within the Ahmadiyya sect. The larger is the Ahmadiyya Muslim Community and the smaller is the Lahore Ahmadiyya Movement. Members of both communities are called Ahmadis, and both live throughout Pakistan. The Pakistani headquarters of both communities are in Punjab. The larger subcommunity in Pakistan has its center in Rabwah, while the smaller subcommunity has its largest population and headquarters in Lahore. Both groups share a strong reverence for their founder, Mirza Ghulam Ahmad; they reject any form of religiously motivated violence, including violent jihad; and they apply metaphor to interpreting parts of the Qur'an. The most striking difference between the subcommunities is the status each grants to Mirza Ghulam Ahmad. While members of the larger one view him as a non-law-bearing prophet, members of the other do not view him as a prophet (Ali 1994).

Official and accurate estimates of the Ahmadi population in Pakistan have been, and continue to be, difficult to obtain because of state persecution. Ahmadis are not permitted to identify as Muslim on the Pakistan census. As a result, government estimates are thought to be considerably lower than the actual number. Additionally, because of concerns about the security of their members, the Ahmadi communities in Pakistan have been hesitant to report figures. The number of Ahmadis in Pakistan is estimated to be roughly 600,000 (Rahman 2014), though there is considerable variation in estimates. The Lahore Ahmadiyya Movement is estimated to be a small proportion of the total Ahmadi population in Pakistan. An estimate of the size of the Lahore Ahmadiyya Community in Pakistan could not be obtained,[1] though the closest estimate of Lahore Ahmadis worldwide is about 30,000 members prior to 2008.

The state, Islamists, and the Pakistani public do not distinguish between the two groups. They view members of both subcommunities as residing "beyond the pale" of Islam and as a deviant, minority group. The state-sanctioned persecution codified in Pakistan's constitutional articles, sections of the PPC, and electoral policies applies to both subcommunities. The public's prejudice is also channeled towards both groups, as are attacks by Islamists.

DEOBANDI ISLAMIST GROUPS

Terrorism against Ahmadis is carried out largely by a number of Deobandi Islamist organizations. While Islamist groups of other Islamic strands, such as Barelvi and Shia, have also been involved in, or at least supported, the persecution of and militancy against Ahmadis, the most dominant Islamist actors responsible for terrorism against Ahmadis have and continue to be Deobandi Islamists. While Deobandi groups have different leaders and exhibit some nuanced variations in their political objectives, they share a similar totalitarian worldview and fundamental theological beliefs. Among the most notable Islamist groups responsible for terrorism against Ahmadis, both historically and today, are Majlis-e Tahaffuz-e Khatm-e Nabuwwat, Majlis-i-Ahrar, the SSP, and, more recently, the TTP and the LeJ.

These groups have carried out attacks against Ahmadis throughout Pakistan. By executing their assaults in different parts of the country, they collectively terrorize Ahmadis in every province. The oldest of these groups is Majlis-i-Ahrar, which goes back to 1929, before the creation of an independent Pakistan. It was formed in Lahore, and after Pakistan declared its independence the organization's raison d'etre became the persecution of the Ahmadiyya community. Focusing all its efforts against the Ahmadis, it began an aggressive public. It was the first organization that publically campaigned for the persecution of Ahmadis in Pakistan, and it was responsible for the first episode of sectarian violence in Pakistan (Saeed 2012, p. 202; Haqqani 2006, p. 77). Like Majlis-i-Ahrar, Majlis-e Tahaffuz-e Khatm-e Nabuwwat is also an old organization with the primary purpose of eliminating the Ahmadi sect. Though headquartered in and a product of Pakistan, the organization has branches all over the world which propagate anti-Ahmadi sentiment and foment violence against Ahmadis. The organization is connected to many other radical Deboandi groups which are also responsible for systematic violence against Ahmadis, including the SSP (Reetz 2008). The SSP is a Punjab-based terrorist organization, formed in 1985. It was established by a Deobandi cleric, Maulana Haq Nawaz Jhangvi (Ahmar 2005, p. 7). It is responsible for publishing the monthly magazine *Paighame Khatme Nubuwwat*.

The two newest Deobandi Islamist organizations, which are responsible for some of the most recent and brutal acts of terror are the LeJ and the TTP. The LeJ was formed in 1996 and is a splinter group of the SSP. It operates out of the Punjab, though its attacks are carried out across the country. It has a strong following in the rural areas of the Punjab (Haqqani 2006, p. 83). It also has a branch that focuses on attacks in the FATA. The TTP is the newest of the Deobandi militant groups, targeting Ahmadis. Established in 2002, it is headquartered in the northwest region of Pakistan: the FATA. Its close affiliate Tehrik-e-Taliban Punjab operates out of Punjab. The TTP and its Punjab affiliate both organize and carry out terrorist attacks primarily within the borders of Pakistan.

THE DEOBANDI THEOLOGY AND ITS IMPLICATIONS FOR AHMADIS

All of these Deobandi groups have a heightened sense of superiority regarding their belief system. They resolutely believe that there is only one correct version of Islam, which is their extremist theological belief system. The Deobandi theology holds that all other Muslims have a corrupted interpretation of Islam and that non-Muslim religious minorities are kafir (non-believers). According to their belief system, both groups should be killed. Their hyperconservative thinking not only renders a complete intolerance of non-Deobandi Muslims but also is oppressive of women. Deobandi groups espouse an intolerant and extreme interpretation of sharia and seek to establish a Sunni caliphate. Deobandi groups also maintain animosity towards the West, its ideologies and its principles.

In many ways the Deobandi theology has a very similar worldview to that of Wahhabism. The major theological difference between the two strands of Islam is that Wahhabism subscribes to the Hanbali school of Islamic thought, while Deobandi follows a very rigid interpretation of the Hanafi school of Islamic thought. However, in terms of the practice of religion, political objectives, and the interpretation of the Qur'an and the ahadith, Wahhabism and Deobandi Islam share many traits. Similar to Wahhabism, the Deobandi ideology pares down religion to what it perceives to be its core beliefs and practices, ridding it of pre-Islamic and local cultural customs and norms. Like Wahhabism, Deobandi Islam subscribes to a very literalist and black-and-white view of the world. The ideology divides the world into two conceptual categories: *Dar al-Islam*, which is translated as the abode of Islam, and *Dar al-harb*, which is translated as the abode of war. The abode of Islam refers to Muslims, narrowly defined by Deobandis, as those adhering to the tenets of Deobandi Islam. The abode of war refers to all non-Muslims, including apostates. According to Deobandi thought, those belonging to the abode of war are the enemies of Islam. It is the duty of those who are part of the abode of Islam to increase the number of Muslims and reduce the number of those belonging to the abode of war by converting non-believers and killing apostates.

The underlying theology that Deobandis adhere to is intolerant of all religious minorities. However, Ahmadis are particularly targeted because unlike other religious minorities or non-believers, they fall into a separate category—that of apostates. According to Deobandi Islamists, Ahmadis are the most reprehensible minority group because their founder, Mirza Ghulam Ahmad, based on his teachings, digressed from the religion of Islam and created what Deobandis believe to be a separate religion. According to the rigid interpretation of the Hanafi variant of sharia that Deobandi Islam subscribes to, the punishment for apostasy is death. Though sharia holds the state, not any type of societal or vigilante group responsible for implementing the punishment, Islamist groups have interpreted the law to extend the responsibility of implementation to non-state actors, such as themselves.

The theological belief which inspires these groups to kill Ahmadis is takfir, which is the practice of declaring a self-identified Muslim as an apostate and then subsequently killing them on the basis of that declaration. These groups render Ahmadis as *wajib-ul-qatl*, or "worthy of death" based on Ahmadis' heterodox theological beliefs. They characterize and encourage the killing of members of the Ahmadi community as a religious duty, incumbent on all Muslims (Hashim 2014). The non-conventional views of Ahmadis are characterized by Deobandi Islamists and clerics as blasphemous and insulting to Islam. Alongside their own direct terrorist attacks on Ahmadis, these Islamist groups spread anti-Ahmadi propaganda and instigate riots. They incite the public to kill Ahmadis, encouraging martyrdom.

In addition to the theological beliefs of Ahmadis, a secondary reason that Deobandi groups cite to justify their targeting of them is the Ahmadi community's pro-West views. The Deobandi theology's belief in a jihad against the West is at odds with the Ahmadi community's commitment to co-existence with other faiths and an unqualified rejection of violence. The Ahmadi community's favorable view of the West is often cited by Islamists as a reason to attack them. Ahmadis have a long tradition of holding a positive attitude towards the West, in part because the religious freedom provided in the West is in consonance with their worldview. The Ahmadi community's founder, Mirza Ghulam Ahmad, spoke favorably about the religious freedom and rule of law provided by the British government and subsequently exhibited great respect for British rule (Ahmad 2007, p. 928). Ahmad specifically rejected the notion of a violent jihad against the British government, which was contrary to the Deobandi notion of jihad against Western powers. Unlike some other immigrant Muslim communities in the West, the Ahmadi community has a history of assimilating in their new homelands, participating both in the politics and the civil society of these countries. For example, the Ahmadi community in the USA formed a bipartisan congressional caucus to focus on alleviating the issues of religious freedom and the violation of human rights globally (Drake 2014). Islamist groups and clerics criticize this type of political and civic participation by Ahmadis abroad, along with their history of positive relations with the West, accusing them of disloyalty and treason. This criticism is part of the smear campaign they wage against the Ahmadi community in order to incite violence.

The influence of Deobandi theology and the empowerment of Deobandi Islamist groups today is largely due to the state support and backing they received during the authoritarian regime of the dictator General Muhammad Zia-ul-Haq. Zia, a follower of the Deobandi school of thought, surrounded himself with Deobandi clerics when in power. He appointed mostly Deobandi members to the Council of Islamic Ideology, which was a central advisory board that influenced his Islamization policies, including those targeting Ahmadis (Rahman 2014, p. 418). Though the legalized state persecution of Ahmadis originated during the previous regime under Zulfikar Ali Bhutto, it proliferated under Zia. Since that time, Deobandi groups have not retreated from politics and the public sphere; in fact, they continue to garner increasing influence in Pakistani society.

STATE-ENDORSED PERSECUTION OF AHMADIS:
ENABLING ISLAMIST TERRORISM

Although Islamist groups target religious minorities other than Ahmadis as well, they are able to carry out frequent attacks against Ahmadis without retribution because the state and the Pakistani public share their anti-Ahmadi sentiment. This widespread discrimination by the state and the public is not present against any other religious minority group to the degree that it is for Ahmadis. Ahmadis are the only religious minority whose religious persecution is officially sanctioned by the state.

Clauses 3(a) and 3(b) of Article 260 of the Pakistani Constitution classify Ahmadis as non-Muslim.[2] Thus, the excommunication of Ahmadis from Islam, which is the primary theological justification for killing them, is sanctioned by the state. Members of the TTP and the LeJ, as well as those of other Deobandi Islamist groups, find validation in their acts because of the legalized status of Ahmadis as non-Muslim.

The state goes beyond the declaration of Ahmadis as apostates by criminalizing their practice of religion. Sections 298-B and 298-C of the PPC forbid Ahmadis from referring to their place of worship as a *masjid* (mosque), reciting the call to prayer (azzan), and referring to themselves as Muslims. Violation of these bans is met with fines and prison sentences.

298-B. Misuse of epithets, descriptions and titles, etc., reserved for certain holy personages or places:

1. Any person of the Quadiani group or the Lahori group (who call themselves "Ahmadis" or by any other name) who by words, either spoken or written, or by visible representation,

    (a) refers to, or addresses, any person, other than a Caliph or companion of the Holy Prophet Muhammad (peace be upon him), as "Ameer-ul-Mumineen", "Khalifatul-Mumineen", "Khalifatul-Muslimeen", "Sahaabi" or "Razi Allah Anho";
    (b) refers to, or addresses, any person, other than a wife of the Holy Prophet Muhammad (peace be upon him), as "Ummul-Mumineen";
    (c) refers to, or addresses, any person, other than a member of the family "Ahle-bait" of the Holy Prophet Muhammad (peace be upon him), as "Ahle-bait"; or
    (d) refers to, or names, or calls, his place of worship as "Masjid"; shall be punished with imprisonment of either description for a term which may extend to three years, and shall also be liable to fine.

2. Any person of the Quadiani group or Lahori group (who call themselves "Ahmadis" or by any other name) who by words, either spoken or written, or by visible representation refers to the mode or form of call to prayers followed by his faith as "Azan", or recites Azan as used by the Muslims, shall be punished with imprisonment of either description for a term which may extend to three years, and shall also be liable to fine.

298-C. Person of Quadiani group, etc., calling himself a Muslim or preaching or propagating his faith:

> Any person of the Quadiani group or the Lahori group (who call themselves "Ahmadis" or by any other name) who, directly or indirectly, poses himself as a Muslim, or calls, or refers to, his faith as Islam, or preaches or propagates his faith, or invites others to accept his faith, by words, either spoken or written, or by visible representations, or in any manner whatsoever outrages the religious feelings of Muslims shall be punished with imprisonment of either description for a term which may extend to three years and shall also be liable to fine.[3]

This state-sponsored oppression of Ahmadis fosters a conducive environment for Islamists to target them. In addition to these particular aspects of the PPC, which explicitly discriminates against Ahmadis, there are other sections as blasphemy laws which are used to discriminate against religious minorities in general but that target Ahmadis most notably.[4]

The severity of Pakistan's persecution of Ahmadis is highlighted by the consistently high scores it receives on religious persecution indices. Pew's Government Restrictions Index scores Pakistan in the top echelon of states with restrictions on religious freedom (Pew 2014). One of the primary sources used by Pew is the US Department of State's annual reports on international religious freedom which stress, in particular, the Government of Pakistan's discriminatory treatment of Ahmadis (US State Department 2014). The legalized persecution of Ahmadis, which is codified in the Pakistani Constitution and the PPC, is not limited to de jure status. The compendium of persecutory laws, those explicitly referring to Ahmadis and the general blasphemy sections of the PPC, are implemented especially against the Ahmadis (State Department 2013). It is this de jure and de facto discrimination, particularly against the Ahmadis, which eliminates any deterrent that might deter Islamists from terrorizing Ahmadis because they can do so without fear of state retribution.

STATE DISENFRANCHISEMENT OF AHMADIS

In addition to these legalized forms of religious persecution, the state also restricts the Ahmadi community's basic political right to vote by adopting electoral laws which amount to practical disenfranchisement of the Ahmadi community. The disenfranchisement policy was adopted in 1985 when Zia mandated a separate electorate for religious minorities, as part of his Islamization of Pakistan. Prior to the separate electoral system, Pakistan had a joint electoral system in which all Pakistani citizens, regardless of their religion, could choose from all eligible candidates running in an election. In the joint electoral system, the religion of the voter and candidate did not matter (Khan 2013). The separate electoral system adopted by Zia created a separate electoral register for minorities. This meant that at the time of voter registration, voters were required to declare their religious affiliation and were given a ballot accordingly. Religious minorities, including Ahmadis, were restricted to voting for candidates from their own religious community. Only 5 percent of National Assembly seats were reserved for all of the minorities, collectively.

This separate electoral system was discriminatory towards all minorities and prevented them from voting for district candidates running in the general election (Farooq 2013). However, the system marginalized Ahmadis in particular because the policy necessitated that in order for Ahmadis to vote, they had to declare themselves as non-Muslim, a notion that they fully reject.

In 2002, Pervez Musharraf reformed the system for all minorities except for Ahmadis. While other minority groups can now vote and run as candidates in the general election alongside Muslim candidates, Ahmadis are still part of a separate electoral register. They have the same two no-win options available to them as they had in the original separate electorate adopted in 1985. To vote as a Muslim and choose from the list of all of the district's candidates, they must renounce their Ahmadiyya affiliation by signing a statement that Mirza Ghulam Ahmad was a false prophet. The other option is to self-declare as non-Muslim and vote in a separate ballot, which is exclusively created for Ahmadis (Younus 2013). Like the state's adoption of the other forms of religious persecution, this policy relegates the Ahmadi community's status to that of second-class citizens. If the state, which is a protector of its citizens, can abuse a segment of its population, then Islamist groups feel entitled to do the same.

ANTI-AHMADI PUBLIC SENTIMENT:
ENABLING ISLAMIST TERRORISM

The Pakistani public's view of Ahmadis is in alignment with the subjugated status granted to the community by the state. The lack of sympathy for Ahmadis enables terrorists to target them without the consequence of a public backlash that could lead to demands on the state to hold the terrorists accountable. There was virtually no public outcry after the 2010 Lahore massacre, and protest attendance by non-Ahmadis was nominal throughout the country (Walsh 2010). The public's lack of concern was reflected in the media. There was effectively no sympathy or compassion expressed for the minority group by media organizations, public figures or analysts invited on news programs. Without the restraint of accountability on either the public or the media, Islamists are able to freely carry out violence against Ahmadis.

The Pakistani public's sanctioning of violence against the Ahmadi community can be best understood if the public's attitude towards Ahmadis and their views about religion are examined in conjunction. According to Pew's public opinion polls, two out of three Pakistanis polled view Ahmadis as non-Muslim, and only 7 percent view Ahmadis as Muslim (Sahgal 2013). Given that Ahmadis self-identify as Muslim, the predominant view of the public suggests that a widespread and deep-seated religious intolerance and narrowmindedness exist in Pakistani society. While these statistics regarding the public's views suggest a strong prejudice against the Ahmadi community, the public's consent to Islamist groups' violence against Ahmadis is corroborated by its views about Islamic law and apostasy.

Public opinion studies indicate that the Pakistani public has a strong attachment to sharia and support for the hudud (penal laws) which prescribe severe corporal punishments. A resounding 88 percent of polled Pakistanis support "making Sharia the official law in their country" (Pew 2013, p. 15). Since the dictatorial regime of Zia, the variant of sharia adopted by the state and implemented in Pakistan is an extreme orthodox version that is followed by Deobandis. Given that Pakistan has already made sharia the law of the land, this statistic suggests support for the existing legal framework. A similarly large majority also support religious courts (Pew 2013, p. 19).

Perhaps most telling is the Pakistani public's views about the hudud. These laws prescribe fixed punishments for particular crimes.

According to sharia, these crimes are considered to be the gravest in Islam and carry severe, corporal punishments. The notable crimes governed by the hudud include theft and robbery, premarital sex, adultery, homosexual relations, alcohol consumption, and apostasy. Among the Pakistanis who support sharia as the law of the land, all of them also support the corporal punishments that it prescribes (Pew 2013, p. 52). Given the Pakistani public's belief that Ahmadis are non-Muslim and their resounding support for sharia, in particular the corporal punishments for crimes such as apostasy, it becomes evident that there will not be a public outcry in response to the attacks carried out by Islamist groups. It is evident that the public at a minimum implicitly supports the Islamists' terrorist activities against the Ahmadi community.

Pakistani society's intolerance of Ahmadis is further captured by Pew's Social Hostilities Index. The index measures religious abuse of and violence against minorities by both societal groups, such as Islamist groups, and as the broader public (Pew 2014). Of all countries, Pakistan has the highest score or, in other words, the highest level of persecution and violence against religious minorities perpetrated by Islamist groups and other individuals in society. Given the public's strong anti-Ahmadi sentiment, the state lacks the incentive to reform the discriminatory laws against Ahmadis. In fact, pandering to anti-Ahmadi sentiment has been a common source of political legitimacy used by state officials throughout Pakistan's history (Rahman 2014). The next section will illustrate how political leaders have adopted each of the state's anti-Ahmadi laws as a strategy to gain the approval of Islamists and the public by responding to their demands for state discrimination against Ahmadis.

Origins of the State's Legalization of Ahmadi Persecution: Pandering to Anti-Ahmadi Sentiment

The adoption of each of the anti-Ahmadi laws, both the constitutional amendments and the PPC sections, was the result of the state capitalizing on the public and Islamists' intolerance of Ahmadis. Passage of the second amendment to the Constitution declaring Ahmadis as non-Muslim occurred under Zulfikar Ali Bhutto in 1974. Though democratically elected, Ali Bhutto was facing a decline in his political legitimacy owing to a number of unpopular political moves. He failed to fulfill his campaign promise of economic development (Rashid 1985, p. 89; Khan 1985, p. 223). Additionally, he marginalized Pakistan's democratic institutions by replacing democratic provincial governments with federal authority (Khan 1985, p. 89). He also promoted one-party rule over which he maintained exclusive power (Eltayeb 2001, p. 74; Noman 1988; Waseem 1989). Facing a severe decline in political legitimacy, Bhutto capitalized on the public's and Islamists' aversion to Ahmadis, and forced the passage of the second amendment to the Constitution. From the perspective of the state, the change officially expelled Ahmadis from Islam by declaring them non-Muslim.

At the time of the adoption, the Pakistan National Alliance, which comprised largely Islamist forces, was running an aggressive anti-Ahmadi campaign. In their usual fashion, the Islamists were organizing large protests and rallies across the country, vocalizing their animosity toward Ahmadis (Haider 2010; Saeed 2007). Pakistan was littered with anti-Ahmadi posters, which prompted the killing of some. There was also widespread public pressure on the Bhutto government to declare Ahmadis as non-Muslim, with notable support from unions and student organizations (Saeed 2012). In this sociopolitical environment, Bhutto pressured the National Assembly to pass the constitutional amendment, marking the adoption of the state's first codified policy of persecution against Ahmadis.

The adoption of the other two anti-Ahmadi laws, which were added to the PPC, were decreed by the authoritarian dictator Zia, who was a strong champion of Deobandi theology. Needing some type of political legitimacy to justify his authoritarian rule, Zia chose Islam-based legitimacy with a strong Deobandi leaning. He Islamized the country, most notably by adopting the extremist version of sharia supported by Deobandi theology. In alignment with Deobandi theology, he adopted the entire compendium of laws, including the penal laws that prescribe severe corporal punishments. In addition to the adoption and implementation of sharia, he greatly expanded the number of Deobandi madrassas, providing them with state funding (Hiro 2012, p. 162). This promoted the spread of Deobandi theology throughout the country and planted the seeds of future generations of Deobandi followers who would continue to carry out attacks against Ahmadis.

In 1984, seven years into his dictatorship, Zia proceeded to issue Ordinance XX, which incorporated the anti-Ahmadi penal laws that incapacitated the ability of Ahmadis to practice their faith. This was a popular strategy because, at the time, Islamist groups were running a vocal anti-Ahmadi campaign and inflaming the public's negative feelings towards the Ahmadi community. The laws were issued by Zia in a time of similar societal unrest that characterized the mass anti-Ahmadi rallies, in which Bhutto forced the passage of the constitutional amendment declaring Ahmadis as kafir.

The strength that societal actors have to influence the state to adopt anti-Ahmadi policies is present today. The exclusion of the Ahmadi community from Musharraf's electoral reforms in 2002 was in response to pressure from Islamists. Musharraf's original reform plan to shift Pakistan's separate electoral system to a joint one incorporated all minorities, including Ahmadis. This was due largely to international pressure from the USA, which petitioned Musharraf to stop the persecution of the Ahmadi community (Younus 2013). However, this pressure was unable to counter the domestic pressure from Islamists who publically criticized the reform plan and questioned Musharraf's political legitimacy. The vocal criticism by Islamists resulted in Musharraf amending the reform to exclude Ahmadis from the joint electoral system. Ahmadis are the only religious minority today who have a separate electoral register.

SYSTEMATIC VIOLENCE AGAINST AHMADIS: AS OLD AS PAKISTAN

Ahmadis have been the victims of violence by Islamist groups since the formation of Pakistan. Some of the earliest experiences of societal persecution began in the early 1950s when the Deobandi group Majls-i-Ahrar, along with members of the JI led by Maududi, began to organize publically and call for both state and societal oppression of Ahmadis. As an organization, the Majlis-i-Ahrar's main objective was the elimination of Ahmadis (Punjab Disturbances Court of Inquiry 1954, p. 12). Both organizations began an active campaign against the Ahmadis with the Majlis-i-Ahrar taking the lead.

Together, both groups led anti-Ahmadi public gatherings such as rallies, street protests, and public sermons. During these gatherings, they demanded the removal of Ahmadis from government positions. This included most notably the Foreign Minister of Pakistan at that time, Muhammad Zafarullah Khan. They also demanded that the state pass discriminatory legislation, marginalizing the Ahmadi community. The groups were successful in mobilizing large crowds, inciting them to act violently against Ahmadis by using vicious and disparaging rhetoric to characterize Mirza Ghulam Ahmad and his followers (Punjab Disturbances Court of Inquiry 1954). During the gatherings, Majlis-i-Ahrar strategically chose to use the most insulting characterizations in Islamic theology to describe the founder of the Ahmadis in order to stir emotions and provoke a religiously conservative Pakistani public to attack Ahmadis. For example, they accused Mirza Ghulam Ahmad of being the dajjal or the "false messiah", which is one of the most loathed characters in Islamic theology. They falsely accused him of committing immoral acts (Punjab Disturbances Court of Inquiry 1954, p. 15) which are viewed as grave sins in Islam. They also defamed him by intentionally misquoting his writings (Saeed 2012). The groups were successful in achieving their aims: their incitement led to widespread atrocities against the Ahmadi community in Punjab, which became known as the 1953 Punjab Disturbances.

Worsening Violence Against Ahmadis and an Absence of Political Will

The early history of violence against Ahmadis set the stage for a continuation and worsening of violence. Since the state's adoption of the anti-Ahmadi penal laws under Zia's regime in 1984, at least an estimated 245 Ahmadis have been killed and an additional 205 physically attacked in violence led by societal groups alone (Hashim 2014). Because of the public's view of Ahmadis, any hardline move against Islamists runs the risk of being perceived as support for the Ahmadi community, which is a liability for elected officials.

The violence perpetrated by followers of Deobandi ideology can be classified into two categories: mass terrorist attacks on Ahmadi mosques, and targeting individual Ahmadis and families, usually outside in public.

Among the attacks on Ahmadi mosques were the October 2000 attacks in Sialkot and Sargodha, when at least ten Ahmadis were shot dead while praying. In 2005, in Mandi Bahauddin Punjab, worshippers in an Ahmadi mosque were gunned down, with eight being killed and another twenty injured. Worshippers in an Ahmadi mosque in Mardan KPK were killed and injured when a suicide bomber detonated his bomb in September 2010.

The worst terrorist attack against Ahmadis, in terms of both scale and sheer brutality, occurred in 2010 in Punjab, which is home to some of the most prominent Deobandi Islamist groups. The 2010 Lahore massacre refers to the coordinated attacks on two Ahmadi mosques. They were carried out by members of the Punjabi Taliban, which is an affiliate of the TTP and has overlapping membership with other Deobandi groups, most notably the LeJ. The Islamist attackers entered two Ahmadi mosques during Friday prayers, launching grenades and firing guns indiscriminately. One of the attacks was carried out at an Ahmadi mosque in the upmarket neighborhood of Model Town, and the second was on an Ahmadi mosque in the older area of Garhi Shahu (Ahmed 2010). The Taliban perpetrators killed close to 100 Ahmadis and severely wounded more than 100 other Ahmadi worshippers in the mosques.

The state's negligence before the 2010 Lahore massacre and the reaction afterwards illustrates the reluctance of the state to vocally condemn and punish Islamist perpetrators of violence against Ahmadis. Prior to the 2010 Lahore massacre, human rights organizations petitioned the regional government to assist the Ahmadi community with security because of an increase in Deobandi Islamist groups' threats and incitement. However, elected officials intentionally dismissed the reports and did not provide any security because of a concern about a backlash from the groups and their supporters (HRW 2012). The same fear of a backlash by the Islamists and the public, which inhibited the state from preventing the attacks in the first place, dictated their behavior after the attacks as well. Even regional elected officials did not visit the attacked sites, nor did they show any dismay in public (Walsh 2010). A month after the attacks, Prime Minister Nawaz Sharif called Ahmadis "brothers of Muslims" in a token attempt to show a minimal degree of sympathy for the victims of the Deobandi terrorist attacks. However, even that cautious statement was met with uproar from the association representing the Deobandi madrassas of Pakistan, Wafaq-ul Madaris-al Arabia. The association reprimanded Sharif for his statement and asked him to withdraw it immediately. It reiterated its position that Ahmadis were kafir and traitors. It added that they could not be brothers of Islam because of their apostate status ("Sharif's Statement" 2010).

The state's indifference to threats of terrorism before the Lahore massacre and its response after are not anomalies. They fit into its consistent pattern of deliberate negligence. Local and global human rights organizations observe and report the state's consistent record of deliberate failure to hold accountable those involved in violence against Ahmadis. They fail to arrest, let alone convict, the criminals, and they are unwilling to stop violent attacks even when law enforcement is at the scene (HRW 2010).

Inaction by Law Enforcement: Enabling Islamist Terrorism

The state's unwillingness to stop societal violence against the Ahmadi community occurs initially at the law-enforcement level. As first responders, law-enforcement actors have the primary designation of stopping unlawful activity. However, Pakistan's law enforcement, in particular the police, intentionally fails to stop violence against Ahmadis. It also deliberately fails to follow up after the attacks have occurred. When, in 2014, a mob of militants attacked the homes, shops, and mosques of Ahmadis in the town of Gujranwala in Punjab, the police were was on site remained completely inactive. They chose to spectate alongside the crowd of onlookers and supporters, while the terrorists plundered Ahmadi homes and shops, and then set them on fire ("Report on the Persecution of Ahmadis" 2015, pp. 7–8). The police intentionally failed to stop the rioters and refused to assist the victims of the attack in any way. The attack led to the deaths of an elderly woman and two children, and left many injured. This complicity by law enforcement in violence against Ahmadis is systematic.

Members of the Ahmadi community are also regularly the victims of individual target killings ("Report on the Persecution of Ahmadis" 2015). These assassinations occur at unexpected times, usually in broad daylight when the victims are going to work or returning home. Most are by gunshot, and the police refuse to respond, allowing the assailants to escape. Among the most gruesome acts of violence that occurred in public was the 1995 stoning to death of two Ahmadis in what is today the KPK. The two Ahmadis were on their way to a court hearing when they were attacked and stoned to death by a violent gang of men inspired by Deobandi ideology. Despite police officers being present, they failed to stop the attacks and the murderers were not charged, let alone convicted. The 2010 Faisalabad murder of three Ahmadis also took place in public, when the victims were gunned down while on their way home from work. About a month later, an Ahmadi man and his son were stabbed and murdered inside their home in Narowal, Punjab. Such attacks are not limited to the KPK and Punjab. In 2015, three Ahmadis in Karachi were shot while on their way home after nightly prayers. The perpetrators of this systematic violence are consistently left alone by law enforcement: they aren't questioned, investigated, or charged for their crimes.

The Media's Dissemination of Anti-Ahmadi Sentiment: Enabling Islamist Terrorism

Along with the state and the public, the media plays a central role in enabling Islamist violence against Ahmadis. Both the state-run and independent media have consistently failed as an institution to highlight the injustices done to the Ahmadi community. The Pakistani media is not merely silent on the issue of systematic persecution and violence against the Ahmadi community; it goes beyond that by actively acting as a vehicle for Islamists. Islamists can easily access the media, using it to spread their militant theology and incite the public to attack Ahmadis. The Urdu-based media in particular is known to instigate violence against Ahmadis, even falsely constructing media stories (Tanveer 2014).

Within the past ten years there has been an upsurge in what is the equivalent to televangelical programs being broadcast on Pakistani television. These center on theatrical clerics who carry substantial influence in a deeply religious society. Among the most popular of the programs are those hosted by self-proclaimed alim (scholar) and former Minister of Religious Affairs Aamir Liaquat. He has a following and carries both religious and political legitimacy with much of the Pakistani public because of his religion-based position in the government. Liaquat has used his show and influence to foster hatred towards Ahmadis. There have been at least two episodes in which he and his guest clerics incited viewers to kill Ahmadis, and within a week of the airing of each, there were attacks on members of the Ahmadi community.

The first incident occurred in 2008. Liaquat devoted one of the episodes of his show, *Aalim Online*, to celebrate the 34th anniversary of the Ahmadis being constitutionally declared non-Muslim under the Bhutto regime ("Report on the Persecution of Ahmadis" 2009, p. 75). During the episode, he and his guest clerics used derogatory and inflammatory language to discuss the Ahmadi community and its founder Mirza Ghulam Ahmad. During their discussion, they called for the killing of Ahmadis by referring to the concept of wajib ul qatl. Given the popularity of Liaquat and the religious legitimacy of clerics in Pakistani society, by invoking the Deobandi-espoused concept of wajib ul qatl, they encouraged the public to murder Ahmadis as an act of jihad. After the airing of the episode, two Ahmadi individuals were murdered in the Sindh province, one within 24 hours and the other within 48 (Asian Human Rights Commission 2008).

The second incident occurred in 2014. Liaquat invited clerics from different strands of Islam for one of his episodes of his daily morning show, *Subh-e-Pakistan*. The clerics ranted about Ahmadis' apostate status, used hateful language to describe the community and their founder, and even accused them of being agents for the West ("Report on the Persecution of Ahmadis" 2015). The hateful speech was led by the Sunni Deobandi and

Barelvi clerics, but the Shia cleric also gestured approval of the Sunni clerics' views (Shia Public Affairs Committee 2014). Following the broadcast, a 27-year-old Ahmadi member in Punjab was shot and killed. Liaquat is not the only media personality who uses his position to enflame societal persecution against the Ahmadis. Other news and talkshow broadcasters also frequently invite clerics, allowing them to use their shows as outlets to incite violence.

Among the other prominent clerics who consistently utilize the media to transmit hatred and instigate violence against Ahmadis is Tahir Ashrafi, a Deobandi cleric and Chairman of the Pakistan Ulema Council. He frequently uses public outlets to disseminate hatred towards Ahmadis. In one of his public speeches, which was widely publicized through social media outlets, he threatened violence against anyone who sought to reform the anti-Ahmadi state laws. In his speech, Ashrafi also threatened the Minister of Minorities Affairs, Shahbaz Bhatti, a Christian and an advocate for reforming Pakistan's blasphemy laws. Only a few weeks after the speech, Bhatti was assassinated by Deobandi militants. The state, in accordance with its tradition of providing immunity from liability to clerics who use media outlets to incite violence against Ahmadis and other minorities, did not question Ashrafi.

CONCLUSION

All religious minorities in Pakistan are the victims of Islamist-instigated violence, led primarily by Deobandi groups. The plight of the members of the Ahmadiyya sect is a particularly bad one because all notable state and societal actors share the Islamists' intolerance for the minority group. As a result, Ahmadis face discrimination from all influential actors in the public sphere and cannot seek refuge from Islamist violence. The involvement of the state, the public and the media in proliferating prejudice against Ahmadis creates a conducive environment for Islamists to plan terrorist attacks and then execute them without having to be accountable for their crimes. Prospects for a reduction in violence against Ahmadis are incredibly grim. Any action taken by the state incurs severe political costs for elected officials because of the public's animosity towards the Ahmadi group. The state and society's encouraging attitude will allow Islamists to continue to commit atrocities against the Ahmadi community without restraint.

NOTES

1. I contacted the central administration of the Lahore Ahmadiyya Movement to obtain an estimate of the number of members but was not given a figure, likely due to security concerns for the community's members.
2. See Pakistan Constitution, Part XII, Chapter 5, Articles 260(3)(a), 260(3)(b).
3. PPC, Part XV, §§ 298B and §§ 298C.
4. See PPC, Part XV, §§ 295, §§ 295A, §§ 295B, §§ 295C, §§ 298, §§ 298A.

REFERENCES

Ahmad, B. (2007). *The great reformer: Biography of Hazrat Mirza Ghulam Ahmad of Qadian*. (H. Rahman, Trans.). Dublin: AAIIL USA Inc.

Ahmar, M. (2005). Sectarian conflicts in Pakistan. *Pakistan Vision, 9*, 1–19.

Ahmed, I. (2010, May 28). Why Taliban attacks two Muslim-minority mosques in Pakistan. *The Christian Science Monitor*. http://www.csmonitor.com/World/Asia-South-Central/2010/0528/Why-Taliban-attacks-two-Muslim-minority-mosques-in-Pakistan. Consulted 12 Aug 2015.

Ali, M. M. (1994). *The split in the Ahmadiyya movement*. Columbus: AAIIL USA Inc.

Ali, M. M. (1996). *True conception of the Ahmadiyya movement*. Columbus: AAIIL USA Inc.

Asian Human Rights Commission. (2008, September 9). Pakistan: Two persons murdered after an anchor person proposed the widespread lynching of Ahmadi sect followers. *Asian Human Rights Commission*. http://www.humanrights.asia/news/urgent-appeals/AHRC-UAC-203-2008. Consulted on 18 Aug 2015.

Drake, M. (2014, February 27). Muslim Group to get own caucus on Capitol Hill. *The Washington Times*. http://www.washingtontimes.com/news/2014/feb/27/small-muslim-offshoot-to-get-own-caucus-on-capitol/?page=all. Consulted on 13 Aug 2015.

Eltayeb, M. (2001). *A human rights approach to combating religious persecution: Cases from Pakistan, Saudi Arabia, and Sudan*. Antwerpen: Intersentia.

Farooq, U. (2013, May 4). The Pakistanis who won't vote. *The Wall Street Journal*. http://blogs.wsj.com/indiarealtime/2013/05/04/the-pakistanis-who-wont-vote/. Consulted 13 Aug 2015.

Faruqui, N. (1983). *Ahmadiyyat in the service of Islam*. Newark: AAIIL USA Inc.

Haider, Z. (2010). *The ideological struggle for Pakistan*. Stanford: Hoover Institution Press.

Haqqani, H. (2006, November 1). Weeding out the Heretics: Sectarianism in Pakistan. *Hudson Institute*. http://www.hudson.org/research/9769-weeding-out-the-heretics-sectarianism-in-pakistan. Consulted 12 Aug 2015.

Hashim, A. (2014, August 7). Pakistan's Ahmadiyya: An absence of justice. *Al Jazeera English*. http://www.aljazeera.com/indepth/features/2014/08/pakistan-ahmadiyya-an-absence-justice-20148616414279536.html. Consulted 12 Aug 2015.

Hiro, D. (2012). *Apocalyptic Realm: Jihadists in South Asia*. New Haven: Yale University Press.

HRW (Human Rights Watch). (2010, June 1). Pakistan: Massacre of minority Ahmadis. https://www.hrw.org/news/2010/06/01/pakistan-massacre-minority-ahmadis. Consulted 18 May 2015.

HRW (Human Rights Watch). (2012, May 27). Pakistan: Prosecute Ahmadi Massacre suspects. https://www.hrw.org/news/2012/05/27/pakistan-prosecute-ahmadi-massacre-suspects. Consulted 11 Aug 2015.

Khan, O. (1985). Political and economic aspects of Islamisation. In M. A. Khan (Ed.), *Islam, politics and the state: The Pakistan experience*. London: Zed Books Ltd.

Khan, A. (2013, March 14). The myth of free and fair elections in Pakistan. *Georgetown Journal of International Affairs*. http://journal.georgetown.edu/the-myth-of-free-and-fair-elections-in-pakistan-by-amjad-mahmood-khan/. Consulted 14 Aug 2015.

Noman, O. (1988). *The political economy of Pakistan 1947–1985*. London: Kegan Paul International.

Pew Research Center. (2013). *The world's Muslims: Religion, politics and society* (The Pew Forum on Religion and Public Life). Washington, DC: Pew Research Center.

Pew Research Center. (2014). *Religious hostilities reach six-year high*. Washington, DC: Pew Research Center.

Punjab Disturbances Court of Inquiry. (1954). *Report of the court of inquiry*. Lahore: The Punjab Disturbances Court of Inquiry Lahore..

Rahman, F. (2014). State restrictions on the Ahmadiyya Sect in Indonesia and Pakistan: Islam or political survival? *Australian Journal of Political Science, 49*(3), 408–422.

Rashid, A. (1985). Pakistan: The ideological dimension. In M. A. Khan (Ed.), *Islam, politics and the state: The Pakistan experience*. London: Zed Books.

Reetz, D. (2008). Change and stagnation in Islamic education The Dar al-Ulum of Deoband after the split in 1982. In F. A. Noor, Y. Sikand, & M. van Bruinessen (Eds.), *The Madrasa in Asia: Political activism and transnational linkages* (pp. 71–104). Amsterdam: Amsterdam University Press.

Report on the persecution of Ahmadis in Pakistan during the year 2008. (2009). *The Persecution of Ahmadis.* http://www.persecutionofahmadis.org/wp-content/uploads/2012/02/ann-report-2008.pdf. Consulted 18 Aug 2015.

Report on the persecution of Ahmadis in Pakistan during the year 2014. (2015). *The Persecution of Ahmadis.* https://www.persecutionofahmadis.org/wp-content/uploads/2010/03/Persecution-of-Ahmadis-in-Pakistan-2014.pdf. Consulted on 11 Aug 2015.

Saeed, S. (2007). Pakistani nationalism and the state marginalisation of the Ahmadiyya community in Pakistan. *Studies in Ethnicity and Nationalism, 7,* 132–152.

Saeed, S. (2012). Political fields and religious movements: The exclusion of the Ahmadiyya community in Pakistan. *Political Power and Social Theory, 23,* 189–223.

Sahgal, N. (2013, September 10). In Pakistan, most say Ahmadis are not Muslim. *Pew Research Center Fact Tank.* http://www.pewresearch.org/fact-tank/2013/09/10/in-pakistan-most-sayahmadis-are-not-muslim/. Consulted 7 Aug 2015.

Sharif's statement on Ahmadis angers clerics. (2010, June 7). *The Express Tribune with the International New York Times.* http://tribune.com.pk/story/19379/sharifs-statement-on-ahmadis-angers-clerics/. Consulted 12 Aug 2015.

Shia Public Affairs Committee. (2014, December 28). Ahmadiyya killings: Call for action against Aamir Liaquat Hussain and GEO TV. *Shiapac.* http://www.shiapac.org/2014/12/28/ahmadiyya-killings-call-for-action-against-aamir-liaquat-hussain-and-geo-tv/. Consulted 18 May 2015.

Tanveer R. (2014, May 22). Intolerance: Violence against Ahmadis is at its peak today. *The Express Tribune with the International New York Times.* http://tribune.com.pk/story/711398/intolerance-violence-against-ahmadis-is-at-its-peak-today/. Consulted 12 Aug 2015.

US Department of State. (2014). *International Religious Freedom Report for 2013 Pakistan.* http://www.state.gov/j/drl/rls/irf/religiousfreedom/index.htm#*wrapper.* Consulted 15 Aug 2015.

Walsh, D. (2010, June 7). Ahmadi Massacre Silence is Dispiriting. *The Guardian.* http://www.theguardian.com/commentisfree/belief/2010/jun/07/ahmadi-massacre-silence-pakistan. Consulted 18 May 2015.

Waseem, M. (1989). *Politics and the state in Pakistan.* Lahore: Progressive Publishers.

Younus, F. (2013, 14 May). Pakistan's Separate but equal elections. *Huffington Post.* http://www.huffingtonpost.com/faheem-younus/pakistans-separate-but-equal-elections_b_3270567.html. Consulted 14 Aug 2015.

CHAPTER 9

Barelvi Militancy in Pakistan and Salmaan Taseer's Murder

Jawad Syed

The tragic murder of Punjab Governor Salmaan Taseer in 2011 has raised questions about the extent of Sunni Sufi or Barelvi extremism in Pakistan.[1] In view of the significant support of Taseer's murderer by a section of Barelvis, in addition to Deobandis and Salafis, there is a need to probe Barelvi militancy in terms of its current capability and future potential. This chapter addresses this issue.

Sunni Sufis and Barelvis are estimated to be 50–60 percent of the Muslim population in Pakistan in contrast with 15–20 percent Deobandis, 15–20 percent Shias and 5 percent Ahl-e-Hadith or Salafis/Wahhabis.[2] Based on an analysis of official statistics on terrorism, Barelvis are the least violent Muslim community. Deobandis, with less than 20 percent of the Muslim population in Pakistan, are responsible for more than 90 percent of militancy, including 100 percent of suicide bombings and other indiscriminate massacres in the country. Barelvis are responsible for less than 1 percent of militancy.[3]

J. Syed (✉)
University of Huddersfield, Huddersfield, UK

© The Editor(s) (if applicable) and The Author(s) 2016
J. Syed et al. (eds.), *Faith-Based Violence and Deobandi Militancy in Pakistan*, DOI 10.1057/978-1-349-94966-3_9

231

IDEOLOGICAL DIFFERENCES

At an ideological level, the Barelvis represent a pluralistic Sufi tradition of Sunni Islam in the subcontinent, characterized by saints and shrines that have been historically welcoming and inclusive towards not only Muslims of diverse sects but also towards non-Muslim communities. In contrast, the Deobandi movement is aligned with Wahhabism and advances a harsh, takfiri (apostatizing) and jihadist interpretation of Islam.[4] The Barelvi movement in India and Pakistan has been vehemently resisting the ultra-orthodox, anti-Sufi, countercultural ideologies of the Deobandis and the Salafis/Wahhabis.[5]

Ahmed Raza Khan Barelvi (1856–1921) founded the Sunni Barelvi movement as a safeguard against Wahhabi-inspired Deobandi literalism in South Asia. It was a mass movement, defending popular Sufism, which grew in response to the increasing influence of Deobandi and Wahhabi ideologies. The Ahl-e-Hadith and Salafis represented Wahhabi ideology. Wahhabi puritanical ideology was also discreetly promoted by the Darul Uloom Deoband,[6] which was founded in India in 1866. Ahmed Raza Khan collected the opinions of leading clerics of Mecca and Medina (before the Wahhabi conquest of those cities) and compiled them into a compendium with the title *Husam-ul-Haramain*, declaring that the Deobandi and Wahhabi beliefs represented an intolerant and distorted deviation from Islamic faith.[7] It is, however, a fact that despite the anti-Deobandi fatwas, the Barelvis and Sufis have never engaged in takfiri-style violence against Deobandis or any other sect. The takfiri jihadist violence against fellow Muslims and non-Muslims remains a hallmark of Deobandis and Wahhabis.

According to numerous fatwas of Deobandi clerics and madrassas (see Table 9.1 for an example), Sunni Barelvi and Sufi practices are tantamount to polytheism and heresy. As a result of these fatwas, key Sunni Sufi shrines in Pakistan and elsewhere have been attacked—for example, Data Darbar in Lahore, Abdullah Shah Ghazi in Karachi, Bari Imam in Islamabad, Jhal Magsi in Balochistan and Rehman Baba in Peshawar. In these and other attacks, thousands of innocent, peace-loving Sunni Sufis have been killed.

Sufism and its local Barelvi traditions have a long history and a large popular following in the subcontinent. Popular Sufi culture is centred on Thursday night gatherings at shrines and annual Urs Festivals (death anniversary of Sufi saint), which feature Sufi music and dance. There is an annual festival of Milad-un-Nabi on the Prophet's birthday, as well as special devotion to Abdul Qadir Gilani, a twelfth-century Sufi saint from Iraq/Iran.

Table 9.1   An example of Deobandi fatwas against Barelvis

Question: 318
1. Is it permissible to pray behind Barelvi [Sufi] imam?
2. What are the main differences between Deobandis and Barelvis?
Answer: 318 7 May 2007 (Fatwa: 620 = 410/H)
1. If he is only Bidati [innovator in religion, a derogatory term used for Sufis and Barelvis by the Deobandis] and does not hold beliefs that lead one to *kufr* (infidelity) then *salah* (prayer) will be valid behind him but will be *makrooh* (undesirable)
2. .... The Barelvis consider it compulsory to adopt the anti-sunnat [i.e., against the traditions of Prophet Muhammad] issues as a symbol of their sect, while the ulema of Deoband reject all these innovations. For details, please see Mutala-e-Barelviat by Allama Dr Khalid Mahmood, Ghalat Fahmiyon ka Izalah, Tuhfatul Jannah Liahlis Sunnah, Fatawa Rahimia v 1, 6, Fatawa Mahmoodiah etc.
Allah (Subhana Wa Ta'ala) knows Best
Darul Ifta
Darul Uloom Deoband

(*Darul Ifta* 2007, May 7. Question 318. http://www.darulifta-deoband.com/home/en/Deviant-Sects/318).

Contemporary Deobandi and Salafi/Wahhabi fundamentalists criticize popular Sufism, which in their view does not accurately reflect "true" or "pure" Islam (Buchen 2011).[8] They also criticize the Sufi traditions of music (*qawwali/sama*) and the *dervish* dance. However, the Sufis/ Barelvis on their part consider their beliefs and rituals to be representative of Islam's inclusive and pluralistic character.

While Deobandis also stake claim to Sufism, they resemble Wahhabis in their opposition to traditional Sufi rituals, such as Urs, Milad-un-Nabi and visiting shrines. Like its ideological variant, Wahhabism, Deobandism shares common roots and an admiration for mediaeval polemicists, and takfiri jihadist clerics such as Ibn Taymiyyah (1263–1328) and Muhammad ibn Abd al-Wahhab (1703–1792). Deobandis eschew the peaceful and culturally rich traditions of commemorating the Prophet Muhammad's birthday and the martyrdom of his grandson, Imam Hussain.[9] The Barelvi Sufi traditions of Milad-un-Nabi and Ashura are meant to sensitize Muslims to the human values of peace and justice, and many Sunni and Shia Muslims worldwide practice both traditions, often together. In contrast, the Deobandi and Wahhabi sects stress a desensitizing and literalist view of Islam with a tendency to apostatize and use violence against differing viewpoints within Islam by misrepresenting them as "polytheism" (shirk) and "innovation" (bidat). The Barelvi belief in the notion of intercession (*wasilah*) is in stark contrast to strong Deobandi aversion to devotional-based spirituality, an aversion that is rooted in mediaeval polemical literature of exclusivism. The Deobandi and Wahhabi view of Sunni Barelvis and Sufis is that they are hippy deviants; their beliefs are not part of mainstream Islam and therefore are not a credible counterpoint to the Deobandi or Wahhabi version of "pure" Islam.[10]

Deobandi "reforms" are aimed at purging Islam of the "impure" traditional practices of Sunni Sufis, Barelvis and Shias, in addition to Hindu, Christian and Judaic influences. However, the Barelvi traditions are not just a reaction to the seemingly intolerant, ultraorthodox and violent view of Islam that is presented by Deobandis and Wahhabis/ Salafis. Barelvis claim that their beliefs and practices are also inspired by earlier Islamic mysticism, egalitarianism and intrafaith harmony. From a critical perspective, Deobandi beliefs may be seen as a colonial apparatus of Saudi Wahhabi beliefs, and they can be traced back to Ibn Taymiyyah and other mediaeval polemics.[11] Armstrong (2014)[12] argues that "although scripture was so central to Ibn Abd al-Wahhab's ideology, by insisting that his version of Islam alone had validity, he had distorted the Quranic message. The Quran firmly stated that 'There must be no coercion in matters of faith' (2:256), ruled that Muslims must believe in the revelations of all the great prophets (3:84) and that religious pluralism was God's will (5:48)".

Historically, Barelvis and other traditional Sufis have shown an inclusive and non-violent approach to other sects and faiths, which is in stark contrast to the takfiri, jihadist and violent character of the Deobandi and Wahhabi movements. The Deobandi ideology of jihad is inspired by the 1831 jihadist militant movement led by Syed Ahmed and Shah Ismail in South Asia who were themselves influenced by the ideology of Muhammad ibn Abd al-Wahhab of Arabia (1704–1792). Politically, Deobandis have oscillated between ascetic and activist covers depending on the sociopolitical context and opportunities, such as access to power and resources, and favourable demographics (Moj 2015).

An Embattled and Disempowered Majority

The Barelvi–Deobandi ideological differences became rather pronounced after Partition in 1947. In terms of population, the Barelvi school was dominant in Punjab while the Deobandi seminaries predominated in the Khyber Pakhtunkhwa (KP) and Balochistan among the Pashtun tribes.[13] During General Zia-ul-Haq's military dictatorship (1977–1988), the Deobandi and Salafi/Wahhabi ideologies received state patronage, in addition to generous financial support from Saudi Arabia.[14] The Barelvis, despite their numerical majority, were increasingly cornered and disempowered.

In 1979 an intense theological debate between a Barelvi scholar and a Deobandi scholar was held in Jhang (Punjab). Known as the "Munazira-e-Jhang", the debate lasted for seven to eight hours. The Barelvi scholar was Muhammad Ashraf Sialvi, who was declared the winner at the end of the debate.[15] The Deobandi participant, Haq Nawaz Jhangvi, would later form an infamous militant organization, the SSP, which has since earned notoriety for killing Shias, Sunni Barelvis and minorities throughout Pakistan.[16] The original manifesto of the founders of the SSP reveals that the outfit was set up principally to wage war on the Barelvis and their Sufi shrines. It has been reported that the original manifesto was "kafir kafir, Barelvi kafir" (Barelvis are infidel), which was changed against Shias only later.[17]

Ironically, while Darul Uloom Deoband opposed the creation of Pakistan in 1947, describing it as sinful and un-Islamic, once the country was established, its clerics initiated a process of hardline takeover. This was witnessed as early as 1949, when leading Deobandi cleric Shabbir Usmani campaigned for the first pro-Sharia legislation (the Objectives Resolution) in Pakistan.[18]

For centuries, even after the arrival of Islam in the eighth century, the spiritual folklore in Punjab, Sindh and other areas of Pakistan has emphasized love and compassion for all. Pakistan, long before its establishment, was the birthplace of Lal Shahbaz Qalandar (1177–1274), Guru Nanak (1469–1539), Shah Hussain (1538–1599), Sultan Bahu (1630–1691), Rehman Baba (1653–1711), Bulleh Shah (1680–1757), Abdul Latif Bhittai (1689–1752) and Waris Shah (1722–1798).[19]

Gradually, and especially in the aftermath of the Afghan Jihad of the 1980s and the increasing influence of Saudi Arabia, sections of the country's population have taken on Deobandi and Salafi puritanism. The Soviet invasion of Afghanistan and the concomitant arrival of Saudi-Wahhabi puritanism further strengthened the militant Deobandi mindset. Fighting the Soviet "infidels" not only armed and trained Deobandi and Salafi radicals; the experience also opened the floodgates of violence against all alleged infidels or lesser Muslims, including Sunni Sufis, Barelvis Shias, Christians, Hindus, Jews and other communities.

In recent decades, Deobandi militant organizations such as the SSP and its splinter militia, the LeJ, have serially attacked not only Shias but also Sunni Barelvis, Sufis, Christians and Ahmadis. The SSP currently operates as ASWJ, which, despite its banned status, continues to function openly.[20] Deobandi militants have seized Barelvi mosques, attacked their shrines and targeted their scholars. There have been numerous attacks on

Sunni Barelvi and Shia processions honouring the birth of the Prophet Muhammad (Milad un-Nabi), and the martyrdom of Imam Hussain (grandson of the Prophet), in different parts of Pakistan.[21] In 2010 there were additional assaults on prominent Barelvi and Sufi shrines, such as the Data Ganj Bakhsh in Lahore (50 killed)[22] and Abdullah Shah Ghazi in Karachi (at least eight killed). In 2011 there was an attack on the Sakhi Sarwar shrine in Dera Ghazi Khan (more than 50 killed). In February 2013 there was another on the Ghulam Shah Ghazi shrine in Shikarpur (four killed).[23]

Indeed, what is commonly (mis)represented or perceived as a sectarian conflict between Sunni and Shia Muslims in Pakistan could be more accurately described as largely one-sided Deobandi attacks on Shia, Sunni Barelvi and other religious communities.[24]

Between March 2005 and April 2011 alone, there were 29 attacks on Sufi shrines.[25] In two years, 2010 and 2011, 128 people were killed and 443 were injured in 22 attacks on shrines and tombs of saints and religious people in Pakistan, most of them Sufi in orientation.[26]

Barelvis commonly point to the Nishtar Park massacre of 2006 as an example of a Deobandi effort to eliminate Barelvis entirely. In that attack, a suicide bomber hit a high-profile congregation, wiping out the Sunni Tehreek (ST's) top leadership, along with other Barelvi leaders. It was later discovered that the attack was the handiwork of LeJ (the militant wing of the SSP).[27]

Moreover, in 2009 a suicide bomber from the TTP, a Deobandi militant outfit, killed a leading Barelvi scholar, Mufti Sarfraz Naeemi, who was well known for his anti-Taliban stance.[28] Other Sunni leaders, including Saleem Qadri, Hanif Billoo, Dr Abdul Qadeer Abbasi, Abbas Qadri, Akram Khan, Pir Samiullah and Mahmood Shah, have been killed and their murder claimed by Deobandi militants. The militants have also killed clerics of their own Deobandi subsect due to political, ideological and other disputes, such as Dr Muhammad Farooq,[29] Maulana Hasan Jan[30] and Shams-ur-Rahman Muawiya.[31]

In a recent video report, Reeves (2014)[32] notes that the most common victims of Deobandi militancy in Pakistan are their fellow Sunni Muslims—that is, Sunni Sufis and Barelvis. Reeves observes that attacks by the Taliban, the SSP/LeJ and other Deobandi groups dominate the headlines relating to Pakistan, yet most Pakistanis follow a different form of Islam that is more moderate and peculiar to South Asia: Barelvi Islam. The report describes how Sufi shrines are venerated by Barelvis who seek

Sufi intercession to Allah, and pray to Allah at the shrines for health and prosperity, rain and bumper harvests. It also describes how Sufi shrines are bombed by Deobandi militants. Other forms of aggression against shrines and saints include digging up tombs to cause damage to them. Reeves (2014) claims that the people are in no doubt about the culprits. They blame ultraconservative Deobandi Muslims, who consider the practice of praying at the shrines to be un-Islamic. He says that the veneration of saints for intercession (wasilah) to God is common in the salvation-oriented Barelvi branch of Islam that is entwined with Sufi mysticism and ancient folk practices. Barelvis are seen as more moderate on most issues than the more puritanical Islamic sects. The report cites Maulana Khateeb Mustafai, a Barelvi cleric, who states that Sufi Islam is under assault at the hands of the Deobandis. In his words, "They infiltrate Barelvi mosques. They have desecrated and demolished countless shrines. Their organizations are getting support from Arab states. That's why this is happening."

Reeves also cites retired Pakistani general Talat Masood, who says, "The money and the financial support that the Deobandis have been receiving is from Saudi Arabia and they flush them with funds."

KEY ATTACKS ON SUNNI SUFIS AND BARELVIS

According to an estimate (see Appendix), more than 600 key Sunni Sufi and Barelvi leaders and activists have been target killed, while the total number of Sufis/Barelvis indiscriminately killed by Deobandi militants may be to the tune of tens of thousands, given the fact that Barelvis constitute a majority of more than 50,000 Pakistanis killed by the TTP/SSP/LeJ militants. The following is an overview of the key attacks targeted at Barelvis only.

18 May 2001

ST leader Saleem Qadri was assassinated by the SSP/LeJ. His successor, Abbas Qadri, and other Sunni Barelvi leaders alleged that certain pro-jihadist elements in the security agencies were patronizing the Deobandi militants. Saleem Qadri was ambushed apparently by a team of six well-trained assassins riding three motorbikes while he was on his way to Noorani Masjid for the Friday congregation. Qadri and five others were killed on the spot, while three others were wounded. The corpse of one of the killers, who was later identified as Arshad alias Polka, an activist of the SSP, was found in the vicinity, apparently killed in a retaliatory shooting by Saleem Qadri's guards.[33]

19 March 2005
A suicide bomber killed 40 at the shrine of Pir Rakhel Shah in Jhal Magsi, Balochistan.

27 May 2005
As many as 20 people were killed and 100 more were injured when a Deobandi suicide bomber attacked a gathering at Bari Imam Shrine during the Urs Festival. According to the police, two SSP activists were arrested from Thanda Pani and two hand grenades were seized from them. The police said that the two men brought the suicide bomber from the north and provided him with boarding at the house of another SSP activist in Rawalpindi before sending the attacker to the shrine.[34]

11 April 2006
A grand Sunni Barelvi congregation celebrating the Milad un Nabi was suicide bombed. The entire Sunni Barelvi leadership of the ST, many of them eminent Sufi and Barelvi scholars, was killed,, including Maulana Abbas Qadri, Akram Qadri, Iftikhar Butt, Mufti Shahid Attari, Dr Abdul Qadeer Abbasi, Hanif Billo (President of the Jamaat Ahle Sunnat) and Hafiz Taqi (leader of the JUP). In total, 57 (including 49 prominent Sunni leaders) were killed, while another 100 were injured. The congregation was celebrating the birthday of the Prophet Muhammad, a custom that Deobandis consider to be un-Islamic. The Deobandi groups, the SSP and the LeJ were the chief suspects, since those killed included the three main leaders of their fiercest rival, ST, and the most prominent Sunni Barelvi group (ICG 2007).

16 December 2008
Pir Samiullah was killed by the Deobandi Taliban in Swat. His dead body was exhumed and desecrated.[35]

17 January 2009
Pir Rafiullah and Pir Juma Khan were killed in Peshawar.[36]

17 February 2009
Pir Syed Phool Badshah Bukhari was killed in Peshawar

18 February 2009
JUP-Noorani's provincial leader Maulana Iftikhar Ahmed Habibi was killed in Quetta, Balochistan.

8 March 2009
Rahman Baba Shrine was attacked.

12 June 2009
Senior Barelvi cleric Dr Sarfraz Ahmed Naeemi, a renowned religious scholar and principal of the Jamia Naeemia, was killed, along with a number of aides and students, in a targeted suicide attack

at his seminary's office in Lahore. Naeemi had supported military action against the Taliban and also issued a decree calling suicide attacks haram (forbidden) in Islam. He had also arranged an anti-Taliban seminar in his madrassa two weeks before his murder. A spokesman for the TTP claimed responsibility for the attack (*Dawn* 2009).[37]

2 September 2009
Hamid Saeed Kazmi was attacked in Islamabad. He sustained injuries but survived.

1 July 2010
Two suicide bombers blew themselves up at the Sufi shrine, Data Darbar shrine in Lahore. At least 50 people died and 200 others were hurt in the blasts.

7 October 2010
In an attack on Abdullah Shah Ghazi shrine in Karachi, 10 people were killed and 50 injured.

25 October 2010
In an attack on the shrine of Baba Farid Ganj Shakar in Pakpattan, five were killed and several injured.

14 December 2010
In an attack on Ghazi Baba shrine in Peshawar, three were killed.

3 April 2011
At the annual Urs Festival of Sakhi Sarwar shrine near D.G. Khan, a twin suicide attack left at least 42 dead and almost 100 injured.

25 February 2013
A blast tore through the Ghulam Shah Ghazi shrine in Shikarpur, killed four.

6 January 2014
Six people were killed near a Sufi shrine in Karachi. Their bodies were found outside the shrine with a note claiming to be from the TTP, threatening that "People visiting shrines will meet the same fate." Two of the men had been beheaded while the rest had had their throats slit (Hassan 2014).[38]

6 September 2014
In Sargodha, Deobandi militants attacked an event of Sufi devotional music (qawwali/samaa) killing a senior Pakistan army official, along with his brother and another person. The devotional music ceremony was in progress at Astana Fazal when the Deobandi militants opened fire at the audience, killing Subhani, the head of the shrine, his brother Brigadier Fazal Zahoor Qadri and Malik Ayub (Dawn 2014)[39]

19 February 2015

Tehsil President of Jamat Ahle Sunnat (JAS, a Barelvi group) Syed Mehmood Shah was gunned down in Mansehra. Local Sunni Barelvi leaders suspected that Deobandi militant outfit ASWJ was involved in this target killing.

22 June 2016

Amjad Sabri, Pakistn's top Sufi singer, celebrated for devotional songs from a centuries-old mystic tradition Qawwali, was shot dead in Karachi. A spokesman for the Pakistani Taliban, Qari Saifullah Mehsud, claimed responsibility for the killing and said Sabri was targeted because the group considered his music blasphemous.

THE BARELVI REACTION

In a relatively recent move that has outraged Barelvis, the SSP started operating as the ASWJ. The Deobandi outfit adopted the new name after it was banned for militant activities, which included sectarian attacks on Shias and Sunni Barelvis. The fact that the Deobandi ASWJ now claimed for itself the title of "Ahl-e-Sunnat" (literally meaning Sunni) was objected to by the Barelvis, because they see themselves as the followers of true and moderate Sunni Islam and the Deobandis as a Wahhabi-influenced deviant group.[40]

During General Zia's military dictatorship and afterwards, the Deobandis enjoyed not only state support[41] but also funding from Saudi Arabia and other Arab countries (which they continue to receive to date),[42] and they were able to expand their influence at the cost of Sunni Sufis and Barelvis. In Karachi and other parts of Pakistan, traditionally Barelvi mosques were gradually taken over by Deobandi clerics and Imams, often associated with the SSP/ASWJ, the JUI and other Deobandi outfits.[43] It was in this context that the ST emerged as Sunni Barelvi resistance to Deobandi militancy.

In response to the target killings of Sunni Barelvis and Sufis, and the forced takeover of Barelvi mosques, the ST cadre and other Barelvis resorted to sporadic violence. However, compared with the Deobandis, the Sunni Barelvis were neither supported by the state nor trained in jihadist camps. Indeed, unlike the SSP/ASWJ/Taliban network's indiscriminate violence, Sunni Barelvi sporadic militancy was limited to Deobandi militant groups and their leaders.

ICG (2007) notes that the ST was founded in the 1990s to defend Barelvi mosques and protect them from takeovers and intimidation by Deobandi groups.[44] The ST was suspected by some sections of the killing of controversial Deobandi cleric Yusuf Ludhianvi in 2000. Ludhianvi was notorious for his support of the Taliban and the SSP/ASWJ, and was also known for his hate speeches against Sufis, Barelvis and Shias. ICG (2007, p. 26) notes that the ST was effectively neutralized by the massacre of its main leaders in the 2006 Nishtar Park bombing in Karachi.

As a matter of record, neither a single incident of indiscriminate attack against Pakistani civilians or security forces, nor an incident of suicide bombing, has been attributed to Sunni Barelvis or Sufis. In contrast, Deobandi militants have killed more than 50,000 Pakistani civilians and security personnel in recent decades. The only exception is the murder of Salmaan Taseer, Governor of Punjab, at the hands of Malik Mumtaz.

MALIK MUMTAZ HUSSAIN, ALIAS MUMTAZ "QADRI"

Some reports about Salmaan Taseer's murder by Malik Mumtaz Hussain Qadri provide a false impression that Sunni Barelvis are equal in terms of violence or militancy to Deobandis or Salafis/Wahhabis. Such an impression is not only statistically weak but also ignores the transnational context that all major terror outfits, including ISIS, Al-Qaeda, Al-Nusra, Boko Haram, Al Shabab, the Taliban and the SSP/ASWJ/LeJ, are a Salafi/Wahhabi and Deobandi phenomenon. Furthermore, these Salafi/Wahhabi and Deobandi militant groups are as much opposed to Christians, Jews, Hindus and other non-Muslims as they are to Sunnis, Sufis, Barelvis and Shias.[45]

To equate the systematic and dominant Deobandi terrorism in Pakistan with rare, isolated incidents of violence by Sunni Barelvis, Sufis or Shias is tantamount to false neutrality. In statistics, an outlier is an observation that is numerically distant from the rest of the data. Grubbs says that "an outlying observation, or outlier, is one that appears to deviate markedly from other members of the sample in which it occurs".[46] Within the context of alleged Barelvi militancy, Taseer's murder at the hands of Malik Mumtaz may be treated as a statistical outlier, especially given the larger context of political instability and the Deobandi-dominated faith-based violence and radicalization.

Punjab's Governor Salmaan Taseer was killed on 4 January 2011 by one of his security guards, arranged for and provided by the Punjab government of Chief Minister Shahbaz Sharif. Malik Mumtaz was reported to be unfit for security duties owing to his extreme religious inclination. Awan (2011)[47] reports that Mumtaz "had a passion for instigating religious debate and on two occasions he had pointed his weapon on colleagues with whom he himself had initiated some controversial debate. He was declared unfit for sensitive duty in a report prepared by the Special Branch of the police. His name was among 11 officers declared 'unsuitable' for high security assignments."

However, the Punjab police ignored the report and he was deployed as a part of Taseer's security team. Other guards say that he had talked of killing the governor but they had taken it as a joke.[48]

According to media reports, Salmaan Taseer was shot 26 times. Surprisingly, none of the Police guards tried to shoot at or stop Mumtaz even after Governor Salmaan Taseer had fallen. In Mumtaz's own confession, he states that he had planned to kill the governor three days earlier and had taken other guards into his confidence so that they would not try to stop him. This would indicate that Mumtaz had prior information about the schedule and movements of the governor and possibly did not act alone. However, the religious leanings of other guards in Governor Taseer's security detail were never questioned.

The ultimate responsibility for Taseer's security lay with the Punjab government, which was led by Taseer's political rivals: Chief Minister Shahbaz Sharif and Law Minister Rana Sanaullah. Both Shahbaz Sharif and Rana Sanaullah are alleged to have had links and/or sympathies with the SSP/ASWJ and the TTP. Taseer also raised this point a few weeks before his murder in an interview with *Newsweek* magazine, during which he categorically condemned the Punjab government regarding its alleged links with banned terror outfits. Taseer said:[49]

I worry about terrorism. The Pakistan Muslim League (Nawaz), which is in government in the Punjab, has old linkages with and a natural affinity for extremist organizations like Sipah-e-Sahaba, Lashkar-e-Jhangvi, Khatm-e-Nubuwwat [an anti-Ahmadi outfit], and so many others. Let's face it: terrorists need logistical support from within—somebody funds them, somebody guides them, and somebody looks after them—and that support is coming from the Punjab. Some 48 terrorists have been released by an antiterrorism court recently because they could not be prosecuted, or rather, there was a failure to prosecute them. This is disgraceful. If the Punjab government was solidly against the militants, this would not have happened. You can't have your law minister [Rana Sanaullah] going around in police jeeps with Ahmed Ludhyanvi [of the outlawed SSP], whose agenda is to declare Shias infidels and close down their places of worship, and then say you want harmony in this province. You can't have the chief minister, who is also the home minister, standing at [Lahore mosque] Jamia Naeemia pleading with the Taliban to please not launch attacks in the Punjab because he shares the same thinking against the U.S. as they do. What message does this send out to the local magistrate and police officer? There has to be zero tolerance toward militants, and the only way you can have this is if the government is totally committed ... Dealing with the militants has to be no holds barred. Their lives should be made hell; they should be prosecuted, and sent to hell where they belong.

Furthermore, Taseer took a bold stance in support of a blasphemy-accused Christian woman, Asia Bibi, and called for the amendment of the law to stop its misuse. Before his murder, a concerted campaign was run against him not only by the ruling PML-N government in Punjab but also by religious clerics of the SSP/ASWJ, the JUI, the JI and other groups. Rana Sanaullah, a senior PML-N leader and a cousin of the former Chief Justice of Pakistan Iftikhar Chaudhry, was allegedly the lynchpin between the PML-N and the SSP/ASWJ. It was Sanaullah who led a sinister campaign against Taseer, casting aspersions on his personal character, family members and religious beliefs.[50]

Taseer visited Asia Bibi in prison and forwarded her clemency appeal to the President of Pakistan. The governor's efforts on Asia's behalf, and his labelling of the existing blasphemy law as a "black law", outraged the religious right wing.

Moreover, a few media anchors and journalists, including Meher Bukhari and Ansar Abbasi, among others, were part of a hateful campaign in the mainstream media in which Taseer was wrongly framed as a blasphemer of the Prophet. Abbasi tried to justify Taseer's murder in a number of his columns and media appearances.[51]

In an interview with Taseer broadcast on Samaa TV on 25 November 2010,[52] the anchor, Meher Bukhari, asked provocative questions, framing Taseer as a proponent of the blasphemy of the Prophet.[53] During the show, which was watched by millions of Pakistanis, Bukhari alleged that Taseer was working on a pro-Western liberal agenda by defending an allegedly blaspheming Christian woman.

Declan Walsh notes in *The Guardian* that Taseer's bold style "brought him into conflict with populist media figures. [In November 2010] Meher Bukhari, a prominent female television anchor, asked Taseer if he wasn't following a 'pro-western agenda' by supporting the Christian woman. Taseer replied: 'If you are asking me if I am a liberal, I am.' " [54]

Meher Bukhari was accused of framing Taseer to increase the ratings of her television programme. Pro-Taliban politicians and media persons made similar provocative statements against Taseer.

By late November 2010, religious groups around the country were staging mass demonstrations against the government to show support for the blasphemy law and to condemn Taseer,[55] with some claiming that the governor himself was guilty of apostasy—a crime punishable by death in Pakistani law.

On 3 December 2010, a Deobandi cleric, Maulana Yousaf Qureshi of the historic Masjid Mohabaat Khan in Peshawar, offered a Rs 500,000 reward for anyone who killed Asia Bibi. Qureshi also warned the government against any move to abolish or change the blasphemy law. He warned: "No president, no parliament and no government has the right to interfere in the tenets of Islam. Islamic punishment (according to Muslim jurisprudence) will be implemented at all costs."[56]

On 31 December 2010, a few days before Taseer's murder, a PML-N leader from Muzaffargarh, Abad Dogar, announced at a public rally a financial bounty of Rs 20 million for anyone who would kill Taseer. Dogar was previously a leader of the banned SSP/ASWJ.[57] The rally was organized by religious hardliners to oppose any move to repeal or amend the blasphemy law. Talking to the media after the rally, Dogar said that he would raise the bounty to Rs 30 million if a resident of his local area, Khangarh, killed Taseer.

It was against this charged background that Malik Mumtaz shot Taseer in the back with 27 bullets from an AK-47 submachine gun in Islamabad. Mumtaz, allegedly a follower of the Barelvi movement Dawat-e-Islami, was quickly disowned and condemned by Maulana Ilyas Qadri, the chief of Dawat-e-Islami. In a video statement, Maulana Ilyas Qadri said that not everyone who wore a green turban represented the Dawat-e-Islami or the Barelvi Sufi movement. He referred to well-known Barelvi books, such as *Bahar-e-Shariat* and *Fatawa Razawiya*, to assert his opinion that taking the law in one's own hands was not permissible, even against one who blasphemed against the Prophet.[58] Dr Tahir-ul-Qadri, Pakistan's most senior Barelvi cleric, bluntly stated that Malik Mumtaz was a murderer who needed to be punished as per Pakistani law. Qadri also said that one might disagree with Taseer's views but whatever he said could not be described as blasphemy. In reference to the murder of Taseer, Qadri further said that even if one commits an act of blasphemy, they need to be dealt with in a court of law, and individuals are not allowed to take the law into their own hands.[59] Another analyst, Tahir Khalil, indicated in the daily *Jang* that "Qadri" was not a part of Malik Mumtaz Hussain's official name.[60] However, the episode seemed to capture at least a section of the generally peaceful Barelvis on a highly sensitive topic—that is, the Prophet's honour and love.

There are conflicting reports about Malik Mumtaz's family background. For example, it has been reported in *The Friday Times* (edited by senior Pakistani journalist Najam Sethi) that Mumtaz is

> a convert from the Deobandi to Barelvi school of thought. His parents and siblings are Deobandi. They live in Rawalpindi and belong to the nearby Bara Kahu area. Mumtaz adopted the name Qadri out of respect for the Barelvi Dawat-e-Islami leader Ilyas Qadri ... The organization [Dawat-e-Islami] has remained non-violent ... At one stage of his police career, Qadri was not as religious. Sometimes he would grow a large beard and sometimes be seen without it (Awan 2011).[61]

Tahir Khalil reported in *Jang* (8 January 2011) that Mumtaz was in touch with some militants based in Kohat, and that in 2002, when he was employed in the Punjab constabulary, he wore a long beard and used to be a staunch Deobandi. Khalil reports that Qadri was not part of his family name but was only due to his recent affiliation with the Dawat-e-Islami, when people started calling him Qadri.[62] Indeed, his brother's name is Dilpazeer Awan, who is not a "Qadri".[63]

The fact is that the Punjab government's senior minister, Rana Sanaullah, other PML-N leaders, pro-Taliban clerics and a few media persons were involved in a defamatory campaign against Taseer before his murder. Despite reports about the suspicious and extreme behaviour of Mumtaz, he was deputed as Salmaan Taseer's bodyguard. Shortly after Taseer's murder, the Chief Justice of the Lahore High Court, Justice Khawaja Muhammad Sharif, a known supporter of the ruling PML-N party, decided to act as defence lawyer for Mumtaz.[64] In his arguments in the Supreme Court, he claimed that Mumtaz was a true lover of the Prophet who could not tolerate the slain governor's stance against the blasphemy law.[65] This indicates that certain powerful players contributed to, or enabled, Taseer's murder.

Clearly the Sharif brothers of the ruling PML-N party disliked Governor Taseer. In a public address in a local mosque, Nawaz Sharif's son-in-law

 **Shehryar Taseer**
@shehryar_taseer

PML-N gives ticket to Sardar Ebad
Dogar (NA-178) an ex SSP leader who
announced 10 Million bounty on
Governor Punjab #SalmanTaseer.

RETWEETS	LIKES
149	5

2:53 PM - 20 Apr 2013

Fig. 9.1 Taseer's family reaction (Taseer, Shehryar. *Twitter.* https://twitter.
com/shehryar_taseer/status/325547862610042880)

and a PML-N politician, Captain (retired) Safdar, declared Mumtaz as a
holy warrior (*mujahid*) and praised Taseer's murder.[66]

Only two years after Taseer's murder, in the 2013 elections, Sardar
Abad Dogar from Muzaffargarh was awarded a PML-N ticket (NA-178)
to contest elections for the national parliament. This is the same person
who had declared that Salmaan Taseer was a blasphemer and announced a
financial bounty for his killer (Mir 2013).[67] Taseer's family also took public
notice of this development (Fig. 9.1).

Some Barelvi leaders used this episode to establish their own credentials as lovers of the Prophet. Hanif Qureshi, a local Barelvi cleric from
Rawalpindi, praised Mumtaz's actions, hailing him as a hero. Mumtaz's
family members were given much appreciation and possibly financial support by those hailing Mumtaz's action.

After Taseer's murder, Barelvi scholars from the Jamaat Ahl-e-Sunnat
Pakistan (JASP) issued a statement that explicitly warned mosque leaders
not to offer Islamic funeral prayers to Salmaan Taseer.[68] It would appear
that a section of Barelvis did not show any hesitation in owning and praising Taseer's brutal murder at the hands of Malik Mumtaz, alias Qadri.

However, in front of the courts, Malik Mumtaz was kissed and decorated with garlands not only by Barelvi groups but also by Deobandi and
Salafi groups, while lawyers belonging to the PML-N and the JI threw
rose petals at him.[69] Only a year before Taseer's murder, many of these

lawyers were a part of the Lawyers Movement for the restoration of the controversial[70] former Chief Justice Iftikhar Chaudhry. This is the same judge under whose controversial tenure the Supreme Court released a number of SSP/ASWJ and Taliban terrorists, including Malik Ishaq, and the extremist bias or fear of some judges was noted by the press[71] and others. Professor Hoodbhoy[72] writes:

> Even when the government plucks up the courage to try terrorists, the judicial system ensures an almost zero-percent conviction rate. Malik Ishaq, who rose to fame as a Shia-killer, was freed after frightened judges treated him like a guest in the courtroom, offering him tea and biscuits.

Iftikhar Chaudhry's restoration as the Chief Justice could not have been possible without the movement led by the PML-N, the JI, the ASWJ and other right-wing parties.

In addition to the Barelvi clerics, the Deobandi and Salafi groups endorsed Mumtaz's actions. According to media reports, numerous Deobandi and Wahhabi (Salafi) organizations participated in rallies to show solidarity with Mumtaz.[73] Several clerics, many of them Barelvis but also including Deobandi and Salafis, signed a fatwa that forbade Muslims from taking part in funeral prayers for Salmaan Taseer. The Deobandi Imam of Badshahi Mosque in Punjab's capital Lahore refused to lead ritual services for Taseer.[74] The JUI-F leader Mufti Mohammed Usman Yar Khan said, "the blasphemer of the Prophet will be punished directly by Allah as per the Quran, so there is no need for any legislation on this matter. Murder of Salmaan Taseer fulfilled the promise Allah of punishing the blasphemer". Another senior Deobandi cleric, Mufti Naim from Jamia Binoria, Karachi, commented, "The blasphemy law was made exactly to prevent such incidents. Else there will be chaos in the country and everyone would kill everyone."[75]

Indeed, it was none other than a Barelvi cleric, Maulana Afzal Chishti, who led Taseer's funeral prayer, which indicated that senior Barelvi leaders such as Tahir-ul-Qadri and Ilyas Qadri were not alone in their condemnation of Taseer's murder.

The cowardly murder of Taseer was a pivotal moment in Pakistan's religiopolitical landscape. As a member of the elite police force, Mumtaz was supposed to be guarding Governor Taseer, but he betrayed the trust of an unsuspecting and brave man. This was a tragic event in Pakistan's short history but the real tragedy lies in its aftermath.

Taseer's murder may be seen as a confluence of events. In the preceding years, the state's decades-long policy of subcontracting its foreign goals in Afghanistan and Kashmir to Deobandi and Salafi militant proxies was unravelling. The radical Lal Masjid's violent standoff[76] in Islamabad and subsequent suicide attacks against security institutions and civilians had revealed the folly of depending on extremist takfiri groups for foreign policy objectives. The Taliban graduates and recruits of radical Deobandi madrassas such as the Lal Masjid, Jamia Haqqania, Jamia Banuri Town and Jamia Khair-ul-Madaris had taken over vast sections of northwestern Pakistan,[77] in spite of a delayed and half-hearted military action against them.[78]

Hamid Saeed Kazmi, a moderate Sunni Barelvi leader and Federal Religious Affairs Minister, was jailed on possibly politically motivated charges made by a JUI-F representative, Azam Swati.[79] In 2009, Kazmi had survived a terrorist attack on his life. The JUI-F is the leading Deobandi religiopolitical party in Pakistan and is known for its sympathies for proscribed militant outfits, such as the Taliban and the SSP/ASWJ. Hamid Saeed Kazmi's imprisonment by a bench headed by the controversial chief justice[80] adversely affected Barelvi support for the then PPP-led coalition government.

In November 2010 a PPP senator proposed legislation in a private capacity on amending the blasphemy law at a time when the government was derailed, its cabinet in tatters and the country in the grip of the Taliban.[81] In effect, there was no popular sentiment to support such an amendment. Governor Taseer, a daring and sincere person, stepped into the fray to support an innocent Christian woman, Asia Bibi, who was jailed on trumped-up blasphemy charges. A hateful and violence-inciting campaign was started against Taseer by pro-Taliban journalists and clerics. They falsely misrepresented Taseer's suggestion to amend the blasphemy law as itself an act of blasphemy.

It was against this backdrop that Taseer was killed. The PPP government in the centre was hobbled, with its own Barelvi leader in jail for possibly politically motivated charges at one end while facing a potential coup on the other. The pro-Taliban lobby had made its trap. In one sweep it had created a campaign to discredit the entire Barelvi Sunni population as extremists while also trying to drive a wedge between the PPP and its traditional Barelvi support base.[82] Needless to say, the Barelvi–PPP partnership against extremism has further deteriorated since.[83]

The most important influential Barelvi clerics, such as Tahir ul Qadri (of the Minhaj-ul-Quran and the Pakistan Awami Tehreek) and Ilyas Qadri (of the Dawat-e-Islami), refused to fall into the trap. However, a few Barelvi clerics, such as Hanif Qureshi and Sarwat Qadri, decided to own and support Malik Mumtaz in a politically expedient and opportunistic manner to exploit the Barelvi notion of the *ishq-e-rasool* (love of the Prophet).

The mainstream media failed to ask tough questions, such as why a known radical such as Malik Mumtaz was included in Taseer's security detail, and why no action was taken against Abad Dogar, who had announced a bounty for Taseer's murder. The PML-N stood to gain from eliminating Governor Taseer, who was a vocal critic of the party's links to and/or sympathies with proscribed Deobandi terror outfits. Not only did his murder remove the PML-N's major political opposition but it also empowered its Deobandi allies by putting Barelvis on the back foot.

Ismail Khan notes that Tahir Ashrafi, the Chairman of the Pakistan Ulema Council, a Deobandi organization, tried unsuccessfully to distance sections of the Deobandis from Malik Mumtaz Qadri, commenting that "sentiments were being exploited" against Taseer. This did not deter the JUI-F, the JI and other Deobandi organizations from organizing massive rallies in support of Malik Mumtaz. Ironically, in 2007, the same Deobandi scholar, Tahir Ashrafi, ruled that Muslims should honour Osama Bin Laden in reaction to the British government's granting of a knighthood to Salman Rushdie.[84] It should be noted that Tahir Ashrafi also delivered a highly provocative speech against Shahbaz Bhatti, the only Christian minister in the Pakistani cabinet, warning him to refrain from any attempt to amend the blasphemy law. In the speech, Ashrafi praised Mullah Omar on his holy war against the USA and pronounced a violent public invective against Shahbaz Bhatti, in which he spoke of "physical elimination" if the minister did not stop opposing the blasphemy law. That speech is still seen as the one that signed Bhatti's murder at the hands of the LeJ/ASWJ in March 2011, but no action was taken against Ashrafi.[85]

At the time of the TTP/SSP's attack on the Data Darbar shrine in July 2010, Taseer stood with Sunni Barelvis and criticized Rana Sanaullah and the PML-N's soft approach with proscribed militant outfits. He visited the injured who had been admitted to Mayo Hospital, Lahore. He said that the provincial government was warned about the attack, but the Punjab chief minister failed to take appropriate action. He also criticized the Punjab government for supporting banned organizations in the province.[86] In response, Rana Sanaullah proceeded to make cheap and personal attacks against the Taseer family. Previously, personal pictures of Taseer's family were paraded and lampooned on social media by his political opponents and right-wing activists.[87]

According to Leena Ghani, a commentator writing in Pakistan's daily *Express Tribune*

No one can deny the fact that a well-planned character assassination of Mr Taseer was a major contributing factor to the build-up behind his eventual assassination. The party [PML-N] succeeded in portraying the Punjab governor as a morally corrupt, alcohol-drinking, west-favouring liberal who had committed blasphemy himself. This started with the Punjab law minister brandishing Mr Taseer's family's private pictures on the steps of the Punjab Assembly and culminated in him insinuating that Mr Taseer had committed blasphemy. After his assassination, the PML-N was quick to distance itself from the whole affair, absolving itself of all responsibility while refusing to condemn the extremism which contributed to the act in the first place.[88]

Taseer was in fact a moderate Muslim with liberal and progressive views. He despised the takfiri attacks on the pluralistic fabric of Pakistan and spoke out against them. Months after Taseer's murder, in August 2011, his son was kidnapped by the Taliban, who sought to exchange him for Malik Mumtaz's release.[89] However, Mumtaz was hanged on 29 Feburary 2016, and Shahbaz Taseer was released a week later by his captors, allegedly in exchange for a hefty ransom.[90]

Mumtaz's execution was protested not only by Barelvis but also by Deobandi organizations, such as the ASWJ, the JUI and the JI.[91] Indeed, some Barelvi sections continue to support Mumtaz, promoting him as a hero. However, even they were not arm-twisting the state—unlike anti-state Deobandi militant groups such as the Taliban, which wanted to barter Malik Mumtaz for Shahbaz Taseer.[92] Notwithstanding the distasteful rallies by the Barelvis in Mumtaz's support, their overall tactics cannot be compared to the kidnapping and suicide attack tactics often used by Deobandi militants in pursuit of their objectives.

The project to challenge the growing takfiri element within the Deobandis by empowering traditional Sunni Barelvis was scuttled with Taseer's assassination. Pro-Taliban and other journalists and commentators have since used this event to discredit Barelvis as being just as extremist as Deobandis. They have achieved this by exploiting the situation and omitting crucial details. For instance, there is no mention of the PML-N leader Abad Dogar, an extremist Deobandi and former leader of the SSP/ASWJ, who offered significant financial rewards for killing Taseer. Both before and after the murder, various Deobandi religiopolitical parties united against Taseer and were the most supportive of his murderer. A former chief justice of the Lahore High Court, Khawaja Sharif, offered his services to defend Taseer's murderer.

While bearing the brunt of Deobandi violence, Sunni Barelvis are now viewed by certain sections of the media as being equal in violence. This is notwithstanding the fact that leading Barelvi clerics such as Tahir ul Qadri, Ilyas Qadri and Afzal Chishti have publicly condemned Taseer's murder. Indeed, a Barelvi cleric Afzal Chishti led Taseer's funeral when most of the other clerics, including Deobandis and Barelvis, had pulled out.

Taseer's murder is being misused as a red herring to discredit the entire Barelvi movement and its historical struggle against takfiri Deobandi and Wahhabi movements. In June 2014, even as the Nawaz Sharif government was trying to avoid military action in North Waziristan and instead pre-ferred dialogue with the Taliban, leading Sunni organizations such as the Pakistan Awami Tehreek (PAT) and the Sunni Ittehad Council (SIC) were prompt to support the proposed military action.[93] However, the Sunni Barelvis paid a heavy price. In June 2014, scores of unarmed activists of the PAT, including women, were beaten and shot outside the Tahir-ul-Qadri's political office in Lahore by the heavy handed action of the Punjab police. More than 80 were injured in addition to 14 being killed[94] by the police. The attackers also included PML-N activists such as Gullu Butt.[95] A judicial commission's report held the Punjab government responsible for the Model Town bloodbath.[96]

According to the *Express Tribune*, more than 40 Deobandi and Wahhabi organizations, along with Barelvi groups, participated in rallies to show their solidarity with Malik Mumtaz:[97]

On Wednesday, more than 40 parties including representatives of Deobandi groups Jamaat-i-Islami, Jamiat Ulema-i-Islam (Fazl and Sami groups), Aalmi Majlis Tahaffuz Khatam-i-Nabuwat, Tanzeem-i-Islami, Tehreek-i-Islami, Ittehadul Ulema Pakistan and Jamia Ashrafia—as well as Wahhabi groups Jamaatud Dawa, Tehreek Hurmat-i-Rasool, and Muttahida Jamiat Ahl-i-Hadith—met to discuss a coordinated response to the sentence. Tehreek Namoos-i-Risalat and Tanzimul Madaris, both Barelvi groups, also attended. The speakers criticised the court's decision to sentence Qadri to death as against Islamic injunctions and the ideology of Pakistan. JI Ameer Syed Munawwar Hassan said that the court's verdict reflected an "unfortu-nate secularist atmosphere" in Pakistan. He urged the participants to unite against the judgement. He said there would be protests all over the country on Friday. Tahaffuz Namoos-i-Risalat Mahaz, an alliance of Sunni Barelvi parties, has already called a strike on Friday. Jamaatud Dawa Ameer Hafiz Saeed said the court's decision was part of "the conspiracy against Islam" and an attack on Pakistan's ideology. He said Muslims should stand up and tell the world that they are ready to die but not ready to allow blasphemy. He said all Muslims felt just like Mumtaz Hussain Qadri about the issue.

After decades of state-sponsored radicalization during and after the Afghan Jihad, one cannot expect its effects not to have seeped into every community in Pakistan, albeit in varying degrees. For decades, and especially after General Zia-ul-Haq's aggressive Wahhabization,[98] everything from textbooks to mainstream media, and most importantly the pulpit, have suffered from intolerant content. During General Zia's military regime, the Deobandi sect was given special preference by the state—an advantage that continued during limited democratic governments in the post-Zia era. After witnessing decades of Deobandi militancy, both as non-state proxies and as discarded anti-state insurgents, one should not expect other faith communities to continue with their traditional pacifism.

Sunni Barelvis witnessed that the law did not work in prosecuting Deobandi militants. If known militants such as Malik Ishaq[99] and Ismatullah Muawiya could get off scot free, and if the state's machinery, including the judiciary, would intervene to overturn convictions and explore technicalities to release the JuD's jihadist leader Hafiz Saeed, how serious was it in trying to curb faith-based militancy?

Deobandi religiopolitical parties provided the cover while Deobandi militant groups, such as the Taliban and the SSP/LeJ, challenged the writ of the state in parts of Pakistan. The impression given to other faith communities was clear. In order for them to survive, they had to eschew their previous tolerant modes of co-existence. In order for them to survive at the political level, they would have to adopt certain postures of intolerant groups, such as the JI, the JUI-F and the SSP/LeJ. To their credit, at least two main leading Sunni Barelvi clerics did not become co-opted. However, a section of the Barelvi leadership fell into this abyss.

In a wider context, Barelvi militancy in Pakistan is almost non-existent, and in its miniscule form it has generally been directed against the forced takeover of Barelvi or Sunni Sufi mosques by the powerful Deobandi lobby. Against this backdrop, the outpouring of support by a section of Barelvis for Malik Mumtaz has been counterproductive in more ways than one. First, it has provided an opportunity to the pro-Taliban and SSP/LeJ lobby to claim that the Barelvis are as violent as the Deobandis. Second, it has dented the indigenous Barelvi and Sufi movement led by moderate clerics such as Dr Tahir ul Qadri, Ilyas Qadri and Sahibzada Hamid Raza against radical Deobandi and Wahhabi ideologies. However, it must be noted that Ilyas Qadri, the head of the Dawat-e-Islami, clearly dissociated himself from Malik Mumtaz's crime. Tahir-ul-Qadri also categorically condemned Taseer's murder. He also called for religious moderation as well as efforts to rein in strife between different Islamic sects.

The Global Context

Taken as a whole, however, Taseer's murder is only one incident of Barelvi militancy, which cannot and must not be compared to more than 60,000 Pakistanis of all faiths and sects killed by Deobandi militants. There is therefore a need to engage with moderate Barelvi and other Islamic scholars in order to highlight and augment strains of moderate Islam against the takfiri jihadism of Deobandi militants. At the same time, Deobandi militancy in Pakistan must be seen in the global context of Salafi/Wahhabi and Deobandi militancy and the attacks on Sunni Sufis, Shias, Christians and other communities in the Middle East, Europe, parts of Africa and elsewhere.

In countries as diverse as Iraq, Syria, Mali, Nigeria and Libya, there have been systematic attacks on Sufi shrines by radical Salafi/Wahhabi militants.[100] There is also some evidence of Pakistan's radical Deobandi support of ISIS militants.[101] The latest incident is the San Bernardino massacre involving Pakistan-origin fanatic Tashfeen Malik, who converted from Barelvi to Deobandi/Wahhabi ideology[102] and conspired with her husband to kill 14 innocent people.

Deobandi and Wahhabi violence against Sunni (Sufi, Hanafi, Maliki etc.) Muslims is ignored or under-reported in mainstream media. The media routinely indulge in Islam vs. the West, Sunni vs. Shia and Saudi vs. Iran binaries in its reports on incidents of violence by terror outfits. Often the same binaries are also reproduced in academic scholarship and policy reports on Islamism and terror. These are mostly not only inaccurate but also counterproductive[103] because of their obfuscating and sweeping nature.

Fernandez (2015) notes that ISIS violence against fellow Sunni Muslims has not been adequately documented. In August 2014, for instance, ISIS killed almost 1,000 male members of the Sheitaat Tribe, a Sunni-Arab tribe in Syria. Many members of the tribe are currently in refugee camps. They, along with Iraqis from Anbar province and other refugees, have their own first-hand stories to tell.[104]

In October 2014, the bodies of more than 150 members of an Iraqi Sunni tribe, which fought ISIS, were found in a mass grave. ISIS militants took the Sunni Arab men from their villages to the city of Ramadi and killed them. In a separate case, witnesses said that they found 70 corpses from the same Albu Nimr tribe near the town of Hit in the Sunni heartland Anbar province. Most of the latter were members of the police or an anti-ISIS Sunni force called Sahwa (Awakening). The Human Rights Ministry of Iraq said at the beginning of November 2014 that the number of people from Albu Nimr tribe killed was 322.[105]

Similar stories are to be told by the Sunni Sufi and Barelvi communities of the KP[106] and Balochistan,[107] who, in addition to the Shias and non-Muslim communities, have suffered the most at the hands of the Deobandi Taliban and SSP/LeJ militants.

Despite its imperfections, Sufi Islam and the enhancement of its pluralistic and inclusive character, not only in Barelvis but also in other Islamic sects, is the only pragmatic and ideological way through which takfiri jihadism by Deobandis and Wahhabis can be dealt with. In Jenkins' words, the best hope for global peace is not a decline or secularization of Islam but rather a renewal and strengthening of its spiritual, mystical and pluralistic dimensions.[108]

Notes

1. Jamal, A. 2011. Sufi militants struggle with Deobandi jihadists in Pakistan. *The Jamestown Foundation*, February 24. http://www.jamestown.org/single/?tx_ttnews%5Btt_news%5D=37562&no_cache=1#.VmwLzd_hDBI

2. Global Security. n.d. Barelvi Islam. http://www.globalsecurity.org/military/intro/islam-barelvi.htm

3. Hussain, S.E. 2010. *Terrorism in Pakistan: Incident patterns, terrorists' characteristics, and the impact of terrorist arrests on terrorism*. PhD Thesis. University of Pennsylvania.

4. Lewis, M.W. 2010. Deobandi Islam vs. Barelvi Islam in South Asia. *Geo Current*. October 7, 2010.

5. Moj, M. 2015. The Deoband Madrassah Movement, Countercultural Trends and Tendencies. Anthem Press.

6. See Manzur Numani's book "Muhammad Bin Abdul Wahab aur Hindustan Kay Ulama Haq", i.e., "Muhammad Ibn Abd al-Wahhab and the rightly guided clerics of India".
7. Sanyal, U. 2010. Devotional Islam and Politics in British India: Ahmed Raza Khan Barelwi and His Movement, 1870–1920. Delhi: Yoda Press.
8. Buchen, S. (2011). Sufism under attacked in Pakistan. *The New York Times*. Times Video, June 6. Available at: http://www.nytimes.com/video/world/asia/1248069532117/sufism-under-attack-in-pakistan.html
9. Fareed, F. 2011. 'Sufi' group rejects Deoband fatwa against celebrating Prophet's birthday. Two Circles, November 10. http://twocircles.net/2011nov10/sufi_group_rejects_deoband_fatwa_against_celebrating_prophets_birthday.html
10. Mohammed, N. 2015. Wahhabi versus Sufi: social media debates. The Times of India, July 19. http://timesofindia.indiatimes.com/home/sunday-times/deep-focus/Wahabi-versus-Sufi-social-media-debates/articleshow/48128165.cms
11. Armstrong, K. 2014. Wahhabism to ISIS: how Saudi Arabia exported the main source of global terrorism. The New Statesman, November 27. http://www.newstatesman.com/world-affairs/2014/11/wahhabism-isis-how-saudi-arabia-exported-main-source-global-terrorism
12. Ibid.
13. Ahmed, K. 2000. Re-assertion of the Barelvis in Pakistan. *The Friday Times*, September 8.
14. *DW* 2012, August 24. The 'Wahabi Republic' of Pakistan. http://www.dw.com/en/the-wahabi-republic-of-pakistan/a-16191055
15. *Munazira-e-Jhang*, Ahlus Sunnah Publications, Jhelum.
16. Khan, I. 2011. The assertion of Barelvi extremism. *Hudson Institute*. http://www.hudson.org/research/9848-the-assertion-of-barelvi-extremism
17. Ibid.
18. *The Friday Times*, 2011, August 26. Constituent Assembly adopts Objectives Resolution (1949). http://www.thefridaytimes.com/beta2/tft/article.php?issue=20110826&page=30
19. Malik, I.H. 2006. Culture and Customs of Pakistan. Greenwood Press, Westport.

20. *Dawn* 2012, March 10. Government bans Ahle Sunnat wal Jamaat, claimsreport.http://www.dawn.com/news/701588/government-bans-ahle-sunnat-wal-jamaat-claims-report

21. *The Express Tribune*, 2013, January 15. Police foil terror plot targeting Eid Milad procession in DI Khan. http://tribune.com.pk/story/498984/police-foil-terror-plot-targeting-eid-milad-procession-in-di-khan/

22. *CNN* 2010, July 2. Explosions at famous shrine in Pakistan kill dozens. http://edition.cnn.com/2010/WORLD/asiapcf/07/02/pakistan.explosions/index.html

23. *The Express Tribune*, 2013, March 4. Shikarpur blast: the pir of the shrine succumbs to injuries. http://tribune.com.pk/story/515690/shikarpur-blast-gaddi-nasheen-of-the-shrine-succumbs-to-injuries/

24. Boone, J. 2015. San Bernardino shooter's 'hardline' Islam not an outlier in native Pakistan. *The Guardian*, December 7. http://www.theguardian.com/us-news/2015/dec/07/tashfeen-malik-pakistan-conservative-islam-isis-san-bernardino-shooting

25. Timeline of attacks on shrines in Pakistan. *Terrorism Watch.* http://terrorismwatch.com.pk/images/Timeline%20Of%20attacks%20on%20Shrines%20In%20Pakistan.pdf

26. Circle (2011). Pakistan Security Analysis Annual Report 2011. *Center for Innovative Research Collaboration and Learning.* Available at: http://www.circle.org.pk/images/Pakistan%20Security%20Annual%20Report.pdf

27. Perwaiz, S.B. 2015. Police finalise 10 cases for trial in military courts. *The News*, August 24. http://www.thenews.com.pk/print/58109-police-finalise-10-cases-for-trial-in-military-courts

28. Ali, Muhammad Faisal. 2009. Suicide bomber kills anti-Taliban cleric Allama Naeemi. *Dawn*, June 13.

29. Perlez, J. 2010. Killing of Doctor Part of Taliban War on Educated. The New York Times, October 8. http://www.nytimes.com/2010/10/09/world/asia/09pstan.html

30. Azami, D. 2013. The 'dissenting' clerics killed in Afghanistan. BBC, November 19. http://www.bbc.co.uk/news/world-asia-22885170

31. *The Express Tribune*, 2014, April 19. Raza Rumi attack perpetrator arrested. http://tribune.com.pk/story/697627/raza-rumi-attack-perpetrator-arrested/

32. Reeves, P. (2014). In Pakistan, Ultra-Conservative Rivals Attack Moderate Muslims. *NPR*, April, 28. Available at: http://www.npr.

org/2014/04/28/307627337/in-pakistan-ultra-conservative-muslim-movement-grows-stronger
33. Siddiqui, T. 2013. KARACHI: SSP activist gets death in Qadri murder case. Dawn, April 12. http://www.dawn.com/news/93946/karachi-ssp-activist-gets-death-in-qadri-murder-case
34. Raja, M. 2011, August 21. Bari Imam Shrine attack 2005: Police await suspects on judicial remand in another case. *The Express Tribune.* http://tribune.com.pk/story/236095/bari-imam-shrine-attack-2005-police-await-suspects-on-judicial-remand-in-another-case/
35. Roggio, B. 2008. Taliban desecrate body of slain opposing tribal leader. *Long War Journal,* December 17. http://www.longwarjournal.org/archives/2008/12/taliban_desecrate_bo.php
36. Bacha, A.H. 2009. PESHAWAR: Another faith healer shot dead in Peshawar. *Dawn,* February 18. http://www.dawn.com/news/343819/peshawar-another-faith-healer-shot-dead-in-peshawar
37. *Dawn* (2009). Suicide bomber kills anti-Taliban cleric Allama Naeemi. *Dawn,* June 13. Available at: http://www.dawn.com/news/848443/suicide-bomber-kills-anti-taliban-cleric-allama-naeemi
38. Hassan, S.R. 2014. Six Pakistanis killed over visit to Sufi Muslim shrine. *Reuters,* January 7. http://www.reuters.com/article/us-pakistan-shrine-beheadings-idUSBREA060FB20140107
39. *Dawn* (2014). Brigadier among three killed in attack on shrine. *Dawn,* September 7. Available at: http://www.dawn.com/news/1130402
40. Mufti Gulzar Naeemi, cited in: Saqib Akbar (ed.), *Pakistan Kay Deeni Masalik (Pakistan's Muslim Creeds), Al-Baseera,* December 2010, p. 13. (cited in Ismail Khan's report for the Hudson Institute).
41. Khosa, T. 2014. The general's pledge. Dawn, December 1. http://www.dawn.com/news/1147948
42. *Dawn,* 2011, May 25. WikiLeaks: 2009: Was Qaddafi funding Sipahe Sahaba? http://www.dawn.com/news/631599/2009-was-qaddafi-funding-sipahe-sahaba
43. Jamal, A. 2011. Sufi Militants Struggle with Deobandi Jihadists in Pakistan. *The Jamestown Foundation.* http://www.jamestown.org/programs/tm/single/?tx_ttnews%5Btt_news%5D=37562&cHash=520e6 5450a; Tanveer, R. 2012. Barelvi leader alleges pro-Deobandi bias in Defence Housing Authority. *The Express Tribune,* March 11. http://

tribune.com.pk/story/348259/barelvi-leader-alleges-pro-deobandi-bias-in-defence-housing-authority/

44. ICG (International Crisis Group) 2007. Pakistan: Karachi's madrasas and violent extremism. *International Crisis Group.* Asia Report N°130—29 March 2007.

45. Syed, J. 2015. From Karachi to San Bernardino: In Quest of an Alternative Discourse on Terrorism. *The Huffington Post*, December 8. http://www.huffingtonpost.co.uk/jawad-syed/san-bernardino-karachi-terrorism_b_8740002.html

46. Grubbs, F. E. 1969. Procedures for detecting outlying observations in samples. *Technometrics* 11 (1), 1–21.

47. Awan, A. 2011. Anatomy of a murder. *The Friday Times*, January 15–21. Available at: http://www.thefridaytimes.com/14012011/page7.shtml

48. Ibid.

49. *Newsweek*, 2011. Key Pakistani governor killed by own bodyguard. January4.http://www.newsweek.com/key-pakistani-governor-killed-own-bodyguard-66815

50. Ghani, L. 2011. The PML-N's duplicity: Letter to the editor. *The Express Tribune*, March 13; Khan, M. 2010. Dealing with the devil. *The Express Tribune*, January 8. http://tribune.com.pk/story/100558/dealing-with-the-devil

51. Pakistan Media Watch, 13 October 2011. Is Khawaja Sharif or Ansar Abbasi defending Mumtaz Qadri? http://pakistanmediawatch.com/2011/10/13/is-khawaja-sharif-or-ansar-abbasi-defending-mumtaz-qadri/; Abbasi, A. 2011. Mumtaz Qadri ko saza, Adalat nay riasat kee nakami nazarandaz kardi. *Jang*, October 10.

52. Pak's Media-Mujahidin Meher Bukhari's venomous attack on Salman Taseer. *YouTube.* https://www.youtube.com/watch?v=b0_plr3mgJw

53. The News Tribe. A short history of Mehar Bukhari. http://www.thenewstribe.com/2012/06/17/a-short-history-of-mehar-bukhari/

54. Walsh, D. 2011. A divided Pakistan buries Salmaan Taseer and a liberal dream. *The Guardian*, January 6. http://www.theguardian.com/world/2011/jan/05/pakistan-salman-taseer-liberal

55. Manzoor, U. 2011. Events that led to Taseer's murder. *The News*, January 06.

56. *The Express Tribune.* 2010. Blasphemy case: Cleric offers Rs500,000 for Aasia's execution. December 3. http://tribune.com.pk/ story/85412/blasphemy-case-masjid-imam-offers-reward-to-kill-aasia

57. *NDTV*, 2011. Pak police arrests man who offered Rs 20 million for killing Taseer. January 5. http://www.ndtv.com/world-news/ pak-police-arrests-man-who-offered-rs-20-million-for-killing-taseer-444084

58. Mumtaz Qadri Qatil hai by Ameer e Ahle Sunnat. YouTube. https:// www.youtube.com/watch?v=lPrBtOnjpBM

59. Ilyas Qadri and Dr Tahir ul Qadri condemn Salmaan Taseer's murder by Malik Mumtaz. *YouTube.* https://www.youtube.com/ watch?v=tat9unKyUO8

60. Khalil, T. 2011. Mumtaz Qadri kay shiddat pasand tanzeem say rabton ka inkishaf. *Jang*, January 8. Available at: Pak.net

61. Awan, A. 2011. Anatomy of a murder. *The Friday Times*, January. Available at: http://www.thefridaytimes.com/14012011/page7.shtml

62. Khalil, T. 2011. Mumtaz Qadri kay shiddat pasand tanzeem say rabton ka inkishaf. *Jang*, January 8. Available at: https://lubpak.com/ wp-content/uploads/2015/01/111.jpg

63. *BBC News* 2011, January 10. Mumtaz Qadri admits killing Governor Salman Taseer. http://www.bbc.co.uk/news/world-south-asia-12149607

64. Syed, J. 2011. Sharif vs Sharif. Daily Times, October 17. http:// archives.dailytimes.com.pk/editorial/17-Oct-2011/view-sharifs-vs-sharif-dr-jawad-syed

65. Malik, S. 2015. Salmaan Taseer kay qaatil Mumtaz Qadri ki nazr saani ki appeal bhi mustarad. *BBC Urdu*, December 14. http://www.bbc.com/urdu/ pakistan/2015/12/151214_mumtaz_qadri_appeal_rejected_zh

66. Captain Safdar Speech in Favour of Ghazi Mumtaz Qadri. *Daily Motion.* http://www.dailymotion.com/video/x3flczi

67. Mir, A. 2013. SSP leader who fixed bounty on Taseer given PML-N ticket. *The News*, May 7. http://www.thenews.com.pk/Todays-News-2-175873-SSP-leader-who-fixed-bounty-on-Taseer-given-PML-N-ticke ; Shehzad, M. 2013. Friends or foes? *The Friday Times*, May 24. http://www.thefridaytimes.com/beta3/tft/article. php?issue=20130524&page=4

68. Siddiqui, Salman. 2011. Hardline Stance: Religious bloc condones murder. *The Express Tribune.* January 5.
69. Shah, S. 2011. Mainstream Pakistan religious organisations applaud killing of Salmaan Taseer. *The Guardian*, January 5. http://www. theguardian.com/world/2011/jan/05/pakistan-religious-organisations-salman-taseer
70. *Dawn*, 2011. Herald exclusive: Not so blind justice. March 21. http://www.dawn.com/news/614820/herald-exclusive-not-so-blind-justice
71. Munawar, H.B. 2011. Lashkar-e-Jhangvi and the "lack of evidence". *Dawn*, July 19. http://www.dawn.com/news/645189/lashkar-e-jhangvi-and-the-lack-of-evidence
72. http://www.viewpointonline.net/2014/03/vp192/religious-persecution-in-pakistan?fb_comment_id=1431405170434729_196791#f13e3c82b4
73. Tanveer, R. 2011. Deobandis, Wahhabis to join Qadri protests. *The Express Tribune*, October 6. http://tribune.com.pk/story/267875/deobandis-wahhabis-to-join-qadri-protests
74. *Pakistan Today.* 2011, January 6. Top prayer leaders deny Taseer his rites. http://www.pakistantoday.com.pk/2011/01/06/national/top-prayer-leaders-deny-taseer-his-rites/
75. Siddiqui, S. 2011. Hardline Stance: Religious bloc condones murder. *The Express Tribune*, January 5. http://tribune.com.pk/story/99313/hardline-stance-religious-bloc-condones-murder
76. Haider, E. 2013. Of holy lies and Lal Masjid. *The Express Tribune*, October 29.
    http://tribune.com.pk/story/624242/of-holy-lies-and-lal-masjid/
77. Craig, T. 2015. The Taliban once ruled Pakistan's Swat Valley. Now peace has returned. *The Washington Post*, May 9. https://www.washingtonpost.com/world/the-taliban-once-ruled-pakistans-swat-valley-now-peace-has-returned/2015/05/08/6bb8ac96-eeaa-11e4-8050-839e9234b303_story.html
78. ICG 2007. Pakistan: Karachi's madrasas and violent extremism. Asia Report N°130 – 29 March 2007. http://www.crisisgroup.org/~/media/Files/asia/south-asia/pakistan/130_pakistan_karachi_s_madrasas_and_violent_extremism.ashx
79. *The Express Tribune*, 2011, February 14. Hajj scam: Kazmi, Swati open unhealed wounds in new war of words. http://tribune.com.

pk/story/118495/hajj-scam-kazmi-swati-open-unhealed-wounds-in-new-war-of-words/

80. *The Express Tribune* 2011, January 28. Hajj scandal: SC dissatisfied over FIA's progress. http://tribune.com.pk/story/109862/hajj-scam-contacts-established-between-kazmi-and-rao-shakeel/

81. *The Express Tribune*, 2010, November 6. Bill to amend blasphemy laws submitted in NA secretariat. http://tribune.com.pk/story/82002/bill-to-amend-blasphemy-laws-submitted-in-na-secretariat/

82. *Dawn*, 2010, April 4. The passion for Bhutto. http://www.dawn.com/news/832627/the-passion-for-bhutto

83. Khan, I. 2011. The assertion of Barelvi extremism. *Hudson Institute.*

84. ibid

85. *Vatican Insider*, 2015, March 9. Pakistan: Impunity reigns in Bhatti's murder case. http://www.lastampa.it/2015/03/09/vaticaninsider/eng/world-news/pakistan-impunity-reigns-in-bhattis-murder-case-RGve1JwekG6Hl1c2KyKU5H/pagina.html ; Tahir Ashrafi Behind The Murder of Shahbaz Bhatti. *YouTube.* https://www.youtube.com/watch?v=33MISggpVvE

86. *The Express Tribune* 2010, July 3. Politicians condemn attack on DataDarbar.http://tribune.com.pk/story/25385/politicians-condemn-attack-on-data-darbar/

87. http://www.tafrehmella.com/threads/governor-punjab-salman-taseer%E2%80%99s-family-wine-dance-pictures-scandal.133686/

88. Ghani, L. 2011. The PML-N's duplicity: Letter to the editor. *The Express Tribune*, March 13.

89. *Christians in Pakistan* 2014, March 31. Pakistan Tehreek e Taliban demands Release of Mumtaz Qadri. http://www.christiansinpakistan.com/pakistan-tehreek-e-taliban-demands-release-of-mumtaz-qadri/

90. Khan, M.I. 2016. Shahbaz Taseer: Why was murdered Pakistan governor's son released? *BBC News*, March 9. http://www.bbc.co.uk/news/world-asia-35768245

91. *The News* 2016. Rallies staged against Mumtaz Qadri's hanging. March2.http://www.thenews.com.pk/print/102212-Rallies-staged-against-Mumtaz-Qadris-hanging

92. *Dunya News* 2014, February 3. TTP prepares demand list for talks: sources.http://dunyanews.tv/en/Pakistan/210820-TTP-prepares-demand-list-for-talks-sources

93. *Minhaj-ul-Quran* 2015, March 6. Speakers at peace seminar pay tributes to Dr Tahir-ul-Qadri. http://www.minhaj.org/english/tid/32157

94. *Daily Times,* 2014, August 26. Punjab CM, govt responsible in Model Town massacre: Qadri. http://www.dailytimes.com.pk/national/26-Aug-2014/punkjab-cm-govt-responsible-in-model-town-massacre-qadri

95. *The Nation,* 2015, September 18. Court smashes Gullu Butt's bail plea. http://nation.com.pk/lahore/18-Sep-2015/court-smashes-gullu-butt-s-bail-plea

96. *Pakistan Today* 2014, August 26. Judicial Commission report holds Punjab govt 'responsible' for Model Town bloodbath. http://www.pakistantoday.com.pk/2014/08/26/national/judicial-commission-holds-punjab-govt-responsible-for-model-town-bloodbath/

97. Tanveer, R. 2011. Deobandis, Wahhabis to join Qadri protests. *The Express Tribune,* October 6. http://tribune.com.pk/story/267875/deobandis-wahhabis-to-join-qadri-protests

98. Hoodbhoy, P. 2009. The Saudi-isation of Pakistan. *The Newsline,* January 3.

99. Ali, K. 2015. Malik Ishaq had serious differences with Ludhianvi: observers. Dawn, August 25. http://www.dawn.com/news/1202616

100. The Muslim 500. Destruction of Sufi Shrines. http://themuslim500.com/2013-2/issues-of-the-day/destruction-of-sufi-shrines

101. Khan, A. 2014. No regret over supporting IS, says Lal Masjid cleric. *The Express Tribune,* December 15. http://tribune.com.pk/story/806711/no-regret-over-supporting-is-says-lal-masjid-cleric/

102. Walsh, D. 2015. Tashfeen Malik Was a 'Saudi Girl' Who Stood Out at a Pakistani University. *The New York Times,* December 6. http://www.nytimes.com/2015/12/07/world/asia/in-conservative-pakistani-city-a-saudi-girl-who-stood-out.html

103. Galloway, G. 2015. Geroge Galloway criticizes Saudi attack on Yemen, debunks the false Sunni-Shia binary. YouTube, March 28. https://www.youtube.com/watch?v=RYPLEMKvq2A

104. Fernandez, A.M. 2015. Four ways to counter ISIS propaganda more effectively. *The Brookings,* November 16. Available at: http://www.brookings.edu/blogs/markaz/posts/2015/11/16-countering-isis-propaganda-fernandez

105. Georgy, M. 2014. Iraq says 322 tribe members killed, many bodies dumped in well. *Reuters,* November 2. http://www.reuters.com/ article/us-mideast-crisis-iraq-idUSKBN0IM0I920141102
106. *Dawn* 2009, June 29. Mastermind of shrine attacks arrested. http:// www.dawn.com/news/942507/mastermind-of-shrine-attacks-arrested
107. *Dawn*, 2005, March 21. Shrine blast toll rises to 40. http://www. dawn.com/news/385987/shrine-blast-toll-rises-to-40
108. Jenkins, P. (2009). Mystical power. *Boston Globe*, January 25. Available at: http://www.boston.com/bostonglobe/ideas/articles/ 2009/01/25/mystical_power/?page=full

APPENDIX: SUNNI SUFI AND BARELVI KILLINGS
IN PAKISTAN

Date	Province	Place	Incident	Killed/ injured
18 December 1986	Punjab	Mananwala	Khalid Mahmood killed	1/0
14 February 1987	Punjab	Tandlianwala	Sher Ali, Javed Iqbal and Babar Hussain killed	3/0
15 November 1989	Punjab	Jhang	Hafiz Muhammad Afzal killed during Milad	1/0
16 February 1991	Punjab	Gujranwala	Rana Shaukat Ali killed	1/0
31 May 1991	Punjab	Sargodha	Imdad Hussain killed in Dhalli area	1/0
15 June 1991	Sindh	Karachi	Abdus Salam Qadri of ST killed	1/0
12 August 1994	Punjab	Gujranwala	Maulana Akram Rizvi killed	1/0
9 December 1994	Punjab	Faisalabad	Abdur Rahman Raza killed	1/0
9 December 1995	Punjab	Wazirabad	Shabbir Hussain Shah killed	1/0
12 January 1996	Punjab	Jhang	Ihsanullah killed	1/0
5 February 1996	Punjab	Layyah	Fazl Husain Fazl killed	1/0
14 July 1996	Punjab	Lahore	Ilyas Qadri attacked, Sajjad Raza and Ahmed Raza killed	2/0
10 December 1996	Punjab	Lahore	Irfan Waraich killed	1/0

Date	Province	Place	Incident	Killed/ injured
10 December 1996	Punjab	Gujranwala	Shahzad Butt, Masood Khalid Mufti and Ismat Noori killed	3/0
17 April 1997	Punjab	Sialkot	Naeem Bhatti killed	1/0
10 July 1997	Sindh	Karachi	Javed Qadri killed	1/0
16 January 1998	Sindh	Karachi	Saleem Qadri killed	1/0
6 February 1998	Sindh	Karachi	Haseeb Khan killed in Shah Faisal Colony	1/0
29 June 1998	Punjab	Bahawalpur	Kaleemullah Khan Saeedi killed	1/0
16 July 1998	Sindh	Karachi	Saleem Qadri killed	1/0
18 July 1998	Sindh	Karachi	Abdul Waheed Qadri of ST killed	1/0
18 April 1999	FATA	Khyber	Pir Baba's shrine attacked	2/6
20 December 2000	Punjab	Sialkot	Mehr Waryam killed	1/0
6 April 2001	Sindh	Karachi	Hafiz Pir Muhammad Piral and Zakir Hussain killed during Milad	2/0
18 May 2001	Sindh	Karachi	ST leader Saleem Qadri assassinated; Anis Qadri, Abid Baloch, Altaf Juneju and Hafeez Qadri killed	6/3
1 May 2002	Punjab	Lahore	Deobandi SSP terrorists killed Dr Murtaza Malik, his driver and a policeman in Gulshan-i-Iqbal	3/0
19 August 2002	Punjab	Muzaffargarh	Shahid Qadri killed	1/0
18 October 2003	Punjab	Sialkot	Irshad Akhtar killed	1/0
9 November 2004	Sindh	Karachi	Kamran Qadri and Meraj Qadri killed	2/0
10 February 2005	Islamabad Capital Territory	Islamabad	Barri Imam's caretaker Akram Raja killed	1/0
19 March 2005	Balochistan	Jhal Magsi	Deobandi suicide bomber killed 50 at the shrine of Pir Rakhel Shah in Jhal Magsi, Balochistan	50/85
18 April 2005	Sindh	Karachi	Tahir Qadri killed	1/0
27 May 2005	Islamabad Capital Territory	Islamabad	A suicide bomber attacked a gathering at Bari Imam shrine during the annual festival	28/100

Date	Province	Place	Incident	Killed/injured
5 June 2005	Sindh	Karachi	Ashraf Qadri, Faiz-ul-Hasan Butt and Danish Qadri killed	3/0
13 August 2005	Sindh	Karachi	Islamic TV channel (QTV's) Maulana Abdul Karim Naqshbandi killed	1/0
12 October 2005	Sindh	Karachi	Muhammad Ali Qadri and Akhtar Shah killed	2/0
30 October 2005	Sindh	Karachi	Nadeem Qadri killed	1/0
5 December 2005	Sindh	Karachi	Maulana Habib-ur-Rehman Saeedi killed	1/0
15 December 2005	Sindh	Karachi	Muhammad Adnan Butt Attari killed	1/0
26 January 2006	Balochistan	Hubb	Grenade attack on a Sufi shrine, Syed Shah Bukhari	3/0
11 April 2006	Sindh	Karachi	A grand Sunni Barelvi congregation celebrating Eid Milad un Nabi suicide-bombed. Entire leadership of the ST was killed, including 49 Sunni leaders and Maulana Abbas Qadri, Akram Qadri, Iftikhar Butt, Mufti Shahid Attari, Dr Abdul Qadeer Abbasi, Hannif Billo, President of Jamaat Ahle Sunnat, Hafiz Taqi, leader of the JUP, and ex-member of the National Assembly	57/150
14 April 2006	Sindh	Karachi	ASWJ bomb scare in Dawat Islami Faizan-e-Madina	30/45
14 April 2006	Punjab	Faisalabad	Maulana Abdul Qadir killed by the SSP/ASWJ .	1/0
10 July 2006	Sindh	Karachi	Driver of the head of ST killed at airport	1/0
12 May 2007	Sindh	Karachi	Sohail Qadri killed	1/0
8 July 2007	Islamabad Capital Territory	Islamabad	Colonel Haroon Islam killed by Deobandi terrorists of Lal Masjid	1/0
28 July 2007	FATA	Khyber	Haji Shah Torangzai Lakro shrine destroyed and converted to Deobandi Mosque	0/0

Date	Province	Place	Incident	Killed/ injured
28 December 2007	FATA	Khyber	Abdul Shakoor Malang Baba's shrine attacked	6/7
3 March 2008	KP	Peshawar	Abu Saeed Baba's shrine attacked by rockets	10/6
18 March 2008	FATA	Bara	Sufi shrine attacked	13/9
26 March 2008	Sindh	Karachi	Noman Qadri killed	1/0
28 March 2008	Sindh	Karachi	Muhammad Ejaz Qadri killed	1/0
30 March 2008	Sindh	Karachi	Faizan Qadri and Awais Qadri of ST killed	2/0
23 April 2008	Sindh	Karachi	Amir Abul Hasan of ST killed in Korangi	1/0
1 May 2008	KP	Peshawar	Ash-hab Baba's shrine attacked	3/0
7 July 2008	Sindh	Karachi	Sufi shrine attacked in Peer Mangu	1/4
19 September 2008	Balochistan	Quetta	Bomb exploded at an Islamic religious school. Victims included Sunni Sufis, Barelvis and Deobandis	5/8
10 October 2008	KP	Swat	Pir Samiullah's brother was killed	1/0
15 October 2008	Sindh	Karachi	Abdus Sattar Qadri of ST killed	1/0
17 October 2008	Sindh	Karachi	Sultan Qadri and Irfan Qadri killed	2/0
19 October 2008	Sindh	Karachi	Noor Muhammad Qadri killed	1/0
28 October 2008	Sindh	Karachi	Wasim Qadri and Fahim Qadri killed	2/0
10 November 2008	Sindh	Karachi	Furqan Qadri killed	1/0
11 November 2008	Sindh	Karachi	Hafiz Farhan Naqshbandi and Asif Qadri killed, Ahmed Qadir and Sajid Qadri injured	2/2
9 December 2008	KP	Buner	Pir Baba's shrine attacked	1/6
15 December 2008	Sindh	Karachi	Muhammad Ali of ST killed	1/0
16 December 2008	KP	Swat	Pir Samiullah was killed by extremist Deobandis; his body was exhumed and desecrated	1/0
17 January 2009	KP	Peshawar	Pir Rafiullah killed	1/0

Date	Province	Place	Incident	Killed/ injured
17 February 2009	KP	Peshawar	Pir Syed Phool Badshah Bukhari killed	1/0
18 February 2009	Balochistan	Quetta	JUP-Noorani's provincial leader Maulana Iftikhar Ahmed Habibi killed	1/0
5 March 2009	KP	Peshawar	Rahman Baba shrine bombed	0/0
7 March 2009	KP	Nowshera	Pir Bahadar Baba shrine attacked	1/12
9 March 2009	Punjab	Faisalabad	Muhammad Anwar Attari of Dawat Islami killed during Milad rally	1/0
9 March 2009	KP	Hazro	Dilnawaz Khan and Waheed killed	2/0
1 May 2009	FATA	Landi Kotal	Amir Humza Shinwari's shrine attacked with rockets	5/0
6 May 2009	FATA	Orakzai	Pir Khayal Muhammad shrine attacked	7/0
8 May 2009	KP	Peshawar	Pir Sheikh Ali Baba or Omar Baba Shrine attacked	6/0
12 June 2009	Punjab	Lahore	Mufti Sarfraz Naeemi killed in a Deobandi ASWJ suicide attack	6/15
2 September 2009	Islamabad Capital Territory	Islamabad	Hamid Saeed Kazmi attacked and injured	0/1
4 December 2009	Punjab	Rawalpindi	Suicide bombing in army mosque in Rawalpindi	37/67
5 January 2010	FATA	Orakzai	Seven shrines attacked; many injured or kidnapped	0/35
1 April 2010	FATA	Khyber	Sufi shrine attacked	10/20
22 April 2010	FATA	Orakzai	Pir Baba Abdul Haq shrine attacked	3/0
20 June 2010	Sindh	Karachi	Firoz Khan of ST killed	1/0
21 June 2010	KP	Peshawar	Pir Baba Umar Mian shrine attacked in Chamkani	11/0
1 July 2010	Punjab	Lahore	Two Deobandi suicide bombers blew themselves up at the Sufi shrine, Data Durbar Complex	50/200
15 July 2010	FATA	Landi Kotal	Haji Sahibzada Siddiq Binor alias Peer Bacha shrine attacked	8/0

Date	Province	Place	Incident	Killed/injured
19 August 2010	Punjab	Lahore	Pir Khaki Shah Rasool shrine attacked in Green Town Bagrian	7/0
20 September 2010	KP	Peshawar	Pir Saalik Shah Baba shrine attacked	3/0
2 October 2010	KP	Mardan	Dr Muhammad Farooq Khan killed	1/0
7 October 2010	Sindh	Karachi	Adbullah Shah Ghazi shrine attacked	21/60
24 October 2010	FATA	Khyber	Syed Muhammad Shah shrine in Pranga bombed	4/0
25 October 2010	Punjab	Pakpattan	Baba Farid Ganj Shakar shrine attacked	11/25
14 December 2010	KP	Peshawar	Ghazi Baba shrine attacked	3/5
3 January 2011	FATA	Waziristan	In South Waziristan, Baba Musa Neeka shrine bombed	4/0
4 February 2011	Punjab	Lahore	Baba Saeen shrine attacked	3/27
5 March 2011	KP	Nowshera	Akhund Panju Baba shrine mosque	13/30
3 April 2011	Punjab	Dera Ghazi Khan	Sakhi Sarwar shrine attacked	62/120
18 April 2011	Punjab	Gujranwala	Ex-Ahle Hadith Omar Farooqi Tauheedi attacked; Hammad Tauheedi killed	1/1
20 April 2011	Sindh	Karachi	Farhan Qadri and his wife killed	2/0
21 April 2011	Balochistan	Quetta	Abdul Kabir Qambrani Qadri, his son Muhamamd Amin, friends Dur Muhammad Khan and Shamsuddin Qadri killed	4/5
24 May 2011	Sindh	Karachi .	Commando Muhammad Rashid Attari killed in ASWJ's attack on Pakistan Naval Station Mehran	1/0
22 July 2011	FATA	Landi Kotal	Kotal Hamza Shinwari shrine attacked	3/0
19 October 2011	FATA	Khyber	Agency Haji Gul shrine near Pir Noor ul Haq Qadri Member of the National Assembly (MNA's) house	2/0
21 October 2011	KP	Swabi	Karim Shah shrine bombed	2/0

Date	Province	Place	Incident	Killed/ injured
1 November 2011	KP	Dera Ismail Khan	Saeedullah Daad Shah shrine bombed	3/0
11 December 2011	FATA	Khyber	Agency Nisar Baba shrine detonated; Sheika Bahadar Bara	4/0
3 February 2012	KP	Peshawar	Phandu Baba shrine attacked at Chamkani	0/0
10 March 2012	Sindh	Karachi	Saleem Qadri killed	1/0
16 April 2012	Sindh	Karachi	Two ST workers, 30-year-old Rashid and 35-year-old Yahya, shot dead in Gulshan-e-Zahoor in Lines Area	2/0
21 June 2012	KP	Peshawar	Shrine of Hazrat Panj Peer attacked	3/0
18 May 2012	Sindh	Karachi	Shehbaz Qadri and Armaghan Qadri killed	2/0
3 May 2012	Punjab	Lahore	Shakil Qadri of ST killed	1/0
13 August 2012	Sindh		Karachi Arif and Sajid Khan of ST killed	2/0
14 August 2012	Sindh	Karachi	Aftab Chishti of the ST District West and Fahim Qadri shot dead in Baldia Town	2/0
5 December 2012	Sindh	Karachi	Zahid Qadri of ST killed	1/0
6 January 2013	Sindh	Karachi	Two ST workers killed: Abdur Razzaq and Muhammad Ali	2/0
26 February 2013	Sindh	Shikarpur	Hajan Shah Huzoori at Marri village killed	4/12
15 April 2013	Punjab	Faisalabad	Sahibzada Haji Fazle Kareem poisoned	1/0
4 May 2013	Punjab	Lahore	ST's Khurram Raza Qadri shot dead	1/0
2 June 2013	Sindh	Karachi	Jawad Qadri and Yasir Qadri killed	2/0
26 August 2013	Sindh	Karachi	Javed Qadri of ST killed in Ranchore Lines	1/0
30 November 2013	Sindh	Karachi	Saleem, a Sufi malang, kidnapped and beheaded	1/0
31 December 2013	KP	Charsadda	Baba sahib shrine bombed	3/0
7 January 2014	Sindh	Karachi	Six Sunni Sufis slaughtered at Ayub Shah Bukhari shrine	6/0

Date	Province	Place	Incident	Killed/injured
10 January 2014	KP	Mardan	Shaheed Ghazi Baba shrine attacked	2/0
3 February 2014	Sindh	Karachi	Kamran Qadri of ST killed in Manghopir	1/0
9 February 2014	Sindh	Karachi	Aastana Per Mehrban Shah, Baldia Town, attacked	8/16
16 February 2014	KP	Peshawar	Peer Israr killed in Shambokhel, Peshawar, with eight relatives and companions	9/0
20 May 2014	Sindh	Karachi	Two brothers, Amanullah Qadri and Ameenullah Qadri of ST, killed in Orangi Town	2/0
17 June 2014	Punjab	Lahore	PAT workers killed by Punjab Police	14/89
23 June 2014	Islamabad Capital Territory	Islamabad	Chan pir shrine attacked near Shahzad Town	2/80
2 July 2014	Sindh	Karachi	Maqsood Qadri target killed; Naeem Qadri injured	1/1
9 August 2014	Punjab	Bhakkar	Sunni Barelvi leader of PAT killed	1/0
9 August 2014	Punjab	Kamoke	Sunni Barelvi leader killed	1/0
20 August 2014	Punjab	Gujranwala	Sunni Barelvi leader of PAT killed: Shoaib	35/1
24 August 2014	Sindh	Karachi	Nazar Hussain Shah dargah attacked in Korangi; another attack in Gizri	1/1
26 August 2014	Balochistan	Mastung	Sheikh Taqi shrine attacked	5/0
28 August 2014	Balochistan	Avaran	Sunni Sufi shrine attacked and Sunnis killed	6/13
31 August 2014	Islamabad Capital Territory	Islamabad	PAT workers killed by PML-N police	4/12
6 September 2014	Punjab	Sargodha	ISI's Brigadier Fazle Zahoor, his brother Fazle Subhani and another Sunni Sufi killed	3/3
18 September 2014	Sindh	Karachi	Dr Shakil Auj killed by Deobandi ASWJ terrorists after an alleged fatwa by Mufti Rafi Usmani	1/0
19 September 2014	Sindh	Karachi	ST worker Meraj Muhammad killed	1/0

Date	Province	Place	Incident	Killed/injured
1 October 2014	Sindh	Karachi	ST worker Muhammad Hussain Qadri killed	1/0
1 October 2014	Sindh	Karachi	Sunni ST worker Hasan alias Lala killed in Godhra camp	1/0
19 October 2014	Sindh	Karachi	Faisal Qadri killed in fake encounter	1/0
20 October 2014	Sindh	Karachi	Afzal Qadri of Sunni Tahreek killed	1/0
1 November 2014	Punjab	Chicha	PAT leader Maulana Hafiz Bashir ul Qadri killed	1/0
12 November 2014	Balochistan	Quetta	2 Sunnis along with 2 Shias and a Hindu killed	2/2
26 December 2014	Sindh	Karachi	Qadir Shah killed in Baldia Town Karachi	1/0
19 February 2015	KP	Abbottabad	Maulana Mehmud Shah Rizvi killed in Mansehra	1/0
2 March 2015	Balochistan	Usta	Ghausia mosque attacked	2/5
18 April 2015	Sindh	Karachi	Sunni Ittehad Council's leader Tariq Mehboob attacked	1/0
29 April 2015	Sindh	Karachi	Prof Syed Abdur Rehman killed	1/0
31 May 2015	KP	Dera Ismail Khan	Deobandi terrorists attacked Sunni Barelvi spiritual leader, Peer Atal Sharif, and his son in a roadside bomb attack	0/2
17 September 2015	Sindh	Karachi	Sunni Sufi shrine Zinda Peer attacked	2/4
22 June 2016	Sindh	Karachi	Famous Sufi singer Amjad Sabri target killed by the Taliban	1/0

Note: This table comprises the most notable incidents only.

Total number of notable Sunni Sufi and Barelvi leaders and activists target killed = 617 (excluding the Sufi/Barelvi deaths in indiscriminate attacks by the TTP/ASWJ).

CHAPTER 10

The Shias of Pakistan: Mapping an Altruistic Genocide

Abbas Zaidi

INTRODUCTION

Altaf Hussain, a resident of Dera Ismael Khan and working in Peshawar as an assistant director of the Anti-Corruption Department, had been receiving threats from members of the proscribed Deobandi group ASWJ. On 13 December 2013, he did not return home from the office. His family members in Dera Ismail Khan contacted him in the evening as per their routine, but his phone was out of reach. They called repeatedly but could not establish contact with him. On the morning of 20 December, they were informed that his corpse had been found outside Mardan. His severed head and body parts were scattered all over the area.

Pakistan's media—print and electronic—uniformly blacked out the story. Only a local Dera Ismael Khan newspaper reported details of the tragedy (Ahmad, 21 December 2013).[1] People outside Dera Ismael Khan learned about Altaf Hussain's fate from Mr Anser Abbas, a family friend of Altaf Hussain. In 2009, Anser Abbas himself was a victim of terrorism when he lost both of his hands in a suicide bombing at a Shia religious procession in Dera Ismael Khan. He now tweets with his feet (Ghani, 10 February 2014).[2] The story of Anser Abbas also went unnoticed in the Pakistan media.

A. Zaidi (✉)
University of New South Wales, Sydney, NSW, Australia

© The Editor(s) (if applicable) and The Author(s) 2016   273
J. Syed et al. (eds.), *Faith-Based Violence and Deobandi
Militancy in Pakistan*, DOI 10.1057/978-1-349-94966-3_10

Here is another case. On the morning of 18 February 2013, Dr Ali Haider left home in his car to drop his 12-year-old son, Ali Murtaza, off at school.[3] As he approached the Forman Christian College (Lahore) underpass, four men riding two motorbikes closed in and sprayed the car with bullets. Once the car had stopped after hitting the roadside, the assassins walked up and shot Haider in the face and head multiple times. After that, they shot his son in the head and rode off. Haider was Pakistan's top eye specialist and at the time of his murder was a professor and Head of the Department of Ophthalmology at Lahore's General Hospital.

Within the month of February, Haider's murder was preceded by murders of hundreds of men, women, boys, girls and infants in various parts of Pakistan. Tragic as these killings were, no one—media, politicians, opinion-makers, social activists, NGOs or human rights organizations (including the Pakistan Human Rights Commission)—pointed out that all the people killed were Shias.

Thus, for a writer or researcher writing in the present or future about faith-based killing in Pakistan and basing their work on journalistic and other sources, the word "Shia" will be non-existent. In other words, no instance of Shia killing being evident, there is, or will be, no such thing as Shia killing, let alone Shia genocide.

This chapter is about Shia genocide in Pakistan. Since most of the available definitions of genocide are too general (see below), I seek to revisit the concept by redefining it with reference to the Shia genocide in Pakistan. I also propose a model of genocide that, it is hoped, will account for the general dynamics of genocide. I would like to make it explicit here that since the proposed definition and model are 'new', they should be noted for their tentativeness.

Another point I should like to make here is that in Pakistan the Shias are not the only community under a genocidal assault. The Ahmadis, Christians, Hindus, and Barelvi Sunnis/Sufis have also been facing extreme persecution at the hands of Deobandi militants. However, the present study is about the Shias only.

METHODOLOGY

Studies carried out on genocide often do not adopt an explicit research methodology.[4] The proposed model aims to account for the dynamics of genocide by drawing on Halliday's Systemic-Functional Linguistics (Halliday 1994). The central contention of Systemic-Functional Linguistics is based on the premise that language references reality, perceived or otherwise, in society. In other words, various happenings are the result of people's engagement with the world around them or the 'goings-on', which, according to Halliday (1994, p. 106), is "people's most powerful impression of experience". This is the ideational function of language that embodies people's experience of the outer and inner worlds (Halliday 1971/1996, p. 58).

Happenings, however, are not immutable; they are given specific meaning by people because they want them to be understood in specific ways and, thus, wishing their interlocutors to take on "a complimentary role". This is the interpersonal or evaluative function. Halliday (1971/1996, pp. 58–59) elaborates on the interpersonal role thus:

> the speaker is using language as a means of his own intrusion into the speech event: the expression of his comments, his attitudes, and evaluations, and also the relationship that he sets up between himself and the listener—in particular, the communication role that he adopts, of informing, questioning, greeting, persuading, and the like.

The happenings and their representations, however, have to be put across in certain ways. In other words, happenings have to be give prominence and foregrounding so that they dominate a given scenario. This is the textual function of language through which language creates "links with itself and with the situation; and discourse becomes possible, because the speaker or writer can produce a text and the listener or reader can recognise one" (Halliday 1971/1996, p. 59).[5]

Based on Halliday's systemic functions, the model given below will endeavour to show how genocide is planned, carried out, and justified. Briefly, a genocide is based on real or imagined happenings rooted in the past or present. "Facts" to incriminate a designated group are positioned in a way which justifies a genocidal campaign. The very act of designating a group (or blaming the victim) is an act of positioning. And, finally, the identity, beliefs and so on of the designated group are foregrounded in various ways to set the focus on its "crimes" and "immorality".

Genocide: The Problem of Definition

"Genocide" is an unfortunate term, which reveals the parochial approach of many a scholarly mind. For instance, Michael Ignatieff (2001, p. 25) refuses to accept that the black slavery which killed millions of African slaves was genocide. In his own words slavery is called genocide, when—whatever else it was—it was a system to exploit the living rather than to exterminate them ... . Genocide has no meaning unless the crime can be connected to a clear intention to exterminate a human group in whole or in part. Something more than rhetorical exaggeration for effect is at stake here. Calling every abuse or crime a genocide makes it steadily more difficult to rouse people to action when a genuine genocide is taking place.

Ignatieff presents a humane view of slavery. By his formulation, the human costs of slavery were just an epiphenomenon. The master was not so bad after all because he wanted his slaves to live a long, healthy life so that he could utilize their bodies. Ignatieff, *inter alia*, is not willing even to give a basic understanding of slavery—"whatever else it was". He is unhappy with calling "every" abuse and crime genocidal. It can be argued that few descendents of the slaves today would find Ignatieff's view of slavery acceptable. It may be asked: What about those slaves who ceased to be "useful" once past their physical prime? Was there a welfare system set up for them by their white masters? What about those who were not "useful" by birth because they had some disability? What if today a descendant of those slaves claims that their treatment constituted genocide? Will they be shut up because their claim (of genocide) is not in line with a definition that Ignatieff constructs?

Another unfortunate aspect of the traditional debate about genocide is its focus on the number of people physically eliminated. Hundreds of thousands of people have to be killed in order to qualify for the title. Otherwise, any debate about their status will hit one definitional snag after another, such as "carnage", "massacre", "violence", "mayhem", "bloodshed", "bloodbath", and even "incomplete genocide". Thus Melson (1992, p. 3) defines partial genocide as "mass murder in order to coerce and to alter the identity and politics of the group, not to destroy it".

As will be seen below, Melson cannot differentiate between mass killing and genocide, a distinction which is made by Waller (2007, p. 14), thus:

Scholars use two terms to classify the collective violence stemming from state-directed terrorism. *Mass killing* means killing members of a group without the intention to eliminate the whole group or killing large numbers of people without a definition of group membership. Collective violence means *genocide* when a specific group is systematically and intentionally targeted for destruction.

Rubenstein (2004, p. 2) gives the following definition of genocide:

> Genocide might then be defined as the deliberate killing of most or all members of a collective group for the mere fact of being members of that group.

This may be called a numbers game—pseudoscientific positivism, at best—according to which the only criterion to qualify for genocide is the number of people killed. What if 49 percent of a targeted group are killed and 51 percent survive? According to Rubenstein's criterion, it will not be considered genocide. Ironically, in the same breath, Rubenstein (2004, p. 2) says:

> Hitler killed far fewer European Jews than the number of Indians of North and South America in the century or so after European discovery in 1492.

Nevertheless, Rubenstein finds the killing of the Jews by the Nazis genocidal, but the killing of enormously far more Native Americans by the European settlers something else.

Many more scholars have been mesmerized by the fetish that genocide is no more than the actual killing of people. Pieter Drost (1959, p. 125), one of the earliest scholars of genocide, defined genocide as

> the deliberate destruction of physical life of individual human beings by their membership of any human collectivity as such.

Thackrah's (2004, p. 104) definition is also about physical annihilation:

> the systematic elimination of a group of people who have been designated by another community or by a government to be destroyed.

Most scholarly works on genocide reference the United Nations definition of genocide. The UN definition of genocide enshrined in the Convention on the Prevention and Punishment of the Crime of Genocide, passed in December 1948, says that any of the following acts committed with intent to destroy, in whole or in part, a national, ethnical, racial, or religious groups, constitutes genocide:

(a) Killing members of the group;
(b) Causing serious bodily harm or mental harm to members of the group
(c) Deliberately inflicting on the group conditions of life calculated to bring about its physical destruction in whole or in part;

(d) Imposing measures to prevent births with the group;
(e) Forcibly transferring children of the group to another group.

Despite some of its good points, the UN definition can be termed selective at best. It was formulated as part of Western powers' agenda to control the world at the end of the Second World War. At the time of its formulation, political groups were deliberately excluded to please the then Soviet Union. Discussing the circumstances which led to the formulation of the UN definition of genocide, Hinton and O'Neill (2009, p. 4) observe:

> The very concept and legal definition of genocide was forged in a highly politicised atmosphere, one that resulted in inclusions and exclusions and a moral gradation of atrocity. The destruction of political groups, while abhorrent, was written out of the convention and became something else, an implicitly lesser crime; cultural genocide similarly dropped from sight, eventually re-emerging in popular discourse as "ethnocide".

Some scholars have tried to obfuscate genocide in pain-and-pleasure, quick-recovery terms. For instance, May (2010, p. 88) contends:

> The lives [of genocide survivors] may well be enormously impoverished, but people will normally be able to form new social relationships and social rules partially to replace those lost by the genocidal campaign. Second, although the lives and deaths of the victims of genocide will be impoverished because of the loss of some group-based identification, perhaps even unaffected by what has occurred in the genocide. And, third, although genocide does affect the meaningfulness of both one's life and death, it is likely that there is still some meaning to life and death ever after genocide.

This is another unfortunate example of how an armchair scholar undermines the whole notion of genocide. Expressions such as "normally", "identification", and "ever after" will sound vacuous, even heartless, to someone who is a member of a group targeted by a genocidal campaign.

The problem with most of the scholars and writers on genocide is that most of them seem to have spent little time with survivors of a genocide. They often rely on second-hand information, and probably lack empathy about the people they study. Another problem is that many scholars do not seem to have properly conceptualized genocide.

Understanding the concept of genocide should involve probing it from various angles, locating it in its sociohistorical perspectives, and trying to uncover hidden histories behind it (see below).

The question is: Who is qualified to define genocide? Usually it is the powerful who dole out the title of "genocide" as a matter of favour or disfavour. Thus the entire Western world led by the USA dubbed Saddam Hussain a genocidal lunatic, but the US-backed President Suharto of Indonesia was applauded for "tackling" communism. The crimes committed in Latin America during the Cold War are not called genocidal because the perpetrators were US allies. The genocidal impulses of US allies such as Augusto Pinochet in Chile, Anastasio Somoza in Nicaragua, and Doc Duvalier in Haiti are "understandable". The contras in Nicaragua could kill countless civilians with impunity (see, e.g., Chomsky and Dietrich 1999; Gellately and Kiernan 2003; Esparza et al. 2009; and Chomsky 2013) without any retribution. Genocide is certainly bad, but as long as the mass murderer is "our son of a bitch", all is fine.[6] This should explain why the Shia genocide has not attracted the attention of the USA and its allies in the West: any talk about the Shia genocide might perhaps create sympathy for Shia Iran. It will certainly incriminate Saudi Arabia, a US ally, which is the moving spirit behind the Shia genocide in Pakistan (see below).

It would not be difficult to see why a number of genocide scholars are fixated on the primacy of numbers in deciding what constitutes genocide. One credible explanation, I would like to argue, is that almost all the studies done on genocide have been ex post facto. It is not usual to report genocide as it happens.[7] The use of the tense in Hinton's (2002a, p. 1) chronicling of the history of genocide should prove this point:

With the rise of the nation-state and its imperialist and modernizing ambitions, tens of millions of "backward" or "savage" indigenous peoples *perished* from disease, starvation, slave labour, and outright murder. Sixty million others *were also annihilated* in the twentieth century, often after nation-states *embarked* upon lethal projects of social engineering intent upon eliminating certain undesirable and "contaminating" elements of population. The list of victim groups during this "Century of Genocide" is long. Some are well-known to the public—Jews, Cambodians, Bosnians, and Rwandan Tutsis. Others have been annihilated in greater obscurity— Hereros, Armenians, Ukrainain peasants, Gypsies, Bengalis, Burundi Hutus, the Ache of Paraguay, Guatemalan Mayans, and the Ogoni of Nigerian. [emphasis added]

This shows the benefit-of-hindsight nature of most of the studies on genocide. It should answer the question about where the present work is located in the corpus on genocide: it describes (is witness to) the Shia genocide as it is being carried out in Pakistan.[8]

It is not that there are no good definitions of genocide; far from it. For instance, Chalk and Jonassohn (1990, p. 23) say:

> Genocide is a form of one-sided mass killing in which a state or other authority intends to destroy a group, as that group and membership in it are defined by the perpetrators.

This definition is not complete but it has a few important points: (1) genocide involves the victim and the perpetrator; (2) there is a power asymmetry between the two groups; (3) there is a formidably powerful institution backing the perpetrator; (4) it is the perpetrator who decides if the victim deserves to live or not; and (5) the victim faces potential destruction.

Shaw (2003, p. 34) defines genocide as:

> Deliberate destruction of a people, principally but only by means of killing some of its members.

There are two outstanding features of this definition. First, genocide is deliberate, and since it is deliberate it is executed over a certain period.[9] In other words, genocide is not a one-off incident. Second, genocide is not just the physical elimination of the victim. As I will try to show below, *genocide can be carried out without actually killing a member of a target group.*

Since this chapter is not about genocide in general but the genocide of the Shias of Pakistan, I would like to end this section with a few relevant remarks.

Given the limitation of the physical-eliminative notion, I propose that genocide be explored in ecological terms. Ecology, I will try to show below, is an all-inclusive concept. The ecology of genocide will include the post-traumatic lives of survivors and also the new (future) stage(s) in the history of genocide. An ecological view of genocide will mean that the notion should be studied phenomenologically: What is it like for the victim to live in a genocidal ecology? What is it like for a Shia to live in a society (i.e., Pakistan) where wall after wall has graffiti declaring *Kafir Kafir Shia Kafir*"[10] What is it like to pass by a mosque or madrassa where loudspeakers at any time of the day shout fatwas that Shias are blasphemers, enemies of Islam, fitnah,[11] Jewish agents, and wajib-ul-qatal?[12] What kind of society do the Shias live in where Shia haters publicly and in the media justify Shia killing by declaring them apostate and heretics, and the state invokes no law to check them? What is the world like for a Shia who has survived a genocidal attack but is physically incapacitated? How does their mind function after escaping death? How many Shia children develop dissociative identity disorder because they live in a society where they are traumatized almost every day? What dreams about their future do they have? How do they regulate their "affective reactions"?[13] What about the families of the Shias killed? How do they act out their lives economically, psychologically, and socially? What happens to their family structure?[14]

Genocide: An Alternative View

It is hoped that the preceding remarks clarify that genocide should not be confined to the people who are eliminated physically. The genocidal killing of members of a designated group at any given time is but a stage in a genocidal campaign. One genocidal act at a given moment brings about many repercussions. One way to engage with the phenomenon of genocide is to understand it in terms of injury recidivism. In their archaeological ethnographic-interpretative work, Harrod, Lienard, and Martin have argued that clinical data world over have shown that people who suffer significant injury are at greater risk of future injuries. This includes a fair amount of accidental trauma too. They (2012, p. 64) further say:

> In intragroup conflict, nonlethal violence is similar to lethal violence in that the desired outcome of confrontation is to gain status or resources through the submission of other individual(s).

The argument of Harrod et al. can certainly be extended to a group that faces persistent discrimination, is regularly demonized, and lives in a state of permanent insecurity because any number of its members can be (indeed, are) fatally attacked without warning.

Most of the studies done on genocide unfortunately fail to address this issue.

Another way of looking at the phenomenon of genocide is not to discuss it in religious phraseology even if the victims are killed in the name of religion. There is no denying the fact that genocide is an ethical issue. It is an extremely emotive issue too, and it evokes the Manichaean binary of good and evil. However, religious or moral metaphors lead to abstractions. Genocide, therefore, should be dealt with as a legal-human issue. Dying a natural death is a basic human right. Someone killed for their beliefs, race, or ethnicity is deprived of their human right of not only living out their natural span of life but also of their dreams, ideals, desires, and visions. Thus genocide is a crime and not a moral aberration. People cannot be prosecuted for their moral shortcomings. It is only when they commit crimes that they can be punished by society.

Last, collateral damage to various possessions of genocide victims should also be taken into account as part of genocide, such as the destruction of the victims' means of livelihood and dwelling.[15] Here is an example, an eyewitness account,[16] of how genocide is a combination of loss of the victim's life and of their possessions:

> We have recently seen a horrible example of the Wahhabis' cruel fanaticism … . Now the enormous wealth that has accumulated in the [mosques of Imam Hussain] … has been exciting the Wahhabis' avidity for a long time. They have been dreaming permanently of the looting of the town and were so sure of success that their creditors fixed the debt payment to the happy day when their hopes would come true. That day came at last … . 12,000 Wahhabis suddenly attacked [the mosque of] Imam Hussain; after seizing more spoils than they had ever seized after their greatest victories they put everything to fire and sword … . Old people, women and children—everybody died at the barbarians' sword. Besides, it is said that whenever they saw a pregnant woman, they disembowelled her and left the foetus on the mother's bleeding corpse. Their cruelty could not be satisfied, they did not cease their murders and blood fl owed like water. As a result of the bloody catastrophe, more than 4,000 people perished. The Wahhabis carried off their plunder on the backs of 4,000 camels. After the plunder and murders, they destroyed the imam's mausoleum, and converted it into a cloaca of abomination and blood. They inflicted the greatest damage on the minarets and domes, believing that those structures were made of gold bricks. (Fatah 2008, p. 146)

Based on my examination of various genocidal campaigns, and with an eye on the Shia genocide in Pakistan, I would like to define genocide as *an altruistic, institutionalized assault on inner and outer lives of a largely defenceless group whose culpability is designated by the perpetrator.*

Below I present five points to clarify the definition. Given the focus of this work, I shall base my discussion mainly on examples from the Shia genocide in Pakistan:

Altruistic: Probably every genocidal campaign is of an argumentative-justificatory nature with moralistic warrants. In the perpetrators' discourse, words such as "killing" or "murder" seldom appear. The alibi for genocide posited is that some act or action taken by the perpetrators is based on some "higher" principle that may be for societal/social or religious/moral good. One way to approach the altruistic nature of genocide is to view it diachronically, which means that genocide is often not a one-off action; it has roots in history. The roots lie in a past incident or incidents which the perpetrator claims to be outrageous and unforgivable.[17] The incident(s) can be of religious, political, economic, or even mythical nature, but the perpetrator claims it/them to be a matter of great significance.

The Shia genocide in Pakistan and elsewhere is based on the claim of the perpetrators that for hundreds of years the former have been insulting some revered personalities of Islam, including some of the wives of the Prophet Muhammad.[18] The Shias are also blamed for waging wars against Sunni rulers in the past,[19] thus the Deobandi claim that the Shias have historically been blasphemers and saboteurs (see below).[20]

Given the altruistic nature of genocide, it can be claimed that it is fundamentally an obliterative project. Thus there is no room for the victim to live with the perpetrator in peaceful co-existence. The only way for the victim to live peacefully is to give up their lifestyle and/or belief system and adopt that of the perpetrator, or live as a second-class citizen.[21] Thus it may be said that genocide is transformative because it seeks the victim's transformation one way or another.[22]

The Shia killers in Pakistan, and elsewhere, are very categorical and uncompromising about wiping the Shias out of existence for being kafir. They openly claim that the Shias should either give up their "blasphemous" beliefs or get ready to be killed.[23]

Institutionalized: The word "institution" covers a large terrain. First, the genocidal mind and intent are rooted in the ideological belief system of the perpetrator. The history of the relations between the perpetrator and the victim is based on and/or backed by widely accepted tracts and edicts that the victim's existence is unacceptable. "Institution" also means a powerful organization, often a state that puts its weight behind the perpetrator. Genocide is not possible without the patronage of a state or a very powerful organization. Sometimes the state itself carries out genocide.[24] However, where a state is weak, non-state actors—states within a state—carry out genocidal violence. Brass (2003) claims that the genocidal violence in Punjab at the time of Partition had nothing to do with the state. He is, if at all, only partially correct. The violence was the result of the established British policy of divide and rule. Besides, at the time of Partition, the British state abandoned people to their fate, giving marauders and assassins complete impunity to act violently.[25]

Historically there have been countless state-sanctioned fatwas against the Shias, declaring them infidels and unworthy of living. It has been because of these fatwas that the Shias have historically been indiscriminately killed, crushed, or pushed to extreme marginality in every society where they have lived with non-Shia Muslims. In Pakistan it is the state itself which has created Shia killers, and has been patronizing them.[26] All the main institutions of the state of Pakistan—such as the army, the judiciary, the press, and the political rulers—are complicit in the Shia genocide.[27] In Saudi Arabia and Bahrain too, it is the state which has been killing Shias with impunity. In the words of Rosen (2006, p. 182),

> In Saudi Arabia, hone to Wahabi Islam, Shias are known as *rafida*, or "rejectionists". A highly pejorative term, it means that Shias are outside Islam. To Shias it is the equivalent of being called "nigger." Zarqawi uses the word to describe Shias, as do many other Sunni radicals in the region. Saudi Arabia's Shias have been persecuted, prevented from celebrating their festivals, and occasionally threatened with extermination.[28]

Inner and outer lives. This is the central point of the definition presented above. As I have tried to show in my discussion of various definitions of genocide, it is wrong to think it only in terms of physical elimination of the victim. The genocidal perpetrator aims to obliterate the victim's inner and outer lives. The perpetrator wants to destroy the culture and the soul of the victim. This is why ethnocide is part of genocide. Indeed, ethnocide is the softer side of genocide because its declared intent is not to kill the victim. Ethnocide

> admits the relativity of evil in difference: others are evil, but we can improve them by making them transform themselves until they are identical, to the model we propose and impose. (Clastres 1994, p. 23)

Thus, if the victim is weaned away from their culture and is made to adopt the culture of the perpetrator, their identity and inner life cease to exist. In addition, as noted above, the victim living in a genocidal society lives in permanent fear and is constantly traumatized. It would not be hard to imagine that in such a condition the victim either becomes defensive with respect to their culture and beliefs, or begins to hate their community, its various practices, and, perhaps, themselves.[29] In any case, they experience helplessness and hopelessness:

> Genocide in the generic sense is the mass killing of substantial numbers of human beings, when not in the course of military action against the military forces of an avowed enemy, under conditions of the essential defencelessness and helplessness of the victims. (Charny 1997, p. 86)

Clastres (1994, p. 44) has also noted:

> Ethnocide is then the systematic destruction of the ways of living and thinking of people different from those who lead this venture of destruction. In sum, genocide assassinates people in their body, ethnocide kills them in their mind.[30]

Whereas Clastres distinguishes genocide from ethnocide, I argue that ethnocide is part of genocide. I draw support for my view, for instance, from Manne, who says:

> A national inquiry last year found that the [Australian] government policy of forced removal was a gross violation of human rights and technically an act of genocide because it has the intention of destroying Australia's indigenous culture by forced assimilation. (R. Manne cited by Martin and Rose 2003, p. 32)

The outer life has at least two aspects. First is the very physical existence which the genocidal perpetrator seeks to eliminate. This is pure murder. However, the other aspect of the outer life is about how an individual functions as part of society. The outer life is also the physical correlative of one's cultural and religious beliefs and practices.[31] In a genocidal situation, the victim faces discrimination in various forms and at various levels. Thus they cannot carry out activities to which they are entitled as humans. The perpetrator robs the victim of their human essence. It is in this context that Card has claimed that genocide is "social death". To cite her,

Specific to genocide is the harm inflicted on its victims' social vitality. It is not just that one's group membership is the occasion for harms that are definable independently of one's identity as a member of the group. When a group with its own cultural identity is destroyed, its survivors lose their cultural heritage and may even lose their intergenerational connections. To use Orlando Patterson's terminology, in that event, they may become "socially dead" and their descendants "natally alienated," no longer able to pass along and build upon the traditions, cultural developments (including languages), and projects of earlier generations. The harm of social death is not necessarily less extreme than that of physical death. Social death can even aggravate physical death by making it indecent, removing all respectful and caring rituals, social connections, and social contexts that are capable of making dying bearable and even of making one's death meaningful. In my view, the special evil of genocide lies in its infliction of not just physical death (when it does that) but social death, producing a consequent meaningless-ness of one's life and even of its termination. (Card 2003, p. 73)

A view of a genocidal campaign carried out in the past or the present will amply show that the perpetrator's intention was as much destroying the mind and soul of the victim as destroying their body. Turkey is one signifi-cant example. It is one country which has historically carried out multiple genocides. The example of Turkey's Kurdish population is relevant here. The Kurds have not been allowed to use their own language for any mean-ingful activity other than day-to-day communication. Turkey did not allow the Kurds to publish anything in their language. They were not allowed to study Kurdish in school. No assault on a culture of a group is as far-reaching and destructive as banning its language.[32] The wholesale killing of the natives by the Conquistadores went hand in hand with the banning of native religious and cultural practices. It would not be hard to argue that a religious-fanatic mind and a genocidal mind are more or less the same in their obsession with destroying the inner and outer lives of the victim group.

In Pakistan, the Shias find it hard to continue to carry out their religious and cultural practices. By holding a religious gathering, they put their lives on the line. Shia mosques, houses, and religious gatherings and processions are routinely bombed. They are allowed to hold gatherings and processions only in those places and areas where they have been doing so for decades. They are required to obtain a licence from the government to stage a pro-cession or hold a gathering, called *majlis*. Having spoken to hundreds of Shias, I can safely claim that since General Zia ul Haq took over in July 1977, they have not been issued a single licence for a religious procession.

The entire cultural and educational scene of Pakistan aims to create a sense of irrelevance, marginality, and inferiority among the Shias. A few examples by way of illustration are in order here, such as the yearly literary festivals held in Karachi and Lahore. Every festival includes sessions on "literature and society" and "literature and politics". In 2012, 2013, and 2014, the two festivals were preceded by Shia killings in Quetta and Karachi. In the various discussions held by the participants, the possibility of striking peace with the Taliban was discussed in a pros-and-cons spirit, but no mention was made of the Shia killings. A few people who tried to raise the issue were asked to leave. The media totally blacked out the fact that anyone tried to say a word about the Shia killings.[33] The Shia identity is so suspect that, even at a book fair, anything suspected to be Shia is not allowed to be displayed or sold. Even at International book fairs, a 'Shia' Iranian bookstall is forced to pack up and leave because there are "Shia books" on sale.[34]

In Pakistan, "religious studies" and "Pakistan studies" are compulsory subjects up to college level. In these two subjects, every effort is made to destroy the Shia identity. In religious studies, students are told that the only proper ways of doing ablution, offering prayers, living like a true Muslim, and burying the dead are the Sunni ways. No recognition is given to the fact that Islam in Pakistan is not monolithic. The Shias constitute 20 percent of Pakistan's population, but in the "Islamic studies" books they are not acknowledged, even as one of the sects making up Islam. In these books, Islam means everything which is non-Shia, even anti-Shia. Even in those areas where they are in the majority, Shia students are forced to read books which explicitly tell them that their way of praying and so forth is not the "proper Islamic" way. In this respect, the case of Gilgit-Skardu is significant where the Shias are in the majority, constituting 75 percent of the population. Shia students have been forced to read Islamic studies books which portray them as heretics. When in 2000 the Shias demanded the removal of controversial content from the textbooks, scores of them, including their community leaders, were killed by the security forces. The Shia areas were placed under curfew and the students were not allowed to enter schools and colleges for a year. Their economic lives were curtailed too. It took them almost five years to change the highly offensive contents.[35]

Apart from the religious rituals, the inner lives of Shias are attacked in another way. Pakistan society is awash with national heroes who happen to be those Muslim warriors who in the past conquered and/or ruled India. As Ahmed has pointed out, every hero promoted in various forums—media, schools, cultural shows and festivals—was a Shia killer.[36] In addition to the warrior-heroes, Pakistani textbooks have "Islamic" heroes too. These are theologians of yore, such as Shah Waliullah and Sheikh Ahmed Sirhindi, who spent their lives preaching not only hatred of Shias but also their physical annihilation.[37] The intensity of anti-Shia curricula in Pakistanis has led to the majority of students of Pakistan's universities regarding the Shias as kafirs.[38]

Largely defenceless. The victim group is largely defenceless.[39] It is possible that the victim can put up a fight in some circumstances, such as a place/area where the victim community has a significant number of people. However, in the overall scenario of genocide, it matters little. The victim group is defenceless and is at the mercy of the perpetrator.

As a result of the incessant killings of Shias, especially Shia doctors in the early 1990s, some Shia youths formed a group called Sipah-e-Muhammad (the Soldiers of Muhammad), which offered resistance to the SSP (the Soldiers of the Companions of the Prophet). Some Shias claim that the Soldiers of Muhammad was created by Pakistan's intelligence agencies to bring a bad name to the Shias to prove that they were also capable of violence. However, even if the Soldiers of Muhammad was a genuinely Shia resistance group, it was officially banned in 2001, and its leaders and activists were either killed or jailed without any legal process or procedure being followed. One of its leaders, Ghulam Raza Naqvi, spent 18 years in jail (1996–2014) without ever being charged. No publication, no human rights group, and no politicians ever raised a voice about him.[40]

Victim's culpability. That the victim's culpability—or crime or sin—is defined by the perpetrator is indicative of the immense power of the latter. One way to do this is to identify the victim in sinful or criminal terms. Dabag (2005, p. 52) has put it clearly thus:

> The exertion of violence and its authorization are also closely related to the construction of collective identity in the perpetrator society. Thus, the study of genocide and identity raises two issues: for the victims, suffering from genocide implies a multitude of discontinuities, injuries, and losses. The experience of extreme physical and psychological violation not only leads to long-term traumatic effects which are passed on to following generations, but also to the radical destruction of their identities. This kind of destruction, however, is not a mere side effect of genocidal violence, but rather its primary objective.

Since the perpetrators are powerful, they can construct 'facts/truths' about their victims which justify genocide.[41] The perpetrator's power to inscribe a specific identity on the victims also robs them of their dignity that, *inter alia*, is a violation of their basic human rights:

> human persons possess an inherent dignity by virtue of the properties of their existent personal being. Simply by being the kinds of creatures they are ontologically, persons are characterized by real dignity. Dignity is not an extra benefit conferred upon persons by social contract or positive law. Dignity is not the culturally relative invention of some people who socially construct it in their minds and discourse. Dignity is a real, objective feature of human personhood. (Smith 2010, p. 434)

The Shias claim to be Muslims because they believe in all of the basic five fundamental doctrines of Islam, like other Islamic sects.[42] However, the Shia killers, given their sheer power and backing by the state of Pakistan,[43] have forced a different identity on them: they are kafir. Had Dr Ali Haider converted to, say, the Deobandi sect of Islam, he would have become a hero, a poster boy of the Deobandis, purified of all sins for having been a Shia in the past, and his life would have been spared. However, he would have ceased to be a Shia. Similarly, if, for the sake of argument, all the Shias of Pakistan were to give up their beliefs as demanded by the Deobandis, they would not be killed, but their Shia identity, and various cultural and denominational practices, would be wiped out of existence. In other words, without a single Shia being killed, the genocide of the Shias would be complete. This should support my claim above that genocide is possible without any actual killing taking place. Reducing the life chances of a group will result in its disappearance qua group eventually. An all-out assault on a group's inner life will obliterate every other aspect of that life.

MODELING GENOCIDE

Consequent to the above discussion, it is perhaps possible to work out a model for the concept of genocide. I propose the following model, which, I would like to claim, covers almost the entire range of the concept (Fig.10.1).

Ideational Grounding

This refers to the provenance and locale of a given instance of genocide. Genocidal violence seeks its justification in some actual or perceived historical incident and is perpetuated on certain people in a

Fig.   10.1   Genocide
model

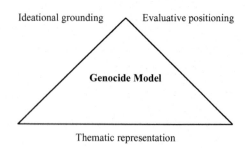

Thematic representation

certain place or places. The grounding can be epistemological. For instance, the genocidal violence against the Shias is as old as the 1400-year history of Islam. The justification for the violence is based upon the persecutors' claim that the Shias insult some companions of the Prophet Muhammad. The 'insult' originated in the succession dispute after the death of the Prophet (for a concise account of the origins of the dispute, see Hazleton 2009). The Shias at that time supported the unsuccessful succession claim of Ali bin Abu Talib, the Prophet's cousin and son-in-law. To this day, the Shias argue that the claim of Ali bin Abu Talib was more legitimate than that of those who succeeded the Prophet.[44]

It is interesting to note that the Shias are killed not because they have any disagreement with other Muslims over any of the fundamentals of Islam; they are killed because they do not accept the legitimacy of some of the companions of the Prophet to rule over more than 1,000 years ago. Thus the Shias and their homes, workplaces, mosques, bodies, ands mind have become hostage to an epistomologial ideational grounding (see below).

Evaluative Positioning

One way of positioning the victims is to deny that their genocide is taking place, or has ever taken place. For instance, an outright denial is made: no such thing as genocide is taking place. This is done by denying the very identity, which is the very cause of genocide, of the victims. Another way of denying genocide is to claim that some people of a certain group are being killed, but they are either killed at random—that is, the killing is not systematic—or the number is too low to qualify as genocide. By not reporting the identity of the victims, the denier puts an irrelevant gloss on the killing in question.

Another way to position an issue in question is to adopt cognitive vagueness about it. This is done by adopting a twisted axiology. In the context of the Shia genocide, it is done in many ways. One way is to explain the Shia genocide by creating a false Shia–Sunni binary—that is, it is a Shia-versus-Sunni conflict. The Shia genocide in Pakistan is being carried out not by Sunnis but by Deobandis. More than 55 percent of Pakistanis are Barelvi Sunnis. The Deobandi Sunnis make up 20 percent. Those journalists who call the Shia genocide a Shia–Sunni conflict are in fact guilty of creating false perspectives from which to view the issue. A few more ways of creating obfuscation are (1) to call the violence against the Shias a ramification of the Iran–Saudi conflict in the Middle East; (2) to claim that the anti-Shia violence is a result of the US drone attacks following 9/11 (since the Deobandi Taliban cannot strike back at the Americans, they attack the Shias); and (3) the Shia killers are well-meaning but misguided Muslims—'our people'—who can be convinced to scale back their 'militancy'.

Validatory hermeneutics, or justification of the Shia genocide, is posited through 'persuasive' argumentation. Such argumentation is based on jurisprudence, theology, and nationalism. In accordance with such validatory hermeneutics, the argument that blasphemers and infidels have to be put to the sword is naturalised. Through the twisted exegesis of 'authoritative' sources, murder is justified. It is also justified because of nationalism: the Shias of Pakistan are 'agents' of Shia Iran who have secretly been gnawing at the foundations of Pakistan.

The justification of genocide is also couched in other terms, such as ridiculing the victims or giving Marxist and psychological explanations of the motives behind killing (see below for more on Marxist view of the Shia genocide).

Thematic Representation

In a genocidal campaign, the victims' beliefs and practices are foregrounded in terms that portray them as hostile to and incompatible with those of their tormentors. The commonalities that can bring the tormentors and their victims together are backgrounded.

There are five basic tenets of Islam: *shahadah* (belief that Allah is the only deity and Muhammad was his messenger); *salat* (daily prayers); *zakat* (charity); fasting; and *hajj* (a Muslim must perform the pilgrimage at least once). There are other tenets that must be accepted: belief in the holy books; belief in the prophets who preceded Prophet Muhammad; belief in the angels; and belief in the Day of Judgment.

All Shias follow the above tenets. However, they do not accept the legitimacy of Abu Bakr, Umer, and Usman, who ruled the Islamic world after the Prophet Muhammad's death. They accept the legitimacy of Ali bin Abu Talib, cousin and son-in-law of the Prophet Muhammad, who succeeded Abu Bakr, Umer, and Usman. The Shias also claim that not all of the companions of the Prophet were perfect human beings who could make no mistakes.

No acknowledgement is made that the Shias believe in the basic tenets of Islam just like the Sunnis. In the genocidal campaign against the Shias, the Deobandis give thematic foregrounding to the Shia 'blasphemy' that is their refusal to accord legitimacy to the abovementioned rulers. The Shia identity created is that of a blasphemer who wants to destroy Islam by undermining some of the companions of the Prophet. It is based upon such identification of the Shias that thousands of Deobandi fatwas exist that apostatize them and call for their physical and social death.[45]

SHIA GENOCIDE IN PAKISTAN

Before 1947, Pakistan was part of India. The Shias were indiscriminately killed by the Muslim rulers of India before the arrival of the British. This is not the place to trace the history of the Shia genocide before 1947, that is, the establishment of Pakistan. The point is that those who became Pakistanis after 1947 were the same people who had lived in undivided India. After the establishment of Pakistan, the Shias were killed for their beliefs, but it was on 3 June 1963 that the very first organized assault was launched on them. It was an Ashura mourning procession which was attacked by a group of Wahhabi Muslims. They attacked Shia men and boys with meat cutters, long knives, and sickles, killing at least 118. Later they cut the Shias into pieces and then collected whatever was left of them and set their remains on fire. Before the police arrived, most of the Shias had been burned to ashes. In those days there was no television channel in Pakistan and there were only a handful of newspapers, mostly controlled by the government. The following day, the Shia killing was reported thus:

> Ashura was marred by sectarian clashes in Lahore and a Khairpur village, Theri, yesterday, taking toll of some lives. Many were injured and admitted to hospitals.

The reporting of the genocidal attack on the Shias of Khairpur is evidence that the denial, obfuscation, and justification of the Shia genocide in Pakistan are not a new phenomenon. The above report gives the impression that (1) two equally powerful parties clashed; (2) the clash was deliberate and planned on both sides; (3) both parties were equally guilty; (4) both parties suffered casualties; and (5) there were not many casualties. In addition, the site of the Shia killing is just 'a' village in a remote and thus unimportant place. To this day, the Theri massacre has not been chronicled or referenced in any Pakistani publication. It is only recently that the Amnesty International has referred to it.[46]

Since 1963 the Shias have been routinely killed, but it was after the 1979 Afghan Jihad, a Saudi–US project, that the Shia genocide was set in a steady motion (Coll 2005). The US objective was to undermine the Soviet Union. For Saudi Arabia, it was an ideal opportunity to spread its exclusivist Salafi/Wahhabi ideology. In the words of Firdous (2009, p. 112),

> The invasion of Afghanistan by the Soviet Union in 1979 can be considered as the starting point of Saudi financing to Sunni Muslims fighting for religious or political goals. That war in particular was the occasion to affirm Wahhabism as the "true belief", in sharp contrast to the atheism promoted by "infidel" communists and the "deviating" Islam followed by Sufis and Shiites.

Since then, Pakistani Shias have been killed in massive numbers. There are various claims that put the number of the Shias killed in tens of thousands. The appendices in this book chronicle incidents of Shia killings, but these numbers are not accurate because they depend on the figures given by Pakistan's mainstream newspapers, but the Pakistani media has been less than truthful about Shia killings. It can safely be assumed that the actual number of Shias killed is far greater than is given in the reports and press data.[47] Based on the analyses presented here and elsewhere in this book, the partiality of the media should be clear. One way to find out about the lies of the Pakistani media regarding the Shia genocide is to compare its reporting to that of Shia websites, and find out how extensively the former under-reports Shia killing. Unfortunately, these websites have been established only recently. The oldest is Let Us Build Pakistan (LUBP), which was set up in 2008. Thus there is no way of finding out how many Shias have actually been killed.

Mutilative Violence and Intellecticide

The individual body, Scheper-Hughes and Lock (1987, p. 31) argue, is:

> the most immediate terrain where social truths and social contradictions are played out … as well as the locus of personal and social resistance and struggle.

Physical violence is symbolic violence too. Killing, in addition to being a physical act, is also an ideological act too. Apart from being killed indiscriminately through remote control and suicide bombings, the nature of selective killing of the Shias is very significant. Selective killing has a duality: the Deobandis kill the finest of the Shia minds. In the early 1990s the Deobandis killed hundreds of the top Shia doctors. The likes of Dr Ali Haider, the advocate Shakir Rizvi,[48] the scholar-theologian Allama Nasir Abbas,[49] Allama Alim-Al Musavi, Professor Dr Shabiul Hassan,[50] the poet and educator Sibte Jafar Zaidi,[51] Professor Dr Shabih of Gujrat University, Sindh High Court lawyer Kausar Saqlain,[52] Professor Saifuddin Jafari,[53] engineer Muntazir Mehdi,[54] Allama Taqi Hadi Naqvi,[55] and the poet Mohsin Naqvi were the very best in their respective professions.[56] By carrying out the Shia intellecticide, the killers want to reduce the Shia community into a semiliterate, insignificant minority which has no cerebral vitality and no ability to perform creatively. In Perez's (2012, p. 26) words,

> By killing young and old alike and reducing them to unrecognized mass, the aggressors create a substantial psychological import on the regional interaction sphere in which they are operating.

The Shia intellecticide is not without its message, and this is the other side of the duality: all of the Shia minds mentioned above were shot in the face and head in such a manner that their faces became a mass of flesh and bone. By killing them in such a brutal manner, the message was clear: their mutilated corpses have been a symbol of total defeat and humiliation of the Shia community.[57] Whereas a mutilated body symbolizes the obliteration of the person killed, to the rest of the victim community it is a message about its helplessness, degradation, and inferiority. The perpetrator's ability to strike at will and get away with it is a taunt, and also a reminder to the victim community about its impotence. By so brutally wasting the finest of the Shia minds, the killers notify their insignificance: they are as expendable as flies. Perhaps what is intellecticide to the Shias is no more than insecticide to the Deobandis.[58] Mutilated corpses of men, women, children, and infants frequently littered on the road are another message: litter. A mutilated corpse symbolizes a posthumous assault on it because it cannot be buried in the normal way. Genocidal killing—that is, killing fellow human beings—is cannibalistic because it feeds the perpetrator's lust for power over the victim. And when the media, the government, and various human rights groups deny, obfuscate, and even justify their genocide, it is a message to the Shias not only that they are an insignificant group, but also that their belief system and culture have no place in Pakistan.

Shia Genocide: Some Examples

Pakistan's mainstream publications and television channels have never taken up the issue of the Shia genocide in a meaningful way. As I try to show here, there is no way for a researcher to find out exactly how many Shias have been killed as a result of the faith-based violence against them. Nishapuri has compiled a list of the Shias killed by the Deobandis and the Salafis from 1963 to May 2015. He claims that more than 25,000 have been killed.[59] Despite being a commendable effort, the list gives only a partial view of the Shia genocide because it is based on published reports in Pakistan's mainstream newspapers. As I have indicated at the beginning of this chapter, and exemplified in Chapter 4 on the media, Pakistan's media goes out of its way not to report Shia killing. These are reported only when a number of Shias are killed, or when they are killed as a result of attacks on their mourning processions. One way to find out if a person who has been killed is a Shia is to look for their surname. Again, Pakistan's media often omits the last name of the victim if they happen to be Shia.[60]

As I have indicated above, the Shia genocide in Pakistan is ongoing, and, given the apostatizing Deobandi-theological foundations, it will go on. Added to this are the anti-Shia pathologies of oil-rich Middle Eastern oligarchies—(*oiligarchies*)—such as Saudi Arabia, Qatar, and the United Arab Emirates, so there may be no abatement in the Shia genocide in Pakistan or elsewhere. The instances of Shia genocide in Pakistan include a campaign against Shia doctors that since the 1990s has resulted in the killing of hundreds of them.[61] The persistence of the campaign has led to Shia doctors changing both their own names and the names of their clinics.[62] Apart from the daily killing of Shias, there are a number of instances where there have been mass killings. Shia people have been taken out of buses, lined up, and killed by the dozen. As they were shot, the camera-men accompanying the assassins recorded the shooting and then proudly uploaded the footage online. Later the 'political' leaders of Deobandi groups proudly referred at public gatherings to the "runs" scored by "our fighters". The Shias have regularly been killed while participating in their mourning processions and even funeral processions (see, e.g., Hassan, 29 December 2009; Kan, 4 September 2010; Qasimi, 7 February 2012; Qureshi, 22 November 2012).

DEOBANDIS

In this chapter I have used the word "Deobandi" to identify the Shia killers. Almost without exception it is the Deobandi sect of Sunni Islam which has been killing the Shias in Pakistan. The Taliban, the SSP, the ASWJ, the LeJ, Jundullah, and the JM are all Deobandi.[63] The LeJ, the main culprit, is an affiliate of Al-Qaeda.[64] All of these groups are officially banned, but are allowed to take part in politics, run for parliamentary seats, and form alliances with major political parties. Those who iden-tify the Shia killers as Sunni deliberately obfuscate the issue to make it look like a Shia–Sunni issue, which is a complete lie. As noted above, the majority of Pakistanis—more than 55 percent of the population—are Barelvi Sunnis, a sub-continental version of the Sufism. They are also routinely killed by the Deobandis.[65]

In Pakistan, more than 90 percent of various acts of terrorism have been committed by Deobandis. Why they have become so powerful is because they are backed by the state of Pakistan and financed by Saudi Arabia and the United Arab Emirates.[66] An account of the extent of Deobandi terror-ism in Pakistan, especially against Shias, is comprehensively recorded and analysed by Hussain (2010) in his doctoral thesis.

Writing in an Indian magazine, Ahmed (20 March 2013) discusses Deobandi fatwas against the Shias:

A number of Deobandi clerical leaders of Pakistan co-signed or confirmed the fatwa against the Shia in 1986. Among them were two well-known names: Muhammad Yusuf Ludhianvi and Mufti Nizamuddin Shamzai … . Fatwas of apostatisation were issued from time to time from all the prominent Deobandi madrasas of Pakistan. Darul Ulum Haqqaniya Akora Khattak of Maulana Samiul Haq (the seminary where the assassins of ex-prime minister Benazir Bhutto have confessed to staying before the attack on her in 2007) issued its own fatwa of apostatisation of the Shia in 1986 saying that eating food cooked by them, attending their funeral and burying them in Sunni graveyards stood banned. Another fatwa from Jamia Ashrafia Lahore, whose leader Maulana Muhammad Malik Kandhalwi, known to be a relative of general Zia, declared the Shias kafir because "they held that the Quran had been tampered with and gave Hazrat Ali a status equal to Prophet Muhammad, claiming that angel Jibreel [Gabriel] had made a mistake while taking wahi [revelation] to the Prophet".

Elsewhere, Ahmed (11 March 2014) reproduces the Deobandi fatwa which has been used to kill Shias in Baluchistan:

All Shia are worthy of killing. We will rid Pakistan of unclean people. Pakistan means "land of the pure" and the Shia have no right to live in this country. We have the edict and signatures of revered scholars, declaring the Shia infidels. Just as our fighters have waged a successful jihad against the Shia Hazara in Afghanistan, our mission in Pakistan is the abolition of this impure sect and its followers from every city, every village, and every nook and corner of Pakistan.

As in the past, our successful jihad against the Hazara in Pakistan and, in particular, in Quetta is ongoing and will continue in the future. We will make Pakistan the graveyard of the Shia Hazara and their houses will be destroyed by bombs and suicide-bombers. We will only rest when we will be able to fly the flag of true Islam on this land of the pure. Jihad against the Shia Hazara has now become our duty.

Marxist Renditions

I am mindful of the fact that some researchers would like to write a Marxist account of the Shia genocide. Some journalists have indeed tried to put a Marxist gloss on it by claiming that in the city of Jang, the working-class Deobandis are killing Shia property owners. However, they cannot even differentiate between peasants and workers. Their journalistic articles are innocent of methodology. Here is one example:

His humble origins have made him anti-feudal and pro-people. He loses no opportunity to criticise the Maliks, the hereditary tribal elders who are traditionally pro-establishment and receive all the benefits doled out by the government. He is keen to highlight the plight of the ordinary tribesmen and motivated to solve the problems confronting the common man. If he has his way, he would like to rob the rich to pay the poor like a modern-day Robin Hood. That explains the reason for young men, mostly jobless, to flock to his banner and make up bulk of his Lashkar-i-Islam outfit.[67]

This is a description of the notorious bandit-cum-murderer Mangal Bagh, who has not only created a state within a state in the Tirah Valley, but has also been responsible for the killing of hundreds of Barelvi Sunnis who in his opinion were not good Muslims. Bagh took active part in the War Afghanistan. In the Tirah Valley, no woman is allowed to step outside her home. Bagh shut down all of the CD shops in the valley and no one is allowed to have a dish antenna. It is noteworthy that the author of the Bagh description is a much-respected leftist writer. In his quasi-Marxist zeal, he has forgotten that the "young men" who "flock to his banner" are enforcers of the sharia which Bagh has imposed in the valley, and not a leftist, progressive revolution. Often these illiterate "young men" act as judges for the sharia 'courts'.

I think a Marxist critique of the Shia genocide will not be very convincing. Often, Marxist critiques are non-contextual because they take the notion of class conflict as monolithic. This brings about analytical simplifications. Pakistan's genocidal mind is intertwined with contemporary (e.g., petrodollars, Wahhabism, and Islam as a failed system) and (trans)historical (Islam in the Indian subcontinent, the British Raj, and the self-hatred of the Muslims of the subcontinent who are not 'genuine' Muslims but converts) issues.[68] I have discussed some of these issues elsewhere.[69]

CONCLUSION

To make them manageable and focused, the definition and the model above have been discussed only with reference to the Shia genocide in Pakistan. I would like to maintain that both the definition and the model can be found useful to understand and analyse other instances of genocide because although every genocide is unique, the "deliberate concealment and or manipulation of facts by the perpetrators is more often the rule than the exception" (Lemarchand 2011, p. vii).

Genocide, as I have indicated above, is a matter of one group's power over another. Why the pathologically brutal physical treatment and the socioeconomic destruction of the Palestinians and the Shias in Israel, Saudi Arabia, and Bahrain is never explored in terms of genocide is because these countries are the protégés of the West led by the USA. The same observation can be made about many other genocides in Burundi (1972), Eastern Congo (1996–1997), South-West Africa (1904), Australia (1970s), and various regions in Europe (gypsies at different times). Lemarchand (2011) terms these and other genocides "forgotten genocides". The unchallenged power of the Deobandi groups is possible only if the Deobandis have the backing of the state, especially the Pakistan Army, which is the de facto ruling elite of the country. Apart from the army, the main backers have been Saudi Arabia and the Pakistan Muslim League (Nawaz Sharif Group). Research on the Deobandi nexus with these actors can be carried out to find out how national/local and international elements have contributed to making Pakistan a land of genocides.

The electronic media's construction of Ahmed Ludhianvi[70] from the chief promoter of the Shia killing to a national political leader is instructive. I remember that when the Geo channel first put Ludhianvi on a talk show, no other guest was willing to sit with him.[71] Now he is an "Islamic scholar" and the voice of the "moderate Sunnis". The electronic media is now more active than the print media in promoting the Shia genocide. Research on its advocacy of the genocide is urgently needed.

There are enormous ethnographic, ethnomethodological, and phenomenological research possibilities regarding the Shia genocide. How the state of Pakistan has allowed the Deobandis to destroy the inner lives of the Shias has never been explored. Some friends have informed me that some Shia and other persecuted community women were forced into prostitution because their men, the breadwinners, were killed. How Shia orphans end up in the child labour market is another significant issue. Ethnomethodological research on Shia killers and Shia haters will unravel the various assumptions underlying the Shia genocide. I hope someone will do ethnographic and ethnomethodological research in these areas.

NOTES

1. Anser Abbas' tweets and details of the local newspaper are discussed in Ahmad's article. Ahmad's was the only blog which raised the issue of Altaf Hussain's murder.
2. Interestingly, the Al-Jazeera interview focuses on his disability but does not say a word about his identity or how/why he became disabled.

3. Dr Ali Haider's other son did not join him that morning to attend school because he was sick. Had he been with him, he would have also been killed.

4. I make no claims to have studied genocide-related sources exhaustively. However, none of the sources given in this chapter is based on explicit methodology.

5. The technical name for these functions is "metafunctions".

6. President Roosevelt's loving characterization of Samoza.

7. I refer to two books in this regard: Chalk and Jonassohn (1990) and Hinton (2002).

8. There is one perceptive article on the Shia genocide in Pakistan. See, for example, Hussain (2 May 2014). See also a short report, "Shia genocide: A crisis in Pakistan", by various authors: https://lubpak.com/wp-content/uploads/2014/05/UN-Report-3-Shia-Genocide.pdf.

9. Schabas (2000) and Levene (2005) have the same view about the deliberateness of genocide.

10. Shias are infidels.

11. Mischief.

12. Deserving death.

13. See Kaplan (2013).

14. The wife and mother of Altaf Hussain, who was beheaded by the Deobandis, lost their minds on finding out about him.

15. A great deal of work can possibly be done on this aspect.

16. This is an account of just one example of how the Wahhabis have been destroying Shia lives and possessions.

17. See, for example, Andreopoulos (1997) and Nhema and Zeleza (2008).

18. This is not true, but this is not the place to discuss the issue. Even if it were true, it does not justify killing from any legal or moral point of view.

19. The Shias' quest has historically been one for legitimacy. This is why they have refused to submit to tyrants and usurpers. For details, see, for example, Halm (2007) and (2007).

20. On the history of Shia–Sunni differences, see Hazleton (2009) and Gonzalez (2013).

21. However, if the basis of genocide is racial, there is probably no escape for the victim.

22. I have avoided this term because it is often used in political science as an antonym to "transition". It is also used in the context of business

studies and entrepreneurship. Thus it does not have the gravity and singularity of "obliterative".

23. This official Deobandi website proudly displays Deobandi fatwas apostatizing the Shias: http://www.darulifta-deoband.org/; and http://www.deoband.org/.

    The most respected official Deobandi website has the following fatwa against the Shias: "Bohras are Shiah. The beliefs and faiths of Shiah found in their books are against the Quran and Hadith. Therefore, they are not Muslims. It is not correct for a Sunni Muslim to get married with a Shiah or Bohra": http://www.darulifta-deoband.com/showuserview.do?function=answerView&all=en&id=519 2&limit=2&idxpg=0&qry=%3Cc%3EFAB%3C%2Fc%3E%3Cs%3EFL S%3C%2Fs%3E%3Cl%3Een%3C%2Fl%3E. See more on this website: http://www.darulifta-deoband.com/.

24. For details, see Jones (2006), Simon (2007), and Cooper (2009).

25. This is not the place to discuss Partition. However, a note should be made that the violence in undivided India started months before Partition. See, for example, Pandey (2004).

26. I will return to this point in the Chapter 18.

27. See Asian Human Rights Commission's report of 23 February 2013; Human Rights Watch report of 27 January (2014), Sharma (2005), and Hussain (2007).

28. See also Wilcke (2009).

29. See, for example, Fisher et al. (2002) and Krippner and McIntyre (2003).

30. My discussion in this section and later on in this chapter will, I hope, clarify the issue.

31. Personally, I am not comfortable about separating culture from religion. I should like to argue that religion subverts culture or even destroys it. However, many scholars would like to separate the two. For example, it could be argued that one can practice Indian culture but observe Islamic beliefs which are external to Indian culture. I do not wish to complicate the issue but hope to take it up in another study, which I plan to do with reference to the anthropology of Islam.

32. See Gunter (2009), Hasiotis and Hasiotis (2010), and Gunes (2013).

33. This comes from a number of friends and respondents who participated in those festivals. A view of the media will show that no reference was made to the Shias, though a lot of space was given to pleas to make peace with the Taliban.

34. "Unfortunate disruption: Iranian bookstall closed," *Dawn*, 10 December 2012: http://www.dawn.com/news/1061596/unfortunate-disruption-iranian-bookstall-closed. The report says, "Buckling under [ASWJ's] pressure, the police confiscated the books while the fair's organisers closed down the stall."

35. Ali has given a detailed account of anti-Shia textbooks, which the Shia students are forced to read in the areas where they are in the majority. See Ali (2008), Nayyar and Salim (2003), and Shehzad (2003).

36. See Ahmed (2011).

37. See Jafri (24 September 2013).

38. See Siddiqa (2010).

39. See Scherrer (2003), and Provost and Akhavan (2010).

40. Only a Shia blog has a raised voice for him. See "Forgotten prisoner: 16 years of imprisonment of SMP Chief Ghulam Raza Naqvi," *Shiite News*, 8 August 2011: http://www.shiitenews.com/index.php/pakistan/3330-forgotten-prisoner-16-years-of-imprisonment-of-smp-chief-ghulam-raza-naqvi--shiite-news-exclusive-report.

41. Thus genocidal violence is considered to be just by the perpetrator and unjust by the victim.

42. These doctrines are (1) belief in the oneness/unity of God; (2) belief in the existence of the angels; (3) belief in the prophets of God; (4) belief in the scriptures; and (5) belief in the Day of Judgement. All Muslim scholars belonging to any school of thought in Islam accept that these are the only five doctrines basic to becoming Muslim. Thus the Shias claim that since they, like the rest of the Muslims in the world, follow the five fundamental tenets of Islam, they are Muslim.

43. This issue has been taken up in another chapters of this book.

44. "Shia" means "a partisan". With reference to Islam, it means "the Partisan of Ali bin Abu Talib".

45. Again, the reader is referred to the following Deobandi websites, where they can read anti-Shia fatwas: http://www.darulifta-deoband.org/; and http://www.deoband.org/.

46. Read an account of the Theri massacre Alo (28 May 2013). The article also reproduces the reporting of the massacre quoted in this section. There is a link in the article to a short documentary which gives details of the Theri massacre.

47. To give a few examples, these Shia killings were never reported by the media:

"3 More Shias Shot Martyred In Pakistan," *Shia Post*, 23 April 2014: http://en.shiapost.com/2014/04/23/3-more-shias-martyred-in-paksitan/.

"Shia Advocate Ghulam Abid Attacked In Shikarpur," *Shia Post*, 23 April 2014: http://en.shiapost.com/2014/04/23/shia-advocate-ghulam-abid-attacked-in-shikarpur/.

"Shia Youth Shot Martyred In Takfiri Terrorist Attack In Karachi," *Shia Post*, 22 April 2014: http://en.shiapost.com/2014/04/22/shia-youth-shot-martyred-in-takfiri-terrorist-attack-in-karachi/.

"Another Professor Shot Martyred By ASWJ-LeJ Terrorist In Karachi," *Shia Post*, 21 April 2014: http://en.shiapost.com/2014/04/21/another-professor-shot-martyred-bu-aswj-lej-terrorist-in-karachi/.

"Shiite Man Shot Martyred In Karachi," *Shia Post*, 21 April 2014: .http://en.shiapost.com/2014/04/21/shiite-man-shot-martyred-in-karachi/.

"One Martyred, Another Critically Injured By ASWJ Terrorists In Karachi," *Shia Post*, 17 April 2014: http://en.shiapost.com/2014/04/17/one-martyred-another-critically-injured-by-aswj-terrorists-in-karachi/.

"Two Shiites Shot Martyred In Quetta," *Shia Post*, 12 April 2014: http://en.shiapost.com/2014/04/12/two-shiites-shot-martyred-in-quetta/.

"Shia Taxi Driver Shot Martyred In Takfiri Terrorist Attack Near Parachinar," *Shia Post*, 10 April 2014: http://en.shiapost.com/2014/04/10/shia-taxi-driver-shot-martyred-in-takfiri-terrorist-attack-near-parachinar/.

"Two Shiites Including A Shia Lawyer Shot Martyred In Karachi," 10 April 2014: http://en.shiapost.com/2014/04/10/shia-lawyer-shot-martyred-in-karachi/.

"Shia Doctor Haider Raza Shot Martyred In Karachi," *Shia Post*, 9 April 2014: http://en.shiapost.com/2014/04/09/shia-doctor-dr-haider-raza-shot-martyred-in-karchi/.

48. He was Lahore's top lawyer and at one time served as the president of the Lahore chapter of the Pakistan ML, Pagara-Juneo Group.

49. Allama Nasir Abbas was a scholar and a *noha* (elegy) reciter par excellence. He was one of the few Shia scholars who did not wear the Iraqi-Iranian style of clothing; he wore Pakistani dress all the time. He described himself as a "cultural Shia".

50. He was the author of more than 50 books on literary criticism. He was a poet and fiction writer too. Newspapers reported his murder but without telling the readers that he was killed because he was a Shia. The newspapers also did not tell their readers that the LeJ had accepted responsibility said that more Shias would be killed. See, for example, "City mourns Dr Shabih's murder," *The Nation*, 20 May 2012: http://www.nation.com.pk/lahore/20-May-2012/city-mourns-dr-shabih-s-murder. *The Nation* report says, "According to details, four masked men riding two motorbikes gunned down Dr Shabihul Hasan by spraying straight bullets on various parts of his body while he was riding his motorcar (LEF-4458) on Friday night. Paramedical staff said that two bullets claimed his life that pierced into his heart and kidney. Shariful Hassan, brother of the deceased professor, alleged that his brother was killed by terrorists."

51. A poet, a reciter of epic poetry, and former principal of Liquatabad College, Karachi.

52. One of the most highly respected and capable legal experts in the Sindh province.

53. He was a professor at the Government College of Technology, Karachi. Not a word was recorded about him in any mainstream newspaper or on any television channel. Only a Shia blog reported his murder. See "Another Professor Shot Martyred By ASWJ-LeJ Terrorist In Karachi," *Shia Post*, 21 April 2014: http://en.shiapost.com/2014/04/21/another-professor-shot-martyred-bu-aswj-lej-terrorist-in-karachi/.

54. A lecturer at NED University in Karachi. The murder of this young Shia intellectual also went unreported. See "Engineer Muhammad Yousuf Shot Martyred In Karachi," *Shia Post*, 13 April 2014: http://en.shiapost.com/2014/04/13/engineer-muntazir-mehdi-shot-martyred-in-karachi/.

55. While reporting his death, *Dawn* did not identify his Shia identity. He was simply referred to as "a religious scholar". See "Religious scholar shot dead in Karachi," *Dawn*, 27 February 2014: http://www.dawn.com/news/1089836/religious-scholar-shot-dead-in-karachi.

56. A partial list of the prominent Shias killed can be found at http://lubpak.com/archives/132675.

57. I want to put this on record: this part of my discussion is completely inspired by Perez (2012).

58. It is no coincidence that, in Karachi, Shias have traditionally been referred to as *khatmal* (bedbugs).

59. The compilation can be accessed at https://lubpak.com/archives/132675.

60. A separate study is required to deal with this issue. I have collected data on it and hope to be able to publish my findings in the future. As a sampler, the reader is directed to an article written by Jibran Nasir, Pakistan's well-known human rights campaigner. This was written about a boy who survived a suicide attack on the Hazara Shias in Quetta. He lost many of his friends and relatives in the attack. All the people named by Nasir in his article are Shia. However, he refers to them by their first name only, thus concealing their Shia identity. See Nasir, Jibran (4 February 2014). Karachi embraced Ibtihaj with love and support but will you do the same, Bilawal Bhutto? *Express Tribune*: http://blogs.tribune.com.pk/story/20888/karachi-embraced-ibtihaj-with-love-and-support-but-will-you-do-the-same-bilawal-bhutto/.

61. Some of the murders have been chronicled at https://lubpak.com/archives/tag/shia-doctors.

62. See, for example, Baloch Saher (31 July 2010) and "Karachi's doctors live in fear after spike in deadly attacks" (16 June 2015). *Dawn*.

63. I should like to point out that it is not possible that every Deobandi wants to kill Shias. However, I can safely say that many of the Deobandis who do not subscribe to the Shia genocide still believe that the Shias are a heretical or deviant community.

64. Pakistan: The militant jihadi challenge, International Crisis Group, *Asia Report No. 164*, 13 March 2009.

65. This is not a research work about the Barelvi–Deobandi issue. The Deobandis have persistently attacked Sunni Barelvi/Sufi leaders and shrines. The high-profile Barelvi leader Mufti Naeemi was killed by a suicide bomber sent by the Taliban. See "Suicide bomber kills anti-Taliban cleric Allama Naeemi," *Dawn*, 13 June 2009: http://www.dawn.com/news/848443/suicide-bomber-kills-anti-taliban-cleric-allama-naeemi. The Sunni Barelvis also claim that the Deobandis wiped out their Karachi leadership in 2006. See "Bomb carnage at Karachi prayers," *BBC News*, 11 April 2006: http://news.bbc.co.uk/2/hi/south_asia/4900402.stm.

66. "US embassy cables: Hillary Clinton says Saudi Arabia 'a critical source of terrorist funding,'" *The Guardian*, 5 December 2010:

http://www.theguardian.com/world/us-embassy-cables-documents/242073.

Walsh, Declan. "Hillary Clinton memo highlights Gulf states' failure to block funding for groups like al-Qaida, Taliban and Lashkar-e-Taiba," *The Guardian*, Monday 6 December 2010: http://www.theguardian.com/world/2010/dec/05/wikileaks-cables-saudi-terrorist-funding.

Cartalucci, Tony, "Destroying a nation state: US-Saudi funded terrorists sowing chaos in Pakistan," *Global Research*, 24 December 2013: http://www.globalresearch.ca/destroying-a-nation-state-us-saudi-funded-terrorists-sowing-chaos-in-pakistan/5323295.

67. Yusufzai (11 May 2008).
68. Manzoor (1993) discusses why Pakistani Muslims are *number do* Muslims, which means "bogus/fake". Also see, Ahmad (1978) and Ahmed (2004).
69. Zaidi (2011).
70. And his Shia-apostatizing ideology.
71. It was Saleem Safi's "Jirga". See http://www.youtube.com/watch?v=krs1VshLYBM.

REFERENCES

Ahmad, I. (1978). *Caste and social stratification among Muslims in India*. New Delhi: Manohar.

Ahmad, L. (2013, December 21). Pakistani media ignores Altaf Hussain Durrani, a Shia police officer beheaded and cut up by Deobandi terrorists. *Let Us Build Pakistan*. http://lubpak.com/archives/298799

Ahmed, K. (2011). *Sectarian war: Pakistan's Sunni-Shia violence and its link with the Middle East*. New York: Oxford University Press.

Ahmed, K. (2013, March 30). Sectarian violence in Pakistan. *Economic and Political Weekly*. http://www.epw.in/commentary/sectarian-violence-pakistan.html

Ahmed, K. (2014, March 11). Hunting the Hazaras. *Newsweek Pakistan*. http://newsweekpakistan.com/hunting-the-hazara/

Ahmed, M. (2004). *Faisalabad Division ke Siasat per Biradarism kay Asraat* [*Effects of the caste system on the politics of Faisalabad*]. Unpublished PhD thesis, Department of Political Science, B Z University, Multan.

Ali, N. (2008). Outrageous state, sectarianized citizens: Deconstructing the 'Textbook Controversy' in the Northern Areas, Pakistan. *South Asian Multidisciplinary Academic Juornal*. Url: http://samaj.revues.org/1172 Accessed on 16 August 2016. DOI : 10.4000/samaj.1172. Online since 31 December 2008, connection on 16 August 2016.

Alo M. (2013, May 28). 50th anniversary of the Theri Massacre. *Let Us Build Pakistan.* http://lubpak.com/archives/266633

Andreopoulos, G. J. (Ed.). (1997). *Genocide: Conceptual and historical dimensions.* Pennsylvania: University of Pennsylvania Press.

Baloch, Saher. (2010, July 31). Surgical strikes. *Newsline.* http://www.newslinemagazine.com/2010/07/surgical-strikes/

Brass, P. (2003). The partition of India and retributive genocide in the Punjab, 1946–47: Means, methods, and purposes. *Journal of Genocide Research, 5*(1), 71–101.

Card, C. (2003). Genocide and social death. *Hypatia, 18*(1), 63–79.

Chalk, F., & Jonassohn, K. (1990). *The history and sociology of genocide.* New Haven: Yale University Press.

Charny, I. W. (1997). Towards a generic definition of genocide. In G. J. Andreopoulos (Ed.), *Genocide: Conceptual and historical dimensions* (pp. 64–94). Pennsylvania: University of Pennsylvania Press.

Chomsky, N., & Dietrich, H. (1999). *Latin America: From colonization to globalization.* Minneapolis: Ocean Press.

Chomsky, N. (2013). *The essential Chomsky.* New York: The New Press.

Clastres, P. (1994). *Archaeology of violence* (J. Herman, Trans.). New York: Semiotext(e).

Coll, S. (2005). *Ghost wars: The secret history of the CIA, Afghanistan and Bin Laden.* London: Penguin.

Cooper, A. D. (2009). *The geography of genocide.* New York: University Press of America.

Crilly, R. (2013, September 10). Only in Pakistan can the Taliban be described as 'stakeholders'. *Daily Telegraph Blog.* http://blogs.telegraph.co.uk/news/robcrilly/100235192/only-in-pakistan-can-the-taliban-be-described-as-stakeholders/

Dabag, M. (2005). Modern societies and collective violence: The framework of interdisciplinary genocide studies. In G. C. Kinloch & R. P. Mohan (Eds.), *Genocide: Approaches, case studies, and responses* (pp. 52–62). New York: Algora Publishing.

Drost, P. (1959). *The crime of state* (Vol. 2). Leyden: A.W. Sythoff.

Esparza, M., Huttenbach, H. R., & Feierstein, D. (2009). *State, violence and genocide in Latin America: The Cold War years.* London: Routledge.

Fatah, T. (2008). *Chasing the mirage: The tragic illusion of an Islamic state.* Mississauga: John Wiley & Sons Canada.

Firdous, K. (2009). Militancy in Pakistan. *Strategic Studies 30* (2): 50–59.

Fisher, A. T., Sonn, C. C., & Bishop, B. J. (2002). *Psychological sense of community: Research, applications, and implications.* London: Springer.

Forgotten prisoner: 16 years of imprisonment of SMP Chief Ghulam Raza Naqvi. (2011, August 8). *Shiite News.* http://www.shiitenews.com/index.php/

pakistan/3330-forgotten-prisoner-16-years-of-imprisonment-of-smp-chief-ghulam-raza-naqvi--shiite-news-exclusive-report-

Gellately, R., & Kiernan, B. (Eds.). (2003). *The spectre of genocide: Mass murder in historical perspective.* Cambridge: Cambridge University Press.

Ghani, F. (2014, February 10). The pain of being disabled in Pakistan. *Al-Jazeera.* http://www.aljazeera.com/indepth/features/2014/02/pain-being-disabled-pakistan-2014249751959749.html

Gonzalez, N. (2013). *The Sunni-Shia conflict: Understanding sectarian violence in the Middle East.* Orange County: East Nortia Media Ltd.

Gunes, C. (2013). *The Kurdish national movement in Turkey: From protest to resistance.* London: Routledge.

Gunter, M. M. (2009). *The A to Z of the Kurds.* New York: Scarecrow Press.

Halliday, M. A. K. (1994). *Introduction to functional grammar.* London: Arnold.

Halliday, M. A. K. (1971/1996). Linguistic function and literary style: An inquiry into the language of William Golding's The Inheritors. In J. J. Weber (Ed.), *The stylistics reader: From Roman Jakobson to the present* (pp. 56–86). London: Arnold.

Halm, H. (2007). *The Shiites: A short history.* Princeton: Markus Wiener Publishers.

Harrod, R. P., Lienard, P., & Martin, D. L. (2012). Deciphering violence in past societies. In D. L. Martin, R. P. Harrod, & V. R. Perez (Eds.), *The bioarchaeology of violence* (pp. 63–80). Gainesville: University of Florida Press.

Hasiotis, A. C., & Hasiotis, A. C. (2010). *The axis of shame: Great Britain, Israel, the United States and Turkey in the Middle East.* Pittsburgh: Dorrance Publishing.

Hassan, A. (2009, December 29). Suicide bomber kills 30 on Shia procession in Karachi. *The Guardian.* http://www.theguardian.com/world/2009/dec/28/pakistan-suicide-attack-kills-30

Hazleton, L. (2009). *After the Prophet: The epic story of the Shia-Sunni split in Islam.* New York: Random House.

Hinton, A. L. (2002a). The dark side of modernity. In A. L. Hinton (Ed.), *Annihilating the difference: The anthropology of genocide* (pp. 1–40). Berkley: University of California Press.

Hinton, A. L. (Ed.). (2002b). *Annihilating difference: The anthropology of genocide.* Berkley: University of California Press.

Hinton, A. L., & O'Neill, K. L. (Eds.). (2009). *Genocide: Truth, memory, and representation.* London: Duke University Press.

Hussain, S. E. (2010). *Terrorism in Pakistan: Incident patterns, terrorists' characteristics, and the impact of terrorist arrests on terrorism.* Unpublished PhD thesis, University of Pennsylvania. The thesis is available online at: http://repository.upenn.edu/edissertations/136

Hussain, W. (2014, May 2). Early warning signs of Shia genocide in Pakistan. *The Diplomat*. http://thediplomat.com/2014/05/early-warning-signs-of-shia-genocide-in-pakistan/

Hussain, Z. (2007). *Frontline Pakistan: The struggle with militant Islam*. London: I.B. Tauris.

Jafri, N. (2013, September 24). Sectarianism in Pakistan: School textbooks and national identity. http://muftah.org/sectarianism-in-pakistan-school-textbooks-national-identity/#.UkjGgdwqY_k.facebook

Jones, A. (2006). *Genocide: A comprehensive introduction*. London: Routledge.

Kaplan, S. (2013). Child survivors of the 1994 Rwandan genocide and trauma-related affect. *Journal of Social Issues, 69*, 92–110.

Karachi's doctors live in fear after spike in deadly attacks. (2015, June 16). *Dawn*. http://www.dawn.com/news/1188546

Khan, B. (2010, September 4). Pakistan suicide bomber kills 43 in Shia parade backing Palestinians. *The Guardian*. http://www.theguardian.com/world/2010/sep/03/pakistan-suicide-bombers-kill-44-at-parade

Krippner, S., & McIntyre, T. M. (2003). *The Psychological impact of war trauma on civilians: An international perspective*. Westport: Greenwood.

Lemarchand, R. (Ed.). (2011). *Forgotten genocides: Oblivion, denial, and memory*. Philadelphia: University of Pennsylvania Press.

Levene, M. (2005). *The meaning of genocide*. London: I.B. Tauris.

May, L. 2010. *Genocide: A normative account*. Cambridge: Cambridge University Press.

Manzoor, A. M. (1993). *The Pakistan problem: Historical background of Punjab and consolidation of Pakistan*. Lahore: The Frontier Post Press.

Martin, J. R., & Rose, R. (2003). *Working with discourse: Meaning beyond the clause*. London: Continuum.

Melson, R. (1992). *Revolution and genocide: On the origins of the Armenian genocide and the Holocaust*. Chicago: Chicago University Press.

Ignatieff, M. (2001, February 26). Lemkin's words. *The New Republic*.

Nayyar, A. H., & Salim, A. (Eds.). (2003). *The subtle subversion: The state of curricula and textbooks in Pakistan, Urdu, English, social studies and civics*. Islamabad: Sustainable Development Policy Institute.

Nhema, A. G., & Zeleza, T. (2008). *The roots of African conflicts: The causes and costs*. Ohio: Ohio University Press.

Pakistan: Shia genocide: Military and militants. (2013, February 23). *Asian Human Rights Commission*. http://www.humanrights.asia/news/ahrc-news/AHRC-ART-021-2013

Pandey, G. (2004). *Remembering partition: Violence, nationalism and history in India*. Cambridge: Cambridge University Press.

Perez, V. R. (2012). The politicization of the dead. In D. L. Martin, R. P. Harrod, & V. R. Perez (Eds.), *The bioarchaeology of violence* (pp. 13–28). Gainesville: University of Florida Press.

Provost, R., & Akhavan, P. (Eds.). (2010). *Confronting genocide.* London: Springer.

Qasimi, H. (2012, February 7). Pakistani extremists film massacre of Shiite minority group. *The Observers.* http://observers.france24.com/en/20120702-pakistan-quetta-extremists-film-massacre-shiite-minority-group-hazara

Qureshi, A. (2012, November 22). Pakistan Taliban suicide bomber kills 23 in Rawalpindi. *The Guardian.* http://www.theguardian.com/world/2012/nov/22/pakistan-taliban-suicide-bomber-rawalpindi

Rosen, N. (2006). *In the belly of the green bird: The triumph of the martyrs in Iraq.* New York: Simon and Schuster.

Rubenstein, W. D. (2004). *Genocide: A history.* New York: Pearson Education Limited.

Schabas, W. (2000). *Genocide in international law: The crimes of crimes.* Cambridge: Cambridge University Press.

Scheper-Hughes, N., & Lock, M. M. (1987). The mindful body: A prolegomena to future work in medical anthropology. *Medical Anthropology Quarterly, 1*(1), 6–41.

Scherrer, C. P. (2003). *Ethnicity, nationalism, and violence: Conflict management, human rights, and multilateral regimes.* London: Ashgate.

Sharma, D. P. (2005). *The new terrorism: Islamist International.* Delhi: APH Publishing.

Shaw, M. (2003). *War and genocide.* Cambridge: Cambridge University Press.

Shehzad, M. (2003). Textbook controversy in Gilgit. *The Friday Times, XV,* p. 19.

Siddiqa, A. (2010). *Red hot chilli peppers Islam—Is the youth in elite universities in Pakistan radical?* Heinrich Boll Stiftung, Foreign-Security Policy Paper, p. 24.

Simon, T. W. (2007). *The laws of genocide: Prescriptions for a just world.* Oxford: Greenwood.

Smith, C. (2010). *What is a person?* Chicago: University of Chicago Press.

Thackrah, J. R. (2004). *Dictionary of terrorism.* London: Routledge.

Unfortunate disruption: Iranian bookstall closed. (2012, December 10). *Dawn.* http://www.dawn.com/news/1061596/unfortunate-disruption-iranian-bookstall-closed

US Embassy cables: Hillary Clinton says Saudi Arabia 'a critical source of terrorist funding. (2010, December 5). *The Guardian.* http://www.theguardian.com/world/us-embassy-cables-documents/242073

Waller, J. (2007). *Becoming evil: How ordinary people commit genocide and mass killing.* Oxford: Oxford University Press.

Walsh, D. (2006, December 6). Hillary Clinton memo highlights Gulf states' failure to block funding for groups like al-Qaida, Taliban and Lashkar-e-Taiba. *The Guardian*. http://www.theguardian.com/world/2010/dec/05/wikileaks-cables-saudi-terrorist-funding

Wilcke, C. (2009). *Denied dignity: Systematic discrimination and hostility toward Saudi Shia citizens*. New York: Human Rights Watch.

Yusufzai, R. (2008, May 11). The man from Bara. *The News*. http://jang.com.pk/thenews/may2008-weekly/nos-11-05-2008/dia.htm

Zaidi, A. (2011). Postcolonial insanity. *Journal of Postcolonial Cultures and Societies, 2*(4), 1–29.

CHAPTER 11

The Intra-Sunni Conflicts in Pakistan

Zulqarnain Sewag

INTRODUCTION

Within most religions there is evidence of infighting and divisions among different sects and denominations. Whether they are Catholics or Protestants, Shias or Sunnis, Sufis or Salafis, Muslims or Christians, Hindus or Muslims, the divisions are not only ideological but sociopolitical as well. At times, these differences manifest into violent conflicts.

Conflict denotes competitive, opposing and antagonistic actions and a struggle for power, or disagreement between people, groups or ideas. Within the world of Islam, much of the faith-related conflict is based on diverse interpretations of Qur'anic injunctions, sunna and hadith (practices and sayings of the Prophet Muhammad).

Pakistan at this juncture is passing through many crossroads with innumerable flashpoints that are jeopardizing its sociopolitical harmony and cultural diversity. National integration is at stake and may gradually erode. In 1947, when Pakistan gained independence from the British Raj, the focus was on protecting the interests of a Muslim minority in the subcontinent. In subsequent years, the emphasis changed towards alienating and apostatizing Ahmadis. In the 1980s

Z. Sewag (✉)
National Defence University, Islamabad, Pakistan

© The Editor(s) (if applicable) and The Author(s) 2016
J. Syed et al. (eds.), *Faith-Based Violence and Deobandi Militancy in Pakistan*, DOI 10.1057/978-1-349-94966-3_11

313

and beyond, further divisions emerged in the shape of not only Sunni–Shia conflict but also an intra-Sunni conflict, such as Barelvis/Sufis vs. Deobandis/Salafis.

This chapter focuses on the growing intra-Sunni differences and conflicts, and how they are influenced by the takfiri (excommunication) ideology. The chapter is divided into two main sections, covering the traditional intra-Sunni conflicts and the modern intra-Sunni conflicts. In the first, the historical roots of the differences and conflicts are traced within the teachings of the four Sunni imams along with an analysis of Salafism and Sufism. In the second section, the roots of such differences are traced in the sociopolitical and religious movements that took place in the region. The chapter also discusses religious-cum-political parties along with their aims, philosophies and differences. It concludes with some recommendations to overcome intra-Sunni conflicts in Pakistan.

Traditional Intra-Sunni Differences

While the mainstream media and academic studies generally focus on the Sunni–Shia divide, there has been relatively less attention given to divisions among different Sunni subsects on the basis of the teachings of the famous four imams and adherence to the practice of the Sihah Sitta (the six authentic books of Hadith). The six authentic books in Sunni Islam are listed below.

1. Sahih Bukhari by Muhammad bin Ismail Al Bukhari (810–870 AD/196–256 AH), born in Bukhara and died in Samarqand
2. Sahih Muslim by Abul Hassan Muslim Al Hajjaj (821–875 AD/206–261 AH), born and died in Nishapur
3. Jame Tirmizi by Abu Esa Muhammad Al Trimidhi (824–892 AD/209–279 AH), born and died in Termez, Iran
4. Sunan Abu Dawood by Abu Daud Suleiman bin Ash'ath (817–889 AD/202–275 AH), born and died in Sistan, Iran
5. Sunan Al Sughra by Abu Adul Rahman al-Nasai (829–915 AD/215–303 AH), born in Turkmenistan
6. Sunan ibn Maja by Abu Abdullah Mohammad ibn Yazid (824–887 AD/201–273 AH)
7. Muwatta Imam Malik by Imam Malik bin Anas (713–795 AD)

It may be noted that some religious scholars include Sunan Ibn-e-Maja in the Siha Sitta in place of Muwatta Imam Malik.

There are indeed differences in the number, method and interpretation of the ahadith (plural of hadith). These differences have grown wider with the passage of time. Also, there is a huge difference in the teachings, practices and interpretations of the four famous imams (jurisprudents) in the Sunni school of thought. The first one is the Hanafi school of thought, whose founder was Imam Abu Hanifa (699–767), and its followers are called Hanafi. The Maliki school of thought was founded by Imam Malik bin Anas (713–795). The Shafi school of thought was founded by Muhammad ibn Idris ash-Shafi (767–819). Imam Ahmad bin Hanbal (781–855) was the founder of the Hanbali school.

There are practical, theological and philosophical variations among these schools of thought. Imam Hanbal was a student of Imam Malik, while Abu Yusuf (Imam Abu Hanifa's disciple) enjoyed Abbasid propagation and patronizing (Kathir). The Abbasid caliphs appointed some of the main followers of the respective schools to key judiciary posts. The Abbasids were hereditary kings and they promoted those jurisprudents who assisted, supplemented and supported their rule. They used to get their actions approved by the religious clerics for public support and legitimacy. They tortured and punished those who disobeyed them.

During Muslim rule in India, a series of interconnected movements took place that included the movement of Sheikh Ahmad Sirhindi (1564–1624), the Fraizi (obligations) movement of Haji Shariatullah (1781–1840), the militant movement of Syed Ahmad (1786–1831) and the Deobandi movement (founded in 1866) immediately after the Indian War of Independence (1857). These movements were puritanical and the latter ones were inspired by the Wahhabi clerics of Saudi Arabia. The roots of Wahhabi, Salafi and Ahl-e-Hadith belong to the Hanbali school of thought, whereas Barelvis and Deobandis trace their roots to the Hanafi school of thought. These schools conflict with each other on various points. The major conflicting problems started when some of the Hanafis visited Mecca and Medina to receive Islamic education where Hanbali and Salafi ideologies were dominant, and on returning to their respective countries they preached what they had been taught there. Thus they were not only confronted by other sects but also by their own fellows.

The Sufi Order and its Opposition by the Ultraorthodox Clerics

Sufis are the mystics who pursued an intuitive and spiritual approach to Islam, whereas Qazis sought firm adherence to the rules of fiqh (jurisprudence) and sharia (Islamic law). The Qazis (preceding the Wahhabis and Deobandis) provided the first element of tension in the Delhi courts (in the Mughal era) as they tried to influence the empire in the direction of strict adherence to sharia. They found some Sufi practices, such as sama (a forerunner of modern day qawwali), objectionable and they influenced the Delhi court to declare a ban on them. A second element of tension was introduced by "reform" movements of the era; similar tensions also took place in the thirteenth century. These movements were puritanical and exclusionary, and were led by ultraorthodox polemical clerics who saw in *tasawwuf* (Sufism) the possibility of social stagnation. Ibn Taymiyya of Damascus (d. 1326) is a central figure for the polemical ultraorthodox reform movements. He aroused the Mamlukes to take a stand against the Mongols, and over the centuries his takfiri ideas travelled to Delhi, where they were pitted against the powerful Sufi movement of the Chishtia Order. Again it was Muhammad ibn Abdul Wahhab in the eighteenth century who linked Sufism with shirk (polytheism). In the subcontinent, Ahmed Sirhindi, Haji Shariatullah, Syed Ahmed, Shah Abdul Aziz (son of Shah Waliullah) and so forth refuted Sufism in many ways.

The following is a brief overview of key Sufi orders. The Chishtiyah order was founded by the Persian saint Mu'in ud Din Chishti (d. 1236 CE) in Khurasan, Iran, and it is highly influential in Indo-Pak subcontinent. The Suhrawardiyah mystical chain was founded by Persian scholar Abu Najib Suhrawardi (d. 1168 CE) in Iraq. It has a strong presence in the subcontinent. The Naqshbandiyah was founded by Baha al Din Naqshband (d. 1389 CE) in Bukhàra, modern-day Uzbekistan. It is popular from China to North Africa, Europe and the USA. The Qadiriyah was founded by Persian scholar and saint Abdul Qadir al Jilani (1077–1166 CE) in Baghdad and its influence stretches from Morocco to Malaysia, and from Central and South Asia to South Africa.

The opposition to some of the moderate, cultural traditions of Sufism came not only from Wahhabis and Salafis, but also from the Deobandi subsect of Hanafism, and from certain sections of the Naqshbandi order. For instance, the leading figure of the Naqshbandi order in India, Ahmed Sirhindi, opposed the Mughal emperor's attempts at interfaith unity between Muslims and Hindus. He specifically opposed marriages between the two faith groups. In hindsight, Ahmed Sirhindi represents the bridge between the Naqshbandi order and the Deobandi school of thought that emerged later. Whether it was opposition to Emperor Akbar's moderate views on interfaith or intrafaith harmony, or the emergence of ISIS in Iraq, some sections of the Naqshbandi order played a role in cooperation with Wahhabis/Salafis based on sectarian prejudice and exclusion. A few Naqshbandis along with the pro-Saddam Baathists are part of the larger ISIS conglomeration. The Naqshbandi order has also played a prominent role among some sections of the Chechen jihadist movement in cooperation with Wahhabis. However, taken as a whole, the Sufi movements, including those of Qadiris, Chsihtis, Suhrwardis and also moderate Naqshbandis, are pluralistic and inclusive in nature.

The Ideology of Ibn Taymiyya

The other thing that made certain Sunni segments inimical towards their fellow Muslims was the influence of Taqi ad-Din Ahmad Ibn Taymiyyah on them. Ibn Taymiyyah studied Hanbalism and greatly influenced Ibn Abdul Wahhab. He banned logic and philosophy from Islamic teachings and practices. He even discouraged the *ijtehad* (independent logical reasoning) and taught his followers to have practical jihad against non-believers. It is reported that all of the terrorist organizations act on the teachings of Ibn Tamiya, especially on the issue of takfir and jihad (Fig. 11.1).

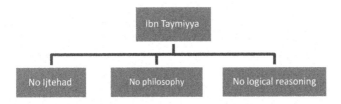

Fig. 11.1 The teachings of Ibn Tamiya

IDEOLOGY OF MUHAMMAD IBN ABDUL WAHHAB

Muhammad ibn Abdul Wahhab had strict views on shirk (polytheism) and Sufism. He gave five elements to define shirk, which are followed by Wahhabis, Ahl-e-Hadith and Deobandis as well. The five elements as described by him are:

1. *Fi-Ilm*: Knowledge, Knowledge of Ghaib (unknown)
2. *Fi-Siffat*: Authority, Someone else has the power
3. *Fi-Ibadat*; Worship, Praying from someone else
4. *Fi-Aadat*; Laws, Believing in Superstitions
5. *Fi-Adab*: Respect, Taking oath of other than God

Ibn Abdul Wahhab, in view of his thoughts on polytheism, banned visiting shrines and ordered the demolition of existing ones. His teachings led to the destruction of Jannat ul Baqi in Medina where the Holy Prophet's family is buried, including his daughter, grandsons, descendants and some companions. Ibn Taymiyyah's innovations also led to the destruction of Jannat al Mualla in Mecca, where the grandfather, uncle and other ancestors of the Prophet were laid to rest. These graveyards were razed in 1925 on the orders of the Saudi king Ibn Saud. These actions of the newly founded kingdom provoked the whole Muslim world against them. Wahhabis consider the Prophet to be dead and forbid anyone from praying to him or seeking his intercession. However, the Sufis claims that the Qur'an recommends intercession via both the Prophet and other exalted personalities. These are the major causes of animosity between Wahhabis/Salafis and other Sunni sects.

THE HISTORICAL CONTEXT IN SOUTH ASIA

Intra-Sunni conflicts in the subcontinent can be traced back to the latter stages of the Mughal era. Zahiruddin Babur, the pioneer of the Mughal dynasty in Hindustan, advised his son and heir, Humayun, to avoid igniting sectarian differences because they weaken Islam (Jaffar 1936; Ali 2012). During the Mughal reign it was Sheikh Ahmed Sirhindi, influenced by the teachings of some Arab scholars, who first decreed that the Shias are infidels and that established Sufi teachings are contradictory to Islamic teachings. After him, this gulf increased over time among Muslims. Ahmed Sirhindi seems to have been a sharia-minded cleric who also claimed to be a mystic. Though he belonged to the Naqshbandia order, he was against the traditional rituals of Sufism being practised and promoted in the region. He attempted to combine Sufism with Mullahism, and tried to bring Sufism into conformity with ultraorthodoxy. His actions clashed with Sufism and were opposed by other Sunni orders.

After the Mughal emperor Shah Jahan, the struggle for kingship started between his sons, Dara Shikoh and Aurangzeb Alamgir. The former was more tolerant of the Hindus, Sufis, Shias and non-Muslims as per the policies of his predecessors, whereas the latter subscribed to the strictly pro-sharia teachings of Ahmed Sirhindi (Jaffar 1936). Aurangzeb's era saw the ascendancy of religious extremism. The clergy were on the side of Alamgir. Alongside political reasons, one dominant element in this fight between the two brothers was religious supremacy. Shia states were taken into central polity, and countless Shia Muslims and Sufis, in addition to Hindus, were killed on the behalf of Aurangzeb. After Aurangzeb's death in 1707, Muslims became the victims of wars among Mughal princes for the sake of kingship. The Mughal empire divided into smaller domains held by various Nawabs and Rajas, and then ultimately by the British colonialists. Muslim communities as a whole descended into political chaos, economic decline and religious bigotry.

THE EMERGENCE OF DARUL ULOOM DEOBAND

After the Indian War of Independence of 1857, Muslims were in decline on all fronts. To meet these circumstances, two major institutions emerged: the Darul Uloom Deoband and Aligarh. The Darul Uloom Deoband was rooted in religious orthodoxy and literalism, whereas Aligarh was a symbol of modernism. The founders of both were Sunnis, but they had wide differences. Thus, for years, the Deoband opposed and criticized Aligarh at every opportunity. One reason was the collection of finances because Muslims were confused about whom to donate to. The formation of the Darul Uloom madrassa took place on 30 May 1867 by Muhammad Qasim Nanotvi along with other clerics, such as Rashid Ahmad Gangohi, Muhammad Yaqub Nanotvi and Fazal al-Rahman Usmani.

The name Deobandi is derived from the name of the town Deoband in which the Darul Uloom seminary is located. The clerics of this seminary sided with the All India Congress. The decree was issued by Rasheed Ahmad Gangohi in favour of joining the congress. Later on the Madrassa at Deoband divided into two: the Usmani group (a tiny section), led by

Shabbir Ahmad Usmani, which supported Quaid e Azam and the Pakistan movement, and the Madani group, led by Hussain Ahmad Madani, which supported the congress. However, as later events proved, this division could well have been a pragmatic approach to ensure that both camps remained connected to competing power centres and exercised influence in the relevant country.

In 1919 the political wing of the Darul Uloom Deoband, the JUH, was constituted by Abdul Mohasim Sajjad, Qazi Hussain Ahmed, Ahmed Saeed Dehlvi, Mufti Muhammad Naeem Ludhianvi and Mufti Kifayatullah, who along with the Madani group opposed the Pakistan Movement. These differences even irked religious tensions as opposite decrees were issued from both sides. The Barelvi clerics in general supported the Pakistan Movement.

The syllabus of the Darul Uloom Deoband madrassa was based on traditional subjects. It was influenced by the teachings of the Wahhabi movement, especially on the subject of jihad, and also in the sectarian and takfiri opposition to Sufis and Shias. Thus syllabus differed in course with all other Sunni sects practised in the Indo-Pak subcontinent as after it Barelvi School emerged with pro-Sufi interpretations. However, the Deobandis claimed to have roots in Sufism, especially in the Naqshbandia order, but their conduct does not prove that claim.

INTRA-SUNNI CONFLICTS IN PAKISTAN

The factional details of major Sunni subsects working in Pakistan, along with religious roots of different schools and their political/religious manifestations, are as shown in Fig. 11.2

In the Barelvi subsect, Jamiat Ulema e Pakistan Noorani Group (JUP-N), the PAT, the JAS, the ST and Dawat e Islami (DI) are included. In the Deobandi subsect, the JUI-F, the ASWJ, the TJ, Lal Masjid and certain proscribed outfits such as the SSP, the LeJ, the HM, the JeM, the TTP, Jundullah, Hizb ul Tahrir and others are included. The JI and Tanzim e Islami of Dr Israr (TI) claim to be non-sectarian but are generally aligned with the Deobandi Taliban.

THE WAHHABIS AND THEIR INFLUENCES IN PAKISTAN

Around the time that the subcontinent was facing a bitter political and economic crisis, there arose a movement in Hejaz (Arabia) with the birth of Muhammad Ibn Abdul Wahhab in 1703, the founder of Wahhabism.

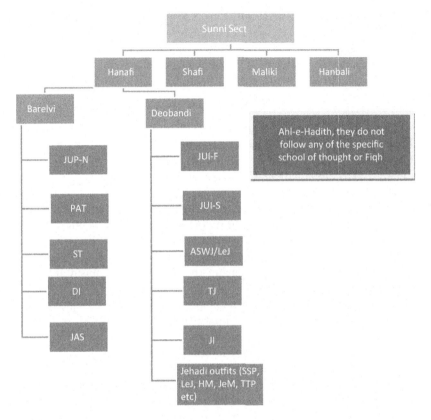

Fig. 11.2 An overview of the subsects of Sunni Islam

This movement is the progenitor of harsh interpretations and connotations of Islam. Ibn Abdul Wahhab labelled Sufism as un-Islamic and Ibn al-Arabi, a legendary Sufi saint, as an apostate. For him, Shias were also apostates. He justified the demolition of the holy shrines (Commins 2006). His movement started exporting harsh ideologies that eschewed peaceful Muslims (Commins 2006) as this movement is denoted as the pioneer in cultivating the seeds of sectarianism in the Islamic world (Blanchard 2008).

Wahhab assisted the Saud family in capturing the areas surrounding Najd. During the nineteenth century, Wahhabi hordes attacked different parts of the Arabian Peninsula, and even Karbala and Baghdad in Iraq, and they were temporarily repelled by the Ottoman general, Mohammad Ali Pasha.

In the latter part of the 1920s, King Abdul Aziz al-Saud, with the assistance of the UK, rebelled against the Ottoman caliphate. Wahhabism was made the official state religion of Saudi Arabia, the country that emerged after Hejaz was captured by the Saud clan and renamed.

WAHHABISM AND THE SOUTH ASIAN CONNECTION

Muhammad ibn Abdul Wahhab and Shah Waliullah (1703–1762) studied under the same teacher in Medina and were influenced by Ibn Taymiyya's takfiri and jihadist ideology. Subsequently, Shah Abdul Aziz Dehlvi (1745–1823), the son of Shah Waliullah, Shah Ismail Dehlvi (1779–1831) and Syed Ahmad Shaheed (1786–1831) planted Wahhabism in the veins of Indo-Pak Subcontinent, and also excommunicated and apostatized both Shias and Sunni Sufis by labelling them as deviants. Dehlvi and Shaheed undertook militant jihad against Sikhs and were killed in Balakot during fighting in 1831. Their jihadist movement replaced the dovish Hanafism with the hawkish Hanbalism, paving the way for Wahhabism and neo-Kharijism in the region.

To expand Wahhabi influence on the soil of Pakistan, Saudi Arabia continues to provide ideological, moral and financial support to hardline elements linked to Wahhabism against all other sects (Yusuf 2012). Iran also supported likeminded groups to counter the financial and ideological support of Saudi Arabia and other Gulf countries (Saima Afzal 2012). It is estimated that, since the 1970s, Saudi Arabia's annual spend on religious propagation abroad has been between $2 billion and $3 billion, which is even more than the Soviet propaganda budget, which was $1 billion per annum (Vallely 2007). The Islamic University of Medina claims to have students from more than 139 countries. Much of its funding is transported through two Saudi-based organizations: the Rabita al-Alami al-Islami (World Muslim League) and the Dar ul-Ifta wal Dawat ul-Irshad. Saudi clerics frequently visit Deobandi and Salafi groups, madrassas and mosques in Pakistan. Literature based on Wahhabi teachings is widespread in bookstores and madrassas across the world.

AHL-E-HADITH

In the words of an Indian-born scholar, Dr Gayatri Chakravorty Spivak, the name Ahl e Hadith means the followers of Hadith. They are the Salafi/Wahhabi of the subcontinent. They are literalist and do not rely on secondary sources of Islamic law. Their male followers do not trim their beards, and they fold their hands above the naval. They believe that other Sunni subsects have betrayed the teachings of the "Righteous Caliphs" as they erred in their blind compliance with Hanafi and other Sunni imams, which, as per the Ahle e Hadith is a violation of the Islamic faith. Furthermore, also as per Ahle e Hadith, Sunni Hanafi beliefs and practices, like those of Sufism, are not in accordance with Islam but akin to shirk (polytheism). The Salafi/Wahhabi further state that the Sunni during prayers fold their hands over the belly instead of the chest, which is against the "true" Islamic practice. Thus all these acts are bidat (impermissible innovation). Ahle e Hadith label themselves as true monotheists. They are influenced by the teachings of Muhammad ibn Abdul Wahhab.

Syed Nazeer Husain from Delhi and Siddiq Hasan Khan of Bhopal transported this school from the Arabian Peninsula to the subcontinent. Maulana Sanaullah Amritsari (1870–1943), a pioneer of the Ahl e Hadith subsect, supported the Deobandi Ulema in the formation of the JUH but was a bitter critique of the Hanafis. The crystallization of the Ahl e Hadith as a distinct sect happened gradually. Hanafis saw it following the path of Wahhabis so they opposed it. A movement in the subcontinent against both Ahl e Hadith and the Saudi government took place in 1926 when Ibn Saud captured Hejaz, while the Hanafis there formed Hizb ul Ahnaf (the Hanafi Army) and Khuddam al Haramain (Servants of the Two Holy Cities) against Saudi rule and decided not to visit Mecca and Medina until the Wahhabis were overthrown.

For the legitimization of his rule, Ibn Saud organized a conference in Najd in 1927, which was attended by many Indian Ahl e Hadith and some Deobandi clerics. The founder, President Muhammad bin Ibrahim Junagarhi (d. 1942) of the All-India Ahl-i Hadith Conference, in a pamphlet declared that, "from every angle, religious as well as political, Ibn Saud is the most well suited to be the servant (ruler) of the Hejaz" (Jalil 2001). The Ahl e Hadith vehemently oppose Sufism (Foundation n.d.).

Salafis take their name from the Salaf (the pious predecessors). They are puritans, strict and literalist, and they are influenced by the teachings of Ibn Taymiyya, Ibn Abdul Wahhab, al-Maqdisi and Imam Ahmed bin Hanbal.

Muhammad Abduh (1849–1905) of Egypt, Muhammad Rashid Rida (1865–1935) from Lebanon, Jamal al-Din al-Afghani (1839–1897), Abdul Aziz bin Abdullah bin Baz (1910–1999) from Saudi Arabia, Sheikh Abu at-Tamimi (1925–2001) from Saudi Arabia, Muhammad

Nasir-ud-Din al-Albani (1914–1999) from Albania, Muqbil bin Hadi al-Khallali (1933–2001) from Yemen and Abdul-Ghaffar Hassan (1913–2007) from Umarpur, Delhi, India, are prominent exponents of the Salafi movement.

Salafis in their takfiri form are generally anti-West and anti-democracy, and call Western imperialists the major conspirator against Muslims. In Pakistan, Farhat Hashmi, a female activist (born in 1957), and Hafiz Muhammad Saeed (born in 1947) are prominent preachers of Salafism. Ehsan Elahi Zaheer (1945–1987) from Sialkot, Punjab, was orthodox Salafi and Ahl e Hadith, and one of the major critic of other sects. He declared Shias and Barelvis to be infidels. Hafiz Zubair Alizai (1957–2013) from Attock, Punjab, was a strong proponent of Salafism. Salafis are generally split into three categories: purists, activists and jihadists. Al-Qaeda, ISIS, Jabhat al-Nusra, Ansar al-Islam, Boko Haram, Ansar al-Shariah, the Armed Islamic Group of Algeria and Al-Shabaab are the notorious jihadi facets of the Salafi movement (Jones 2014). Their conduct towards both Muslims and non-Muslims is very harsh.

As a minor difference, Wahhabism was a pared-down form of Islam which cast off the influence of modernity, whereas Ahl-e-Hadith tried to reconcile Islam with modernism (Stanley 2005). These were the efforts of King Faisal of Saudi Arabia, who assisted cross-pollination between Ibn Abd al-Wahhab's teachings on oneness, polytheism and transgression, and Salafi interpretations of ahadith. Some of the Salafis included Ibn Abdul Wahhab in the list of Salaf. Thus the monarch was able to bridge the gap (Beling 1980).

CONFLICT BETWEEN DEOBANDIS AND AHL-E-HADITH

Rasheed Ahmad Gangohi as the principal of Darul Uloom Deoband praised the Wahhabi ideology but some of his students differed in their views. Hussain Ahmad Madani (1879–1957), who also remained the head of the madrassa at Deoband, wrote a polemical tract entitled "Al-Shahab al-Saqib". In this he claimed that Muhammad bin Abdul Wahhab actually preached falsehood, killed numerous Sunni Muslims and forced many others to accept his false creed. He also presented Wahhab as a tyrant, a traitor and despicable (Faizi 1986).

Ahmed Raza Khan, the leader of the Barelvis, in his book *Husam al-Harmayn*, termed Deobandis as Wahhabi and infidels. However, Muhammad Zakariya, Ilyas Kandhalavi and Yusuf Kandhalavi, the founding members of the Deobandi-related TJ, openly declared themselves as Wahhabis.

However, to improve relations with Saudi Arabia, in 1978 a staunch Saudi supporter and prominent Deobandi, Manzur Numani (d. 1997), wrote a book entitled *Sheikh Muhammad bin Abdul Wahhab ke Khilaf Propaganda aur Hindustan Ke Ulema-e-Haq par uskay Asrat* (The Propaganda against Sheikh Muhammad bin Abdul Wahhab and Its Impact on the True Clerics), which changed the situation further (Naumani 1998). In the book he appreciated and legitimized the teachings and preaching of Ibn Abdul Wahhab (Darul Ifta 2012). His work further bridged the gap between Deobandis and Wahhabis. During the First Gulf War in 1990–1991, there emerged a split within Wahhabism: both inside Saudi Arabia and outside owing to the permission by the Saudi king to allow American troops to protect the holy places in Mecca and Medina. After 9/11, the international political scenario once again united these old allies.

In the 1990s, Sayyid Talib ur Rahman, a Saudi-based Pakistani Ahl e Hadith scholar, wrote a book entitled *Ad-Deobandia*, in which he concluded that Deobandis are apostates and Barelvis are grave worshippers (Rahman 1990). A series of books was published against Deobandis. The group organized a two-day Tahaffuz-i Sunnah Conference in Delhi in the middle of 2001 at which, without criticizing the Saudi regime, Ahl e Hadith were declared a product of a sinister imperialist conspiracy. After the conference, a list of 50 points was recorded that argued that Ahl e Hadith had violated both the Qur'an and sunna (Shahjahanpuri 2001). It was mentioned in a pamphlet that Ahl e Hadith were part of a global conspiracy to call other Muslim sects infidels (Bulandshahri 2001). In different decrees issued from the Darul Ifta in Madrassa Deoband, Ahl e Hadith, the JI, Shias and Barelvis are said to be the followers of an un-Islamic path and thus deviants. However, in recent decades, Deobandi clerics of India and Pakistan have grown closer to the Saudi government and its official Wahhabi clergy.

THE IRANIAN REVOLUTION, AFGHAN JIHAD AND SAUDI FUNDING

In 1979, two major incidents, the Iranian Revolution and the Soviet invasion of Afghanistan, occurred that not only affected the sociopolitical dynamics in the region but also had a substantial impact on the sectarian dynamics in Pakistan and beyond. Some pro-Saudi Sunni groups in Pakistan did not accept the Iranian Revolution and practically participated in the Afghan Jihad. The other mild and moderate Sunni factions, on the other hand, were not too concerned about the Iranian Revolution and even remained indifferent to the Afghan Jihad. This attitude created a divide within Sunni subsects, which is still present. The Soviet invasion of Afghanistan can be considered as the starting point of Saudi funding to Sunni Muslims—mostly Deobandi and Salafi/Wahhabi Muslims—competing for religious or political influence. That war in particular was an event to affirm Wahhabism as the true belief, in sharp contrast to the alleged promotion of atheism by the Communists and the competing version of Islam followed by Barelvis, Sufis and Shias (Firdous 2009). It is widely believed that Salafis seek to preserve Saudi interests in Pakistan (Waseem 2004). Pakistan was directly affected by its role in the proxy war in Afghanistan, and it has still failed to come out of this quagmire. Many radical Deobandis and Salafis received their training during the Afghan Jihad. After the war, they directed their jihad against the non-Deobandi and non-Salafi sects instead (Dotani 2011).

Saudi Arabia, and to a lesser extent Iran, allegedly provided financial and infrastructural support to Deobandi/Salafi and Shia madrassas, respectively, in what has been termed a proxy war in Pakistan (Waseem 2004). While there is no scale of comparison between alleged Iranian funding versus Saudi funding, the overall effect was particularly devastating for Sunni Barelvis/Sufis and Shias. The state exclusively backed Saudi-financed militias, which disavow defining this phenomenon as a "proxy war". This has destabilized the harmonious setup of the country. Saudi and other Middle Eastern countries finance only those specific Sunni groups that propagate their agenda—that is, Deobandi and Salafis.

On 22 May 2011, British newspapers *Dawn* and *The Guardian*, reported that nearly $100 million in annual funding was provided to Deobandi and Ahl e Hadith clerics and seminaries, as well $6,500 per person to the families of "martyrs" who conducted suicide attacks or died while attacking the security forces. This funding goes to Southern Punjab and is provided by Saudi Arabia, the United Arab Emirates, Qatar and Kuwait. Funding is also given to certain seminaries and clerics based in Gujranwala, KPK and FATA (Miller 2012; Moniquet 2013). Wahhabism is alleged to have direct links with terrorism and is a fanatic Islamic sect that sponsors terrorist activities around the globe (Malhotra 2011).

In Afghanistan, the Saudi government financed Deobandi outfits such as Gulbuddin Hikmatyar's Hizb-e-Islami over others. The idea was to overcome Iran in a post-Soviet Afghanistan that was to be subjugated by forces friendly to their US/Saudi/Pakistani benefactors (Irfani 2004). On both sides of the Durand Line the creation of jihad nurseries made it the central hub for transporting sectarian hate from the shores of Baluchistan to the rest of the country (Human Rights Watch 2005). Dr Ayesha Siddiqa writes that Al-Qaida, the TTP, Jundullah, the SSP, the LeJ, the HUJI, the JeM, the ASWJ and so forth have common objectives and are on the same page in calling other sects infidels. They have same Deobandi ideology and channels, and all are anti-Shia, anti-moderate Sunnis.

DEOBANDIS IN PAKISTAN

In present-day Pakistan, Deobandis are in dominant positions in most spheres of influence. Though Barelvis and Deobandis are followers of Imam Abu Hanifa, they differ in practice. For example, Deobandis are opposed to traditional Sufi rituals. At times, these differences turn into conflicts and ultimately into clashes. They are also manifested in beliefs and practices such as prayer timings, Friday prayers, and the length and importance of Taraveeh prayers. Other significant conflicting connotations relate to ritual Sufi practices as well as the notions of jihad and ijtihad.

Extremism could be a possible outcome of fundamentalism, whereas violence is an explicit form of extremism. The Taliban and other hardliners are associated with the mantle of Deobandi and takfiri (excommunicator) beliefs. Deobandis term Barelvis as "irredeemable heretics". The majority of Sunni Muslims in Pakistan are considered to be Barelvis.

As per a University of Pennsylvania study, close to 90 per cent of terrorist activities in Pakistan are carried out by Deobandis. The Punjabi Taliban, the SSP, the LeJ and so on, who are all Deobandis, also threaten Jamat ud Dawa and the LT, and label them as establishment puppets owing to the latter's compliance. Extremist Deobandis also oppose those Deobandis and Barelvis who condemn attacks on civilians and the security forces. Maulana Hassan Jan (Deobandi) in Peshawar on 17 September 2007 and Dr Sarfraz Naeemi (Barelvi) in Lahore on 12 June 2009 were killed as a result of their moderate views and decrees against the Taliban and suicide bombings. Maulana Fazal-ur Rahman, the chief of the JUI-F, has also faced a suicide attack in this connection.

Famous Deobandi seminaries in Pakistan are:

- Jamia Uloom ul Islamia (Binori Town), Karachi
- Darul Uloom Haqqania, Akura Khattak
- Darul Uloom Karachi
- Jamia Ashrafia, Lahore
- Jamia Binoria al-Aalmia, Karachi
- Ahsan-ul-Uloom, Karachi
- Jamiatur Rasheed, Karachi, Karachi
- Ashraf ul Madaris, Karachi
- Khair-ul-Madaris, Multan

ATTACKS ON SUFI SHRINES

KPK and the FATA have borne the brunt of faith-based violence at the hands of the TTP. Similarly, Lashkar-e-Islam has frequently attacked and desecrated the tombs of great Sufi saints, such as Hazrat Rahman Baba, Abdul Shakoor Malang Baba in Peshawar on 18 December 2007, Hazrat Abu Saeed Baba in Bara Khyber Agency on 3 March 2008, Mian Umer Baba on 8 May 2009, Ashaab Baba in Peshawar in May 2008 and Bahadur Baba in Nowshera on 7 March 2009.

The shrine of Hazrat Sayyid Ali Tirmizi, commonly known as Pir Baba, in Buner was locked while the mausoleum of the famous freedom fighter Haji Sahib Tarangzai in Mohmand was captured and converted into the Taliban's headquarters. The attacks on shrines have also taken place in other provinces of Pakistan.

In July 2010, the tomb of Data Ganj Bakhsh in Lahore was bombed and around 45 devotees were killed. In the same year, the shrines of Abdullah Shah Ghazi in Karachi and Sheikh Farid ud Din Ganj Shakar in Pakpattan were attacked, killing 9 and 7 pilgrims, respectively. Among the justifications for attacking Sufi tombs is the allegation of polytheism, Sufi's inclination towards Shia'ism, and their acceptance and welcoming of all people, irrespective of their religion, sect, creed or race. In the ongoing War on Terror, the USA considers Sufi shrines as a potential force against terrorism, thus it has given $1.5 million for their renovation and preservation since 2001.

Here's a list of some other attacks on Sufi shrines

- On 18 September 18 2015 the Shrine of Zinda Pir located in Mehran Town, Korangi industrial area, Karachi was attacked, as a result of which two people were killed.

- On 10 January 2014 in Mardan, two caretakers were killed in the shrine of Shaheed Ghazi Baba.
- On 9 February 2014, 8 people were killed and 16 injured as a result of firing on the Astana Jalali Baba in Karachi.
- On 26 February 2013 the shrine of Pir Hajan Shah Huzoori at Marri village near Shikarpur was destroyed by a planted explosive device as a result of which 4 people died and 10 were injured.
- On 3 November 2012 the shrine of Phandu Baba at Chamkani, near Peshawar, was bombed. As a result it was partially destroyed.
- The shrine of Hazrat Kaka Sahib at Nowshera was blown up by a bomb. As a result, four people were killed.
- On 21 June 2012 the shrine of Hazrat Panj Peer (the shrine of five saints) in Peshawar was hit by a bomb on a donkey cart, as a result of which three people were killed.
- On 2–3 April 2011 in a suicide attack on Sakhi Sarwar in Dera Ghazi Khan, around 50 people were killed and 100 were injured (Akbar n.d.).
- On 14 December 2010 in Budh Bheer area, Peshawar Ghazi Baba Shrine was attacked.
- On 25 October 2010 in Pakpattan district, Punjab, the Baba Fareeduddin Ganjshakar Shrine was attacked, as a result of which 7 people were killed and 25 were injured.
- On 14 October 2010 in Landi Kotal, a subdistrict of Khyber, a shrine was attacked with no causalities being reported.
- On 7 October 2010 in Karachi, the Hazrat Abdullah Shah Ghazi Shaheed shrine was bombed, as a result of which 9 people were killed and 75 were wounded.
- On 19 August 2010 in the Green town area of Lahore, a shrine was attacked and two devotees were killed.
- On 15 July 2010 in Landi Kotal, Khyber, a shrine was targeted with no human loss.
- On 1 July 2010 in Lahore, the Data Ganj Bakhsh Shrine was bombed, as a result of which 45 devotees were killed and 175 were injured.
- On 21 June 2010 in the Chamkani area of Peshawar, the Shrine of Mian Umer Baba was bombed.
- On 22 April 2010 in Landi Kotal, another mausoleum was attacked, as a result of which 1 person was killed and 6 were injured.
- On 21 April 2010 in Orakzai Agency, a shrine was attacked, as a result of which nine people were injured.
- On 5 Januuary 2010 in the Satori Khel area of Orakzai, seven shrines were bombed.

- On 8 May 2009 in Peshawar. Sheikh Omar Baba's shrine was targeted.
- On 5 March 2009 in the Hazarkhwani area of Peshawar, the famous Pashtun traditional Islamic poet Rahman Baba's shrine was attacked.
- In May 2008 in Peshawar, the shrine of Ashaab Baba was attacked.
- On 7 March 2009 in Nowshehra, the shrine of Bahadur Baba was attacked, as a result of which one person died.
- On 3 March 3 2008 in Bara subdistrict, Khyber, the 400-year-old shrine of Abu Saeed Baba was bombed, as a result of which 10 people were killed.
- On 9 December 2008 in Buner, the shrine of Hazrat Pir Baba was attacked, as a result of which 1 person was killed and another 4 were injured.
- On 18 December 2007 on GT Road, Peshawar, the shrine of Abdul Shakoor Malang Baba was targeted, as a result of which 4 devotees were killed and 1 was wounded.
- On 27 May 27 2005 in Islamabad, the Bari Imam Shrine was bombed, as a result of which 25 devotees were killed and 100 were injured.
- On 20 March 2005 in Jhal Magsi, Kachi district/Baluchistan, the Urs of Sufi saint Pir Syed Rakheel Shah Shrine was bombed, as a result of which 40 devotees were killed and 15 were injured (Table 11.1).

Source: Pakistan Security Report 2010, by Pakistan Institute for Peace Studies (PIPS), January 2011 and Daily the News, *Daily Express Tribune* 2014 Reports.

Table 11.1 Attacks on Sufi shrines

Year	No. of shrines attacked
2005	2
2006	1
2007	2
2008	3
2009	5
2010	18
2011	5

Source: Pakistan since 9/11, a Statistical Report of a Decade of the War on Terror, Circle, Centre for Innovative Research, Collaboration and Learning, www.circle.org.pk

TABLIGHI JAMAT

The TJ is the Deobandi missionary wing. Its inception was aimed at ostensibly responding to Hindu and Christian missionaries but, after the independence of Pakistan, its members started travelling from village to village to teach "true Islam". Its headquarters are situated in Raiwind near Lahore. The group's members officially portray themselves as simple missionaries, but in the recent past many cases have been reported where militants sought accommodation and hideouts in the Tablighi Markaz at Raiwind.

LAL MASJID (RED MOSQUE)

The mosque gets its name from the interior and exterior red colouring. It is a government mosque built in 1965 in Islamabad, and the designated cleric is supposed to be appointed by the government, receiving pay and privileges from the federal exchequer. Maulana Abdullah, from a poor peasant family of Rajan Pur district, Punjab, and a graduate of the Deobandi madrassa Jamia Uloom ul Islamia, Binori Town, Karachi, was appointed as its first imam. He had close ties with General Zia ul Haq and with other high-ranking officers and bureaucrats. During the Soviet–Afghan War, the Red Mosque played a vital role in recruiting and training radicals to fight against the Soviet forces. After his assassination in 1998, his sons Abdul Aziz Ghazi and Abdul Rashid Ghazi took over the reins of the mosque.

The assassination of Maulana Abdullah was a turning point for the relations between the Red Mosque and the military. The new chiefs of the mosque, the Ghazi brothers, made it the centre of radicalization to form a caliphate. They created direct links with terrorist organizations against the civilians and law-enforcement agencies. In 2007, the students and clerics of Lal Masjid forcibly occupied a children's library and some other government buildings in Islamabad, then set about implementing their sharia "code" through acts of violence and property destruction. After months of protracted negotiations (instead of enforcing the writ of the state), on 3 July 2007 a clash erupted in which Ghazi Abdul Rasheed was killed while his other brother Ghazi Abdul Aziz was arrested while fleeing in a burqa. The aftermath of the clash proved to be fatal. A Ghazi force was established to take revenge, which started massive attacks on civilians and the security forces, and which is still active today (Gishkori 2015). Lal Masjid also has a seminary for women, called Jamia Hafsa. As per a freely available and widely circulating video clip, the students of the seminary were filmed paying an oath of allegiance to and praying for the success of ISIS and its caliph Abu Bakr Al Baghdadi. Apart from Deobandis, Wahhabis and Ahl e Hadith, all other Sunni sects have conflicts with the ideology and practices of this mosque. Its future role is likely to be continued antagonism and violent confrontation with the Constitution of Pakistan.

HIZB UT-TAHRIR

Hizb ut Tahrir (HT), a Sunni Muslim international pan-Islamic organization, was founded by Taqqiuddin al-Nabhani in Jerusalem in 1953. It now has more than a million members based in more than 50 countries. Not unlike Salafis, the core philosophy of the organization is to re-establish a sharia-based caliphate and keep on proselytizing Islam all over the globe. It has taken inspiration from Syed Qutb, a leading follower and scholar of Ibn Tamiya and Ibn Hanbal. It bitterly opposes democracy and other political systems. Though it strives for the unification of Muslims, it considers many of the Muslim sects to be transgressors. Currently it has heavily invested in jihad and is supporting the Syrian rebels and jihadists against the Bashar Assad's regime. Its charter stipulates that non-Muslims cannot participate in the selection of the caliph but they will be given rights as enshrined in the Charter of Medina of the seventh century. Ahmed Rashid, a renowned analyst, writes in his book *Jihad: The Rise of Militant Islam in Central Asia* that HT has strong links with the Islamic Movement of Uzbekistan. It has been banned in Pakistan since 2004 but it openly publicizes its agenda through pamphlets in distributed in mosques and markets. It has planned many attacks in Pakistan, including those on General Pervez Musharaf, PIPS, Islamabad, and Shamsi Air Base in Baluchistan. A serving Pakistani Army officer, Brigadier Ali Khan has been detained in connection with HT (Rana 2011; Aman 2011).

JAMAAT-E-ISLAMI

The JI was founded on 26 August 1941 by Sayyid Abul Aala Maududi. It was opposed to the creation of Pakistan. After independence, it gained momentum gradually and remained at the heart of many political and religious movements in the country. After General Zia ul Haq took over the reins of the country, the JI became his ideological and political arm. JI members were inducted in the federal cabinet and gifted the slots of information and broadcasting; production; and water, power and natural resources (Nasr 1996; Haqqani 2005). The incumbent ruling PML-N and the JI were both nurtured and nourished under the umbrella of General Zia ul Haq. There has been a strong nexus between the JI and the PML-N, which can even be witnessed today. The JI not only has close ties with Tehreek-e-Nafaz-e-Shariat-e-Muhammadi (TNSM) of Sufi Muhammad but also with other radical organizations, such as the TTP, the ASWJ and al-Qaeda. Some critics call the JI the mother of all banned, sectarian and terrorist outfits. The remarks of the previous JI chief, Munawar Hassan, about the TTP showed that his party adheres to the TTP's ideology. He called the killed members of the TTP martyrs, whereas he has derided the Pakistani soldiers fighting for the protection of their coutnry (Mir, The Jihadi face of the Jamaat: Is the alliance with the establishment over now? 2013).

As far as the JI's relations with al-Qaeda are concerned, Khalid Sheikh Muhammad, the number three in Al-Qaida, was arrested from the house of a female office bearer of the JI women's wing (Group 2003). Islami Jamiat e Tulba (IJT), the student wing of the JI, was found guilty of having links with al-Qaeda. The terrorists captured from the boys' hostels of Punjab University, Lahore, revealed these links.

Attaur Rehman, alias Umer alias Ibrahim aka Zubair, a Karachi University graduate and former IJT member, was arrested in 2004 in connection with masterminding an attack on General Ahsan Hayat. Hayat was the corps commander in Karachi and as a result of that attack on his car, there were significant casualties. Attaur Rehman was also the founder of Karachi-based Jundullah in 2003. Jundullah is the organization which claimed responsibility for killing 10 foreign climbers on 23 June 2013 at a base camp of the Nanga Parbat in the north of Pakistan.

Engineer Ahsan Aziz, a member of JI, joined al-Qaeda and was killed in a drone attack in North Waziristan in 2012. His funeral prayer was led by JI chief Qazi Hussain Ahmed along with Syed Salahuddin, the chief of the Hizb ul Mujahedeen. Major Adil Abdul Qudoos (a former major of the Pakistan Army) was an active member of the JI. Along with his father Abdul Qudoos Khan, his brother Ahmed Abdul Qudoos and his wife Farzana Qudoos, he was killed in a drone attack on the Afghan border on 11 November 2014 (Mir, Drone deaths underline JI's Jihadi links, 2014a). It was also reported that thousands of JI members received training and fought alongside Arab and other transnational mercenaries during the Soviet-Afghan War in the 1980s. The JI also has close ties with the banned ASWJ (Mir 2014b).

THE BARELVIS

Ahmed Raza khan (1856–1921) laid the foundation of the Hanafi Barelvi school of thought in 1904 to resist the intolerant Wahhabi and anti-Sufi ideologies of the Darul Uloom Deoband. He rejected militant jihad against the British in opposition to the Deobandi view. To muscularly assert the Barelvis as a counterforce to Deobandi obscurantism, Ahmed Raza Khan issued decrees regarding the infidelity of Wahhabis, Deobandis and Ahle e Hadith. In a wider context, his stance was in reaction to the takfeer of the Sunni Sufis by Ibn Taymiyyah and Muhammad ibn Abd al-Wahhab, and later attacks by the Darul Uloom Deoband. The Barelvi school is syncretic and dynamic in nature, like the subcontinent from where it originates, primarily because it does not harshly oppose local and diverse cultures. In contrast, the Deobandi School seems to be strict and barren, like the foreign Arab lands from where it seeks its inspiration. Barelvis also rejected the violent jihad, including the one that took place in Afghanistan. In the post-9/11 War on Terror, they have supported the Pakistani state and have issued decrees calling terrorists who have attacked civilians and the security forces khawarij and takfiris (excommunicators).

Among the Sunni organizations, the PAT, the SIC, the ST and the DI are relatively moderate. They generally do not label any Muslim fellows as an infidel and resort to violence against them. The PAT is the political wing of the Minhaj ul Quran. It came into being in 1989 under Dr Muhammad Tahir ul Qadri, its main leader and founder. This movement believes in Islamic democracy, social justice and moderation. It has networks in other countries. The ST was founded in 1990, mostly as a counter against the oppression and exploitation of the Deobandis. During the 1990s and 2010s, there has remained a one-sided turf war between the Deobandis and Barelvis regarding the forcible takeover of Barelvi mosques by Deobandis. Saleem Qadri, the ST's founding leader, was killed in a sectarian attack by the Deobandi SSP/ASWJ in May 2001. A major sectarian attack on the ST was witnessed in 2006 when its religious congregation was attacked in Nishtar Park, Karachi.

The DI is another religious organization. Founded during the 1980s by Maulana Ilyas Attar Qadri, its teachings are based on the interpretation of Imam Ahmad Raza khan Barelvi (1856–1921). The prime philosophy of the DI lies in the saying "I must strive to reform myself and people of the entire world" (Table 11.2).

Table 11.2   Differences between Sunni Barelvi and Deobandi sects

Issue	Barelvi	Deobandi	Nature
Sufi lineage	Believe in all spiritual orders	Same	No difference
	Perform rituals at shrines	Reject traditional Sufi rituals	Difference and conflict
	Consider shrines as reference (Waseela)	Reject Sufi shrines	Conflict, it may take violent form
	Importance of mysticism	Literalist sharia is more important	Difference
Jihad	Jihad against self, the greater jihad	Militant jihad against non-believers, the greater jihad Tablighi Jamaat calls Jihad against self the greater jihad	Conflict both inter -Sunni and intra-Deobandi
The mosques	Mosque as social institution	Mosque as social as well as source of learning (control over bigger/strategic mosque for control over masses and finances); mosque as centre for radicalization	Conflict, it may become violent
Seminaries	Character-building	Produce jihadi nursery, processions, subscriptions	Conflict, turn into violence
Religious Decrees	More of religious nature	More of political nature	Conflict, may be violent
Suicide attack	Forbidden	Mixed opinion	Conflict

The Barelvis and Deobandis have both similarities and differences. Both are the followers of Imam Abu Hanifa but they adhere to significantly different interpretations of the Hanafi teachings. Barelvis believe in all Sufi lineages and pray with their reference; Deobandis claim to believe in all spiritual orders but do not pray through intercession or wasilah. Barelvis view the struggle against the self as the greater jihad but the Deobandis consider armed conflict with the non-believer or kafir the greater jihad. Barelvis consider the mosque as a centre and a social institution where preaching and rituals are performed. Deobandis describe mosques as a very strategic point. They make the mosque the source of earning and view it as a physical point within different geographical zones to control the masses. The Deobandi strive to control and take over the pulpit of major mosques. Barelvis call seminaries a place of character-building.

For the Deobandis, mosques and their adjoining madrassas are of integral importance as jihadi nursery, providing manpower for protests and processions, and funds to run the group's affairs. The decrees issued by the Barelvis are generally religious and spiritual in nature, whereas those issued by the Deobandis are mostly political. Another conflict between the Barelvis and the Deobandis is regarding suicide attacks: the former totally forbids them or allows them only when the state is at war with anti-state enemies, whereas the latter has a different opinion. Deobandis differ regarding the definition of the enemy. They justify the use of suicide attacks against all those whom they consider to be enemies, whether Muslims or non-Muslims (Table 11.3).

Wahhabi/Ahl e Hadith ideology has many differences with all other Sunni sects. The Ahl e Hadith do not believe in any specific school of jurisprudence. Though the name indicates adherence to the ahadith, the group sticks to the Holy Qur,an in a very strict sense, along with its own choice of ahadith. Wahhabi and Ahl e Hadith both deny logic, as was Ibn Taymiyya's position whereas, other Sunni sects believe in all schools of

Table 11.3   Differences between Wahhabi/Ahl-e-Hadith and other Sunni sects

Issue	Wahhabi/Ahl e Hadith	Other Sunni sects	Nature
Belief in school of thought or fiqh (jurisprudence)	Do not follow any specific imam or fiqh	Belief	Difference in the belief that jurisprudence/fiqh is based on the reasoning of the jurist, so not binding, claim Wahhabis
Attitude towards other sects (Shias, non-Muslims)	Strict attitude; takfir of Shia and Sufis	Mild and cooperative	Conflict that even turns into clashes
Belief in spiritual orders	Rejection of sufism	Firm belief	Conflict
Interpretation of Islamic teachings (prayer, fasting, traveeh, juma, pilgrimage, etc.)	Rigid	Moderate	Difference
Islamic punishments Hudud and other (apostil, blasphemy)	Strict compliance	Mild compliance	Difference
Jihad	Practice	Mix	Difference
Ijtehad	Focus on primary source	Both primary and secondary	Difference

thought and the books of the hadith. The attitude of the Wahhabis/Ahle e Hadith is harsh towards other Muslim sects, including the rest of the Sunnis, whereas other Sunnis have a relatively positive relationship with both believers and even, in many cases, non-believers. The Wahhabis do not believe in the spiritual orders whereas other Sunni Muslims not only keep faith in them but adhere to their teachings as well.

Wahhabi and Ahl e Hadith are very rigid in their practice of the Islamic obligations. They differ in their timings and methods with other Sunni sects. The Wahhabi and Ahl e Hadith are also very strict in their Islamic punishments, whereas other Sunni segments have only mild compliance. They also practice and preach fighting with the sword or with modern weapons, but all other Sunni factions prefer fighting to discipline one's own inner self. On the issue of ijtehad, the Wahhabi and Ahl e Hadith rely on the Qur'an as the primary source whereas all other Sunni sects believe in both primary and secondary sources of Islamic law.

THE ISSUES OF TAKFIR AND KHARUJ

Takfir means the act of declaring a Muslim to be outside the creed of Islam, whereas *kharuj* denotes armed rebellion against the state. An important question to raise is what circumstances force a kharuj (i.e., defence) for the enforcement of sharia, against Muslim governments supporting aggression and oppression or on the basis of takfir (disbelief)? There is a common understanding and voice of the majority that Islam does not allow any armed rebellion which results in bloodshed. Similarly, Islam has a simple and clear definition of a Muslim. Therefore calling anyone an infidel on the basis of ideological or faith-based differences or owing to personal grievances is illegitimate, un-Islamic and forbidden. Thus attacks on civilians or law-enforcement agencies, or rebellion against the government, is not allowed in Islam. This belief rejects all of the theories and claims of the extremist organizations, as well as their interpretations of attacking those outside their own faith. Al-Qaeda, influenced by Wahhabism, introduced its takfiri agenda, which claims that members of other strains of Islam are deviant apostates and are worthy of death. This slogan was soon supported by likeminded Deobandi groups, such as the TTP, the SSP, the LeJ, the LT, Jamat-ud-Dawa, the ASWJ, the JM and the HT, who are now applying this ideology to the killing of ordinary people.

Attacks on Civilians and the Security Forces

The hardliners and extremist organizations that attack civilians and the law-enforcement agencies claim that they so because these individuals/bodies support their enemies—that is, the West. Recently, in an interview with Saleem Safi on a *Geo TV* talkshow, "Jirga", the previous chief of JI, Munawar Hassan, said that he considers the Taliban to be martyrs, but he was not sure about the casualities of the security forces. From 2003 to 2015, fatalities of 20,720 civilians and 6,320 personnel of the security forces have been recorded in violent terrorist attacks. From 2002 to 2015, 425 suicide attacks took place in which 6,411 people belonging to all sects were killed (Portal 2015) (Fig. 11.3).

Sectarian Trends after 9/11

The 9/11 attacks have changed the traditional parameters of sectarian rifts. Now the traditional Shia–Sunni conflicts have transformed into Intra-Sunni, Deobandi/Salafi vs. Barelvi/Sufi conflicts. At times they may also take the shape of a personal or political rivalry which is linked with religion and sect. The book *Muslim World after 9/11* describes different

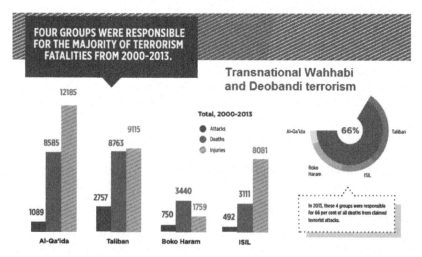

Fig. 11.3 Transnational Wahhabi and Deobandi terrorism (*Source*: Adapted with some changes from GTI 2014)

factors behind Muslim radicalism and sectarian violence, including the conditions, processes and catalyst events (David Thailer, 2004). When the Government of Pakistan decided to join the War on Terror, almost all Deobandi militant groups went against the security forces and civilians, and started bombing the ordinary masses and personnel of military and paramilitary forces. The LeJ formally split into two groups headed by Asif Chotu and Asif Ramzi. The first was tasked to target Shias and other like-minded people, and the other was assigned to attack foreigners. Now a lot of its factions are operating in Karachi and other parts of the country, and they have strong links with all other international terrorist organizations. The ST emerged as another contender in the arena of sectarian violence, especially after the bomb blast of Nishtar Park, Karachi, in 2006. Again, on 27 February 2010, the milad programmes of the SIC were attacked in Faisalabad and Dera Ismail Khan. On 6 February 2013, more than 50 religious clerics from the SIC issued a decree, calling the terrorists transgressors. In 2007 in Khyber, FATA, emerged as another flashpoint when there a war started there between Lashkar e Islam, supported by Deobandis, and Ansar ul Islam, supported by Sunnis/Barelvi. In the current scenario there are many non-state actors with diverse interests, with the possible involvement of foreign actors. ISIS is another threatening group that is trying to spread from Iraq and Syria to Afghanistan and Pakistan.

THE INCREASING ROLE OF THE SEMINARIES

At the inception of Pakistan, the number of religious seminaries (madrassas) was fewer than 300 but now it is more than 40,000, most of them following Deobandi ideology. As per estimates, millions of students are studying in the religious seminaries. The number of affiliated seminaries with Ittehad-e-Tanzeemat-e-Madaris Pakistan (ITMP) is around 35,337, whereas the religious and interior ministries reveal that approximately 8,249 seminaries across the country are unregistered (Tribune n.d.). As per the data provided as of 30 December 2014 by the Provincial Home/Auqaf departments to the Ministry of Religious Affairs, the number of registered madrassas operating in Baluchistan is 13,000, in Punjab 16,000, in KPK 3,136, in Sindh 2800, and in Islamabad Capital Territory 401. However, the Ministry of Religious Affairs has only 26,131 seminaries on its record, of which 14,768 are in Punjab, 7,118 in Sindh, 2,704 in Baluchistan, 1,354 in KPK and 187 in Islamabad. On the basis of data provided by the provincial Auqaf Departments, the ministry estimates that there are 125,000 mosques operating in the country, of which 810 are in Islamabad.

The unregistered seminaries as per the senior official of the ministry comprise 4,135 in KP, 2,411 in Punjab, 1,406 in Sindh and 266 in Baluchistan. There are 31 unregistered seminaries in Islamabad and all are built on encroached land, including some registered on state land. The saddest aspect of the lawlessness is that, as per the officer, these seminaries have never cooperated with government officials when it comes to registration owing to differences in curricula, beliefs and thoughts. The Deobandis are fewer in population but the number of their religious seminaries is greater than those of even the Barelvis, who are estimated to make up three-quarters of the Sunni population in the country. In Pakistan, 20 percent of the population considers themselves to be Deobandi but they own and operate 65 percent of the religious seminaries. On the other hand, the Barelvis have a 25 percent share of the madrassas, Ahl al-Hadith has 6 per cent and the Shias have only 3 percent. The number of Deobandi seminaries in 1988 was 1,779, and this had increased to 7,000 by 2002. Following state support during and after General Zia ul Haq, the number of Deobandi seminaries ballooned to 64 percent of the total (Mansoor 2015).

A joint survey conducted by Islamabad police and Islamabad Capital Territory administration in the wake of the Peshawar carnage revealed that out of 179 registered madrassas in Islamabad, at least 109 belong to Deobandis, 50 to Barelvis, 7 to Ahl-e-Hadith and 3 to Shias. Moreover, there are 84 illegal Deobandi madrassas, 68 Barelvis, 2 Ahl-e-Hadith and 6 Shia. This number does not include the 72 day-scholar Qur'anic institutes. Some 31,769 students are enrolled in Islamabad alone. Among them, 17,382 belong to the districts of Islamabad and Rawalpindi, while the other 14,377 hail from KPK, Azad Kashmir, Gilgit-Baltistan and FATA.[1] Interestingly, the total number of schools and colleges run by the government in the federal capital is 422, whereas the number of seminaries is 401 (Hussain 2015).

CONCLUSION

If the intra-Sunni conflicts are not addressed, they may become more severe and increasingly devastating. Therefore Pakistan today needs a coherent strategy and national solidarity to address the takfiri ideology, which creates differences among fellow Muslims and is injurious to the country's multicultural social fabric. The takfiri ideologies of radical Deobandi militants view Sufi teachings as bidat and shirk while treating the Shias as kafir. The terrorist conviction rate in Pakistan is only 4 per cent owing to a lack of modern technology and methods available to law-enforcement agencies, threats to the judiciary, the absence of a witness-protection programme and a passive prosecution system. Though military courts have been established in this regard, there remain issues of bureaucratic hurdles, and lack of will and enforcement. There is a need for a fully functional system that could not only protect judges and witnesses but also expedite the prosecution system. Radical Deobandi and Salafi madrassas and clerics should be engaged in these reforms, monitoring and legal/punitive measures in order to contain the sectarian violence, including intra-Sunni violence, in Pakistan. The Government of Pakistan has devised a National Action Plan against terrorism but this deals only with the issue of Talibanization, and to some extent hate speech and jihadi literature. It does not fully cover the main elements, such as the takfiri curricula and fatwas, which are fuelling sectarian strife and the anti-Sufi and other forms of terrorism in the country. The funding channels of these extremist organizations should be curtailed, as well as laws enforced to prevent militant outfits from operating with new names. The state must ensure that each citizen has equal rights and responsibilities. It must not accommodate a culture of favouritism on the basis of faith, sect, caste, language or ethnicity. It must halt the swiftly spreading takfiri ideology. This is the only way that Pakistan can get rid of sectarian and takfiri terrorism.

NOTE

1. Holy Cows in Islamabad, Pakistan http://tribune.com.pk/story/820454/holy-cows-in-capital-majority-of-madrassas-operating-illegally/ visited on Friday, October 23, 2015.

REFERENCES

Afzal, S. Iqbal, H. Inayat, M. (2012, November–December). Sectarianism and its implications for Pakistan security: Policy recommendations using exploratory study. *Journal of Humanities and Social Science (JHSS)*, *4*(4): 19–26.

Akbar, S. (n.d.). Series of worldwide destruction of shrines. Retrieved October 22, 2015, from Albasirah: http://www.albasirah.com/en/articles/religious/379-series-of-worldwide-destruction-of-shrines.html

Ali, D. M. (2012). Almiya e Tawreekh.

Aman, S. (2011, July 05). Protect Pakistan from Hizb ut-Tahrir. Retrieved October 26, 2015, from The Express Tribune: http://blogs.tribune.com.pk/story/6777/protect-pakistan-from-hizb-ut-tahrir/

Angel M Rabasa, B. C. (2004). Muslim world after 9/11. Monica: RAND.

Beling, W. L. (1980). *Pan-Islamism, King Faisal and the modernisation of Saudi Arabia*. London: Westview Press.

Blanchard, C. M. (2008). *The Islamic traditions of Wahhabism and Salafiyya*. Washington, DC: Congressional Research Center.

Bulandshahri, M. H. (2001). *Tawassul-o-Isteghasiya Baghayr Allah Aur Ghayr Muqallidin Ka Mazhab*. New Delhi: Farid Book Depot.

Commins, D. (2006). *The Wahabi Mission and Saudi Arabia*. London/New York: I.B. Tauris.

Darul Ifta, D.U. (2012, December 12). Opinion about Muhammad ibn Abdul-Wahhab. Retrieved October 26, 2015, from Darul Ifta, Darul Uloom Deoband. http://darulifta-deoband.org/showuserview.do?function=answerView&all=en&id=37703

Dotani, A. N. (2011). The impact of Afghan crisis on Pakistani Society since 1979 till date. In Presented at the international conference, Doshisha University, Kyoto, pp. 6–7.

Faizi, M. u.-R. (1986). *Shaikh Muhammad bin 'Abdul Wahhab Ke Bare Mai Do Mutazid Nazren*. Varanasi: Jami'a Salafiya.

Firdous, K. (2009). Militancy in Pakistan. *Institute of Strategic Studies*, 112–129.

Foundation, A.-H. (n.d.). Sufism: Its origins. Retrieved October 26, 2015, from Ahya Organization. http://www.ahya.org/amm/modules.php?name=Sections&op=viewarticle&artid=145

Gishkori, Z. (2015, January 22). Intelligence update: Ghazi Force is gaining ground, says reports. Retrieved October 29, 2015, from The Express Tribune: http://tribune.com.pk/story/825538/intelligence-update-ghazi-force-is-gaining-ground-says-reports/

Group, S.A. (2003, May 29). Jamat-e-Islami, HizbuL Mujahideen & Al Qaeda. Retrieved October 23, 2015, from South Asia Analysis Group: http://www.southasiaanalysis.org/paper699

GTI (Global Terrorism Index) (2014). Global Terrorism Index 2014. Vision of humanity. Available at: http://www.visionofhumanity.org/sites/default/files/Global%20Terrorism%20Index%20Report%202014_0.pdf; http://www.visionofhumanity.org/sites/default/files/Global%20Terrorism%20Index%20Report%202014_0.pdf

Haqqani, H. (2005). *Pakistan: Between mosque and military*. Washington, DC: Carnegie Endowment for International Peace.

Hashmi, G. M. (2014). Sectarian Conflicts: A dominant threat to Pakistan's Internal Security. *Journal of Political Studies*, 21(1): 103–118.

Human Rights Watch. (2005). *Blood stained hands: Past atrocities in Kabul and Afghanistan's legacy of impunity*. New York: Human Rights Watch.

Hussain, D. (2015, January 12). Holy cows? In capital, majority of madrassas operating illegally. Retrieved October 23, 2015, from The Express Tribune: http://tribune.com.pk/story/820454/holy-cows-in-capital-majority-of-madrassas-operating-illegally/

International Crisis Group. (2005). *The sate of sectarianism in Pakistan*. Islamabad: International Crisis Group.

Irfani, S. (2004). *Religious radicalism and security in South Asia*. Honolulu: Asia-Pacific Center for Security Studies.

Jaffar, S. M. (1936). *The Mughal Empire from Babar to Aurangzeb*. Peshawar: Sadiq Muhammad Khan, Kissa Khawani Bazaar.

Jalil, A. M. (2001). *Imam Muhammad bin 'Abdul Wahhab Ki Da'wat Aur 'Ulama-i Ahl-i Hadith Ki Masa'i*. Varanasi: Idara al-Bahuth al-Islamiya.

Jones, S. G. (2014). *A persistent threat: The evolution of al Qa'ida and other Salafi Jihadists*. Washington, DC: RAND, National Defence Research Institute.

Malhotra, V. P. (2011). *Terrorism and Counter Terrorism in South Asia and India: A Case of India and her neighbours*. New Delhi: Vij Books India Pvt Ltd.

Mansoor, H. (2015, July 31). Report on state of madressahs in Pakistan launched. Retrieved October 23, 2015, from Daily Dawn: http://www.dawn.com/news/1197466/report-on-state-of-madressahs-in-pakistan-launched

Miller, J. S. (2012). *Facebook Fatwa: Saudi Clerics, Wahhabi Islam, and social media*. Washington, DC: Foundation for Defense of Democracies.

Mir, A. (2013, November 12). The Jihadi face of the Jamaat: Is the alliance with the establishment over now? Retrieved October 23, 2015, from The News International: http://www.thenews.com.pk/todays-news-2-213835-the-jihadi-face-of-the-jamaat-is-the-alliance-with-the-establishment-over-now

Mir, A. (2014a, November 11). Drone deaths underline JI's Jihadi links. Retrieved October 23, 2015, from The News International: http://www.thenews.com.pk/Todays-News-13-34264-Drone-deaths-underline-JIs-Jihadi-links

Mir, A. (2014b, November 03). Most of Jundallah members had association with JI, IJT. Retrieved October 23, 2015, from The News International: http://www.thenews.com.pk/Todays-News-2-282162-Most-of-Jundallah-members-had-association-with-JI-IJT

Moniquet, C. (2013). *The involvement of Salafism/Wahhabism in the support and supply of arms to rebel groups around the world*. Belgium: Directorate-General for External Policies of the Union.

Nasr, S. V. (1996). *Mawdudi and the making of Islamic revivalism*. New York: Oxford University Press.

Naumani, M. (1998). *Sheikh Muhammad bin Abdul Wahab ke Khilaf Propaganda aur Hindustan Ke Ulema-e-Haq par uskay Asrat*. Lucknow: al-Furqan Book Depot.

Portal, S. A. (2015, October 18). Fidayeen Attack in Pakistan. Retrieved October 23, 2015, from South Asia Terrorism Portal. Available at: http://www.satp.org/satporgtp/countries/pakistan/database/Fidayeenattack.htm

Rahman, S. T. (1990). *Ad-Deobandia*. Karachi: Dar ul-Kitab wa'l Sunnah.

Rana, M. A. (2011, July 10). The Hizb ut-Tahrir threat. Retrieved October 26, 2015, from Daily Dawn: http://www.dawn.com/news/643016/the-hizb-ut-tahrir-threat

Shahjahanpuri, S. M. (2001). *Qur'an-o-Hadith Ke Khilaf Ghayr Muqallidin Ke Pachas Masa'il*. New Delhi: Farid Book Depot.

Stanley, T. (2005). Understanding the origins of Wahhabism and Salafism. *Terrorism Monitor, 3*(14): 8–10.

Tribune, E. (n.d.). The revolution within. Retrieved October 22, 2015, from (http://tribune.com.pk/story/825216/the-revolution-within/)

Vallely, P. (2007, November 1). Wahhabism: A deadly scripture. Retrieved October 25, 2015, from The Independent, UK: http://www.independent.co.uk/news/uk/home-news/wahhabism-a-deadly-scripture-398516.html

Waseem, M. (2004). *Religious radicalism and security in South Asia*. Honolulu: Asia-Pacific Center for Security Studies.

Yusuf, H. (2012). *Sectarian violence: Pakistan's greatest security threat?* Oslo: Norwegian Peacebuiding Resource Center.

CHAPTER 12

Genealogical Sociology of Sectarianism: A Case Study of Sipah-e-Sahaba Pakistan

Tahir Kamran

On 7 Muharram 1969, a mourning procession emerged from the Imambargah Muhajirin after *fajr* (morning) prayer in Jhang, a city located in the south east of Pakistani Punjab. After passing through many narrow lanes, it was scheduled to end at Imambargah-i-Qadeem. One of the important points of en route was Khewa gate (one gate among three of the city), which was renamed Bab-i-Umar in the same month. Two mosques—Masjid-i Taqwa (of Deobandi *maslak* [denomination]) and Masjid-i Ahl-i Hadith—were located on the very route of the procession. A day prior to the procession, a huge billboard (depicting Bab-i-Umer) was erected there. The district administration was in a quandary about the potential powder-keg situation. Daunted, it promptly brokered a deal between the Sunni and Shia ulema, the key feature of which was that while the procession would take its usual route, the board would be covered with a piece of cloth. Unfortunately, as the procession came close to the gate, someone unveiled the board. Subsequently, a processionist, Ashraf Baloch, an underling of the Sial biraderi from Jhang city, soaked his shirt in the nearby drain and hurled

T. Kamran (✉)
Department of History, Government College University, Lahore, Pakistan

© The Editor(s) (if applicable) and The Author(s) 2016   345
J. Syed et al. (eds.), *Faith-Based Violence and Deobandi Militancy in Pakistan*, DOI 10.1057/978-1-349-94966-3_12

it at where the name "Umar", the second caliph of Muslims, was written. It was an act of utter desecration for the Sunnis. Tumult ensued. By the time the fury had subsided, six people had lost their lives, including Mawlana Shirin, a *khatib* and prayer leader of Masjid-i-Taqwa.[1] It was the first instance of the two sects colliding head on in the city. Although General Yahya Khan's coincidental takeover and declaration of a state of emergency on the very day of the Bab-i-Umar incident prevented further loss of life, many Sunni clerics launched a strong campaign in condemnation of the Shia. This had a significant impact on the general public, and more so, on the future electoral politics because it changed the sociopolitical matrix of Jhang in particular and Punjab in general. The anti-Syed group capitalized on the Sunnis' charged sentiments. It paraded the widows of those killed in the incident in black mourning dress in the Sunni-congested areas of the city.[2] This fanned sectarian emotions and overturned the political chessboard. As a consequence, the sectarianism (anti-Shia impulse) became a decisive factor in the forthcoming elections, held in 1970, in all three National Assembly constituencies of Jhang district. Of course, the politics of Jhang have not been the same since.

The Bab-i-Umar incident became one of the many factors that led to the birth of the SSP and its militant orientation. However, this aggressive posture of the militant Deobandi faction cannot be attributed completely to the religioideological divide. In fact, many other causes can be identified that help to unpack the apparently uniform sociology of the organization. This chapter seeks to analyse the multiple faces of the SSP, which can be associated primarily with the elements/components involved in the party. The chapter is divided into two sections. The first explores the genealogical transformation of Ahrar's anti-Shia sentiments, which were finally resurrected in the form of the SSP in September 1985. The grave impact of that legacy was compounded by the Iranian Revolution, and Zia-ul Haq's anti-Shia policies, which added the violence and regimentation of the organization. But why did Jhang of all places became the epicentre of anti-Shia militancy? I also address this question in the first section (although it is in its own right a separate topic for research) by exploring the emergence of wealthy but politically under-represented Sunni classes in the city. The second section traces the modes of violence used by this militant outfit and the effect that they had on the electoral results.

GENEALOGICAL TRANSFORMATION

On 6 September 1985, Maulana Haq Nawaz Jhangvi (1952–1990), along with Maulana Zia-ur-Rehman Farooqi (d. 1997), Maulana Eesar-ul-Haq Qasmi (d. 1991) and Maulana Azam Tariq (1962–2003), established the Anjuman Sipah-e-Sahaba which was soon after its inception was renamed as the SSP. The SSP's ideologies link the emergence of their organization with such events as a *tabbara* campaign conducted in Hassu Balail, Kaki Nau and Rodu Sultan, small towns in Jhang district, allegedly at the behest of Shia landlords against the companions of the Prophet. They also attached extraordinary significance to the Bab-i-Umar incident, which took place in 1969. From the outset, the SSP adopted an aggressive posture towards the Shia, particularly its Athna-i-Ashari branch. This was seen at the Kul Pakistan Difa-i-Sahaba Conference (All Pakistan Conference for the Defense of Prophet's Companion) held on 7 February 1986 at Chandan Walla Mohalla, Jhang Sadar. Haq Nawaz Jhangvi[3] presented a welcome address, which amounted to an indictment against the Shia community at large. In Punjab, the tradition of indicting the Shia sect is not a new phenomenon, and its genealogy may be traced to Ahrari's condemnation of the Shia community. From its very inception, the movement's leaders, such as Haq Nawaz Jhangvi, have acknowledged and eulogized the legacy of Atta Ullaha Shah Bokhari and his colleagues in Majlis-e-Ahrar (established in 1929). However, one must not lose sight of the fact that Haq Nawaz Jhangvi tried to subject Barelvis to his exclusionary axe. Barelvis being more inclusive, they have been indicted of heresy by both Deobandis and Wahhabis. In view of that, along with Manzoor Ahmad Chinioti, another Deobandi cleric known for his antipathy for Ahmedis, Jhangvi locked his horns with his Barelvi counterparts, Ashraf Siavi and Abdur Rasheed Rizvi, in the outskirts of Jhang city, Naul Wala Bangla, on 27 August 1979.[4] That event, known as Munazara-i-Jhang, had the theme *Gustakh Kaun?* (Who is blasphemous?) *Deobandi ya Barelwi* (Deobandi or Barelvi?). It lasted for seven to eight hours and some of the witnesses reported that Jhangvi and Chinoti lost the debate.[5] Nevertheless, Jhangvi's denunciatory tone and tenor towards the Barelvis continued until the early 1980s. However, he was later circumspect and avoided antagonizing them, primarily for electoral reasons. That strategy paid him a handsome dividend. But before bringing the SSP into our investigative focus, it would be pertinent to put violent streak of the Deobandis into perspective. We must therefore shift our gaze for a while to Majli-i-Ahrar, which was the major source of inspiration for the SSP.

With the emergence of Majlis-i-Ahrar-i-Islam,[6] a party composed of Punjabi dissidents of the Khilafat Movement, Punjab witnessed a puritanical and agitational style of politics in the 1930s. Most of the leaders were firebrand orators who could spellbind their audiences for hours. The individual profile of the Ahrar leaders suggests it as a composite organization representing all Muslim sects. However, the core ideology and principal leaders, such as Ata Ullah Shah Bukhari and Habib-ur-Rehman Ludhianvi, adhered to Deobandi Islam. Although a detailed account of the Deobandi creed has already been provided in earlier chapters, it would not be out of place to reiterate its emphasis on religious exclusion through takfir. In a nutshell, one can say with a measure of certainty that Walliullah's thought, after shedding its Sufi content, was adopted by Deobandis from 1867. It was the puritanical, scriptural reimagining of Islam. The denomination had its political articulation in such organizations which were inherently anti-Shia, such as Majlis-Ahrar (1929), Majlis-i-Tehafuz-i-Khatam-i-Nubuwwat (1949) and the SSP (1985). Its puritanical interpretation of the Islamic foundational text(s) is quintessentially anti-Shia, and this created fissures within the dominant Sunni Islam. Takfir denotes excommunication, or the declaration of a person or group of people to be non-Muslim. Although instances of takfir can be gleaned from the early history of Muslims, they started featuring regularly in the Muslim discourse from the last quarter of the nineteenth century.[7] Deobandi clerics were at the centre of the trend of issuing takfiri fatwas. Though not a takfiri treatise as such, Rashid Gangohi's *Hadayatush Shia* (Advice to the Shia) is the first published account where one can detect its presence. Deobandi clerics, such as Abdul Shakoor Lukhnavi and Manooz Naumani, not only built their respective careers on denouncing Shias but left behind a strong legacy.[8] What's more, those in the vanguard of the Deobandis condemned the more flexible Sufi tradition, the shrine culture, music and multireligious gatherings, which were at odds with the Deobandi zeal to purify religion. Since the Muslim peasantry were well integrated into the local customs and convention, the Deobandis and other groups influenced by them did not accept their version. Thus Ahrar, a Deobandi faction, had entrenched following lower-middle echelon of the urban Muslim populace, and particularly the artisans of Lahore, Amritsar and Sialkot districts of Punjab. Ahrar leaders such as Chaudhry Afzal Haq and Sahibzada Faiz-ul-Hasan, mostly subscribed to an ideology that had tangible Marxist content.[9] Iftikhar Malik holds that Ahrar imbibed the "impact of the October Revolution in Russia (1917)". Therefore Ahrar managed to carve out a constituency for itself in the urban lower middle classes of Punjab. In addition, it drew immense support from central Punjab because of the presence of large Kashmiri Muslim communities in such cities as Amritsar, Lahore and Sialkot. In fact, large numbers of Kashmiri Muslims migrated to these cities from Kashmir because of the "autocratically wayward methods of administration" of the Dogra rulers of the princely state. Killing a cow was a cognizable offence punishable with seven years of rigorous imprisonment. A special tax was levied on the slaughter of goats and sheep, even at Eid, a Muslim religious festival. If a Hindu embraced Islam, he had to forfeit all his inherited property. Many Muslim places of worship were either closed down forcibly or confiscated by the state. Majlis-i-Ahrar was the first among the Muslim political groups to raise its voice against these "atrocities" of the state against Muslims. A large number of Ahraris forced their way into Kashmir ostensibly to rescue Muslims from the oppressive rule of Maharaja Hari Singh(1925–1948), and a large number of the group's followers were arrested. Majlis-i-Ahrar could not achieve its objective of freeing its brethren from the oppressive Dogra rule. However, it secured extraordinary political mileage out of the agitation. Now it was reckoned to be the champion of downtrodden Muslims.

The movement for the rights of poor Muslims in Kapurthala State raised its profile and popularity even further. The princely state of Kapurthala, situated on the west bank of the river Bias, in Punjab had the support of 57 percent of the Muslim population, but it was ruled by a Sikh: Maharaja Jagjeet Singh. The vast majority of Muslims were peasants, living in abject misery. Some 60 percent of the state's revenue was accrued through the taxes paid by Muslim peasants. Moreover, Hindu moneylenders subjected the poor peasantry of the Begowal and Bholeth areas to merciless economic exploitation. So the situation was ripe for Ahrar to intervene immediately after its Kashmir campaign, which had won it a tremendous accolade as champion of the Muslims. The upward swing in Ahrar's popularity continued until the Masjid Shahid Ganj incident in Lahore in 1935, which irreparably undermined its political standing in the province. That mosque was built in the seventeenth century by Abdullah Khan, who was a personal attendant to Prince Dara Shikoh, the son of Emperor Shahjehan. Adjacent to the mosque was a *kotwali* (police station), where some Sikhs were executed by Mughals as a result of an insurgency. Later on, Sikhs built Gurdwara at the site of Kotwali during Ranjit Singh's reign, which was expanded in a due course to encompass the mosque. The issue remained dormant for almost a century, but in the 1930s the contesting claims over the site drew the Sikhs and Muslims apart. Ahrar kept itself aloof from that contentious issue, which was exploited by people like Zafar Ali Khan, the editor of the famous *Zamindar*. Ahrar's neutrality had a sapping affect on its popularity.[10] After the Shahid Ganj incident, the situation was quite chequered for Ahrar because its electoral strength was undermined quite considerably. Nevertheless, the impact of some of its leaders (particularly Bokhari) had a lasting resonance, culminating in the politics of religious exclusion, which became its hallmark in the days to come.

The anti-Shia turn came in Ahrar's political ideology with the advent of the Madeh-i-Sahaba Movement (1937–39) in the UP, which widened the sectarian chasm between the Sunnis and the Shias.[11] A large number of Ahraris from Punjab travelled to Awadh especially to court arrest. Awadh had a concentration of influential Shias who invariably resorted to tabbara, a practice of ridiculing the first three caliphs, causing sectarian antagonism. Hence the UP government clamped a ban on tabbara. In retaliation, the Shia resorted to "tabbara agitation". To counter that agitation, Majlis-i-Ahrar started a practice of reciting Madh-i-Sahaba, wherein Ahrari operatives recited verses praising the "four rightly guided caliphs". That situation exacerbated the sectarian tension. However, sectarian animosity was papered over in the 1940s as the Pakistan Movement gained momentum, thus mitigating the sectarian sentiments. Ahrar subsequently reinvented itself in a changed scenario by putting forth its offshoot, Majlis-i-Tahafuz-i-Khatam-i-Nubuwwat (MTKN, Organization to Protect Finality of Prophethood), in 1949. That organization spearheaded the anti-Ahmadi movement in 1953 and virtually shook the very foundations of the state. Despite its inability to achieve its objective of casting Ahmadis out of Islam, MTKN nevertheless lent vigour and vitality to the Deobandi groups.[12] One impact of the Deobandi denominations acquiring vigour was the exacerbation of sectarian differences as they kept recurring, as in 1963 the Sunni attacks in Their, near Khairpur, Sindh, and then in Lahore. These acts of violence, according to Hassan Abbas, "had a major impact on Shia thinking".[13] Obviously such a sectarian tendency finally culminated in the establishment of the SSP.

This resurrection of the Ahrar model in the form of the SSP would not have been possible without the Iranian Revolution in 1979. This had emboldened Pakistan's Shias so that they "abandoned the Shia tradition of political quietism".[14] SSP spokesmen were quite strident in pointing out a huge amount of Shia literature being produced in Urdu and being distributed freely through the consistently widening network of Iranian cultural centres. In that literature, "Sahaba (or the companions of the Prophet, Abu Bakr, Omer and Uthman) were denigrated in utterly brazen way".[15] They had been alleged to curse Sahaba publically, a practice which was called tabbara, which caused disquiet among the Sunnis. Thus not only "awakened" but "emboldened" in the wake of the revolution's success in Iran, Shias were visibly vociferous in putting forward demands for "rights and representation", evincing firm belief in Khomeini's support, which he quite generously extended to them.

This favourable international environment encouraged membership of Shia political movements sponsored both financially and politically by Tehran. TNFJ was one such organization having monetary and political ties with Tehran. Proselytization to Shia'ism was yet another impact of "Shia Revivalism" being vigorously pursued, evoking as a consequence a sharp Sunni counterpoise. Qasim Zaman, while drawing on the claim made by Sayyid Arif Husayn Naqvi, finds "considerable evidence of Shii [sic] proselytization especially in rural and small towns of the Punjab".[16] Furthermore the compulsory deduction of zakat (tithe) from bank accounts also became a reason for defections from the Sunni ranks. Many non-practising Sunnis converted to Shia'ism just to avoid having zakat deducted from their yearly savings.[17] With the Shia revival in Iran, as Nasr puts it, "the years of sectarian tolerance were over. What followed was a Sunni-versus-Shia contest for dominance, and it grew intense."[18] Nasr's assertion seems quite sweeping as the phenomenon of sectarian differentiation had been inextricably complex, emanating from the interplay of myriad currents and crosscurrents. Nevertheless, the Iranian Revolution and the impact it had on the Pakistani Shias spurred a Deobandi reaction which had up until then been sporadic. Manzur Naumani's book *Irani Inqilab: Imam Khumayni aur Shi'iyyat*, published in 1984 with its preface written by Abul Hassan Nadwi, represents a concerted response to the mounting Iranian influence in Pakistan. Later on this book "became the gospel of Deobandi militant organizations that in 1980s mushroomed across Pakistan to press the fight against the Shia".[19] Naumani was funded by Saudi charity Rabita Alam Islami (World Islamic League). He therefore wrote to the Deobandi seminaries of both India and Pakistan, eliciting their juristic opinion on Shia belief. Thus, in 1986, he managed to wangle fatwas out of them, declaring Shias kafir. In 1993, Naumani produced a volume of those fatwas entitled *Khomeni Aur Shia Kay Barah Main UlemaKaraam Ka Mutafiqqa Faisala* (Consensual Verdict of the Ulema on Khomeni and the Shia). Major Deobandi clerics from Pakistan who responded to the call of Naumani included Muhammad Yousaf Ludhianvi and Mufti Nizamuddin Shamzai. Similar fatwas came from Dar ul Ulum Haqqaniya, Akora Khattak, which not only apostatized Shias but exhorted on Sunnis not to eat food cooked by them or to attend their funeral. None of them can even be buried in a Sunni graveyard.[20] Sectarianism lies at the heart of the SSP's goals. Out of the eight aims spelt out by the founding members of the SSP, five are aimed at circumscribing, if not completely extirpating, Shia'ism from Pakistan. Hussain Haqqani has explored the role of the Zia regime in sponsoring such organizations as the SSP as a counterpoise to the Shia ascendancy. He maintains that

> The Zia-ul-Haq regime saw the SSP as a check on the rise of Shia influence and gave it a free hand. Soon covert links had been established between the SSP and Pakistan's Inter-Services Intelligence (ISI), which managed official Pakistani support of jihadi operations in Afghanistan and Indian-controlled Kashmir. SSP cadres attended Afghan Mujahideen training camps and returned to kill Shia leaders within Pakistan. The rise of the Taliban in the 1990s further deepened the ties among Pakistan's various jihadi groups, Deobandi madrassas and Sunni
> sectarian organizations such as the SSP.[21]

Similarly, a retired police officer, Mr Tariq Khosa, who served in Jhang in the early 1980s, revealed in his article "The Miasma of Hate", published in *Dawn* (5 December 2015), that when Haq Nawaz Jhangvi was arrested on the charge of conflagrating anti-Shia sentiment through his speeches, Zia ul Haq interceded and secured Jhangvi's release.[22] Zia lent unequivocal support to the SSP after he had a "bad meeting" with Khomeini. He used the SSP to resist Shia mobilization and contain Iranian influence. Thus state patronage and foreign funding provided a favourable environment for the expansion of such organizations as the SSP and the LeJ.[23] In 1991 the SSP held the Haq Nawaz International Conference in Islamabad. Maulana Abdul Qadir Azad, an employee of the Government of Punjab, and khateeb of Badshahi Mosque Lahore, was one of the speakers. Similarly, Senator Sami-ul-Haq's participation in the conference points to the state's favourable disposition towards the SSP.[24] Maulana Abdul Hafeez Makki,[25] a scholar from Saudi Arabia, was the chief guest, which fully illustrates the extraneous sources of support furnished to the SSP.

The need to counter a "Shia threat" in Pakistan was realized by the Zia regime when the Shia protested about the zakat and usher ordinance promulgated in 1979. This formed a crucial element in the state-sponsored Islamization process. It brought Shias out in protest in unprecedented numbers. The parliament in Islamabad was laid siege by more than 50,000 Shias from all over Pakistan in July 1980.[26] They came together under the banner of Wafaq-e-Ulema-e-Shia Pakistan. The Imamia Student Organization (ISO)[27] played a pivotal role in making the whole episode in Islamabad a remarkable success. The convergence of such a huge number of Shias in the federal capital was made possible largely because of the ISO's unflinching endeavours. Thus it was brought home to the government that "the mode of Zakat collection enumerated in the Ordinance was not in conformity with their beliefs and demanded that Shias should be treated in accordance with their personal law".[28] The two-day siege of the parliament house in Islamabad forced Zia-ul-Haq to amend the ordinance in what is known as the "Islamabad Pact". On 27 April 1981, the Finance Ministry exempted Shias from zakat.[29] Immediately afterwards the Shia clergy thought of constituting an organization with the expressed objective of averting the danger of the blatant "Sunnification"[30] of Pakistan and safeguarding the interests of their community. Hence the TNFJ[31] came into being in 1979 in Bhakkar, under the leadership of Mufti Jaffar Hussain.[32] It asked for the recognition of Shia law by the courts, and the formation of Shia Waqf Boards and separate Islamic studies courses for Shia students. The TNFJ became palpably assertive in its political stance when Arif-ul-Hussaini succeeded Jaffar Hussain as its leader in 1984.[33] Here it is important to mention Saudi Arabia's encouragement of the Zia regime to proclaim the edict of zakat. The Arab scholar Maruf Dualibi came to Pakistan at the behest of the Saudi government to impose the anti-Shia laws that Pakistan otherwise was not keen to enforce. He was the one who framed the Zakat and Ushr Ordinance. Khaled Ahmed reveals that the King of Saudi Arabia gave Zia the seed money to start the system of zakat in Pakistan, on the condition that part of it would go to the Wahhabi party, the Ahl-e-Hadith.[34] In 1993 its armed offshoot by the name of Sipah-i-Muhammad Pakistan (SMP) emerged, under the leadership of Ghulam Reza Naqvi, the then district President of Tehrik-i-Jafaria Jhang. By the end of 1994, the SMP had established its headquarters at Thokar Niaz Beg, a suburb of Lahore which possessed a sizable Shia population.

The abovementioned complexities beg a question: Why did the Jhang district become a breeding ground for the birth of the SSP, and why not any other part of the country? The very sociology of the district provides the answer. Contemporary scholarship has largely ignored the sociology of spaces occupied by the victimizer and victims in favour of metanarratives (e.g., the influence of outside forces, the role of the Iranian Revolution or Reagan's administration, Zia's Islamization or a lack of democratic values). The Jhang district divides central from southern parts of the Pakistani Punjab. The district is largely dominated by the Shia landlords who derive their legitimacy from the shrine practices and the claim of having an association with the family of the last prophet of Islam.

Almost 18 biraderis inhabit rural Jhang, Sials being the most influential because of their numbers, affluence and political clout.[35] The Syeds are also politically powerful and wealthy. Jhang is overwhelmingly a rural district in population terms. Nevertheless, migrants from East Punjab form an important group in Jhang City. They are drawn from the trading and weaving communities. Despite their wealth, these communities were traditionally not very well represented in the realm of power politics, dominated by the local landholders.

Jhang's history, until the reign of Walidad Khan Sial (d.1747) in the early eighteenth century, is shrouded in "Cimmerian darkness". However the accounts of the Greek historians Arrian and Curtius, along with those of the Chinese pilgrim Hwen Thsang, allude to its very remote history that goes certainly as far back as fourth century BC when this territory had its first taste of marauding at the hands of Alexander in 327 BC.[36] Despite Jhang's ancient past, the documented sources with some "validity claim" do not go beyond the eighteenth century, when the Sial rule was firmly in place. Therefore histories of the Jhang and Sial tribes are inextricably enmeshed. Consequently the adage "the history of Jhang is the history of the Sial"[37] has a substantial element of veracity in it.

Rai Mal Khan's (d. 1503) assumption of leadership ushered in an era of Sial supremacy in Jhang. He meted out a crushing defeat to the ruling Nauls, and rebuilt the city in 1462, which had been devastated in the battle. Sial rule reached its zenith during the reign of Walidad Khan (1717–1747), spanning over three decades. His legacy was sustained by his successors until Ranjit Singh's rise to power in Punjab. Ahmed Khan, the last Sial chieftain, after offering stiff resistance to the Sikh army, was eventually cowed in 1810. Consequently, Sial suzerainty over Jhang was ended. After Punjab's annexation in 1849, Sial chief Ismael Khan was co-opted by the British. He was duly rewarded for the services he discharged in 1857.

Thus the political importance of the tribe remained throughout the colonial period as its chiefs fitted very well into the client–patron network, set up by the British. Sials continued to be influential after independence, despite the fact that the Sial chief, Inayatullah Khan, had opposed the idea of Pakistan in 1947. Currently, Amanullah Khan is one of the many claimants of the Sial leadership but the internecine conflicts among the Sials have weakened their power relative to that of the Syeds in local politics. Apart from the Bharwana Sials of Tehsil Jhang and the Janjiana Sials of Shorkot, all leading Sials are Shias.

The prominent Syed families are those of Rajoa in Tehsil Chaniot and Shah Jiwana in Tehsil Jhang. However, Syeds have marked their presence in Shorkot and Uch. Most of them can trace their descent to Sher Shah, Sayyid Jalal-ud-Din Surkh Bukhari.[38] They own large tracts of land in Jhang and Chiniot. Both of the Syed families enjoyed full patronage of the British as a reward for the "good service" that they rendered as and when it was needed. Sayed Muhammad Ghaus, Syed Charagh Shah, Sardar Hussain Shah and Syed Ghulam Abbas among the Rajoa Syeds held positions of pre-eminence during British rule. Currently, Sardarzada Zafar Abbas is the leading figure among the Rajoa Sayeds. Similarly, Syed Khizar Hayat from the Shah Jiwana Syeds, who "have always been of importance", was virtually reared up by the British through the Court of Wards. His younger brother, Mubarak Shah, and Syed Raja Shah's son, Abid Hussain, shot to the position of political renown that still resonates in his daughter-cum-legatee, Abida Hussain, and her cousin but political adversary, Faisal Saleh Hayat. Both of these Syed families are Shia, so many political analysts looked askance at them for manoeuvring sectarian loyalties for political gain. The emergence of Abid Hussain on the political scene consigned Sials to the position of insignificance, particularly from the days in the run-up to the creation of Pakistan up to the 1970 elections. Abid Hussain was a close associate of Muhammad Ali Jinnah in the 1940s and used his influence quite sagaciously to earn ministerial positions in the 1950s. In the political arena, Sials had no leader who could match Abid Hussain in terms of political insight and stature.[39]

Syed–Sial factional rivalries have contributed to sectarianism. At times the internecine conflict within the Syed (Shia) clan has emerged on the political surface of Jhang, leading to asituation which was capitalized by the Sunni faction in and around Jhang. In Jhang, the politics of sectarian differentiation first emerged during the 1951 Punjab election. Ironically, the two Syed families, Shah Jiwana and Rajoa, close relatives yet political adversaries, in order to undermine each other politically, lent unswerving support to non-Syed and Sunni candidates. Abid Hussain successfully lured Pir of Sial Sharif into throwing in his lot for Maulana Muhammad Zakir, who pulled off a victory against Rajoa candidate Sardar Ghulam Muhammad Shah from the Chiniot constituency. Similarly, Rajoa Syeds went all out in support of Maulana Ghulam Hussain against Mubarak Ali Shah, a candidate of Shah Jiwana group from the Jhang constituency. Despite the Shia–Sunni differences being considerably whipped up in the run-up to the electoral contest, Mubarak Ali Shah nevertheless secured a comfortable victory.[40] Sectarianism was thus used as a ploy by Shia Syed families as part of their factional rivalries. The power politics articulated in intraclan divergence was transformed into interclan rivalry within the span of two decades. Hence the Syed in-fight gave way to a Sial–Syed contest for power. As we shall see below, biraderi rivalries intersected with sectarianism not just in electoral contests but also in outbreaks of violence, such as the Bab-i-Umar episode. This can be understood as a major turning point in the rise of sectarianism in Jhang.

Over a period of time, the urban commercial classes emerged, who were primarily Sunni by sect and were marginalized in the power structure of the district. To carve out new spaces within the existing power structure, local traders and bazaar merchants largely supported and funded the establishment of the SSP and its offshoot, the LeJ. Such sociology of the organization, in fact, not only displaced biraderi influences on the political landscape of the district but also tilted it towards violence which more or less became a definitive pattern in future elections in the district.

However, a more obvious militant element in the SSP entered in the late 1980s. The end of the War in Afghanistan resulted in the disbandment of a large number of well-trained militants. Some of these mujahideen were attracted to organizations such as the SSP, which readily employed them. The SSP was a cash-rich organization because of its indirect funding from Saudi Arabia and Iraq. Popular philanthropy, much of which came from Deobandi sources, also swelled its coffers. Mariam Abou Zahab furnishes us with an interesting link between the SSP and the drugs mafia. Since Jhang is at the crossroads of drug and arms distribution networks, it was financially viable for mafia groups to maintain a certain level of tension. They kept on stoking the sectarian differentiation, not allowing calm to last long enough, which did not serve their financial interests well. Heroin smuggling increased manyfold.[41] Drug and alcohol trafficking witnessed an increase of 250–300 percent after the sectarian violence had taken Jhang into its fold.[42]

The Deobandi madrassa union, Wafaq-al-Madaris, which has its head office in Multan, along with the Khair-ul-Madaris seminary, the national centre for Deobandi instruction, openly supported the SSP.[43] Young zealots mostly recruited from the seminaries were sent for training in the art of violence in Afghanistan. Therefore sectarian militancy escalated to a considerable extent. The LeJ, under the leadership of Riaz Basra, comprised those militants who were instructed in the use of explosives and guerrilla tactics. They went to Afghanistan for training in a camp in Sirobi, near Kabul, run by the Taliban Minister Maulvi Hameedullah.[44] They were not only growing in fighting power but multiplying in numbers. Animosh Roul mentions five splinter groups of the SSP besides the LeJ: Jhangvi Tigers, Al Haq Tigers, Tanzeem ul Haq, Al Farooq and Al Badr Foundation.[45]

Modes of Violence

Like most of the militant struggles, the anti-Shia campaign of the SSP thrived on the spilling of human blood. The cult of the martyr was very effectively deployed by the successors of Haq Nawaz, which enhanced not only the SSP's electoral standing but also its renown. Ironically, Shia influence implicitly permeated into the SSP's overall schema as the Shia theological discourse is structured around the cult of the martyr. Scores of martyrs and the ongoing sectarian strife afforded the SSP "functional utility"[46] that contributed immensely to perpetuating its hold.

Sectarian killing began with the murders of Ehsan Ellahi Zaheer in 1987 and TNFJ leader Allama Arif-ul-Hussaini in 1988. Haq Nawaz himself did not have many days to live. On 22 February 1990, his tumultuous life and career came to an end.[47] The SSP's rhetoric had always been aggressive, but now its deeds matched its words. Eventually, in 1996, the LeJ was to emerge as an armed offshoot of the SSP. Militancy not only intimidated Shias but also increased the SSP's electoral support. From the very outset, the SSP leadership sought influence in the National Assembly in order to amend the Constitution so that there could be a Sunnification of the Pakistani state. On that occasion the government of Punjab was visibly perplexed about the law and order situation during the period of mourning because this followed hard on the heels of the murder of Haq Nawaz. As a pre-emptive measure, the government called together urban notables and leaders of the SSP for negotiation. Malik Saleem Iqbal, the Health Minister of Punjab, presided over the proceedings on 16 July 1990. Members of the Jhang district administration, the SSP leadership and other important persons were made part of the negotiations and taken into confidence. Thereby an *aman muahida* (peace agreement) was concluded to the satisfaction of the government.[48] However, only a few days after the agreement, a bomb exploded at chowk Bab-i-Umar in Jhang city, killing 3 Sunnis and injuring 28. This effectively sabotaged the peace efforts. The very site of the bomb explosion was not far from Aman ullah Khan Sial's *haveli* in Jhang. As already mentioned, Amanullah Khan is a leader of a Sial clan in Jhang and adheres to the Shia. This is highly suggestive of the fact that the efforts to bring peace to the conflict-ridden city were stymied because the important biraderis, like Sials and Syeds, had been excluded as stakeholders in the whole process.

In these circumstances, the SSP did expand far beyond its roots in sectarian rivalries and biraderi politics in Jhang. It organized itself remarkably well at the district and tehsil levels. According to one estimate, the SSP had 74 district and 225 tehsil level units before it was proscribed on 12 January 2002. It also ran 17 branches in foreign countries, including Saudi Arabia, Bangladesh, Canada and the UK. With its 6,000 trained and professional cadres and 100,000 registered workers,[49] it was the best-knit and best-organized Islamic party in Pakistan after the JI. The SSP's growing influence was accompanied by its association with violence. While Jhang was the scene of many sectarian killings, they spread to other areas of Punjab and beyond. Although the SSP attempted to distance itself from the activities of the LeJ, it was never done convincingly. The LeJ had links with "international terrorist" movements which culminated in the banning of both organizations by President Musharraf in response to the post-9/11 situation. Support for the SSP and the LeJ has as a result been driven underground.

The Taliban had been a great source of inspiration for the SSP's leaders, who sought to replicate their policies in Pakistan. In October 2000, Azam Tariq, while speaking at an International Difah-e-Sahaba Conference in Karachi, said that "the SSP aims to transform 28 large Pakistani cities into model Islamic cities where television, cinema and music would be banned".[50] Azam Tariq was an ardent supporter of jihad in Indian-controlled Kashmir. When Masud Azhar founded the JM in the aftermath of his release in Kandahar, following the hijacking of an Indian aircraft in December 1999, Azam Tariq pledged to send 500,000 jihadis to Jammu and Kashmir to fight the Indian security forces.[51]

The SSP extremists had two major styles of operation: targeted killings and indiscriminate shootings at places of worship. A number of leading Shias were assassinated. By 1992 the SSP activists had gained access to sophisticated weapon systems. Saudi Arabia was the major source of funding as Iran provided financial support to Shia outfits. In June 1992, the SSP adherents used a rocket launcher in an attack which killed five police personnel.[52] The attempted assassination of Prime Minister Nawaz Sharif in January 1999 is yet another example of their zeal for resorting to violence. Sharif was lucky that the bomb planted beneath the bridge on Raiwind Road on the route to his residence exploded prematurely, but it was a clear testimony of how lethal the sectarian terrorists had become.

During the 1990s, Iranian officials functioning in various capacities in Pakistan became the victims of SSP militants. Most prominent among them was Agha Sadiq Ganji, Iranian Consul General, who was gunned down on 19 December 1990 by a young lad from Jhang, Sheikh Haq Nawaz.[53] Ganji was widely believed by SSP supporters to have masterminded Haq Nawaz Jhangvi's murder. However, there was no tenable evidence of his involvement other than his presence in Jhang on the day of the murder. Muhammad Ali Rahimi, an Iranian diplomat, was another victim of a targeted killing in Multan in 1997. The Iranian Cultural Centre at Lahore was set ablaze the same year in January. This was in retribution for the assassination of Zia-ur-Rehman Farooqi along with 26 others at the Lahore Session Court. Five members of the Iranian armed forces were fatally ambushed in Multan in September, sparking off a serious diplomatic row between Islamabad and Tehran. The targeting of Iranians was apparently meant to convey the message to Shia militants that not even their "patrons" were safe.[54]

Sectarian polarization enabled the SSP to increase its vote bank. This has similarities with the way in which communal violence in a number of UP towns has strengthened the hold of the BJP. In the central Jhang constituency in the 1990 election, Maulana Esar-ul- Qasimi, Haq Nawaz' s successor and vice patron, secured victory with a considerable majority. As the IJI candidate for the National Assembly, he obtained 62,486 votes. He also stood as an independent candidate on a Provincial Assembly seat and defeated IJI ticket holder and favourite Sheikh Iqbal by a margin of almost 10,000 votes.[55]

Nawaz Sharif's crackdown on militancy during 1997–1999, together with the general disapproval of violence and militancy, saw a considerable decline in sectarian killing in Punjab. From January 1999 to December 2000, not a single incident of sectarian violence was reported. The military takeover on 12 October 1999 may be one of the reasons that militant groups had assumed a low profile. However, the next elections held in

2002 under military rule reversed the process. Azam Tariq won the election, though he was in jail. Both the LeJ and the SSP, along with their Shia rivals the SMP and the TNFJ, had been banned by Pervez Musharaf on 14 August 2001 and in 2002, respectively.[56] Nevertheless, Tariq was allowed to contest the elections as an independent candidate. This decision evoked sharp reaction from many quarters. Tariq's victory was quite unexpected. In fact, it fits well into the pattern in Pakistan where representatives of religious militant outfits tend to do well in the conditions of "guided democracy" because of the marginalization of mainstream parties. However, after 9/11, such figures as Azam Tariq have had to act circumspectly. After securing election victory instead of siding with the opposition alliance of the religious party Muttihidda Majlis-i-Ammal, Tariq went along with the pro-Musharraf Muslim League (Quaid-i-Azam) and managed to secure the release of the imprisoned SSP activists. In October 2003, Tariq was killed in Islamabad, his death most foretold in the history of Pakistan, according to *The Daily Times*, Lahore. There had been 20 previous attempts on his life. Tariq's murder may be a death knell to the SSP or Millat-i-Islamya (a name given to the organization after it was proscribed in 2002). Later on its was renamed the ASWJ, with Ahmed Ludhyanvi as its leader. The resulting leadership vacuum has rendered the organization rudderless. Consequently its immediate future seems bleak. Having said that, sectarianism remained a recurring feature in Pakistan, but after 9/11 its frequency waned marginally. In these years, the LeJ widened the scope of its violence, making Barelvis (Sunni Sufis) its prey, and the massacre in Nishtar Park, Karachi, in 2006, killing around 50 people, its illustration. In that ghastly act, a suicide bomber hit a high-profile congregation convened by the ST, wiping out its top leadership. In 2009, renowned Barelvi scholar from Jamia Naeemia, Lahore, Mufti Sarfraz Naeemi, was assasinated by the TTP. Naeemi was known for his anti-Talban views, which he articulated in a vociferous manner. Ismail Khan in his study on Barelvis reveals that between March 2005 and April 2011 alone, as many as 29 attacks on Barelvi shrines were carried out by the TTP and its various offshoots.[57]

However, after the Lal Masjid incident in 2007, as Arif Rafiq asserts, the sectarian frenzy reached alarming proportions, particularly after the advent of the TTP. In 2010, in total 57 attacks were orchestrated by various factions against each other, killing 509 people. In 2013, according to PIPS, sectarianism resulted in 658 casualties in which 471 were Shias and 99 Sunnis.[58] However, the Sunni death count also includes the Sunnis killed as a result of Deobandi militancy against Barelvis.

In the garrison city, Rawalpindi, 13 attempted targeted killings were registered in the first 11 months of 2014.[59] In April of the same year, the Interior Ministry shared with the members of the Senate that sectarian violence had caused 2,090 deaths in the previous five years.[60] These statistics prove the extent of sectarian fissures, posing existential threat to the very state. Remorsefully, Pakistan has so far failed to find a tangible antidote to that anathema, in which, one may assert, the Deobandi creed and its adherents have a major role to play.

CONCLUSION

Main merney ko pher raha houn, merney ko (I am looking for death only) because the Shia are using abusive language for the companions of the prophet, said Haq Nawaz in one of his addresses to his devotees.[61] The very sensibility of the top brass set the agenda for a militant struggle against the Shia sect. However, such unflinching commitment to the cause of Shia elimination or the Sunnification of Pakistan does not subscribe only to ideological commitment. While tracing the genealogical sociology of the SSP, this chapter contends that the old conflicts compound and re-emerge in a new context. In other words, the movement operated at different levels in order to serve the interests of various groups and stakeholders. At the local level, the SSP may be viewed as a struggle of the emerging commercial class primarily comprising immigrants and marginalized locals against the Shia landlords. However, this violent struggle never totally replaced biraderi politics. But within the national and international context, the SSP became an instrument of the Pakistani state and of Saudi Arabia to counter Iranian influence within the country, and to help in the Talibanization of Afghanistan.

The new modalities (e.g., violence and election politics) were deployed by the militant organization to further their interest in the public domain. Other Sunni religious political parties also provided legitimacy to this violence in the name of religion. The stage was set by the Bab-i-Umar incident, but the old legacies of Ahrar also inspired the struggle against the Shia sect. Shias were the focus for sectarian militancy in the wake of the Afghan Jihad and the Iranian Revolution. The proliferation of madrassas with foreign funding provided much-needed cadres for the SSP. As many studies suggest, soon after the birth of the SSP it proliferated to other parts of the country, such as Multan, Faisalabad, Sargodha and Bahawalpur. Karachi, too, was hit ominously hard by the sectarian menace.

Acknowledgements: I am grateful to Dr Hussain Ahmad Khan for his constructive criticism, which helped me immensely in formulating the arguments in the text.

NOTES

1. The whole event was narrated by Sayyid Thana al Haqq Tirmidhi, an
   eyewitness to the episode, August, 2006.
2. Ibid.
3. "Haq Nawaz Jhangvi was born in 1954 in the town of Jhang. After
   completing his primary education in Arabic and Theology, he left for
   Multan where he studied in the renowned Islamic University, Khair-
   ul-Madaris. He qualified as an Islamic Scholar/Alim in 1972 from this
   university at the tender age of 19. After which he once more returned
   to his home town, Jhang." For a detailed profile and speeches, see
   "Haq Char Yaar::: Sayings of Maulana Haq Nawaz Jhangvi Shaheed
   (r.t.a)", http://www.kr-hcy.com/shaheed.shtml, accessed on 5
   December 2008.
4. The Manazara was held under the official auspices. Professor Taq ud
   Din Anjum, Mr Manzoor Khan (advocate) and Ghulam Bari (school-
   teacher were the judges). For further details, see Maulana Khursheed
   Hassan Khawar, *Tariekhi AurAdeemul Misal Mubaesah ki Rodad:
   Manazara-i-Jhang* (Silanwali: Manzar-e-Ashraful Ulma, 2014).
5. Ibid.
6. For the causes of the emergence of Majlis-i-Ahrar, see Jan Baz Mirza,
   Karwan-i-Ahrar, vol. i (Lahore: Maktaba-i-Tabsara, 1975), pp. 81–84.
7. Tahir Kamran, "Takfir and Terrorism", *The News on Sunday*, Lahore,
   June 22, 2014.
8. Tahir Kamran, "More Thoughts on Takfeer", *The News on Sunday*,
   Lahore, June 29, 2014.
9. Iftikhar Haider Malik, *Sikander Hayat Khan: A Political Biography*
   (Islamabad: National Institute of Historical and Cultural Research,
   1985), p. 55.
10. Abdullah Malik, *Punjab ki Siyasi Tehreekain* (Lahore: Kausar
    Publishers, 1986), pp. 194–204. Also see David Gilmartin, *Empire
    and Islam: Punjab and the Making of Pakistan* (London: University
    of California Press, 1988), pp. 99–107.
11. Shia here denotes the Ithna-I-Ashari or Twelvers. They believe in the
    institution of Imamat whereby the twelve imams are considered as the
    true representatives of Islam as against Khilafat or Khulfa-i Rashidin.

See John L. Episto, *What Everyone Needs to Know about Islam* (New York: Oxford University Press, 2002), pp. 45–47.

12. Tahir Kamran, "The Pre-history of the Religious Exclusionism in Contemporary Pakistan: Khatam-e-Nubuwwat, 1889–1953", *Modern Asian Studies*, Cambridge University Press, doi:1017/Soo26749X14000043.

13. Hassan Abbas, *Shiism and Sectarian Conflict in Pakistan*, Occasional Paper Series, West Point, Combating Terrorism Centre, 2006, pp. 22–23.

14. Here political quietism denotes *taqiyyah* or dissimulation. See Ian Talbot, "Understanding Religious Violence in Contemporary Pakistan: Themes and Theories" in R. Kaur (ed.), *Religion, Violence and Mobilization in South Asia* (New Delhi: Sage Publications, 2005), p. 154.

15. Sahaba or the companions of the Prophet (Abu Bakr, Omer and Usman) are held in a high esteem by the Sunnis, whereas Shias condemn them as usurpers. Shias consider Ali, the cousin and son-in-law of the Prophet, as the rightful heir of the Prophet instead of the first three caliphs. Interview with Maulana Ilyas Balakoti, Jhang, August 2006.

16. Sayyid Arif Husayn Naqvi, *Tadhkira-yi Ulama-i-Imamiyya-i Pakistan* (Islamabad: Markaz-i Tahqiqat-i Farsi-yi Iran wa Pakistan, 1984) quoted in Qasim Zaman, "Sectarianism in Pakistan: The Radicalization of Shii and Sunni Identities", *Modern Asian Studies*, Vol. 32(3), (1998), pp. 689–716.

17. Hussain Haqqani, "Weeding out the Heretics: Sectarianism in Pakistan", *Current Trends in Islamist Ideology* vol. 4, Hudson Institute Washington D.C. November, 2006 in http://www.futureofmuslimworld.com/research/pubID.58/pub_detail.asp, Accessed on, 3rd March 2008.

18. Vali Nasr, *The Shia Revival: How conflicts Within Islam Will Shape the Future* (NY: W.W. Norton & Company, 2006), p. 148.

19. Ibid.

20. Khaled Ahmed, "When Madrasa Challenges the State", *Indian Express*, 14th February, 2015.

21. Haqani, "Weeding out the Heretics".

22. Mr Tariq Khosa also declared the same before the Senate Committee on Defense and Defense Production. See Christophe Jaffrelot, *Pakistan Paradox: Instability and Resilience* (Random House India, 2015), p. 488 fn.

23. Encouragement from successive regimes, an unremitting flow of foreign funds (especially from Saudi Arabia) and the absence of governmental oversight have been cited as the principal factors in the dramatic rise in the numbers of madaras (European Commission 2002) quoted in Ali Riaz, *Global Jihad, Sectarianism and the Madrassahs in Pakistan* (Singapore: Institute of Defence and Strategic Studies, 2005), p. 5.

24. *Zindgi* (Lahore, 8–14 June 1991).

25. Ibid.

26. See Azmat Abbas, *Sectarianism: The Players and the Game* (Lahore: South Asia Partnership, 2002), p. 7. However Nasr gives the figure of 25,000 Shia activists who gathered in Islamabad. Nasr, *The Shia Revival*, p. 161.

27. A group of students from Lahore University of Engineering and Technology founded the ISO on 22 May 1972 to provide an all-Pakistan Shia platform. Dr Majid Noroze Abidi and Ali Reza Naqvi were among the founders. They focused on religious and social issues, including aid for poor students. The numerical strength and organizational capability of ISO leaders became evident during the 1979–1980 agitation of Shias against Zia's Zakat and Usher Ordinance. See Abbas, p. 9.

28. Ibid.

29. Muhammad Amir Rana, "Evolution of militant groups in Pakistan(4)", *Conflict and Peace Studies*, vol. 6, no. 1, January-June 2014, p. 117.

30. Seyyed Vali Reza Nasr, "Islam, the State, and the Rise of Sectarian Militancy in Pakistan", in Christophe Jaffrelot (ed.), *Pakistan: Nationalism Without a Nation* (London: Zed Books, 2001), pp. 87–90.

31. The TNFJ was renamed Tehrik-e-Jafria Pakistan in a convention held in March 1993 at Faisalabad. See Abbas, *Sectarianism*, p. 8.

32. Jafar Hussain (1916–83) was born in Gujranwala, educated in Lucknow and Najaf, in Southern Iraq, and he then taught at a Shia seminary in his native city. He served on various government committees, including the Council of Islamic Ideology. Zaman, "Sectarianism in Pakistan", pp. 694–695.

33. Allama Arif Hussain Al Hussaini was a Turi Pushtun from the Shia stronghold of Parachinar in Northern Pakistan. He received instruction from Najaf and Qum, and was sent to Pakistan by the Iranian government in 1978. According to his official biography, he was expelled from Iran before the revolution. Abbas, *Sectarianism*, p. 8.

34. Khaled Ahmed, *Sectarian War, Pakistan's Sunni-Shia Violence and its Links to the Middle East* (Karachi, Oxford University Press, 2013), p. 29.

35. Siddiq Sadiq, *Jhang: The Land of Two Rivers* (Jhang, 2002), p. 40.

36. *Gazetteer of the Jhang District 1883–84* (Lahore: Sang-e-Meel Publications, 2000), p. 23. Some old material collected from Shorkot mound in Jhang district—that is, an agate seal in pictographic language is supposed to be 10,000–15,000 years old. For reference, see Sadiq, *Jhang*, p. 67.

37. *Gazetteer of the Jhang District* 1883–1884, p. 27.

38. Bilal Zubairi, *Tazkira i Auliyia i Jhang* (Jhang: Jhang Adabi Academy, 2000), p. 213.

39. Abid Hussain came into the political limelight in 1936 when as a student leader he presented a welcome address to Muhammad Ali Jinnah in Lahore. Jinnah was there to preside over a meeting of the Muslim Students Federation. Later he was elected Chairman of the Jhang Board (1937–54). He became Member of Legislative Assembly (MLA) in 1946 and a member of the Punjab Assembly in 1951. In 1954 he joined the cabinet of Muhammad Ali Bogra as Minister of Agriculture. Later he joined the Republican Party and became its secretary general. Ayub Khan disqualified him under an Elected Bodies Disqualification Order (EBDO). Therefore he could not contest the 1962 and 1965 elections. The last election he contested was in 1970, which he lost against JUI candidate Ghulam Haider Bharwana. He died in 1971. Sadiq, *Jhang*, pp. 217–218.

40. Naseer Ahmed Saleemi, "Jhang Mein Shia Sunni Tanaziah: Aghaz Sey Anjam Tek". *Zindagi* (Lahore:14–20 December 1991), pp. 19–21.

41. Mariam Abou Zahab, "The Sunni-Shia Conflict in Jhang (Pakistan)", Magnus Marsden, ed. *Islam and Society in Pakistan: Anthropological Perspectives* (Karachi, Oxford University Press, 2010), p. 173.

42. Khalid Hussain, 'Live and Let Die', The Friday Times, 3–9 September 1992, in ibid.

43. International Crisis Group 'The State of Sectarianism in Pakistan', p. 15.

44. Owais Tohid, 'An Eye for an Eye, In Death, as in Life Interview-Qari Shafiqur Rehman', October 2003, http://www.newsline.com.pk/newsoct2003/stopoct1.htm accessed on 17 Oct 2007.

45. Animosh Roul, *Sipah-e-Sahaba: Fomenting Sectarian Violence in Pakistan* 'Terrorism Monitor' vol. 3(2) (January 27, 2005).

46. Paul R. Brass, *The Production of Hindu-Muslim Violence in Contemporary India*. Seattle: University of Washington Press, 2003), p. 377.

47. Maulana Zia ur Rehman Faruqi became the Chief Patron of the SSP after Haq Nawaz Jhangvi's assassination. Before that he was imam and khateeb of a mosque run by Auqaf Deptt at Sumundri, Faisalabad. *Zindagi* (Lahore, 14–20 March 1991).

48. Along with Malik Saleem Iqbal, Arshad Lodhi (Deputy Commissioner, Superintendent of Police), people who took part in the negotiations were Maulana Rashid Ahmad Madni, Mohalla Chandanwalla, Dildar Ali (Secretary, Anjuman-i-Tajran), Haji Muhammad Ali (President, Anjuman-i-Tajran), Mian Iqbal Hussain, Muhammad Zahur Chuhan (Advocate), Sheikh Muhammad Iqbal (Chairman, Municipal Committee, Jhang), Muhammad Farooq (President Anjuman-i-Tajran, Jhang City), Muhammad Rafique Saqi (General Secretary, Anjuman-i-Tajran Jhang City), Muhammad Aslam (Joint Secretary, Anjuman-i-Tajran, Jhang City) and Maulana Esar ul Qasimi. See *Aman Muahida (Manzur Shuda) Zilai Intizamia wa membraan e Committee Anjuman-i-Sipah-i-Sihaba wa Muazizeen-i-Jhang* (Jhang: 1990).

49. Ibid. Also see the SSP, Terrorist Group of Pakistan, South Asia Terrorism Portal, 21 June 2004, http://www.satp.org/satporgtp-Pcountries/Pakistan/terroristoutfits/ssp.htm accessed 23 February 2007.

50. The SSP, Terrorist Group of Pakistan, http://www.satp.org/satporgtp/countries/Pakistan/terroristoutfits/Ssp.htm accessed 3 March 2007.

51. In the Spotlight: Sipah-i-Sahaba Pakistan (SSP) (July 9, 2004), http://www.cdi.org/.../friendlyversion/printversion.cfm, accessed on 3 March 2007.

52. The SSP, Terrorist Group of Pakistan, http://www.satp.org/satporgtp/countries/Pakistan/terroristoutfits/Ssp.htm accessed on 3 March 2007.

53. *Zindagi, Lahore* (14–20 December 1991), Sheikh Haq Nawaz was later hanged in Mianwali jail on 28 February 2001. Kaka Balli, kin of Amanullah Sial, was convicted to life imprisonment for the assassination of Haq Nawaz Jhangvi. The SSP, Terrorist Group, see also Abbas, p. 13.

54. Tohid, "An Eye for an Eye, In Death, as in Life Interview-Qari Shafiqur Rehman".

55. *General Elections Report*, p. 243. He contested that election from the JUI (Sami ul Haq Group) quota. See *Zindagi* (Lahore, 14–20 March 1991).
56. For further details, see Ch Akhter Ali, "Reference under 6(2) of the Political Parties Act (as amended)", Supreme Court of Pakistan, Islamabad, 29 January 2002.
57. Ismail Khan, The Assertion of Barelvi Extremism, Hudson Institute, http://www.hudson.org/research/9848-the-assertion-of-barelvi-extremism.
58. *Pakistan Security Report-*2013, Islamabad, Pak Institute for Peace Studies, 2014, p. 25, cited in Jaffrelot, *The Pakistan Paradox*, p. 492.
59. Mohammad Asghar, "Target Killings rise in Rawalpindi as sectarian hatred is fanned", *Dawn*, 15 November 2014 (http://www.dawn.com/news/1144577).
60. Irfan Ghauri, "Sectarian Violence: over 2,000 people killed in 5 years, Interior Ministry tells Senate", *The Express Tribune*, 24 April 2014 (http://tribune.com.pk/story/699/sectarian-violence-over-2000-people-killed-in-5-years-says-interior-ministry/).
61. See the complete text of Haq Nawaz's speech at http://www.kr-hcy.com/wasiyat/index.shtml, accessed on 05 December 2008.

CHAPTER 13

Islamization and Barelvis in Pakistan

Thomas K. Gugler

Jihad today is a crisis phenomenon. As Muslim jurists lost their traditional authority, jihad became secularized, its rhetoric revolutionary and
its war practices individualized.[1] At the same time the survivability of
individuals and organizations of irregular warfare is highly dependent on
the support of a regular power. The irregular is forced to legitimize itself
through the regular.[2] Clausewitz claimed that "war is an instrument of
policy"[3] in the famous Chapter 6B of the eighth book of *On War*. He
explained that although irregular warfare has its specific grammar, it has
no independent logic. Irregular warfare is in its central character shaped
and led by policy itself.

A Pew research poll conducted in 2013 found that 91 percent of
Pakistani respondents believe that the country is headed in the wrong direction.[4] Pakistan has become an excessively violent country over the past
decade, and it has seen militants increasingly relying on crime, narcotraf-
ficking and smuggling to augment their financial base. Jihadists in Pakistan
have observed the territorial conquests made by their counterparts in Iraq
and Syria, and the huge media coverage of their decapitations and other
actions, with a mixture of envy and admiration. The rise of ISIS is increasing
the pressure on more traditional militant outfits, such as Al-Qaida and the

T.K. Gugler (✉)
Centre for Islamic Theology, University of Muenster, Muenster, Germany

© The Editor(s) (if applicable) and The Author(s) 2016
J. Syed et al. (eds.), *Faith-Based Violence and Deobandi
Militancy in Pakistan*, DOI 10.1057/978-1-349-94966-3_13

Taliban, not to lose their share and to retain hard resources, such as funding sources and members. In September 2014, ISIS propaganda appeared in Urdu, Dari and Pashto. In mid-October 2014, six top commanders of the TTP, comprising five TTP district chiefs and the TTP's official spokesman, Shahidullah Shahid, pledged allegiance to the ISIS leader, al-Baghdadi.[5] Their statement said: "All Muslims in the world have great expectations of you [...] We are with you, we will provide you with Mujahideen and with every possible support." In January 2015 it also released a video message that showed Shahidullah Shahid with dozens of militants. At the end of the video they killed a person, apparently a Pakistani soldier. Several of these individuals, meanwhile, officially represent the ISIS leadership for the Khorasan Shura—the ISIS leadership council for Afghanistan and Pakistan.[6] However, their statement was rejected by another section of the TTP, which asserted their leader Mullah Fazlullah's allegiance to Mullah Muhammad Omar, the apparently dead Afghan Taliban leader.[7] Under Mullah Fazlullah, the former head of the Swat Taliban who—unlike his predecessors Hakimullah Mehsud (killed in November 2013) and Baitullah Mehsud (killed in August 2009)—is not a member of the influential Mehsud clan, the TTP has suffered fragmentation as a result of discord among its leaders.[8]

The above development indicates at least some fissures within the TTP, a radical Deobandi-led militant outfit, in terms of support for ISIS. The matter was further compounded when other radical Deobandis started pronouncing their support for ISIS. For example, a video statement released by the female students of the Jamia Hafsa (a Deobandi madrassa) in Islamabad paid allegiance to the ISIS Caliph Abu Bakr al-Baghdadi, inviting him to help and lead their movement in Pakistan. The statement was publicly owned and endorsed by Maulana Abdul Aziz, a senior Deobandi cleric of Islamabad's Lal Masjid (Red Mosque). Aziz said that he respected ISIS because of the similarity in their missions. He said that although he and his madrassa students had no direct link with the leadership of ISIS, they have deliberated on this issue and decided to promote the mission and message of ISIS. Commenting on a video released on 26 November 2014 by the Jamia Hafsa madrassa students declaring their support for ISIS and its chief Abu Bakr al-Baghdadi, Aziz said that the female students had prepared the video with his consent. The principal of the madrassa, Umm-e Hassan, reportedly endorsed this action, saying that the girls were justified in declaring support for ISIS (Khan 2014).[9]

While radical Deobandi outfits are dominant players in incidents of violence and militancy in Pakistan, and some of them also identify with

ISIS, it is important to note that, demographically, Deobandis represent a numerical minority among Pakistan's Sunni Muslims. Indeed, the major ideological challenge to terrorism within Pakistan comes from Barelvis, the traditional Sufis, who despite their numerical majority are an increasingly under-resourced and beleaguered community. In the last few years, a rising number of Barelvis have been killed by radical Deobandi outfits operating as the TTP, the SSP/ASWJ, the LeJ and numerous other groups or aliases with blurring boundaries and shared membership. According to Deobandi ideology, as is evident through numerous fatwas issued by the Dar al-Uloom Deoband and other seminaries in India and Pakistan, certain Sufi practices of the Barelvis, such as visiting shrines, *wasilah* (intercession), *milad al-nabi* (birthday of Prophet Muhammad), urs (anniversary of Sufi saints) and qawwali (devotional music) are tantamount to shirk (polytheism) and/or bidat (innovation). Against this backdrop, and also in response to the out-right condemnation of terrorism by the Barelvis, Sufi shrines and leaders of the Barelvis have been targeted—for example, the attacks on Data Darbar in Lahore, Abdullah Shah Ghazi in Karachi, Jhal Magasi in Balochistan and Rehman Baba in Peshawar, the massacre of the ST's leadership in Karachi, and the target killings of Abbas Qadri, Sarfraz Naeemi and several other Barelvi/Sufi leaders. Haider (2011)[10] reports a revealing statistical picture of the Deobandi militancy in Pakistan. He notes:

> The network of sectarian violence in Pakistan has its roots in the Deobandi sect. Syed Ejaz Hussain, who is a deputy inspector general of police, for his doctoral thesis in criminology at the University of Pennsylvania analysed the demographic and religious characteristics of the 2,344 terrorists arrested between 1990 and 2009 in Pakistan. These terrorists were the ones whose cases were forwarded to the courts after the police were satisfied of their guilt based on their preliminary investigation. The sectarian breakdown of the arrested terrorists revealed that more than 90 per cent were of the Deobandi sect.

In light of the above, it is important to contextually understand and constructively engage with all religious communities to eliminate terrorism. In this pursuit, indeed, the Sunni Barelvis, the largest component of the Muslim population in Pakistan, are most relevant.

Any debate about the South Asian issue of Barelvis versus Deobandis is intrinsically tied to the US or Western debate about Sufis versus Salafis/Wahhabis and Deobandis. Some analysts claim that Sufism frees people and that the Sufi dimension of Islam is more inclusive and pluralistic and hence conducive to democracy. Reading through security reports on Muslim countries, in particular those authored in a spirit of neo-Protestant interventionism, one could get the impression that some think tanks or foundations may seek to refashion Sufism into a post-*tariqa* (Sufi order) and fiqh-based ideology. No matter how much one tries to avoid labels such as Salafi or Wahhabi, because they have hardly any explanatory usefulness (in particular the pejorative term Wahhabi is imposed on Deobandis and Ahl-e Hadith [Salafi] by their opponents), the ongoing debates about the local level can hardly be disconnected from the dominant discourse. Self-identifying Salafis disagree among each other about who rightfully can claim the label "Salafi". Similarly, some Deobandis have claimed the term "Sufi" for themselves, although Deoband-based Shaykh al-Hadith Nasir Ahmed Khan admits that the decline of tasawwuf is the single most significant change to be observed inside the Dar al-Uloom Deoband since the 1930s.[11]

Indeed, despite their claim to Sufism, a rising number of Deobandis resemble their Salafi counterparts in their rejection of traditional Sufi practices, which they label as shirk (polytheism) and haram (forbidden). While radical Deobandis in Pakistan continue to attack Sufi shrines and folk Sufis and Barelvis, their counterpart Salafis (ISIS) in Iraq and Syria are doing the same. In this respect, both ISIS and radical Deobandis draw inspiration from the destruction of the shrines of Baqi (Medina), Mualla (Mecca) and Karbala (Iraq) at the hands of the forces of Muhammad ibn Abd al-Wahhab and his followers.

In response, some Barelvis in Pakistan are trying to preserve their traditions by reviving the *malfuzat* (compilation of the discourses of a Sufi) readings at dargahs (shrines), expanding the Barelvi madrassas and promoting the Sufi rituals. Collective memory is constantly revised and modified. In order to not reproduce the impression of an easy answer to the quite complicated and somehow weird political question of who is a "good Muslim" and who is a "bad Muslim" (Mamdani 2005), I chose to start with a very brief introduction about their more or less specific beliefs.

DEOBANDI AND BARELVI BELIEF SYSTEMS

The "purist" "reform" movement of Deoband, deriving its name from the location of the seminary founded in May 1866, aims to purify South Asian Islam from alleged Hindu and Sikh influences, in addition to polytheistic Shia and Sufi influences, and it demands a reorientation of Islamic practice towards the way it is attributed to the companions (Sahaba) of the Prophet.

In ideological variance to Deobandism, there was a coalition of Sufi shrines and schools around 1880 around the person of Ahmad Raza Khan (1856–1921) in Bareilly, a city located today in the Indian state of Uttar Pradesh (Sanyal 2011). Their purpose was to defend the traditionalist ritual practices performed at Sufi shrines. After 1890, they quickly expanded their pir-based networks throughout South Asia to unify Sufi sympathizers and oppose the Deobandi outfits, such as the Dar al-Uloom Deoband and the Nadwat al-ʿUlamā. Followers of the Barelvi school of thought (maslak) refer to themselves as *Ahl-e Sunnat wa Jamāʿat*, people of the sunna and the majority community, or the *Sawād-e Azam* (great majority) of the Sunni sect. The name ASWJ has been hijacked by the radical Pakistani Deobandi outfit the SSP, which has been condemned and rejected by the Barelvis. The Barelvis preach practices close to popular Islam and Sufism, encouraging folk rituals revolving around saints, their shrines and their graves. Their main focus is on the veneration of the Prophet Muhammad, who is considered to possess specific special qualities (*ʿilm-i ghaib* - Knowledge of the unseen world, sole preserve of God, *ḥāḍir-o nāẓir* - Despite the physical death of the Prophet Muhammad, he is present as a conscious being, *nūr-i muhammadī* - Light of prophet Muhammad). Love for the prophet, *ʿishq-i rasūl*, is hence essential for the Barelvi concept of Islamic piety.

At the beginning of the twentieth century, Deobandis and Barelvis engaged in fatwa wars, challenging each other's version of Islam in written statements. It must be understood that Deobandis and Barelvis are not monolithic entities. Indeed, both movements developed relatively differently in Pakistan compared with in India, and in both countries there are different subgroups—institutions, organizations and movements—with specific purist, political or sectarian agendas and differing opinions, emphases and approaches towards Islamic piety and activism.

In particular, in Pakistan, some Deobandi-affiliated groups began in recent years to attack Sufi shrines—for example, the Data Darbar (July 2010) and Sakhi Sarwar shrines (April 2011). Deobandis consider Barelvis to be at best uneducated[12] grave worshippers, idolaters, polytheists or even crypto-Hindus. The Barelvis too have a long tradition of mistrust and open hatred against Deobandis and Salafis (not to mention Ahmadis), whom they consider to be kafir (unbelievers) and blasphemers of the Prophet (Okarvi 2002), as they perceive them to suffer from a lack of respect for the Prophet. However, this Barelvi mistrust against Deobandis is for the most part symbolic and does not systematically translate into organized violence. These polemical sectarian semantics of disrespect and abuse often remain peripheral in everyday life as the radical rhetorics of the Barelvi preachers are in practice counterbalanced by local and context-oriented blessing pirs:

> While the maulvi preaches, the pir blesses. Perhaps for this reason the ulama may well prefer saints who are safely interred in their graves. There is also a difference in tone and ideology between saint and maulvi. Whereas Barelvi ulama are strident and militant, advocating Islamic radicalism and revolution, saints are soft spoken and peace promoting [...] This stridency of the Barelvi ulama stems from the intercalary position they occupy in the Sufi cult system, placed in the middle between saints and followers. This is particularly true of the more educated ulama who hold important positions in major mosques or educational institutions and political organisations. The ulama compensate for the weakness of their authority through their strident tones. At the urs it is almost impossible even for a native Urdu speaker to understand parts of the ulama's speeches, once they take off in flight.[13]

A key difference between the more emotional Barelvi lovers of the Prophet and the rather puritanical monotheistic interpretation of Deoband is the extraordinary status attributed to the Prophet Muhammad owing to the central role that respect for the Prophet takes in the Barelvi belief systems. In contrast, Deobandis and Salafis usually treat the Prophet in an ordinary manner. Raza Khan's most famous fatwa, *Ḥusām al-Ḥaramain*, published in 1906, expressis verbis mentions the Deobandi founding fathers *Muḥammad Qāsim Nānautawī* (1833–1877), *Rashīd Aḥmad* Gangohī (1829–1905) and Ashraf ʿAlī Thānwī (1863–1943) among the *Wahhābīya Shaiṭānīya*, unbelievers and Satanists[14]:

> It is also true that these sects are confident of infidels, who are their main sources of support and allies who are enemies of Islam. They are making blasphemous statements and creating sacrilege faiths in order to create disunity amongst the Muslims and erase Islam and the Muslims from the surface of the Earth.[15]
>
> Loyalty to Allah is useless without love for the Prophet.[16]

Similar anti-Barelvi fatwas were issued by the Dar al-Uloom Deoband. Indeed, it is not unusual in Deobandi madrassas to refer to Barelvis as grave worshippers and polytheists.

This difference—love for the prophet—unfolds in a variety of beliefs, which in their various forms became the centre of debates among various reformist agents.

(i) *Intercession*: Using a medium of Sufi saints to seek help from Allah. Although salvation and spiritual support can only come from Allah, Barelvis allow and encourage the faithful to ask the saints, as wasilah or intercession, for blessings from Allah. Accordingly there is a special status of the prophets and awliya (saints):

> The distinguished Prophets and illustrious Awliya enjoy a very special proximity with Allah and are therefore, Divinely blessed to assist fellow creation. This assistance can be of a spiritual or physical nature and can be rendered while they are alive and even after their death. These Elite Servants of Allah offer their help only by the Command of Almighty Allah.[17]

Deobandis are more sceptical of intercessors and consider the seeking of assistance from the deceased a sign of polytheism.

(ii) *Saying "Yā Muhammad!" and "Yā Rasūl Allāh!"*:
The invocation of the Prophet is allowed and encouraged among Barelvis, whereas Deobandis consider such invocations to be shirk (polytheism) because, to them, the additional "Yā!" (Oh!) implies the presence of the person being invoked, yet the Prophet has died. Thus Deobandi mosques do not display signs saying "Yā Rasūl Allāh!", but these are usually evident in Barelvi mosques.

(iii) *"Death" of the prophet*[18]:
Barelvis believe that the prophet Muhammad has died, but at the same time continues to live, and from his grave he passes the invocational prayers of the Muslim ummah. For this reason he is able to appear in dreams and visions.

(iv) *Wasilah—Intercession*[19]:
For Barelvis the intercession via the prophet Muhammad is a *conditio sine qua non* to seeking proximity to God[20]:

> Only the Prophet can reach God without intermediaries. This is why, on the Day of the Resurrection, all the prophets, *walis* (intermediary), and ulema will gather in the Prophet's presence and beg him to intercede for them with God.[21]

For Barelvis, approaching Allah (*tawassul*) means to supplicate to Allah through the Prophet or another living or deceased saint. That is, the Muslim seeks the wasilah of a saint, who is considered to be specifically close to Allah or the Prophet Muḥammad and requested to function as an intercessor:

O Allāh! I ask You with the wasīla of the Prophet. Ya Muḥammad! I am making du'ā' to Allāh Most High with your wasīla, so that Allāh Most High may accept my du'ā'. O Allāh! Make Prophet as my interceder.[22]

Deobandis consider this practice to be polytheism, as per their belief Allah alone is worthy of worship and third parties cannot support or increase the likelihood of acceptance of any prayer.

(v) *Nūr—Divine light*[23]:

Barelvis consider the Prophet Muhammad not only as human (*bashar*) but also as *nūr-i khudā*, the light of God.

Undoubtedly, there has come to you from Allah a light and a Book, luminous.[24]

According to Barelvi beliefs the light of the Prophet was created before the creation and is hence timeless. That means that the Prophet was initially created from the light of God, and after that the creation was unfolded out of this light. *Nūr-i Muḥammadī* is the first manifestation of the divine light, and out of that everything else was created dependent on it. The dictum of the Prophet's infallibility originates from this concept, which is again rejected by Deobandis. Deobandis consider the Prophet as solely bashar (human) or *insān-i kāmil* (the perfect human). The debate about this question resulted in the famous fatwa war about whether the Prophet as perfect beauty or a figure of light could have had a shadow, which the Barelvis deny.

(vi) *'Ilm-i ghaib—knowledge of the unseen*[25]:

Knowledge of the unseen, the past and future, is for Deobandis one of the exclusive qualities of Allah: "Who indicates that anybody other than Allāh possesses 'ilm-i ghaib, is indeed a kāfir [...] friendship and sympathy with him are totally harām."[26] Barelvis, however, believe that (1) Allah can reveal parts of this knowledge to selected prophets; and that (2) Allah has provided his most beloved Prophet Muhammad as the only one to have full access to this knowledge, and that the Prophet Muhammad did pass it on to selected successors. To declare the Prophet Muhammad devoid of this knowledge is considered to be blasphemous by Barelvis.

(vii) *Ḥāḍir-o nāẓir—presence of the Prophet, who views all actions*[27]:
As light the Prophet is eternally omnipresent, hence he is present (*ḥāḍir*) and witness and viewer (*nāẓir*) of all human deeds. Ḥāḍir, present, means in regard to the Prophet because he has a supercreational knowledge of the nature of things (*al-ʿilm al-ḥuḍūrī*). Barelvis believe that the Prophet can be present at the same time at different locations and is able to view the whole of creation inside his grave in his palm.

(viii) *Bidʿa—Innovation*:
Innovation is a highly ambivalent term and, according to Deobandi and Salafi beliefs, is mostly understood as opposite to sunna, tradition or customs of the Prophet. There is a distinction between *bidʿa sayyia*, a bad innovation, which is contradicting a sunna, and *bidʿa ḥasana*, a good innovation in harmony with sharia—for example, the insertion of vocalization signs in the Qurʾan, mosque minarets, Friday sermons in a language other than Arabic, calling for prayers with loudspeakers or making pilgrimage by plane. The circumambulation of a grave, urs celebrations and a celibate lifestyle are innovations that are usually heavily criticized by Deobandis.[28] Barelvis regard several purist Deobandi teachings as historically new, with little foundation in the historical Islamic teachings.

(ix) *Mīlād al-Nabī—Birthday of the Prophet*:
On 12 Rabīʿ al-awwal, Barelvis celebrate the birthday of the Prophet through processions and gatherings during which *durūd* (*taṣliya*) are sent—that is, salutations are offered to the Prophet Muhammad, donations are collected for the needy, and the deeds and virtues of the Prophet are commemorated. According to the Barelvis, this is clearly a pious act. Deobandis reject the milad rituals, considering them un-Islamic, and they argue[29]:

If at the same point of time different birthday congregations take place, will Muhammad be present at all locations or not? He has to decide according to his preferences where to go and where not to go. If he would be present at all locations, how could he be at a thousand places, while his existence is one?"[30]

Quite famous is the online fatwa given by the Deobandi Mufti Taqi Usmani, who likens milad to Christian Christmas celebrations,[31] against which he levels the same arguments to identify them as non-biblical and un-Christian, as he does against milad to consider it non-Qur'anic and un-Islamic.

(x)   *Idkhāl at-Tawāb—Raising the spiritual status of the deceased*:
Barelvis believe that spiritual benefits as well as the forgiveness of sins can be generated and asked for on another's behalf, including when someone has already passed away. The means for attaining that higher spiritual status are, for example, prayer, giving donations, reciting the Qur'an and making an additional hajj in the name of that person. Deobandis and Salafis consider it impossible to produce spiritual benefits through one's own deeds for another Muslim (in particular someone who has died). However, Barelvis usually fix a date for a meeting dedicated to this purpose after someone has died. Guests gather to donate for the needy in the name of the deceased, the Qur'an is recited and so on.

(xi) *Taʿwīz—Amulet locket*:
The *taʿwīz* is a *duʿāʾ*, a verse of the Qur'an or of the ahadith, written on a repeatedly folded piece of paper worn in a locket around the neck. As an amulet it can, for instance, unfold healing powers for sick people, protective powers for children or repel evil. Alternatively a *duʿāʾ* can be blown into the face of those seeking help or assistance. Deobandis reject this practice, treating it as a Hindu or polytheist influence.

(xii) *Travelling to the grave of the Prophet*:
Masjid al-Nabawī, the Prophet's mosque with the green dome in Medina, should be visited only with the intention of performing prayers according to Deobandi scholars. On that occasion one may visit the grave of the Prophet. However, Barelvis allow and stress that Muslims travel to Medina with the intention of visiting the grave of the Prophet.

The Holy Prophet said in a hadith that "Whoever will visit my grave, it is like he who has visited me in my life time."[32]

Deobandis consider travelling to graves parallel to Hindu pilgrimages and so consider the custom to be un-Islamic:

The Holy Apostle had cursed the Jews and Christians, for they made the graves of their Prophets mosques.[33]

Clearly, in their rejection and condemnation of the Barelvi belief system and traditional Sufi rituals, there is not much difference in the position of the Deobandis and so-called Salafis/Wahhabis. The Barelvis are antagonists to the Deobandi "reformers" in the sense that they subscribe to shrine rituals and ritual worship of intercessors between Muslims and Allah (such as urs, celebrating the anniversary of the death of popular saints, and *milād al-nabī*, the birthday of the Prophet Muhammad), and at the same time they are reformist in their emphasis on individual responsibility for salvation. These debates are not distinctive for the Islamic periphery or for South Asia; comparable debates shape Islamic history anywhere in the Muslim world, including the history of Arab Islam (see Meier 2002).

The Rise of Deobandis and
the Barelvi Revival in Pakistan

Pakistan has nationalized Indian Islam. Some therefore think that "its true home remains with the Muslim minority of India, which thus portends the future of Islam itself as a global entity".[34] Indeed, the traditionally most authoritative institutions of the Sunni schools of thought remained in India after Partition. The Barelvis were among the first to support the Pakistan Movement and the demand for an independent Islamic state. In contrast, the Dar al-Uloom Deoband and the majority of Deobandi clerics opposed the creation of Pakistan and interpreted the project of establishing a Muslim state as an obstacle against the Islamization of India as a whole. Ironically, Islamic state politics in Pakistan was mostly in favour of Deobandi, and more recently Ahl-e Hadith/Salafi, institutions. Only a few Deobandi clerics decided to support the Pakistan Movement, but they were highly influential. The increasing Saudi influence too helped the Deobandi clerics and madrassas. In the 1960s, King Faisal of Saudi Arabia decided to construct a national mosque for the people in Pakistan, which was completed in 1986. Although the majority of Sunni Muslims in South Asia subscribe to Barelvi beliefs, and Deobandis at first did not support the Pakistan Movement, the military dictator Zia ul Haq (1977–1988) forged a strong alliance between the military and Deobandi institutions and movements (e.g. the TJ). Already in 1975, the Afghan Hizb-i Islami had begun in Pakistan to bring Islamist students and the ulema together to organize resistance against the regime in Kabul.[35] In 1978, Peshawar-based Hizb-i Islami and the JI founded the Harakat-i Inqilab-i Islami (Movement for the Islamic Revolution). During the late 1970s and 1980s, the Deobandi madrassas in that area systematically recruited mujahideen for the jihad in Afghanistan after the Soviet invasion in 1979. The Deobandi clerics benefited in particular from foreign funding from the Kingdom of Saudi Arabia as well as other Arab states. Pakistan's ISI supported the mostly Deobandi mujahideen because they seemingly fitted into Pakistan's military ideology of developing "strategic depth" against India—that is, to install a pro-Pakistan government in Kabul and "create a Muslim region capable of standing up against India economically, demographically and perhaps even militarily".[36] The Pakistani intelligence service favoured mostly the Hizb-i Islami, which established itself in the refugee camps also to assassinate its political adversaries such as the leftists, nationalists and royalists. The Talibanization of Afghanistan has become the most successful foreign policy project in the history of Pakistan. The support of the country has been vital for the survival and revival of the Taliban, not only after the North Atlantic Treaty Organization (NATO)-led International Security Assistance Force (ISAF) mission. Already in 1999 about a third of Taliban fighters were foreigners (i.e., either Pakistani or passing through Pakistan).[37] To date, foreign funding of educational institutions is probably the single most important factor that enables radical Islamic elements to confront the state and threaten the peaceful co-existence of citizens in Pakistan. The Deobandis in Pakistan were used by state agencies to create the Taliban, and at least eight ministers of the Islamic Emirate of Afghanistan graduated from Deobandi madaris in Pakistan. The Taliban has been supported by state agencies that wish to transform Afghanistan to a client state and military hinterland. The question of the future of Afghanistan is hence deeply interwoven with the dynamics of Pakistan.

This alliance between Pakistan's state agencies and Deobandi madaris and Ahl-e Hadith institutions had consequences for Barelvis as well. Zia's focus on sharia impacted on the processes of redefining the saints of Pakistan (Ewing 1983). It was under the charismatic JUP leader Ahmad Shah Nurani that Pakistan's Barelvis agreed to enhance their status and reimagine their collective identity to foster their project for the Islamization of society after the Multan Sunni Conference in October 1978.[38] 1980 was an important year for Barelvi renaissance in Pakistan.[39] Until October 1981, Minhaj ul-Quran (MQ) and the DI were established with headquarters in Lahore and Karachi, respectively.[40] Both Barelvi organizations effectively turned into truly transnational movements for Barelvi revival with centres in about 100 countries each. While the MQ maintains a television presence through QTV, DI runs its own television channel, Madani channel. The return to fundamentalism then is an effort to restore threatened certainties and thus major religious traditions generated by powerful revival movements.[41]

India strikingly lacks homegrown Islamic militancy and "democratic reality appears to be the antidote to totalitarian theories of any kind".[42] One could question, of course, whether it is indeed "democracy" or rather the minority status of Muslims in India that highlights a common identity, as Muslims, between the Deobandis and Barelvis there (cf. Schnabel et al. 2013). Apparently the problematic factor that led to the massive level of Islamist militancy in Pakistan may be the state support given to jihadism, in which Pakistani Deobandi clerics and madrassas played the role of willing partners and benefited a great deal in terms of their access to power, money and other resources, thus expanding their madrassa network and influence.

STATE-SPONSORED JIHADISM

The military dictator Zia ul-Haq (1977–1988) explained in an interview with *The Economist* that "Pakistan is, like Israel, an ideological state. Take out the Judaism from Israel and it will fall like a house of cards. Take Islam out of Pakistan and make it a secular state; it would collapse."[43] Pakistan remains an ideological state that does not seek security but yearns for an irrational and unrealistic parity with India.

Pakistan's north-western frontier is historically no frontier at all. The problems of Afghanistan therefore cannot be separated from those of Pakistan, and vice versa. The Durand Line has never been accepted as a border by Afghanistan. Every day about 60,000 people cross the porous 2,640 km-long Durand Line, which is not marked by any natural border, such as a river or a mountain (ICG 2014). The TTP leader, Mullah Fazlullah, appears to coordinate his attacks in Pakistan from the Afghan side, and the command and control centres of the three main militant groups of Afghan insurgents, Mullah Omar's Quetta Council (the remnants of the Islamic Emirate of Afghanistan), Gulbuddin Hekmatyar's Hizb-e Islami and the Al-Qaeda-linked Haqqani network, are based in and operate from Pakistan. Hence the US government created the concept of "AfPak" to denote the geographic, cultural and religious entity encompassing both countries that contributes to their geographical incoherence as separate states.[44]

The USA and the Kingdom of Saudi Arabia financially supported Pakistan's jihad against the Soviets in Afghanistan which unfolded after 1979. Pakistan installed the Taliban regime in Afghanistan during the 1990s to win strategic depth against India as well as to make sure nobody else could play the Pashtun card, as some demanded an independent state of Pashtunistan in the area. The establishment of the Taliban regime in Afghanistan remains the most successful foreign policy project in the history of Pakistan. The infamous Maktab ul-Khidmat, led by the Jordanian-Palestinian Muslim Brother Abdullah Azzam and the Saudi national Osama Bin Laden in Peshawar, as well as several other outfits and networks for the global recruitment of mujahideen, kept on operating after 1990, bringing Muslim men to AfPak for jihadi training. After the fall of Kabul, several militant outfits with thousands of activists regrouped against Pakistan's eternal political arch foe, India, turning Pakistan into the world's most important epicentre of transnational terrorism. Between 1990 and 1994 approximately 10,000 militants were trained in the camps in Afghanistan, mostly for the JI, the JM and the LT (at that time operating as Jamaat ud-Dawa and now renamed Filah-e Insaniat Foundation) for their missions in Kashmir, where new jihadi camps were built in the Pakistan administered part. In January 2012, Hafiz Saeed praised Pakistan for the freedom that jihadi activists enjoy: "Pakistan is unmatched in terms of the freedom it allows for the pursuit of jihad and for the spread of Islam."[45]

The military's national ideology developed a policy of "strategic depth", aimed at creating a client state in Afghanistan that could be used as a "military hinterland". The relations between the two countries are hence tense, characterized by mutual mistrust and viewed through a narrow security prism. Afghanistan's close ties with India are largely motivated by hostility towards Pakistan. The Pakistani military high command continues to hedge its bets, either actively or tacitly supporting a resurgent insurgency that threatens to undermine Afghanistan's transition. The classified NATO report, *State of the Taliban 2012: Detainee Perspectives*, evaluates more than 27,000 interrogations with insurgents and concludes that ISI support has been critical to the survival and revival of the Taliban:

> The Government of Pakistan remains intimately involved with the Taliban. In the opinion of Taliban personnel, a primary mission of ISI is to insure that Pakistan-based militant groups' activities remain externally directed. Pakistan remains fundamentally opposed to GIRoA [Government of the Islamic Republic of Afghanistan] [...] In meetings with Taliban leaders, ISI personnel are openly hostile to ISAF and the government of Afghanistan. ISI officers tout the need for continued jihad and expulsion of "foreign invaders" from Afghanistan.[46]

The downsizing of the US–NATO security umbrella in Afghanistan seemingly heightened both Pakistan's and Afghanistan's incentives to use insurgent proxies for leverage against one another. The next phase of the conflict could have consequences that extend far beyond the region. Facing its militarily much stronger arch-enemy, India, in the east and a weak and strongly tribal society in Afghanistan in the west, Pakistan's military has had little choice but to support terrorist outfits to secure strategic depth in Afghanistan and to draw India in a low-intensity conflict. Some analysts call this Pakistan's geostrategic curse. As shown earlier, Barelvis didn't benefit from these processes that relocated resources as well as symbolic capital.

Cultural environment enables and restricts human activity. There is no evidence that Islamic solidarity provides inoculation against sectarian or ethnic conflict: "In this context nationalism is clearly a more benign form of political identity than Islam: at least in principle sectarian divisions should not matter in a national context, whereas they can hardly fail to matter in a religious one."[47] Islam has a proven insufficiency in gluing together Pakistani society.

The use and misuse of religion by the state and the military undermined its potential to emerge as a strong, tolerant and democratic state.[48] Pakistan's military ideology of creating a manageable chaos in Afghanistan and pulling India into a low-intensity conflict resulted in processes of radicalization and militarization among Deobandi and Ahl-e-Hadith institutions. Thus jihadism and militant sectarianism became a core element in Deobandi and Ahl-e-Hadith interpretations of Islam in Pakistan. Although Shias and Sunni Barelvis have not been immune to activist groups engaging in sectarian violence, the notion of a militant jihad against "unbelievers" is not an integral element of their belief systems. Shia or Sunni Barelvi versions of Osama Bin Laden, Mullah Omar or Hafiz Saeed are hence indeed unthinkable.

THE WAHHABI FACTOR

"Salafabism"—the term for an influential trend of the gradual merging of Salafism and Wahhabism that began in Pakistan in the late 1970s—is probably the best label for the contemporary crisis of conscience in Pakistan, which enabled the ugly face of Islam with its shocking acts of violence to attract an astonishingly high level of passive tolerance, if not active support, in civil society. In particular, state leaders such as General Zia ul Haq and Nawaz Sharif received significant financial backing from the Kingdom of Saudi Arabia.

Among the Islamic belief systems in Pakistan the Ahl-e-Hadith are closest to the Wahhabi or Salafi understanding of Islam that is prevalent in Saudi Arabia. However, their reach in Pakistani society is rather limited, although their institutions do attract youngsters from a Sunni Barelvi or Deobandi background as well. Deobandis, in particular those with a more conservative understanding of their *aqida* (belief), have then been the second choice for partnership of Saudi activists. Barelvis, Shias and Ahmadis clearly belong to the opponents of Wahhabi beliefs.

Asif Ali Zardari, the Pakistani president from 2008 to 2013, and allegedly a Shia or Barelvi, was not seen as a qualified leader for the country in Riyadh. The Saudis wished for a return to military rule at that time.[49] "We in Saudi Arabia are not observers in Pakistan, we are participants", commented the Saudi ambassador to the USA, Adel al-Jubeir, in 2007. The Saudis supported Nawaz Sharif, their "honoured guest" during his exile from Pakistan, who was democratically re-elected as Pakistan's prime minister in July 2013.

Interior advisers and ministers in Pakistan have long criticized the Saudi role in funding radical religious seminaries inside Pakistan. A cable suggests that annually about $100 million find their way from Gulf countries to jihadist networks in Pakistan.[50] Recently revealed official documents indicate that the problematic Islamic seminaries are often the ones that benefit the most from foreign funding, mostly from Gulf countries.[51] More than 70 percent of Pakistani children study part-time in madrassas.[52] On 29 January 2015, the Pakistani senate discussed the issue, and immediately after the 12/16 Peshawar massacre there was a tendency to take action: "Foreign funding to seminaries is very dangerous. It has triggered sectarian war in Pakistan. It must be blocked on a now or never basis", commented Senator Tahir Mashhadi.[53] This news has been heard with much hope in Afghanistan, which suffers considerably from Pakistan-backed proxies. There, the Saudi funding of religious seminaries in Pakistan is perceived as an existential threat to the future of a peaceful Afghanistan.[54]

The Saudi impact, however, does not just stretch across the political elite, the military, conservative madaris and the export of cheap labour forces. Saudi Arabia is the country that employs the largest number of Pakistani labour migrants and is the largest remittance provider to Pakistan—more than $5.6 billion during the fiscal year from July 2014 to June 2015 (another $6.3 billion to be added as remittances from the other Gulf Cooperation Council [GCC] countries). One of the largest universities in Pakistan (with about 30,000 students), the IIU in Islamabad, is headed by a Saudi national, who allegedly speaks neither English nor Urdu. Extremist ideology is imported also under the cover of modern education.[55] The Saudi-funded university intentionally promotes (sectarian) Salafi, takfiri and Ikhwani doctrines.[56] And this is only what happens in the spotlight. What about the Saudi impact on the CII?[57] Why has an enlightened intellectual like Muhammad Khalid Masud been pressured to step down as its head? Saudis seemingly view Pakistan's military and nuclear arsenal as part of its own repertoire of assets.[58] Why did Pakistani officers train ISIS troops to fight in Syria against Bashar al-Assad? Why did thousands of Pakistani Sunni soldiers—most of them from the Pakistani Navy—join the Saudi attack on Yemen in 2015, even though Pakistan's parliament decided otherwise? And who is to blame for all these developments? Is it the Saudis who seek to expand their influence in the region by means of realpolitik, or is it the Pakistani political and religious elites who sell off the military, religious and human resources of Pakistan along with its dīn (religious code of life).

For Saudis there is sufficient reason for optimism to further expand the Wahhabi impact in state and society, mosque and madrassa, with their "preferred figure", Nawaz Sharif, in office, and the military—their long-term cooperation partner—increasingly taking full control of counterterrorism policy.

A Game Changer?

On 16 December 2014, seven Deobandi militants affiliated with the TTP, at least one of them trained in a madrassa, attacked the APS in Peshawar, killing 145 people, 133 of them children—all boys, mostly shot in the head. The attack has been described in the media as Pakistan's 9/11 and a potential game changer in the way that state agencies cooperate or engage with terrorist networks. Unlike his predecessor, General Kayani, Pakistan's current army chief, General Raheel Sharif, decided to initiate a bold military operation, Zarb-e Azb, against the TTP/LeJ militant outfits hiding in the Waziristan region. He also expanded the operation to other parts of the country, including Karachi, Quetta and South Punjab. A similar change in tone was evident at the political level: "There is no distinction now between good and bad Taliban," claimed Nawaz Sharif in a blunt confession that must have shocked the military on the day after the massacre, and he further emphasized that Pakistan would "continue the war against terrorism until the last terrorist is eliminated."

Indeed, it is not the civilian government's decision to deal with—either support or neutralize—the jihadist militant outfits. However, the military is facing increased pressure to deliver, and has yet to prove its ability to liberate areas such as Swat and Waziristan from the clutches of the Taliban. More recently, in 2015, Pakistani police, with the military in the background, killed a notorious terrorist, Malik Ishaq Deobandi, the head of the LeJ and the vice president of the ASWJ.

With the Peshawar school massacre it became evident that the military cannot control the Deobandi militancy that it helped to enable for jihadist purposes in Afghanistan and Kashmir.

On 17 December 2014, Nawaz Sharif ended the moratorium on the death penalty in terror-related cases. However, the vast majority of the 300 executions (from the massacre until the beginning of December 2015) have been for crimes unrelated to terrorism. Teachers have been given gun training and allowed to take firearms into classrooms in KPK. Immediately after the Peshawar school massacre, the Pakistan Air Force carried out retaliatory unmanned aerial vehicle attacks and airstrikes using F-16 and JF-17 jets to bomb hideouts close to the Afghan border. Other security agencies launched several operations for targeted killings as well as arrests. In January 2015 more than 10,000 people were arrested on various charges after the 20-point "National Action Plan"[59] anti-terrorism programme was announced a week after the massacre. Up to May 2015, 49,000 suspects had been arrested, but only 129 belonged to the TTP. The Haqqani network was officially banned in January 2015, but not yet targeted in the ongoing operations in North Waziristan. Controversially, the idea of an amnesty plan for banned militant organizations has been debated. On 6 January 2015, the parliament adopted the Twenty-First Amendment Bill and the Army Act Amendment Bill, which aim to set up constitutionally protected and speedy military courts to conduct proceedings in cases related to terrorism. At least nine military courts have been established since January 2015. Chief of Army Staff, General Raheel Sharif, said in December 2014: "The enemy lives within us and looks like us. The challenge is huge." However, the Pakistani military is organized and trained for warfare with India, not for a counterinsurgency in the forbidding geography of the Afghanistan–Pakistan border. While recent steps seem to indicate at least a partial willingness on the part of the state to take the War on Terror more seriously, at the same time the government lacks sufficient capacity.

In July 2015 the ICG criticized that the National Action Plan does not seem to be a coherent strategy but a hastily conceived wish list devised for public consumption.[60] The TTP's strongest ally and enabler, the Deobandi militant group the SSP, continues to operate by its new name, ASWJ, and its madrassas and mosques have been given police protection.

STATE-SPONSORED SUFISM

The USA has recently become another bidder on the religious markets in Pakistan. Sufis are often portrayed as pluralists. The traditional Sufi communities such as the Barelvis may be the natural enemy of Deobandi and Salafi militancy, but this does not mean that they are "the natural ally of those who are opposing Salafism, especially when they are opposing Salafism for their own reasons".[61] It is, however, a fact as is also evident from the statistical data, that unlike Deobandi and Salafis, the Barelvis are not involved in systematic incidents of violence and terrorism in Pakistan or elsewhere, although all faith groups and sects have an extremist fringe. As Sufis are generally peaceful (not necessarily pacifist), several American analysts have called for their empowerment to oppose radical Deobandism and Salafism.

Given that the Barelvi ideology is the subcontinental form of traditional Sufism, governments in India, the USA and Pakistan are considering supporting and strengthening Barelvi institutions. A heritage report (Curtis and Mullick 2009) concluded that the USA should actively help to revive Pakistan's pluralist traditions to fight extremism. The security analysis of the World Organization for Resource Development and Education (Mirahmadi et al. 2010) strongly recommended the international donor community to financially assist Barelvi institutions in Pakistan:

> Across Pakistan more generally, it is also important to note that many of the Jamaat Ahle Sunnat (Barelvis) institutions lack international standards of excellence because of financial limitations and a lack of exposure to proper training and capacity building. International donors should be advised of these limitations and should work to strengthen their core abilities because of their massive grassroots appeal and credibility.[62]

Some observers criticized the US policy of pushing Pakistan towards state-sponsored Sufism because it politicizes Islam further.

Looking at the developments in the world during the last decade, governments would probably be well advised to not try to (mis)use specific religious traditions for the advancement of their own political objectives. While pluralistic traditions should be encouraged, it is important not to expose these vulnerable communities in the face of better armed and trained Deobandi militants. Instead, the government should focus on increased security for and preservation of the Barelvi shrines, leaders and institutions.

Pakistan's Barelvi organizations formed a SIC launching the Save Pakistan Movement to fight Talibanization in 2009. Around the same time the parliament revived the National Sufi Council established under Musharraf in 2006, which had become dormant and ended up organizing music festivals and printing calendars, under the new name of Sufi Advisory Council. The SIC supported military operations against the Taliban.[63]

The TTP then in turn intensified attacks against popular Sufi shrines. On 1 July 2010, two suicide bombers attacked the Data Darbar shrine of the eleventh-century saint, Ali Hujwiri, in Lahore, killing 45. Similar attacks have been carried out by Deobandi militants against the Ahmadis, Christians and Shia Muslims of Pakistan.

Although there is no ideology of jihadism among Barelvis and this group is in general peaceful, there are a number of caveats. Barelvis are not necessarily aloof from politics.

LOVING THE PROPHET: CARTOON AFFAIRS

Germany has until today not witnessed any successful Islamist attack targeting Germans. On 20 March 2006, 28-year old Amir Cheema, a Pakistani student of textile management at the Niederrhein University of Applied Sciences in Mönchengladbach, entered the Axel-Springer publishing house in Berlin with the intention of stabbing the editor in chief of *Die Welt*, Roger Köppel, for reprinting some of the Danish cartoons. He was overpowered by security guards in the building. On 3 May 2006, during pretrial confinement in Moabit prison in Berlin, he hanged himself with a noose made from his clothes. Amir Cheema was allegedly a Barelvi. Apparently the love of the Prophet is a subject on which Barelvis become impassioned. Another important case in this regard is that of Malik Mumtaz Qadri in Pakistan.

A HUMAN RIGHTS APPROACH TO THE FUNDAMENTAL RIGHT OF RELIGIOUS FREEDOM

Pakistan's blasphemy laws deeply shape the Pakistani (mis-)understanding of the human right of religious freedom. From 1999 to 2010, Pakistan annually proposed a resolution combating defamations of religions, in particular against Islamophobia, at the United Nations Human Rights Council (UNHRC) in Geneva, which led to intense and controversial debates.[64] It was finally rejected in 2011. The resulting UNHRC resolution 16/18, "Combating intolerance, negative stereotyping and stigmatization of, and discrimination, incitement to violence, and violence against persons based on religion or belief", has to be understood in the context of the Rabat Plan of Action (on the prohibition of advocacy of national, racial or religious hatred that constitutes incitement to discrimination, hostility or violence), which clearly recommends that "States that have blasphemy laws should repeal them, as such laws have a stifling impact on the enjoyment of freedom of religion or belief, and healthy dialogue and debate about religion." Pakistan's approach to misinterpreting religious freedom caused severe damage to the reputation of the fundamental human right to freedom of religion or belief in the international arena and

> it cannot be emphasized enough that freedom of religion or belief does not provide respect to religions as such; instead it empowers human beings in the broad field of religion and belief. The idea of protecting the honour of religions themselves would clearly be at variance with the human rights approach. (see A/68/290)[65]
>
> As a human right, freedom of religion or belief does not protect religions per se (e.g. traditions, values, identities, and truth claims) but aims at the empowerment of human beings, as individuals and in community with others […] The interpretation of religious traditions is not the business of the State and should be left to the followers of the various convictions, who are the rights holders of freedom of religion or belief.[66]

CONCLUSION

The contestation of the traditional Sufi ideology versus Deobandi or Salafi ideology has become politically loaded and increasingly complex. Since the 1930s there has been a decline in formal teaching of Sufism or tasawwuf in Deobandi seminaries. With the increasing Salafi/Wahhabi and Saudi influence, the once existing institution of the Deobandi khanaqh is disappearing. During the second part of the twentieth century, Deobandis increasingly propagated an anti-*tarīqah* (Sufi method) and anti-Sufi message, targeting in particular systems of shrine-centred Islamic authority. The Islamization politics under Zia ul-Haq favoured Deobandis and Ahl-e-Hadith (and their madaris produced mujahideen for the jihad in Afghanistan), and systematically discriminated against Sunni Barelvi institutions. The easy access to weapons in the years of the jihad led to a militarization even of those Deobandi groups that formerly subscribed to a sectarian agenda—for example, the SSP/ASWJ. In the late 1980s, Deobandis and Barelvis were fighting over mosques and madaris in particular in Karachi. The financial support from private persons and Islamic foundations from GCC countries to Deobandi and Ahl-e-Hadith institutions in Pakistan resulted in a further Wahhabization and conservative radicalization of those institutions. Militant attacks against Sufi shrines have increased in recent years, and it seems difficult today to imagine a revival of the traditional and peaceful pluralism of Islam that once existed in Pakistan. Fighting extremism is a difficult task in a country with a weak rule of law. However, foreign countries should not get involved in political projects for the support of any specific belief systems, which are necessarily in violation of the fundamental human right of freedom of religion or belief. Instead the focus should be on the elimination of the support available to radical Deobandi and Salafi madrassas and outfits from Saudi Arabia, other Gulf countries, and from within the Pakistani establishment. Countries which get involved in such projects should be held accountable, and the foreign funding of radical madaris must be stopped. The vast majority of Muslims in Pakistan are moderate and wish nothing more than progress towards a more peaceful society. It is this civil society that deserves more attention and secured rights. Barelvis indeed deserve more attention in publications on Islam in Pakistan and, sure enough, Barelvi belief systems are the backbone of everyday Islam all over South Asia.

Notes

1. Ess 2012: 120.
2. Schmitt 2010: 77–78.
3. Clausewitz 1963: 216–221.
4. Richard Wike: "What Pakistan Thinks," May 10, 2013, available at http://www.pewglobal.org/2013/05/10/what-pakistan-thinks/.

5. Zahir Shah Sherazi, "Six Top TTP Commanders Announce Allegiance to Islamic State's Baghdadi," *Dawn*, October 14, 2014, http://www.dawn.com/news/1137908. The five commanders were the TTP amir for Orakzai Agency, Saeed Khan; the TTP's Kurram chapter chief, Daulat Khan; Fateh Gul Zaman, the TTP head in Khyber; the TTP's Peshawar amir, Mufti Hassan; and the TTP's Hangu chief, Khalid Mansoor.

6. "Islamic State Appoints Leaders of 'Khorasan Province,' Issues Veiled Threat to Afghan Taliban," *Long War Journal*, January 27, 2015, http://www.longwarjournal.org/archives/2015/01/islamic_state_appoin.php.

7. "TTP Announces Sacking of its Spokesman," *Dawn*, October 21, 2014, http://www.dawn.com/news/1139316.

8. "The Taliban," Council on Foreign Relations website, http://www.cfr.org/terrorist-organizations-and-networks/taliban/p35985#!/ [accessed February 12, 2015].

9. Khan, A. 2014. No regret over supporting IS, says Lal Masjid cleric. *The Express Tribune*, December 15. Available at: http://tribune.com.pk/story/806711/no-regret-over-supporting-is-says-lal-masjid-cleric/.

10. Haider, M. 2011. An incurable disease. *Dawn*, October 5. www.dawn.com/2011/10/05/an-incurable-disease/.

11. Geaves 2015: 191.

12. Suhaïl 2002.

13. Werbner 2003: 257.

14. Raza 2005: 32–50.

15. Raza 2005: 71.

16. Raza Khan 1996: 13.

17. Raza Khan 2007: 6.

18. Ammar 2001: 29–34.

19. Raza Khan 1897 and Raza 2005c: 1–25.

20. Sanyal 1996: 132.

21. Riza Khan cited by Sanyal 1996: 153.

22. Hadith cited by Ammar 2001: 38 and Raza Khan 2007b]: 11–13.

23. Raza 2005b: 52–113 and Raza Khan 1903.

24. Qur'an 5: 15.

25. Ammar 2001: 51–58. Raza Khan 1996: 25–33.

26. Fatāwa-yi Rashīdīya Vol. II, p. 14, cited by al-Qādirī 1992: 55.

27. Haddad 2003: 36–51.
28. Qasmi 2008: 33–34, 66 and 84–88.
29. "Imdad Allah saw nothing wrong with ceremonies intended to bless the souls of the dead, or those commemorating the birthday of the Prophet Muhammad—at which the Prophet himself was believed to make an appearance, with people standing in his honor—or the death anniversaries of Muslim saints, especially at their shrines [...] As he explained to Gangohi, his own view was that ceremonies honouring the Prophet or commemorating the dead were not necessarily objectionable in themselves, as long as they were not turned into religious obligations." (Zaman 2007: 24). Not all Deobandīs found friendly words to express their doubts about this position (Zaman 2007: 82).
30. Ashraf ʿAlī Thānwī in Fatāwa-yi Imdādīya, Vol. II, p. 58, cited by al-Qādirī 1992: 158. Similarly Fatāwa-yi Imdādīya, Vol. IV, p. 58, cited by al-Qādirī 1992: 169–170.
31. Usmani, Mufti Taqi: "Rabi'ul-Awwal", http://www.albalagh.net/general/rabi-ul-awwal.shtml [09.10.2015].
32. Raza 2005d: 53.
33. Qasmi 2008: 61.
34. Devji 2013: 250.
35. Dorronsoro 2005: 81.
36. Dorronsoro 2005: 145.
37. Dorronsoro 2005: 236.
38. Malik 1990: 43.
39. Philippon 2011: 78.
40. Gugler 2011: 99.
41. Berger 2014: 9, 21.
42. Metcalf 2014: 30.
43. Cited in Devji 2013: 4.
44. Kaplan 2012: xvi.
45. Tanveer, Rana: "Free to pursue jihad: Saeed appreciates Pakistan's unique freedoms," The Express Tribune, January 1, 2012, http://tribune.com.pk/story/315046/jud-chief-appreciates-freedom-in-pakistan.
46. "State of the Taliban," January 6, 2012, available at http://s3.documentcloud.org/documents/296489/taliban-report.pdf.
47. Cook 2014: 38.
48. Paul 2015: 148.

49. Declan Walsh: "WikiLeaks cables: Saudi Arabia wants military rule in Pakistan," *Guardian*, December 1, 2010, http://www.theguardian. com/world/2010/dec/01/saudis-distrust-pakistan-embassy-cables.

50. "Extremist Recruitment on the Rise in Southern Punjab" (cable, dated November 13, 2008), WikiLeaks, http://www.wikileaks.org/ plusd/cables/08LAHORE302_a.html.

51. "Details of Financial Aid Being Received by Seminaries in 2013–14," available at https://www.scribd.com/doc/254073491/Details-of- financial-aid-being-received-by-seminaries-in-2013-14   [accessed October 1, 2015].

52. Nelson 2014: 164.

53. Zahid Gishkori: "Year 2013–14: 80 Seminaries Received Rs300m in Foreign Aid," *The Express Tribune*, January 29, 2015, http://tri- bune.com.pk/story/829407/year-2013-14-80-seminaries- received-rs300m-in-foreign-aid/.

54. Massud Ebady: "A Weak Saudi Kingdom Can Mean Afghanistan's Silver Lining," *Khaama Press*, January 28, 2015, http://www. khaama.com/a-weak-saudi-kingdom-can-mean-afghanistans- silver-lining-9285.

55. Shafqat, Amna: "Islamic University Islamabad: My education in a Saudi funded university," *Pak Tea House*, February 11, 2015, http:// pakteahouse.net/2015/02/11/islamic-university-islamabad- my-education-in-a-saudi-funded-university.

56. Haq, Riazul: "Questionable activities: IIUI promoting extremist doc- trines, says intelligence agency," *The Express Tribune*, May 13, 2015, http://tribune.com.pk/story/885224/questionable-activities-iiui- promoting-extremist-doctrines-says-intelligence-agency.

57. Ahmed, Khaled: "Losing their Religion: Pakistan's runaway Council of Islamic Ideology," Newsweek, March 22, 2014, http://news- weekpakistan.com/losing-their-religion.

58. Alam, Kamal: "Saudi Arabia has devastated Pakistan's history of reli- gious tolerance and diversity," *Muftah*, June 3, 2015, http://muftah. org/saudi-arabia-has-devastated-pakistans-history-of-religious- tolerance-and-diversity/#.VhrDYeztlBf.

59. Anup Kaphle: "Pakistan Announces a National Plan to Fight Terrorism, Says Terrorists' Days Are Numbered," *Washington Post*, December 24, 2014, http://www.washingtonpost.com/blogs/ worldviews/wp/2014/12/24/pakistan-announces-a-national- plan-to-fight-terrorism-says-terrorists-days-are-numbered/.

60. ICG 2015: i.
61. Sedgwick 2015: 117.
62. Mirahmadi et al. 2010: 23.
63. "Fatwa for Jihad against America," *The Nation*, September 26, 2011, http://nation.com.pk/lahore/26-Sep-2011/Fatwa-for-Jihad-against-America.
64. See Commission on Human Rights resolutions 1999/82, 2000/84, 2001/4, 2002/9, 2003/4, 2004/6, 2005/3; General Assembly resolutions 60/150, 61/164, 62/154, 63/171, 64/156, 65/224; Human Rights Council resolutions 4/9, 7/19, 10/22, and 13/16.
65. Bielefeldt 2014: 190.
66. Bielefeldt 2014: 176f.

BIBLIOGRAPHY

al-Qādirī, Arshad. (1992). *Zalzala*. Dilhī: Maktaba Jām-i Nūr (1972).

Ammar, A. (2001). *Traditional scholarship & modern misunderstandings. Understanding the Ahle al-Sunnah. Bristol*. Bristol: Islamic Information Centre.

Benard, C. (2003). *Civil democratic Islam: Partners, resources, and strategies*. Santa Monica: RAND Corporation.

Berger, P. L. (2014). *The many altars of modernity: Toward a paradigm for religion in a pluralist age*. Berlin: De Gruyter.

Bielefeldt, H. (2014). *Freedom of religion or belief: Thematic reports of the UN special Rapporteur 2010–2013*. Bonn: Verlag für Kultur und Wissenschaft.

Butt, I. H. (Ed.). (2013). *Securing a frontline state: Alternative views on peace and conflict in Pakistan*. Islamabad: Heinrich-Böll-Stiftung.

Cook, M. (2014). *Ancient religions, modern politics: The Islamic case in comparative perspective*. Princeton: Princeton University Press.

Curtis, L., & Mullick, H. A. H. (2009). *Reviving Pakistan's pluralist traditions to fight extremism*. http://www.heritage.org/Research/Reports/2009/05/Reviving-Pakistans-Pluralist-Traditions-to-Fight-Extremism

Devji, F. (2013). *Muslim Zion: Pakistan as a political idea*. London: Hurst.

Dorronsoro, G. (2005). *Revolution unending: Afghanistan, 1979 to the present*. New York: Columbia University Press.

Ewing, K. (1983). The politics of Sufism: Redefining the saints of Pakistan. *The Journal of Asian Studies, 42*(2), 251–268.

Fair, C. C. (2014). *Fighting to the end: The Pakistan army's way of war*. New York: Oxford University Press.

Gayer, L. (2014). *Karachi: Ordered disorder and the struggle for the city*. Noida: HarperCollins.

Geaves, R. (2015). The contested Milieu of Deoband: 'Salafis' or 'Sufis'? In L. Ridgeon (Ed.), *Sufis and Salafis in the contemporary age* (pp. 191–216). London: Bloomsbury.

Gugler, T. K. (2011). *Mission Medina: Da'wat-e Islāmī und Tablīġī Ğamā'at.* Würzburg: Ergon.

Gugler, T. K. (2012). From Kalashnikov to keyboard: Pakistan's Jihadiscapes and the transformation of the Lashkar-e Tayba. In R. Lohlker (Ed.), *New approaches to the analysis of Jihadism: Online and offline* (pp. 37–62). Vienna: Vienna University Press.

Gugler, T. K. (2013). Angriff auf die Ambiguitätstoleranz: Pakistans Barelwiyat zwischen Prophetenliebe und Sufislamismus. In J. Kursawe & V. Brenner (Eds.), *Konfliktfaktor Religion? Die Rolle von Religionen in den Konflikten Südasiens* (pp. 131–152). Baden-Baden: Nomos.

Gugler, T. K. (2015). Barelwis: Developments and dynamics of conflict with Deobandis. In L. Ridgeon (Ed.), *Sufis and Salafis in the contemporary age* (pp. 171–189). London: Bloomsbury.

Haddad, G. F. (2003). *Mawlid: Celebrating the birth of the Holy Prophet (saw).* Karachi: Barkati Publishers.

ICG (International Crisis Group). (2014). *Resetting Pakistan's relations with Afghanistan.* Brussels: International Crisis Group.

ICG (International Crisis Group). (2015). *Revisiting counter-terrorism strategies in Pakistan: Opportunities and pitfalls.* Brussels: International Crisis Group.

Kaplan, R. D. (2012). *The revenge of geography: What the map tells us about coming conflicts and the battle against fate.* New York: Random House.

Khan, a. (2014). *No regret over supporting IS, says Lal Masjid cleric.* 814 The Express Tribune, December 15. available at: http://tribune.com. 815 pk/ story/806711/no-regret-over-supporting-is-says-lal- 816 masjid-cleric/

Knight, M. M. (2015). *Why I am a Salafi.* Berkeley: Soft Skull Press.

Madsen, S. T., Nielsen, K. B., & Skoda, U. (Eds.). (2012). *Trysts with democracy: Political practice in South Asia.* New Delhi: Anthem.

Malik, J. (1990). The luminous Nurani: Charisma and political mobilisation among the Barelwis in Pakistan. In P. Werbner (Ed.), *Social analysis 28, special issue: Person, myth and society in South Asian Islam* (pp. 38–50). Adelaide: University of Adelaide.

Mamdani, M. (2005). *Good Muslim, bad Muslim: Islam, the USA, and the global war against terror.* New Delhi: Permanent Black.

Meier, F. (2002). *Nachgelassene Schriften: Band. 1. Bemerkungen zur Mohammedverehrung.* Leiden: Brill.

Metcalf, B. D. (2014). Islam and democracy in India. In R. Jeffrey & R. Sen (Eds.), *Being Muslim in South Asia: Diversity and daily life* (pp. 18–41). New Delhi: Oxford University Press.

Mirahmadi, H., Farooq, M., & Ziad, W. (2010). *Traditional Muslim networks: Pakistan's untapped resource in the fight against terrorism.* Washington, DC: WORDE.

Muedini, F. (2015). *Sponsoring Sufism: How governments promote "mystical islam" in their domestic and foreign policies.* New York: Palgrave.

Nelson, M. J. (2014). Ilm and the individual: Religious education and religious ideas in Pakistan. In R. Jeffrey & R. Sen (Eds.), *Being Muslim in South Asia: Diversity and daily life* (pp. 161–180). New Delhi: Oxford University Press.

Okārvī, K. N. (2002). *Deoband se Bareilly: Ḥaqāʾiq.* Dihlī: Islāmik Pablisharz.

Paul, T. V. (2015). *The warrior state: Pakistan in the contemporary world.* New York: Oxford University Press.

Philippon, A. (2011). *Soufisme et politique au Pakistan: Le mouvement barelwi à l'heure de la guerre contre le terrorisme.* Paris: Karthala.

Qasmi, M. A. (2008). *What is Sunnat and What is Bidat? Innovation in Islam.* New Delhi: Adam Publishers.

Raza, I. A. (2005a). *Husam al-Haramain.* Stockport: Raza Academy Publication.

Raza, I. A. (2005b). *Search for the truth* (Vol. I). Stockport: Raza Academy Publication.

Raza, I. A. (2005c). *Thesis of Imam Ahmad Raza.* Durban: Barkaatur-Raza Publications.

Raza, I. A. (2005d). *Did Wahabiyyah existed in the time of the Prophet and Sahabah?* Stockport: Raza Academy Publication.

Raza Khan, I. A. (1897). *Forty Ahadiths on the intercession of the Holy Prophet (saw).* Mumbai: Tehreek-e-Fikr-e-Reza.

Raza Khan, I. A. (1903). *Manba al-Manīya. Divine vision.* Mumbai: Raza Academy.

Raza Khan, I. A. (1996). *The essentials of the Islamic faith. The importance of the highest respect for Allah Ta'ala and the Prophet (saw).* Lahore: Vision Islamic Publications (1908).

Raza Khan, I. A. (2007a). *Beacons of hope. The blessings of assistance from the solicitors of divine aid.* Mumbai: Raza Academy (1893).

Raza Khan, I. A. (2007b). *The validity of saying Ya Rasoolallah.* Mumbai: Raza Academy.

Sanyal, U. (1996). *Devotional Islam & politics in British India. Ahmad Riza Khan Barelwi and his movement, 1870–1920.* Delhi: Oxford University Press.

Sanyal, U. (2011). Barelwīs. In *Encyclopedia of Islam 3, 2011–1* (pp. 94–99). Leiden: Brill.

Schmitt, C. (2010). *Theorie des Partisanen: Zwischenbemerkung zum Begriff des Politischen.* Berlin: Duncker & Humblot.

Schnabel, N., Halabi, S., & Noor, M. (2013). Overcoming competitive victimhood and facilitating forgiveness through re-categorization into a common victim or perpetrator identity. *Journal of Experimental Social Psychology, 49*(5), 867–877.

Sedgwick, M. (2015). Sufis as 'Good Muslims': Sufism in the battle against Jihadi Salafism. In L. Ridgeon (Ed.), *Sufis and Salafis in the contemporary age* (pp. 105–117). London: Bloomsbury.

Suhaïl, D. A. A. (2002): *Barelwīyat kā ḍehnī Safar.* Deoband: Dār al-Kitāb.

van Ess, J. (2012). *Dschihad gestern und heute.* Berlin: De Gruyter.

von Clausewitz, C. (1963). *Vom Kriege.* Reinbek: Rowohlt.

Weismann, I. (2015). Modernity from within: Islamic Fundamentalism and Sufism. In L. Ridgeon (Ed.), *Sufis and Salafis in the contemporary age* (pp. 9–31). London: Bloomsbury.

Werbner, P. (2003). *Pilgrims of love. The anthropology of a global Sufi cult.* Bloomington: Indiana University.

Yusuf, M. (2014). Introduction. In M. Yusuf (Ed.), *Pakistan's counterterrorism challenge* (pp. 1–14). New Delhi: Foundation Books.

Zaman, M. Q. (2007). *Ashraf 'Ali Thanawi. Islam in modern South Asia.* Oxford: Oneworld.

CHAPTER 14

Fighting the Takfiris: Building an Inclusive American Muslim Community by Countering Anti-Shia Rhetoric in the USA

Raza Mir and Mohammad Ali Naquvi

On 5 February 2006, the annual Ashura procession in New York was wending its way down Park Avenue when it met with a group of young men who began shouting anti-Shia slogans, cursing the mourners and showering them with leaflets that pronounced the verdict of apostasy on all Shia Muslims. The situation became extremely volatile despite a sizeable police presence, as Shia youth, initially bemused by the protesters, began to get agitated. Luckily the situation was defused, but the altercation perhaps inaugurated the emergence into the public sphere of an organized anti-Shia sentiment in the USA. What had hitherto been seen only in the comments section of web-based articles and on other social media outlets was manifesting itself in the public sphere.

R. Mir (✉)
William Paterson University, Wayne, NJ, USA

M.A. Naquvi
Mohsena Memorial Foundation, Trenton, NJ, USA

© The Editor(s) (if applicable) and The Author(s) 2016   399
J. Syed et al. (eds.), *Faith-Based Violence and Deobandi Militancy in Pakistan*, DOI 10.1057/978-1-349-94966-3_14

The Shia community across North America roundly condemned this act, in several statements.[1] Perhaps hyperbolically, it referred to its antagonists as "Al Qaeda terrorists", though it turned out that the protesters were affiliated with a Salafi outfit called Islamic Thinkers Society,[2] an ultraconservative group that is based in New York and is affiliated with Al-Muhajiroun, a pro Al-Qaeda British extremist group. The group's website contains boilerplate denunciations of Shias as non-Muslims and support for ISIS.

As canaries in cages go, this is a worrisome development, which foretells of an emerging and slowly growing anti-Shia mobilization in the USA. This is unfortunate because intra-Muslim relations in the USA are marked for the most part by peaceful co-existence and mutual respect. There are, however, several increasing signs that some of the more militant extremists have begun to ratchet up the rhetoric against minority Muslims, such as the Shia, in the digital realm, in the financial arena (through supporting anti-Shia extremism in South Asia and the Middle East) and through these occasional face-offs that threaten to become violent. Among Shia groups, this form of militant anti-minorityism is referred to as the takfiri wave, referring to the penchant of these groups for tarring minorities with the label of apostasy (kufr).

The takfiri brush occasionally tars some Sunni groups, such as Sufis and Barelvis, as well, but much of the ire of these groups is directed at Shias, perhaps mirroring current geopolitical currents. Most takfiri ideologues in the USA subscribe to either the Deobandi or the Salafi ideologies, with Deobandis predominating among South Asian communities and Salafis predominating in the communities of Arab or Middle Eastern origin.

In this chapter we attempt to accomplish three things. The first is to map the arc of this growing anti-Shia rhetoric in the USA, which can trace horizontal transnational connections to similar, well-developed movements in South Asia and the Middle East. We tease out the linkages between these groups and their counterparts, such as the LeJ, the SSP the Taliban and ISIS. We also attempt to link the more militant anti-Shia movements in the USA to a subtler form of exclusion and disengagement—for example, the reluctance of Islamic studies departments across the country to include discussions of Shia fiqh while teaching Islamic jurisprudence, or in more extreme cases making wildly erroneous (and perhaps mischievous) links between the Shia faith and terrorism. The reluctance of some mainstream American Muslim organizations to support mobilizations against anti-Shia violence is another example of the mainstreaming of anti-Shia rhetoric in Muslim America.

The second section of this chapter is devoted to providing a counterexample, that of pan-Islamic harmony. It is fair to say that there are several examples of pan-Islamic inclusivity in the USA, which often run afoul of the takfiris. We will point towards several such examples where diverse Muslim communities have gathered together and organized in the spirit of harmony and communal sharing. In this regard it is important to note that all groups that are supportive of social justice, civil liberties and democratic rights are natural allies. To that end, we also point briefly towards non-Muslim groups that have rallied against the takfiris and made common cause with beleaguered Muslim groups, though we eschew any detailed discussion of this solidarity to stay within the remit of our chapter.

In the final section, we offer suggestions about how Muslim groups that are opposed to Salafi and Deobandi ideologies can assist in developing intrafaith initiatives and the marginalization of these extremist outfits, whose anti-Shia rhetoric is the tip of a very dangerous iceberg that threatens the foundations of religious freedoms for Muslims in the USA, and ends up legitimizing and strengthening the dangerous currents of Islamophobia that are increasingly becoming the norm there.

SHIAPHOBIA AND ANTI-SHIA RHETORIC

The dominant problem concerning Muslims in the USA continues to be that of rampant Islamophobia, a racist tendency that tars Shias and Sunnis alike, and denies any intra-Islamic heterogeneity in its construction of Muslims as a monolithic people, devoid of history and multiple identities (Mir et al. 2015). However, recent political events in the Middle East have brought a lot of sectarian tensions within Muslims to the fore, particularly in the shape of rising Salafi/Wahhabi and Deobandi puritanism, which manifests itself as an intolerance towards both intra-Islamic heterogeneity and non-Muslim faiths. We explore the roots and modes of this intolerance below.

Transnational Connections

The violent strains of anti-Shia sentiment in other parts of the world, such as Pakistan (Zahab 2004), Syria (Kazimi 2006), Saudi Arabia (Shakdam 2014) and the UK (Richards 2007), are well explored in other chapters. However, it would not be wrong to say that "Shiaphobia" is setting down roots in different parts of the intellectual and political sphere

(Patterson 2015), and that many terrorist groups operating in these parts of the world target the Shias as their primary quarry. Mainstream scholars and commentators focus primarily on the ways in which these groups target Westerners and espouse hatred for modernist ideologies, but it is instructive to note that within the takfiri sphere of influence, Shias (and, to a lesser extent, other Muslim minorities) remain the primary target, of both their doctrinal hatred and their practiced violence. For instance, the reporter Ben Taub has recounted in an extensive *New Yorker* article how ISIS kidnappers release their Christian hostages when the ransom is paid, but kill Shia hostages regardless (Taub 2015).

Overview of American Shiaphobia

The situation in the USA vis-à-vis intra-Islamic sectarian conflict appears relatively better than in the Middle East and South Asia. Shias and Sunnis have histories of working together, perhaps as a consequence of having to deal with the broader problem of Islamophobia. However, the current forms of sectarian conflict in the Middle East and South Asia have strained at the fabric of this togetherness. For example, Anwar al-Awlaki, the Yemeni-American Al-Qaeda recruiter who was killed by the USA in 2011, routinely peppered his anti-US talks with long diatribes against Shias.[3] The Canadian Muslim preacher Bilal Phillips often excoriates Shias as non-believers.[4] Likewise, Western preachers who claim that Sufism is not Islam[5] are extremely popular in the USA, and websites that denounce Barelvis as an "extreme Sufi sect" that is beyond the pale of Islam[6] find favor among those in the USA who subscribe to takfiri ideologies. This discrimination even extends to non-traditional realms—for example, the Washington DC-based Center for Islamic Pluralism published a 2008 report entitled *Black America, Prisons and Radical Islam*, in which it alleged that Muslim prison chaplains in the USA were, among other things, spreading anti-Shia propaganda.[7]

It is not our intention in this chapter to highlight all of the examples of anti-Shia rhetoric in the Muslim sphere. A careful analysis of the internet, including the comments section of a variety of Salafi/Wahhabi websites, will quickly underscore the growing strain of Shiaphobia in mainstream US circles. In this section we focus on those aspects of anti-Shia rhetoric in the USA which are far more muted but nonetheless emerge in a variety of intellectual and political realms. It is useful to remember at this stage that those who denounce the Shias also routinely denounce Sufis and Barelvis similarly, and to that extent any takfiri outfit is inimical to all of these groups. For geopolitical reasons, Shiaphobia is the flavor of the month among these outfits, their hostility to other Muslim groups notwithstanding.

History and Background

Anti-Shia sentiments in mainstream US spheres have a decades-long history. Shias, who were coming into their own in the 1970s, had flown under the radar of the mainstream US consciousness. This changed quite substantially with the 1979 Iranian Revolution and the subsequent US hostage crisis (Farber 2002). Much of the resentment against Muslims in the USA was focused on the Iranians, and by extension the Shiites were presented in the mainstream press as some sort of a violent and messianic cult. Subsequently the October 1983 bombing of the US Embassy in Beirut, where the primary suspect was Hezbollah, another organization with Shia roots, strengthened the general suspicion of Shias in the mainstream US consciousness. President Reagan's support of the mujahideen fighting the Soviets in Afghanistan, which became an integral part of US policy in the late stages of the Cold War (Mamdani 2004), was yet another alienating scenario since many of these fighters were Salafi and Wahhabi fundamentalists, whose hatred of Shias and Sufis/Barelvis was legion. Additionally, the USA had special diplomatic relationships with the Saudi regime, another government that persecuted Shias, denying them their civil liberties and religious freedom. Finally, in the Iran–Iraq War that broke out in 1980, the USA supported the regime of Saddam Hussein, who was a known oppressor of Shias. It would be generally accurate to say that the decade of 1980s was politically difficult for American Shias, as they walked the delicate balance between the emerging Islamophobia of the American mainstream and a perception of pro-Wahhabi diplomatic positions assumed by the US government.[8] While Saddam Hussein fell out of favor with the US after 1990, the tide did not change substantially. For example, there was hardly any public reaction in the USA when the Taliban, the newly emerging rulers of Afghanistan, slaughtered thousands of Hazara Shias in 1998 (Rashid 2001).

However, subtle shifts in the broader geopolitical discourse have created some issues for the Islamic community in the USA. In an about face that is arguably as reductive as past anti-Shia sentiment, political commentators routinely refer to violent acts perpetrated on innocent civilians by terrorist outfits such as ISIS as the handiwork of "Sunni extremists" (Bryen 2015). This, of course, feeds into the dominant rhetoric of the violent extremists, who attempt to draw a false Islam–West binary, which excludes Islamic minorities from its formulation.

The Modus Operandi of American Shiaphobia

The Shiaphobia wave in the USA is muted compared with that in other parts of the world, but it is exerted through more subtle forms of anti-Shia sentiment that are arguably more insidious than open confrontations. Some of the problems include the following:

1. *(Mischievously) erroneous depictions of the events of Karbala*: The Islamic world is characterized by a consensus that Imam Husayn's martyrdom at Karbala on 10 Muhurram, 61 AH, was a paradigmatic event in Islamic history, where the forces of Yazid were characterized as the epitome of evil, and the army of Imam Husayn was understood as the paragon of moral fortitude, religious forbearance and social justice. However, in the recent past, tendencies have emerged that attempt to underplay the importance of this event, the role of Husayn in Islamic history, and Yazid's infamy and tyranny. For instance, when one of the co-authors of this chapter studied Islamic jurisprudence at the American University in Cairo in 2008 as part of a summer law program, the director of the program presented a published paper of his own on the last day of class. The thesis of this paper was that today's modern-day suicide bombing originates from Husayn's stand at Karbala because he knew he was going to die. This representation of Imam Husayn's death as a suicide has a shameful history in *Wahhabi* ideology, which the professor has adopted lock stock and barrel (Freamon 2003). In that context, one can clearly read similar malafide intentions in the revisionist accounts emerging from Salafi scholars that depict Imam Husayn as having erred in taking on the forces of Yazid, the assertion that Yazid was a just king who was appalled to learn that his generals had over-reached at Karbala[9] and so forth. The intention here is not to debate the authenticity of these statements but to depict them as acts of mischief aimed at undermining the Islamic consensus that had been cemented over centuries, and which allowed Muslims of all sects to observe the events of Karbala as a tragedy.

2. *Oppression through Exclusion*: It has been well documented by scholars working in the field of ethnic studies that exclusion by marginalization constitutes a powerful strategy whereby dominant groups render minorities near powerless (Lewis 2005). If one can develop a corpus of work that systematically excludes and ignores the marginalized groups in a community, the act renders those groups invisible. Ideology works primarily through the process of universalizing sectional interests, and presenting the views of dominant groups as the official account of history and principle. To that end, many Salafi groups have embarked on a process where discussions of Islam ignore its diversity, and systematically exclude Shias, Sufis and Barelvis from their analysis. For example, classes entitled "Islamic Jurisprudence" on college campuses across the country overwhelmingly teach the four Sunni *madhabs* (sub-sects or schools of jurisprudence) with little to no mention of the Jafari school of jurisprudence. Even the fairly progressive Zaytuna College of Hayward, California, which recently became a US-accredited liberal arts college that offers a BA in Islamic law and theology, did so without including Shia jurisprudence in the curriculum.[10] The Salafi intellectuals in the Western space thus seek to redefine Islam according to their strict principles of austerity, which indirectly abets fatwas that are subsequently issued by extremist clerics declaring minority groups as apostates (and, therefore, legitimate targets of violence).

3. *Inability or Unwillingness to Support Oppressed Shias and Sufis*: Arguably, most Sunnis are as disgusted by anti-Shia violence as any Shia. However, mainstream Islamic organizations are often slow to condemn the violence or to label it as such. This is consistent with studies in other spheres that suggest that mainstream majority communities are a bit blind to anti-minority prejudice, For example, when Hurricane Katrina hit the Gulf Coast of the USA in 2005, psychologists analyzed how the response of White liberal groups tended to be slower to condemn the racially discriminatory nature of the government response (Adams et al. 2006). A similar situation has emerged in the USA where mainstream Islamic groups, while being opposed to anti-Shia violence, are slower to recognize its urgency and its hateful nature. For instance, an event entitled Pakistan in Crisis: Gender, Minority Rights & Shia Genocide was organized by one of the co-authors in 2013 at New York University, and multiple Muslim and other campus organizations co-sponsored the event. However, the undergraduate Muslim Student Association refused to associate with the event, saying that it did not

agree with the term "genocide" in the title. Unfortunately, the principle of moral hazard begins to apply here. If the selective beheading of Hazara Shias in Afghanistan, or the bombing of Shia mosques in Kuwait and Sufi shrines in Pakistan, are not condemned by Muslim groups in the same way that they condemn, say, the murder of innocent civilians in Paris, it presents a picture of disunity, and suggests that violence against Muslim groups in the name of Islam is not as prevalent or abhorrent.

4. *Shutting Shias out of the Governance of Pan-Islamic University Bodies:* Historians of minority mobilization have noted that while minorities are often welcomed into the rank and file of mainstream organizations, their exclusion from positions of leadership in these institutions remains a marker of their overall marginalization (Arnesen 1998). An unfortunate development in the Muslim world in the USA has been the subtle exclusion of Shia groups from the leadership, and sometimes the membership, of student organizations that claim to speak for Islam. For example, most observant Shia students of Rutgers University are associated with an organization called Ahlul-Bayt Student Association (ABSA). It is a relatively recent part of the student government umbrella of organizations and, according to its Shia members, it was principally created because the existing Muslim student group, the Rutgers University-Muslim Students Association (MSA), began to cool towards, and eventually marginalized, its Shia members, particularly as broader political strains between Shias/Sufis and Salafis began to be felt worldwide. By some accounts, the student group attempted to rewrite its constitution to ensure that Shias were not eligible for a post on its governance council and refused to fund any Muharram programming using the MSA budget. Some Shia Rutgers students then used the student life initiatives at the university to register ABSA, an organization that attempts to be inclusive of all Muslims but certainly has a strong Shia influence. Sadly, this is indicative of the experience of many Shia Muslims on various campuses around the country. The dispersion within the Muslim organizations in the USA has an unfortunate side-effect of fragmenting a minority population, thereby weakening its power of advocacy and mobilization. And, arguably, doing so in the formative college years where Shia and Sunni Muslims are more likely to interact on a regular basis, this initiates young people for a life of disunity in their future Muslim communities as working adults with families.

5. *Direct Confrontations with Shias:* Perhaps as a direct consequence of the above, we have begun to see direct verbal and digital confrontations within Islamic groups, with the takfiris playing their favorite card, the edict of apostasy. For instance, respected ideologues, such as the current Dean of Academic Affairs at the Houston-based Al-Maghrib Institute, have been on record denouncing Shias (and Sufis) as "heretics" (Elliot 2011). We have already discussed how revisionist histories of the events of Karbala attempt to absolve Yazid of culpability in the death of Imam Husayn. Of course, the transnational character of the internet ensures that American residents routinely participate in chats that accuse Shias of being the true killers of Imam Husayn, be they hosted in the UK[11] or South Asia. The current US entente with Iran and the Iraqi Shias following the threat of ISIS has arguably fractured the relations between Shias and Sunnis further. In general, a variety of American social scientists have called for greater engagement of the US government with Shias (Rhode 2013), which has angered the takfiri lobby further.

It is very important to contextualize these acts of intellectual hostility. Prima facie, the disagreements between different sects of Islam in the USA are minor compared with the heated rhetoric in far-off lands such as Pakistan and Syria. Moreover, in the USA and in most parts of the world, relations between Islamic communities are civil and cordial, with a shared Islamic ethos predominating over any differences in jurisprudence. Many of the sectarian conflicts between Muslim groups have origins that are deeply embedded in political economy rather than religious difference. At the level of interaction between civilian groups, one rarely encountered much tension until the advent of an aggressive strain of Wahhabi proselytizing around the 1980s. This, of course, has a history that is unrelated to theological differences but is primarily geopolitical in character. The pressures on the Saudi monarchy escalated in the 1980s on several counts, including the Iranian Revolution of 1979, which was followed by Khomeini's popular call for an anti-imperialist pan-Islamic identity, the emergence of violent extremists within the kingdom that led to the siege of the Holy Mosque in Mecca in the late 1970s (Wright 2006), and a call towards Arab nationalism on the part of those who sided with Iraq in the Iran–Iraq War. In a search for legitimacy, Saudis began a grand project of Salafi/Wahhabi appeasement, which included global outreach towards diasporic Muslims, seeking to convert them towards Salafi ideals.

Mosques were promised funding if they adhered to Salafi principles and invited Salafi preachers to become their spiritual leaders. While this was more pronounced in South Asia and the Far East, similar strategies were also adopted in the West, including the USA. In South Asia, one can map a clear intensification in the vilification of Ahmadis, Barelvis and Shias in the 1980s, a strain that had to be felt among the diasporic communities in other parts of the world. For example, when one of the co-authors traveled to Chile in 2010 and met with leaders of a local Shia center in Santiago, the founder relayed a story that is all too familiar in Muslim communities: the first mosque in the city was started by Shias and Sunnis together but eventually, due to Saudi funding and the installation of a Salafi preacher, the Shias were slowly pushed out and had to establish a center of their own.

We argue that these developments have had a disproportionate effect on the Shia–Salafi dynamic in the USA. As Benedict Anderson argues in his book, *Imagined Communities*, diasporic groups construct their identities in the absence of a lived experience of sharing, and therefore exert disproportionate pulls on their home environments, fueled by the power of print media as well as circuits of financial repatriations (Anderson 2006). Since the advent of the internet, a variety of options have become available to such groups, including the recruitment of ISIS conscripts through social media, the uploading of hypercritical videos, and the proxy arguments between religious groups in religious forums (Callimachi 2015). It is important to understand that much of the hysteria about "terrorist funding" and "extremist chatter" in the mainstream press within US circles is no more than an Islamophobic response to religious self-expression by Muslims. Nonetheless, the extreme end of these spaces does harbor a hateful rhetoric that is then deployed to justify, and occasionally fund, global anti-Shia violence. Within the US space it is an extremely difficult ethical terrain for principled Shia activists. On the one hand, they need to speak out against radical anti-Shia outfits that seek to politicize the interdenominational differences, often through the simple-minded reiteration of the canard that Shias are not Muslims, and through the attribution of all manner of unsubstantiated beliefs and practices to Shias. In many ways it is as much an act of "race-making" as anti-black rhetoric in the USA (see, e.g., Omi and Winant 2014 on racial formation in the USA; it could well be a template for the formulation of a Shia identity through the practices of representation).

On the other hand, the much more urgent dilemma in the USA is the ongoing and pervasive project of Islamophobia, which uses very much the same templates at a more macrolevel, and makes no distinctions between intra-Islamic heterogeneity, thereby posing an existential danger to all Muslims, ironically including the Salafis and Deobandis as well (Gottschalk and Greenberg 2008). The imperative of combating Islamophobia makes intra-Muslim dialogue and inclusivity even more urgent, especially in the USA. For example, in the aftermath of the attacks in Paris in November 2015, a dangerous strain of right-wing reactionary discourse emerged. Led by respected politicians who were running for the presidency of the USA, they began to demand that the USA should only accept Christian Syrian refugees (Davidson 2015), making the outrageous and unconstitutional demand that the USA start keeping tabs on its entire Muslim population by requiring ID cards and maintaining a database of all Muslims (Ballhaus 2015), and spreading the false narrative that US mosques were hotbeds of terrorism sheltering "sleeper cells" of people planning attacks on the USA (Hohman 2015). The opposition to the proposed Islamic Community Center named Park 51 in New York, scurrilously labeled the "Ground Zero Mosque" by extremists of various stripes (Carlin and Khan 2011), is a stark reminder that within the USA the strains of Islamophobia are on the rise, getting more virulent, and internecine Muslim conflicts play into the hands of those very illiberal groups that are determined to strip Muslims of their democratic rights and civil liberties.

To summarize, while these tensions within Islamic sects in the USA are relatively minor compared with those in other parts of the world, they nonetheless present a deterioration, which does not bode well for the future of the Muslim community. Much of the blame for this lack of inclusivity between the denominations can be laid at the door of the takfiris, who take their cues from horizontal transnational connections to parts of the world where these tensions are much more pronounced, especially in the contemporary era. These differences are exacerbated by the limited interactions between these denominations, which is even more pronounced in the virtual realm, where echo chambers amplify the differences and make the denunciations of Shias more sharp-edged, illiberal and violent. However, intra-Islamic tensions in the USA are far weaker than the dominant tension that afflicts American Muslims equally—that of virulent, violent and state-sanctioned Islamophobia. To that end we argue that the Muslims of the USA are in a position to provide templates whereby Muslims of different sects can cooperate, and perhaps work together on common causes. These examples of coordinated action have the potential to inform and inspire other parts of the world as well.

SHIA–SUNNI COOPERATION AGAINST TAKFIRIS

Whereas there has been a rise in anti-Shia sentiment in the USA due mainly to developing crises and geopolitics in the Middle East, the Iranian nuclear deal, and a perceived "Shia Revival" in the region (Nasr 2006), it is also important to highlight examples of Shia–Sunni cooperation in light of rising extremism, takfirism and the rise of ISIS. It is important not to view these different forms of illiberalism in the Islamic world as separate entities but to see them as a confluence of strands. For example, there is a lot that the South Asian Deobandis have in common with the Taliban and Salafis from a philosophical standpoint. Their understanding of Islam is predicated far more on the vilification of Islamic minorities than on the separation of Islam from other faiths. To that end, the pronunciation of edicts of apostasy against Muslim minorities is their stock in trade, and thus the term takfiris is appropriate to describe them. However, many Muslim scholars who take religious study seriously have sounded clarion calls for unity between different Islamic groups. They argue that this unity must not be predicated upon the dissolution of differences between the different groups, but rather to acknowledge them, honor them and then look for ways in which they can make common cause based on shared principles, practices and socio-religious amity. Recently a Shia scholar and the only active mujtahid in North America, Sayyid Sulayman Hassan Abidi, President of Ahlul Bayt Seminary in Streamwood, Illinois, made an eloquent plea among Shia congregants to work for Shia–Sunni unity based on the same principles.[12] Sheikh Hamza Yusuf, an influential American Sunni scholar and Co-founder of Zaytuna Institute, has made similar pronouncements asking for intra-Islamic unity.[13] One can find numerous instances of such calls for unity, and we would like in this chapter to focus on a few other examples where such initiatives have been made, in both the oratorical and the organizational space in the USA.

Muharram in Manhattan and the Role of Chaplains

The first and most shining example of this is the Muharram in Manhattan program at the Islamic Center of New York University (ICNYU).[14] The program was set up in 2010 despite initial reluctance from the ICNYU leadership. The first year started as one majlis[15] to gauge reaction to such an event in a predominantly Sunni Muslim, albeit academic, environment on campus. Although the center is located at an academic institution, it serves the local New York City Muslim population, with programming almost every day. The initial majlis was well received, and in the second year the program was split between ICNYU, Columbia University (sponsored by the MSA), and a local community organization called Alwan for the Arts with a total of five majlises. In its third year the program ran for nine days, split between ICNYU and Park51 Community Center, alias the "Ground Zero Mosque". This allowed the program to provide important crossovers between student groups and community outfits, and also to counter some of the notoriety associated with the Park51 center. This helped it to develop organically, based on the needs of different audiences.

The idea was to develop an all-English Muharram program during the first 10 days of Mohurrum observance, not only for Shia Muslims but also for all those who had an interest in learning about the events of Karbala. Speakers varied from the noted author of *The Tragedy of Karbala*, Syed-Mohsin Naquvi, to the former Iraqi Ambassador to the UN, Hamid Al-Bayati, as well as other Shia and Sunni scholars. After six years the program has now matured and runs similarly to Muharram programs around the world, where one speaker is invited to talk for the first 10 days leading up to Ashura, and amateur poets recite lamentations before and after the main lecture. The stark difference in this program, though, is that the entire observance, including the poetry, is done in English and at least half the audience are non-Shia. In fact, a handful of people over the years have been reported to convert to Shiaism after learning about Karbala and Shia Islam because of the Muharram in Manhattan program, with many Shias who had otherwise lost interest in the observance within an *imambara* (Shia mosque and the attached hall for religious gatherings) atmosphere returning to their roots because they felt more comfortable in this novel environment.

In its fourth year, the entire program was held at ICNYU, and a Muharram fund was established at the university where donors could directly contribute. This is the first predominantly Sunni center in North America, and perhaps the world, with a dedicated fund for Shia programming. In fact, just before the start of the last Muharram, on 9 October 2015, in his Friday khutba, Muslim Chaplain Imam Khalid Latif delivered a more radical different and enlightening take on the observance than the Sunni community is used to hearing.[16]

He said in part:

I would encourage those of us who are not familiar with the tragedies that take place in the month of Muharram to take the time to go and understand and read our history. And that's a Muslim history, not a Sunni or a Shia history. And to be able to relate and connect to every character that is there and to understand really, what are they made of? That they were able to move forward in the face of such atrocity, in the face of such challenge, and still say that the next world is more important than this one. That Allah is greater than all of this. That I will not compromise on my relationship with the Divine for anything of this dunya (world). It's for you and me to take from, not from anybody else. It's for you and me to reflect on, to make the individual decision. And it starts in being honest with yourself. Do you really believe that honesty drives you? Do you believe that integrity drives you? ... I would encourage that you engage and take in some capacity. Push your comfort zone, and not for anybody else's sake. Not to prove that you are somehow open-minded and you will be present in gatherings. Let this Muharram be about your heart ... and yield to the idea that there is immense opportunity for gain and rejuvenation. We just have to decide whether it's something we want to take for ourselves or not.

Imam Khalid Latif is not the only religious leader to use the metaphor of Karbala as a symbol of Islamic unity. A few days after his sermon, in October 2015, the Sunni Muslim Chaplain at Princeton University, Imam Sohaib Sultan, released a video on the commemoration of Muharram with a strong intrafaith focus, saying in part[17]:

And the women were taken into a state of bondage and enslaved. And it is the women like Zainab, may God be pleased with her, the granddaughter of the Prophet (pbuh), who survived that incident. And she against all odds tells the story and carries on the legacy of Imam Husayn, which was really the message of Imam Hasan, which was really the message of Imam Ali, which was really the message of our beloved messenger Muhammad, peace and blessings be upon him. So this month of Muharram, we recommit ourselves to standing with those who are oppressed, with feeding those who are hungry, with giving water to those who are thirsty, with giving shelter to those who are homeless, with clothing those who are naked. And this month we are forced to answer this very simple question, "do we stand with the oppressed or do we stand with the oppressors?" Let this question guide our lives and our spirits and our souls and all of our affairs.

Community Organizing, Social Justice and the Law

Another example of Shia–Sunni cooperation is the coming together of 37 Muslim organizations in New Jersey, both Shia and Sunni, to issue a joint statement against takfirism and, specifically, ISIS. This led to the formation of a group called the Shia-Sunni Alliance of New Jersey, which continues to cooperate in sharing information and planning joint initiatives that bring communities together. The philosophy behind the group is to strengthen the mainstream Muslim community with inclusivity as a foundational principle, which will help to marginalize extremist takfiri elements. Initially there was reluctance by some organizations to sign the statement because they did not want to lose support from donors that mihht identify with the Wahhabi doctrine. Ultimately, however, positive peer pressure won them over.[18]

As mentioned earlier, mainstream US groups working for civil liberties have cooperated with Shia and Sunni Muslims, working in concert for the common cause of safeguarding their citizenship rights. A good example of this phenomenon was the lawsuit filed by Muslim advocates and the secular Center for Constitutional Rights in June 2012, *Hassan* vs. *City of New York*, against the New York Police Department for spying on Islamic schools, Muslim businesses and mosques in New Jersey.[19] One of the 11 plaintiffs in the case is the largest Shia masjid in New Jersey, and the head plaintiff named in the title is an observant Shia and Iraq War veteran. In October 2015, Judge Thomas L. Ambro wrote a blistering decision for the USA Court of Appeals for the Third Circuit saying in part:

> What occurs here in one guise is not new. We have been down similar roads before. Jewish-Americans during the Red Scare, African-Americans during the Civil Rights Movement, and Japanese-Americans during World War II are examples that readily spring to mind. We are left to wonder why we cannot see with foresight what we see so clearly with hindsight—that "[l]oyalty is a matter of the heart and mind[,] not race, creed, or color."[20]

Although the case is ongoing, this latest decision shows the positive effects of intrafaith organizing against Islamophobic policies for American Muslims as a whole and, ultimately, all communities of color.

In line with this strategy are various social justice movements in the country, such as Muslims for Ferguson,[21] that are bringing American Muslims together with African-American communities against police brutality, demanding law-enforcement reform and accountability. Specifically, a newly founded social services center in Trenton, New Jersey, the Husayn Center for Social Justice, is bringing together Shia, Sunni and African-American communities to further diversify this work under broad Islamic principles to help the marginalized and underprivileged in society. As a first-of-its-kind Muslim social institution, it holds great promise to accelerate already existing movements and bring more Muslims of all backgrounds together to inform the American public about the true spirit of Islam through social action. Institutions like these are essential to indirectly defeat the strain of takfirism that exists in the Muslim diaspora.

Academic Institutions as Incubators of Change

The role of New York University (NYU) and Princeton University in providing safe spaces for ecumenical and inclusive chaplains such as Imam Khalid Latif and Imam Sohaib Sultan cannot be understated. Other academic institutions have also participated in these incipient attempts to create spaces where all Muslim groups can operate together. One hopes that these bodies function as incubators, allowing younger Muslims to gain valuable experience of working together, an experience that they can then take forward into the world at large.

Along with sermons, a constructive role is being played by academic conferences. For example, various universities conduct Prophet Muhammad Day and Husayn Day events, where people of different religious persuasions can reflect on the broader social impact of these Islamic personages respected by a great majority of Muslims. From discussing and celebrating religious figures, this approach is slowly moving towards addressing issues of potential conflict as well. For instance, a conference hosted in April 2015 by Bayan Claremont College in California, entitled Sectarian Peace/Conflict in Religions: The Middle East and the Globe, provided a great framework for what such Muslim institutions can do to foster cooperation among different Muslim communities. The stated purpose of the conference was as follows:

> Sectarian tension is a reality of all religious traditions that leads to myriad forms of interactions among coreligionists ranging from tolerant coexistence to most impulsive violence. The emergence of sects seems to be inevitable, for the fundamental teachings of any religion allows multiplicity of interpretations. The irreducible plurality of possible interpretations of

religious teachings indicates that sects will always exist and the well-being of a particular religious tradition will depend on maintaining a comprehensive framework in which the difference of opinion is perceived as legitimate and, moreover, a source of richness. Muslim history provides ample examples of peaceful coexistence among sects and schools of thought showing that constructing such an inclusive framework is possible, both theoretically and practically, within Islamic tradition. At this particular point in history, however, sectarian violence seems to have escalated among Muslims. This conference aims to look at the political-economic-textual root causes of sectarian hubris, the recent rising wave of sectarian violence in the Middle East, and its possible impact on Muslims residing in other parts of the globe. The conference will also attempt to offer a road map to transcend the predicaments of the current sectarian strife.

And as we write this chapter, plans are under way by a major predominantly Sunni Muslim organization, Muslim Community Network (MCN), to put on a workshop in New York City for the Muslim community to counter increasing anti-Shia rhetoric in mosques following the Iran nuclear deal and rising sectarianism in the Middle East. The goal is to eventually generate a statement of mutual respect and inclusion to be signed by American Muslim organizations, Shia and Sunni, across the city.

As more and more individual Muslims, groups and organizations see the urgent need and utility of intrafaith community-building, it would be useful to provide specific ideas whereby different groups can make intra-Muslim collaboration a part of their activism. In the next section we discuss different ways in which such collaboration can be made possible. Our focus here is the USA, though the template could be used in other geographic spheres.

Towards an Inclusive American Muslim Community

In the earlier two sections, we identified and described two competing strains among Muslims in the USA. The first can be referred to as "sectism" (Watt 2005), a process whereby one sect ideologically arrogates to itself the right to define the entire religious space. Within the USA, the takfiri groups have attempted, with marginal success, to speak for Muslims in general (Sagini 2014). This process demands an "other", which can then be vilified and expelled from the self-drawn boundaries of religion, a rhetorical move that fans the flames of sectarian violence in other parts of the world. For the most part, Shias, along with other disenfranchised Muslim minorities, stand in for this "other." It is worthwhile noting that extreme ideologies have always functioned similarly in all spheres, be they Nazis in Germany, ultraxenophobic Hutus in Rwanda, or the Ku Klux Klan in the southern USA in the late nineteenth century. Their modus operandi is to designate a minority as standing in for the absence of purity in society, and enact ritualized violence against it in the name of "protecting the pure". The response to this violence must necessarily be made at multiple levels, including the intellectual, for unless one halts its momentum, it typically accelerates its way to genocide (Werbner 1997). The specter of genocide haunts Islamic minorities, especially in certain vulnerable geographies, and we underestimate the rhetorical power of these violent groups at our own peril.

However, attempts and practices by takfiris to justify their violent depredations in the name of religious practice have not gone uncontested. The second strain of organizing we have described here relates to direct collaboration among different denominations within Islam, which interrupt the talk of one group being right and the other being wrong, and focus instead on a shared ethos within Islam. For instance, Shias and Sunnis throughout the USA have engaged in the process of productive dialogue, friendly relations and mutual respect, adding a vital counterweight to these illiberal tendencies. We have attempted in the earlier section to acknowledge and highlight some of these interdenominational initiatives.

Here we attempt to offer a brief manifesto for the emergence of an inclusive American Muslim community. This community must be predicated upon a joint effort by Shias, Sunnis and concerned non-Muslims to take on the divisive agenda of the takfiris. So:

1. We first propose that every Islamic conference conducted in the USA needs to have a main session entitled "Understanding Shiaism", where they invite a Shia scholar to explain the fundamentals, clear up misconceptions, and take questions from the audience with a strong moderator who can handle hecklers in the audience. The issue should be framed as one of religious freedom within Islam and the US Constitution. Unfortunately, mainstream "Islamic" conferences in the USA have a default Sunni template, usually dominated by Salafi and Deobandi clerics, which is counterproductive. This act of acknowledging and honoring Muslim minorities in these spheres will have the effect of introducing the participants of these conferences to the

diversity within the religion in an atmosphere of civility and legitimacy, thereby predisposing them towards an understanding of the beliefs of different minority groups.

2. We propose that, in the academic arena, classes named "Islamic jurisprudence" in Western universities must include Shia law in their syllabus. If the professor is not trained in it, a visiting lecturer should be invited to teach those classes. It is important to reiterate that one of the constituents of the rainbow that represents Islamic jurisprudence is the *Jafari fiqh*, (Shia Islamic jurisprudence), followed by more than 350 million Muslims. Islamic jurists ignore it at their own peril, the peril of being incomplete and therefore not legitimate in its claims to being "Islamic."

3. As the numerically dominant group, the onus is on the Sunni community to reach out to Shia centers in their area to hold joint events, such as Eid celebrations. Especially on festive occasions, a space can be opened up for harmonious interaction, rather than atomized events in denomination-defined spaces, where the separation of Sunnis and Shias becomes needlessly reinforced at the sociocultural level. Likewise, one must understand that Sufi practices in Islam have a long history and are not incompatible with Islamic beliefs. The spread of Islam to different parts of the world, especially Turkey, Central Asia and South Asia, was accomplished by Sufi saints, which of course led to syncretic practices being adopted by these groups as multiple cultures came under the Islamic banner. Just as Muslims all over the world subscribe to different cultural practices relating to food, marriage ceremonies, dress and social gatherings, so too their modes of worship exhibit diversity. However, none of these deviate from generalized Islamic principles, and recognition of this diversity is essential to intra-Islamic harmony.

4. In the same vein, we recommend that predominantly Sunni organizations that aspire to an "Islamic" imprimatur must reach out to representatives from diverse Shia communities and invite them onto their boards to make sure any distinct needs and concerns of the local Shia community are being heard and addressed. Of course, there will be organizations that are predominantly related to a particular sect, and one need not seek diversity in those outfits, but any organization that seeks to speak for the Muslim community at large must make a conscious effort to diversify their membership, their leadership and their field of activism so as to begin creating an inclusive American Muslim narrative.

5. Shia organizations need to police their own communities to ensure that the rhetoric from their pulpits does not degenerate into name-calling against Islamic historical figures revered by Sunnis. This is an ongoing project, with edicts from various Shia leaders proscribing vituperations against historical figures that are revered by other Muslim groups. Similarly, Sunni organizations need to call upon their leadership to halt name-calling of Islamic figures that are revered by Shias. In South Asia in particular, Deobandi clerics often refer to Hazrat Abu Talib, the uncle of the Prophet Mohammad, as a kafir, which is primarily a mischievous ploy aimed at taunting Shias. Such practices need to be condemned by all Muslim groups.

6. Finally, it is essential that all Muslim organizations unequivocally condemn takfirism jointly, wherever it comes from. One of the falsehoods perpetrated in the Islamophobic sphere is that moderate Muslims are slow to condemn terrorism and violence by Muslims. That is of course a false assertion,[22] but a joint response by all Muslims, led by Sunni groups, against anti-Shia violence will go a long way towards creating an atmosphere of inclusion.

Takfiri groups do no favors to Islam. They vitiate the atmosphere within Muslim communities, fan the flames of Islamophobia, and produce an atmosphere of mistrust and hatred. All right-thinking Muslims in the USA need to unite and produce a measured response to these hate-fueled tendencies. Our commitment as activists working for social justice demands this response, and it has the potential to produce traditions of inclusiveness in other parts of the world as well.

NOTES

1. One statement can be seen here: http://al-huda.al-khoei.org/news/63/ARTICLE/1117/2006-02-07.html.
2. The website of the group is at http://islamicthinkers.com/. Their views on Shias can be accessed at http://islamicthinkers.com/welcome/?p=1177. Their statements in support of ISIS can be seen at http://islamicthinkers.com/welcome/?p=1256.
3. Many such sermons survive in the public realm as videos. For example, see https://www.youtube.com/watch?v=jk9jWp9oa48.
4. See https://www.youtube.com/watch?v=3hnIERpeFDI.
5. See https://www.youtube.com/watch?v=atKMRZ5snTA.

6. See http://islamqa.info/en/150265.
7. See http://www.islamicpluralism.org/CIPReports/CIPPrisonReport. pdf.
8. Of course, this perception was inaccurate. As Mahmood Mamdani points out, the US relationship with Islamic extremists throughout the Middle East and South Asia was an extension of their determination to win the Cold War by "all means necessary" (Mamdani 2004, p. 13). However, it is accurate to say that the USA was willing to tolerate excesses against Shia minorities by the ruling classes of Saudi Arabia and Iraq, and the militias of Afghanistan, in favor of anti-communist cooperation.
9. See https://www.youtube.com/watch?v=nm7mKOTZ0qQ, which shows a video of the US ideologue Yasir Qadhi, expounding on these assertions in an articulate, if wildly inaccurate, assertion. The fact that this video has been viewed more than 250,000 times reflects not only its power but the emerging rhetoric of urbane apologetics regarding the role of Yazid in Karbala, and subtle attempts to undermine the well-accepted idea in Islamic history across sects that the sacrifice of Imam Husayn was a paradigmatic event in Islamic history.
10. See https://www.zaytuna.edu/academics/bachelors_program.
11. For example, see http://www.exploring-islam.com/hussain-and-yazid. html.
12. See https://www.youtube.com/watch?v=QGFt8gFGG20.
13. See https://www.youtube.com/watch?v=Ai3vPxJwNUY.
14. See http://muharraminmanhattan.com/.
15. A majlis is a gathering that observes the events of Karbala. It is quite common all over the world to have these events in the first 10 days of the month of Mohurrum.
16. See https://www.youtube.com/watch?v=Teyuo5yobGg.
17. See https://vimeo.com/142318008.
18. The full statement with signatures can be found at: http://www.iscj. org/Resources/Announcements/Joint%20Shia%20Sunni%20 Statement.pdf?hc_location=ufi.
19. See https://www.muslimadvocates.org/endspying.
20. Seehttp://www.muslimadvocates.org/files/Hassan-3rd-Cir-Ruling-10-13-15.pdf.
21. See https://www.facebook.com/Muslims4Ferguson/.
22. See http://theamericanmuslim.org/tam.php/features/articles/muslim_voices_against_extremism_and_terrorism_part_i_fatwas/0012209 for an incomplete list of Muslim responses to terrorism.

REFERENCES

Adams, G., O'Brien, L. T., & Nelson, J. C. (2006). Perceptions of racism in Hurricane Katrina: A liberation psychology analysis. *Analyses of Social Issues and Public Policy, 6*(1), 215–235.

Anderson, B. (2006). *Imagined communities: Reflections on the origin and spread of nationalism.* London: Verso Books.

Arnesen, E. (1998). Up from exclusion: Black and white workers, race, and the state of labor history. *Reviews in American History, 26*(1), 146–174.

Ballhaus, R. (2015, November 20). Donald trump draws fire for comments on Muslim database. *The Wall Street Journal.* Archived at http://blogs.wsj.com/washwire/2015/11/20/donald-trump-draws-fire-for-comments-on-muslim-database/. Accessed 20 Dec 2015.

Bryen, S. (2015, November 4). Sunni extremists may have downed Russian airbus. *San Diego Jewish World.* Archived at http://www.sdjewishworld.com/2015/11/04/sunni-extremists-may-have-downed-russian-airbus/. Accessed 20 Dec 2015.

Callimachi, R. (2015, June 27). ISIS and the lonely young American. *New York Times.* Archived at http://www.nytimes.com/2015/06/28/world/americas/isis-online-recruiting-american.html. Accessed 20 Dec 2015.

Carlin, N., & Khan, H. (2011). Mourning, memorials, and religion: A psychoanalytic perspective on the Park51 controversy. *Religions, 2*(2), 114–131.

Davidson, A. (2015, November 16). Ted Cruz's religious test for Syrian refugees. *The New Yorker.* Archived at http://www.newyorker.com/news/amy-davidson/ted-cruzs-religious-test-for-syrian-refugees. Accessed 20 Dec 2015.

Elliott, A. (2011, March 20). Why Yasir Qadhi wants to talk about Jihad. *New York Times.* Archived at http://www.nytimes.com/2011/03/20/magazine/mag-20Salafis-t.html. Accessed 20 Dec 2015.

Farber, D. (2002). *Taken hostage: The Iran hostage crisis and America's first encounter with radical Islam.* Princeton: Princeton University Press.

Freamon, B. K. (2003). Martyrdom, suicide, and the Islamic law of war: A short legal history. *Fordham International Law Journal, 27,* 299–369.

Gottschalk, P., & Greenberg, G. (2008). *Islamophobia: Making Muslims the enemy.* New York: Rowman & Littlefield.

Hohman, L. (2015, January 15). Sheriffs sound off on jihad training camps in the US. *WND.* Archived at http://www.wnd.com/2015/01/sheriffs-sound-off-on-jihad-training-camps-in-u-s/. Accessed 15 Jan 2015.

Kazimi, N. (2006). Zarqawi's Anti-Shia legacy: Original or borrowed? *Current Trends in Islamist Ideology, 4,* 53–72.

Lewis, G. (2005). Welcome to the margins: Diversity, tolerance, and policies of exclusion 1. *Ethnic and Racial Studies, 28*(3), 536–558.

Mamdani, M. (2004). *Good Muslim, bad Muslim: America, the cold war, and the roots of terror.* New York: Doubleday.

Mir, A. Toor, S. & Mir, R. (2015). Of Race And Religion: Understanding the Roots of Anti-Muslim Prejudice in the US. In Bendl, R., Bleijenberah, I., Henttonen, E., and Mills, A. J. [Eds.] *The Oxford Handbook of Diversity in Organizations.* Oxford, Oxford University Press (pp. 499–517).

Nasr, S. W. (2006). *The Shia revival: How conflicts within Islam will shape the future.* New York: WW Norton Press.

Omi, M., & Winant, H. (2014). *Racial formation in the United States.* New York: Routledge.

Patterson, M. (2015). The Shi'a spring: Shi'a resistance and the Arab spring movement in the GCC states. *Mathal, 4*(1), 3–27.

Rashid, A. (2001). *Taliban: Militant Islam, oil and fundamentalism in Central Asia.* New Haven: Yale University Press.

Rhode, H. (2013). *The U.S. role in the Sunni-Shi'ite conflict.* Archived at http://www.gatestoneinstitute.org/3708/the-us-role-in-the-sunni-shiite-conflict. Accessed 20 Dec 2015.

Richards, J. (2007). Contemporary terrorist threats in the UK: The Pakistan dimension. *Journal of Policing, Intelligence and Counter Terrorism, 2*(1), 7–33.

Sagini, M. M. (2014). *Globalization: The paradox of organizational behavior: Terrorism, foreign policy, and governance.* New York: University Press of America.

Shakdam, C. (2014). *Saudi Arabia's escalating campaign against Shia Muslims.* Archived at http://www.internationalpolicydigest.org/2014/05/26/saudi-arabias-escalating-campaign-shia-muslims/. Accessed 20 Dec 2015.

Taub, B. (2015, June 1). Journey to Jihad why are teen-agers joining ISIS? *The New Yorker.* Archived at http://www.newyorker.com/magazine/2015/06/01/journey-to-jihad. Accessed 20 Dec 2015.

Watt, D. F. (2005). Attachment mechanisms and the bridging of science and religion: The challenges of anthropomorphism and sect-ism. *The Psychoanalytic Review, 92*(2), 191–221.

Werbner, P. (1997). Essentialising essentialism, essentialising silence: Ambivalence and multiplicity in the constructions of racism and ethnicity. In Werbner, P., and Modood, T. [Eds.] *Debating cultural hybridity: Multi-cultural identities and the politics of anti-racism.* London: Zed (pp. 226–254)..

Wright, L. (2006). *The looming tower: Al-Qaeda and the Road to 9/11.* New York: Vintage Books.

Zahab, M. A. (2004). The Sunni-Shia Conflict in Jhang (Pakistan). In Ahmad, I. and Riefled Helmut [Eds.] Lived Islam in South Asia. New Delhi: Social Science Press (135–148).

CHAPTER 15

The "Othering" of the Ahmadiyya Community in Bangladesh

Humayun Kabir

INTRODUCTION

In 1987 a group of students from local madrassas accompanied by some lay Muslims, instigated by their ulema (Islamic clerics), forcefully occupied an Ahmadi mosque in Kandipara, Bangladesh. Kandipara is a locality of Brahmanbaria, an east-central district town of Bangladesh, where the country's first Ahmadiyya Jamaat was established in 1912 (see Kabir 2009, pp. 419–421). This incident was one of the earliest examples of persecution of the Ahmadiyya community in the 1980s. That decade was characterized by a surge in anti-Ahmadiyya movements paralleling the increasing visibility of the ulema. During this period, Islamists mobilized into newly formed political fronts, adding to the influence of the dominant Islamic political party—Bangladesh Jamaat-e-Islami (BJI).[1] Added to this was the reinstatement of Islam as a political force and rhetorical discourse of the state ideology.[2] As the Islamic political groups gained strength, the anti-Ahmadiyya hatred campaigns characterized by violence also gained strength. The more the secular-liberal mainstream political groups allied with Islamic political forces, the greater was the visibility of persecution of the Ahmadiyya community in Bangladesh.

H. Kabir (✉)
North South University, Dhaka, Bangladesh

© The Editor(s) (if applicable) and The Author(s) 2016
J. Syed et al. (eds.), *Faith-Based Violence and Deobandi Militancy in Pakistan*, DOI 10.1057/978-1-349-94966-3_15

423

Throughout the 1990s and 2000s, the Ahmadis, a small minority with an estimated 100,000 followers, were subject to various forms of persecution, including harassment, assault, violent attacks, excommunication, bombing, killing, vandalism and obstruction of burial, primarily by religious clergy and Islamists. In Brahmanbaria, the place from where the Ahmadiyya religious doctrine spread to other parts of the country, an estimated 25,000 Ahmadis live in an environment of cultural alterity in which they are constantly constructed as an "other". Following the Pakistani model (where Ahmadis were declared non-Muslim by a constitutional amendment in 1974), the religious clergy and Islamists in Bangladesh are demanding similar measures. Their principal demand is to expel Ahmadis from Islam by legal means. The anti-Ahmadiyya activism includes preaching, propagation, demonstration, agitation and attacks aimed at the construction of Ahmadis as an "other" and as a "must be obliterated and excluded group of people from the name of Muslim".[3] In Brahmanbaria, as elsewhere in contemporary Bangladesh where the Ahmadis are dispersed, religious clerics are active in warding off all forms of visible and public religious activity of the Ahmadiyya community through different resistive and violent measures. Organized and violent forms of resistance against the followers of Ahmadiyya increasingly restrict their freedom to practice their religion.

Of all sectarian, subsectarian and maslaki (denominational groups) offshoots of Islam in South Asia, the Ahmadiyya community has been historically subject to "othering" by Sunni, Shia and other mainstream Muslims who are strongly antithetical to the Ahmadis' belief in the prophethood of Mirza Ghulam Ahmad (1835–1908) after Muhammad, the seal of all prophets in Islam (see Friedmann 2003). However, the process of "othering" as a form of competition and branding one's own school of thought as the "true" and "authentic" representative of Islam has been a trend among various offshoots of Sunni Islam, such as Deobandi, Barelvi and Ahl-e-Hadith. The trend dates back to the nineteenth and twentieth centuries when Islamic revivalist-reformist movements resulted, in response to and following interaction with various transformative forces. Colonial encounter, the birth of nation-states, the impact of religious majoritarianism, communalism and Islamism all began to have an indelible effect on the perception and construction of Muslim selfhood. What is distinctive is that earlier the nature of such contestation, as delineated later in the case of Brahmanbaria, was limited to theological debates (bahas) and religious argument, preaching and propagation activities, which were less violent in nature, but now it has become intolerant and hostile, at least in the case of Bangladesh. The process of "othering" the Ahmadiyya community needs to be located and understood in this shifting trend. What characterized this shift of contestation from mere theological debates to more politically informed Islamic movements and activism is the causal effect of multiple forces: the rise of Islamism; the increasing visibility and involvement of religious preachers, clerics and reformers in politics; the desecularization of the state; and transnational links between Islamic forces.

The nature of the "othering" process among Muslims by Muslims since the nineteenth and twentieth centuries has not always been constant, but I do not decipher the differences here. Rather, what I attempt to explicate is the persecution of the Ahmadiyya community's case in a wider historical-political context of South Asian Muslims' sectarian and "quasi-sectarian"[4] strife and contestation. In doing so I limit my discussion to Deobandi Islam, a school of thought or maslaki strand primarily associated with the Darul Uloom Deoband madrassa founded in 1866 in northern India. The followers of this strand are dispersed across South Asia and beyond, with their own "universe" through religious teachings and allegiance to Deobandi doctrinal thought (see Metcalf 1982; Haroon 2008; Reetz 2007; Zaman 2007). The Deobandi school of thought, I contend, began to gain its institutional strengths and ideological foothold through the foundation of various prototyped Deobandi seminaries from the early twentieth century in Bengal. With a process of contextual adaptability and gradual increase in the number of Deobandi madrassas, the Bengali Deobandis—those who returned from a Deoband seminary after their educational mission—continue to maintain an allegiance to the Urdu-speaking elite Deobandi scholars of northern India. This also includes those who succeeded the Deoband returnees and received advanced Islamic education in prototyped Deobandi madrassas, in either Bangladesh or Pakistan. Over time, these generations of clerics have worked to institutionalize and instrumentalize Deobandi Islam to correct and perfect Bengali Muslims' "Hinduized" and popular folk Islam (see Ahmed 1996, pp. 39–105; Banu 1992, pp. 35–42; Uddin 2006, pp. 41–76; Kabir 2015, pp. 7–11). But many of the successors of the earlier generation of Bengali Deobandis stepped up from their primary involvement in preaching and teaching Islam to negotiating with the state for the "protection" of Islam. This gradual transition from piety to politics, facilitated by several interconnected factors, including the rise of the political platform for Deobandi scholars and a growing nexus between mainstream and Islamic political forces, paved the way for sectarian strife in Bangladesh from the 1980s. In this context the Ahmadiyya community was targeted as the extreme "other", though other groups practising popular and folk Islam have also been persecuted. As I describe in this chapter, the transposition of sectarian strife in Bangladesh is also linked to the political rise of Bengali Deobandis from the 1980s. The chapter explores the dynamics of transnational, national and local contexts in relation to a widely known anti-Ahmadi movement—the International Khatme Nabuwat Movement Bangladesh (IKNM)—a Deobandi outfit operating in other parts of South Asia with various names, aiming to declare Ahmadis "non-Muslim" and to prohibit their right to various Islamic practices and rituals. Although the IKNM, founded and led by Deobandi scholars, and its affiliated organizations are unsuccessful thus far in excluding Ahmadis from the Muslim fold, their concerted activism over the years is contributing to the hatred and violent campaigns against Ahmadis. Grassrootization of the persecution of Ahmadis, I argue, is the result of the nexus between Islamists and liberal democratic parties which tends to legitimize the imposition of monolithic and monoreligious culture by undermining the plural and syncretized religious tradition in Bangladesh.

THE JOURNEY OF THE AHMADIYYA JAMAAT IN BANGLADESH

The Ahmadiyya Jamaat was founded in Qadian, India, by Mirza Ghulam Ahmad (1835–1908) as a reform movement within Islam and "as a reaction to the eclipse of Islam by the west in the 19th century and the successful evangelism carried out by British missionaries amongst the Indian population" (Valentine 2014, p. 101). In Bangladesh (then a part of India), the Ahmadiyya Jamaat was first established in the district town of Brahmanbaria in 1912 when a saintly scholar, Maulana Abdul Ohayed, embraced Ahmadiyya doctrine and began to preach it among the local Muslims. Maulana Ohayed was a noted Islamic scholar who received Islamic education under the religious mentorship of Maulana Abdul Hayy of Farangi Mahall in Lucknow, India. On his return to Brahmanbaria he started to serve as a qazi (a judge who delivers judgement according to Islamic law) and as "Head Maulana" of a high school. Additionally he was the khatib (prayer leader) of Brahmanbaria Jame Mosque. It is believed that Maulana Ohayed, after hearing about Mirza Ghulam Ahmad's acclaimed prophecy, started to communicate with the founder in 1903.[5] In the initial period, as a Sunni Muslim scholar, he was rather curious about the basis on which Ahmad claimed himself as a promised messiah, *mujaddid* (expected reformer) and *mahdi* (redeemer). The theological debate, argument and counterargument between Maulana Ohayed and Mirza Ahmad were exchanged through letters for several years.[6] After the death of Ghulam Ahmad in 1908, Maulana Ohayed travelled to Qadian in 1912 and met the first caliph of the Ahmadiyya Jamaat. Then he embraced the Ahmadiyya doctrine. After returning to his hometown, Brahmanbaria, where he was highly revered and acknowledged for his excellence in Islamic knowledge, many other lay Muslims followed him and eventually the Ahmadiyya community began to spread across the locality. Although four other Muslims from various localities embraced the Ahmadiyya creed in different incidents from 1903 to 1909, the foundation of the Ahmadiyya Jamaat in Brahmanbaria in 1912 by Maulana Ohayed was the beginning of the journey of Ahmadis in Bangladesh (*Ahmadiyya Bangla* 2008).

The first jamaat of the country remained active until 1936, when it was shifted to Calcutta for some years. Finally it moved to Bakshibazaar, Dhaka, where the community purchased land in 1946.[7] However, the Ahmadiyya community in Brahmanbaria still maintains a jamaat which takes care of organizing religious activities, providing social services to the community, and preaching and propagating the Ahmadiyya doctrine. Now the Ahmadiyya Jamaat has 103 branches and 425 community neighbourhoods where Ahmadis reside. There are 65 *moballeg* (preacher), who are assigned to serve the community in different zones and regions (*Ahmadiyya Bangla* 2008).

DEOBANDIS' RESISTANCE AGAINST AHMADIYYA IN BRAHMANBARIA: FROM THEOLOGICAL DEBATE TO VIOLENT ATTACKS

Historically speaking, the resistance against the Ahmadiyya community is intricately interconnected with the proliferation and institutionalization of Deobandi thought in Bangladesh. As part of their reformist augmentation in nineteenth- and twentieth-century Bengal, the Urdu-speaking Deobandis, whom the Bengali Deoband returnee revered, were concerned about making the lay Bengali Muslim aware of "correct" and "perfect" Islamic beliefs and practices and also persuading them to abandon certain practices deemed as "un-Islamic". Against this backdrop, Jamia Islamia Yunusia Madrasa, one of the largest Deobandi madrassas, was founded in 1914 at Kandipara in Brahmanbaria, just years after the foundation of the country's largest and first Deobandi madrassa—Al Jamiatul Ahlia

Darul Uloom Muinul Islam, popularly known as Hathazari—in 1901 in Chittagong. The foundation of Yunusia Madrasa was credited to Maulana Abu Taher Muhammad Yunus, a northern Indian Deobandi scholar who came to Brahmanbaria after receiving prophetic order in a vision, and after whom the madrassa was named (Kabir 2009, pp. 418–419). When the Ahmadiyya community began to evolve after Maulana Ohayed's return from Qadian in 1912, as a follower of Mirza Ghulam Ahmad, Maulana Yunus arrived as a counterforce in order to safeguard further conversion of Muslims to Ahmadis in the locality. The ulema associated with Yunusia Madrasa believed that the madrassa was established to fend the Muslims off the "Qadiani"[8] fetna (evil ideology):

> When Mirza Ghulam Ahmad, the founder of Ahmadiyya Muslim community, claimed himself as a Prophet, the news was also spread in Brahmanbaria. Probably it was in the early twentieth century. At that time, a man, namely Syed Abdul Ohayed, popularly known as *"Boro Moulavi"* [senior Islamic theological expert], after whom a locality of Brahmanbaria Municipality was named as *"Moulavi Para"*, and who was the prayer-leader (*Imam*) of Brahmanbaria Jamia Mosque, was sent to investigate the matter of the prophecy of Mirza Ghulam Ahmad at Qadian in India by some local influential Muslim followers. When *Boro Moulavi* came back to Brahmanabaria, it was found that he became a follower of Ahmadiyya. Then he was sacked from his prayer job at mosque. However, he preached and pleaded with the doctrine of Ahmadiyya in Brahmanbaria. As a result, a number of Sunni Muslim followers became Qadiani here. At that time, a Deobandi follower, Maulana Yunus, came to Brahmanbaria to save the Sunni Muslim from the evil doctrine of Ahmadiyya.[9]

The arrival of a northern Indian Deobandi scholar in a distant locality such as Brahmanbaria adduced the Deobandis' early reformist programme aimed at safeguarding the sacrosanct boundary of Sunni Islam. Mufti Muhammad Nurullah (d. 2009), a Bengali Deoband returnee who served as a muhtamim (director) of the Yunusia madrassa for years, narrates how Maulana Yunus was able to dissuade the Ahmadiyya followers in Brahmanbaria using theological expertise:

> Maulana Yunus was one of the repudiate caliphs [spiritual successor] of Maulana Hussain Ahmed Madani of Deoband Madrasa at that time. Once, Maulana dreamed prophet Muhammad (S). The prophet ordered him to go to Brahmanbaria town and said "there Qadianipeople are slaying my

Khatme Nabuwat [finality of prophethood] tradition and making my *ummat* [follower] *murtad* [apostate]. Go there and establish a madrasa in which *ilme din* [Islamic knowledge] will be imparted." Maulana Yunus came here according to the prophetic order he received in a vision. He was very competent in rhetorical argument. Nobody could defeat him in *munzara* or *bahas* [theological debate]. He was able to convince theologically many Qadiani Muslims for their misguidance. He was invited in many villages to convert the misguided Qadiani families. A serial of *tawba* [repentance for sin] was going on in many Qadiani families from one village to other ... Finally, he decided to stay here in an attempt to establish a madrasa. He consulted with his spiritual guide Maulana Hussain Ahmed Madani of Deoband Madrasa. Then he established the madrasa here.[10]

Yunusia Madrasa, with its Deobandi Islam as an important theological doctrine and ideological foundation, evolved in reaction to the conversion of local Muslims to Ahmadiyya and remained operative as a centre not just for Islamic learning but for resistance against further conversion of Muslims to Ahmadiyya, and delimiting the Ahmadis presence and religious activities in the locality. The contributions of several other Bengali Deobandis, who joined Yunusia Madrasa upon Maulana Yunus's call after their successful educational and religious mission at Deoband, in maintaining the theological and ideological positions against Ahmadis, are highly acknowledged and praised by the contemporary ulema and their disciples associated with the madrassa. As I was told, Maulana Tazul Islam, a man of Brahmanbaria, returned from Deoband with excellent academic achievements, succeeded Maulana Yunus as muhtamim, and had been a reformer and saviour of local Muslims against Ahmadiyya's erroneous doctrine. Other Bengali Deobandis who served the madrassa include Maulana Muhammadullah Hafezzi Huzur (1895–1987), Maulana Shamsul Haq Faridpuri (1895–1969) and Maulana Abdul Ohab Pirji (1890–1976), whom the contemporary Bengali Deobandis revered as iconic figures for their religious and scholarly devotions to Islam and for contributions to the foundation of Deobandi madrassas in various parts of the country. Many of their followers and successors were in the forefront of anti-Ahmadi movements later, particularly from the 1980s. They institutionalized and symbolized the ideological basis of Deobandi Islam in Brahmanbaria as a counterforce to Ahmadiyya and other reprehensive innovation (bidat) in Islam as well.

The deliberate foundation of Yunusia Madrasa at Kandipara, with its visibility and huge infrastructure, including a multistorey seminary complex with more than 1,000 students, unwittingly rendered an invisible threat to the tiny Ahmadiyya minority in the locality. The more the Yunusia Madrasa was glorified and iconized, the more the local Ahmadiyya community felt threatened. Over the course of time, Yunusia Madrasa produced thousands of graduates, of whom many founded prototyped madrassas in and outside the locality, and these, and other similar types of madrassas as well, are connected to Yunusia Madrasa through a board of education (*edara-e-talim*), which eventually recognized it as a custodian of Islam, in particular Deobandi Islam. The ulema and the madrassas centred on Yunusia Madrasa often launch activism such as protests, agitation and street rallies if they find something that breaches the sanctity of Islam, particularly Sunni Islam.[11]

The religious verdicts (fatawa) of northern Indian Urdu-speaking Deobandis—the religious gurus and icons of the ulema of Yunusia Madrasa—such as the eminent Deobandi scholar Maulana Shabbir Ahmad Usmani (1886–1949), declared Ahmadis as apostate, and an apostate, according to their interpretation of sharia law, is subject to the death penalty (Friedmann 2003, pp. 29, 154). Interestingly the same Deobandi cleric, Shabbir Ahmed Usmani, had also signed a fatwa declaring the Shias outside the fold of Islam (Merchant 1990). The Bengali Deobandis in Brahmanbaria, and elsewhere in the country as well, promote and circulate the ideological stance of Urdu-speaking Deobandis' notions about Ahmadiyya through vernacularized forms of writing. For instance, religious sermons of Maulana Muhammad Yusuf Ludhianvi's (1932–2000, a Pakistani Deobandi cleric prominently known for his takfiri (apostatizing) fatwas against Ahmadis and Shias and his intolerant views about Sunni Barelvis/Sufis), against Ahmadiyya have been circulated in the form of a translated booklet among the ulema circle and their disciples. The booklet constructed Ahmadis as *zindiq* (heretics whose teachings endangered the Muslim community) and apostate, whose punishment is execution (Ludhianvi 2000).

Despite such theological and ideological connections to the Deobandis, the "othering" process led by the early generation of Bengali Deobandis in Brahmanbaria was less violent in character; rather, it was largely a theological war between the custodians of Sunni Islam and the local Deobandis and Ahmadis. With some exceptions in the 1930s and 1960s, the violent attacks against the Ahmadiyya community in Brahmanbaria locality were less visible until the late 1980s. As I have described elsewhere, in 1987 the followers of Yunusia Madrasa mobilized and led an angry mass under the banner of Tahafuzz-e Khatme Nabuwat Jubo Songhothon (TKNJS [Organization of the Youth for the Protection of Finality of Prophethood]) that forcefully occupied Masjid Mubarak of the Ahmadiyya community in Kandipara. After the occupation of the mosque, which was renamed Masjid Fatah (conquered mosque), and the threats posed by the attackers under the patronage of local Bengali Deobandis, an estimated 200 Ahmadis reconverted from Ahmadiyya belief to Sunni Islam by declaring not to believe in the prophecy of Mirza Ahmad in a legal edict in the local court.

A new madrassa, Al-Jamiatul Islamia Tazul Uloom Tahafuzze Khatme Nabuwat Madrasa (TKNM) was gradually founded in the place of the occupied mosque, which was named after Maulana Tazul Islam, the second muhtamim (administrator) of Yunusia Madrasa, for acknowledging his contribution to the reformist activities against Ahmadiyya in the locality (Kabir 2009, pp. 419–421; see also Persecution of Ahmadis, 22 November 2011). Now the Ahmadis at Kandipara perform their religious practices in a separate mosque, and the TKNM is located just on the other side of the mosque. Both the TKNM and the TKNJS, which are theologically and ideological indoctrinated by Yunusia Madrasa and receive patronage from the religious leadership of the madrassa, exert vigilance against Ahmadiyya, in particular the fact that Ahmadis pose as Muslims through various religious activities.

Since the incident of 1987, the Ahmadis cannot call azzan (call to prayer) using a loudspeaker. The community could not observe *salana jalsa* (annual community congregation) for more than two decades. In 2006, when they prepared to celebrate salana jalsa after an interlude of 21 years, the Mufti of Yunusia Madrasa vowed to disrupt the programme by announcing a three-day *tafsir mahfil* at Masjid Fatah, located in close proximity to the place where the Ahmadiyya's programme was planned. To avoid a possible clash between the followers of the TKNJS and the Ahmadis, the local administration imposed a legal bar that eventually foiled the programme (*Daily Star*, 21 May 2006). The local administration asked the Ahmadiyya community to ensure that its programme would not provoke and hurt mainstream Muslims. This was a difficult requirement because the mainstream religious clerics and their followers were provoked by the very fact that the Ahmadis pose as Muslims. In another incident in 2010, when the Ahmadiyya community planned to celebrate salana jalsa, members of the TKNJS staged demonstrations for several days, chanting slogans: "take lethal weapons, take axes, and decapitate the Qadianis" (Persecution of Ahmadis, 22 November 2011; *Daily Star* 20 March 2010a). The TKNJS vowed to disrupt the Ahmadis' jalsa and submitted a written demand to the local administration to ban the "anti-Islamic activities" by the Ahmadis which, they warned, could undermine law and order in the locality. Failing to safeguard the religious rights and freedom of the Ahmadis, the administration imposed several conditions on them, such as stipulating that "the program must be held inside the Ahmadiyya mosque", "Ahmadis will not be allowed to use [a] microphone", "the sound of the program must not go outside", "there should not be any sort of provocative comments and wrong religious interpretations", "the discussion must be confined to the teachings of [the] Holy Prophet" and so on (Persecution of Ahmadis, 22 November 2011; *Daily Star* 20 March 2010a).

Reports suggest that the persecution of the Ahmadiyya community has been a frequent phenomenon in Brahmanbaria and elsewhere in the country. However, the incidents of violent attacks increased in the early 2000s when the Islamists for the first time allied with the Bangladesh Nationalist Party (BNP)-led government (in power 2001–2006). For example, in October 2004 some 900 people of the Sunni sect, of whom many were brandishing machetes and axes, led by a local imam (prayer leader), razed an Ahmadiyya mosque, vandalized houses and attacked local Ahmadis in a locality in Brahmanbaria. The attack, which left 11 Ahmadis including 6 women injured, was made under the banner of the Deobandi outfit the International Tahafuzze Khatme Nabuwat Committee, Bangladesh (*Daily Star*, 30 October 2004). In another incident in June 2005, anti-Ahmadi bigots exploded nearly two dozen bombs at Kandipara, targeting mainly the Ahmadiyya community. They also torched the Ahmadiyya mosque there (*Daily Star* 25 June 25 2005a). In the same year, several bombs were planted secretly in the yard of an Ahmadiyya woman's house, severely injuring her (*Daily Star* 16 August 2005b). In addition to violent attacks, the Ahmadiyya community in Brahmanbaria has been subject to other forms of persecution. In 2006, for instance, when an elderly woman of the Ahmadiyya community died, villagers obstructed her burial on the grounds that she was a follower of an "infidel" was not allowed to be buried in a Muslim graveyard. However, with the intervention of the local administration, she was buried within 28 hours of her death (bdnews24. com, 17 January 2006).

The case of Brahmanbaria suggests that earlier the Bengali Deobandis' resistance to the Ahmadiyya was largely based on theological debates and reformist programmes, but later it turned to violence and force against the community. The persecution of the Ahmadiyya community in Brahmanbaria aims to undermine the visible presence of Ahmadis as a Muslim population. "Posing as Muslims" by Ahmadis was made a punishable offence in Pakistan after the introduction of General Ziaul Haq's (in power 1978–1988) Ordinance XX (Valentine 2014, p. 106), whereas the Ahmadis' visibility in the religious sphere is objectionable and punishable without any legal bar in Bangladesh. The cause needs to be explicated in relation to the grassrootization of the anti-Ahmadi hatred campaign, which flourished simultaneously with the rise of Islamism and the sensitization of Islam as an ideological discourse in state and non-state arenas since the 1980s in Bangladesh.

From Piety to Politics: Desecularization, Islamism and the Bengali Deobandis

Although denominational differences continued to exist as embodied by diverse Islamic institutions, movements and religious leaderships, such sectarian variations did not lead to violent strife in Bangladesh until recently. This is unlike Pakistan, where the radicalization of sectarian identity resulting from a milieu of sociopolitical and religious developments has been a regular phenomenon for many decades. The intolerant religious environment in Bangladesh began to evolve from the mid-1980s, when denominational differences were reinvigorated by the Islamists, particularly targeting the Ahmadiyya community (Riaz 2009, p. 87). Why did persecution against the Ahmadiyya community gain ascendancy in the 1980s? There are multiple contributing factors, including the desecularization of the Bangladeshi state, the reinstitution of Islam as an important identity marker of the state, the rise of Islamism along with the shifting roles of the religious clergy from religious preachers to political actors, and the increasing connectivity with Muslim countries and Islamic movements that facilitated the importation of transnational Islamic ideas to the tradition of local syncretized Islam.[12] Additionally, the sensitization of Islam as an ideological discourse in state and non-state arenas through various activism and movements has made deep inroads into the evolution of intolerant attitudes towards other denominational groups of Islam in Bangladesh since the 1980s.

After the birth of Bangladesh in 1971, secularism as a state principle was enshrined in the first Constitution of Bangladesh, and it "was the logical outcome of a situation where Bengalis were being oppressed in the name of religion" during the period when Bangladesh was part of Pakistan (Mohsin 2004, p. 471). The constitution of 1972 drew the principle of secularism as not having a complete absence of religion but, rather, prohibition of religion for the use of political purposes and of all forms of communalism (Mohsin 2004, pp. 470–471). Secularism as enshrined in the Constitution shielded the rise of Islamism and communalism, though Islam remained a salient feature of Bengali Muslims' social and cultural lives. The Islamic political parties which were operating in former East Pakistan disappeared from the visible political scene in post-independence Bangladesh. The JI, which made concerted political efforts and collaborated with the Pakistani Army during the Bangladesh War of Independence, went into hiding, and its political leadership were dispersed for fear of prosecution against their alleged roles in the war.

But secularism did not last for long in the wake of a military regime. Almost at the same time, when "Islamic authoritarianism" in Pakistan was gaining ground under the military ruler President General Muhammad Zia-ul-Haq (in power 1978–88) (Esposito and Voll 1996, p. 105), President General Ziaur Rahman (in power 1977–1981), the first military ruler of Bangladesh, orchestrated a desecularization process—the obliteration of the secularism principle from the Constitution, the introduction of popular Islamic phrases in the Constitution, the invention of "Bangladeshi" nationalism in close association with Islamic sentiments against "Bengali", reinstating Islamic political parties in the name of political liberalization, and extending ties with the Muslim states on the basis of Islamic solidarity (Kabir 2015, pp. 60–61; see also Kabir 1995, pp. 196–202). However, neither Ziaur Rahman's desecularization policy, characterized by popular Islamic rhetorical agenda, nor his newly founded political party—the BNP, whose foundation was based on "liberal Islamic nationalism" (Mohsin 2004, p. 475)—envisioned establishing a Sharia-based state in Bangladesh, and thereby the structuralization of Islam in the state in the forms of legal enactment was far behind the case of Pakistan.

Nevertheless, the transformation of the state from a pro-secular to a desecular ideological direction had an unequivocal and indelible impact on the sanctity of Islam in political culture and on the rise of Islamism in later years in Bangladesh. The ulema, including Deobandis, who were largely occupied in Islamic reformist programmes, such as preaching and teaching Islam, began to organize under certain political platforms, joining the bandwagon with those Islamic political groups, such as the BJI, which took a stance against the Bangladesh War of Independence on the grounds that the division of Pakistan would undermine Islamic solidarity. Ziaur Rahman masterminded the orchestration of the Islamization policy, which enabled an increase in the number of Bangladeshi migrant workers, and visits of state dignitaries to the Middle East. This marked the beginning of channelling money, resources, aid, charity and transnational Islamic ideas from Saudi Arabia and other Middle Eastern countries to Bangladesh. In this context, some Bengali Deobandis primarily associated with various prototyped Deobandi madrassas in the country stepped up from their initially defined zone—community-based religious institutions and organizations—to the space of political battlefield as Islamists. The dual identity of many of the Bengali Deobandis, as religious reformers and political actors, gave birth to a crisscross relationship between piety and politics, or religion and power. In this context, the Bengali Deobandis began to organize themselves politically under the leadership of Maulana Hafezzi Huzur (1895–1987), an eminent mystic leader who served at Yunusia Madrasa after his return from Deoband and contributed significantly to the proliferation of Islamic education through the foundation of Deobandi madrassas in the country.[13]

Hafezzi Huzur's political visibility, beginning from 1978 at the age of 82, was symbolized by many of his followers—Deobandis and mystic groups—who instrumentalized the rise of political Islam under his leadership as an alternative force beyond BJI, whose theological perspective they denounced as *Mawdudi fitnah* (Mawdudi, the founder of BJI, chaos) (see Kabir 2015, p. 64). Largely backed by his followers, the religious clergy of the Deobandi madrassas, and mystic leadership and disciples, Hafezzi Huzur contested the presidential elections in 1981 and 1986. His newly founded political party, the Bangladesh Khelafat Andolon (BKA [Bangladesh Caliphate Movement]) established in 1981, was creating a platform for connecting not just the ulema with a madrassa background but also other pro-Islamic groups. The symbolization of Hafezzi Huzur as a political, not just as a spiritual, leadership was possible in a context in which the country experienced a vacuum of a democratic political environment before and after the takeover of the state power by military ruler President General Hussain Muhammad Ershad (in power 1983–1990). He maintained the Islamization policy of his predecessor, President Ziaur Rahman, sought support from mystic leaders (pir) by making frequent visits to their sites, declared Islam as the state religion, and even aimed to introduce Arabic learning as compulsory in school education (Riaz 2004, pp. 37–39). Hafezzi Huzur's contestation in a presidential election and his formation of a new political party—BKA—helped him to connect with the leadership of Muslim countries in the Middle East, as evinced from his visits to Saudi Arabia, Iraq and Iran, where he met high-level state dignitaries.

The political context that began to move gradually from Islamic rhetorical ideology to the rise of the organized force of political Islam reconfigured the evolution of the anti-Ahmadiyya movement in a new fashion in the 1980s. For instance, Majlis-e Tahafuzz-e Khatme Nabuwat (Assembly for the Protection of the Finality of Prophethood), the main anti-Ahmadi organization that was influenced by its counterpart in Pakistan, joined the Combined Action Committee in an allied Islamic political force of nine parties in 1984 led by Hafezzi Huzur and the BKA to launch a movement against the military ruler, President Ershad, for the foundation of an Islamic state in Bangladesh (Ismail 2005, p. 227). The alliance, mainly dominated by ulema with a Deobandi madrassa background, The alliance, mainly dominated by ulema with a Deobandi madrassa background, spearheaded the anti-Ahmadi movement, in parallel with the rise of Bengali Deobandis in politics. It is reported that draft legislation for declaring Ahmadis "non-Muslims" was framed in 1988, the year when President Ershad constitutionally adopted Islam as the state religion (Hossain 2004, p. 91).

Growing factionalism within the Deobandis and a sharp distinction between Deobandis and mystic groups began to emerge in the years after Hafezzi Huzur's death, leading to the fragmentation of the Deobandis' political platform. For instance, Maulana Fazlul Karim (known as Chormonai pir), who was a disciple of Hafezzi Huzur, founded a separate political party in 1987, the Bangladesh Islami Shasontantra Andolon (Bangladesh Islamic Constitutional Movement [ISA]), renamed the Islamic Andolon Bangladesh (Islamic Movement Bangladesh) in 2008. Similarly, Shaikhul Hadith Allama Azizul Haq (1919–2012), a prominent Deobandi and founder rector of a large Deobandi madrassa in Dhaka (Jami'a Rahmania Arabia), founded in 1986, formed Bangladesh Khelafat Majlis (Bangladesh Caliphate Assembly [BKM]) in 1989. Previously he served as a deputy (naib amir) under Hafezzi Huzur's political leadership and contributed to the foundation of the ISA before forming the BKM. By the 1990s, the Bengali Deobandis, which already had several political parties based on the leadership of the rectors of various Deobandi madrassas united under an allied political platform—Islami Oikyo Jote (IOJ [United Islamic Front])—led by Mufti Fazlul Haque Amini[14] (1949–2012) and operated from the madrassa he headed—Jamia Qurania Arabia, known as Lalbagh Madrasa, Dhaka.

Despite fragmentation within Islamism and competition among three major Islamic political fronts—Jamaat, Deobandis, and mystic leader-based political parties—and despite unsuccessful attempts on all Islamic fronts to establish *Islami hukumat* (Kingdom of Islam), the Islamists' success can be highlighted by what Riaz and Fair (2010) contend:

> Islamists have scored a victory on many fronts: making Islam as a political ideology in a nation which came into existence on a basis of secularist principles; emerging in a formidable force in Bangladeshi politics; making Islam an integral part of the political discourse, and creating an environment within which a menacing militancy can flourish, to name but few (p. 60).

The unsuccessful efforts to establish Islamism as a totalizing project to Islamize Bangladeshi society often united the Islamists, despite their differences in leadership, theological doctrine and ideological orientation, in protecting the sanctity of Islam, in particular Sunni Islam. The Islamists target the state as a central force that can ensure the sanctity of Islam without being an Islamic state in nature. On the other hand, the Deobandis whose political parties are less well organized and limited within the ulema and madrassa circles, in this sense traditional in nature, compared with the BJI, whose organizational strength is rooted to its followers coming from the modern-educated urban petty bourgeoisie class, often galvanize the cause of sanctity of Islam through street demonstrations, protests and rallies. By showcasing their presence publicly, on the one hand, the Deobandi political leadership aimed to legitimize and gain their political leadership along with its counterpart, the BJI. On the other hand, however, they were able to sensitize the sanctity of Islam in Bangladeshi public life. In this emerging political context, the persecution of the Ahmadiyya community has been legitimized since the 1980s and throughout the 1990s and 2000s, as shown by various forms of religiopolitical activism that aimed to protect the sanctity of Islam against "blasphemous" issues.

Reportedly, the first draft legislation for declaring the Ahmadiyya community as "non-Muslim" was framed in 1988, and also in the late 1990s, though not enacted (Hossain 2004, p. 91). In 1993 a private lawyer filed constitutional litigation seeking Ahmadis to be declared as "non-Muslim" under the constitutional provisions that enshrined Islam as the state religion and stated fraternal relations with the Muslim states based on

Islamic solidarity. The pleader, in support of his constitutional litigation, referred to the case of Pakistan, where Ahmadis were declared as "non-Muslim". In response to this litigation, the High Court proclaimed that the Constitution of the country had "not empowered the Government to decide or declare who is Muslim and who is not" and added that "the Government has no obligation or power to decide or declare any persons or group of persons as non-Muslims in order to safeguard sanctity of [the] State religion" (Hossain 2004, p. 91).

In the same year, Motiur Rahman Nizami, one of the top leaders of the BJI, currently imprisoned and sentenced to death for his roles in crimes against humanity under a war trial, placed a "blasphemy" bill modelled on Pakistani law in the parliament, creating "insult to the Koran" and "insult to the Prophet" as new offences for which life imprisonment and the death sentence were proffered as the maximum punishments (Hossain 2004, pp. 91–92). Although these efforts were in vain, the Islamists appeared to be an important political force that grounded "Islamic sensibility" as an inescapable discourse in both state and non-state arenas (van Schendel 2009, p. 253), and the government, considered as liberal and democratic after the ousting of the last military ruler, President Ershad, in 1990, cannot ensure the religious rights and a persecution-free environment to Ahmadis. When, for the first time, a coalition of Islamists, including the BJI and the IOJ, became part of the government led by the BNP (from 2001 to 2006), movements for the persecution of the Ahmadiyya community increased significantly, demanding that the state and the Islamists connected to state power implement some legal measures to exclude the Ahmadis from the Muslim fold. In an anti-Ahmadiyya drive, Maulana Mahmudul Hasan Mamtaji, an Islamic religious cleric associated with a Deobandi madrassa in Dhaka, and reportedly known for his hatred campaign and violent activism against Ahmadis under an allied organization (Khatme Nabuwat Andolon Coordination Committee), demanded that the Islamists connected to state power fulfill their pledge: that is, declaring the Ahmadiyya community as "non-Muslims": "Since they promised an Islamic society, Motiur Rahman Nizami, Fazlul Haq Amini, Delwar Hossain Sayeedi (and MPs of Jamaat-e-Islami and other Islamic parties) must place a bill in this regard in Parliament" (*Daily Star*, 27 December 2003b).

The Islamists who were able to connect themselves as "kingmaker" to the liberal-democratic political forces and to state power, in a divisive and hatred propagandist politics between the Awami League and the

BNP, are often successful in making the state loyal to Islamic sensibility in political and public lives, which eventually promotes Islam as a mono-lithic and monoreligious tradition by undermining the diverse nature of religious practices of the Muslim community in Bangladesh. In the wake of a heightened upsurge of the anti-Ahmadi movement led by the ideo-logues of the IOJ and Khatme Nabuwat during the BNP-led Islamic alli-ance government (2001–2006), the government banned all publications of the Ahmadiyya community, as authorized in a press release from the Home Ministry in January 2004. "The ban has been imposed in view of objectionable materials in such publications that hurt or may hurt the sen-timents of the majority Muslim populations in Bangladesh" (*BBC News*, 9 January 2004; see also HRW 2005, pp. 29–33). The secular-liberal groups and civil society vehemently opposed the ban as a fundamental breach of constitutional rights, and later it was lifted after the High Court of Bangladesh issued an order against it. The ban against the constitutional rights that guarantee every religious community or denomination's rights to "profess, practise or propagate any religion" and "establish, maintain and manage its religious institutions" (Article 41.1, Part 3) insists that the state bows to the majority ideology.

RADICALIZATION AND GRASSROOTIZATION OF "OTHERING" AHMADIYYA

In addition to the rise of Islamism and the nexus between Islamists and secular-liberal mainstream political forces that paves the way to a gradual increase and strength of anti-Ahmadiyya movement, Bengali Deobandis interaction with transnational theological scholars and institutions rein-vigorated the vendetta against the Ahmadiyya community in Bangladesh. Maulana Obaidul Haq (d. 2007), a Deobandi scholar appointed as chief clergy (*khatib*, prayer leader) of Baitul Mukarram, the national mosque in Dhaka, by President Ershad in 1984 who remained in the post until his death in 2007, pioneered the anti-Ahmadi campaign and movement by utilizing his symbolic power as an spokesman of Islam and networks with theologians of Muslim countries. Maulna Haq received advanced Islamic education from Deoband seminary of India, devoted many years to teaching Islam to Deobandi madrassas including in Pakistan, and was involved in Nejam-e Islam, an Islamic political party founded by a Bengali Deobandi in 1953 (now a part of the IOJ) (see Ashraf 2008). He headed the IKNM from the 1980s. In 1993, under Haq's leadership, the IKNM held a conference in Dhaka that Islamic theologians from Saudi Arabia, Pakistan and India, and representatives from the BJI and the BNP attended.

The conference pushed its anti-Ahmadi demands—declaring Ahmadis officially as "non-Muslims", banning their publications and removing those Ahmadis serving in high-ranking government's posts. Endorsed by the top-ranking leaderships of the BJI, the conference participants vowed to observe a "demand day" for pressuring the government (HRW 2005, pp. 10–11). On another occasion, while the chief imam of the Masjid-e Nawabi (the Prophet's Mosque) was on a tour of Bangladesh from Saudi Arabia in 1997, the IKNM organized a large-scale public meeting in Dhaka. The chief imam condemned the founder of Ahmadiyya Jamaat,Mirza Ghulam Ahmad, as a traitor, "misleading others by their self-made and false Quranic commentary", and the meeting demanded a ban on the use of Qur'anic passages and Islamic terminology on Ahmadi mosques, the prohibition of the burial of Ahmadis in Muslim graveyards, and a ban on and confiscation of all Ahmadi publications, including the Ahmadi version of the Qur'an (HRW 2005, pp. 11–12). Another international conference, headed by Maulana Haq, held in Dhaka with participation from Egypt, India, Pakistan and the UK, urged for the excommunication of the Ahmadis in Bangladesh (HRW 2005, pp. 13–14).

The importation of transnational Islamic ideas into Bangladesh was channelled through the visits of Islamic theologians from Muslim countries to Bangladesh, and vice versa. It is very likely that Maulana Haq's active and vehement opposition to Ahmadis was fomented not just by his theological indoctrination with Deobandi Islam like other contemporaries of his age but also by his connection to Aalmi Majlish-e Tahafuzze Khatme Nabuwat (*aalmi,* international) or Majlish-e Tahafuzze Khatme Nabuwat, the anti-Ahmadi outfits led by Deobandi theologians in Pakistan since the 1950s, during and after his teaching service at Darul Uloom Karachi madrassa. On the other hand, Maulana Haq was a widely known and much revered theologian for his position as chief imam of the national mosque, which symbolically represented him as an authority of Islam, though officially there is no authorized spokesman of Islam in Bangladesh. Therefore Maulana Haq's public presence, through the IKNM, as a vehement denouncer of the Ahmadi people, inspired other religious clergy to join and strengthen the anti-Ahmadi movement from the late 1980s and throughout the 1990s and 2000s. The gradual proliferation of Qaumi madrassas indoctrinated by Deobandi Islam and operated by Deobandi scholars-cum-political leaders with their theological and ideological connectivity began to appear in the battle against the Ahmadis with various organizational offshoots and religiopolitical activism beyond the capital city of Dhaka. Therefore the spread of the anti-Ahmadi hatred campaign and movement from the centre to the periphery and from a circle of religious and political leaderships to local religious clergy outside Dhaka—a process which I coin in the phrase "grassrootization"—was the result of a cumulative effect of interaction of transnational and local Islam, the spiritual and ideological connectivity of the Deobandis through their religious institutions and political platforms, and public religious sermons, meetings and propagation against the Ahmadiyya community jointly with various Islamic political forces. Intrinsic to the grassrootization process of the anti-Ahmadi movement is the increasing participation of common Muslims in various localities, primarily attracted in the name of the sanctity of the finality of prophethood and mobilized by local religious clergy associated with madrassas and mosques.

The unsuccessful bid to target the state to declare Ahmadis non-Muslims and to exclude them from visible religious spaces and institutions despite protests, processions and street rallies, and despite endorsement from the top Islamic leadership in and outside the country, led to the evolution of the radicalization of the anti-Ahmadi movement characterized by violent attacks either by mob or by clandestine militant groups. In many cases, violent attacks organized publicly are orchestrated and mobilized by local religious clerics affiliated with Islamic political parties. However, clandestine attacks on Ahmadis were increasingly reported from the beginning of the 2000s. The radicalization of "othering" Ahmadis, in parallel with the grassrootization of anti-Ahmadi hatred campaign, began to reconfigure the persecution of the Ahmadiyya community in two forms: first, publicly visible incidents of forceful intimidation and occupation of Ahmadi religious spaces and institutions and attacks on Ahmadis by local religious clergy, often backed by Islamists and the religious leaderships of a particular community; and, second, the violent attacks by clandestine militant Islamic groups which began to emerge from the late 1990s and early 2000s.

According to the Ahmadiyya community, 12 persons had been "martyred" for the propagation of the "true" message of Islam in Bangladesh from 1963 to 2003 (Ahmadiyya Bangla 2008). One of the bloodiest incidents was a bomb attack on about 100 Ahmadis attending Friday prayer at a mosque in the southern town of Khulna, leaving six Ahmadis killed and several others injured (*BBC News* 10 October 1999). In another attack, led by a local leader of the BJI in 2003, Shah Alam, president and prayer leader of the local Ahmadiyya community in the Jhikargacha subdistrict of Jessore, was beaten to death during the month of Ramadan. Prior to the attack, a local BJI leader incited other Sunni Muslims to attack the Ahmadis, which he dubbed as a form of jihad and thus not punishable. The human rights activists who visited the area after the killing found that Shah Alam and his family faced harassment in various forms (HRW 2005, pp. 20).This was one of many attacks on the Ahmadiyya community at the local level, often mobilized by the followers of Islamists. The top leadership of the Islamic political parties often ideologically inspire their followers at the local level by denouncing the Ahmadiyya community publicly. For instance, Matiur Rahman Nizami, the amir of the BJI and currently sentenced to death for crimes against humanity in the Bangladesh War of Independence (1971), made an oblique reference to the Ahmadiyya community when he was a minister of the BNP-led allied government (in power 2001–2006). At a public rally he referred to Ahmadis as "misguided followers" of a "fake" prophet and as kafir (infidels) (Bdnews24.com 3 May 2005a).

By the early 1990s, paralleling the establishment of political Islamic forces in Bangladesh from three main fronts—the BJI, Deobandis and the mystic leadership-based political parties—the grassrootization of hatred campaigns against and attacks on the Ahmadiyya community had reportedly increased, and intrinsic to this was a gradual participation of local Sunni Muslims who had hitherto been less concerned about "othering" and less violent against the Ahmadis. As many local communities and their leadership are increasingly affected by the politicization and exploitation of Islam as a means to gain power, the persecution of the Ahmadiyya community has gradually increased in various localities. Paralleling such grassrootization of resistance against the Ahmadis, radicalization of the anti-Ahmadi movement began to reconfigure with forceful intimidation and violent attacks. In October 1992, for instance, a huge procession attended by more than 1,200 people attacked the main Ahmadiyya complex in Dhaka and ransacked rooms, burnt hundreds of books (including copies of the Qur'an), looted valuables, detonated crude bombs and set the building on fire, leaving 20 Ahmadis injured (HRW 2005, p. 10). Attacks on Ahmadis and their place of worship, street processions and rallies, and public religious sermons with hate speeches by religious clergy had been frequent phenomena after the demilitarized political context in

1991, the beginning of parliamentary democracy in Bangladesh. This facil-itated the construction of Ahmadis as a religious "other" whose visibility and presence as Muslims were being challenged, not just in a particular locality but across the country. The construction of "otherness" against the sanctity of Islam helped to spread the hatred against the Ahmadiyya community among local religious clergy, the political leadership and even lay Muslims. As a result, the Ahmadiyya community is also often subjected to ill-treatment, denial of education, excommunication and other forms of discrimination.

Reportedly, for example, the Ahmadiyya community in the village of Uttar Bhabanipur in the south-western Kushtia district were ostracized by villagers when local Islamic leaders with the support of BNP and BJI lead-ers forbade 17 Ahmadi families from trading goods, sending their children to school and harvesting their crops. The families were excommunicated from their own village for 25 days (HRW 2005, p. 20). In another inci-dent, the male members of the Ahmadiyya community in the village of Ghatail in Tangail district left their homes and were afraid to return after a series of attacks on them by local religious clergy, allegedly patronized by the leaders of the local BNP and BJI. The prayer leader of the mosque of Ghatail subdistrict town had been campaigning against the Ahmadis under Imam Parishad (Prayer Leaders Council). A member of the Ahmadiyya community was reported to have informed that local "bigots hanged sign boards at different places in the village saying Kadianis [Ahmadiyyas] have no iman [faith]. They are infidel. No rickshaw puller should carry them and no shopkeeper should sell any items to them" (*Daily Star* 25 August 2010b).

The anti-Ahmadi movement acquired renewed vigour when the Islamists shared the state power of the BNP-led allied government with the BJI and the IOJ. Many Islamists, including the madrassa-centric Deobandis whose support was essential to the victory of the BNP and its allied Islamic forces against the Awami League in 2001 election, expected that their long-cherished demand—declaring Ahmadis "non-Muslims"—would be tabled and fulfilled by their leaders enjoying the post of state power. However, the Deobandis and other Islamists remaining outside state power reinvigo-rated the anti-Ahmadi demonstrations, rallies and attacks in the early years of the 2000s in order to pressure the government, including the Islamists in power, to take legal measures against the Ahmadis. In November 2003, when a virulent campaign to pressure the government to declare Ahmadis non-Muslims was launched under the leadership of Maulana Mahmudul

Hasan Mamtazi, a Deobandi theologian and the Amir of Hifazate Khatme Nabuwat Andolon Coordination Committee (HKNAC), an alliance of an anti-Ahmadi outfit and a mob of nearly 5,000 with bamboo and wooden sticks and brickbats attempted to occupy a mosque of the Ahmadiyya community at Nakhalpara i the Tejgaon area in Dhaka, leaving 50, including policemen, injured (*Daily Star* 22 November 2011). Earlier, Maulana Mamtaji orchestrated and mobilized several hundred followers who were successful in capturing the mosque forcefully for some time, though they could not hold it owing to the intervention of law-enforcement personnel, and vehement opposition from civil society and human rights activists.

The anti-Ahmadi movement received new vigour due to support from other organisations and groups such as the Amra Dhakabashi, a socio-cultural organisation led by Maulana Mamtazi. Through a series of protests that often turned violent, the religious clergy associated with Deobandi madrassas, Islamists from various political parties and several other organizations including Aamra Dhakabasi threatened the BNP-led allied government with Islamists in following Pakistan where Ahmadis have been categorised as non-Muslim. The HKNAC leader warned that the preceding "government failed to return to power as it shut down 250 madrassahs and the ruling alliance will face the same fate if they do not meet our demands" (*Daily Star* 27 December 2003). Maulana Mamtazi continued to urge the people to wage jihad against the Ahmadis. It was in this context that the BNP-led Islamist government bowed to the anti-Ahmadi demand when it banned Ahmadiyya publications in 2004, as discussed earlier. During this period, however, paralleling the increasing anti-Ahmadi movement, the militant Islamists with their own agenda—the establishment of a Sharia-based Islamic state—appeared after several clandestine attacks against the government and secular-cultural groups (see Riaz 2008). Of many such incidents, Jamiatul Mujahideen's attack with 450 small bombs targeting government officials and offices across the country in August 2005 was most notable. The BNP-led allied Islamists government had to face redoubled pressures—the violent attack on the Ahmadiyya minority community and the clandestine militant groups' attack on government offices and officials. This suggests that the threat of Islamists remains unstoppable, impassable and inescapable because political Islam has been legitimized by non-Islamic mainstream political forces.

The political dynamics of Bangladesh moved to a new stage, a detailed discussion of which is beyond the scope of this chapter. Suffice it to note here that the persecution of the Ahmadiyya community seems insurmountable partly due to the grassrootization of the hatred against the Ahmadiyya in various communities, and partly owing to the nexus between Islamists and religious clergy, and between Islamists and mainstream political parties, and to a political culture blended with politics and religion. The religious clergy and the Islamists often brand the present Awami League government as "anti-Islamic" and the "enemy" of Islam because it restored the "secularism" principle of the first Constitution of Bangladesh; albeit a fusion of religion and secularism since Islam as a state religion was retained in the Constitution. The secular policy of the Awami League, which critics consider to be a "new brand of secularism" or "ultra-secularism" because of its policy to "minoritise Islam" (Islam 2011), could not ensure the freedom of the Ahmadiyya community (see AHRC 2011). In February 2011, when the Ahmadiyya Muslim Jamaat prepared to observe the 87th annual convention of the community with the participation of 8,000 followers, including international attendees, in Gazipur, a district close to Dhaka, the local administration imposed a legal bar against the convention in response to the opposition and protests of the religious clergy in the area (*Daily Star* 7 February 2011). The state's intervention, which aimed to reduce the possibility of attacks on Ahmadis, inadvertently served the interests of the anti-Ahmadis, whose resistance delimits the freedom of religious practices of the Ahmadiyya community in Bangladesh.

CONCLUSION

The Bengali Deobandis, whose revivalist-reformist ideology was largely shaped by a connection with the northern Indian Urdu-speaking Indian Deobandis and their institution—Darul Uloom Deoband seminary—were successful in adopting the theological doctrine and ideological orientation in the Bangladeshi context. In the process of contextual adoptability of Deobandi Islam, the Bengali Deobandis turned to become an important religiopolitical force aiming to safeguard the sanctity of Islam, in particular Sunni Islam. Historically, these Deobandi theologians challenged the Ahmadiyya doctrine and beliefs as part of "correcting" and "perfecting" Bengali Muslims, as discussed in the case of Brahmanbaria. Owing to their strength, gradually gained through the proliferation of Deobandi madrassas throughout the country, and through the establishment of Deobandis' political platform, their reformist programme became more aggressive, violent and political in nature, endorsed and patronized by other Islamic groups. It is not just the Ahmadiyya community whom they target but also other forms of practice and groups which they deem to be anti-Islamic. The diverse and rich Islamic tradition in Bangladesh embraces devotion to Sufi shrines, mystic religious institutions and persons; the culture of mystic minstrels; audible and visible celebrations of Shia festivals; and so on. An attempt to establish a more orthodox and puritanical Islam, influenced partly by the importation of transnational Islamic ideas and partly by the rise of Islamism and clandestine Islamic movement, leads to an incipient religious environment that seems to be increasingly hostile and intolerant towards others.

Although the radicalization of "othering" the Ahmadiyya was more pronounced than for other religious minority groups and practices within the broader Islamic and Muslim cultural traditions, a growing sectarian, subsectarian and differentiation with "other" practices and traditions has become plausible and conceivable in recent years in Bangladesh. For example, the Baul, the mystic minstrel known for their melodious mystical songs and esoteric practices against the orthodox and institutional religious practices, has been part of Bengali cultural tradition for centuries. Now the religious clergy, backed by Islamists, question their practices, and often the mystic minstrels have been persecuted for their non-conformity to Islam (*Daily Star* 24 August 2014). The symbolization and representation of Baul and their one-string musical instrument (*ektara*) is part of Bengali cultural festivals. In 2008, when the government planned to erect a Baul sculpture at a cross-section of the road near the international airport in Dhaka, religious clergy and their disciples from a nearby Deobandi madrassa launched a movement against it on the grounds that the erection of a human figure was impermissible in Islam. The Deobandi Islamist Mufti Fazlul Haq Amini promised that all statutes would be demolished if an Islamic government came into state power. Eventually the government did not erect the statues as part of representing the spirit of mystic minstrels as symbols of Bengali culture; instead an Islamic monument was built (Kabir 2012, pp. 30–34).

The tolerant and accommodative nature of the Islamic tradition in Bangladesh has been under constant threat, particularly so in recent years, as reportedly attacks on popular folk Islamic practices, such as devotion to Sufi shrines, have also taken place in recent years. For instance, two devotees were slaughtered by unknown assassins inside a Sufi shrine in Chittagong, the port city of the country, in 2014 (*The Express Tribune*

4 September 2015). Also, bombs are often hurled at *mazars* (mystic/Sufi mausoleums) in order to defeat the "polytheistic rituals", as dubbed by orthodox religious clergy and Islamists. A series of bomb attacks on an often-visited mazar in Akhaura, Brahmanbaria, left 1 dead and 100 injured in 2005 (Bdnews24.com 12 August 2005b).

The Shia community, unlike its counterpart in Pakistan, has not been targeted for persecution so far, and its religious practices and rituals are largely attended by many Sunni people. Despite attacks on folk Islamic practices and institutions, the dominant syncretistic and folk Islamic traditions remain popular among Bengali Muslims. Therefore observing the Shia rituals of Muharram and visiting the religious sites of Shia—that is, imambara—is not alien to large numbers of Sunni Muslims who are frequent visitors to Sufi shrines. Moreover, the Shia community was negligible in size compared with the Sunni community, so they do not pose a threat to the Sunni religious and Islamic leadership. Therefore a distinct Shia identity was markedly unnoticeable in comparison with that of the Sunnis, which may be the reason for less politicization and radicalization of the Shia identity. However, the subsumed Shia identity in the folk Islamic tradition, alongside the Sunni-majority population, seems to have been undermined by a recent bomb attack on this tiny minority community. In October 2015, when the Shia community with thousands of Sunni Muslim devotees was preparing to start an annual rally on the occasion of Ashura at its historic site—Hussaini Dalan, old Dhaka—sudden bomb explosions before dawn killed a Sunni boy and injured nearly 100. ISIS reportedly took responsibility for the attack. However, the government dismissed this on the grounds that ISIS presence in Bangladesh was absurd (*BBC News* 24 October 2015). Thus diversity within Islam and the Muslim community in Bangladesh is being undermined with the rise of an intolerant and hostile religious environment.

In this context, the persecution of the Ahmadiyya community may become more virulent if the Islamic forces, both legitimate and illegitimate, find a congenial political context for their agenda. Of all "other" Islamic groups and practices, the danger of persecution of the Ahmadiyya community stems from the fact that it is visibly legitimized because the state's efforts often favour the demands of the anti-Ahmadi outfits and delimit the religious rights and freedom of the Ahmadiyya community. The leadership of the Ahmadiyya community views the threats and resistance against them as an "anti-Bangladeshi" element, imported from Pakistan. The ideological foothold of undivided Pakistan (1947–1971), against which Bangladesh struggled and fought for independence—that is, the use of Islam to legitimize the exploitation of Bengali people—has been a boomerang that passed through desecularization policy, the hybridization of Islam and religion, the establishment of political Islamic forces, and popularizing Islamic discourses in post-1980s Bangladesh. This eventually led to an environment where Ahmadiyya's as well as other non-orthodox groups' religious practices, rituals and festivals are increasingly challenged. Although sectarian and subsectarian strife have not been dominant so far, it is likely that a closer relationship between publicly visible anti-Ahmadi outfits and clandestine militant Islamic groups will lead to heightened violent persecution of the Ahmadiyya community in Bangladesh. This is bound to happen if the state fails to demarcate the boundary between religion and politics, and the political leadership, both Islamic and non-Islamic, bow to popular Islamic demands on the basis of majoritarian theory.

NOTES

1. For the Islamic political fronts beyond the BJI, evolved in the 1980s under the leadership of Bengali Deobandi scholars and Sufi master, see Kabir (2015).
2. Since the birth of Bangladesh in 1971, the role of Islam in the formation and evolution of the state can be underlined in three distinct paradigms: disintegrative, rhetorical and fusion. The disintegrative paradigm under which the state adopted secularism as a state principle and proscribed political exploitation of religion was undermined when the desecularization—that is, adaptation of Islam as a state ideology and reinstitution of Islamic political parties—was deliberately promoted by the military regime (1977–1990). The rhetorical paradigm began to transform into the fusion paradigm when the government revived secularism as a state principle but retained Islam as a state religion (Kabir, 2015, pp. 59–62).
3. Conversation with a Mufti (jurist-consult), Jamia Qurania Arabia madrassa, Lalbagh, Dhaka, September 2009.
4. Metcalf (1982, p. 264) coined the term to denote the theological distance and difference of various offshoots of Sunni Islam.
5. Maulana Abdul Awal Khan Chowdhury, member of Ahmadiyya Jamaat, recorded interview, September 2009, Bakshibazaar, Dhaka.
6. Interview with Hazrat Maulana Mufti Muhammad Nurullah (d. 2009), a Deoband returnee scholar, and Principal of Jamia Islamia Yunusia Madrasa, Brahmanbaria, August, 2008.

7. Interview with Maulana Abdul Awal Khan.
8. "Qadiani" refers to the Ahmadiyya followers, with derogatory connotations, because the founder of Ahmadiyya Jamaat was from Qadian, India.
9. Recorded interview with Maulana Abdus Sattar, former graduate of Yunusia Madrasa and teacher of Al-Batul Girls' Madrasa, Brahmanbaria, October, 2005.
10. Recorded interview with Mufti Muhammad Nurullah, Director of Yunusia Madrasa, Brahmanbaria, September, 2004.
11. In 1998, when a national NGO organized a fair for its clients, mostly impoverished rural women, in Brahmanbaria town, many ulema and their disciples started to resist the fair as "un-Islamic" in nature because it allowed the intermingling of men and women in a public place, which, according to them, is not permitted in Islam (see Kabir, 2012, pp. 26–30).
12. Inclusive to the nature of Islam in Bangladesh is "an amalgam of Buddhist, Hindu, and local syncretistic practices, combined with Sufi-inspired Islam and Shia practices" (Ahmed 1983, p. v). For detail about syncretistic tradition, see Roy (1983)
13. On the political rise of the Bengali Deobandis and Maulana Hafezzi Huzur, see Kabir (2015, pp. 62–66).
14. He received advanced theological education at a Pakistani Deobandi seminary, the Jamia Uloom-e Islamia Madrasa of Banoori town, Karachi. He founded a political party—Islamic Morcha—which joined the IOJ in 1996.

References

Ahmadiyya Bangla. (2008). Bangladeshe Ahmadiyyat[Ahmadiyya in Bangladesh]. Retrieved August 30, 2015, from http://www.ahmadiyyabangla.org/Ahmadiyyat-in-Bangladesh.htm.

Ahmed, Rafiuddin. (1996) [1981]. *The Bengal muslims 1871–1906: A quest for identity*. Delhi: Oxford University Press.

Ashraf, J. A. (Ed.). (2008). *Akashchuwa Minar: Jatiya Khatib Hazrat Maulana Obaidul Haq Smorone*. Dhaka: Madrasa Faizul Uloom.

Asian Human Rights Commission/AHRC. (2011). Bangladesh: Government fails to protect freedom of religion and assembly of Ahmadiyya community. Retrieved October 3, 2015, from http://www.humanrights.asia/news/urgent-appeals/AHRC-UAC-042-2011

Banu, U. A. B. R. A. (1992). *Islam in Bangladesh*. Leiden: Brill.

BBC News. (1999, October 10). Six die in Bangladesh bomb attack. Retrieved October 2, 2015, from http://news.bbc.co.uk/2/hi/south_asia/469548.stm

BBC News. (2004, January 9). Bangladesh bans Islam sect books. Retrieved October 15, 2015, from http://news.bbc.co.uk/2/hi/south_asia/3382931. stm

BBC News. (2015, October 24). Dhaka blasts: One dead in attack on Shia Ashura ritual. http://www.bbc.com/news/world-asia-34625375

Bdnews24.com. (2005a, May 3). Nizami makes oblique reference to Ahmadiyyas: Says followers of 'so-called prophet' are 'Kafir'. Retrieved September 30, 2015 from http://bdnews24.com/politics/2005/05/03/nizami-makes-oblique-reference-to-ahmadiyyas-says-followers-of-so-called-prophet-are-kafir

Bdnews24.com. (2005b, August 12). Bomb blast in Shrine in Akhaura: One killed, 100 injured. Retrieved September 30, 2015, from http://bdnews24. com/bangladesh/2005/08/12/bomb-blasts-in-shrine-in-akhaura-one-killed-100-injured-updated

Bdnews24.com. (2006, January 17). Zealots obstruct burial of elderly Ahmadiyya woman in Brahmanbaria. Retrieved October 2, 2015, from http://bdnews24. com/bangladesh/2006/01/17/zealots-obstruct-burial-of-elderly-ahmadiyya-woman-in-brahmanbaria

Esposito, J. L., & Voll, J. O. (1996). *Islam and democracy*. New York: Oxford University Press.

Friedmann, Yohanan. (2003) [1989]. *Prophecy continuous: Aspect of Ahmadi religious thought and its medieval background*. Berkley: University of California Press.

Haroon, S. (2008). The rise of Deobandi Islam in the north-west frontier province and its implication in colonial India and Pakistan 1914–1996. *Journal of Royal Asiatic Society, 18*(1), 47–70.

Hossain, Sara. (2004). 'Apostates', Ahmadis and advocates: Use and abuse of offences against religion in Bangladesh. Retrieved October 17, 2015, from http://www.wluml.org/sites/wluml.org/files/import/english/pubs/pdf/wsf/10.pdf

HRW (Human Rights Watch)/Asia. (2005). *Breach of faith: Persecution of the Ahmadiyya community in Bangladesh*. New York: Human Rights Watch.

Islam, M. S. (2011). "Minority" Islam in Muslim majority Bangladesh: The violent road to a new brand of secularism. *Journal of Muslim Minority Affairs, 31*(1), 125–141.

Ismail, M. M. (2005). Hafezzi Huzur (RA) er Jiboner Tritiyo Karmasuchi Jihad Fi Sabilillah. In H. H. Parishad (Ed.), *Hafezzi Huzur Smarok Grantha* (pp. 170–256). Dhaka: Hafezzi Huzur Parishad.

Kabir, M. G. (1995). *Changing face of nationalism: The case of Bangladesh*. Dhaka: University Press Limited.

Kabir, H. (2009). Replicating the Deobandi model of Islamic schooling: The case of a Quomi madrasa in a district town of Bangladesh. *Contemporary South Asia, 17*(4), 415–428.

Kabir, Humayun. (2012). *Politics of Islam, the state, and the contested cultural identity: Ulama's activism in postcolonial Bangladesh.* A scholarly peer-reviewed pamphlet. Alexandria: Bibliotheca Alexandrina.

Kabir, H. (2015). Beyond Jamaat-e-Islami: The political rise of the Deobandis, the mystic leaders, and Islamism in Bangladesh. In I. Mattson, P. Nesbitt-Larking, & N. Tahir (Eds.), *Religion and representation: Islam and democracy* (pp. 50–77). New Castle: Cambridge Scholars Publishing.

Ludhianvi, Maulana Muhammad Yusuf. (2000). *Qadiani abong onnano kafirder modhe parthoko* [the difference between Qadiani and other infidels]. (Mufti Muhammad Abdullah). Dhaka: Batil Protirodh Library.

Merchant, L. (1990). *Jinnah: A judicial verdict.* Karachi: East–west Publishing Company.

Metcalf, B. D. (1982). *Islamic revival in British India Deoband, 1860–1900.* New Delhi: Oxford University Press.

Mohsin, A. A. (2004). Religion, politics and security: The case of Bangladesh. In S. P. Limaye, R. G. Wirsing, & M. Malik (Eds.), *Religious radicalism and security in South Asia* (pp. 467–488). Honolulu: Asia-Pacific Centre for Security Studies.

Reetz, D. (2007). The Deoband universe: What makes a transcultural and transnational educational movement of Islam. *Comparative Studies of South Asia, Africa and the Middle East, 27*(1), 139–159.

Riaz, A. (2004). *God willing: The politics of Islamism in Bangladesh.* Lanham: Rowman and Littlefield.

Riaz, A. (2008). *Islamist militancy: A complex web.* London: Routledge.

Riaz, A. (2009). Interactions of 'transnational' and 'local' Islam in Bangladesh. In P. Mandaville, F. a. Noor, A. Horstmann, D. Reetz, A. Riaz, et al. (Eds.), *Transnational Islam in South and Southeast Asia: Movements, networks and conflict dynamics.* Washington: The National Bureau of Asian Research.

Riaz, A., & Fair, C. C. (2010). *Political Islam and governance in Bangladesh.* London: Routledge.

Roy, A. (1983). *The Islamic Syncretistic Tradition in Bengal.* Princeton, New Jersey: Princeton University

The Daily Star. (2003a, November 22). Bid to capture Ahmadiyya mosque turns violent. Retrieved September 29, 2015, from http://www.thedailystar. net/2003/11/22/d3112201033.htm

The Daily Star. (2003b, December 27). Bigots demand bill declaring Ahmadiyyas non-Muslims. Retrieved August 30, 2015, from http://archive.thedailystar. net/2003/12/27/d3122701077.htm

The Daily Star. (2004, October 30). Ahmadiyya mosque razed, 12 houses robbed in B'baria 11 including 6 women injured. Retrieved September 30, 2015, from http://archive.thedailystar.net/2004/10/30/d4103001044.htm

The Daily Star. (2005a, June 25). Ahmadiyya area in B'baria bombed, mosque torched. Retrieved September 30, 2015, from http://archive.thedailystar. net/2005/06/25/d5062501022.htm

The Daily Star. (2005b, August 16). Blasts at Ahmadiyya house injures woman, bombs were planted, two suspects arrested. Retrieved October 2, 2015, from http://archive.thedailystar.net/2005/08/16/d5081601097.htm

The Daily Star. (2006, May 21). Section 144 bars Ahmadiyyas from holding religious festival in B'baria. Retrieved September 30, 2015, from http://archive.thedailystar.net/2006/05/21/d60521012714.htm

The Daily Star. (2010a, March 20). Cops dictate terms for Ahmadiyya programmes. Retrieved September 30, 2015, from www.thedailystar.net/newDesign/news-details.php?nid=130840

The Daily Star. (2010b, August 25). Tangail Ahmadiyyas left to live on nerves. Retrieved September 30, 2015, from http://archive.thedailystar.net/newDesign/news-details.php?nid=152200

The Daily Star. (2011, February 7). Bigots foil Ahmadiyya convention. Retrieved October 20, 2015, from http://archive.thedailystar.net/newDesign/news-details.php?nid=173186

The Daily Star. (2014). Souls of bauls bleeding. Retrieved October 20, 2015, from http://www.thedailystar.net/souls-of-bauls-bleeding-38412

The Express Tribune. (2015, Sep 4). 'Trained assassin' kills two at Bangladesh shrine. Retrieved October 30, 2015, from http://tribune.com.pk/story/950769/trained-assassin-kills-two-at-bangladesh-shrine/

The Persecution of Ahmadis. (2011, November 22). In *The situation in Brahmanbaria, Bangladesh.* Retrieved September 15, 2015, from https://www.persecutionofahmadis.org/the-situation-in-brahmanbaria-bangladesh/

Uddin, S. M. (2006). *Constructing Bangladesh: Religion, ethnicity, and language in an Islamic nation.* Chapel Hill: The University of North Carolina Press.

Valentine, S. R. (2014). Prophecy after prophet, albeit lesser prophets? The Ahmadiyya Jamaat in Pakistan. *Contemporary Islam, 8*(2), 99–113.

van Schendel, W. (2009). *A history of Bangladesh.* Cambridge: Cambridge University Press.

Zaman, M. Q. (2007). Tradition and authority in Deobandi madrasas of South Asia. In R. W. Hefner & M. Q. Zaman (Eds.), *Schooling Islam: The culture and politics of modern Muslim education* (pp. 1–39). Princeton: Princeton University Press.

CHAPTER 16

Hidden in Plain Sight: Deobandis, Islamism and British Multiculturalism Policy

Sam Westrop

For decades, government, media and much of academia have treated Muslims as one homogenous bloc. Those who concern themselves with the question of Islam, especially regarding the problems of extremism and terrorism, have largely ignored the realities of religious, cultural and ethnic diversity among British Muslims. The distinct failure to consider British Islam's various constituents is all the more astounding when one considers the amount of attention that it otherwise receives. The fundamental failure to delve deeper—to examine and define British Islam—has been deftly exploited by Islamist and ultraconservative Islamic groups, who have asserted themselves as political and religious representatives of British Muslims, to little protest from an ill-informed political and intellectual elite.

Deobandi clerics, in particular, have discovered a polity that is not just uncertain of how to respond to Islam but is also not sure what British Islam is, and whom it represents. Although Deobandi Islam has various shades, few scholars would dispute that it is ultimately an ultraconservative branch of Sunni Islam, whose clerics propagate ideas that sharply, and sometimes violently, clash with tolerant, democratic standards. In the UK, the imposition of the Deobandi orthodoxy is most clearly seen within

S. Westrop (✉)
Gatestone Institute, New York, NY, USA

© The Editor(s) (if applicable) and The Author(s) 2016   453
J. Syed et al. (eds.), *Faith-Based Violence and Deobandi Militancy in Pakistan*, DOI 10.1057/978-1-349-94966-3_16

chaplaincy programmes. In schools, prisons, universities and hospitals, Deobandi clerics are entrusted with the welfare of young British Muslims by policy-makers who are oblivious to the politics of British Islam.

Today the make-up of British Islam partly reflects the competing schools of thought within South Asian Islam. As within South Asia, the two dominant groups are the Deobandi and Barelvi denominations, which together command a clear majority of British mosques. In the late nineteenth century, the Barelvi movement grew in response to the perceived threat of Deobandi puritanism. Today these tensions continue to dominate political and religious discourse in South Asia, as well as the fractious development of British Islam. Barelvi Muslims represent the traditional or cultural Sufi practices of Islam, such as the milad (the birthday of the Prophet), qawwali (devotional music), urs (death anniversary of a Sufi saint) and other festivals. However, Deobandis, despite their claim to Sufism, reject these Sufi practices, declaring them un-Islamic and polytheistic (Moj 2015). Philip Lewis (2014, p. 237) notes that gradual "Talibanisation" has made Barelvis "bitterly hostile" to British Deobandis of Pakistani origin. Whereas the Barelvis "emphasize love and spirituality", writes Innes Bowen (2014, p. 4), the Deobandis place "more stress on orthodoxy and knowledge of Islamic texts". Although Deobandi Islam grew out of the Sufi tradition, its founding ideologues were influenced by Wahhabism and thus quickly denounced particular Sufi traditions—such as the visiting of shrines or the celebration of the Prophet Muhammad's birthday—as idolatrous.

In this sense, Deobandi Islam shares certain outlooks with its puritanical cousins, Arabia's Salafists, who also condemn Sufi veneration of the Prophet as a challenge to the monotheistic principles of Islam. Although the founding ideologues of both the Salafist Wahhabis and the Deobandis took inspiration from the thirteenth-century revivalist scholar Ibn Taymiyyah, there remain key jurisprudential differences. As we will discover, the alliance between today's Deobandis and Salafists is not particularly the result of any religious accord but of strategic necessity and financial influence. Although Salafist movements are spreading across the globe, in the UK it is the Deobandis who maintain a firm hold over British Muslims.

In 2014, data collected by Mehmood Naqshbandi (2014) concluded that of the UK's 1,740 mosques, 754, or 43.3 percent, were Deobandi. Three Deobandi institutions in particular, and their networks, are perceived as the most influential: the missionary organization TJ, the seminary

Darul Uloom Bury and the clerical body Jamiat Ulama-e-Britain (JUB). Naturally, they propagate the same theology and there is a great deal of overlap between these networks. There is also some overlap with British Islamist movements, including the South Asian Islamist group JI, and Saudi-backed Salafist organizations.

As we shall see, British Deobandis were emboldened by the protests against Salman Rushdie, which demonstrated to Deobandi institutions the value of outrage in the name of Islam. We will look at the institutions that make up British Deobandi Islam, as well as the ideas and rhetoric discussed by Deobandi seminaries, schools and their clerics. We shall examine the link between British Deobandi Islam and terrorism, and the Deobandi relationship with Islamism. And we will discuss the reasons why some Deobandi clerics no longer advocate complete seclusion from society, and why Deobandi Islam has become such a dominant force within British Islam.

British Deobandis are connected to extremist movements in South Asia as well as the proliferation of extremist thought among young British Muslims. By appointing Deobandi scholars to mentor young Muslims through the chaplaincy system, partly in an effort to combat extremist views, the authorities risk reinforcing the very cause of the problem. Further investigation of the influence of the Deobandi movement in the UK affords us an opportunity to explore the roots of Islamic extremism as well as expose the serious flaws in our attempts to tackle it.

THE RUSHDIE AFFAIR

British Deobandis first asserted themselves as a voice of British Islam during the 1989 protests against Salman Rushdie's novel *The Satanic Verses*. After Iran's Ayatollah Khomeini issued his infamous fatwa against Rushdie, some prominent British Islamists remember the protests as a moment of focused unity for British Muslims. Inayat Bunglawala, a prominent British Muslim commentator, was a student at the time. He recounts: "I felt a thrill. It was incredibly uplifting. The fatwa meant that as British Muslims we did not have to regard ourselves just as a small, vulnerable minority; we were part of a truly global and powerful movement" (Malik 2010, p. 18).

The sense of a unified Muslim voice might have been felt among some laypeople, but among the leaders of British Muslim sects the reality was perhaps the opposite. The protests against Rushdie marked a powerful change in the perception and practice of Islam in the UK. Across the world, in fact, Rushdie did not offer a target for a united Islamic undertaking but a means by which individual Islamic movements could assert their own dominance. As Kenan Malik (2010, p. 18) notes, the Iranian fatwa was a brazen challenge to Saudi influence: Khomeini's "bold action seemed to contrast with the spinelessness of the Saudis". It offered Muslims around the world a "new moral and religious struggle to restore their pride".

Religious outrage as a means to achieve political dominance was also played out in the UK. Competing protest and friction between the country's Deobandi, Barelvi and JI institutions served to fuel *The Satanic Verses* anger. The initial campaign against the book was coordinated by the United Kingdom Action Committee on Islamic Affairs (UKACIA), a Saudi-backed organization run mostly by JI operatives. While the Jamaatis and the Saudis were appealing for Muslim governments to ban the book, collecting petition signatures and lobbying British politicians, it was actually British Deobandis who organized the first public protest in the UK. In December 1988, 7,000 British Muslims marched through the city of Bolton (Lustig et al. 1989). The large number of Deobandi mosques gathered grassroots support with ease. The JI, which had political institutions but few mosques, was unable to garner such support. But the Deobandis, without the political influence and media contacts enjoyed by the JI, failed to attract the attention of the media to their protest.

A month later, on 14 January 1989, there was another demonstration in Bradford, organized by the Bradford Council of Mosques. This time the protest received worldwide attention. A crowd of 1,000 Muslims arrived at the city hall, where the book was doused with petrol and set alight (Hadfield 1989). Some of Bradford's elected councillors attended the demonstration and advocated that the book be banned. The Bradford Council of Mosques comprised representatives of Deobandi and Barelvi mosques and associations. During the Rushdie affair, its president was Sher Azam, who is today a committee member of Jami'at-i Ulama Britannia, a prominent Deobandi institution. In contrast with Bolton, the Deobandis in Bradford enjoyed a close relationship with local decision-makers. The Bradford Council of Mosques was, in fact, subsidized by the local authorities, which, in accordance with multiculturalist policy, had delegated the provision of certain social services among Bradford Muslims to the Bradford Council of Mosques. Giles Kepel (2004, p. 136) notes that the political dominance of this Deoband-led council meant that "the only option for the Indian/Pakistani youth of Muslim origin ... who felt culturally attacked by *The Satanic Verses*, was therefore to sign up for the campaign organized by the Bradford Council of Mosques and other local Islamic associations". Amateur film of the book-burning was passed to the media, which was broadcast by television stations across the world. The JI groups were not happy with the Deobandi success. Representatives of the Islamic Foundation, a prominent JI organization, later claimed that the demonstration was "staged … to spread a negative image of Islam" (Ahsan and Kidwai 1991, p. 41). The battle against Rushdie was also a battle for the leadership of British Islam.

Over the following months, a number of British Islamic movements competed to demonstrate their outrage, while Islamic regimes abroad competed to demonstrate their influence. Both Iran and Saudi Arabia funded British protests. Iran reportedly gave $1 million for a demonstration outside Parliament (Pipes 2009, p. 164), during which the novel and effigies of its author were burnt. Once Khomeini had issued his fatwa, Giles Kepel (2004, p. 139) writes, he "was effectively proclaiming himself the spiritual guide of all Muslims and thereby wresting the leadership role from the Saudis". Despite the Iranian backing for protests, few British Shiites took part in the anger. While young Muslims such as Inayat Bunglawala may have felt empowered by apparent Muslim unity in outrage, Sunni Islamic leaders, whether in Bradford, the UK or internationally, saw each other not as comrades but as rivals. And although Iranian money may have found its way into the pockets of British Islamic groups, officials from the Deobandi-led Bradford Council of Mosques lamented that Iran's fatwa had "pulled the rug from under our feet" (Kepel 2004, p. 140).

British Deobandis learned an important lesson from the Rushdie affair. By protesting against Rushdie, Deobandi leaders had accrued some legitimacy as a voice of British Islam. Gradually discarding the complete isolation of the past, a section of the UK's Deobandi movement cautiously began to involve themselves in a few public endeavours. Deobandi mosques and associations may have lacked the political contacts that the JI groups enjoyed, but whereas the JI had lobby groups and media savvy, the Deobandis had religious and community institutions—they had grassroots power.

BRITISH DEOBANDI INSTITUTIONS AND THEIR CLERICS

In contrast with the political Islam of the JI or the Muslim Brotherhood, which have, on occasion, actively rejected the influence of ulema, religious institutions are the key to the Deobandi movement's power, and the most important institution within Deobandi Islam is the seminary. During British colonial rule in the nineteenth century India, these seminaries were created by Muslims, explains Philip Lewis (2002), in order to survive without political power. In the UK the first Deobandi seminary was established in Bury in 1973. Darul Uloom al-Arabiya al-Islamiya, also known as Darul Uloom Bury, was the project of Sheikh Yusuf Motala, who acted on the instructions of his mentor, Sheikh Mohammad Zakariya (1898–1982). In 1976 the Bury seminary received more than £40,000 from Saudi "philanthropists" (Inter-Islam). Then, in 1982, a second seminary, the Institute for Islamic Education, was opened in Dewsbury. The Dewsbury seminary, also known as Darul Uloom Dewsbury, became part of the headquarters of the Deobandi missionary organization, the TJ. These two seminaries, in Bury and Dewsbury, have come to represent the two main strains of Deobandi Islam in the UK today.

The journalist Innes Bowen (2014) writes that, according to Dewsbury graduate Mushfiq Uddin, there are 22 Deobandi seminaries in the UK, 15 of which are offshoots of Darul Uloom Bury. Sophie Gilliat-Ray (2006, p. 58), meanwhile, claims that Bury "acts as the mother madrasah" to only "five other *dar ul-uloom* in Britain". The seclusion of Deobandi seminaries means that gathering accurate figures is difficult, especially as many seminaries are unregistered. Philip Lewis (2014, p. 238) believes there are 24 registered seminaries in the UK, comprising "sixteen Deobandi, five Barelvi, one Shi'ite, one of the Muslim Brotherhood and one founded by the late sheikh Dr Zaki Badawi". Along with unregistered seminaries, these figures do not include the growing number of part-time seminaries. Ebrahim College, for example, is an institution in Whitechapel that applies modern learning methods to traditional Deobandi teachings. Their offered courses even include online components, and the college is attempting to accredit its qualifications through the University of Gloucestershire. Mushfiq Uddin, who is chief executive of the Ebrahim College, regards his "college's connection to Deoband as an academic connection, rather than a sectarian or political one" (Bowen 2014, p. 20). In 2013, Ebrahim College publicized its courses at the Global Peace and Unity conference, an event organized by Muslim Brotherhood and JI officials.

The curriculum followed by seminaries, some Muslim commentators have argued, perpetuates Deobandi insularism. Musharraf Hussain, a government advisor on mosques, has claimed that "too many seminary students studied a narrow syllabus and inhabited a cocooned world". These graduates, he argues, are "without sufficient communication skills, without leadership skills and without a good understanding of British culture. The people coming out of British seminaries are detached because they can't fit in" (Gest and Norfolk 2008). Deobandi schools also appear to inculcate pupils with a complete devotion to Islam and a rejection of the outside world. The Institute of Islamic Education, a school in Dewsbury run by the Deobandi missionary sect the TJ, has warned that pupils caught "socialising with outsiders ... will be expelled if there is no improvement after cautioning" (Tubb 2015). At Tauheedul Islam Girls' High School, a state-funded school in Blackburn, schoolgirls were ordered "to wear the hijab outside the school and home" and "not bring stationery to school that contains un-Islamic images" (Griffiths et al. 2013). Visitors to the school included the Saudi cleric Sheikh Abdul Rahman al-Sudais, who has referred to Jews as "pigs" and "scum of the human race". Al-Sudais has blamed the "sins" of women, such as "unveiling, mingling with men, and being indifferent to the hijab", as the cause for natural disasters (Bradley 2006, p. 170). At the Jameah Girls' Academy in Leicester, girls as young as 11 are required to wear the *niqab* (the full-face covering). The schools' patrons have included Mufti Muhammad ibn Adam Al-Kawthari, a Deobandi cleric who has ruled that women should not leave the home, cannot refuse their husbands' demands for sex and should be stoned to death if they commit adultery (MacEoin 2009).

While institutions such as Ebrahim College appear to transcend the usual Islamic divisions and austere restrictions, most British Deobandis remain rooted in tradition. Nevertheless, the Bury network is not entirely of a single mind. Tensions between ulema have persistently arisen over the question of collaboration with the outside world. To some extent, the infamous book burnings during the Rushdie affair widened these internal divisions further. But such discord has always existed. In colonial India, the Deobandi ulema were, at times, split between those who supported working within a secular state and those who advocated establishing a separate Muslim state. Today in the UK, Deobandi clerics are, likewise, seemingly divided into those who want to isolate themselves from society and those who want to cultivate an Islamic influence over the laws and institutions under which they live. Barbara Metcalf (2011) notes of Deobandi movements in South Asia, "None of the Deobandi movements has a theoretical stance in relation to political life. They either expediently embrace the political culture of their time and place, or withdraw from politics completely." However, all of the groups associated with this movement continue to propagate Deobandi ideology and support each other while making use of the resources in their relevant domains. Notwithstanding their pragmatic differences, the pursuit of Islamic sharia remains their shared goal.

Today, some representatives of Deobandi organizations can be found involved with a number of interfaith bodies; Deobandi mosques are affiliated with Islamist-run umbrella organizations, such as the Muslim Council of Britain; and Deobandi schools have shown a greater willingness to open their doors occasionally to the curious visits of journalists or other faith leaders, especially in the wake of the Trojan Horse scandal, in which the British media uncovered extremist Islamist involvement in Birmingham schools. These examples of public contribution, however, do not seem to represent a broader ethos of openness and inclusion. They are, at best, a means for politicians to stave off concerns with the topical problems of extremism and radicalization; and a means for Deobandi Islam to gain influence over British Muslims by asserting its role as a voice of British Islam. Meanwhile, a considerable number of Deobandi ulema continue to warn Muslims not to mix with the kufr (a derogatory term for non-Muslims) and to reject the iniquities of Western mores.

Mufti Saiful Islam, for example, is a graduate of Darul Uloom Bury and Director of Jamiah Khatamun Nabiyeen, a Deobandi school in Bradford. He warns Muslims against imitating the kufr, and condemns anyone who buys or accepts Christmas presents (Lewis and Birt 2011). Other graduates of Darul Uloom Bury offer similar warnings. Mahmood Chandia, who is the proprietor of Madrasatul Imam Muhammad Zakariya, a Deobandi secondary school in Bolton, has preached that Jews use music as a "Satanic web" to corrupt young Muslims (Norfolk 2007b). Sheikh Ahmed Ali, who runs the Al-Mahadul Islami seminary in Bradford, heralded the 9/11 attacks as a "return to Islam: sisters are wearing hijab … the lion is waking up" (Norfolk 2007b).

Riyadh ul Haq, who runs the Al Kawthar Academy, is "widely seen", writes Innes Bowen (2014, p. 21), "as a potential successor to the principal of Darul Uloom Bury, Sheikh Yusuf Motala". Haq urges Muslims to be "steadfast" against the West's "persecution of the Muslims", and its "enmity, hostility, hatred of the *ummah*" (Lewis and Birt 2011). Haq describes the Taliban as "the only group of people upon the earth who are establishing the Sharia and the law of Allah". He claims that "the Jews … have monopolised everything: the Holocaust, God, money, interest, usury, the world economy, the media, political institutions … they monopolised tyranny and oppression as well. And injustice." And he warns

Muslims: "do not align yourselves with the kuffar" (Norfolk 2007c). The Inter-Islam website, which is run by members of the Darul Uloom Bury network, contains hundreds of lectures, notes and religious texts that echo the isolationist, anti-Jewish and anti-Western rhetoric of senior Deobandi clerics. It publishes religious texts that foretell a Muslim slaughter of the Jews come the Day of Judgement, and warns Muslims not to befriend Christians or "imitate the disbelievers" (Inter-Islam).

Aggressive Deobandi ideas are not just propagated by clerics at the seminaries. The Khatme Nubuwwat Academy, for example, is a Deobandi group in London. Its website states that the organization serves to "create awareness about the Qadiani (Ahmadiyya)", a much-persecuted Muslim minority sect, which the website refers to as "traitors both to Islam and to India" (Khatme Nubuwwat Academy). According to *The Independent* (Taylor 2010), Suhail Bawa, an imam at the group's mosque, has claimed that Ahmaddiyas are behind terrorist attacks in Pakistan, adding that "This will become apparent very soon to you all that Qadiani themselves are behind this whole conspiracy. [They] are responsible for whatever has happened in Lahore. This is all Qadiani conspiracy. They now come to television programs to try to falsely demonstrate their victimisation." According to one report, the Khatme Nubuwwat Academy also works in Pakistan to bring about the death penalty for non-Muslims. *The Express Tribune* (2012), an affiliate of *The New York Times*, has reported that Khatme Nubuwwat was actively supporting the prosecution of Asia Bibi on the charge of blasphemy: " 'We will chase her through hell ... don't worry about the money, hiring best lawyers,' Salam told *The Express Tribune*, quoting the son of Khatm-e-Nabuwat's London chapter's leader."

Foreign Deobandi lecturers, popular among the Bury network, conduct regular speaking tours in the UK. Ismail Menk, for instance, is a Zimbabwean cleric who studied at Darul Uloom Kantharia, a Deobandi seminary in India. He has been frequently invited to the UK by Muslim student societies and various Islamic charities to give lectures and speak at fundraising events. Menk's hostility to Western liberalism is unmistakable: he argues that democracy will lead to bestiality (Mufti Ismail Menk on Democracy and Freedom of Speech 2014), and he describes homosexuals as "filthy" and worse than "dogs and pigs" (Gay Muslims: Best Response Mufti Ismail Menk 2013).

In contrast, the push within British Deobandi Islam to work with the outside world is perhaps best represented by Ibrahim Mogra, another graduate of Darul Uloom Bury. Mogra is also the Assistant Secretary

General of the Muslim Council of Britain (MCB), an umbrella organization otherwise dominated by representatives of the JI. Mogra has become a public face of the MCB, conducting media interviews and appearing at press conferences organized jointly with other faith leaders. His media savvy and prominent political connections are a far cry from the Deobandi book burnings and street demonstrations during the Rushdie protests. In addition, Mogra is a regular speaker at interfaith dialogue events. He is a member of the Congress of Imams and Rabbis for Peace, as well as the Christian Muslim Forum. Mogra is one of a number of Deobandi clerics who recognize the value of working with decision-makers, with media and representatives of other religious groups. This inclusive approach is perhaps a response to the call of the Deobandi cleric Abul Hasan Ali an-Nadwi, who, in a speech before Darul Uloom Dewsbury in 1982, urged Muslims to engage with their non-Muslim hosts (Damiel 2013):

> You should leave an imprint on the host community of your usefulness. You must demonstrate your existence here is more beneficial than that of the native people. You must impart on them the lessons of humanity. You should demonstrate how noble and principled you are, and that there cannot be found more upright humans elsewhere besides you. You need to establish your worth, that you are a blessing and mercy for this country. However if you decide to live in an enclosed environment content with your Prayers and Fasting, apathetic to the people and society you live in, never introducing them to the high Islamic values, and your own personal qualities, then beware lest any religious or sectarian flares up. In such a situation you will not find safety.

Communication, however, does not mean integration. Even Ibrahim Mogra, who is frequently portrayed as a voice of moderation, has clearly expressed that Muslims should work with the outside world, but only to fix their "corrupt society" through the introduction of Islam. In 2002, addressing a Deobandi Youth Tarbiyyah Conference, Mogra (2002) encouraged Muslims to be "proactive": Muslims should vote, put up candidates, become school governors, "be involved in community projects", and "engage in mainstream politics and activities". He also warned Muslims against working with the security services. He tells his audiences that the West despises Islam, and that Muslims should not succumb to Western culture but resist it. He nevertheless believes that some limited engagement affords Muslims an opportunity to demonstrate the virtues of Islam and expose the failure of the West's "so-called progress ... We can point out to them [that] what they call backwardness is good for society."

Mogra is not the only public face of British Deobandi Islam. In an interview with Innes Bowen (2014, p. 14), Islam Ali Shah, a committee member of the JUB, explains that his organization works "to educate Muslims in Britain; to provide chaplaincy services to Muslims in prison or hospital; ... to ensure that mosques know how to comply with UK laws and regulations; and to advise Muslims about what is and what is not permissible". Most significantly, the "organisation's leaders have also been involved in some interfaith meetings". The JUB is a network of Pakistani Deobandi scholars and an offshoot of the JUI), Pakistan's leading Deobandi political party. One of the JUI's leaders has been described in Pakistan as a "patron of jihad". In 2007, a senior JUI leader, Fazlur Rehman, told *The Times* (Norfolk 2007a) that his organization and the British JUB "have a unanimity of thought and ideology". The general secretary of the JUB, Sheikh Mohammad Ismail, is a graduate of a Deobandi seminary in Pakistan described by the ICG as "the fountainhead of Deobandi militancy countrywide", whose students have "spread a web of similar jihadi madrassas across Karachi and beyond" (Norfolk 2007a). Other JUB officials include Ayub Laher, who is also an executive committee member of the Inter Faith Network for the UK, a taxpayer-funded umbrella group for interfaith organizations across the country. Laher is also a governor of the Carlton Bolling College, a Bradford state school that was implicated in 2014 as part of media and government investigations into extremism in schools. Media investigations (*BBC News* 2014) found that school staff segregated male and female students, drove out non-Muslim officials and altered the curriculum to accommodate hardline Islamic values. Whereas once these Deobandi clerics would have preached isolation from British society, it appears, as with Islamist movements such as the Muslim Brotherhood, that Deobandi organizations are now preaching interfaith and providing chaplaincy services by day but promoting hardline beliefs at night. Increasingly certain sections of the British Deobandis have become, entryist political movements.

There are some among British Deobandi who recognize the dangers of isolation. Sheikh Musa Admani, a Deobandi cleric in London, has said that the "subtle demonization" of British society instilled in young children in schools and seminaries may ultimately contribute to the problem of violent Islamic extremism (Bowen 2014).

If Ayub Laher, Ibrahim Mogra and Musa Admani are the friendly faces of British Deobandi Islam, then who are their polar opposites? Who are the committed isolationists? Certainly the clerics cited earlier, such as

Mahmood Chandia, warn about the evils of kufr, the West and the Jews, but they do not totally reject the societies in which they live. Chandia, for instance, concedes that a good education provides a means for Muslims to influence the institutions that shape society. He encourages Muslims to become school governors, judges, academics and journalists (Lewis 2004). Chandia himself is a lecturer at the University of Central Lancashire. The most important voice of isolationism, in fact, is the TJ, the Deoband's missionary movement.

Simply put, the TJ is a "world-wide movement which seeks to revive Islam by encouraging Muslims to lead their lives in accordance with the injunctions of Islamic law" (Sikand 1998). In practice, however, it serves to bring ordinary Sunni Muslims into the Deobandi fold. In the UK the first Tablighi seminary, the Institute for Islamic Education, was established in Dewsbury in 1982, under the management of Muhammad Ishaq Patel, a Tablighi leader in the UK. The TJ is not, however, separate from the Deobandi Bury network. The head of Darul Uloom Bury, Yusuf Motala, actually established the Bury institution on the orders of Muhammad Zakariya, the author of one of the TJ's most important texts, *Fazail-e-Amaal*. Philip Lewis and Jonathan Birt (2011, p. 109) claim, in fact, that, "even if the two movements are formally separate, the Tablighi Jamaat has been essential in supporting the rapid institutionalization of the Deobandi movement". As with Darul Uloom Bury, the Tablighis have enjoyed financial support from Saudi Arabia. In 1978 the construction of the TJ mosque in Dewsbury was subsidized by the World Muslim League, a Saudi organization that funds Salafist causes (Alexiev 2005). Wahhabi support for Tablighi missionary work has led mosques aligned with Saudi Arabia and the South Asian Ahl-e-Hadith movement in the UK to permit Tablighi activists to conduct activities from their mosques.

Tablighi rhetoric seems to be as exclusivist and illiberal as the Deobandi Bury network. A prominent Tablighi cleric, Ebrahim Rangooni, has declared that the TJ will "rescue the *ummah* [global Muslim community] from the culture and civilisation of the Jews, the Christians and enemies of Islam" so as to "create such hatred for their ways as human beings have for urine and excreta" (Nahid Kabir 2012, p. 152). Rangooni also warns about the "dangers" of Muslim children being educated by the "enemies of Allah" in non-Muslim schools: "Save your progeny from the education of school and college in the same way as you would save them from a lion or a wolf … To send them in the atmosphere of college is as dangerous as throwing them into hell with your own hands" (Sikand 1998).

Despite this paranoid, insular perspective, the TJ has often been described as a quietist movement that "remains aloof from worldly involvement, including, of course, all political affairs" (Sikand 2006). While the Deobandi Bury network sends its graduates to work in hospitals, prisons and even, as we have seen, at interfaith events, the TJ, on the other hand, remains a highly private network of missionaries, who, on occasion, have even eschewed computers and written records. As Innes Bowen (2014, p. 39) notes, "there is no major doctrinal dispute between the Tablighi Jamaat and the mainstream Deobandi movement in Britain, just a difference in method when it comes to encouraging religious observance".

Some critics, however, do not believe that the TJ is simply a benign missionary movement. Alex Alexiev (2005) writes that the West has dangerously misunderstood the TJ. The Tablighis, he writes, have

> always adopted an extreme interpretation of Sunni Islam, but in the past two decades, it has radicalized to the point where it is now a driving force of Islamic extremism and a major recruiting agency for terrorist causes worldwide ... Perhaps 80 percent of Islamist extremists in France come from Tablighi ranks, prompting French intelligence officers to call Tablighi Jamaat the "antechamber of fundamentalism".

Is the TJ in the UK a radicalizing force? For that matter, what involvement do British Deobandis as a whole have in the jihadist threat?

From Radical to Terrorist

Over the past few decades, a growing number of terrorist acts and terrorist groups have been linked to the UK's Deobandi networks. During the 1990s, Deobandi groups in the country were visited by fundraisers from the Taliban and the Kashmiri jihadist group the HUM. An English-language version of a Taliban/SSP publication, *Dharb-e-Momin* (Shield of the Believer), was commonly found in Deobandi mosques (Bowen 2014). *The Times* has reported that another Deobandi terror group, the JM, is thought to receive £5 million a year from British Muslims (Norfolk 2007a). In November 2003, the founder and head of Darul Uloom Bury, Sheikh Yusuf Motala, was held at Heathrow for seven hours under the Terrorism Act, although no charges or accusations were ever levelled against him. More importantly, however, a number of notorious British terrorists have been involved with the TJ and other Deobandi groups, including three of the July 2007 bombers, Richard Reid, Zacarias Moussaoui, and several of those involved with the airline bomb plot in 2006 (Bowen 2014). In 2003, after the arrest of a Deobandi student on suspicion of a terrorist offence, anti-terrorist police raided Jamiatul Ilm wal-Huda, a Deobandi seminary in Blackburn. The student, Saajid Badat, was later sentenced to 13 years in jail for planning to explode a passenger plane (*BBC News* 2005). And amid the growing number of British Muslims fleeing for Syria and Iraq to fight with ISIS, a significant number of recruits have emerged from Deobandi areas of the UK. Talha Asmal, an ISIS recruit and the UK's youngest suicide bomber, grew up in Saville Town, a part of Dewsbury almost entirely under the thumb of Deobandi institutions (Halliday 2015). Similarly, Khadija, Sugra and Zohra Dawood were three sisters who fled to Syria in 2015. They are the daughters of Mohammad Dawood, an imam at the Deobandi's Nusrat-e-Islami Mosque in Bradford (Fielding 2015).

It seems likely that the isolationist, anti-Western rhetoric preached by Deobandi ulema, seminaries and mosques contributes to the growing willingness of young British Muslims to commit violent acts. But in those instances of Deobandi involvement, there is also an element of radicalization of ordinary Muslims of other denominations. In the case of the 7/7 bomber Mohammed Siddique Khan, for example, although the media pointed out that he had worshipped at the TJ mosque in Dewsbury (Laville 2006), few mentioned that Khan was originally from a Barelvi family. This may well reflect the gradual radicalization of ordinary Sunni Muslims that has been taking place in recent decades owing to the increasing resources and influence of the Salafi and Deobandi ideologies in Islamic madrassas, mosques, literature and the media. But it is also important to note the overlaps with other denominations and sects. As Kenan Malik (2010, p. 108) writes, "For Siddique Khan the pull of fundamentalism came from several directions." His wife's family were from the Indian Deobandi tradition, while, in addition, "radical Islamist groups such as Hizb ut-Tahrir organized at Leeds Metropolitan University where both he and Patel were students". Another of the 7/7 bombers, Jamal Lindsay, regarded himself as a Salafist, and yet, reports Innes Bowen (2014, p. 43), he "rarely worshipped at his local Salafi mosque but chose instead to go with his Salafi jihadi mentor to a Tablighi Jamaat mosque because … they had identified it as a place where they might find people who they could convert to their far more radical belief system".

British Deobandi institutions are not the only bad apples on the tree. Islamist and Salafist groups and clerics have also been implicated in the radicalization of young British Muslims. In Cardiff, the sermons of Salafist preachers have been blamed for the radicalization of three young British Muslims: the brothers Nasser and Aseel Muthana and their friend, Reyaad Khan. The distraught father of the Muthana brothers told the *Daily Telegraph*, "Behind this are Islamic radicals, hiding behind the scenes, influencing the minds of young people. ... Someone is persuading them, brainwashing them, helping them travel, arranging tickets." Another anonymous source quoted by *The Telegraph* claimed that the three young Muslims were radicalized at the Al Manar Centre, an Islamic institution in Cardiff (Sawer and Mendick 2014). Clerics who have preached at the Al Manar Centre include Mohammad Al Arifi, a Salafist preacher banned from the UK, who has declared:

> There is no doubt that a person whom Allah enables to sacrifice his soul, and to fight for the sake of Allah, has been graced with a great honour ... Devotion to Jihad for the sake of Allah, and the desire to shed blood, to smash skulls and to sever limbs for the sake of Allah and in defence of His religion, is, undoubtedly, an honour for the believer. (MEMRI 2010)

Another regular Al Manar speaker, however, is Haitham Al Haddad, a British preacher who has described Jews as "apes and pigs" and "enemies of God" (RNW Media). Haddad, however, claims to represent both Salafist and Deobandi Islam, which he argues should not be seen as an "oxymoron", and says that the unity of these two schools of thought "equips the *ummah* with the necessary tools to free its thinking from narrow-mindedness, partisanship, shallowness, ignorance, and an inferiority complex" (Haddad 2009).

Deobandi Islam provides the raw, fundamental piety to which some terror recruits are initially drawn. It is not the sole recruiting ground for Islamist terror but it is evidently an important launching pad. Although Deobandi clerics such as Riyadh ul Haq preach the glory of martyrdom, the real threat that Deobandi Islam poses is not the explosive act of violence but the pernicious effect of extremism. The primary problem with the Deobandis, including British Deobandis, is not one of jihad but one of segregation. Greater violence and civil disorder will ultimately be the consequence of a far broader problem—that the single largest Islamic sect in the UK largely advocates isolation, hatred for non-Muslims (as well as minority Muslim sects) and a steadfast rejection of liberal democracy.

DEOBANDIS, ISLAMISTS AND THE PUBLIC SECTOR

If we accept the comments made by clerics such as Ibrahim Mogra (2002)—that limited engagement is a means to fix a "corrupt" and arrogant West—then where Deobandi ulema do appear to embrace mainstream society it is perhaps only to further a Deobandi agenda. Consequently, some critics may well be cautious of the increasing number of Deobandi clerics employed by the public sector, particularly within chaplaincy programmes.

As previously noted, it is difficult to establish the exact number of Deobandi seminaries in the UK. Across the country's Islamic sects, Philip Lewis and Jonathan Birt (2011, p. 97) note that

> a 2003 survey shows us that there are nearly 2,500 young men studying in seminaries ... A reasonable estimate is that currently around 140 *ulema* graduate in Britain every year ... Around 80 per cent of the current graduates are Deobandi—well out of proportion to the size of their natural constituency—and this clear majority is likely to be even more dominant given the fact that, with a single exception, the Barelwi [seminaries] function more as preparatory schools for further basic and advanced study abroad.

Consequently "there are far more graduates being produced than available imamate positions allow ... Thus the graduates, the vast bulk of them Deobandi, have and will continue to have to look outside the traditional forms of employment."

During the 1990s, a growing Muslim prison population brought about a need for Muslim prison imams. For the surplus of unemployed Deobandi clerics, prison chaplaincy was an obvious career prospect. Maqsood Ahmed, the first Muslim Adviser to Prisons, appointed by the Ministry of Justice in 1999, was even invited to Darul Uloom Bury to address students about the life of a prison imam (Gilliat-Ray 2006). In their study of Muslim chaplaincy, Sophie Gilliat-Ray et al. (2013, pp. 9–10) conclude that, consequently, "some of the first appointments of Muslim chaplains in both the prison and health contexts were among individuals from the Deobandi school of thought, and graduates of British Islamic seminaries". By 2009 there were 203 Muslim chaplains employed by the Prison Service and, "as a result of the early formation of Deobandi seminaries in Britain, many of these chaplaincy posts have been taken up by graduates of these institutions" (Gilliat-Ray 2012, p. 173).

From the start, however, prison chaplaincy drew in some hardline clerics. In June 1991, *Muslim News* dedicated a full page to the increasing

Muslim prison population. It featured an interview with Dr Ijaz Mian, who was attending to Muslim inmates in a number of prisons (Dhalla 1991). At the time, Mian was an imam at the Lewisham and Kent Islamic Centre. He would later be filmed by an undercover documentary team advocating the introduction of religious police to regulate Islamic behaviour, and telling his congregants at the Ahl-e-Hadith mosque in Derby, "You cannot accept the rule of the *kaffir*. We have to rule ourselves and we have to rule the others" (Doward 2007).

Allegations of extremism among prison imams have continued to surface over the years. In December 2001, three prison imams were suspended after allegedly circulating anti-US literature among Muslim prisoners in the wake of the 9/11 attacks. Paul Goodman MP (HC Deb 2006–2007) has noted that Muktar Said Ibrahim, who took part in the July 2007 terrorist attacks in London, is "alleged to have been indoctrinated in Feltham or Aylesbury young offenders institutions", where these suspended imams had worked. Some studies report that officials suspected Abdul Ghani Qureshi, the father of one of the suspended imams, had himself radicalized the convicted Al-Qaeda "shoe bomber", Richard Reid, when he preached at the same Feltham prison where Reid had been incarcerated (Hamm 2007, p. 30).

Today, problems still abound. Prison chaplains include Deobandi clerics such as Azadul Hussain, a graduate of a Deobandi seminary in London who has circulated, on social media, far-right conspiracy theories that blame the deposal of the Egyptian Muslim Brotherhood on a Jewish conspiracy (Hussain 2013). He is also a supporter of radical Islamist groups, such as CAGE and HT (Westrop 2014). Other prison chaplains include Yusuf Az Zahaby, a Deobandi scholar who is a "leading member of the Islamist organisation Al Hikma Media", where his colleagues include "Shady Suleiman, who promotes killing women who engage in premarital sex", and the Salafist campaigner "Abdur Raheem Green, who condones beating women to 'bring them to goodness' " (Gibbons 2014).

Amid concerns about radicalization in prisons, the government claims that chaplaincy is an important weapon in the battle against extremism, but it does not monitor the influence of Deobandi clerics within chaplaincy programmes: "The Prison Service employs skilled Imams, from a range of backgrounds, who are able to challenge and address extremist ideology regardless of faith or ethnic background" (Ford 2012). The Ministry of Justice has also declared that it does not "hold data" on its chaplains' religious affiliations, stating instead that "Muslim Chaplains are employed to meet the religious and pastoral needs of prisoners and are required to meet specified eligibility criteria and be assessed on skills and competencies: there is no requirement that relates to specific denomination" (Ministry of Justice 2012). Moreover, taxpayer-funded investigative reports of chaplaincy programmes fail to mention any of British Islam's various sects (Faith Matters 2010). As long as the authorities treat British Sunni Islam as a single homogenous bloc, it is hardly surprising that particular sects are keen to assert themselves as the leaders of British Islam. In the case of chaplaincy, British Deobandi have seen an opportunity to advance the reach of their institutions in lieu of the political influence enjoyed by the JI groups.

Not everyone, however, is ignorant of the overwhelming Deobandi influence. The academic Sophie Gilliat-Ray, for instance, is a prolific researcher of Muslim communities in the UK. She has written a great deal about prison chaplaincy and is a member of the Home Office's Task Force on Preventing Extremism. Gilliat-Ray et al. (2013, p. 63) contends, however, that Deobandi influence over chaplaincy is beneficial: "If numerous different schools of Islamic thought began to contest 'what counts' as Muslim chaplaincy practice, or challenged prevalent ideas about the practice of Islam in British public institutions, this sphere of religious work would then become disruptive and more difficult to manage."

Evidently, Muslim advisers to the government have also been aware of the Deobandi link to prison chaplaincy. It is no coincidence that Maqsood Ahmed, the first Muslim adviser to the Prison Service, chose to solicit candidates for chaplaincy from Darul Uloom Bury (Gilliat-Ray 2006). Today the recruitment of Muslim chaplains is managed by Ahtsham Ali, the current Muslim adviser to the Prison Service. In 2011, a Home Office committee examining the "roots of violent radicalization" questioned Ali about the role of prison chaplaincy. He was asked, "How do you ensure that extremist imams are not brought into prison roles?" In response, Ali explained that "All recruitment for employed Muslim chaplains has to take place through myself. I have to be present at every single recruitment board and I have been present at every board for the past eight years since I have been in post. Each individual has to have credible qualifications through seminaries" (Home Office 2011). Before his work with the Prison Service, however, Ahtsham Ali worked for a number of JI organizations. He was previously the President of Young Muslims UK, a Jamaati youth group whose publications, under Ali's direction, were criticized by the Institute of Jewish Affairs (1995, p. 242) as "couched in anti-Semitic terms". In 1994, while in charge of Young Muslims UK, Ali gave an interview to *Q News*, in which he defended his organization's "working relationship" with the HT (Asghar 1994).

Ahtsham Ali is not the only Jamaat-associated official to oversee Deobandi influence in the chaplaincy. In 2003 the Markfield Institute of Higher Education established a Certificate in Muslim Chaplaincy. It is there that "many of the religious scholars who contribute to the programme have trained within Deobandi seminaries in Britain, and are connected to the associated scholarly networks" (Gilliat-Ray et al. 2013). The Markfield Institute is, in fact, a branch of the Islamic Foundation, the leading publisher of books by the JI ideologue, Abul Ala Maududi. The Islamic Foundation's current chairman, Khurshid Ahmad, was vice-president of the Pakistani branch of the JI political party. He has described the Taliban as "refulgent and splendid", and has warned of the "implication of Europe's being in the clasp of Jews" (Ahmad 2003a, b).

A similar relationship between political Islam and Deobandi Islam was observed during the Trojan Horse scandal. House of Commons (2014), Peter Clarke (2014), whom the government appointed to investigate allegations of extremism in Birmingham schools, concluded that Islamist plotters relied on Islamic preachers from the "Salafi, Deobandi spectrum". The ringleaders of the Trojan Horse plot, the inquiry's report further reveals, advocated working with Al Hikma, an organization run by preachers such as Shaykh Yusuf Az Zahaby, a Deobandi prison chaplain. Lucy Michael (2011) has observed that, in Manchester, JI and Muslim Brotherhood groups organize political activities, while the religious element is provided by Deobandi organizations. In contrast with the rivalry during the Rushdie protests, the JI and British Deobandis have since established a symbiotic relationship.

Whether seminaries, youth groups or chaplain networks, both the JI and the Deobandis have recognized, writes Pnina Werbner (1996, p. 108), the value of

> forming associations for young Muslims, thereby drawing them away from a
> 'sinful' Western popular culture ... The present popular Islamic radicalism in
> Britain thus draws on discourses formulated by groups such as the Jamaat-i-
> Islami, but fused with an eclectic range of Western liberal discourses as well
> as values grounded in Sufi popular Islam.

This collaboration is not limited to British Deobandi clerics. The leading Pakistani Deobandi scholar, Taqi Usmani, serves on the International

Advisory Council of the JI-run Markfield Institute of Higher Education. Patrick Sookhdeo (2008, p. 107) notes that

> Taqi Usmani asserts than an aggressive expansionist military jihad should be waged by Muslims against non-Muslim lands to establish the supremacy of Islam worldwide. He argues that Muslims live peacefully in countries such as Britain, where they have the freedom to practice Islam, bur only until they gain enough power to engage in battle.

As with the Rushdie affair, while the JI wields the political influence, the Deobandis provide the grassroots, clerical support—a fundamentalist religious foundation on which political Islam can build its ideas.

The UK's Deobandi institutions have prospered within the state multiculturalism model. Although the Deobandi seminaries were originally designed simply to replicate the Gujarati Indian model of religious schooling, since the Rushdie affair, Deobandi groups have also become important middlemen between British Muslims and government. The demonstrations in Bradford, along with racial and religious strife in other British cities, hastened the introduction of multiculturalist policies, both locally and nationally. As the academic Lorenzo Vidino (2010, pp. 135–137) notes, "The British multicultural model has traditionally relied heavily on community leaders who act as trusted intermediaries between the community and the state, to whom the latter can delegate the administration of various services." Local authorities entrusted groups such as the Deobandi-led Bradford Council of Mosques with the provision of certain social services. The government thought, Vidino explains, that it could use Islam as an "antidote to social malaises that plagued the Asian community". And the funds that Islamic organizations received from government allowed them to "significantly alter the balance of power [within the Muslim community] as secular organizations struggled to compete".

British state multiculturalism has mostly subcontracted its dealings with British Muslims to groups dominated by the JI and the Muslim Brotherhood, which were better organized and more familiar with government bureaucracy. Eventually, however, Deobandi groups also recognized an important opportunity to establish their own schools, community associations and chaplaincy programmes. Deobandi-run groups such as the Muslim Chaplains' Association are employed by local authorities to manage counterextremism work (Tower Hamlets Council 2008). Ultimately the government's injudicious delegation of power has entrusted Deobandi clerics with the welfare of young Muslims, and allowed Deobandi schools and seminaries to instill a generation of children with hardline ideas.

British multiculturalism policy treats British Islam as a single homogenous bloc, and it pigeonholes British Muslims into a single identity. By claiming to be the voice of that bloc, unrepresentative Islamist groups have been able to assert themselves as the voice of British Muslims. But the Islamist need for a theological foundation—the clerics and seminaries with which the JI and the Muslim Brotherhood mostly do not bother—has meant that Deobandi Islam has also benefited from establishment ignorance. In contrast, the significant Barelvi population, as well as the many various smaller Muslim sects, are perceived to lack legitimacy and thus exert very little influence over the state's treatment of British Islam.

The reliance on Deobandi groups has been defended by academics such as Gilliat-Ray (2012, p. 88), who argues, with little foundation, that "The well-organized system of Deobandi education for young Muslims, relying upon a carefully constructed curriculum, appears to provide a bulwark against the influence of more 'radical' groups." She has even invited Deobandi clerics such as Muhammad ibn Adam Al-Kawthari to address her students as an "expert" voice of British Islam. Al-Kawthari advocates the killing of adulterers (Kawthari 2004), encourages Muslims to engage in acts of jihad (Student Rights 2012) and claims that "We live in an age where evils such as incest among the non-Muslims is becoming common" (Kawthari 2014). For the most part, however, government and media remain oblivious to the diversity of British Islam and the complexity of its denominational politics. The failure of the government to address the dominance of Deobandi chaplains in British prisons, and its willingness to accept JI groups and activists as gatekeepers to chaplaincy programmes, are further examples of this artless approach.

WHITHER BRITISH ISLAM?

A decade ago the great worry among British politicians was the influence of foreign imams—clerics unable to speak English, and whose attitudes towards the West were a cause for concern. The preferred alternative discussed in Parliament and by journalists at the time was a new generation of home-trained ulema. Since then, however, the growth of Deobandi seminaries and the surplus of Deobandi clerics have not counteracted extremist influence; they have made the problem worse. Whereas foreign imams were unfamiliar to younger British Muslims, today's imams and chaplains are young graduates of the British Deobandi system, who manage to preach the same isolationist message at the mosque while able to work a room at an interfaith event, and they can appeal to a generation of British Muslims prone to the growing problem of radicalization.

Although the Deobandi missionary organization, the TJ, prefers segregation from British society, other Deobandi institutions, established around Darul Uloom Bury, do not advocate complete isolation. Experimentation with the outside world is now partly encouraged by Deobandi seminaries, which produce graduates who are employed outside Deobandi networks, especially within taxpayer-funded chaplaincy programmes. The growing influence of Deobandi clerics within the public sector is not because Deobandis represent the majority of British Muslims but because Deobandi institutions are better organized and more deeply established—a state of affairs with which Barelvi Muslims and other smaller Muslim sects have been unable to compete. Although the Barelvis represent a dominant majority of Sufi Muslims, the financial resources and growing political savvy of the Deobandis have left the Barelvis weak. Deobandi mosques benefit from Saudi patronage, such as the Al Farouq Masjid mosque in Walsall, which allegedly received £5 million from a Saudi "oil millionaire" (West and Knowsley 1997). But Deobandis have also benefited from the state. Under British multiculturalism policy, Deobandi institutions have been appointed, in tandem with Islamist organizations, as the guardians of British Muslims—delegated by local authorities and central government with the provision of community services.

Following the Rushdie protests, political Islam, such as the Islamist group JI, collaborates with and empowers Deobandi organizations because the Deobandi strain of Islam is regarded as suitably austere to accommodate Islamist endeavours. Some parts of the public sector employ Deobandi chaplains with the approval and support of groups run by the JI, such as the Muslim Council of Britain and the Islamic Foundation. From the perspective of Islamist and Salafist movements, Deobandi Islam offers a solid foundation upon which the ideals of political Islam can be constructed. In 1997 a report in the *Sunday Telegraph* even claimed that "the Saudis are refusing to finance new mosques unless they belong to the Taliban's Deobandi school of Islam" (West and Knowsley 1997).

Despite British Deobandis' tentative exploration of the outside world, the reality of Deobandi seminaries and their teachings remains difficult to research—they are, for the most part, closed off to external study. It is not at all apparent that Deobandi Islam is the only basis for violent Islam. But, arguably, the jihadist threat is something of a distraction. The real crisis for British Islam, and for British society, is the unmistakeable lack of integration, the long-term consequences of which appear far more dangerous than the immediate problem of Islamist violence. The priority for policymakers now is to examine properly the diversity and denominational politics of British Islam and challenge—or, at the very least, not facilitate—the dominance of the Deobandi school of thought.

Undoubtedly the Deobandi movement fuels extremist narratives within British Islam. Research by Mehmood Naqshbandi (2014) has revealed that almost half of British mosques are part of the Deobandi movement. The leader tipped next to run Darul Uloom Bury, the Deobandi cleric Riyadh ul Haq, is not a promising appointment. Haq's intense anti-Semitism, sympathy for the Taliban and warnings for Muslims to be "steadfast" against the West's "persecution of the Muslims" (Lewis and Birt 2011) do not suggest a more moderate future for such a significant contingent of British Islam. Since the Rushdie affair, some Deobandi networks have operated as entryist political movements and should be treated as such. That some graduates of Deobandi seminaries, in contrast with the complete isolation of the past, are now working in chaplaincy programmes, occasionally speaking with the media, and are involved with interfaith dialogue initiatives, should not alone be cause for celebration. Without a public rejection of widely held anti-Western, anti-Jewish, anti-democratic and exclusivist ideals propagated by Deobandi clerics, institutions and community organizations, the authorities should be far more cautious about appointing Deobandis to public positions, and should be wary of the Deobandi movement's poisonous effect on the increasingly urgent need for greater integration between British Muslims and British society.

Few doubt that the government understands that there is a problem. Prime Minister David Cameron, in his speech to the Conservative Party in October 2015, explained that "in some madrassas, we've got children being taught that they shouldn't mix with people of other religions; being beaten; swallowing conspiracy theories about Jewish people. These children should be having their minds opened, their horizons broadened, not having their heads filled with poison and their hearts filled with hate" (Sellgren 2015). While the government may recognize that the UK is under threat, it has failed to understand who poses that threat. Recently proposed counterextremism measures by the Conservative government feature crude methods of censorship that feed into a governmental obsession with the effect of social media. Such proposals will do very little to counteract the pernicious effect of Deobandi ideologues, who do their worst work offline.

If the government is to challenge extremist strains of Islam, it must understand those different strains. It must no longer, for example, appoint Islamic chaplains to a prison without even examining their religious denomination. Extremist influence can be tackled without censorship. Funding from the Arabian Gulf can be monitored and blocked if necessary, mosques that fund terrorism can be shut down, representatives of fundamentalist sects should be banned from public positions and chaplaincy programmes, and a thorough census of British Islam should be conducted. British Muslims are not either wholly victims or perpetrators; they are adherents to dozens of diverse groups, sects and political and religious movements, all of which display different attitudes towards extremism, terrorism, integration and the West. Deobandi Islam poses a very particular problem. If it is to be solved, it must be understood.

References

Ahmad, K. (2003a, September). Israel, Pakistan and the Muslim world. *Tarjuman Al Quran*. Jamaat-e-Islami Pakistan.

Ahmad, K. (2003b, July). Musharraf, Taliban and the implementation of Shariah Bill in NWFP. *Tarjuman-ul-Quran*. Jamaat-e-Islami Pakistan.

Ahsan, M., & Kidwai, A. (1991). *Sacrilege versus civility*. Markfield: Islamic Foundation.

Alexiev, A. (2005). Tablighi Jamaat: Jihad's stealthy legions. *Middle East Quarterly, 12*(1), 3–11.

Asghar, W. (1994). A conversation with Ahtisham Ali. *Q News*. Available from: http://standforpeace.org.uk/wp-content/uploads/2014/05/Ahtsham-Ali-Q-News-1994.pdf. Accessed 30 July 2015.

BBC News. (2005). Shoebomb plotter given 13 years [Online]. *BBC News*, 22 April. Available from: http://news.bbc.co.uk/1/hi/uk/4474307.stm. Accessed 29 July 2015.

BBC News. (2014). Bradford school governors 'promoted Islamic agenda' [Online]. *BBC News*, 10 June. Available from http://www.bbc.co.uk/news/uk-27779832. Accessed 28 July 2015.

Bowen, I. (2014). *Medina in Birmingham, Najaf in Brent: Inside British Islam*. London: Hurst.

Bradley, J. (2006). *Saudi Arabia exposed: Inside a kingdom in crisis*. New York: Palgrave Macmillan.

Clarke, P. (2014). *Report into allegations concerning Birmingham schools arising from the 'Trojan Horse' letter*. London: HMSO.

Damiel, I. (2013). Message for Muslims in the west by Shaykh Syed Abul Ḥasan'Alī Nadwī [Online]. Available from: http://propheticguidance.co.uk/message-for-muslims-in-the-west-by-shaykh-syed-abul-%E1%B8%A5asanali-nadwi/. Accessed 28 July 2015.

Dhalla, M. (1991, June 21). Doing time at HM's pleasure. *Muslim News*, p. 5.

Doward, J. (2007, January 7). Revealed: Preachers' messages of hate. *The Guardian* [Online]. Available from: http://www.theguardian.com/media/2007/jan/07/broadcasting.channel4. Accessed 30 July 2015.

Faith Matters. (2010). Faith leadership through Chaplaincy [Online]. Available from: http://faith-matters.org/2010/12/07/faith-leadership-through-chaplaincy-experiences-from-muslim-communities-summary-of-issues-and-recommendations-from-consultations-with-chaplains-sector-leaders-and-communities/. Accessed 30 July 2015.

Fielding, J. (2015, June 21). Jihadi John SPOTTED: Terrorist fled to Libya after he was unmasked as 26-year-old Londoner. *Daily Express*.

Ford, R. (2012, June 7). Muslim extremists at top-security jail are spreading fear among inmates and staff. *The Times*. [Online]. Available from: http://www.thetimes.co.uk/tto/news/uk/article3437862.ece. Accessed 31 July 2015.

Gay Muslims: Best response Mufti Ismail Menk. (2013). [Online] Available from: https://www.youtube.com/watch?v=sWFLF-CY-Eg. Accessed 29 July 2015.

Gest, J., & Norfolk, A. (2008, January 7). British imams 'failing young Muslims'. *The Times* [Online]. Available from: http://www.thetimes.co.uk/tto/faith/article2098879.ece. Accessed 29 July 2015.

Gibbons, K. (2014, July 14). Prison imams linked to Islamic radicals, [Online]. *The Times*. Available from: http://www.thetimes.co.uk/tto/news/uk/article4146755.ece. Accessed 13 July 2015.

Gilliat-Ray, S. (2006). Educating the Ulema: Centres of Islamic religious training in Britain. *Islam and Christian-Muslim Relations, 17*(1), 55–76.

Gilliat-Ray, S. (2012). *Muslims in Britain*. Cambridge: Cambridge University Press.

Gilliat-Ray, S., Ali, M., & Pattison, S. (2013). *Understanding Muslim chaplaincy*. Farnham: Ashgate Publishing.

Griffiths, S., Kerbaj, R., & Graham, G. (2013, September 29). Pupils ordered to wear Hijab out of school. *Sunday Times*.

Haddad, H. (2009, August 25). Hanafi Salafism: An oxymoron? *Islam21C* [Online]. Available from: http://www.islam21c.com/theology/174-hanafi-salafism-an-oxymoron/. Accessed 8 August 2015.

Hadfield, G. (1989, January 15). W H Smith ban on Rushdie book. *The Sunday Times*.

Halliday, J. (2015, June 15). Open outpouring of grief' in home town of Britain's youngest suicide bomber. *The Guardian*.

Hamm, M. (2007, December). Terrorist recruitment in American Correctional Institutions: An exploratory study of non-traditional faith groups. [Online]. Available from: https://www.ncjrs.gov/pdffiles1/nij/grants/220957.pdf. Accessed 30 July 2014.

HC Deb (House of Commons debate). (2006–2007) 19 July 2007 c168WH.

Home Office. (2011). House of Commons oral evidence taken before the Home Affairs Committee: Roots of violent radicalisation. Great Britain Home Office [Online]. Available from: http://www.publications.parliament.uk/pa/cm201012/cmselect/cmhaff/uc1446-v/uc144601.htm. Accessed 30 July 2015.

House of Commons. (2014). *Report into allegations concerning Birmingham schools arising from the 'Trojan Horse' letter.* London: HMSO.

Hussain, A. (2013). *Facebook* [Online]. Available from https://www.facebook.com/azadul.hussain/posts/10203699730001715. Accessed 13 May 2013 (screenshots with author).

Institute of Jewish Affairs. (1995). *Antisemitism world report 1995.* London: Institute for Jewish Policy Research.

Inter-Islam [Online] Available from: http://www.inter-islam.org/Pastevents/darululoom.html. Accessed 28 July 2015.

Inter-Islam [Online] Available from: http://www.inter-islam.org/Prohibitions/Imitating.html. Accessed 28 July 2015.

Kabir, N. (2012). *Young British Muslims: Identity, culture, politics and the media.* Edinburgh: Edinburgh University Press.

Kawthari, M. (2004, October 20). The legal penalty for fornication. *Darul Iftaa* website [Online]. Available from: http://www.daruliftaa.com/node/5657?txt_QuestionID. Accessed 8 Aug 2015.

Kawthari, M. (2014). The Fiqh of covering one's nakedness (Awra): A detailed explanation. *Web Archive* [Internet Archive]. Available from: http://web.archive.org/web/20140221162043/http://qa.sunnipath.com/issue_view.asp?HD=1&ID=2039. Accessed 8 August 2015.

Kepel, G. (2004). *Allah in the West.* Cambridge: Polity Press.

Khatme Nubuwwat [Online] Available from: http://www.khatmenubuwwat.org/. Accessed 8 Aug 2015.

Laville, S. (2006, August 18). Suspects linked to hardline Islamic group. *The Guardian* [Online]. Available from: http://www.theguardian.com/uk/2006/aug/18/terrorism.world. Accessed 30 July 2015.

Lewis, P. (2002). *Islamic Britain.* London: I.B. Tauris.

Lewis, P. (2004). New social roles and changing patterns of authority. *Archives De Sciences Sociales Des Religions, 49*(125), 169–187.

Lewis, P. (2014). Imams in Britain: Agents of de-radicalisation? In F. Peter & R. Ortega (Eds.), *Islamic movements of Europe* (pp. 237–240). London: I.B. Tauris.

Lewis, P., & Birt, J. (2011). The pattern of Islamic reform in Britain. In M. Van Bruinessen & S. Allievi (Eds.), *Producing Islamic knowledge: Transmission and dissemination in Western Europe* (pp. 91–120). London: Abingdon.

Lustig, R. et al. (1989, February 19). War of the word. *The Guardian* [Online]. Available from: http://www.theguardian.com/uk/1989/feb/19/race.world. Accessed 30 July 2015.

MacEoin, D. (2009). *Music, chess and other sins: Segregation, integration, and Muslim schools in Britain*. London: Civitas.

Malik, K. (2010). *From Fatwa to Jihad*. London: Atlantic Books.

MEMRI (The Middle East Media Research Institute). (2010). Saudi Cleric Muhammad Al-Arifi: 'The desire to Shed blood, to Smash Skulls, and to sever limbs for the sake of Allah is an honor for the believer' [Online]. Available from: http://www.memri.org/report/en/print4523.htm. Accessed 8 August 2015.

Metcalf, B. (2011). "Traditionalist" Islamic activism: Deoband, Tablighis, and Talibs [Online]. Available from: http://essays.ssrc.org/10yearsafter911/traditionalist-islamic-activism-deoband-tablighis-and-talibs. Accessed 31 July 2015.

Michael, L. (2011). Islam as rebellion and conformity: How young British Pakistani Muslims in the UK negotiate space for and against radical ideologies. *Religion, State and Society, 39*(2–3), 209–227.

Ministry of Justice. (2012). Freedom of information request [Online]. Available from: https://www.justice.gov.uk/downloads/information-access-rights/foi-disclosure-log/prison-probation/foi-75784.doc. Accessed 30 July 2015.

Mogra, I. (2002). The Terrorism Act 2000 and our responsibilities as Muslims. *Youth Tarbiyyah Conference* [Online]. Available from: http://www.inter-islam.org/Audio/ytc2k2/ytc2k2-19.rm. Accessed 26 July 2015.

Moj, M. (2015). *The Deoband madrassah movement: Countercultural trends and tendencies*. London: Anthem Press.

Mufti Ismail Menk on democracy and freedom of speech. (2014). [Online] Available from: https://www.youtube.com/watch?t=204&v=0Q2du4yoFfY. Accessed 29 July 2015.

Naqshbandi, M. (2014). UK mosque statistics. [Online]. Available from: http://www.muslimsinbritain.org/resources/masjid_report.pdf. Accessed 15 July 2015.

Norfolk, A. (2007a, September 7). Two faces of British youth in thrall to sinister Muslim sect. *The Times*.

Norfolk, A. (2007b, September 7). Hardline takeover of British mosques. *The Times*.

Norfolk, A. (2007c, September 7). The homegrown cleric who loathes the British. *The Times*.

Pipes, D. (2009). *The Rushdie affair: The novel, the Ayatollah, and the West*. London: Transaction Publishers.

RNW Media. Cleric did say "Jews are descendants of apes and pigs" [Online]. Available from: https://www.rnw.org/archive/cleric-did-say-jews-are-descendants-apes-and-pigs. Accessed 7 August 2015.

Sawer, P., & Mendick, R. (2014, June 21). From a Cardiff bedroom to Syrian battlefield: Trail of Jihadist brothers. *The Daily Telegraph*.

Sellgren, K. (2015). David Cameron: Prime Minister warns over extremist teaching. *BBC News* [Online]. Available from: http://www.bbc.com/news/education-34464137. Accessed 1 November 2015.

Sikand, Y. (1998). The origins and growth of the Tablighi Jamaat in Britain. *Islam and Christian–Muslim Relations, 9*(2), 171–192.

Sikand, Y. (2006). The Tablighi Jamaat and politics: A critical reappraisal. *Muslim World, 96*(1), 175–95.

Sookhdeo, H. (2008). *Faith power and territory: A handbook of British Islam.* Virginia: Isaac Publishing.

Student Rights. (2012, July 12). Cardiff University, Muhammad Ibn Adam Al-Kawthari and freedom of expression [Online]. Available from: http://www.studentrights.org.uk/article/1941/cardiff_university_muhammad_ibn_adam_al_kawthari_and_freedom_of_expression. Accessed 8 August 2015.

Taylor, J. (2010, October 21). Hardliners call for deaths of Surrey Muslims. *The Independent.*

The Express Tribune. (2012, January 21). Aasia Bibi's case: Weighed down by guilt, blasphemy accuser mulls pulling back [Online]. Available from: http://tribune.com.pk/story/324943/aasia-bibis-case-weighed-down-by-guilt-blasphemy-accuser-mulls-pulling-back/. Accessed 8 August 2015.

Tower Hamlets Council. (2008). Tower Hamlets prevent action plan April 2008–March2011[Online].http://www.towerhamlets.gov.uk/idoc.ashx?docid=6dc3cc64-4fba-450a-93d6-aa336891ba03&version=-1. Accessed 12 June 2015.

Tubb, G. (2015, July 25). Faith school bans pupils from meeting outsiders. *Sky News* [Online]. Available from: http://news.sky.com/story/1524949/faith-school-bans-pupils-from-meeting-outsiders. Accessed 26 July 2015.

Vidino, L. (2010). *The new Muslim brotherhood.* New York: Columbia University Press.

Werbner, P. (1996). The making of Muslim dissent: Hybridized discourses, lay preachers and radical rhetoric among British Pakistanis. *American Anthropological Association*, 102–122.

West, J., & Knowsley, J. (1997, July 27). British Muslims ordered to adopt Taliban teachings. *Sunday Telegraph.*

Westrop, S. (2014, June 16). Extremist Chaplains and prison radicalization. *Gatestone Institute* [Online]. Available from: http://www.gatestoneinstitute.org/4357/uk-muslim-prison-chaplains. Accessed 30 July 2015.

CHAPTER 17

Violence and the Deobandi Movement

Liyakat Takim

In recent times there has been much discussion about violence in Islam. Especially in the media, Islam has been depicted as intrinsically violent and militant. As a matter of fact, the media has, at times, instilled a fear of Islam. This chapter will initially examine the genesis and development of the Deobandi movement in the Indian subcontinent. It will then focus on the theme of violence that has permeated the movement. Violence, in the context of this chapter, refers to the exertion of physical force so as to injure or cause harm. This chapter will examine the tendency and pattern in the Deobandi outfits to use violence in pursuit of their Islamist, jihadist and sectarian objectives.

In the face of British colonialism and a concomitant desire to preserve Muslim values from being eroded, a group of prominent Indian scholars founded the Deobandi movement in 1867 in Uttar Pradesh, North India. This was part of a series of revivalist movements that were sweeping British India during the time. Scholars including Muhammad Qasim Nanotwi (d. 1880), Rashid Ahmad Gangohi (d. 1905) and Haji Muhammad Abid (d. 1912), among others, agreed to establish an Islamic seminary known as Darul Uloom Deoband.[1] Deoband was chosen because it was a center

L. Takim (✉)
McMaster University, Hamilton, OH, Canada

© The Editor(s) (if applicable) and The Author(s) 2016
J. Syed et al. (eds.), *Faith-Based Violence and Deobandi Militancy in Pakistan*, DOI 10.1057/978-1-349-94966-3_17

481

of Muslim culture. In addition, many families from Deoband had reportedly served the Mughal Empire. It was also in close proximity to the former Mughal capital of Delhi.

Deobandi scholars claim that they responded to colonialism by reforming facets of the Islamic religious tradition in striving to maintain the Muslim identity in the face of colonialism. However, not unlike the Wahhabis of Saudi Arabia, Deobandi "reforms" seem to be directed against Sufi and other traditions of Islam rooted in the Indian subcontinent. It is a fact that Deobandi icons such as Shah Waliullah invited an Afghan ruler, Ahmed Shah Abdali, to attack Hindus, Sufis and Shias in order to "revive the glory of Islam".[2] The jihadist militancy of Syed Ahmed and Shah Ismail, against Sikhs and local Pashtuns, weakened and fractured the indigenous communities of Punjab and the NWFP while strengthening the British rulers. It could be argued that due to their sectarian and takfiri (apostatizing) intolerance towards Sufis, Shias and other Islamic denominations, the Deobandis furthered the cause of British colonialism. Their regressive and ultraorthodox ideology and tactics halted Muslim progress in the fields of education and enlightenment. While reformers such as Sir Syed Ahmed Khan—the founder of the Aligarh Muslim University—stressed modern education after the failed revolt against the British colonialists, the founders of the Deoband madrassa stressed regressive, insular, sectarian and exclusionary tactics.[3]

Owing to the growth of Deobandi and other similar movements, nineteenth-century Indian Islam saw a new emphasis on the study of hadith; it founded new madrassas to preserve and propagate its ideology during colonial rule.[4] Gradually the Deobandi movement expanded to different parts of India. By the end of the nineteenth century there were more than a dozen schools known as Deobandi, from Peshawar to Chittagong to Madras. By 1967, Darul Uloom had reportedly graduated 3,795 students from present-day India, 3,191 from Pakistan and present-day Bangladesh, and 431 from multiple other countries, such as Afghanistan, China and Malaysia. Around the same time, the Deobandis had founded 8,934 schools throughout India and Pakistan.[5]

Darul Uloom center continues to serve as an active place for the teaching of the Islamic tradition. Since it was established, more than 65,000 Muslims are believed to have studied there.[6] As I shall discuss, the exponential growth of such seminaries in Pakistan, together with the incorporation of extremist elements in its curriculum, has been a major factor in precipitating acts of violence in the last few decades.

THE DEOBANDI IDEOLOGY (MASLAK)

Central to the Deobandi teaching is reverence for the Prophet Muhammad, his companions, and those scholars who interpreted the religious tradition. In fact, the exaltation of the companions is a distinctive feature of the Deobandis. According to them, the Prophet Muhammad identified the true path to salvation as "The one that I and my Companions follow". After love for the Prophet the Deobandis maintain that a cardinal principle of faith is to love all the companions.[7] Therefore, in many ways, the actions and statements attributed to the companions become normative. Owing to the exalted status that they enjoy, the companions also become models of correct demeanor.

The primary objective of the Deobandi movement is to inculcate "correct practice" in Muslims and a proper interpretation of Islamic law. A salient feature of Deobandi ideology is the stress on studying prophetic traditions (ahadith) in their seminaries. Students are required to study all six of the Sunni canonical hadith works in one year. After eight years of training in the traditional Islamic sciences, students at the madrassa graduate and become ulema. These scholars are then encouraged to take up positions as teachers, writers, debaters with rival Muslims and non-Muslims, prayer leaders, and guardians at mosques and shrines.[8]

In the field of jurisprudence, Deobandis follow the Hanafi madhab and claim that Abu Hanifa's (d. 767) legal rulings were premised on prophetic traditions rather than on mere arbitrary reasoning (ijtihad), personal opinion (ra'y), analogy (qiyas), or juristic preference (istihsan). Deobandi scholars have further argued that the Hanafi madhab is in complete accordance with the Qur'an and the ahadith.[9] Deobandis also strongly advocate the doctrine of *taqlid* (imitation). They believe that a Muslim must adhere to one of the four schools (madhabs) of Sunni law and discourage interschool eclecticism. One of their main opposing groups are the Ahl-e-Hadith, who are also known as the *ghair muqallid* (those who reject taqlid), because they use the Qur'an and ahadith exclusively. The Ahl-e-Hadith do not recognize practices of erstwhile or contemporary Muslims that are not premised on the revelatory sources. They even reject the rulings of the classical schools of law on the same principle, insisting that the Qur'an and ahadith are the exclusive and directly accessible sources of guidance. The Ahl-e-Hadith accuse those who accept the rulings of a scholar or legal school of blind imitation, and frequently demand scriptural evidence for every argument and legal ruling.[10]

Another feature of the Deobandi movement is its claim to spiritual practices and devotional exercises. However, such a claim is hard to maintain given the fact that the Darul Uloom Deoband and its senior clerics are staunch opponents of traditional Sufi rituals, such as milad-un-nabi (celebrating the Prophet's birthday), qawwali (devotional music) and visiting shrines. The founders of the Deobandi movement, Rashid Ahmad Gangohi and Muhammad Qasim Nanotvi, reportedly studied Sufism under Haji Imdadullah Muhajir Makki.[11] However, the Deobandi approach to Sufism seems to be influenced by the Wahhabis, who reject traditional Sufi rituals and instead prefer literal sharia interpretations. Indeed, Deobandis condemn some Sufi practices, such as shrine-based customs, including the urs (annual death anniversary celebrations), the *fatiha* food offerings for the dead (distributed after reciting the opening chapter of the Qur'an) and the elaborate ceremonies associated with birth, marriage and death.[12] The Deobandis are to be distinguished from the Barelvis (Sunni Sufis of the subcontinent), who affirm the authority not only of the Prophet but also of the saints and holy people, whom they revere as sources of religious guidance and vehicles of mediation between God and human beings.

THE ROLE OF THE MADRASSA IN THE DEOBANDI MOVEMENT

An important consideration in examining the Deobandi movement is the role of the madrassa in promulgating and disseminating its teachings. The madrassa does not appear to have been a major institution in pre-colonial India. Students would learn informally from teachers who would then issue a certificate of completion and permission to transmit their teachings. The modern madrassa, as a formal academic institution equipped with classrooms and a standardized curriculum, was a product of the colonial period.[13]

As the Deobandi movement spread, it established seminaries across the Indian subcontinent to disseminate its interpretation of Islam. The education provided in the seminaries was primarily religious. It is important to note that in Pakistan, as in many developing countries, education is not mandatory. The World Bank estimates that only 40 percent of Pakistanis are literate, and that many rural areas lack public schools. Madrassas, on the other hand, are located all over the country and provide not only free education but also free food, housing and clothing.[14] In the poor areas of southern Punjab, madrassas funded by the Sunni Deobandi sectarian political party the SSP (see below) reportedly even pay parents to send their children.[15]

In the 1980s the Pakistani president, General Mohammad Zia-ul-Haq (d. 1988), supported the madrassas so as to gain the confidence of religious parties for his rule. Zia also wanted to recruit troops for the Soviet-Afghan War.[16] At the time, many madrassas were financed by the zakat (the Islamic tithe collected by the state), giving the government some form of control over them.[17] However, despite their denial, Darul Uloom Deoband and other Deobandi madrassas enjoyed patronage and support not only from the Pakistani establishment during and after General Zia-ul-Haq's military rule but also from the Saudi government.[18] Increasingly, more religious schools are funded privately—by wealthy Pakistani industrialists at home or abroad, by private and government-funded NGOs in the Persian Gulf states and Saudi Arabia, and by Iran. As we shall see, without state supervision, these madrassas are able to preach a very parochial and, at times, violent version of Islam.

DEOBANDIS AND POLITICS

In the aftermath of the Sepoy Mutiny in 1857, the Deobandi ulema pragmatically acquiesced in the face of British colonialism and power. They focused instead on religious education and on training religious leaders to serve the Muslim community. When the Indian nationalist movement spread after the First World War, a large group of Deobandi scholars formed the political party the JUH in 1919. Later they supported the anti-colonial nationalist movement and opposed the creation of Pakistan. These scholars included Abdul Mohasim Sajjad, Hussain Ahmed Madani, Ahmed Saeed Dehlvi and Mufti Muhammad Naeem Ludhianvi.[19]

In essence, these Deobandi scholars agreed with Gandhi and the Indian National Congress in opposing British rule and in demanding independence. They advocated a notion of Indian nationalism in which Hindus and Muslims constituted a single nation united in the struggle against the British.[20] The Jamiat view is that Muslims and non-Muslims have entered a mutual contract in India since independence to establish a secular state. Thus Indian Deobandi teachers, religious leaders and politicians were actively committed to a secular, democratic polity. The leadership of the Deobandi activists was especially committed to preserving "minority cultural rights" in such matters as India's constitutional guarantee to each religious tradition to follow separate family law. Their primary focus was religious education.[21] This stance is, however, in contrast with the sectarian role played by the Darul Uloom Deoband during Sunni–Shia riots in Lucknow in 1930, and also in view of numerous anti-Barelvi, anti-Shia and anti-Ahmadi fatwas by top Deobandi clerics of that era.

At the time of independence, most Deobandis, including the JUH, opposed the Partition of India and saw the creation of Pakistan as a Western plot to weaken the newly created Indian state. Foremost among the politically active figures was Mawlana Husain Ahmad Madani, who engaged in a public exchange with Muhammad Iqbal over the priority of territorial rather than religious identity for statehood.[22] In this context of suspicion and discrimination, Muslim Indian leaders, including Deobandis, intensified their stance as committed participants in India's particular style of a secular, democratic state. Indeed, some have argued that given the strength of both explicit and "soft" Hindu nationalism, or "Hindutva", it is India's Muslims who are most ardently keeping alive the ideals of the country's founding "Nehruvian secularism", committed to the Constitution and to legal processes, as their best hope of flourishing as equal citizens.[23]

Partition in 1947 caused a few Deobandi scholars to migrate to Pakistan. Some of them supported Muhammad Ali Jinnah's Muslim League and his vision of a separate Muslim political entity. Led by Shabbir Ahmad Usmani (1887–1949), these scholars formed the JUI in 1945 in Calcutta. Other figures in the movement included Mufti Muhammad Shafi, Ihtishamul Ḥaqq Thanvi and Abdulḥamid Badaʿuni (d. 1969). In contrast to the JUH's pro-secular stance in alliance with the Indian National Congress, the JUI actively campaigned for the implementation of Islamic sharia law in Pakistan. In both countries, a section of Deobandis pragamatically aligned with the ruling party—that is, with the Indian National Congress in India and with the Muslim League in Pakistan. Thus they adopted a pro-secular or pro-Islamist stance in response to the changing sociopolitical landscape. However, in both countries they continued to maintain close links with the Saudis.

Although they were politically active, the JUI in Pakistan never enjoyed popular support because most Pakistanis did not support their myopic vision of an Islamic state and a narrow interpretation of Islamic praxis. The JUI forged alliances with any party that was politically expedient for it. In the 1970s, for example, it allied with a Pashtun regionalist party in opposition to Zulfikar Ali Bhutto's PPP, a party that was, in principle, liberal socialist. In the mid-1990s, in contrast, it allied with that same PPP, now led by Benazir Bhutto (d. 2007), the daughter of the former prime minister, Zulfikar Ali Bhutto (d. 1979).[24]

Deobandis have a strong influence in Pakistan, not only at the political level but also in educating the next generation of Pakistanis. This is confirmed by the following figures. Some 20 percent of Pakistan's Sunni Muslims would consider themselves Deobandi, and, according to Heritage Online, nearly 65 percent of the total seminaries in Pakistan are run by Deobandis, 25 percent by Barelvis, 6 percent by Ahl-e-Hadith and 3 percent by various Shia organizations.[25] It is within the confines of the madrassas that they operate and through the genre of students they train that the Deobandis exert most influence on Pakistani society.

VIOLENCE AND THE DEOBANDI MADRASSA

In the 1970s the looming war against the Soviet Union led to further recruitment by the Deobandi seminaries in the Pashtun areas of Pakistan. According to a World Bank report, enrollment in the seminaries increased after 1979, coinciding with the start of the Soviet-Afghan War. Many of these students included a number of the Afghan fighters who were trained in Deobandi seminaries. They were financed by Americans who supported the war against the Soviets in Afghanistan for their own geopolitical interests. Saudi Arabia also spent millions of dollars and trained teachers who then indoctrinated madrassa students in Wahhabi ideology. The Saudis targeted the Deobandi seminaries because they comprised the most popular schools in the Pashtun belt.[26]

It is in the madrassas in Pakistan that the Deobandis promote their own version of jihad. These schools indoctrinate their students on the merits of fighting against the Hindus in Kashmir or against Muslims of other sects, whom they label as unbelievers owing to their perceived heresy. Pakistani officials estimate that 10–15 percent of the country's tens of thousands of madrassas espouse such extremist ideologies. There is a palpable attempt to spread this ideology abroad. Many of the militant groups associated with radical madrassas regularly proclaim their plans to bring jihad to India proper as well as to the West, which they believe is run by Jews. A Deobandi offshoot, the JM, is known for conducting terrorist operations in India and elsewhere.[27]

It would be wrong to depict the Deobandis as a monolithic group that espouses a militant ideology. Some Deobandi scholars, especially those in India, have denounced terrorism. In response to the increasing acts of violence, in February 2008 the seminary at Deoband hosted a conference

of some 10,000 Islamic scholars from across the nation. They unequivocally denounced all forms of terrorism, proclaiming that the killing of
innocent people was against the core principles of Islam. The declaration stated that Islam has taught its followers to treat all mankind with
equality, mercy, tolerance and justice.[28] The conference also strongly condemned acts of violence on the part of Americans and others in Iraq and
Afghanistan, which speakers labeled the real "terrorism", as well as implications of covert action in oppressing Muslims in places such as India as
part of a worldwide campaign against Muslims.

Furthermore, on November 3, 2009, a group of JUH Deobandi scholars condemned suicide bombings and attacks targeting innocent civilians.
They also argued that equating jihad with acts of terrorism and the killing
of innocent civilians is incorrect—"Jihad is basically a constructive phenomenon"—and that the misrepresentation of jihad should be avoided.[29]

Violence and the Deobandi Movement

While the ulema of India were denouncing violence in the name of Islam,
some ulema of the JUI in Pakistan were doing the exact opposite. Many
of the Pakistani ulema defended the militant groups in Afghanistan since
they were fighting the Soviet Union's hegemonic interests. As a matter
of fact, the Deobandis were especially supportive of the Taliban, which
shared their sectarian orientation and vision of an Islamic state. It was
from the seminaries in Pakistan that the Deobandis promoted their version of jihad in the name of Islam.

Pakistan's Interior Minister, Moinuddin Haider, for one recognizes
these problems. "The brand of Islam they are teaching is not good for
Pakistan," he says. "Some, in the garb of religious training, are busy
fanning sectarian violence, poisoning people's minds." In June, Haider
announced a reform plan that would require all madrassas to register with
the government, expand their curricula, disclose their financial resources,
seek permission to admit foreign students and stop sending students to
militant training camps.[30] There is little doubt that extremist and, at times,
militant ideology is being taught in some of the madrassas. This is corroborated by Mujibur Rehman Inqalabi, the SSP's second in command.
He is quoted as stating that Haider's reform plan is "against Islam", and
he complains that where states have taken control of madrassas, such as in
Jordan and Egypt, "the engine of jihad is extinguished". The USA is right,
he said, "*Madrasahs* are the supply line for jihad."[31]

From the 1980s on, the number of seminaries in Pakistan increased exponentially. Initially, as I discussed, the madrassas were used to mobilize support for the regime of Zia ul-Haq (in power 1977–1988), who was, in fact, particularly sympathetic to the Deobandi approach. The seminaries were not only a resource in domestic and foreign politics but at times found themselves engaged in a proxy war as both the Saudis and the Iranians tried to disseminate their ideologies in Pakistan. It was in this atmosphere of politics and education that the genesis of the Taliban is to be found.

When the Soviet Union withdrew from Afghanistan, the Taliban based their rule on the strict ideological basis furnished by the Deobandi ulema. The surge in the number of madrassas in Pakistan in the 1980s coincided with the influx of some 3 million Afghan refugees. The madrassas, which were located along the Afghan–Pakistan border, provided the only available education for many of those refugees. The Pakistani Deobandis forged close ties with the Afghan Taliban, especially as many Taliban leaders and fighters had studied in Deobandi seminaries. Mulla Omar (d. 2015), the head of the Taliban, was a product of a Deobandi seminary.[32] Even Hakimullah Mehsud, the new commander of the TTP, studied in a Deobandi seminary in Hangu District of the NWFP. He reportedly abandoned his studies and was heavily influenced by Salafism.[33]

The Madrasa Haqqaniya, in Akora Kathak near Peshawar, has trained many Taliban leaders.[34] According to Jeffery Goldberg, the Haqqania Madrasa is, in fact, a jihad factory

> This does not make it unique in Pakistan. There are one million students studying in the country's 10,000 or so *madrasas*, and militant Islam is at the core of most of these schools. Many *madrasas* are village affairs, with student bodies of 25 or 50. Some of the *madrasas* are sponsored by Pakistan's religious parties, and some are affiliated with the mujahedeen groups waging jihad against India in the disputed province of Kashmir. Haqqania is notable not only because of its size, but also because it has graduated more leaders of the Taliban, Afghanistan's ruling faction, than any other school in the world, including any school in Afghanistan.[35]

Theirs was, according to Ahmed Rashid, a long-time observer, "an extreme form of Deobandism, which was being preached by Pakistani Islamic parties in Afghan refugee camps in Pakistan".[36] Their parochial and often distorted vision of Islam emphasized personal behavior, detailed ritual observances, hatred of the West, a disdain for local cultural practices and the confinement of women to their homes.

After the withdrawal of the Soviet Union and the continued infighting of the Afghan mujahideen, the Taliban established itself in Afghanistan and ruled as the Islamic Emirate of Afghanistan from September 1996 until December 2001, with Kandahar as the capital. While in power, it enforced a strict interpretation of sharia law—one that many Muslim leaders condemned. The Taliban was also denounced for its brutal treatment of women and other minorities. The majority of its leaders were influenced by Deobandi fundamentalism, while Pashtunwali, the Pashtun tribal code, also played a significant role in the Taliban's legislation.[37]

The Taliban's support for Osama Bin Laden after the events of 9/11 and its refusal to give him up to the Americans led to the US invasion of Afghanistan and the Taliban's removal from power in 2001. However, despite this, it has remained an active force in Afghanistan and Pakistan, and has continued its acts of terrorism, frequently killing innocent fellow Muslims. The marriage between the Deobandis and the Taliban gave rise to Sunni extremism during the Soviet–Afghan War in the 1980s, an alliance that continued even after the Soviets were expelled from Afghanistan. As Vali Nasr says,

> Many other South Asia's Sunni extremists, responsible for violence in Kashmir or against Shias and other minorities in Pakistan, hail from the Deobandi tradition, while Ahl-e-Hadith inspires the jihadi fighters of the Lashkar-e Tayiba (Army of the Pure) organization, which has fought in Kashmir.[38]

Another movement that espoused an extremist and militant Deobandi ideology is the TTP, sometimes known as the Pakistani Taliban. This is an umbrella organization of various Islamist militant groups based in the north-western FATA along the Afghan border in Pakistan. In December 2007 about 13 groups united under the leadership of Baitullah Mehsud to form the TTP. Among the group's stated objectives are resistance against the Pakistani state, enforcement of its interpretation of sharia and a plan to unite against NATO-led forces in Afghanistan. It should be noted that the TTP is not directly affiliated with the Afghan Taliban movement led by Mulla Omar. The two groups differ in their histories, strategic goals and interests, although they share a primarily Deobandi interpretation of Islam and are predominantly Pashtun.[39]

The Role of the Mosques in Promoting Violence

In examining the connection between the Deobandis and violence, it is essential to consider the role of their mosques in promoting acts of terrorism. The Deobandis reportedly control around 45 percent of the UK's mosques and nearly all of the British-based training of Islamic scholars.[40] In 2006 *The Daily Mail* connected the terror-linked mega mosque (Markazi Masjid) of the Deobandis and the TJ in Dewsbury, UK, to the 7/7 bombers who were responsible for terrorist acts in London. "The mosque is run by Tablighi Jamaat, a radical Islamic movement believed by intelligence agencies to be a fertile source for recruiting young extremists", the report stated.[41]

The role of mosques in promoting violence is further highlighted in another report. In 2006 *The Times* stated, "Several of the suspects arrested in August over the alleged plot to blow up transatlantic airliners had attended meetings of Deobandi Tablighi Jamaat, which French intelligence has labelled an 'antechamber of fundamentalism'. The FBI says that it is a fertile breeding ground for al-Qaeda." In 2007 *The Times* reported:

> One of the suicide bombers who attacked London in July 2005, Shehzad Tanweer, studied at the Deobandi seminary in Dewsbury and Mohammad Sidique Khan, the leader of the 7/7 terror plot, was a regular worshipper at the adjoining mosque.[42] The mosque authorities have denied these accusations. Richard Reid, the shoe bomber, was said to have been influenced by Tablighi Jamaat, several of whose adherents were also among those arrested over an alleged plot to blow up transatlantic airliners.

A key element here appears to be the connection between Tablighi mosques and violence. A *Telegraph* article from 2006 calls the TJ the "Army of Darkness" and says of the group:

> with increasing and alarming frequency, the name of Tablighi Jamaat is cropping up in the worldwide fight against terrorism ... Several of those arrested on August 9 in connection with the alleged plot to blow up airliners en route from Britain to America, had attended Tablighi study sessions in Britain[43]... The group's ideal of a world governed by an ultra-conservative, neo-medievalist form of Islam, in which women are subservient and all laws and customs are based on religious dictates, is barely distinguishable from the wish lists of al-Qaeda and the Taliban.

In the UK the group is run from the 3,000-capacity Markazi Mosque in Dewsbury—built with funds from Saudi Arabia—which also functions as the TJ's European headquarters.[44]

Deobandi mosques, madrassas and preachers who promote acts of violence have also reached out to Muslims in the West. The recent number of Muslim youth who have shown willingness to join ISIS and have committed acts of terror in the West demonstrates not only the effectiveness of the Deobandi/ISIS propaganda but also the vulnerability of the minds of the youth who have been led to believe that blowing themselves up and killing others will send them straight to heaven. The Deobandis have targeted not only non-Muslims but also fellow Muslims living in their midst.

DEOBANDIS AND SECTARIAN WARFARE

The exponential growth of such Deobandi acts of violence in Pakistan is interwoven with their sectarian hatred of Sunni Sufis, Barelvis and Shias, along with other sects and communities. Sectarian dispute is a competition for religious legitimacy. Different groups contest the right to speak for Islam and the right to decide who is a Muslim. Deobandi schools teach not only what Islam is but also what it is not. They delineate sectarian boundaries and parameters, emphasizing, in the process, who is and who is not a Muslim.

The Iranian Revolution of 1979 was bound to appeal to many Muslims, especially as it had defied a major superpower of the time and because Ayatullah Khomeini (d. 1989) had characterized the USA as the great Satan. Khomeini also wanted to export the revolution, calling on Muslims abroad to rise against their rulers. Deobandi leaders saw this as a threat because the revolution was intertwined with the spread of Shia'ism. Muhammad Manzur Numani is a senior Deobandi leader. The title of his work, *Khomeini, Iranian Revolution and the Shi'ite Faith*, indicates the aspects that worry him most. In fact, he starts his work with a critique of the revolution and then proceeds to refute various aspects of Shia beliefs and practices. As he states, "Khomeini's revolution is based totally on the foundation of Shi'ite religion ie, upon its doctrines of Imamate, *Ghaibate Kubra* (major absence) of [the] Imam-i-Akhiruzzaman (the Imam of the last phase—the awaited Mehdi) and, during this absence, the establishment of *wilayat-ul-faqih* (the rule of the *mujtahid*)."[45]

In response to a Saudi request[46] to contain the increasing threat from the Iranian Revolution, in 1984, Numani published a book entitled

Iranian Revolution: Imam Khomeini and Shiism (Irani Inqilab: Imam Khomeini awr Shi'iyyat). The preface was written by a popular and erudite Indian religious scholar, Abu al-Hasan 'Ali Nadwi (d. 2000), one of the most senior religious leaders of India. Nadwi was an adviser to the Saudi Islamic World League.[47]

Both Numani and Nadwi felt threatened not only by the Iranian Revolution but also, more importantly, by the appeal of Shia'ism, especially because its revolutionary message could attract the Sunni youth. Hence they and other Sunni scholars sought to expose what they claimed to be the "real" face of Shia'ism, exporting, in the process, their writings and sectarian literature abroad. The book further attacked the Shias for their "unIslamic practices and beliefs". Soon, Numani's book became a bestseller throughout the Sunni world. With Saudi support, it was translated from Urdu into English, Arabic and Turkish, and was made available for wide circulation.[48] Such rhetoric was bound to fan sectarian flames.

Sipah-e-Sahaba

The Deobandi and Ahl-e-Hadith (Salafi)) madrassas became the center of opposition to the Shias, while at the same time the ulema in these madrassas had ties with Saudi ulema.[49] This opposition was channeled through groups which, inspired by Deobandi rhetoric and ideology, resorted to militancy to counteract what they perceived to be the Shia threat. The SSP (soldiers of the companions of the Prophet) is a Deobandi Pakistani organization and a formerly registered Pakistani political party. It was established during the time of General Zia al-Haq in Pakistan in the early 1980s by Mawlana Haq Nawaz Jhangvi. Its stated goal was to deter the spread of Shia influence in Pakistan in the wake of the Iranian Revolution. The organization was banned by President General Pervez Musharraf in 2002 as a terrorist organization under the Anti-Terrorism Act of 1997.[50] In October 2000, Mawlana Masood Azhar, the founder of the JeM, was quoted as saying that "Sipah-e-Sahaba stands shoulder to shoulder with Jaish-e-Muhammad in Jehad." This coalition further demonstrates the extent of the Deobandi network in Pakistan. A leaked US diplomatic cable described it as another SSP breakaway Deobandi organization.[51]

As the name indicates, the SSP posited itself as the vanguard of the companions, a position that inevitably entailed opposition to and confrontation with the Shias. It tried to combat the Shias at different levels. The SSP resorted to publishing anti-Shia literature, highlighting elements in Shia texts that were bound to anger Sunnis. These include the denigration of the companions in general and the Prophet's wife, 'A'isha, in particular. The SSP also quoted Shia hadith and tafsir literature that pronounced the Qur'an to be incomplete. This would vindicate its contention that Shia'ism has transgressed beyond Islamic parameters. The SSP further highlighted traditions that claimed that the imams were superior to all prophets apart from the Prophet Muhammad. What it failed to point out was that the Shias themselves do not consider their texts to be completely authentic. In fact, they reject many traditions such as those that suggest that the present Qur'an is incomplete.[52]

For the SSP, the danger of Shia'ism lies not only in its heretical beliefs and practices but also in its proselytism, especially in urban areas. The Shias, it claims, are not only ignorant of true Islam but are responsible for disseminating their ignorance. This has led many Sunnis to stray from the "true Islam". For the Deobandis and the SSP, confronting and combating Shia'ism is not only necessary it is a religious obligation.[53]

LASHKAR-E-JHANGVI

The SSP has a more militant offshoot, the LeJ, which was established in 1994. The most potent aspect of the SSP movement was the militant attacks against the Shias and the subsequent Shia retaliation. The SSP and the LeJ, which later became part of the Al-Qaeda network in Pakistan, attacked Shia targets especially in their holy places and mosques.[54]

The emergence of the Taliban in Afghanistan in 1994 saw a new wave of persecution against the Hazara Shias in Afghanistan. In August 1998, when Taliban forces entered the multiethnic northern Afghan city of Mazar-i Sharif, they killed at least 2,000 civilians, the majority of them Hazaras.

A number of Pakistanis, including members of the SSP and of the LeJ, fought on the side of the Taliban in Mazar-e Sharif. The links between these Afghan and Pakistani Sunni militant groups and the flood of Hazara into Balochistan prompted a rise in persecution of the Hazara in that province too. The Hazara Shia community is concentrated in Quetta and is estimated to be around 500,000. It has to be remembered that the LeJ is an entirely Deobandi group, which has also killed hundreds of Sunni Sufis and Barelvis, in addition to thousands of Shias. Responding to the increased acts of violence, General Pervez Musharraf banned the LeJ in 2002. However, this has not deterred the group from continuing its sectarian attacks across Pakistan.

The various groups affiliated to the Deobandis in Pakistan have engaged in sectarian warfare with the Shias. A 62-page HRW report, *"We are the Walking Dead": Killings of Shia Hazaras in Balochistan, Pakistan,* documents Deobandi militant group attacks on the mostly Shia Hazara community in Balochistan. Since 2008, several hundreds of Hazara have been killed in steadily worsening targeted violence, including two bombings in the provincial capital, Quetta, in January and February 2013, which killed at least 180 people. "Sunni (Deobandi) extremists have targeted Hazara with guns and bombs while they participate in religious processions, pray in mosques, travel to work, or just go about daily life," said Brad Adams, Asia director. This has led to large numbers of Hazaras fleeing Pakistan for refuge in other countries. HRW interviewed more than 100 survivors, members of victims' families, law enforcement, security officials and independent experts for the report.[55]

The increase in Deobandi militant activities has meant that, since 2008, Pakistan's Shia Muslim community has been the target of an unprecedented escalation in sectarian violence. The LeJ has claimed responsibility for most attacks. On January 10, 2013, the suicide bombing of a snooker club in Quetta frequented by Hazaras killed 96 people and injured at least 150. Many of the victims were caught in a second blast 10 minutes after the first, striking those who had gone to the aid of the wounded. On February 17, 2013, a bomb exploded in a vegetable market in Quetta's Hazara Town, killing at least 84 Hazara and injuring more than 160. The LeJ claimed responsibility for both attacks, the bloodiest from sectarian violence in Pakistan since independence in 1947.[56] Moreover, in addition to the Hazaras, Shias of other ethnic groups, such as the Balochs, Pashtuns and Punjabis, have been attacked in Quetta as well as in other parts of Pakistan.

Such attacks were not confined to the Shia community. There have been numerous assaults on Sunni Sufi and Barelvi shrines and leaders in which thousands of people have died. Responsibility for these has been claimed by the Taliban (TTP), the LeJ and other Deobandi militant outfits.[57] Non-Muslims have suffered too. Entire Christian villages were destroyed in 2009 and in 2013, with no one being held to account. The Pakistani Taliban took credit for the murder of Shahbaz Bhatti in 2011, an advocate of reform of the country's blasphemy laws, as he left his Islamabad home, leaving flyers at the crime scene in an upmarket part of Islamabad.[58] In September, splinter groups from the Pakistani Taliban carried out twin suicide bombings on All Saints Church in Peshawar, which killed 119 Christians as they left their Sunday service.[59] Even the Sunni Muslim majority has not been spared from the onslaught. The Pakistani Taliban targeted politicians deemed to be "secular" during the run-up to the May election and afterwards.[60]

According to Knox James, the Pakistan Religious Violence Project that he directed for the US Commission on International Religious Freedom (USCIRF) documented a staggering number of attacks against religious communities over a 30-month period. Between January 2012 and June 2014, two reports recorded 325 instances of targeted violence against religious groups, resulting in more than 3,000 causalities with over 1,100 deaths. The Shia community was hardest hit, with 857 individuals killed in 131 separate suicide bombings and targeted shootings. The Pakistani Taliban and the LeJ repeatedly claimed responsibility for these acts.[61] The violence has been felt by the Ahmadis too, a group that has been declared as heretical by the Deobandis and other Muslim groups. The Ahmadis are regularly assassinated in drive-by shootings and their mosques attacked.[62]

It is important to note that these acts of violence have not been confined to Pakistan because the militant groups are now exporting their version of jihad all over the world. The Khudamudeen Madrasa, according to its chancellor, is training students from Burma, Nepal, Chechnya, Bangladesh, Afghanistan, Yemen, Mongolia and Kuwait. Out of the 700 students there, 127 are foreigners. Nearly half of the student body at Darul Uloom Haqqania, the *madrassa* that created the Taliban, is from Afghanistan. It also trains students from Uzbekistan, Tajikistan, Russia and Turkey, and it is currently expanding its capacity to house from 100 to 500foreign students, its chancellor said. According to the US State Department, Pakistani groups and individuals also help to finance and train the Islamic Movement of Uzbekistan, a terrorist organization that aims to overthrow secular governments in Central Asia.[63]

The extent of the violence can be discerned from the following report. Global Index notes that, in 2013, the country with the second largest increase in numbers of deaths was Pakistan. The country saw a substantial increase in the number of deaths per attack. In particular, the second and third biggest terrorist groups, the LeJ and Jundallah, averaged 20 more fatalities per attack in 2013 than in the previous year. This highlights the growing lethality of the Deobandi militant groups.[64]

An important consideration is the financial support of these groups. Most of their funding comes in the form of anonymous donations sent directly to their bank accounts. The LT (Army of the Pure), a rapidly growing Ahl-e-Hadith (Wahhabi) group, raises funds on the internet. The LT and its parent organization, Markaz ad-Da'wa Wal Irshad (Center for Islamic Invitation and Guidance), have raised so much money, mostly from sympathetic Wahhabis in Saudi Arabia, that they are reportedly planning to open their own bank.

Many of the families of the so-called "martyrs" receive financial assistance from the militant groups. The Shuhda-e-Islam Foundation, founded in 1995 by the JI, claims to have dispensed Rs13 million rupees to the families of martyrs. It also claims to provide financial support to some 364 families by paying off loans, setting them up in businesses or helping them with housing. Both the LT and the HA have established charitable organizations that reward the families of martyrs. Although these foundations provide a service to families in need, they also perpetuate a culture of violence.[65]

TABLIGHI JAMAAT

An offshoot of the Deobandi movement, the TJ movement, began in the late 1920s with Maulana Muhammad Ilyas Kandhlawi (d. 1944), whose family had long associations with Deoband and its sister school in Saharanpur, Mazaahiru'l-`Ulum. Its inception is believed to be a response to Hindu reform movements, which were considered to be a threat to vulnerable and non-practicing Muslims. Maulana Ilyas' strategy was to persuade Muslims to reform themselves and help fellow Muslims to practice a more strict and austere adherence to Islam. The Tablighi movement gradually expanded from a local to a national organization, and finally to a transnational movement with followers in more than 150 countries.[66]

The essential principle of the movement is that every Muslim can be a vehicle for disseminating the values and practices of Islam.[67] For the Tablighis, Muslims ought to spend a portion of their time spreading the word of Islam, wherever they may be. The Tablighi movement permeates mainstream Muslim life by using mosques as the base for their activities.[68] Over time, specific mosques throughout the world have come to be known as "Tablighi mosques". They try to spread Islam among Muslims and even use the hajj (pilgrimage) season to convert Muslims towards their ideas. Tablighis prefer face-to-face encounters and relationships to communicate their message.

With no formal bureaucracy or membership records, it is hard to calculate the number of participants over time, but at the end of the twentieth century, annual meetings of perhaps 2 million people would congregate for three-day meetings in Raiwind, Pakistan and Tungi, Bangladesh; large regional meetings were regularly held in India; and other convocations took place in North America and Europe—for example, in Dewsbury, the site of a major seminary associated with Tablighi activities in the North of England. These convocations were considered to be moments of intense blessings as well as occasions to organize tours. They also gave evidence of the vast numbers touched by the movement.[69]

Being influenced by traditional Islam, Tablighis have confined themselves largely to the ritualistic elements. This has meant that they have been largely apolitical. Owing to their emphasis on purity, personal contact and a return to the practices of the Prophet, they have been successful in attracting adherents to their movement, thus bringing Muslims of other denominations to the Deobandi ideology. Many Muslims of the diaspora do not have access to the traditional Islamic sciences offered in Muslim schools of learning or madrassas. By preaching to the Muslim laity in mosques, workplaces and universities, the Tablighis fill a particular void. Their effectiveness essentially stems from their ability to provide an intensive religious training for individuals who have never attended traditional places of Islamic learning. An increasing number of conversions in both Europe and the USA are the result of the proselytizing activities of the Tablighis.[70] However, as I have discussed, an increasing number of Tablighi mosques have been accused of preaching hatred in their study sessions. Some of the recent perpetrators of violence had reportedly frequented Tablighi mosques and may have been radicalized there.

In response to this movement, the Salafis have disagreed vehemently with the Tablighis. A fatwa from Sheikh Bin Baz in 1997 explicitly stated that the Tabligh was one of the 72 heretical sects of Islam. A Salafi website enumerates a list of deviant sects. This includes the TJ and Deobandism.[71] Wahhabis and Salafis are also critical of the Tablighis' "innovations", especially as they lack a centralized religious leadership. They also criticize the Tablighis for their encouragement of laypersons to propagate Islam and their view that one does not need to be very learned to preach.[72]

CONCLUSION

Movements such as the Deobandis and other Islamic fundamentalism groups represent a trend of clinging on to, or returning to, sacred texts or the "true", "original" or "essential" religion as a way to revolt against aspects of secularism and modernity. Movements such as the Deobandis also call into question the validity and legitimacy of secular governments and react strongly against religious and social pluralism. Instead they want to recreate the idealized environment of the Prophet and an understanding of faith as exemplified by the early generation of Muslims. They also want to purify Islam from cultural and extraneous accretions. The Deobandis reject the compromises with liberal values and secular institutions, and they refuse to observe the boundaries that secular society has imposed around religion. For them, religion is not a peripheral element that can be divorced from daily life.

Ultimately, such movements not only oppose the Western powers but also challenge the authority of local governments that have desacralized the public arena. The Deobandis want to place religion at the center of personal and public life and to impose their brand of a very austere and rigid Islam on the populace. In the attainment of their idealized socioreligious goals, some of the groups affiliated with the Deobandis have resorted to extremist and militant means, in the process contravening some of the very principles of human rights that Islam enunciates. It is this dichotomy that has yet to be resolved.

NOTES

1. Ira M. Lapidus, A History of Islamic Societies (Cambridge: Cambridge Univ. Press, 2002), 626. See also Barbara Metcalf, "Deobandis" *The Oxford Encyclopedia of the Modern Islamic World* http://www.oxford-islamicstudies.com/article/opr/t236MIW/e0187?_hi=0&_pos=2.

2. Upadhyay, R. 2003. Shah wali ullah's political thought—Still a major obstacle against modernisation of Indian Muslims.—See more at: http://www.southasiaanalysis.org/paper629#sthash.FsFO56IS. dpufSouth Asia Analysis Group. http://www.southasiaanalysis.org/paper629.

3. Moj, Muhammad. 2015. The Deoband Madrassah Movement: Countercultural Trends and Tendencies. Anthem Press.

4. Muhammad Qasim Zaman, *The 'Ulama' in Contemporary Islam: Custodians of Change* (Princeton: Princeton University Press, 2002), 14.

5. Luv Puri, The Past and Future of Deobandi Islam. See also Barbara Metcalf, Islamic Revival in British India: Deoband, 1860–1900 (New York: Oxford University Press, 2004), 136. Jocelyne Cesari, *When Islam and democracy Meet: Muslims in Europe and the United States* (New York: Palgrave Macmillan, 2004), 93.

6. Jocelyne Cesari, *When Islam and Democracy Meet*, 93.
7. Ebrahim Moosa, Deobandi School, *The Oxford Encyclopedia of Islam and Law*, http://www.oxfordislamicstudies.com/article/opr/t349/e0090?_hi=1&_pos=1.
8. Barbara Metcalf, "Traditionalist" Islamic Activism: Deoband and Deobandis, Ten Years Later: http://essays.ssrc.org/10yearsafter911/%E2%80%9Ctraditionalist%E2%80%9D-islamic-activism-deoband-and-deobandis-ten-years-later/ Accessed August 15, 2015.
9. Zaman, *The Ulama in Contemporary* Islam, 24.
10. Ibid.
11. Brannon Ingram, Sufis, Scholars and Scapegoats: Rashid Ahmad Gangohi and the Deobandi Critique of Sufism, *Muslim World*: 2009 (99:3): 479. See also Barbara Metcalf, "Deobandis".
12. Barbara Metcalf, "Deobandis" http://www.oxfordislamicstudies.com/article/opr/t236/e0187?_hi=2&_pos=2#match.
13. Barbara Metcalf, "Traditionalist" Islamic Activism: Deoband and Deobandis, Ten Years Later. http://essays.ssrc.org/10yearsafter911/%E2%80%9Ctraditionalist%E2%80%9D-islamic-activism-deoband-and-deobandis-ten-years-later/.
14. Jessica Stern. "Pakistan's Jihad Culture." *Foreign Affairs* 79, no. 6 (November/December 2000): 115–26.
15. Barbara Metcalf, "Traditionalist" Islamic Activism: Deoband and Deobandis, Ten Years Later http://essays.ssrc.org/10yearsafter911/%E2%80%9Ctraditionalist%E2%80%9D-islamic-activism-deoband-and-deobandis-ten-years-later/ Accessed August 15, 2015.
16. Jessica Stern. "Pakistan's Jihad Culture." *Foreign Affairs* 79, no. 6 (November/December 2000): 115–26.
17. Ibid.
18. *Arab News* 2014, February 18. Al-Asheikh acknowledges Deobandi contribution http://www.arabnews.com/news/527401.
19. "Why did the Pak Mawlana visit Deoband?" Rediff India Abroad. July 18, 2003. http://www.rediff.com/news/2003/jul/17pak1.htm. Retrieved August 15 2015.
20. Christophe Jaffrelot, *A History of Pakistan and Its Origins* (Anthem: South Asian Studies, 2004), 224.
21. Barbara Metcalf, "Traditionalist" Islamic Activism: Deoband and Deobandis, Ten Years Later http://essays.ssrc.org/10yearsafter911/%E2%80%9Ctraditionalist%E2%80%9D-islamic-activism-deoband-and-deobandis-ten-years-later/ Accessed August 15, 2015.

22. Barbara Metcalf, "Deobandis".
23. Barbara Metcalf, "Traditionalist" Islamic Activism: Deoband and Deobandis, Ten Years Later http://essays.ssrc.org/10yearsafter91 1/%E2%80%9Ctraditionalist%E2%80%9D-islamic-activism-deoband-and-deobandis-ten-years-later/ Accessed August 15, 2015.
24. Barbara Metcalf, "Traditionalist" Islamic Activism: Deoband and Deobandis, Talibs http://essays.ssrc.org/sept11/essays/metcalf. htm Accessed August 15, 2015.
25. https://en.wikipedia.org/wiki/Deobandi#cite_note-33.
26. Luv Puri, The Past and Future of Deobandi.
27. *BBC News* 2002, February 6. Jaish-e-Mohammad: A profile. http://news.bbc.co.uk/1/hi/world/south_asia/1804228.stm.
28. Barbara Metcalf, "Traditionalist" Islamic Activism: Deoband, Tablighis, and Talibs, http://essays.ssrc.org/sept11/essays/metcalf. htm.
29. Luv Puri, The Past and Future of Deobandi Islam.
30. Jessica Stern "Pakistan's Jihad Culture." *Foreign Affairs* 79, no. 6 (November/December 2000): 115–26.
31. Jessica Stern "Pakistan's Jihad Culture." *Foreign Affairs* 79, no. 6 (November/December 2000): 115–26.
32. Luv Puri, The Past and Future of Deobandi Islam.
33. Ayaz Mir, "Chevalier Of The Undead," Outlook India, November 2, 2009.
34. See Jeffrey Goldberg, "Jihad U.: The Education of a Holy Warrior." *The New York Times Magazine* 25 June 2000. http://www.nytimes. com/2000/06/25/magazine/inside-jihad-u-the-education-of-a-holy-warrior.html. Accessed August 15, 2015.
35. Ibid.
36. Barbara Metcalf, "Traditionalist" Islamic Activism.
37. http://en.wikipedia.org/wiki/Deobandi.
38. Vali Nasr, *The Shia Revival: How Conflicts Within Islam Will Shape the Future* (New York: W.W.Norton, 2006), 101.
39. Carlotta Gall, Ismail Khan, Pir Zubair Shah and Taimoor Shah (26 March 2009). "Pakistani and Afghan Taliban Unify in Face of U.S. Influx". *New York Times.* Retrieved August 15, 2015.
40. Innes Bowen, British Mosques aren't that Moderate After all, 14 June 2014 http://www.spectator.co.uk/features/9230671/who-runs-our-mosques/.

41. Greenhill, Sam; Clark, Laura (21 October 2006). "Veil teacher link to 7/7 bomber". *Daily Mail*. Retrieved August 15, 2015.
42. Norfolk, Andrew (21 October 2006). "How bombers' town is turning into an enclave for Muslims". *The Times*. Retrieved 15 October 2010.
43. https://lubpak.com/archives/337987.
44. https://lubpak.com/archives/337987.
45. Mohammad Manzur Nomani, Khomeini, *Iranian Revolution and the Shi'ite Faith* (London: Furqan Publications, 1988), 17.
46. Khaled Ahmed, 2014. The Lucknow Connection. The Indian Express, May 12. http://indianexpress.com/article/opinion/columns/the-lucknow-connection/.
47. Vali Nasr, *The Shia Revival: How Conflicts Within Islam Will Shape the Future* (New York: W.W.Norton, 2006), 164.
48. Ibid., 165.
49. Ibid., 162.
50. https://en.wikipedia.org/wiki/Sipah-e-Sahaba_Pakistan#cite_note-Raman-1. See also http://isianalysis.blogspot.com/2009/04/musharrafs-ban-analysis-18-1-2002.html.
51. "2009: Southern Punjab extremism battle between haves and have-nots". *Dawn.com* (Dawn Media Group). 2011-05-22. Retrieved August 15, 2015.
52. Muhammad b. Muhammad al-Mufid, *Awa'il al-Maqalat fi al-Madhahib wa'l Mukhtarat* (Tabriz, 1950), 94–5.
53. Muhammad Qasim Zaman, *The Ulama in Contemporary Islam*, 121–2.
54. Ibid., 119–122.
55. http://www.hrw.org/news/2014/06/29/pakistan-rampant-killings-shia-extremists.
56. http://www.telegraph.co.uk/news/worldnews/asia/pakistan/9794542/Pakistan-suffers-bloodiest-day-in-years-after-Quetta-snooker-hall-attack.html.
57. Owais Tohid 2010. In Pakistan, militant attacks on Sufi shrines on the rise. Reuters. http://www.csmonitor.com/World/Asia-South-Central/2010/1105/In-Pakistan-militant-attacks-on-Sufi-shrines-on-the-rise.
58. http://www.theguardian.com/world/2011/mar/02/pakistan-minister-shot-dead-islamabad.

59. http://www.theguardian.com/world/2013/sep/23/pakistan-church-bombings-christian-minority.
60. http://www.reuters.com/article/2013/05/09/us-pakistan-election-idUSBRE94807320130509.
61. Thames, Knox. "Pakistan's Dangerous Game with Religious Extremism." *The Review of Faith & International Affairs* 12, no. 4 (2014): 40–48.
62. http://www.rferl.org/content/pakistan-ahmadis-persecution-violence/24992861.html.
63. Jessica Stern. "Pakistan's Jihad Culture." *Foreign Affairs* 79, no. 6 (November/December 2000): 115–26.
64. http://www.visionofhumanity.org/sites/default/files/Global%20 Terrorism%20Index%20Report%202014_0.pdf.
65. Jessica Stern. "Pakistan's Jihad Culture." *Foreign Affairs* 79, no. 6 (November/December 2000): 115–26.
66. Barbara Metcalf, "Traditionalist" Islamic Activism: Deoband and Deobandis, Ten Years Later http://essays.ssrc.org/10yearsafter911/ %E2%80%9Ctraditionalist%E2%80%9D-islamic-activism-deoband-and-deobandis-ten-years-later/.
67. Jocelyne Cesari, *When Islam and Democracy Meet*, 94.
68. See Barbara Metcalf, "New Medinas: The Tablighi Jama'at in America and Europe," in Barbara Metcalf ed., *Making Muslim* Space, 113.
69. Barbara Metcalf, "Traditionalist" Islamic Activism: Deoband and Deobandis, Ten Years Later http://essays.ssrc.org/10yearsafter911/ %E2%80%9Ctraditionalist%E2%80%9D-islamic-activism-deoband-and-deobandis-ten-years-later/.
70. Jocelyne Cesari, *When Islam and Democracy Meet*, 94.
71. Olivier Roy, *Globalized Islam*, 244–5, fn. 26.; www.allaahuakbar.net.
72. Ibid., 238.

CHAPTER 18

Pakistan's Counterterrorism Strategy: A Critical Overview

Naeem Ahmed

INTRODUCTION

On 13 May 2015, the Ismaili Shiite community was targeted in Safoora Goth, Karachi, in one of the most organized and ruthless terrorist attacks in the history of the city, killing 43 commuters (*Dawn* 14 May 2015). According to Raja Umer Khattab, an official of the Counter-Terrorism Department of Sindh Police, the militants who were involved in the incident were inspired by ISIS and wanted to establish their link with the group (*Dawn* 2 July 2015). Although the investigation into the case is in progress, and five suspects have been arrested, the fact is that since 9/11, Pakistan has been experiencing acute internal security problems in the form of growing anti-state and sectarian terrorism, unleashed by the domestic terrorist network of militant jihadi and sectarian groups, following the Deobandi takfiri ideology that not only emphasizes a strict interpretation of Islam but also declares those Muslims who do not follow such an interpretation as non-believers.

It is true that the military operations in the tribal areas have shattered the terrorist network of Al-Qaeda and the TTP. However, the security operations have not seriously undermined the ability of terrorists, particularly the TTP, to plan and execute terrorist attacks. The terrorists' network,

N. Ahmed (✉)
Department of International Relations, University of Karachi, Karachi, Pakistan

© The Editor(s) (if applicable) and The Author(s) 2016
J. Syed et al. (eds.), *Faith-Based Violence and Deobandi Militancy in Pakistan*, DOI 10.1057/978-1-349-94966-3_18

their strength and their structure have so far remained intact. Moreover, these operations have not reduced the bigger threat, which is now emanating from the TTP-linked urban-based militant sectarian groups. There is also a need to construct an ideological counterpart to military operations in order to rein in Islamist militancy. Eradicating terrorists will not suffice to eliminate terrorism. There is a need to uproot the jihadist ideology and replace it with a moderate, all-encompassing, pluralistic alternative.

Although Pakistan's counterterrorism strategy mainly focuses on the use of military force in the FATA[1] and Provincially Administered Tribal Areas (PATA),[2] against the Pakistani Taliban and Al-Qaeda militants, it ignores the approach of countering the very ideology that provides inspiration and religious authenticity to the terrorists to attack the civilian and military targets. Moreover, Pakistan's counterterrorism strategy is also not devised to counter the terrorist network that has now shifted from the tribal areas to the urban centres, which are now producing well-educated and ideologically committed terrorists. This has resulted in making Pakistan's counterterrorism strategy ineffective and counterproductive in achieving significant outcomes.

While Pakistan's counterterrorism strategy has so far remained incapable of eliminating the homegrown terrorist network, its success largely depends on taking strong measures to neutralize violent extremist ideology that creates ideologically motivated hardcore terrorists. These measures include reforming madrassas that have become the nurseries of extremism and terrorism; establishing a punitive regime by improving the criminal justice system and further strengthening the anti-terrorism regime; launching counter-radicalization programmes to prevent potential terrorists; introducing reforms in the public education sector that currently promote religious hatred and the enemy image of neighbouring countries; and, most important, redefining the country's India-centric national security paradigm, which aims to seek support from militant jihadi groups.

Analysing Pakistan's counterterrorism strategy, this chapter assesses the measures which have so far taken by the Pakistani state to fight the home-based militant jihadi and sectarian outfits, inspired by takfiri ideology. Moreover, it focuses on the coercive aspects of Pakistan's counterterrorism strategy that are based on the traditional mode of warfare in which excessive use of force is resorted to, while ignoring long-term effective measures which require containment of the violent extremist ideology that produces terrorists. Such a policy goes beyond the launching of security operations, and convicting and executing "terrorists" through military courts, or trying them in Anti-Terrorist Courts (ATCs) under anti-terrorism laws. Therefore such a policy needs to create an alternative narrative which offers political and socioeconomic opportunities.

The chapter is divided into five parts. The first discusses takfiri ideology with respect to various developments that have occurred in the Muslim world. The second part deals with Pakistan-based militant jihadi and sectarian groups that follow takfiri ideology. The chapter then analyses Pakistan's counterterrorism strategy. It then evaluates the strategy. The last part offers recommendations regarding the formulation an effective counterterrorism strategy for Pakistan.

THE IDEOLOGICAL THESIS OF TAKFIR

Takfir is an act of a Muslim excommunicating another person or group, where the target is usually apostatized before being killed. It means that the person or group first undergoes the process of takfir before it is targeted. According to Olivier Roy, "The proponents of Takfir usually support jihad as a permanent and individual duty, for the very reason that there is no longer a true Islamic ruler or even a true ummah that could call for Jihad" (Roy 2004, p. 244). In other words, since jihad cannot be waged against Muslims, the act of takfir is the first and most important step of jihadism, whose ideological superstructure is based on religious superiority (*The Nation* 16 April, 2015).

Takfiris are highly influenced by the writings of the thirteenth-century Hanbali theologian, Ibn Taymiyyah, who "for the first time aggressively practiced the principle of Takfir to recognize Muslim resistance against the Tartars, and [also] against those Muslims who placed obstacles in the way of Islamic resistance against the invaders" (Shahzad 2011, p. 147). To him, jihad was justified against the domestic rulers who did not obey the sharia (Islamic) law. Later, during the twentieth century, some radical Islamists used this pretext and launched movements against their own rulers, whom they considered to be Westernized autocratic rulers who did not practise Islam (*Beacham's Encyclopedia of Terrorism* 2011). Important among them were Hasan al-Banna, an Egyptian revolutionary leader and theologian who founded the Muslim Brotherhood in 1928; Syed Qutb (1906–1966), an Egyptian ideologue of the fundamentalists and also an active member of the Muslim Brotherhood; and Abul A'ala Maududi, an eminent South Asian religious scholar who established the JI in 1941. The fundamentalist teachings of these ideologues have largely contributed to shaping the radical attitude of Muslim societies and mobilized millions of Muslims all over the world. They illustrate a discourse which has provided Islamists with an identity, a purpose and a methodology to accomplish their objectives.

The main focus of al-Banna's teachings was to eliminate all of the social, political and economic evils which had crept into Egyptian society at that time due to Westernization. His plan was first to reform the Egyptian socioeconomic and political system, and then to spread his message all over the world. Moreover, he emphasized the liberation of Muslim societies from the influence of the West and its materialistic values, and the revival of Islam by establishing an Islamic state under the rule of a caliphate, which is the icon of Islamic unity (*Beacham's Encyclopedia of Terrorism* 2011).

Syed Qutb was strongly inspired by the teachings of al-Banna and wanted to materialize al-Banna's dream of Islamizing Egyptian society and establishing an Islamic state in Egypt. He pointed out both the internal and the external enemies. With respect to internal enemies, he believed that Muslim societies had been passing through the "new age of ignorance" (*jahiliyya*). According to him, "new *jahiliyya* had engulfed the Muslim peoples and the new pharaohs, who were ruling them" (Bernard Lewis 2004, p. 68). To Syed Qutb, the Muslim rulers, particularly of the Middle Eastern region, were politically corrupt and apostate because they were the accomplices of the enemy. Therefore it was Muslims' religious duty to overthrow those corrupt rulers and establish the sharia-based Islamic state. To him, the threat of the external enemy—that is, the West—was alarming (*Beacham's Encyclopedia of Terrorism* 2011).

Although Maududi opposed the Pakistan Movement on the grounds of territorial nationalism espoused by the All India Muslim League, once Pakistan had been created he aspired to make it a sharia-based Islamic state. He firmly believed that progress could only be achieved if Islamic laws were followed. According to him, the future of Muslims lay in the unity of the Islamic ummah, which was only possible by adhering to their past. Moreover, he believed that it was the religious duty of all the Muslims to wage jihad, against not only corrupt rulers but also external enemies, particularly those who had occupied Muslim territories.

Four major developments in the Muslim world in the late 1970s and early 1980s persuaded the Islamists to assert their power in domestic, regional and international politics. First, Iran's Islamic Revolution in February 1979 not only toppled the pro-West Shah's regime, and consequently threatened the status quo-oriented Arab monarchies and Israel, but also created enthusiasm among the Islamists, even though they belonged to different and opposing sects, to bring such a revolution to their own countries. Second, the siege of the Grand Mosque in Mecca in November 1979 demonstrated resentment against the Saudi Royal family, which is also the custodian of the holy places of Islam: Mecca and Medina. Although the rebellion was brutally suppressed, it provided zeal and ideological inspiration to the Islamists, particularly thousands of Muslim youth, to wage "jihad" against an "atheist" state on behalf of the Muslim state. When in December 1979 the Soviet Union invaded Afghanistan, a third development occurred in the Muslim world that intensified the Islamists' struggle to revive the institution of the caliphate. And, finally, the assassination of the Egyptian President, Anwar al-Sadaat, in 1981, demonstrated the disapproval of the Muslim ruler, who made peace with an enemy state (i.e., Israel,) which had occupied the territory of the Muslims.

According to Saleem Shahzad, "In this highly charged ultra-radical political atmosphere a new generation of radical Muslims was reared" (Shahzad 2011, p. 132). The Soviet-Afghan War provided an opportunity to these highly charged radicals to not only make themselves battle-hardened jihadis but also mingle with each other and be influenced by each other's ideas. Several thousand Pakistanis, who mostly belonged to various Deobandi madrassas, religiopolitical parties (e.g., the JI, the JUI-F and the JUI-S), and militant jihadi and sectarian outfits (e.g., the HUJI and the SSP), also waged the Afghan Jihad, along with the Arab mujahideen. It is notable that it was from the Soviet–Afghan War that Al-Qaeda emerged, though in a very rudimentary form.

The Soviet withdrawal from Afghanistan, and later the union's disintegration in December 1991, was considered to be a great victory by the Islamists, who were now enthusiastic about celebrating the triumph of, in their eyes, having defeated one of the superpowers. However, the First Gulf War (1990–1991) changed the whole Islamist discourse. Saudi Arabia and other smaller Arab states, including Kuwait and Jordan, sought the USA's assistance to drive the Iraqi forces out of Kuwait, as well to ensure their own security vis-à-vis Saddam Hussain's Iraq. The presence of US forces in the Muslim holy land was a turning point where the Islamists took up arms not only against the West, including the USA, but also against their own rulers, who were considered to be the allies of the West against a Muslim country—Iraq—and thus were declared apostate. The events of 9/11 and the US invasion of Afghanistan, being supported by Pakistan with significant logistical assistance, set the stage, according to Shahzad, for the division between the Muslim state and the Muslim militants (Shahzad 2011, p. 132).

In terms of ideology, Al-Qaeda is the current and continued manifestation of the radical ideas of Ibn Taymiyyah, Hasan al-Banna, Maulana Maududi and Syed Qutb. Pan-Islamism is an important part of Al-Qaeda's worldwide campaign. The main ingredients of this campaign are based on anti-Americanism and overthrowing the ruling elite of the Muslim World. In Al-Qaeda's juridical bifurcation of the world into Dar-ul-Harb and Dar-ul-Islam, the Muslim states fall into the former category. States such as Saudi Arabia, Egypt and Pakistan are the "allies of Satan" because the ruling elite in these countries are the allies of the USA (*Beacham's Encyclopedia of Terrorism* 2011).

Shahzad believes that Al-Qaeda organized the 9/11 attacks in order to provoke the USA to target Afghanistan, which would follow a certain Muslim backlash and would eventually lead to a direct confrontation between the West and the Muslim world. Moreover, Al-Qaeda's second objective, Shahzad opines, was to discredit the Muslim ruling regimes by creating contradictions inherent in their political alliances with the West, and, once that allegiance was exposed, takfir would be the important weapon to isolate the Muslim rulers from their masses (Shahzad 2011, p. 138), who would be enraged by the atrocities of the US-led coalition of forces against a Muslim country, Afghanistan, and later on Iraq.

An Overview of Pakistan-Based Militant Deobandi Takfiri Groups

There are numerous Deobandi takfiri militant groups operating in Pakistan. According to Ayesha Siddiqa

> The Deobandi militants refer to jihadi outfits, who subscribe to and are guided by Deobandi ideology, which, in turn derives its strength from the revivalist movement started in Deoband, India by a Muslim scholar Shah Waliullah (1703–1762). The movement aimed at reforming Islamic practices with the purpose of improving the depravation and poor conditions of Muslims. One of the ideas was to stop people from Sufi practices which were seen as taking Muslims away from Islam (Siddiqa 2013, pp. 5–6).

Later, this ideology was employed in the Soviet–Afghan War in the 1980s to motivate people in the name of jihad against the Soviet Union.

Moreover, it was also used to counter the Shiite's growing assertion, which was inspired by the Iranian Revolution, in Pakistan. Frédéric Grare believes that the Wahhabi outfit Jamaat Ulema-e-Ahl-e-Hadith (Society of the Ulema of the People of the Hadith) was the first Sunni sectarian organization that launched an anti-Shiite movement in Punjab after the Iranian Revolution. It not only denounced Shia'ism as heresy but also questioned the loyalty of the Shiites towards Pakistan (Grare 2007, p. 129). The group soon lost its importance.

Two major Pakistan-based Deobandi militant outfits, which were established in the 1980s and played a significant role in the Soviet–Afghan War, were the HUJI and the SSP. The HUJI was founded in the early 1980s by Qari Saifullah Akhtar. Belonging to the Deobandi school of thought, the HUJI describes itself as "second line of defence for every Muslim", with the aim of establishing Islamic rule by waging war (HUJ 2012). Qari's HUJ had very close links with the Afghan Taliban. Even he was a crucial figure in Mufti Nizamuddin Shamzai's efforts to get Osama Bin Laden and Mullah Umar together as partners in jihad (*Daily Times* 9 August 2004).

The other militant Sunni–Deobandi outfit was the SSP, which also fought in Afghanistan but has traditionally focused on targeting the Shiites. It was formed in 1985 by the late Maulana Haq Nawaz Jhangvi, the vice-president of the JUI-F, Punjab, who was the first Pakistani cleric to demand publically that Shiites be declared a non-Muslim minority (Grare 2007, p. 130). The main reason behind the creation of the SSP was to counter the growing influence of Shiites in Pakistan and the region, particularly after the Iranian Revolution in 1979. The SSP had established links with Al-Qaeda during the Soviet–Afghan War (Siddiqa 2013, p. 6). It has also operated as a political party and contested elections. After its banning in 2002, it resurfaced as the ASWJ. In addition to targeting Shiites, the ASWJ has carried out terrorist attacks on Sunni-Barelvis, who have also, in retaliation, taken up violence against the Deobandis. The Sunni–Deobandi and Sunni–Barelvi clashes are more about taking control of mosques. Moreover, the ASWJ and its associated outfits have unleashed frequent terrorist attacks on Sufi shrines. These have included Data Ganj Bakhsh in Lahore in June 2010, Abdullah Shah Ghazi in Karachi in October 2010 and Sakhi Sarwar in Dera Ghazi Khan in April 2011.

However, a dissident group emerged in the SSP in 1996 when its Central Secretary of Information (media representative), Riaz Basra, founded the LeJ. Basra believed that the SSP had abandoned the mission of Maulana

Jhangvi. The LeJ also has links with the Taliban and Al-Qaeda, and it has used Al-Qaeda training camps in Afghanistan (Stenersen 2009, p. 12). Siddiqa believes that the Deobandi militant groups—the SSP, the LeJ and their various offshoots (e.g., the HuM and Harkat-ul-Ansar)—are viewed as a security risk because of their sectarian ideology. She also thinks that the LeJ is considered to be the lynchpin of Al-Qaeda, and this was probably one of the reasons that Pakistan's intelligence agencies created the JeM in 2000 by dividing the HuM (Siddiqa 2013, p. 6). Although the JeM mainly focuses on Kashmir, it also has a broader agenda, which is to some extent close to Al-Qaeda's global vision. While speaking at a mosque in Karachi in January 2000, Maulana Masud Azhar vowed to destroy India and the USA. He said, "We will not rest in peace until India and America are destroyed" (Hussain 2000, p. 20). He added, "The liberation of Kashmir is a part of our main objective of destroying India" (Ibid.). Moreover, the JeM established its links with the SSP, whose former amir, Maulana Azam Tariq, had promised full support to the JeM (Rana 2004, p. 221). Maulana Tariq helped the JeM to establish new mosques and recruitment centres for those wanting to fight in Kashmir (Gul 2002, p. 104).

The most notorious terrorist group, the TTP, which has carried out deadly attacks on military and civilian installations, and the people of Pakistan, was established by Baitullah Mehsud in South Waziristan in December 2007. Currently led by Mullah Fazlullah, son-in-law of Tehrik-e-Nifaz-e-Shariat Mohammedi's Maulana Sufi Mohammad, it is an umbrella organization of various Pashtun militant groups, based in Pakistan's tribal areas, and breakaway factions of militant jihadi and sectarian groups. The aim of the TTP is "to enforce Shariah and to unite against the NATO forces in Afghanistan and do defensive Jihad against the Pakistan army" (*Daily Times* 16 December 2007). Although the TTP has shown its allegiance to Mullah Omar, it never merged into the organizational structure of the Afghan Taliban; rather, it established a separate identity (Abbas 2008). The TTP today is facing a two-pronged threat for its survival: one, the comprehensive security operation, particularly the Zarb-e-Azb (name of Holy Prophet's sword), in North Waziristan, and the frequent US drone attacks that have considerably undermined the strength and infrastructure of the TTP in the FATA region; and two, the major splits in the ranks of the TTP, as many commanders have joined ISIS, which has, reportedly, shown its presence in Afghanistan and Pakistan.

ISIS originated from the current crises in Iraq and Syria, where it built its power on the historic rivalry between Sunni and Shiite Muslims by exploiting the Sunni's anger at the Shia-dominated government, which was established after the ousting of Iraq's Saddam Hussain. However, the footprints of the terrorist outfit have emerged in Afghanistan and Pakistan as well. In the case of Afghanistan, ISIS has gained ground in the three Afghan provinces of Nangrahar, Helmand and Ghazni by driving out the Afghan Taliban, thus making the Afghan Civil War more complex and brutal because the Taliban has been struggling to maintain unity in its ranks amid continuous defections to ISIS (Hussain 2015). It is with reference to this growing threat that the Afghan President, Ashraf Ghani, also sees ISIS as a greater threat to Afghanistan than the Taliban (Hussain 2015).

Similarly, ISIS may have found a foothold in Pakistan, though the Pakistani authorities continue to deny the presence of the terrorist group in the country. The Safoora Goth incident is a case in point. Moreover, a close link between ISIS and Pakistan-based religious militant groups was established when the breakaway factions of the TTP, which have taken sanctuary in Afghanistan's Nangrahar province, also joined ISIS (Hussain 2015). In October 2014, Shahidullah Shahid, a former spokesman for the TTP who was later killed in a US drone strike in Nangrahar province in July 2015, along with five other senior TTP leaders, declared allegiance to ISIS (*The Express Tribune* 14 October 2014). Unlike Al-Qaeda, ISIS uses the internet and social media networks to spread its ideology and attract well-educated youth from around the world.

Another takfiri terrorist group, known as Jundallah, mainly operates in Pakistan's Baluchistan province. Linked with Al-Qaeda and the TTP, it is an Iranian Baluch dissident group which was established in 2003 (Karthikeya 2009). It advocates the rights of the Iranian Sunni Muslims and has carried out several terrorist activities in the Iranian Sistan-Baluchistan province.[3] Although Jundallah is mainly active there, "its footprints have been traced to the Shikarpur terrorist incident, which indicates [an] expansion in its reach" (Moini 2015).

PAKISTAN'S COUNTERTERRORISM STRATEGY[4]

In 2014, two major events brought a significant change to Pakistan's counterterrorism strategy. One was the terrorist attack on Jinnah International Airport, Karachi, on 8 June that resulted in the launching of a much-awaited security operation, Zarb-e-Azb, against local and foreign militants in North Waziristan (*Dawn* 16 June, 2014). The other was the most ferocious terrorist attack on the APS on 16 December, in which more than 150 people, including 130 schoolchildren, lost their lives (*News International* 17 December 2014). The TTP took responsibility for the attack. As an immediate response, the government launched the National Action Plan, which was announced by the Prime Minister, Nawaz Sharif, in his speech to the nation on 25 December. The main aspects of the 20-point plan included establishing military courts,[5] to be headed by military officers; setting up special anti-terrorism force; prohibiting armed organizations and preventing the operation of banned groups under another name; and strengthening and activating the National Counter-Terrorism Authority. To give legal cover to the military courts, the parliament, on 6 January 2015, unanimously passed the 21st Constitutional Amendment Bill (*News International* 7 January 2014).

An analysis of Pakistan's counterterrorism strategy, which it adopted as a result of becoming an ally of the USA in the War on Terror after 9/11, shows that it has been based on coercive measures, which comprise both military and non-military options. The military options include heavy-handed security operations against militants in the tribal areas, and low–intensity, swift operations in the settled areas, particularly in the major cities, to apprehend various leaders of Al-Qaeda and the Taliban. Non-military options comprise legislative aspects, under which different governments in Pakistan, since 9/11, have introduced anti-terrorism legislation in the form of various presidential acts and parliamentary laws to curb the menace of terrorism carried out by homegrown militant jihadi and sectarian groups.

The story of Pakistan's military operations in the tribal areas began when it became part of the US-led Operation Enduring Freedom in Afghanistan, which demanded that it would halt the infiltration of militants into its tribal areas. However, Pakistan's military, since 2002, has conducted a number of small and large operations against the militant groups in the tribal areas. These have included al-Mizan (Justice) in South Waziristan (2002); Operation Kalosha in South Waziristan (March 2004); operation Zalzala (Earthquake) in South Waziristan (January 2008); Sirat-e-Mustaqeem (Right Path) in Khyber (June 2008); Operation Sher Dil (Lion Heart) in Bajaur (September 2008); Rah-e-Haq (True Path) in Swat (2007); Rah-e-Rast (Just Path) in Swat (May 2009); Rah-e-Nijat (Path of Salvation) in South Waziristan (October 2009); Koh-e-Sufaid (White Mountain) in Kurram (July 2011); Zarb-e-Azb in North Waziristan (June 2014); and operation Khyber II in Khyber (March 2015).

The main aspect of Pakistan's security operations in the tribal areas is the use of full-scale vigorous military force against the militants by employing heavy artillery and fighter jets (Jones and Fair 2010, p. 46). Although it is claimed that Pakistan's military has cleared most of the tribal areas of the militants, the terrorist network, which has now expanded to the major urban centres, has not been completely eliminated. Not only are the pitched battles between the militants and security forces in the tribal areas still going on, but major cities of the country are continuously witnessing the scourge of terrorism, mainly carried out by militant sectarian outfits, which have links with the TTP, Al-Qaeda and ISIS.

Similarly, Pakistan's anti-terrorism legislation, dealing with the militant jihadi and sectarian organizations and individuals, comprises various amendments to the Anti-Terrorism Act (ATA) of 1997, as well as the introduction of new laws to make the anti-terrorism regime more stringent. The ATA, which is the basic anti-terrorism structure of Pakistan, was promulgated to eradicate sectarian terrorism from the country during the 1990s. Under the act, ATCs were created to ensure speedy trials. However, the ATA required some amendments in light of the changing security scenario after 9/11. As a result, in January 2002, the government introduced the Anti-Terrorism (Amendment) Ordinance 2002, which called for the targeting of the entire terrorist network with severe punishment, including the death penalty for those involved in aiding and abetting terrorism. Similarly, in November 2002, another amendment was made to the Ordinance of 2002, which authorized the police to hold a suspect for up to 12 months without filing any criminal charges (Anti-Terrorism [Amendment] Ordinance 2002). Moreover, the Anti-Terrorism (Second Amendment) Act 2004, promulgated in January 2005, incorporated further modifications to the ATA of 1997, which enhanced the powers of the ATCs to try offences related to kidnapping for ransom, as well as use of firearms or explosives by any device, including bomb blast, in a place of worship or court premises (Anti-Terrorism [Second Amendment] Act 2004).

The extraordinary security situation which Pakistan faced in the form of a severe backlash from the terrorists after the Red Mosque operation in Islamabad in 2007, and military operations in Swat and South Waziristan in 2009, required further amendments to the ATA 1997. As a result, in October 2009, the government issued the Anti-Terrorism (Amendment) Ordinance, which permitted the extrajudicial confession before the responsible investigative security personnel in the ATCs. Moreover, the remand period was extended from 30 to 90 days, and the burden of proof was shifted to the accused (Kheshgi 2009). Moreover, through a special presidential order, the Ordinance was extended to the PATA, and it established new ATCs in Peshawar and the Malakand region (Yusuf 2010, p. 23).

In the wake of the deteriorating security situation in the country, the government, in June 2011, promulgated the Regulations Action in Aid of Civil Powers 2011 for the FATA and PATA regions, which authorized the armed forces to imprison a suspect until the continuation of action in aid of the civil power. Moreover, the regulations also gave "a set of offences, punishable with death penalty or imprisonment for life or up to 10 years along with fine and forfeiture of property" (*Dawn* 12 July 2011). Under the regulations, notified internment centres were established near the Pakistan–Afghan border at Landi Kotal to detain persons accused of terrorism (Iqbal 2013).

Similarly, the Investigation for Fair Trial Bill 2012, which was passed in December 2012, authorized the government to intercept the private communications of an individual who is deemed likely to be, or is suspected of, engaging in preparations to conduct an act of crime or terror (*The Business Recorder* 21 December 2012). In March 2013 the Parliament passed the Anti-Terrorism (Amendment) Bill 2013, which not only empowered the government to seize property of any person involved in financing terrorism but also extended the definition of terrorism through an amendment in Section 6 of the ATA of 1997, according to which the threat of terrorism would now include "intimidating and terrorizing the public, social sectors, business community and preparing or attacking the civilians, media persons, government officials, installations, security forces or law enforcement agencies" (*Pakistan Today* 14 March 2013). It also prohibited the issuance of passports, arms licences and credit cards to the activists of banned outfits, as well as barring the leaders of the outlawed groups from travelling abroad (*News International* 13 March 2014).

In July 2014, Pakistan's Parliament passed the Protection of Pakistan Bill 2014, which aims to give law-enforcement agencies more power to counter terrorism, and with legal backing to increase the likelihood of conviction. The bill designates a person an "enemy alien" if their identity is not ascertained and if they are involved in waging war or insurrection against Pakistan depredation on its territory. It also authorizes a law-enforcement official, not below grade 15, to shoot on sight a terror suspect, to search any premises and make a non-bailable arrest, without a warrant, of a person who has committed, or is likely to commit, a scheduled offence,[6] which is punishable with imprisonment for up to ten years.

In the case of banning terrorist groups, since 9/11, 45 groups have been outlawed in different phases. These include the LeJ and the SM, a Shiite militant outfit (August 2001), the JeM, the LeT, the SSP, the TJP, the TNSM and the TIP (January 2002), Al-Qaeda (March 2003), Millat-i-Islamia Pakistan (formerly the SSP), Khuddam-ul-Islam (formerly the JeM) and Islami Tehrik-e-Pakistan (formerly the TJP) (November 2003), Lashkar-e-Islami, Ansar-ul-Islam, Haji Namdar Group and the TTP (2008), the ASWJ (formerly the SSP) (2012), and Jama'at-ud-Dawa (formerly the LT) and the Haqqani Network (2015).

Although the anti-terrorism legislation in Pakistan (since 1997) is a "bold departure from the normal legal system" (Kennedy 2004, p. 390), it has yet to prove its effective implementation in the prevention of continuous acts of terrorism, though the pace has slowed down because of the Zarb-e-Azb operation. The tedious aspects of the anti-terrorism regime are its failure to try suspect terrorists speedily, and to ensure the enforcement of the ban on militant outfits that have resurfaced with new names, thus exposing the weakness of the state to establish its writ and authority.

An Evaluation of Pakistan's Counterterrorism Strategy

Pakistan's counterterrorism strategy, which is mainly based on coercive measures, has proved ineffective in not only countering but also eradicating the homegrown hazard of terrorism as it does not focus on counterextremism and counter-radicalization approaches. Rather, it revolves around Pakistan's strategic interests in the region, especially vis-à-vis India[7] and Afghanistan.[8]

Moreover, for Pakistan the growing Indian influence in Afghanistan is also a the major concern, and to deter it is its major strategic interest. This can only be achieved by supporting the elements which can counter the India-friendly Afghan government. It is for this reason that Pakistan's military have still been distinguishing between "good Taliban" and "bad Taliban" by avoiding targeting the former (including the Haqqani Network) in its security operations in tribal areas, in spite of enormous US pressure.

It is true that Pakistan has dealt with the domestic sectarian terrorist groups, such as the SSP and the LeJ, heavy-handedly "through arrests, targeted assassinations, and aggravated inter-group massacres" (Tellis 2008, p. 9), but several members and leaders of these outlawed Deobandi sectarian outfits have been spared because of their overlapping membership of "good Taliban" militant groups, which are fighting in Indian-held

Kashmir and in Afghanistan, and are considered to be "strategic assets" by the military. They also use the same training camps and resources and, to a large extent, have the same ideological inspiration (Mir 2005). These multiple links have made the government's task to eliminate terrorism difficult, and thus made Pakistan's counterterrorism strategy less effective.

RECOMMENDATIONS

Although the security operations in the tribal areas may play a significant role, and should not be underestimated, as in the purging of terrorists' ideologue and chief architects, such as Malik Ishaq, nevertheless, a peaceful Pakistani society without extremist ideology demands countering the Islamists' narrative which has indoctrinated the youth into the destructive jihadist path. Until this is realized, the extremist ideology will continue reverberating among the most vulnerable segments (i.e., the youth) of Pakistani society. Following are some recommendations to make Pakistan's counterterrorism strategy more effective and result-oriented.

Reforming Madrassas

Combating terrorism, extremism and radicalization in Pakistani society strictly demands reforming and regulating the madrassa sector, which constantly produces ideologically indoctrinated radicals along sharp sectarian lines by giving an apocalyptic and limited worldview to the students. Although the madrassa reforms measures are not a new phenomenon in Pakistan,[9] the National Action Plan recommends mapping the religious seminaries by creating "a list of registered and unregistered madrasas and an audit of accounts, with the government assuming responsibility for routing foreign funding" (ICG 2015, p. 12).

The exact number of madrassas in Pakistan is not known. However, a rough estimate suggests that around 30,000, both registered and unregistered, are operating in the country (*Dawn* 10 August 2015). Alarmingly, 11,000 Deobandi madrassas in Pakistan have been identified as sensitive (ICG 2015, p. 12). Moreover, since the launching of the National Action Plan, the law-enforcement agencies have placed 30 religious seminaries in the "suspect" category and these have been closed, according to the Interior Minister, Chaudhary Nisar Ali Khan (*Dawn* 10 August 2015). Among them, 2 are from Punjab, 15 from Sindh and 13 from KPK. No seminary in Balochistan has been placed in this category (*Dawn* 10 August 2015).

The frightening aspect of the madrassas is that they promote extremist ideology, which incites their students to jihad. According to Ayesha Siddiqa

> Religious seminaries are not significant due to the number of Jihadis they produce, but are central to the production of the ideology that feeds the Jihadi, even if said Jihadi is in fact educated in public schools and universities. The madressa denotes an essential power base that contributes ideology and the sustained supply of a narrative into society, which in turn, feeds both radicalism and militancy in Pakistan (Siddiqa 2015).

Although a number of alleged terrorists arrested for carrying out or planning terror attacks have been associated with jihadi madrassas, the policy-makers rarely pay attention to their teachers and mentors, who generally play the role of a facilitator and bring them into contact with the militant organizations. The ongoing security operation in Karachi has also excluded jihadi madrassas (ICG 2015, p. 12). Therefore, in order to counter the very poisonous ideology which gives birth to terrorism, the government needs to take serious measures for the reforming and regulation of madrassas at the earliest opportunity. In the first place, the syllabi of madrassas need the detailed attention of policy-makers. In other words, what is taught in madrassas needs to be checked and changed in order to prevent the production of ideologically driven zealots. Second, the income sources of the madrassas need strict scrutiny because there are reports of foreign funding. According to a Punjab Police report, which it presented to the Senate Committee, at least 950 Punjab-based madrassas received hundreds of millions of rupees (millions of dollars) since 1980s from Qatar, Kuwait, Saudi Arabia and 14 other Muslim and non-Muslim countries (ICG 2015, pp. 16–17). Moreover, there is no audit of the madrassas' domestic sources of income because they receive generous donations in terms of zakat (religious tax). Since there is no audit of their income, there is no mechanism for tracing its use, including in terrorism activities.

Third, although the NAP bans hate speeches and extremist material, the government needs to ensure the effective implementation of the ban to avoid the provocation of violence against other sects.

Establishment of a Punitive Regime

Although Pakistan is well equipped with the anti-terrorism laws, and the legal tools to prosecute and punish terrorists have expanded in recent years, particularly under the ATA, the scourge of terrorism has not been curbed. The country has been witnessing a continuous wave of terrorism, carried out by the domestic sectarian and jihadi outfits. It therefore requires an effective anti-terrorism regime with punitive measures to destroy the terrorist infrastructure and bring the terrorists to justice.

First, there is a need to reform Pakistan's criminal justice system by improving the investigation and prosecution processes by allocating ample resources to the police, as well as equipping them with modern techniques of investigation by providing rigorous training to enhance their investigative capacity. With the faulty investigation process and corruption in the police, which still relies on "eyewitness accounts" for evidence, the probability of the abuse of law increases, thus fostering the opportunity for victimization of the suspect at an alarming level (ICG 2015, p. 19). Although the government has created an alternative special police force, known as the Counter-Terrorism Force (CTF), in all provinces under the National Action Plan on a three-year contract, there is a need to improve and strengthen the existing police structure by providing much needed resources and training, rather than creating a parallel militarized policing system. Moreover, the civilian law-enforcement agencies need to be empowered and held accountable for enforcing the law (ICG 2015, p. 20).

Second, Pakistan's existing anti-terrorism regime needs to be reformed because it has proved inefficient in convicting individual terrorists and terrorist organizations. The lack of a witness-protection programme causes serious security problems for the witness, who often does not appear in court. As a result, several suspect terrorists have been acquitted. According to a report by the ICG, the conviction rates remain around 5–10 percent (ICG 2015, p. 19). There is thus a need to establish a robust protection programme to ensure effective protection for the judges, witnesses and prosecutors.

Third, the ATCs were created in an extraordinary situation with the purpose of ensuring speedy trials for terrorists, but a shortage of funds and staff, as well as heavy case loads, have affected the staff's working conditions. Moreover, the frequent amendments to the ATA have expanded the range of criminal activities, such as kidnapping for ransom; gang rape; arms trafficking; and attacks on government buildings, hospitals, schools and media persons. Such crimes could, otherwise, be tried in the regular courts under the PPC and. Consequently, the burden of ATCs has not only further increased and caused a backlog of pending cases but also slowed the process of the prosecution of high-profile terrorists and thus affected the very efficacy of the ATA. To make the ATCs more effective and results-oriented, there is a need not only to allocate adequate funds but also to lessen their burden by amending the 1997 ATA. To achieve this the act of terrorism needs to be redefined by including only those acts which are larger in scale with an intention to create fear and insecurity among the people, or which are against the security of the state.

Lastly, the tribal areas of Pakistan, especially the FATA, need the serious attention of the policy-makers. This requires the introduction of political and socioeconomic reforms in the FATA. Although in August 2009 the government announced a reform package for the FATA,[10] no concrete steps have so far been taken to address the grievances of the tribal people. As a first step the government needs to extend complete political rights to the FATA by merging it with KPK. Moreover, there is a need to repeal the Frontier Crimes Regulation (FCR)[11] and to replace it with the Criminal Procedure Code of Pakistan. This would then lead to the application of the ATA regime to the terrorists/militants who belong to the FATA region as they cannot legally be tried under the current anti-terrorism laws. These individuals have to be transported to their respective agency, where they can be tried under the FCR. However, with the introduction of the Action in Aid and Civil Power Ordinance, these militants can also be tried under the ATA if they are arrested during security operations in the tribal areas. For this, the arrested suspect militant needs to be transferred from the crime scene and handed over to the police for investigation. This creates another problem. The military personnel captured the suspected militant and handed him over to the police which relied on the evidences provided by security agencies. Police did not conduct any investigation. This weakens the case when the state prosecutor files the challan in court against the arrested militant. Such a weakness in the case could easily be exploited by a defence lawyer. Consequently the suspect militant could avoid conviction or receive bail before the conclusion of the trial.

Counterextremism Programmes and Learning from Others' Experiences

Although the use of military force is a fundamental component of counterterrorism strategy to fight the emerging peril of terrorism, there are limitations to this policy. According to Laura Dugan and Gary LaFree, professors of criminology and criminal justice at the University of Maryland, "over the long term, harsh counterterrorism measures can have a backlash effect" (Stern 2010, p. 1). This is also true in case of Pakistan, whose counterterrorism strategy has been relying on the use of lethal force to combat the threat of terrorism, but with limited success. There is therefore a need to launch counter-radicalization programmes to prevent the emergence of future terrorists. It must be noted that the support for militant jihadi and sectarian groups in Pakistan is waning, particularly after the APS attack. So if a counter-radicalization programme of Muslim extremists, particularly the youth, were ever possible, this is the right time to try. To achieve this objective, the government needs to take the following measures. First, for the successful counter-radicalization programme, it needs to identify the real causes which motivate an individual to join a terrorist organization. Second, the media should be used to counter the homegrown radical extremists. It is said that the media, particularly electronic media, plays a significant role in exacerbating terrorism because terrorists try to publicize their goals by affecting a large audience in an effort to bring about fundamental political change. Therefore the government needs to implement strict measures to check the contents of any programme, website and so forth to determine whether it serves the motives of the terrorists, without undermining the right to freedom of expression. In this regard the media need to encourage broadcasting programmes which give a liberal and pluralistic image of Pakistani society and at the same time discourage any extremist tendencies in the country.

Pakistan can also learn from the experiences of the other countries which have launched counter-extremism and counter-radicalism programmes in order to prevent not only violence in their societies but also the emergence of future terrorists. The counter-extremism programmes of the countries in the West, particularly the UK and the USA, focus mainly on community-based approaches, which specifically concentrate on Muslim immigrants in order to integrate them into Western society by developing intercommunity harmony. Under the British counter-radicalization programme, youth centres have been established that are supported by the Muslim Contact Unit, part of the Special Branch of London's Metropolitan Police, which works with leaders of the Muslim community there, including Islamists, to isolate and counter supporters of terrorist violence (Stern, p. 4). Similarly, the US counterextremism programme, which was initiated mainly by the Homeland Security Department, consists of three key objectives: to understand violent extremism by assessing the threat it poses to the nation as a whole and within specific communities; to support local communities by strengthening relationships with communities that may be targeted for recruitment by violent extremists; and to support local law enforcement in order to deter and disrupt recruitment or individual mobilization for terrorism (Countering Violent Extremism 2015). However, since the Western models of countering violent extremism are in a rudimentary form and focus mainly on Muslim communities, there is a great opposition from various Muslim organizations, such as the Islamic Shura Council of Southern California, the MSA of the West Coast and the United States Council of Muslim Organizations (Brief on Countering Violent Extremism 2015). The concerns of these organizations is that such a government-initiated programme is divisive, futile and founded on the premise that one's faith determines one's inclination towards violence.

Since the case of Pakistan, which is predominantly a Muslim-majority state, is different from those of Western countries, it would be dangerous to replicate a Western model of countering violent extremism. On the other hand, Pakistan may be able to indigenize these models while keeping in mind the dynamics of the society and the particular problems that it faces.

Reforming the Education Sector

To counter the challenge of sectarian militancy, Pakistan needs to reform its impoverished public education system. Although there is no direct link between sectarian militancy and the education system, however, it has been ascertained that the country's education system has been radicalizing many young people while failing to equip them for the job market (ICG 2014, p. 1). According to a report by the ICG, Pakistan's deeply flawed curriculum contributes to the spread of violence and extremism (ICG 2014). Moreover, the report further says that Pakistan has the second highest number of out-of-school children in the world, with 22 percent of those that the country is constitutionally obliged to educate still being deprived of schooling. In addition, expenditure on education remains the lowest in its region (ICG 2014).

Although after the 18th constitutional amendment the provinces have been empowered to devise their education policy, planning and curriculum, a lot of work still needs to be done. Pakistan needs to revise the national curriculum, which promotes xenophobia, religious intolerance, centralized state ideology, national cohesion at the expense of regional diversity and popular opposition to its main enemy, India, against which support for jihadi outfits is in Pakistan's strategic interests (ICG 2014, p. 3). Therefore to create a tolerant and peaceful Pakistani society, the policy-makers need to invest in the public school system and other education projects to counter the current militant discourse of an internal cultural and religious civil war and a clash of civilizations abroad (Waseem 2011, p. 19).

Redefining Strategic Policy

One of the major flaws in Pakistan's counterterrorism strategy is that it is locked into the good Taliban–bad Taliban dichotomy. An effective and productive counterterrorism strategy for Pakistan necessitates discarding the notion of favourites and launching an across-the-board security operation against all militant organizations which are involved in unleashing terrorism within and outside the country. To achieve this objective, Pakistan needs to redefine its strategic policy, which revolves around seeking the support of militant jihadi groups, vis-à-vis its eastern and western neighbours—India and Afghanistan. Such a shift in Pakistan's strategic policy should emphasize improving relations with India and Afghanistan by focusing more on cooperation on mutual security issues to establish peace in the region, and expanding economic ties for the socioeconomic development of the region.

CONCLUDING ANALYSIS

An analysis of Pakistan's current counterterrorism strategy shows that it has proved to be less effective in combating the threat of terrorism by eradicating the terrorist network of homegrown militant jihadi and sectarian outfits. It mainly focuses on "ad hoc, reactive, moment-to-moment, incident-to-incident based approaches" (*The Express Tribune* 2013) through the excessive use of military force in the tribal areas and the adoption of a coercive legal framework under the ATA to contain terrorism. Moreover, the strategy has also remained less efficient in targeting religious extremism, which is deeply ingrained in Pakistani society.

Consequently the terrorist network has not only expanded, particularly to urban centres, but also, over a period of time, become more lethal and ruthless. This is evidenced by the APS attack and the Safoora carnage, where the terrorists targeted the most vulnerable segments of society—the schoolchildren and the minority Ismaili Shiite community in the urban centres of Peshawar and Karachi, respectively.

It is high time that the government recognizes that the root cause of terrorism lies in extremist thought, particularly in takfiri ideology, advocated by the terrorist groups, which are associated with various Deobandi madrassas and also have links with Al-Qaeda and, more recently, ISIS. The TTP's link with ISIS is the most disturbing development, not only for Pakistan but also for the whole region, because it shows that the Middle Eastern radical militant group is spreading its ideological influence to South Asia, particularly Pakistan. This also means that the Pakistani Taliban have been transforming themselves from a local tribal-based group to a much more systematic and refined organization with the objective of establishing a Muslim caliphate through global jihadism. Therefore it is clear that the scourge of terrorism in Pakistan can only be eliminated if the very ideology of violent extremism and radicalism is countered.

NOTES

1. According to Article 246 of the 1973 Constitution of Pakistan, the areas included in FATA are the tribal areas adjoining the districts of Peshawar, Kohat, Bannu, Lakki Marwat, Dera Ismail Khan, Tank and seven tribal agencies of Bajaur, Orakzai, Mohmand, Khyber, Kurram, North Waziristan and South Waziristan.
2. Similarly, the PATA comprises the districts of Chitral, Dir and Swat (which includes Kalam), Malakand, the tribal area adjoining Mansehra district and the former state of Amb; Zhob district, Loralai district (excluding Duki Tehsil), Dalbandis Tehsil of Chagai district, and Marri and Bugti areas.
3. In May 2009 in a suicide attack inside a mosque in Zahedan, the capital of Iran's Sistan-Baluchistan province, 25 people were killed and 130 injured (Karthikeya 2009). In October 2009 in a suicide bombing in Sarbaz, Sistan-Baluchistan, 29 people, including six commanders of the Iranian Revolutionary Guards, were killed (Qadir 2012). Similarly, in December 2010, a suicide bomber killed 41 people in Chahbar, a south-eastern Iranian province of Sistan-Baluchestan (*The Guardian* 15 December 2010). Then in October 2012, a suicide bomber blew himself up outside a mosque in Chahbar, killing two members of the Basij (volunteer forces) (*The Tehran Times* 19 October 2012).
4. A major portion of this section has been taken from Ahmed Naeem 2015, 'Pakistan: In Search of Counterterrorism Strategy?', *BIISS Journal*, Vol. 36, no. 1, pp. 61–70.

5. It should be noted that the military courts were banned in Pakistan by the Supreme Court in February 1999.

6. Scheduled offences include waging war or threatening the security of Pakistan; crimes against ethnic, religious and political groups or minorities, including offences based on discrimination, hatred, creed and race; use of arson, fire-bombs, suicide bombs, biological weapons, chemical weapons, nuclear arms, plastic explosives on public places, government premises, historical places, business concerns; killing, kidnapping, extortion, assault or attack of members of Parliament, judiciary, executive, media, and government employees, including the armed forces and law-enforcement agencies, foreigners or internationally protected persons, welfare workers; attacks on communication and interaction lines, energy facilities, aircraft, airports, flight crew, gas or oil pipelines, national defence installations; cyber crimes; attack on mass transport systems, maritime navigation; hostage taking; and violence transcending national boundaries (Protection of Pakistan Ordinance 2013).

7. In the case of India, Pakistan's strategic interests rest mainly in Kashmir, which the latter considers to be an "unfinished agenda" of the Partition Plan of June 1947. Pakistan's failure to achieve Kashmir's independence from India through wars and bilateral negotiations compelled the former to adopt the policy of engaging the latter in a low-intensity conflict by using militant jihadi groups as its proxies. Moreover, water is the most pressing threat between the two countries.

8. With reference to Afghanistan, Pakistan's strategic interests are linked with the issues of the Durand Line and Pakhtunistan.

9. The Pakistani state started reforming the madrassa sector in the 1960s, when Jamia Islamia Bahawalpur was established in 1963 with the purpose of harmonizing modern and traditional education. However, the programme failed because of bureaucratic sluggishness. Then in 1970 the government established an ulema academy to train and educate imams and khateebs. This also failed to take off. In the 1990s, Benazir Bhutto's government introduced some reforms by making it compulsory for foreign students to obtain a no-objection certificate for studying in the Pakistani madrassas. Bhutto also suspended the zakat to madrassas (for details, see Siddiqa 2015). Immediately after taking over the state apparatus in a military coup, General Pervez Musharraf realized the need to reform madrassas. As a result, in December 1999, a working group was formed "to suggest

ways and means to improve the existing madrasas and to secure fuller coordination among the madrasas and the national education system without affecting the autonomy of madrasas". Similarly in March 2001, "the cabinet decided to set up one model madrasa each in Karachi, Sukkur and Islamabad. As a result, in August 2001, an ordinance was issued to establish a Pakistan Madrasa Education Board (PMEB), for these model religious schools." (ICG 2002, p. 24). The purpose of the PMEB was to improve and secure the uniformity of standards of education and to integrate the system of Islamic education imparted in madaris within the general education system throughout the country (*Dawn* 10 August 2015).

10. The package included political, judicial and administrative reforms for the tribal areas, allowing political activities in FATA, setting up an appellate tribunal, curtailing arbitrary powers of political agents, giving people the right to appeal and bail, excluding women and children from the territorial responsibility clause and envisaging the audit of accounts by the auditor general. The package also envisaged extension of the Political Parties Order of 2002 to the tribal areas and changes in the century-old anachronistic Frontier Crimes Regulation (FCR) to make it responsive to human rights (*Dawn* 14 August 2009).

11. The FCR is a distinctive array of laws, designed by the British in 1848, to handle the affairs of the FATA. The FCR is built on the notion of "collective responsibility" doctrine, according to which the responsibility of the crime is bestowed on the entire tribe. The Government of Pakistan holds its writ on the tribal agencies through political agents.

REFERENCES

Abbas, H. (2008). A profile of Tehrik-e-Taliban Pakistan. *The CTC Sentinel, 1*(2), 1–4. Retrieved from the CTC Sentinel Website: http://www.ctc.usma.edu/wp-content/uploads/2010/06/Vol1Iss2-Art1.pdf.

Ahmed, N. (2015). Pakistan: In search of counterterrorism strategy? *BIISS Journal, 36*(1), 61–70.

Anti-Terrorism (Amendment) Ordinance. (2002). Retrieved from the Senate Website: https://www.unodc.org/tldb/showDocument.do?documentUid=2300&node=docs&cmd=add&country=PAK

Anti-Terrorism (Second Amendment) Act, 2004, Gazette of Pakistan, Extraordinary, Part II. (2005). Retrieved from the Senate Website: https://www.unodc.org/tldb/showDocument.do?documentUid=9928&q=anti-terrorism%20legislation%20in%20Pakistan&edit_btn=SEARCH

Grare, F. (2007). The evolution of sectarian conflicts in Pakistan and the ever-changing face of Islamic violence. *Journal of South Asian Studies, 30*(1), 127–143.

Gul, I. (2002). *The unholy alliance: Pak-Afghan relations under the Taliban.* Lahore: Vanguard.

Harkat-ul-Jihad-i-Islami (HUJI). (2012). Retrieved from http://www.satp.org/satporgtp/countries/india/states/jandk/terrorist_outfits/HuJI.htm

Hussain, Z. (2000, February). In the shadow of terrorism. *The Herald.*

Hussain, Z. (2015, July 15). The looming IS threat. *Dawn,* p. 8.

ICG (International Crisis Group Report). (2002). *Pakistan: Madrasas, extremism and military.* Retrieved from http://www.crisisgroup.org/~/media/Files/asia/south-asia/pakistan/Pakistan%20Madrasas%20Extremism%20And%20The%20Military.pdf

ICG (International Crisis Group Report). (2014). *Education reforms in Pakistan.* Retrieved from www.crisisgroup.org/~/media/Files/asia/south-asia/pakistan/257-education-reform-in-pakistan.pdf

ICG (International Crisis Group Report). (2015). *Revisiting counter-terrorism strategies in Pakistan: Opportunities and pitfalls.* Retrieved from http://www.crisisgroup.org/~/media/Files/asia/south-asia/pakistan/271-revisiting-counter-terrorism-strategies-in-pakistan-opportunities-and-pitfalls.pdf

Iqbal, N. (2013, March 26). Swat Taliban, Afghan govt nexus may give rise to terrorism, SC told. *Dawn.*

Jones, S. G., & Fair, C. C. (2010). *Counterinsurgency in Pakistan.* Retrieved from the RAND Corporation Website: http://www.rand.org/content/dam/rand/pubs/monographs/2010/RAND_MG982.pdf

Karthikeya, R. (2009, August 7). Jundullah a wedge between Iran, Pakistan. *Asia Times.* Retrieved from http://www.atimes.com/atimes/South_Asia/KH07Df04.html

Kennedy, C. H. (2004). The creation and development of Pakistan's anti-terrorism regime, 1997–2002. In S. P. Limaye, R. G. Wirsing, & M. Malik (Eds.), *Religious radicalism and security in South Asia* (pp. 387–411). Honolulu: Asia-Pacific Center for Security Studies.

Kheshgi, K. (2009, November 6). Anti-terror ordinance may be extended to Malakand. *The News International.*

Lewis, B. (2004). The Crisis of Islam: Holy War and Unholy Terror. New York: *Random House Trade.*

Mir, A. (2005). *Sectarian monster.* Retrieved from the South Asia Intelligence Review Website: http://www.ict.org.il/Article.aspx?ID=920

Moini, Q. A. (2015, March 6). A major catch. *Dawn.*

Protection of Pakistan Ordinance, Gazette of Pakistan, Extraordinary, Part-I. (2013). Retrieved from the National Assembly Website: http://www.na.gov.pk/uploads/documents/1383819468_951.pdf

Qadir, M. (2012, February 19). Pakistan mulls crackdown on Jundullah. *Daily Times.*

Rana, A. M. (2004). *A to Z of Jehadi organizations in Pakistan.* Lahore: Mashal Book.

Roy, O. (2004). *Globalized Islam: The search for a new ummah.* Lahore: Alhamra.

Shahzad, S. S. (2011). *Inside Al Qaeda and the Taliban: Beyond Bin Laden and 9/11.* London: Pluto.

Siddiqa, A. (2013). *The new frontiers: Militancy and radicalism in Punjab.* Retrieved from https://lubpak.com/wp-content/uploads/2014/07/db3.pdf

Siddiqa, A. (2015, March 1). The madressa mix: Genesis and growth. *Dawn Special Report,* pp. 6–7.

Stenersen, A. (2009). Are the Afghan Taliban involved in international terrorism. *CTC Sentinel, 2*(9), 1–5. Retrieved from the CTC Sentinel Website: www.mercury.ethz.ch/serviceengine/Files/.../CTCSentinel-Vol2Iss9.pdf.

Stern, J. (2010). *Deradicalization or disengagement of terrorists: Is it possible?* Retrieved from Hoover Institution Website: www.hoover.org/sites/default/files/research/.../futurechallenges_stern.pdf

Tellis, A. J. (2008). Pakistan's record on terrorism: Conflicted goals, compromised performance. *The Washington Quarterly, 31*(2), 7–32.

The Council on American-Islamic Relations (CAIR). (2015). *Brief on Countering Violent Extremism (CVE).* Retrieved from http://www.cair.com/government-affairs/13063-brief-on-countering-violent-extremism-cve.html

The Homeland Security Department. (2015). *Countering Violent Extremism.* Retrieved from http://www.dhs.gov/topic/countering-violent-extremism

The News International (2014). *Country shuts down today to mourn deaths.* December 17. Available at: https://www.thenews.com.pk/archive/print/642280-country-shuts-down-today-to-mourn-deaths

Waseem, M. (2011). *Patterns of conflict in Pakistan: Implications for policy.* Retrieved from the Brookings Website: http://www.brookings.edu/~/media/research/files/papers/2011/3/01-pakistan-waseem/01_pakistan_waseem.pdf

Yusuf, H. (2010). Pakistan's anti-terrorism courts. *The CTC Sentinel, 3*(3), 22–25. Retrieved from the CTC Sentinel Website: https://www.ctc.usma.edu/v2/wp-content/uploads/2010/08/CTCSentinel-Vol3Iss3-art1.pdf.

INDEX

Note: Page numbers with "n" denote notes.

© The Editor(s) (if applicable) and The Author(s) 2016
J. Syed et al. (eds.), *Faith-Based Violence and Deobandi Militancy in Pakistan*, DOI 10.1057/978-1-349-94966-3

Printed by Printforce, the Netherlands